John Patrick, William Wake, Henry More

A Brief Discourse of the Real Presence of the Body and Blood of Christ in the Celebration of the Holy Eucharist

wherein the witty artifices of the Bishop of Meaux and of Monsieur Maimbourg are

obviated, whereby they would draw in the Protestants to

John Patrick, William Wake, Henry More

A Brief Discourse of the Real Presence of the Body and Blood of Christ in the Celebration of the Holy Eucharist
wherein the witty artifices of the Bishop of Meaux and of Monsieur Maimbourg are obviated, whereby they would draw in the Protestants to

ISBN/EAN: 9783337392611

Printed in Europe, USA, Canada, Australia, Japan

Cover: Foto ©Lupo / pixelio.de

More available books at **www.hansebooks.com**

Imprimatur.

Ex Ædib. Lambeth. Jul: 2. 1686.

Guil. Needham R^{mo} in Christo Patri ac D. D. Wilhelmo Archiep. Cantuar. à sacr. Domest.

A BRIEF DISCOURSE
OF THE
Real Presence
OF THE
Body and Blood of CHRIST
In the Celebration of the
HOLY EUCHARIST:
WHEREIN

The Witty Artifices of the Bishop of *Meaux* and of Monsieur *Maimbourg* are obviated, whereby they would draw in the Protestants to imbrace the Doctrine of

Transubstantiation.

Henry More

John 6. v. 54, 63.

Ὁ τρώγων μου τὴν σάρκα, καὶ πίνων μου τὸ αἷμα, ἔχει ζωὴν αἰώνιον.
Ἡ σὰρξ οὐκ ὠφελεῖ οὐδέν. Τὰ ῥήματα ἃ ἐγὼ λαλῶ ὑμῖν, πνεῦμά ἐστι καὶ ζωή ἐστιν.

Calvin. Instit. lib. 4. cap. 17.

In sacra sua Cœna jubet me Christus sub Symbolis panis ac vini corpus ac sanguinem suum sumere, manducare ac bibere. Nihil dubito quin & ipse verè porrigat & ego re ipsam. Tantùm absurda rejicio quæ aut cælesti illius Majestate indigna, aut ab humanæ ejus naturæ veritate aliena esse, apparent.

The Second Edition

LONDON,
Printed for *Walter Kettilby* at the *Bishop's Head* in St *Paul's* Church-Yard, MDC LXXXVI.

A BRIEF DISCOURSE OF THE 𝕽eal 𝕻resence.

CHAP. I.

1. The occasion of writing this Treatise. 2. The sence of the Church of England *touching* Transubstantiation. *3. Three Passages in her* Articles, Liturgie *and* Homilies *that seem to imply a* Real Presence. *4. A yielding, at least for the present, that the Church of* England *is for a* Real Presence, *but of that Flesh and Blood of Christ which he discourses of in the sixth Chapter of St.* John*'s Gospel, though she be for a* Real Absence *of that which hung on the Cross. 5. That our Saviour himself distinguishes betwixt that Flesh and Bloud he bore about with him, and that he there so earnestly discourses of. 6. That this Divine Food there discoursed of, the* Flesh *and* Blood *of* Christ, *is most copiously to be fed upon in the Holy* Eucharist, *and that our* Communion-Service *alludes to the same, nor does by such a* Real Presence *imply any* Transubstantiation.

B   1. THE

A brief Discourse of   Chap. I.

1. THE occasion of writing this short Treatise was this. I observing the Papers here in *England*, published in behalf of the Church of *Rome*, and for the drawing off People from the Orthodox Faith of the Church of *England*, which holds with the ancient pure Apostolick Church in the *Primitive* Times, before that general *Degeneracy* of the Church came in, to drive at nothing more earnestly, than the maintaining their grand Error touching the Eucharist, *viz.* their Doctrine of *Transubstantiation*; Into which they would bring back the *Reformed* Churches, by taking hold of some Intimations, or more open Professions of theirs, of a *Real Presence* (though they absolutely deny the *Roman* Doctrine of *Transubstantiation*) and thus intangling and insnaring them in those free professions touching that Mystery of the *Eucharist*, would by hard pulling hale them into that rightfully-relinquish'd Errour, for which and several others, they justly left the Communion of the Church of *Rome*: I thought it my Duty, so far as my Age, and Infirmness of my Body will permit, to endeavour to extricate the *Reformation*, and especially our Church of *England*, from these Entanglements with which these witty and cunning Writers would entangle Her, in Her Concessions touching that mysterious Theory; and to shew there is no clashing betwixt her declaring against *Transubstantiation*, and those Passages which seem to imply a *Real Presence* of the Body and Blood of Christ at the Celebration of the Holy *Eucharist*.

2. Concerning which, that we may the more clearly judge, we will bring into view what She says touching them both. And as touching the former
(Article

CHAP. I. *the* Real Presence.

(Article 28.) her words are these: "Transubstanti-
"ation (or the change of the substance of Bread and
"Wine in the Supper of the Lord) cannot be proved
"by Holy Writ; but it is repugnant to the plain
"words of Scripture, overthroweth the nature of
"a Sacrament, and hath given occasion to many Su-
"perstitions.] And in the latter part of the *Rubrick*
at the end of the *Communion-Service*, She says, "That
"the Sacramental Bread and Wine remain still in
"their very natural Substances, and therefore may
"not be adored (for that were Idolatry to be abhorred
"of all faithful Christians) and the *natural* Body and
"Bloud of our Saviour Christ are in Heaven and not
"here, it being against the *Truth* of Christ's *natural*
"Body to be at one time in more places than one.]
This is sufficiently express against *Transubstantiation*.

3. Now those passages that seem to imply a *Real Presence* in the *Eucharist* are these. In the above-named Article 28. *The Body of Christ*, saith our Church, *is given, taken, and eaten in the Supper only after an Heavenly and Spiritual manner. And the mean whereby the Body of Christ is received and eaten in the Supper, is Faith.* Against which our Adversaries suggest, That no Faith can make us actually receive and eat that, which is, God knows, how far distant from us; and that therefore we imply that the Body of Christ is *really present* in the *Eucharist*. Another Passage occurs in our *Catechism*, where it is told us, *That the inward part of the Sacrament, or thing signified, is the Body and Bloud of Christ*, which are verily *and* indeed *taken and received by the faithful in the Lord's Supper.* Where [verily] and [indeed] seems to imply a *Real Presence* and Participation of the Body and Bloud of Christ. The last place shall be that in the *Homily*, of *worthy receiving* and reverend esteeming of the Sacra-

B 2 ment

ment of the Body and Bloud of Chrift. The words are thefe, "But thus much we muft be fure to hold, "that in the Supper of the Lord there is no vain Cere- "mony, no *bare Sign*, no *untrue Figure* of a *thing abfent.* "But as the Scripture faith, The Table of the Lord, "the Bread and Cup of the Lord, the Memory of "Chrift, the Annunciation of his Death, yea the *Com- "munion of the Body and Bloud of the Lord, in a mar- "vellous Incorporation,* which by the *Operation of the "Holy Ghoft* (the very bond of our conjunction with "Chrift) is through Faith wrought in the Souls of the "faithful: Whereby not only their Souls live to Eter- "nal Life, but they furely truft to win their Bodies a "Refurrection to Immortality.] And immediately there is added, "The true underftanding of this Fru- "ition and Union which is betwixt the Body and the "Head, betwixt the true Believers and Chrift, the an- "cient Catholick Fathers both perceiving themfelves, "and commending to their people, were not afraid to "call this Supper, fome of them, the Salve of Immor- "tality, and Sovereign Prefervative againft Death; "others the *Deifick Communion*, others the fweet "Dainties of our Saviour, the Pledg of Eternal Health, "the Defence of Faith, the Hope of the Refurrection; "Others the Food of Immortality, the Healthful "Grace, and the Confervatory to everlafting Life.] There are fo many high Expreffions in thefe paffa- ges, that our Adverfaries who would by this Hook pluck us back again into the Error of *Tranfubftanti- ation*, will unavoidably imagine and alledg from hence, that if we will ftand to the Affertions of our own Church, we muft acknowledge the *Real Prefence* of the Body and Blood of our Saviour in the Sacrament.

4. And let us be fo civil to them as, at leaft for the prefent, to yield, that underftanding it in a due fenfe,

CHAP. I. *the* Real Presence. 5

sense, we do acknowledge the *Real Presence*. But it does not at all follow from thence, that we must hold that that very Body of Christ that hung upon the Cross, and whose Blood was there shed, is *really* present in the Sacrament; but that our Church, speaking *conformably* to *Christ's Discourse* on this Matter in the sixth of *John*, and to the ancient *primitive* Fathers, whose expressions do plainly allude to *that Discourse* of our Saviour's in the sixth of S. *John*, doth assert both a *Real Presence* of the Body and Blood of Christ to be received by the faithful in the *Eucharist*, and also a *Real Absence* of that Body and Blood that was crucified and shed on the Cross. And this seems to be the express Doctrine of our Saviour in the above-mentioned Chapter of S. *John*, where the *Eternal* Word incarnate speaks thus——

John 6. v. 51. *I am the living Bread which came down from Heaven*, (viz. the Manna which the Psalmist calls the Food of Angels, also) *if any eat of this Bread, he shall live for ever* (viz. of this true *Manna*, of which the Manna in the Wilderness was but a Type) *and the Bread that I will give is my flesh* (which therefore still is that *immortalizing* Manna, the true Bread from Heaven) *which I will give for the life of the World*, that the whole Intellectual Creation may live thereby, it being their vivifick Food. For as you may gather by *vers.* 62, 63. he does not understand his flesh that hung on the Cross. And it was the ignorance of the *Jews* that they thought he did: and therefore they cryed out on him, saying, *v.* 52. *How can this man give us his flesh to eat?* And that is because they took him to be a mere man, or an ordinary man, not the incarnate *Logos*. Which Logos *Clemens Alexandrinus* calls ἄνθρωπον ἀπαθῆ, *the impassible man;* and *Trismegistus*, τ̀ τῦ Θεῦ παῖδα ἄνθρωπον ἕνα θελήματι Θεῦ, that

one

one man the Son of God born of him, which he says is ὁ γενεσιυργὸς τῆς παλιγγενεσίας, *the Author of Regeneration*, as having the *Life* in him, the Ζωὴ, *John* 1. *v*. 4. and this Ζωὴ or *Life* the *Divine* or Spiritual *Body*, one necessary Element of *Regeneration*, which mystery we cannot here insist upon. But in the mean time let us observe our Saviour's Answer to this Scruple of the *Jews*; He is so far from receding from what he said, that he with all earnestness and vehemency asserts the same again.

Then Jesus said unto them, Verily, verily I say unto you, except you eat the flesh of the Son of man (that is of the *Messias*, or the *Word Incarnate*) *and drink his blood, you have no life in you. Whoso eateth my flesh and drinketh my blood hath Eternal Life, and I will raise him up at the last day. For my flesh is meat indeed, and my blood is drink indeed. He that eateth my flesh and drinketh my blood, dwelleth in me and I in him. As the living Father hath sent me and I live by the Father, so he that eateth me* (*viz*. that eateth his flesh and drinketh his blood) *even he shall live by me. This is that bread that came down from Heaven, not as your Fathers did eat Manna, and are dead; he that eateth of this Bread, shall live for ever.*

5. This is that *earnest*, *lofty* and *sublime* discourse of our Saviour touching his *real* Flesh and Blood, that the scandal given to the Jews could not drive him off from; and persisting in it, he gave also offence to his Disciples, that muttered and said, *This is an hard saying, Who can hear it?* Wherefore I must confess ingenuously, that it seems to me incredible, that under so *lofty mysterious* a Style, and *earnest* asseveration of what he affirms, though to the scandal of both the *Jews* and his own *Disciples*, there should not be couched some most weighty and profound Truth

concerning

concerning some *real* Flesh and Blood of his, touching which this vehement and sublime Discourse is framed, which is a piece of that part of the Christian Philosophy (as some of the Antients call Christianity) which *Origen* terms σοφία. The *Object* of this *eating* and *drinking* is the *Flesh* and *Blood* of Christ: But to rectifie the errour of his Disciples, he plainly affirms, that he doth not mean what he said, of the Flesh and Blood he then bore about with him. In *verse* 61, 62, 63. *Does this offend you* (saith he to them) *what and if you shall see the Son of Man ascend up where he was before* (then my particular *natural* Body will be far enough removed from you, and your selves then from so gross a conceit as to think I understand this of my *natural, particular* Body or Flesh.) No, says he, *the flesh profiteth nothing, it is the spirit that quickens; the words that I speak unto you, they are spirit and they are life,* that is to say, they are concerning that *spiritual* Body and *Life* or *Spirit* that accompanies it (*That which is born of the flesh is flesh, and that which is born of the spirit is spirit*) the both *seed* and *nourishment* of those that are *Regenerate*; the Principles of their *Regeneration,* and the *Divine Food* for their *Nutrition,* whereby they grow up to their due stature in Christ.

6. And where, or where so fully is this *Divine Food* to be had, as in that most solemn and most devotional approaching God in the Celebration of the *Communion* of the *Body* and *Blood* of *Christ*, where we both testifie and advance thereby our *spiritual union* with him, according as he has declared in *John* ch. 6. *He that eateth my flesh, and drinketh my blood, dwelleth in me, and I in him.* Upon which our *Communion-Service* thus glosses: That if with a true penitent heart and lively faith we receive this Holy Sacrament,

Sacrament, we then spiritually eat the Flesh of Christ and drink his Blood, we dwell in Christ and Christ in us, we are one with Christ and Christ with us. And whereas the Adversaries of our Church object, We cannot eat the Flesh of Christ and drink his Blood, in the Celebration of the Lord's Supper, unless his Flesh and Blood be really present; we do acknowledge that *that* Flesh and Blood which our Saviour discourses of in St *John*, and which our *Liturgie* alludes to, as also those notable sayings of the Fathers above cited out of the *Homily*, touching the *worthy receiving the Lord's Supper*, is *really present* in the Eucharist. And that there is that which Christ calls his *Flesh* and *Blood*, distinct from that which he then bore about with him, and was crucified on the Cross, he does most manifestly declare in that Discourse in St *John*, as I have already proved. So manifest is it, that the *Real Presence* does not imply any *Transubstantiation* of the Bread and Wine into the Body and Blood of Christ.

CHAP. II.

1. *The Bishop of Meaux his establishing* Transubstantiation *upon the literal sense of* [This is my Body]. 2. *That according to the literal sense, the Bread that Christ blessed was both* Bread *and the* Body of Christ *at once, and that the avoiding that absurdity cast them upon* Transubstantiation. 3. *That* Transubstantiation *exceeds that avoided Absurdity, as contradicting the* Senses *as well as* Reason, *and labouring under the same Absurdity it self*. 4. *Further Reasons why the* Road *of the literal sense is to be left, and that we are to strike*

into

into the Figurative, *the former contradicting the Principles of* Physicks, 5. *Of* Metaphysicks, 6. *Of* Mathematicks, 7. *And of* Logick. 8. *That* Transubstantiation *implies, the same thing is and is not at the same time.* 9. *A number of Absurdities plainly resulting from* Transubstantiation.

1. AND therefore to prop up this great mistake of *Transubstantiation*, they are fain to recur and stick to a *literal sense* of those words of our Saviour [This is my Body] which I finding no where more handsomely done than by the Right Reverend Bishop of *Meaux*, I shall produce the Passage in his own words (that is, the translation of them) in his *Exposition of the Doctrine of the Catholick Church*, Sect. 10. The Real Presence, says he, of the Body and Blood of our Saviour is solidly established by the words of the Institution [This is my Body] which we understand *literally* ; and there is no more reason to ask us why we fix our selves to the proper and *literal* sense, than there is to ask a Traveller why he follows the *high Road*. It is their parts who have recourse to the *Figurative* sense, and who take by-paths, to give a reason for what they do. As for us, since we find nothing in the words which Jesus Christ makes use of for the Institution of this Mystery, obliging us to take them in a *Figurative* sense, we think that to be a sufficient Reason to determine us to the *literal*.

2. In answer to this, I shall, if it be not too great a Presumption, first accompany this venerable Person in this *high Road* of the *literal* sense of the words of Institution [This is my Body] and then shew how this *Road*, as fairly as it looks, is here a mere *Angiportus* that hath no *exitus* or Passage, so that we must be forced to divert out of it, or go back again.

First

First then, let us take this supposed *high Road*, and say, the words [This is my Body] are to be understood *literally*. Wherefore let us produce the whole Text, and follow this kind of Gloss, *Luke* 22. 19. *And he took bread, and gave thanks, and brake it, and gave unto them, saying, This is my Body, which is given for you, This do in remembrance of me. Likewise also the cup after supper, saying, This cup is the New Testament in my blood, which is shed for you.* Now if we keep to the mere *literal* sense, *This Cup* (as well as, This Bread is the Body of Christ) must be really the *New Testament* in Christ's Bloud, which is a thing unavoidable if we tye our selves to the *literal* sense of the words. But why is not the *Cup*, the *Bloud* or *Covenant* in Christ's Bloud? but that a *Cup* and *Bloud* are *Disparata*, or in general, *Opposita*, which to affirm one of another is a Contradiction; as if one should say, a *Bear* is a *Horse*: and therefore we are constrained to leave the *literal* sense, and to recur to a *figurative*. But precisely to keep to the institution of that part of the Sacrament that respects Christ's Body; It is plain that what he took he gave thanks for, what he gave thanks for he brake, what he brake he gave to his Disciples, saying, *This* (which he took, gave thanks for, brake, and gave to his Disciples, *viz.* the above-mentioned *Bread) is my Body*. Wherefore the *literal* sense must necessarily be, *This Bread* (as before it was *This Cup*,) *is my Body*. Insomuch that according to this *literal* sense it is both *really Bread* still, and *really the Body* of *Christ* at once. Which, I believe, there is no *Romanist* but will be ashamed to admit. But why cannot he admit this but that *Bread* and the *Body* of *Christ* are *Opposita*, and therefore the one cannot be said to be the other without a perfect repugnancy or contradiction to humane Reason; as

absurd

absurd as if one should say, a *Bear* is a *Horse*, or a *Rose* a *Black-bird*; whence, by the bye, we may note the necessary use of Reason in Matters of Religion, and that what is a plain *Contradiction* to humane Reason, such as, a *Triangle* is a *Circle*, or a *Cow* an *Horse*, are not to be admitted for Articles of the Christian Faith. And for this Reason, I suppose, the Church of *Rome* fell into the Opinion of *Transubstantiation*, (from this *literal* way of expounding these words [This is my Body]) rather than according to the genuine leading of that way, they would admit, that what Christ gave his Disciples, was both *real Bread* and the *real Body* of Christ at once.

3. But see the infelicity of this Doctrine of *Transubstantiation*, which does not only contradict the inviolable Principles of *Reason* in humane Souls, but also all the *outward* senses, upon which account it is more intolerable than that Opinion which they seem so much to abhor, as to prefer *Transubstantiation* before it, though it contradict only *Reason*, not the *outward Senses*, which rightly circumstantiated are fit Judges touching sensible Objects, whether they be this or that, Fish or Fowl, Bread or Flesh. Nay I may add, That these Transubstantiators have fallen over and above that contradiction to the rightly circumstantiated senses, into *that very absurdity*, that they seemed so much to abhor from, that is, the confounding two *opposite Species* into one *Individual Substance*, *viz.* that one and the same Individual Substance should be really both *Bread* and *Christ's Body* at once. But by their transubstantiating the *Individual* Substance of the *Bread* into the *Individual* Substance of *Christ's Body*, they run into this very Repugnancy which they seemed before so cautiously to avoid; two Individual Substances (as *species infimæ*) being *Opposita*,

Opposita, and therefore uncapable of being said to be the same, or to be pronounced one of the other without a *Contradiction*. It is impossible that the Soul of *Socrates*, for example, should be so transubstantiated into the Soul of *Plato*, that it should become his Soul, insomuch that it may be said of *Socrates*'s Soul, that it is the Soul of *Plato*; and there is the same Reason of transubstantiating the Substance of the Bread into the Substance of the Body of Christ. So that the *Substance* of the *Bread* may be said to be the *Body* of *Christ*, or the *Substance* of his Body, *which* it must either *be*, or be *annihilated*, and then it is not the *Transubstantiation* of the *Substance* of the *Bread*, but the *Annihilation* of it, into the *Body* of *Christ*.

4. And having rid in this fair-promising *Road* of the *literal* sense, but thus far, I conceive, I have made it manifest, that it is not *passable*, but that we have discovered such difficulties as may very well move me to strike out of it, or return back. And further, to shew I do it not rashly, I shall add several other Reasons, as this venerable Person (that thinks fittest to keep in it still) doth but rightfully require; as declaring, It is their parts who have recourse to the *Figurative* sense, and who take by-paths, to give a reason why they do so. Wherefore besides what I have produced already, I add these, transcribed out of a Treatise of mine, writ many years ago. Besides then the Repugnancy of this Doctrine of *Transubstantiation* to the common sense of all men, according to which it cannot but be judged to be *Bread* still, I shall now shew how it contradicts the Principles of all *Arts* and *Sciences* (which if we may not make use of in Theology, to what great purpose are all the Universities in *Christendom*?) the Principles, I say, of *Physicks*, of *Metaphysicks*, of *Mathematicks*, and of *Logick*.

Logick. It is a Principle in *Physicks*, That that Internal space or place that a Body occupies, is equal to the Body that occupies it. Now let us suppose, that one and the same Body occupies *two* such internal places or spaces at once. This Body therefore is equal to two spaces which are double to one single space; wherefore the Body is double to that Body in one single space, and therefore one and the same Body *double* to *it self*, which is an enormous *Contradiction*.

5. Again in *Metaphysicks*, the body of Christ is acknowledged *one*, and that as much as any one body else in the World. Now the *Metaphysical* Notion of [one] is to be *indivisum à se* (both *quoad partes* and *quoad totum*) as well as *divisum à quolibet alio*; but the body of Christ being both in Heaven, and without any continuance of that body, here upon Earth also, the whole body is divided from the whole body, and therefore is entirely both *unum* and *multa*, which is a perfect contradiction.

6. Thirdly, In the *Mathematicks (Concil. Trident. Sess.* 13.) the Council of *Trent* saying, that in the separation of the parts of the *species* (that which bears the outward show of Bread and Wine) that from this division there is a parting of the whole, divided into so many *entire* bodies of Christ, the body of Christ being always at the same time equal to it self; It follows, that a *part* of the division is *equal* to the *whole* that is divided, against that common Notion in *Euclid*, That the whole is bigger than the part.

7. And lastly, In *Logick*, it is a Maxim, That the parts agree indeed with the whole, but disagree one with another; but in the abovesaid division of the Host or Sacrament, the parts do so well *agree*, that they are intirely the *same individual thing*. And
whereas

whereas any Division, whether *Logical* or *Physical*, is the Division of some *one* into *many*, this is but the Division of *one* into *one* and *it self*, which is a perfect contradiction.

8. To all which you may add, That the *Transubstantiation* of the Bread and Wine into the Body and Blood of Christ implys, that the same thing both *is* and *is not* at the *same time* (which is against that Fundamental Principle in *Logick* and *Metaphysicks*, that both parts of a contradiction cannot be true) which I prove thus. For that *Individual* thing that can be made, or is to be made of any thing, is not; the progress in this case being, *à privatione ad habitum*, as the Schools speak, and the *terms* of Generation or of being made, *viz. à quo* and *ad quem* being *Non esse* and *Esse*, or *Non-existent* and *Existent*; so that that passing, is from *Non-existent* to *Existent*. Now the *individual* body of Christ is *to be made* of the Wafer consecrated, for it is turned into his *Individual* Body. But his *Individual* Body was before this Consecration; wherefore it both *was* and *was not* at the same time. For in the making thereof there was a passing from the *terminus à quo*, which is the *Non-existency* of the thing to be made, to the *terminus ad quem*, to the *Existency* of it, which yet was in Being before.

9. These difficulties are sufficient to shew that this *high Road* of the *literal* sense taken to establish *Transubstantiation* is not passable, so that there is a necessity of diverting or going back. Nor will it be much needful to hint briefly these or other like absurdities more intelligible to the *vulgar* capacity, such as, That the same Body at the same time is greater and lesser than it self; Is but a foot distant from me or less, and yet many thousand miles distant from me: That

That one and the same Person may be intirely present with himself, and some hundred thousand miles absent from himself at once: That he may sit still on the Grass, and yet journey and walk at the same time: That an organized body that hath head, feet, hands, &c. is intirely in every part of it self, the comely parts in the more uncomely: That the same Body now in Heaven may really present it self on Earth without passing any space either directly or circuitously: That our Saviour Christ *communicating* with his Disciples in the last Supper, swallowed down his whole intire Body, limbs, back, belly, head and mouth and all into his stomach, which might amuze and puzzle one to conceive how it was possible for his Disciples not to miss the sight of his hands and head, though his cloaths were still visible as not being swallowed down into his stomach. Or, whether our Saviour swallowed down his own Body into his stomach or no, this puzzle will still remain, how his Disciples could swallow him down without his cloathes, he being still in his cloaths; or how they could swallow him down in his cloaths, the bread being not transubstantiated into his cloaths, but into his body only. These and several such Absurdities it were easie to enumerate. But I hope I have produced so much already, that I may, and any one else, be thought to have very good cause to leave this *high Road* of the *literal* sense, and betake our selves to that more safe path of the *Figurative*, whereby *Transubstantiation* with all its Absurdities is avoided.

CHAP.

CHAP. III.

1. *An evasion of the Incredibility of* Transubstantiation *drawn from the* Omnipotency *of God.* 2. *Ans. That it is no derogation to God's* Omnipotency *not to be able to do what it implies a contradiction to be done.* 3. *If this* Transubstantiation *had been fecible, yet it had been repugnant to the* Goodness *and* Wisdom *of Christ to have effected it.* 4. *A marvellous witty device of taking away all the Absurdities of* Transubstantiation, *by giving to Christ's Body a* supernatural manner of existence. 5. *That the neat Artifice of this* Sophistry *lies in putting the smooth term of* supernatural *for* counter-essential *or* asystatal. 6. *That it is an* Asystatal *manner of Existence, proved from the Author's description thereof in several particulars. Arguments from the* multiplication *of Christ's Body, and difference of time of its* production. 7. *From* Non-extension *of parts.* 8. *From* Independency *of place.* 9. *To make a body* independent *of* Place *as unconceivable as to make it* independent *of* Time. 10. *The Argument from being* whole *in every* part *of the Symbols.*

1. **O**UT of which Absurdities the most witty evasion offered to our consideration that I have met with, is in that ingenious and artfully composed Treatise, entitled, *A Papist mis-represented and represented.* In his Chapter of the Eucharist toward the end, it is well worth the transcribing that I may offer some brief Answers to the things there comprized. "The Papist represented, *saith he (pag.* 11. *lin.* "22.) not at all hearkning to his Senses in a matter
"where

"where God speaks; he unfeignedly confesses, that "he that made the World of nothing by his sole "Word, That cured Diseases by his Word, That "raised the Dead by his Word, That expell'd Devils, "That commanded the Winds and Seas, That mul-"tiplied Bread, That changed Water into Wine by "his Word, and Sinners into Just Men, cannot want "Power to change Bread and Wine into his own "Body and Blood by his sole Word.

2. It is an invidious thing to dispute the Power of the Eternal *Logos* or *Word Incarnate*, who is God of God, very God of very God, and therefore *Omnipotent*, and can do all things that imply no *Contradiction* to be done, as most certainly none of these things there specify'd do imply it. But things repugnant to be done, we may, and that with due reverence, declare God cannot do. As the Apostle does not stick to say, *God cannot lie*, Heb. 6. 18. And why is it impossible for God to lye, but that it is *repugnant* to the Perfection of his Nature, and particularly that Attribute of his *Veracity*? Nor will any adventure to affirm that he can make a Globe or Cylinder which shall be equidistant from, or touch a Plane though but in half of their Spherical or Cylindrical Superficies: or a Circle from whose Center the lines drawn shall be unequal, or a Rectangle Triangle, the Power of whose *Hypotenusa* shall not be equal to both the Powers of the *Basis* and *Cathetus*. And in fine, there are fixt and immutable Idea's of things, and such necessary and inseparable respects and properties of them, that to imagine them *mutable*, or that God can change them, is to disorder and change the *Eternal* and *Immutable* Intellect of *God* himself. Of which those indeleble and necessary Notions, which the minds of all mankind are conscious to themselves

themselves of, if they be but awakened into free attention thereto, is but a compendious *Transcript*.

And therefore God his being not able to do any thing that is a *Contradiction* to those Eternal Idea's and Habitudes of them in his own mind, is no lessening of his *Omnipotency*; but to imagine otherwise, is to dissolve the Eternal Frame of the Divine Intellect, and under a pretence of amplifying his *Omnipotency*, to *enable* God to *destroy himself*, or to make him so *weak* or *impotent* as to be *capable* of *being destroyed* by himself, which is a thing impossible.

3. But suppose the *Eternal Word Incarnate* could have turned the Bread and Wine into his own *Individual* Body and Bloud, and the thing it self were fecible, though it seems so palpably contradictious to us: yet there would be this difficulty still remaining, that it is repugnant to his *Wisdom* and *Goodness* so to do (as the Apostle says, it is impossible for God to lye) in that manner he is supposed to have done it, that is, in declaring a thing is done that is repugnant so apparently to our Intellectual Faculties, and leaves so palpable an assurance to all our Senses, though never so rightly *circumstantiated*, that it is not done, but that it is *still Bread*; and yet that these *species* of Bread and Wine should be supported by a Miracle, to obfirm or harden us in our unbelief of this Mystery of *Transubstantiation*. How does this sute with either the *Wisdom* of God, if he would in good earnest have us to believe this Mystery; or with his *Goodness*, to give this Scandal to the World, for whom Christ died, and to occasion so bloudy Persecutions of innumerable innocent Souls, that could not believe a thing so contrary to all Sense and Reason, and indeed to Passages of Scripture it self, whose Pen-men he did inspire? Wherefore this is a
plain

plain Evincement, that our Saviour meant *figuratively* when he said [This is my Body] and that his Disciples understood him so (there being nothing more usual in the Jewish Language than to call the *Sign* by the *Name* of the thing *signified*) and that this *literal* Gloss has been introduced by After-ages without any fault of our Saviour. But in defence of the literal sense which he would have to infer *Transubstantiation*, our Author holds on thus, *viz.*

4. " That this may be done without danger of
" multiplying his Body, and making as many Christs
" as Altars, or leaving the right hand of his Father,
" but only by giving to his Body a *Supernatural manner*
" *of Existence*, by which being left without *Extension*
" *of Parts*, and rendred *independent of Place*, it may be
" one and the same in *many* places at *once*, and *whole*
" in every *part* of the Symbols, and not obnoxious
" to any Corporeal Contingencies. And this kind of
" Existence is no more than what in a manner he be-
" stows upon every *glorified* Body, than what his
" *own Body* had when born without the least violation
" of his Mother's Virginal Integrity; when he rose
" from the Dead out of the Sepulchre without re-
" moving the stone; when he entered amongst his
" Disciples, the Doors being shut.

5. This is, as I said, a witty contrived evasion to elude the above-mentioned Repugnancies I have noted, and exquisitely well fitted for the amusing and confounding of more vulgar and weak minds, or such as have not leisure to consider things to the bottom, and for the captivating them into a profession of what they have no determinate or distinct apprehension of; by *distinctions* and *exemplifications* that give no real support to the cause they are brought in for to maintain.

For first, to pretend that by a *supernatural manner*

of *Existence* a Body may be in more places than one at once, at the right hand of God the Father in Heaven, and on the Altar at the same time, &c. The Artifice of the Sophistry lies in this, that he has put a more *tolerable* and *soft* expression in lieu of one that (according to his explication of the matter) would sound more *harsh*, but is more *true* and *proper* in this case. For this manner of Existence of a Body which he describes is not simply *supernatural*, which implies it is a Body still, as a Mill-stone by a supernatural power held up in the Air is a Mill-stone still, though it be in that supernatural condition: But the condition he describes is such, as is not only *supernatural* but *counter-essential* or *Asystatal*, that is, *Repugnant* to the very Being of a Body, or of any finite substance in the Universe. It is as if the Mill stone were not only *supernaturally* supported in the Air, but were as *transparent*, as *soft* and *fluid*, and of as undetermined a shape as the Air it self, or as if a right-angled Triangle were declared to be so still, though the *Hypotenusa* were not of equal power with the *Basis* and *Cathetus*, which is a thing impossible: But if instead of a *supernatural manner of existence*, it had been said, an *Asystatal* manner of existence, that is, an Existence repugnant to the very Being of a Body or any finite substance else, it would have been discovered to be a contradiction at the very first sight, and therefore such as ought to be rejected, as well as the affirming that what Christ gave was *really* Bread and *really his Body* at once.

6. And now, notwithstanding this *soft* and *smooth* term of [supernatural] that it is an *Asystatal* manner of Existence, that is here given to the Body of Christ, may appear from our Author's description thereof. For in virtue, he saith, of this *supernatural manner of existence*,

existence, there may be a *Transubstantiation* without danger of *multiplying* Christ's Body, and making as many Christs as Altars. But it is impossible this Absurdity should be avoided, supposing *Transubstantiation*. For there is not a more certain and infallible sign of two bodily Persons being *two* bodily Persons, and not the *same* Person, than distance of Place, wherein they are separate one from another, and consequently *two*, not *one* Body; and this is the very case in *Transubstantiation*, which manifestly implies, that the Body of Christ is in many thousand distant places at once. Which imagined condition in it is not *supernatural* but *Asystatal*, and *contradictious* to the very Being of any finite substance whatever, as has been intimated and firmly proved before, *Chap.* 2.

And as *distance* of *place* necessarily infers difference of Bodies or Persons, so does also *difference* of *time* of their *Production*. That which was produced, suppose sixteen hundred Years ago, and remains so produced, cannot be produced suppose but yesterday, or at this present moment, and so be sixteen hundred Years older or younger than it self. This is not only *supernatural* but *Asystatal*, and implies a perfect contradiction; but yet this is the very case in *Transubstantiation*. The Body of Christ born suppose sixteen hundred Years ago, is yet produced out of the *Transubstantiated* Bread but now or yesterday, and so the same Body is sixteen hundred Years older or younger than it self, which is a perfect *Contradiction*.

7. Secondly, The Papist represented declares, That the Body of Christ by virtue of this *supernatural manner of Existence*, is left without *Extension of Parts*, which is a perfect contradiction to the very nature and essence of a Body, whose universally acknowledged Definition is τὸ τριχῇ διάστατον ἀντίτυπον, implying,

plying a *Trinal impenetrable dimension* or extension. Besides, did Christ's Body at his last Supper, so soon as he had *Transubstantiated* the Bread into it, lose all extension of parts? What then filled out his cloaths as he sat with his Disciples at Table? or how could the Jews lay hold on Christ's Body to Crucifie it, if he had no extension of parts to be laid hold on? How could there be hands and feet and organization of parts, either at the *Table* or on the *Cross*, if there were no extension of parts to be organized? And lastly, being the *Transubstantiated* Bread is the very *Individual* Body of Christ, if they would have this being left without extension of parts, to be understood of it, how can the very same *Individual* Body of Christ have Extension of Parts and have no Extension of Parts, have Organization of Parts and have no Organization of Parts at once? So that the condition of Christ's Body here supposed is plainly *Asystatal*, not as is *smoothly* expressed only *Supernatural*.

8. Thirdly, Whereas the *Papist Represented* declares, that this *Supernatural* Manner of Existence of Christ's Body renders it *Independent of Place*, what can the meaning of that be, but that by vertue of this priviledge it might exist without any *Place* or *Ubi*, which Bodies in their natural condition cannot? But this clashes with the very Story of our Saviour Christ, who was certainly in the Room in which he ate the Passover with his Disciples, after he had *transubstantiated* Bread into his *Individual* Body, and therefore it did not exist *Independently of Place* in virtue of any such *Supernatural Manner of Existence* as is imagined. And as this does not agree with matter of Fact, so it is a perfect contradiction to the Essence of any Body or finite Substance to be exempted from all connexion with *Place* or *Ubi*, but a *finite* Substance must be in a

definite

definite Ubi, and while it is in such a definite *Ubi*, it is impossible to conceive that it is in another *Place* or *Ubi*, whether *intra* or *extra mænia Mundi*. He that closely and precisely considers the point, he will not fail, I think, to discern the thing to be impossible. And what contradiction it implies, I have demonstrated above. So that we see there can be no such *Supernatural Manner* of Existence conferred on a Body in making it *independent* of *Place* or *Ubiety*, as to capacitate it to be one and the same Body in diverse places at once; but that this supposed *Supernatural Manner* is truly an *Asystatal Manner*, and such as is *repugnant* to the very *Being* of a *Body*, or any *finite* Substance whatsoever.

9. To make a body in this sense *independent of Place* or *Ubiety*, is as unconceivable as to make it *independent* of *Time*, which yet would so compleat this impossible *Hypothesis*, that under this pretence when a thing has such a *Supernatural Existence* as exempts it from all connexion with or relation to *Time*, but supposes it utterly independent thereof, as was explained before touching *Place*, we may suppose what we will of a Body, that it may be *Bread* and *not Bread* at the same time, that it may be at *Thebes* and at *Athens* at the same time, as we ordinary mortals would phrase it, sith it is lifted up above all Relation and Connexion with *Time*, nor hath any thing to do with any Time. But yet this assuredly is not a mere *Supernatural Manner of Existence*, but plainly *Asystatal*, and such as if God could cause, there would be no *Eternal* and *Immutable* Truths, but under a Pretext of exalting the *Omnipotence* of God, they would imply him *able to destroy his own Nature*, which would argue an *Impotency* in him, and to extinguish and confound the *Inviolable* Idea's of the Divine Intellect, as I intimated above.

10. And

10. And, Fourthly and lastly, That in vertue of this *Supernatural Manner of Existence*, the Body of Christ should be *whole* in every *part* of the Symbols, and thereby become not obnoxious to any corporeal Contingences; (which is said, I suppose, to avoid the Absurdity of grinding a pieces the Body of Christ with our Teeth when we chew the supposed Species) thus to exist *whole in every part*, is not a mere *Supernatural Manner of Existing*, but *Asystatal*, and implies either that the least part of Christ's Body is as big as the whole, or that the whole Body is God knows how many thousand times bigger than it self. For certainly the whole Body comprized under the whole *Bread* or Species of Bread, is many thousand times bigger than one particle thereof no bigger than a Pins point. Besides that this making the Body of Christ *whole* in *every part*, takes away all possibility of distinct *Organization* of his Body, unless you will have every Pins point of it to have Head, Feet, Hands, Arms, and the rest of the Parts of an humane Body, or have the same *Individual* Body *organized* and *unorganized* at the same time, which are as palpable *Contradictions* as any can occur to the understanding of a man.

And thus much I thought fit to intimate touching this Witty Distinction of a *Natural* and *Supernatural Manner of Existence of a Body*, and to shew that this pretended *Supernatural* Manner of the Existence of Christ's Body, arising from the Bread *transubstantiated*, as the *Papist Represented* describes it, is indeed an *Asystatal Manner of Existence*, and *inconsistent* with the Being of any *Body*, or *finite Substance* whatsoever.

CHAP.

CHAP. IV.

1. *The* Supernatural Manner of the Exiſtence *of a Body conſiſting in* Non-extenſion *of* Parts, Independency of Place, *and being* whole *in every* Part. 2. *The firſt exemplification of ſuch a Manner of Exiſtence in* Glorified Bodies, *not to reach the Caſe.* 3. *Nor the ſecond, in* Chriſt's Body *born without the leaſt Violation of his Mothers Virginal Integrity.* 4. *Nor the third, in* Chriſt's *riſing out of the Sepulcher* without *the* removing of the ſtone. 5. *Nor the fourth, in* Chriſt's *entring amongſt his Diſciples the* doors being ſhut. 6. Tranſubſtantiation *implying a number of contradictions as harſh as that of the ſame body being both* Chriſt's Body *and* Bread *at once, and there being no* ſalvo *for them but this device of a* ſupernatural manner of Exiſtence, *and this ſo plainly failing, it is impoſſible that* Tranſubſtantiation *ſhould be the true* mode of the Real Preſence.

1. IT remains now that we only touch upon lightly the *exemplifications* of this *ſupernatural manner of Exiſtence* of a Body, conſiſting in theſe peculiarities, *Non-extenſion* of parts, *Independency* of *Place*, and being *whole* in *every part,* and to note how none of theſe inſtances reach the preſent caſe.

2. As firſt that of a glorified Body. What Scripture, Reaſon or Authority ever ſuggeſted to us that the *glorified Body* of Chriſt himſelf, much leſs every glorified Body, is without *extenſion of parts*, has no relation to or connexion with *Place*, or is *whole* in every *part?* For without extenſion of Parts it cannot be ſo much as a *Body.* And were not *Moſes* and *Elias* together with Chriſt at his Transfiguration on Mount

Mount *Tabor*, at least *lively Figures* of the state of a *glorified Body*? but it is evident by the description, that they had extension of parts, else what should shining Garments do upon what is unextended, and what glory can issue from a single Mathematical point as I may so call it? And in that they were on Mount *Tabor* together, it is manifest they had a connexion with or dependency on *Place*, nor did exist without being in some *ubi*. And that the glorified Body of Christ is in Heaven not on Earth, is plain from *Act.* 3. 21. And touching his Body he rose in, and therefore was his Resurrection-Body, *Matt.* 28. 6. the Angel says, *He is not here, for he is risen*; which had been a mere *Non sequitur*, if his Body could have been in more places than one at once, which property the *Papist represented* gives it upon account of *Transubstantiation*. And for as much as the *Transubstantiated* Bread and the Body of Christ is one and the same *Individual* Body, and that this that is once Christ's Body never perishes, it is evident, that the Body he rose in, being one and the same Body with the *Transubstantiated* Bread, must have the capacity by this *supernatural manner of Existence* above described, to be in more places than one at once, which is a perfect contradiction to the Angels reasoning: *He is not here, for he is risen*, and gone hence. For according to this *supernatural manner of Existence*, which they suppose in Christ's Body upon the account of *Transubstantiation*, he might be both there and gone thence at once.

3. The Second Instance of this *supernatural manner of existence* of a Body, is Christ's Body born without the least violation of his Mothers Virginal Integrity, which is such a secret as the Scripture has not revealed, nor any sufficient Authority assured us of: The

Mother

Mother of Christ still continuing a Virgin, because she had nothing to do with any *man*, though that which was conceived in her by the overshadowing of the Holy Ghost came out of her Womb in the same circumstances there, that other humane Births do. But suppose the Body of Christ pass'd the wicket of the Womb without opening it, as the Sun-beams pass through a Crystal or Glass, does this import that his Body is either *Independent* of *Place*, or is devoid of *Extension*, or *whole* in every *Part*? surely no, no more than that light that passes through the pores of the Crystal: so that there is nothing repugnant to the nature of a Body in all this. No *Non-extension*, no *Independency* of *Place*, no *penetration* of corporeal *Dimensions*, nor any being *whole in every part*.

4. The Third Instance is *Christ's rising* out of the Sepulcher *without removing the Stone*. But this Instance may very justly be rejected, it disagreeing with the very History of the *Resurrection*, which tells us the *Stone was removed*, Matt. 28. 2. *And behold there was a great Earthquake, for the Angel descended from Heaven, and rolled back the Stone from the door, and sate upon it.* Wherefore we see the Stone was removed. Nor can I imagine why this should make a third Instance, *viz.* Christ's Body passing out of the Sepulcher, the Stone unremoved from the door thereof, unless from an heedless reflection on the fore-going verse (where *Mary Magdalen* and the other *Mary* are said to go to see the Sepulcher) and connecting it to an ill grounded sense with what follows in the second verse, *And behold there was a great Earthquake*; as if it were implyed that the Earthquake and the rolling away the Stone were at that very time that these two Women went to see the Sepulcher, and Christ having risen before, that it would follow that he rose before the Stone of

the Sepulcher was removed; but this is a mistake. For agreeably to *Vatablus* his Gloss (who for *erat* [*& ecce erat terræ motus magnus*] puts *fuerat*, and for *descendit, descenderat*, and for *devolvit lapidem, devolverat*) which implies the thing done before these Women came to the Sepulcher; it is manifest out of the other Evangelists that the matter was altogether so; for *Mark* 16. 2. it is said of the two abovesaid parties, That very early in the morning, the first day of the week, they came unto the Sepulcher at the rising of the Sun, and they said among themselves, Who shall roll us away the Stone from the door of the Sepulcher? and when they looked they saw the Stone was rolled away, *&c.* And it is expresly said in *Luke*, That they found the Stone rolled away from the Sepulcher. And the like is recorded in St *John*, ch. 20. So that it is a plain case, the Stone was rolled away before their going to the Sepulcher.

What time therefore can we imagine more likely of this rolling away the Stone and terrible Earthquake, than at the very *Resurrection* of Christ, who rose in this awful terrour to the Keepers, the Earth quaking, and the two Glorious Angels officiously opening the stony door of the Sepulcher, that the King of glory might pass out, without any further needless or useless Miracle, such as he ever declined in his life time, before his Death and Resurrection? Wherefore this third Instance, it is plain, cannot with any shew be accommodated to the present case, it being raised out of a mere mistake of the Story.

5. The Fourth and last Instance is, *Christ's entring amongst his Disciples, the doors being shut*, recorded *John* 20. 19, and 26. there the Disciples are said to be gathered together privately or secretly for fear of the *Jews*, for which cause they lockt or bolted the doors with-

with-infide, that no man might fuddenly come upon them. But while they were in this privacy or clofeneſs, Chriſt, notwithſtanding, *ſuddenly* prefented himſelf in the midſt of them, for all this clofeneſs or ſecrecy, and not without a Miracle, fuppofing himſelf or ſome miniſtring Angel to unlock or unbolt the door fuddenly, and ſoftly, *ſine ſtrepitu*, which upon this account would be more likely, in that if he had come in, the doors being ſtill ſhut, that might have ſeemed as great an Argument to *Thomas* that he was a *Spirit*, as the feeling his Hands and Side that he was *no Spirit*. Wherefore, I conceive, it is no fufficiently firm Hypotheſis, that Chriſt entred among his Diſciples, the doors in the mean time, at his very entrance, remaining ſhut. But fuppofe they were ſo, this will not prove his Body *devoid* of *Extenſion*, to be *independent* of *Place*, and *whole in every part*, more than his paſſing the wicket of the Womb, like light through Cryſtal, did argue the ſame in the ſecond Inſtance. But the truth of the bufineſs will then be this, That he being then in his *Reſurrection-body* (even that wherewith he was to aſcend into Heaven, which yet he kept in its *Terreſtrial* Modification, and Organization, for thoſe ſervices it was to do amongſt his Diſciples while he converſed with them after his Reſurrection upon Earth; as he made uſe of it in a particular manner to St *Thomas*) he had a Power to modifie it into what Confiſtencies he pleaſed, Aerial, Ætherial, or Cœleſtial, it remaining ſtill that *Individual* Body; that was crucified. This therefore might eafily paſs through the very Pores of the door, and much more eafily betwixt the door and the ſidepoſts there, without any inconvenience more than to other Spiritual Bodies. For the *Reſurrection-body* is an Heavenly and Spiritual Body, as St *Paul* himſelf expreſly declares.

But

But yet as truly a Body as any Body elſe; that is, it hath *impenetrable Trinal Dimenſion*, is not without *Place* or *Ubiety*, nor *whole* in *every part*. This very Story demonſtrates all this, That his Body is not *without Place:* For it ſtood in the midſt of the Room amongſt his Diſciples. Nor the *whole in every part*; For here is diſtinct mention of Chriſt's Hand and his Side, as elſewhere of his Fleſh and Bones, *Luke* 24. 26. which would be all confounded, if every part were in every part. . And if there be theſe diſtinct parts, then certainly his Body hath *Extenſion*; and this ingeniouſly excogitated Diſtinction of the *Natural* and *Supernatural Manner of Exiſtence* of a Body, can by no means cover the groſs Repugnancies, which are neceſſarily imply'd in the Doctrine of *Tranſubſtantiation.*

6. A Doctrine raiſed from the *literal* ſenſe of thoſe Words [This is my Body] which *literal* ſenſe if we were tyed to, it would alſo follow that that which Chriſt gave to his Diſciples was as well *Real Bread* as his *Real Body:* [This] plainly referring to what he took, what he bleſſed, and what he gave, which was *Bread*, and of *this* he ſays, *This is my Body*. Wherefore adhering to the *literal* ſenſe, it would be both *Real Bread* and the *Real Body* of Chriſt at once. But this, as being a Repugnancy, as was noted above, and Contradiction to the known inviolable and immutable Laws of *Logick* and humane Reaſon, is juſtly rejected by the Church of *Rome*, for this very Reaſon, that it implies a Contradiction, that one and the ſame Body ſhould be *Bread* and the *Real Body* of Chriſt at once. Wherefore *Tranſubſtantiation* containing, as has been proved, ſo many of ſuch Contradictions, every jot as repugnant to the inviolable and immutable Laws of *Logick*, or humane

Reaſon

Reason (that unextinguishable Lamp of the Lord in the Soul of man) as this of the same Body being *Real Bread* and the *Real Body* of Christ at once: And there being no *Salvo* for these harsh Contradictions, but the pretence of a *Supernatural Manner of Existence* of a Body, which God is supposed to give to the Bread transubstantiated into the Body of Christ, that is, into the very *Individual* Body of Christ, they being supposed by *Transubstantiation* to become one and the same Body; I say this neat distinction of a *Supernatural Manner of Existing* being plainly demonstrated (so as it is by the *Papist Represented*, explained) not to be a mere *Supernatural Manner of Existence*, with which the *Being* of a *Body* would yet consist, but a Counter-essential, Asystatal, and Repugnant manner of Existence, inconsistent with the *Being* of a *Body*; and none of the Instances that are produced as Pledges of the truth of the Notion or Assertion at all reaching the present Case, it is manifest, that though there be a Real Presence of Christ's Body and Bloud in the Celebration of the Holy Eucharist, acknowledged as well by the Reformed as the Pontifician Party, that it is impossible that Transubstantiation, which the Papist represented here declares, should be the true mode thereof.

CHAP. V.

1. *The Author's excuse for his civility to the Papist Represented, that he shews him that the Road he is in is not the way of Truth touching the mode of the Real Presence.* 2. *That the Bishop of* Meaux *makes the Real Presence the common Doctrine of all the Churches*

as well Reformed as Un-reformed, and that it is acknowledged to be the Doctrine of the Church of England, though she is so wise and so modest as not to define the mode thereof. 3. The sincere Piety of our Predecessors in believing the Real Presence, and their unfortunateness afterwards in determining the mode by Transubstantiation or Consubstantiation.

1. AND therefore the *Papist Represented*, being in so palpable a mistake, and by keeping to the *literal sense* having so apparently wandred from the path of Truth, I hope my thus industriously and carefully advertizing him thereof for his own good, will be no otherwise interpreted than an Act of Humanity or common Civility, if not of indispensable Christianity, thus of my own accord, though not *Roganti*, yet *Erranti comiter monstrare viam*, or at least to assure him that this of *Transubstantiation* is not the right Road to the due understanding of the manner or mode of the Real Presence of the Body and Bloud of Christ in the Celebration of the Holy Eucharist.

2. Which Opinion of the Real Presence the Bishop of *Meaux* declares to be the Doctrine of all the Churches as well Reformed as Unreformed; as I must confess I have been of that perswasion (ever since I writ my Mystery of Godliness) that it is the Doctrine of the Church of *England*, and that the Doctrine is true. And this I remember I heard from a near Relation of mine when I was a Youth, a Reverend Dignitary of the Church of *England*, and that often, *viz.* That our Church was for the *Real Presence*, but for the manner thereof, if asked, he would answer, *Rem scimus, Modum nescimus*, We know the *thing*, but the *mode* or manner thereof we know not.

And

And the assurance we have of the thing is from the common suffrage of the ancient Fathers, such as the above-cited place of our Homilies glances at, and from the Scripture it self, which impressed that Notion on the minds of our Pious Predecessors in the Church of God.

3. For I do verily believe, that out of mere Devotion and sincere Piety, and out of a Reverend esteem they had of the Solemnity of the Eucharist, they embraced this Doctrine as well as broached it at the first. And if they had kept to the profession of it in general, without running into *Transubstantiation* or *Consubstantiation*, and had defined no further than the plain Scriptural Text in the sixth of St. *John* and the Suffrages of the Primitive Fathers had warranted them, *viz.* That there was a twofold Body and Bloud of Christ, the one *Natural*, the other *Spiritual* or *Divine*, which we do really receive in the Holy Communion (within which limits I shall confine my self here without venturing into any farther curiosities) it had been more for the Peace and Honour of the Christian Church, and it might have prevented much scandal to them without, and much Cruelty and Persecution amongst our selves: The History of which is very horrid even to think of. But though there have been these Mistakes in declaring the Mode, yet the thing it self is not therefore to be abandoned, it being so great a Motive for a Reverend approaching the Lord's Table, and duly celebrating the Solemnity of the Holy Eucharist. Nor can we, as I humbly conceive, relinquish this Doctrine of the Real Presence of the Body and Bloud of Christ, without the declining the most *easie* and *natural* sense of the Holy Scripture, as it stands written in the sixth Chapter of St. *John*.

CHAP. VI.

1. Gratian *his distinction of the Flesh and Blood of Christ into* Spiritual *or* Divine, *and into that* Flesh *that hung on the Cross, and that Blood let out by the Lance of the Souldier.* 2. *The same confirmed out of* S. Austin, *who makes the* Body *and* Blood *of* Christ *to be partaken of in* Baptism, *and also from S.* Paul *and* Philo. 3. *Other Citations out of* Philo *touching the* Divine Logos *agreeable with what* Christ *says of himself in his Discourse* John 6. *And out of which it further appears that the Antient Fathers ate the same Food that we, the Divine Body of Christ, but not that which hung on the Cross.* 4. *A strong Confirmation out of what has been produced, that* Gratian *his distinction is true.* 5. *The first Argument from our Saviour's Discourse, That he meant not his Flesh that hung on the Cross, because he says, that he that eats it has Eternal Life in him.* 6. *The second, because his Flesh and Blood is the Object of his Discourse, not the Manner of eating and drinking them.* 7. *The third, because of his answer to his murmuring Disciples, which removes his Natural Body far from them, and plainly tells them,* The Flesh profiteth nothing. 8. Gratian's *distinction no novel Doctrine.*

1. OUT of which sixth Chapter of S*t* *John*, that is manifest which a Member of the *Roman* Church herself, has declared; an eminent *Canonist* of theirs, *Gratian*, in [*Canon dupliciter*] as it is cited by *Philippus Mornæus*, lib. 4. *De Eucharistiâ*, Cap. 8. *Dupliciter intelligitur Caro Christi, & Sanguis :* vel Spiritualis *illa atque* Divina *de quâ ipse dicit,* Caro mea verè
est

Chap. VI.   *the Real Presence.*

est Cibus, & Sanguis meus verè est Potus, & nisi manducaveritis Carnem meam, & biberitis Sanguinem meum, non habebitis Vitam Æternam; *vel caro quæ* Crucifixa *est, & sanguis qui militis* effusus est *lanceâ*. I the rather take notice of this Passage, because he makes use of the very Phrases which I used without consulting him in my Philosophical Hypothesis of the great Mystery of Regeneration, calling that Body or Flesh which Christ so copiously discourses of *John* 6. *Spiritual* or *Divine*, which he plainly distinguishes, as Christ himself there does, from that Body that hung on the Cross, and that Blood that was let out by the lance of the Souldier.

2. For we cannot be *Regenerate* out of these in Baptism, and yet in the same place S. *Augustine* says, We are partakers of the Body and Blood of Christ in *Baptism*; and therefore as *Terrestrial* Animals are not fed (as they say the *Chamæleon* is) of the Air, but by food of a *Terrestrial* Consistency, so our *Regeneration* being out of *spiritual* Principles, our *inward man* is also nourished by that Food that is *Spiritual* or *Divine*. And that is a marvellous passage of S. *Paul*, 1 *Cor.* 10. where he says, *The Fathers did all eat the same spiritual meat, and did all drink the same spiritual drink, for they drank of that spiritual Rock that followed them, and that Rock was Christ*, where S. *Austin*, *Anselm*, *Thomas Aquinas*, and others, as you may see in *Jacobus Capellus*, avouch, That the ancient Patriarchs ate the same Spiritual Food that we, which therefore must be the Flesh and Blood of Christ, in that sense Christ understands it in, *John* 6. And that passage of *Philo* (that *Grotius* notes on the same place) is worth our taking notice of, and that in two several Treatises of his he interprets the *Manna* of the Θεῖος Λόγος, the *Divine Logos*, which agrees hugely well with our

F 2   supposing

supposing that the Flesh and Blood of which our Saviour saith, it is *meat indeed*, and *drink indeed*, he speaks this as he is the *Eternal Logos*, to whom appertains the universal *Divine Body*, as being the Body of his Ζωή, *Life* or *Spirit*, as I have noted in my *Analytical* account of the forepart of the first Chapter of St *John*'s Gospel. See my *Scholia* at the end of my *Enchiridium Ethicum*.

3. And it is marvellously applicable to our purpose what *Philo* says on that Passage of *Deuteronomy*, Chap. 32. ver. 5. *He made him to suck Honey out of the Rock, and Oyl out of the Flinty Rock* (in his Περὶ τοῦ τὸ χεῖρον τῷ κρείτλονι φιλεῖν ἐπιτίθεσθαι) where he says the Rock signifies ἢ στερράν κ̀ ἀδιάκοπτον σοφίαν Θεοῦ. *The solid, steady and infrangible Wisdom of God*; implying the *Immutableness* and Unalterableness of the Natures, Properties, and Respects of the *Idea's* of things in the *Divine* Intellect, The τὰ ἀεὶ ταυτὰ κ̀ ὡσαύτως ἔχοντα, not to be changed or violated for any superstitious purposes whatsoever, as I have intimated before. Wherefore as St *Paul* calls *Christ*, who is the *Eternal Logos*, a Rock, so does *Philo*, by saying, that Rock *Moses* mentions in his Song is the *steady, solid and infrangible Wisdom of God*. Which therefore is that *Essential* Wisdom, the same that the *Divine Logos*, or second *Hypostasis* of the Trinity.

And not many lines after in the same Treatise, the Lawgiver, says he, ἢ πέτραν ταύτην καλεῖ μάννα ἢ πρεσβύτατον τῶν ὄντων, λόγον θεῖον, calls this Rock Manna *the Divine* Logos *that was before all Beings*, and without whom nothing was made that was made, as St *John* testifies. And in his [Περὶ τοῦ τίς ὁ τῶν θείων πραγμάτων κληρονόμος.] speaking of *Israel*, which he would have signifie one that sees God: *He*, says he, *lifting up his Eyes to Heaven sees, and thence receives*,

Chap. VI. *the* Real Presence.

ceives, (τὸ μάννα τ̈ Θεῖον λόγον τ̈ οὐράνιον. τ̈ φιλοθεάμενω ψυχῆς ἄφθαρτον τροφὴν) *the Manna, the Divine Logos, the Heavenly incorruptible Food of the Soul devoted to Holy Speculation.* Which Passages I could not forbear to produce, they having so great an Affinity with that which our Saviour professes of *himself*, that he is this *Bread from Heaven*, the *true Manna*, and *incorruptible Food* of the *Soul*, whereby she is nourished to *Eternal Life*, *John* 6. Out of all which may be more easily understood how the Fathers did all eat the same Spiritual Meat, and drink the same Spiritual Drink, which cannot well be conceived but of such a *Divine Body* and *Bloud of Christ*, as is universal, not restrained to his *particular* humane Nature, but belonging to him as he is the Eternal *Logos*, in whom is the Ζωὴ *Life* or *Spirit*, which goeth along with the Divine Body of this Life or Spirit of Christ, and consequently is rightly called his *Body*. Which being the necessary Principles of *Regeneration* (for *ex eisdem nutrimur ex quibus constamus*) and there being no *Salvation* without *Regeneration*, and no *Regeneration* continued and advanced without *congenerous* Food; we must necessarily conclude with Saint *Paul*, that, *The Fathers all ate the same Spiritual Meat, and drank all the same Spiritual Drink*, Water, Honey, Oyl out of the same *Rock*, Christ, the *Eternal* Word or *Logos*. And certainly that Body and Bloud of Christ out of which the Fathers were *Regenerate*, and by which they were *fed*, cannot be the very Body and Bloud of Christ which hung on the Cross, and whose Bloud was there let out by the Lance of the Souldier that pierced his side: and therefore there was a Body and Bloud of Christ before he was incarnate, for the Regenerate Souls of the antient People of the *Jews* to feed upon, belonging to him as

he

he is the Eternal *Logos*; in whom is the Life and that Spirit of which it is said, That which is born of the Flesh is Flesh, and that which is born of the Spirit is Spirit. Which things are more fully treated of in Παλιγγενεσία, or a Philosophical Hypothesis touching the great Mystery of Regeneration.

4. Wherefore there is all the Reason in the World, if not plain Necessity to admit, what we cited out of *Gratian* that famous *Canonist* of the Church of *Rome*, That we are to understand that there is a *twofold Flesh and Bloud* of *Christ*, either that *Spiritual* and *Divine Flesh*, of which he himself says, *My Flesh is Meat indeed, and my Bloud is Drink indeed*, and, *Unless you eat my Flesh, and drink my Bloud, ye shall not have Everlasting Life* ; Or *that Flesh* which was *crucified*, and *that Bloud* that was let out of his side by the *Lance of the Souldier*, which we shall now endeavour briefly to demonstrate out of that Discourse of our Saviour in the sixth of S. *John*.

5. First then, That the Flesh of Christ that hung once on the Cross, and into which the *Bread* of the *Romanists* is supposed to be *Transubstantiated* in the Sacrament of our Lord's Supper, is not the Flesh here meant, is plain from what is said thereof in this sixth Chapter of S. *John*, ver. 54. *Whoso eateth my Flesh and drinketh my Bloud hath Eternal Life.* But every one that eateth the Bread transubstantiated into the Body of Christ, that once hung upon the Cross, in the *Roman* Communion, has not Eternal Life in him. Nay if that Souldier that pierced our Saviour's Side, and let out his Bloud with his Lance, had drunk also thereof, and cut some piece of his Flesh from his Body and eaten it, is any one so fond as to think, that he thereby would have been made Partaker of Eternal Life ? But if Christ meant that Body

or

or Flesh of his and not some other that is rightly also called his Flesh or Body, it would follow, that that Souldier by doing that savage and inhumane act, would have obtained Everlasting Life. Wherefore it is plain from hence, that there is *another* Body or Flesh of Christ, and *another* Bloud, distinct from that Bloud that was shed on the Cross, and from that Body that hung there, which our Saviour aims at in his Discourse.

6. Secondly, It is plain that our Saviour's Discourse in that Chapter (he passing from that *temporal* Food which he had lately procured for the multitude, to a *Spiritual* and *Eternal*) has for its Object or Subject not the *Manner* or Way of receiving his Body and Bloud, as if it were meant of that very Flesh and Bloud on the Cross, but that it was to be received in a *Spiritual Manner*, which Interpreters, several of them, drive at; but the Object of his Discourse is his *very Flesh* and *Bloud it self*, to be taken (as the Fish and Loaves were wherewith he lately fed them), or it is *himself* in *reference* to this *Flesh* and *Bloud* which belongs to him as he is the *Eternal Word*, and in this sense he says, *He is the Bread of God that cometh down from Heaven, and giveth Life to the World*, ver. 33. And ver. 48. Ἐγώ εἰμι ὁ ἄρτος τῆς Ζωῆς, *I am the Bread of Life*; and speaking of the *Manna* he presently adds, *Your Fathers ate Manna, and yet died*, viz. the natural Death, the natural *Manna* being no Preservative against the natural Death. And ver. 51. Ἐγώ εἰμι ὁ ἄρτος ὁ ζῶν, as before he called himself ὁ ἄρτος τῆς Ζωῆς. For in him is the Ζωή (*John* 1.) or *Life* and *Spirit*, and this *Spirit* or *Life* in the *Divine Body*. I am the living Bread coming down from Heaven (as the Manna is said to do, and to which *Philo* compares the *Divine* Logos) *if any one eat of this Bread he shall*

shall live for ever. He speaks not of the *manner* of eating of it, but of the *Bread it self* to be eaten, and yet immediately thereupon he calls *this Bread* his *Flesh*, which he says, *he will give for the Life of the World,* that is, to the end that they may be enlivened thereby, he thus communicating to them his *Divine* Body and Spirit together. And then presently upon the *Jews* striving amongst themselves and saying, How can this man give us his flesh to eat? (the reason whereof was because they took him to be a *meer* man, and thought that Christ himself understood it of his *humane Flesh*) he affirms with greater earnestness and vehemency, *Verily, verily, I say unto you, unless ye eat the Flesh of the Son of Man (viz.* of the *Messias,* who is the *Logos* incarnate) *and drink his Blood, ye have no Life in you. Whoso eateth my Flesh, and drinketh my Blood, hath Eternal Life, and I will raise him up at the last day. For my Flesh is meat indeed, and my Blood is drink indeed.* And so all along to the very end of his Discourse, he speaks of a *real eating his Flesh,* and *drinking his Blood,* not of the *Manner* of eating, as if it never came nigh them, but only they *thought* of *Flesh* and *Blood* God knows how far distant from them, and so ate the *humane* Flesh of Christ by meer thinking of it, and drank his Blood after the same *imaginary* Manner, which would I think, be a very *dilute* and *frigid* sense of such high and fervid Asseverations of our Saviour, if the Mystery reached no farther than so.

7. But Thirdly and lastly, That it does reach further than so, is exceeding evident from what our Saviour utters upon his Disciples being scandalized at this strange Discourse of his, *ver.* 61. *When Jesus knew in himself, that his Disciples murmured at it, he said unto them, Does this offend you? What if you shall see the Son of man ascending where he was before?* which he must

must needs underſtand of his *particular* viſible Body which he bore about with him, and which his humane Soul did actuate, and which was appropriated to his *humane* nature, which is *finite* and circumſcribed. It is an *Elliptical* ſpeech of his, but thus naturally to be ſupplyed, as I have alſo noted above, as if he ſuppreſſed by an *Apoſiopeſis* this *objurgatory* ſenſe inſinuated thereby. Will you then imagine ſo *groſly* as if I underſtood it of this very Fleſh I bear about with me, when as this *particular body* of mine after my *Aſcenſion* into Heaven will be removed at a *vaſt diſtance* from you? I tell you, *this Fleſh of mine*, as to this purpoſe I have all this time driven at, *profiteth nothing*, you cannot feed of it at ſuch a diſtance if it were to be fed on.

The Text runs thus, *verſ.* 63. τὸ πνεῦμά ἐςι τὸ ζωοποιοῦν, *it is that quickening ſpirit* I aim at in my diſcourſe, that *Divine* or *Spiritual Body* of mine. ἡ σὰρξ ὐκ ὠφελεῖ ὐδέν, *that Fleſh*, which you underſtand and are ſo ſcandalized at the eating thereof, *profiteth nothing* as to this purpoſe, nor has the Blood taken in your ſenſe any thing to do here. *The words that I ſpeak unto you they are ſpirit and they are life.* The Object of thoſe words ſpoken is my *Spiritual Body* and *Blood*, not as I am a *Man*, but the *Eternal Word*, the Divine *Logos*, which contains in it the Ζωὴ or *Spirit*, and my *Divine Body univerſal*, that belongs to that my *Life* or *Spirit*. This is the true Myſtery of the Matter, for by theſe two things aſſerted by our Saviour, 1. That we are to eat his Fleſh and drink his Blood as we hope ever to have Eternal Life. 2. And his declaring his Fleſh profiteth nothing, it is manifeſt that that diſtinction of *Gratian* is true, which he ſeems to have taken out of S. *Hierom* or ſome other ancient Father, who tells us the Fleſh and Blood of

Chriſt

Christ is twofold, the one *natural* and which he bore about with him and hung once on the Cross, the other *Spiritual* and *Divine*, which we may really eat and drink, that is, *really receive* and draw in at the Celebrating the Holy *Eucharist* by a sincere, fervid and devotional Faith. And consequently there is a *Real Presence* of the Body and Blood of Christ in partaking of the Lord's Supper, whereby our Souls are nourished to Eternal Life.

And in that, he says, his *natural* Flesh profiteth nothing to this purpose (for it cannot be said that it profiteth nothing at all, since in vertue of the *Crucifixion* of that *Flesh*, and *Effusion* of that *Blood* on the Cross, we have the remission of our Sins) Christ plainly infers that he has (which cannot be well understood but as he is the *Eternal Logos*) *another Flesh*, viz. that *Spiritual* and *Divine Flesh*, which is mainly profitable for *this* purpose, for the maintaining, perfecting and renewing the *inward man*, that he may attain to his due growth in Christ.

And lastly, How can Christ say, his Flesh that was Crucified on the Cross *profiteth nothing*, when by being *meditated upon* at the Solemnity of the Holy Eucharist, and also at other times, it may serve to kindle and inflame our Love and Devotion towards him, and so urge us to greater degrees of *Repentance* and *Mortification*, and *serious Holiness*; it therefore being useful and profitable for *all this*, I say, why does he then affirm *it profiteth nothing*, but that he does on purpose advertise us that it profiteth nothing *as to the present case* he has spoke to all this while, *viz.* to be the *real meat* and *food* of the *inward man*, and to be *really received* into him, to maintain and encrease those *Divine* Principles in him out of which he is *regenerated*? This his *particular Flesh* and *Blood*, that
hung

hung on the Cross, cannot be profitable for, nor can be come *at*, at such a distance, to be taken in and received; which therefore plainly implies *those other*, which were mentioned above out of *Gratian* (the *Divine* or *Spiritual* Flesh and Bloud of Christ only) to be properly useful to this purpose.

8. And for this Divine and Spiritual Flesh and Bloud of our Saviour, distinguished from his natural; besides St. *Hierome*, you have also the Suffrage of *Clemens Alexandrinus*, in his *Pædagogus*, lib. 2. cap. 2. Διττὸν ᾖ τὸ αἷμα τȣ̃ κυρίȣ, τὸ μὲν γάρ ἐςιν αὐτȣ̃ σαρκικὸν ᾧ τ̃ φθορᾶς λελυτρώμεθα, τὸ ᾖ πνȣματικὸν, τȣτέςιν ᾧ κεχρείσμεθα. The Bloud of our Lord is twofold, the one carnal, by which we are redeemed from corruption; the other Spiritual wherewith we are anointed, and by virtue of drinking thereof we attain to incorruption. Καὶ τȣ̃τ' ἔςι πιεῖν τὸ αἷμα τȣ̃ Ἰησȣ̃ τ̃ κυριακῆς μεταλαβεῖν ἀφθαρσίαι. And as he makes the Bloud of our Lord twofold, so we may be sure he makes his Body or Flesh, because his Mystical Body and Bloud go together. According to that which Mr *Pelling* in his Pious and Learned Discourse of the Sacrament, quotes out of S. *Ambrose*, who, says he, speaking of that Body which is received in the Eucharist, calls it the spiritual Body of Christ, the Body of a Divine Spirit; and he does confidently affirm of all the Antients who have either purposely interpreted, or occasionally quoted the Words of Christ, in the sixth of S. *John*, touching the eating his Flesh and drinking his Bloud, that they all understand him to speak of a Spiritual Flesh and Bloud, distinct not only from the Substance of the Holy Elements, but also from that natural Body of Christ which he took of the Substance of the Holy Virgin, *pag.* 233. So little Novelty is there in this distinction of the

Body and Bloud of Chriſt into Natural, and Spiritual or Divine.

CHAP. VII.

1. *An Apology for being thus operoſe and copious in inculcating the preſent Point from the uſefulneſs thereof.* 2. *The firſt uſefulneſs in that it defeats* Monſieur de Meaux *his* Stratagem *to reduce us to* Tranſubſtantiation, *as if no* Real Preſence *without it.* 3. *The ſecond uſefulneſs, for the rectifying the Notion of* Conſubſtantiation. 4. *The third for more fully underſtanding the Myſtery of the* Euchariſt, *with Applications of it to ſeveral Paſſages in our* Communion-Service. 5. *The fourth for a very eaſie and natural Interpretation of certain Paſſages in our* Church-Catechiſm. 6. *The priviledge of the* faithful Receiver, *and of what great noment the Celebration of the* Euchariſt *is.* 7. *The laſt uſefulneſs in ſolidly reconciling the* Rubrick *at the end of the* Communion-Service, *with that noted Paſſage in our* Church-Catechiſm.

1. THE Reader may haply think I have been over operoſe and copious in inculcating this Diſtinction of *Gratian*'s, touching the Body and Bloud of Chriſt in the Holy *Euchariſt*: But the great uſefulneſs thereof, I hope, may apologize for this my extraordinary diligence and induſtry. For the Notion being both true and unexceptionable, and not at all claſhing, ſo far as I can diſcern, with either the *Holy Scripture*, or *right Reaſon* and *ſolid Philoſophy*, to ſay nothing of the Suffrage of the Primitive

tive Fathers, but rather very agreeable and consentaneous to them all; and also having, as I said, its weighty usefulness, it was a Point, I thought, that was worth my so seriously insisting upon; and as I have hitherto endeavoured faithfully to set out the *Truth* thereof, I shall now, though more briefly, intimate its *Usefulness*.

2. And the first Usefulness is this, Whereas that Reverend Prelate the Bishop of *Meaux* tugs so hard to pull back again the Reformed Churches to the Communion of the Church of *Rome*, by this *Concession*, or rather *Profession* of theirs, that there is a *Real Presence* of the Body and Bloud of Christ at the Celebration of the *Eucharist*, to be received by the *faithful*, and that therefore they must return to the Doctrine of *Transubstantiation*, as if there were no other Mode of a *Real Presence* to be conceived but it: the force of this Inference is plainly taken away, by this Distinction that *Gratian*, one of their own Church, hath luckily hit upon, or rather taken out of some antient Father, and is more fully made out in this Discourse, that there is a *Spiritual* and *Divine Body* of Christ, distinct from that *particular* Body of his that hung on the Cross, which the faithful partake of in the Lord's Supper. Whence it is plain there is no need of *Transubstantiation*, which is incumbred with such abundance of *Impossibilities* and Contradictions.

3. Secondly, This Notion of ours is hugely serviceable for the rectifying of the Doctrine of *Consubstantiation* in the *Lutheran* Church, who are for an *Ubiquity* of the *particular* Body of Christ that hung on the Cross, which assuredly is a grand Mistake. But I believe in the Authors thereof there was a kind of *Parturiency*, and more confused *Divination* of that

Truth,

Truth, which we have so much insisted upon, and their Mistake consists only in this, that they attributed to the *particular* Body of Christ, which belongs to his *restrained* and circumscribed *humane* Nature, that which truly and only belongs to his *Divine Body*, as he is the *Eternal Logos*, in whom is the *Zōn*, the *Life* or *Spirit* of the *Logos*, to which Spirit of *his* this Body belongs, and therefore is rightly called *his Body*, as appertaining to *his* Spirit. For this Body, this *Divine* and *Spiritual* Flesh, as *Gratian* calls it, is every where present, though not to be received as the Food of the *Inward man*, but only by the *Faithful* and *Regenerate*; so that according to this Notion there may be a *Consubstantiation* rightly interpreted, that is a *Compresentiation*, or rather *Compresentiality* of both the *Real Bread* and *Wine*, and the *Real Body and Bloud of Christ* at once; so that they both may be *really* and *indeed* received by all true Believers. And *Lutheranism* in this Point thus candidly interpreted, will prove a sound and unexceptionable *Doctrine*. And I charitably believe, the first Authors of it, if they had fully understood their own meaning, meant no more than so. And I wish I had as much reason to believe that the *Pontificians* meant no more by their *Transubstantiation*, but a *firm* and *fast* hold of the *Real Presence*. I hope the most ingenuous of them at this time of the day mean no more than so, *viz*. That they are as well assured of the *Real Presence* of the Body and Bloud of Christ to be received in the Celebration of the *Eucharist*, as if the very Bread was turned into his Body, and the Wine into his Bloud by a miraculous *Transubstantiation*.

4. Thirdly, It is from this Notion or Distinction of the antient Fathers, as I hinted above, of the Body and Bloud of Christ into Natural and Spiritual or Divine,

CHAP. VII. *the Real Presence.* 47

Divine, that we have ever been well appointed to give a more full and distinct account of the nature of the Solemnity of the *Eucharist* as it is celebrated in our Church, it plainly comprizing these two things. The first the *Commemoration* of the *Death* of *Christ*, of the breaking his Body or Flesh, *viz.* the wounding thereof with Nails and Spears. The other, The partaking of the *Divine Body* and *Blood* of Christ, by which our *Inward Man* is nourished to Eternal Life: which our *eating* the *Bread* and *drinking* the *Wine* are Symbols of. Both which in our *Communion-Service* are plainly pointed at. The first fully, in the Exhortation to Communicants, where it is said, *And above all things you must give most humble and hearty thanks to God the Father, the Son, and the Holy Ghost, for the Redemption of the World by the* Death *and* Passion *of our Saviour Christ, both God and Man, who did humble himself even to the* Death *upon the Cross for us miserable sinners* —— And to the end we should always remember the exceeding great love of our Master and only Saviour Jesus Christ thus dying for us, and the innumerable benefits, which by his *precious Blood-shedding* he hath obtained to us, he has instituted and ordained Holy Mysteries as pledges of his Love, and for a continual remembrance of his *Death*. And in the Prayer of Consecration, the Celebration of the Eucharist is again said to be a *continued* or *perpetuated Commemoration* of Christ's *precious Death* till his coming again.

But now for our receiving the *Spiritual* and *Divine* Body and Blood of Christ, such passages as these seem to intimate it. In the *Exhortation* to the *Communicants*, it is there said, if with a true penitent heart and lively faith we receive this Holy Sacrament, then we *spiritually eat the flesh of Christ and drink his blood,*

blood, then we *dwell in Christ and Christ in us*, we are *one with Christ* and *Christ with us*. This passage plainly points to our Saviour's Discourse, *John* 6. *verf*. 56. where he says, *He that eateth my flesh and drinketh my blood, dwelleth in me and I in him*. And he thus dwelling in us, he enlivens us, we becoming *one* with *Christ* in a manner as the Soul and Body makes *one*, as it followeth in the next verse, *As the living father has sent me, and I live by the father, so he that eateth me shall live by me*, and so we become *one with Christ* and *Christ with us*, we living by Christ as he by his Father; that is to say, as Christ lives by his Father, so we live by the Spirit of Christ dwelling in us, *Rom.* 8. 11. which *Spirit* or *Life* of Chirst always implies the *Divine Body*. As he that is joined unto the Lord in this Body is one Spirit, 1 *Cor.* 6. 17. Now this Exhortation so plainly alluding to this passage of our Saviour's Discourse, which speaks not of his *particular* natural Flesh, but of that which is his *Spiritual* or *Divine* Flesh, it is plain that the genuine sense of the *Exhortation* in this place is, that we *really* though *spiritually* (that is by a fervent and devotional Faith) eat or *receive* the *real* Body and Blood of Christ, *viz.* that *Divine* and *Spiritual* Body and Blood of his above-mentioned. And this passage of our Saviour's Discourse is again alluded to in the Prayer immediately before the Prayer of *Consecration* in these words, "Grant us therefore, Gracious Lord, so to *eat the Flesh* of thy Dear Son Jesus Christ, and *to drink his Blood*, that our sinful Bodies may be made clean by his Body, and our Souls washed through his most precious Blood, and that we may evermore *dwell in him* and *he in us*, John 6. 56. And these two places so plainly alluding to our Saviour's Discourse in the sixth of St *John*, it is very easie and natural

to

to conceive, that what occurs in the *Thanksgiving* after our receiving the Sacrament, does sound to the same purpose. " Almighty and everlasting God, we most heartily thank thee for that thou dost vouchsafe to feed us who have duly received these Holy Mysteries, with the *Spiritual Food* of the most *Precious Body* and *Blood* of thy Son and our Saviour Jesus Christ——The words even of themselves do very naturally point at a *real* though *spiritual* partaking or *receiving* into us the Body and Blood of Christ, namely, of that Flesh and Blood which our Saviour discourses of, *John* 6. And therefore we may be much more assured that they do so, if we take notice, the sense is so back'd and strengthned by the other two Passages which do plainly relate to the Body, or Flesh and Blood Christ discourses of, in the sixth of St *John's* Gospel.

I will only add one Consideration more, and that is from the Title of our *Communion-Service*. Can there be any more likely reason why the Lord's Supper is called THE HOLY COMMUNION, than that it refers to that of St *Paul*, 1 Cor. 10. 16. *The Cup of Blessing which we bless, is it not the Communion of the Blood of Christ? The Bread which we break, is it not the Communion of the Body of Christ? Because there is one Bread, we being many are one Body. For we are all partakers of that one Bread.* Which is that Bread from Heaven, which our Saviour discourses of in the sixth of S. *John*. But the Words I have chiefly my Eye upon are those: The Cup being called κοινωνία τῦ αἵματ۰, the *Communion of the Blood*; and the Bread, κοινωνία τῦ σώματ۰, the *Communion of the Body* of Christ; and the word κοινωνία, in all likelyhood, having the same sense that it had, 2 *Pet.* 1. 4. in θείας κοινωνοὶ φύσεως, where we are said to be called to the *Participation*

cipation of the *Divine Nature,* Communion here in S. *Paul's* Epistle to the *Corinthians* must *naturally* imply our *real* receiving or *partaking* of the Body and Blood of Christ in the celebrating of this Holy Communion, and that by thus partaking of that *one* Divine Body and Blood of his, signified by the eating and drinking the Bread and Wine, we, though *many,* become *one Body*: not in a *Political Sense* only, but, if I may so speak, Divinely *natural,* we being made *all* Members of that *one* Universal *Divine Body* of Christ, as he is the Eternal *Logos,* and so becoming κοινωνοὶ ϑείας φύσεως, 2 *Pet.* 1. 4.

Wherefore, That Passage in St *Paul's* Epistle to the *Corinthians,* does marvellous-fully set out the Nature of that part of the Lord's Supper, that is distinguished from the *Commemoration* of his *Death,* and gives the most genuine Reason of its being called the *Holy Communion,* it implying the *real Communication of* that *one* Divine Body of Christ to the faithful, and their *real Union* thereby with Christ and with one another, which is a full and perfect Holy Communion indeed.

5. Fourthly, This Notion of the Fathers touching the *Spiritual* or *Divine* Body and Bloud of Christ, affords us a very easie and natural Interpretation of that Passage in our *Church-Catechism,* touching the Sacrament of the Lord's Supper, where to the Question, *What is the inward part, or thing signified?* It is answered, "The Body and Bloud of Christ which "are *verily* and *indeed* taken and received by the faith- "ful in the Lord's Supper. In the Answer to a former Question, *Why was the Sacrament of the Lord's Supper ordained?* it is answered, "For a continual "Remembrance of the Sacrifice of the *Death* of "Christ, and the *Benefits* received thereby. One eminent

minent benefit whereof is the *Remission of our sins* through the *Bloud* of Christ shed on the Cross, for without bloud there is no Remission; the *other* is the *feeding* of the *Regenerate* Soul, or *Inward man,* by the *Real,* but *Spiritual* or *Divine Body* and Bloud of Christ, which contains in it our thorough *Sanctification*, which is also a fruit or benefit of the Sacrifice of the *Death* of Christ, forasmuch as we had not been capable of Regeneration and of growth and degrees of Sanctification by the feeding on and *really* receiving the *Spiritual* and *Divine* Body of Christ, without our *Reconciliation* by his Bloudshed on the Cross, which our Church here calls the *Sacrifice* of the *Death* of Christ.

. Now as in this Answer there is contained that great Benefit of the *Remission of our sins* in the Bloud of Christ, and thereby of our *Reconciliation* to God; so in the Answer *mentioned before* is contained that singular Benefit of *perfecting* our *Sanctification* by the nourishing and corroborating our *inward man* by eating or partaking of the *Spiritual* or *Divine* Body and Bloud of our Saviour, which are *verily* and *indeed* taken and received by the faithful in the Lord's Supper.

. [Verily] that is to say, ἀληθῶς or ἀληθινῶς, *truly*, in counterdistinction to *Typically*, or Symbolically, the *Bread* and *Wine* being but *Types* or Symbols of this. Touching which in the Answer to the Question, *What are the Benefits whereof we are made Partakers thereby?* it is said, *The strengthening and refreshing our Souls by the Body and Bloud of Christ, as our Bodies are by the Bread and Wine,* viz. which are but *Types* of the *true*, spiritual or *Divine* Body and Bloud of Christ, but they have a very handsome Analogy the one to the other. But we proceed to the following words [And indeed] that is to say, ὄντως or τῷ ὄντι, reverâ, or *really*,

H 2 not

not as one sceptically would make us to profess, that this *real* participation of the Body and Bloud of Christ, has no *reality* any where but in our *phancy*, which we call *Faith*. To which sense the Translator of the *peaceable method for the re-uniting Protestants and Catholicks*, speaks in his *Preface* to his *Translation*. To which exception, this Notion of the Primitive Fathers, according to which our Communion-Service is framed, and our Homilies allude to, and we so much insist upon, is not liable. [By the Faithful] and that *only* by them, which Body and Bloud the *Faithful* do not receive by champing it with their Teeth, and swallowing it down their Throat; But by a fervid and living devotional *Faith* more than ordinarily kindled at the Celebrating the Holy Eucharist, they draw this D*ivine* and *Celestial* Food (the true *Manna* from Heaven) into their Hearts, whereby their *inward man* is fed and strengthened, and nourished up to Eternal Life, and so the *New Birth* getting growth daily, arrives at last to the due measure of the stature of Christ.

6. This is the Priviledge of the *faithful* Receiver. But for those that are devoid of this *true* and living *Faith*, though the *Divine* Body and Bloud of Christ is every where present to the faithful, yet they who are *unregenerate*, and consequently devoid of the Divine Life, are capable of no union therewith, nor of any growth or strength therefrom. But it is like the light shining into a *dead* man's eye, of which there is no *vital* effect. But for those who are *regenerate*, and consequently have a *real* hunger and thirst after the *Righteousness* of God, though the great Feast upon this Heavenly Food is more especially and copiosely injoyed in the Celebration of the Holy *Eucharist*, yet they may in some good measure draw it in day by day

day by Faith and Devotion, as without the *Presence* of the *Bread* and *Wine* we may at any time *devotionally* think of the Sacrifice of the Death of our Saviour. But certainly this solemn Institution of Celebrating his last Supper, being particularly and earnestly injoyn'd us by *Christ*, if we conscientiously observe the same, it will have a more than ordinary efficacy in us for the ends it was appointed.

7. Sixthly and lastly, as those words of the *Catechism* [the Body and Bloud of Christ which are *verily* and *indeed* taken and received, *&c.*] have, considered in themselves, a very easie and natural sense so explained, as we have according to the Analogy of the Doctrine of the Primitive Fathers and our Church's Homilies that allude to them, explained them; so do they not at all clash with those words of the *Rubrick* affixed at the end of the *Communion Service*, where it is affirmed, " That the Sacramental Bread " and Wine remain still in their very *natural* sub- " stances, and therefore may not be adored (for that " were Idolatry to be abhorred of all faithful Christi- " ans) and the *natural* Body and Bloud of our Savi- " our Christ are in *Heaven*, and *not here*, it being a- " gainst the *truth* of Christ's *Natural* Body to be at " one time in more places than one. There is, I say, in this no contradiction to what occurs in the *Catechism*, which affirms that there is a *Real Presence* of the Body and Bloud of Christ, which are *verily* and *indeed* taken and received by the Faithful in the Lord's Supper, though here a *Real Presence* is denied of the *natural* Body of Christ. But it is to be considered that this Affirmation and Negation is not of the same Body of Christ, and therefore can be no contradiction; and further to be observed, how the very *Rubrick* suggests to us this distinction of the *Na-*

tural

tural Body of Christ (which is appropriated to his *particular* Soul, and which hung on the Cross and was Crucified) and his *Divine* or *Spiritual* Body, the Body of the *Essential Life* or *Spirit* of the Eternal *Logos*, and therefore rightly termed the Body of the *Logos* incarnae, or of Christ.

And therefore when passages of the Ancient Fathers in the Primitive Times, before the degeneracy of the Church came in, may some of them favour a *Real Absence*, other a *Real Presence* of the Body and Blood of Christ, according as different places of the Scripture might occur to their minds touching this matter, the controversy might well be composed by distinguishing betwixt the *Natural* Body of Christ and his *Divine* or *Spiritual* Body; According to the former whereof is the *Real Absence*, according to the latter the *Real Presence* of Christ's Body and Blood, to be received by the Faithful in the Celebration of the Holy Eucharist.

CHAP. VIII.

1. *Monsieur* Maimbourg *so cunning and cautious as not to attempt to bring the Protestants to* Transubstantiation *by their common consent in the* Real Presence, *but by a more general* Maxime, *which, he says, we are all agreed in.* 2. *The aforesaid* Maxime *with the Explication thereof.* 3. Six Supposals *surmiz'd for the strengthening this Engine for the pulling the Protestants into the belief of* Transubstantiation. 4. *A* Counter-Engine *consisting of* sixteen common Notions, *in which, not only the Romanists and we, but all mankind are agreed in.* 5. *An Examination of the strength of*
Monsieur

Monsieur Maimbourg's *Engine, by recurring upon occasion to these* Common Notions; *The* first Prop *examined,* viz. *the Churches* Infallibility *by* assistance *of the* Spirit, *and discovered to be weak from the* Dissention *of Churches in matters of* Faith *in his sense.* 6. From *the promise of the Spirit being* conditional. 7. *And* from *the* Predictions *in the Prophetical Writings, of a general* Degeneracy *of the Church.* 8. *The Examination of the* second Prop, *that would have* Transubstantiation *believed upon the* Synodical *decision of a* fallible *Church.* 9. *The Examination of the* third Prop, *that would have the* Synodical *decision pass into an* Article *of* Faith. 10. *The* fourth Prop *examined by defining truly what* Heresy *and* Schism *is.* 11. *The* fifth Prop *further explained by Monsieur* Maimbourg, *in two Propositions.* 12. *An Answer to the two Propositions.*

1. I Have, I hope, by this time sufficiently proposed and confirmed both the Truth and Usefulness of the distinction of the Body and Blood of Christ (which occurs in the Primitive Fathers) into Natural, and Spiritual or Divine. From whence it may plainly appear to any pious and unprejudiced Reader, that the Inference of a *Transubstantiation* of the Bread and Wine into the *Real Body* and Blood of Christ, from a *Real Presence* of them in the Lord's Supper, is very weak and invalid. Which Monsieur *Maimbourg* (as well as the Bishop of *Meaux,* formerly Bishop of *Condom*) though he take special notice of in his *Peaceable Method, viz.* that this *Real Presence* of the Body and Blood of Christ in the Lord's Supper, is generally acknowledged by the Protestants, *Chap.* 3. whom he will have to hold, *That the Sacrament is not a Figure or empty Sign without Efficacy,* but they do maintain,

maintain, saith he, that it does communicate unto us in a most *real* and *effectual* Manner, the *Body* of Jesus Christ to be the *Food* of our Souls; And he will have Monsieur *Claud* himself acknowledge, that before this Novelty of *Transubstantiation* was introduced, every one believed that *Jesus Christ* is *present* in the *Sacrament*, that his Body and Blood are there *truly* received by the faithful; yet he is so wise and cautious as not to trust to the strength of this Engine for the pulling us back into a belief and profession of that incredible Hypothesis, but according to the Fineness of his wit, has spread a more large Net to catch us in and carry us captive, not only into this gross Errour of *Transubstantiation*, but into all other Errours which the Church of *Rome* has broached, or may hereafter broach and propose as *Articles of Faith*. And therefore it is a point worth our closest consideration.

2. His general *Maxim* is this, That that Church in which are found two Parties concerned, has ever had the power to determine all differences, and to declare that as *matter of Faith*, which before there was no obligation to believe, and that we are bound to acquiesce in her Decisions, under Penalty of being *Schismaticks*.

By the Church her declaring as *matter of Faith* (which seems to sound so harshly) he does not mean, That the Church has Authority to frame *New Articles of Faith*, (*pag.* 17.) but that She is to act according to a *Rule*, which is *Holy Scripture*, and *Tradition* truly and purely *Apostolical*, from which we have also received the Holy Scripture it self. And *(pag.* 18.*)* The Church never did make, and undoubtedly never will make any *New Articles* of *Faith*, since it is not in her power to define any thing but according to the *Word of God*, which she is always to consult with, as
with

with her *Oracle*, and the *Rule* she is bound to follow.

His meaning therefore must be this, That besides those plain and Universally known Articles of the Christian Faith, and acknowledged from the very beginning of Christianity, such as are comprised in the Apostles Creed, there have been, and may be other Articles of Faith more obscurely and uncertainly delivered in Scripture, which, until the Church in a lawful Synod or Council has determined the sense of those places of Scripture that appertain to the Controversie, men have no obligation to believe, but go for the present, for but uncertain and indifferent Opinions. But when once the true Church, in which the Parties differing in Opinion are, and her lawful *Representative* assisted by the Holy Ghost, (as is affirmed *Chap.* 2. *pag.* 28.) a *Canonical* Assembly, which alone has full Power and Sovereign Authority to say juridically (*Chap.* 4. *pag.* 27.) *It seemed good to the Holy Ghost and to us*, has given definitive Sentence touching the Controversie, that which before was but an *indifferent Opinion*, becomes now *Matter of Faith*, and is to be received as an *Article of Faith* by the Dissenting Party, upon penalty of being *Schismaticks* and *Hereticks*. This I conceive to be his precise meaning.

But the great Artifice of all is, that he will have this meaning of his to be the *general* Opinion also of the Protestant Churches. Who can, says he, *(page* 27.) question, but the Protestant Churches of *England, France, Germany,* and *Switzerland* and the *Low Countries* do hold as a Fundamental *Maxim*, that in such Controversies as do arise concerning Doctrine in Matters of Religion, the true Church of which the Dissenting Parties are Members, has full and sovereign power to declare according to the Word of God, *what is of Faith,* and that there is an Obligation of

I   standing

standing to her Decrees, under pain of being *Schifmaticks*? And *(page* 35.*)* I demand, faith he, nothing more for the prefent: I will content my felf with what themfelves do grant; That that Church of which the Parties contefting are Members, (be fhe *fallible* or *infallible*) has full power to decide Differences, and her Decrees do oblige under the Penalty of being *Schifmaticks*.

3. Now from this general *Maxim* granted, as he conceives, on both fides, and which he does chiefly endeavour to prove from the carriage of the Synod of *Dort*, toward the *Arminians* (all which things to repeat here would be too moliminous and inconfiftent with the Brevity I intend, a full Anfwer to Monfieur *Maimbourg*'s *Method* requiring fome more able Pen) he declining, I fay, all difpute touching the *Merit* of the Caufe, the point of *Tranfubftantiation*, he would hence draw us in, to the imbracing that Doctrine merely becaufe we were once of that Church that has *Synodically* determined for it, and confequently reconcile us to all the reft of the Errours of the Church of *Rome*. But that we may not fo eafily be taken in this *Net*, or pulled in by this *Engine*, we will firft examine the *Suppofals* that fupport the ftrength of it, or of which it does confift.

The firft and chiefeft whereof is, That fuch Synods to whofe definitive fentence he would have us ftand, are affifted by the Holy Ghoft.

The fecond, That whether they be or be not, we are to ftand to their determination.

The third, Whatever Matters of *Opinion* (as they are for the prefent but fuch) are decided by fuch a *Synod*, pafs into *Articles of Faith*.

The fourth, That thofe that will not clofe with thefe Decifions, be they what they will, they are
guilty

guilty of *Schism*, as being bound to assent.

The fifth, That these decisive Synods or Assemblies, are to decide according to the Rule of the Word of God.

The sixth and last, That both the Protestants and Papists are agreed in all these.

4. Now before I examine these *Particulars*, these *Supposals*, *Parts* or *Props* of his general *Maxim*, by which he would draw the Protestants again into the Church of *Rome*, and make them embrace *Transubstantiation*, and all other Superstitions and Errours which they have *Synodically* decided *for matters of Faith*: I will, following the very method of this shrewd Writer, propose not only *one* Maxime, but *several Maximes*, wherein both the *Romanists* and *We*, and indeed all Mankind are agreed, and which therefore I will, instead of *Maximes*, call *Common Notions*, in allusion to those of *Euclid*. And the first shall be this,

I. That which in it self is false, no declaring or saying it is true can make it true.

II. Whatever is plainly repugnant to what is true, is certainly false.

III. Whatever is false, can be no due Article of a true Faith or Religion.

IV. The Senses *rightly circumstantiated* are true Judges of their Object, whether such an Object be Earth, Air, Fire, or Water, Body or Spirit, and the like.

Besides that this is a *Common Notion* with all Mankind, the Incarnate Wisdom himself has given his suffrage for it, in his arguing with S[t] *Thomas*, *John* 20. *ver.* 27. *Then saith he to Thomas, Reach hither thy finger, and behold my hands, and reach hither thy hand and thrust it into my side, and be not faithless but believing.*

ving. What is this but the appealing to the truth of Senſe by our Saviour himſelf? And *Luke* 24. ver. 29. *Behold my hands and my feet that it is I my ſelf, handle me and ſee; for a Spirit has not fleſh and bones as ye ſee I have.* Here is an Appeal both to *Senſe* and *Reaſon* at once, and that about the *very Body* of Chriſt, touching which the great Controverſie is raiſed.

V. An Eſſence or Being that is *one*, ſo long as it remains ſo, as it is *diſtinct* from *others*, ſo it is *undividable* or inſeparable from *it ſelf*.

VI. The Whole is bigger than the Part, and the Part leſs than the Whole.

VII. In every Diviſion, though the Parts agree with the Whole, yet they diſagree amongſt themſelves. So that the Part *A*. is not the very Part *B*. nor the Part *B*. the very Part *C*. nor can each Part be truly and adequately the Whole by the foregoing Common Notion.

VIII. The *ſame* Body cannot be actually a *Cube* and a *Globe* at once, and there is the ſame reaſon of any other different Figures of a Body.

IX. No Revelation, the Revealing whereof, or the manner of the Revealing whereof is *repugnant* to the *Divine Attributes*, can be from God.

X. No *Tradition* of any ſuch Revelation can be true, for as much as the *Revelation* it ſelf is *impoſſible*.

XI. No Interpretation of any Divine Revelation that is repugnant to rightly circumſtantiated Senſe and pure and unprejudiced Reaſon, whether it be from a private or publick hand, can be any Inſpiration from God.

XII. No Body can be bigger and leſs than it ſelf at once.

XIII. That Individual Body that is already, nor ceaſeth to be, cannot be made while it is already exiſting.   XIV. One

XIV. *One* and the *same* Body cannot be both *present* with it self and many thousand miles *absent* from it self at once.

XV. One and the same Body cannot be shut up in a Box, and free to walk and run in the Fields, and to ascend into the very Heavens at the same time.

XVI. And lastly (to omit many other such self-evident Truths or *Common Notions*) it is impossible, that a man should swallow his whole Body, Head, Feet, Back, Belly, Arms, and Thighs, and Stomach it self, through his Mouth, down his Throat into his Stomach, that is, every whit of himself into one knows not what of himself, less than a Mathematical Point or nothing. For if all be swallowed, what is there left of the man for it to be swallowed into, but a mere *Point*, or rather *nothing*?

5. Certainly all the World, as well *Papists* as *Protestants*, as soon as they do but conceive the meaning of the Terms, will assent to the Truth of these Propositions at the very first sight; which therefore has made me call them *Common Notions*. Let us now apply our selves to the use of them in the examining the strength of Mr *Maimbourg*'s general *Maxime*, wherein he will have the Papists and Protestants agreed.

The first Prop thereof is, That the *true* Church is *infallible* by the promise made to her of being *assisted by the Holy Ghost*. But here I demand whether this Promise be made to the *Universal* Church, or any *Particular* Church or Churches throughout all Ages. That it is not made to the *Universal* Church *throughout all Ages*, is plain, in that the Parts thereof have been and are still divided in several *matters of Faith*. That no such Promise is made to any *Particular* Church or Churches, is plain from hence, that *these* Churches *are not named* in any part of the Scripture;

which

which omission is incredible, if there had been any such entailment of *Infallibility* upon any *Particular* Church or Churches. But of all Churches, I humbly conceive, it is *impossible* it should be the Church of *Rome*, unless it be possible that all those *Common Notions* which I have set down, and in which all the World, even the Church of *Rome* her self, if they will speak their consciences, are agreed, be false, which they must be if *Transubstantiation* be true. And therefore let any man judge whether is the more likely, *viz.* That *Transubstantiation* should be false, or those *Common Notions* not true.

6. Again, How does it appear that this Promise of the assistance of the Holy Ghost is not *conditional*? Indeed Christ says, *John* 16. 13. *When the Spirit of truth is come, he will guide you into all truth,* viz. the same Spirit that is promised, *Chap.* 14. *ver.* 15, 16, 17. But the words of this pretended *Charter* of *Infallibility* are there set down more fully: *If ye love me, keep my commandments; And I will pray the Father, and he shall give you another Comforter that he may abide with you for ever, even the Spirit of truth whom the World cannot receive.*—— The Promise of the assistance of the Holy Ghost for the infallibly concluding what is true, even from the words of this pretended *Charter* of *Infallibility*, is *conditional*; that is to say, if they so *love* Christ as to *keep his commandments,* and become not worldly and carnal, (for the World cannot receive this Spirit of truth) then this Spirit which leadeth into all truth shall assist them. Wherefore as many as Christ sends this *infallible* Spirit to, he *first* fits them for it by *mortifying* the *Spirit* of the *World* in them, and making them *Members* of his *truly Holy* Church; for the calling themselves *Holy Church*, makes them never a jot the more Holy, if they really be not so, by the first Common Notion. And

And besides, If the Words of this *Charter* of *Infallibility* had not been so express, yet in common sense and reason this condition would necessarily have been understood. Forasmuch as nothing can be more absurd than to imagine the *Assistance* of the *Holy Ghost* to be so *cheap* and *trivial* a thing, as to be procured for the concluding Controversies arising or set on foot in the Church, which are needless and frivolous, or more for satisfying *Curiosity* than *Edification*, and which tend to *Division*, and tearing the Church violently into parts, which was *one* before and in a *salvable* condition without this Decision, as Monsieur *Maimbourg* confesses himself: Or that the Holy Ghost will *assist* such *Assemblies* as are *worldly* and *carnally* minded, and are called to conclude for the *worldly* Advantage and Interest of a worldly Polity, who for the upholding and increasing their *Temporal* Empire (whereby they Lord it over the World, and ride on the necks of Kings and Princes) call themselves *Spiritual*. Certainly when all Christian Truth tends to real and indispensable Holiness, if mankind were not left to the liberty of their own Will, but Christ would have them so *infallibly* wise, he would all along have prepared them for it, by making them unexceptionably Holy, that they might become wise in his own Way and Method.

7. And lastly, There being *Predictions* in *Daniel* and the *Apocalypse* of an *Antichristian* State in the Church to come (in which there will be such a general Apostasie from the Apostolick Purity) even according to their own Interpreters, I demand what assurance we have that these Times came not (in a very great measure) upon the Church, some hundreds of Years before *Transubstantiation* was concluded on by the Roman Church, which therefore must much invalidate

the

the pretence of the *Infallibility* of any such Councils. And our Church of *England*, as all know, in her *Homilies*, whether by *inspiration* or by *mere* solid *Reason* and Judgment, refers the vision of the seventeenth Chapter of the *Apocalypse*, to the Church of *Rome*. And, I hope, to any unprejudiced Reader, that has leisure to examine things, I have even demonstratively made out that truth in my *Exposition* of the *Apocalypse*, and most punctually and distinctly of all in my *Joint-Exposition* of the thirteenth and seventeenth Chapters thereof, *Synops. Prophet.* Book 1. Chap. 11, 12, 13, &c. with the *preparatory* Chapters thereto. Let any one read them that please, and in the due fear of God consider them.

Wherefore, to conclude, touching this first Prop of his general *Maxim*, whereby he would insinuate that *Synods*, to whose definitive Sentence he would have us to stand, are *assisted* by the *Holy Ghost*, it does not only not underprop, but undermine his grand *Maxim*. Forasmuch as we have no assurance that those *Roman* Councils which have concluded for *Transubstantiation* were assisted by the Holy Ghost, but rather quite contrary.

8. The second *Prop* is, That whether a Synod be or be not assisted by the Holy Ghost, we are to stand to their determination. If the *Synod* be not assisted by the Holy Ghost then they are *fallible*, and may be in the wrong: so that the sense is, whether the *Synod* determine *right* or *wrong*, yet we are to stand to their determination. Which as odly as it sounds, yet in some sober sense, I must confess ingenuously, for ought I know, may be true, that is, in such things as are *really disputable*, and which for no sinister base design, but merely for the peace of the Church and Her Edification, it has been thought fit to make a *Synodical* Decision

Decision of the Controversie. But is this colour enough for the Church of *Rome*'s Determination to be stood to? Of making the Bread in the Sacrament to be *transubstantiated* into the very Body of Christ that hung on the Cross at *Jerusalem* (and has ever since his Ascension been in Heaven) by the Priest's saying over it, *This is my Body*, the Bread still remaining Bread to all outward appearance, as before, so that Christ is fain to be at the expence of a perpetual Miracle to make the *transubstantiated* Bread look *like* Bread still, though it be *really* the Body of Christ that hung on the Cross at *Jerusalem*. Which, as I have noted above, is against his Wisdom and Goodness, in that, if *Transubstantiation* be a true Article of the Christian Faith, this is the most effectual way imaginable to make men, if left to their own free thought, *to mis-believe it*, however force and cruelty might constrain them to *profess* it: And so it is against *his Goodness*, to expose so great a part of his Church to such bloody Persecutions as this Article has occasioned in the Christian World. That Christ should do a perpetual Miracle not that will confirm mens Faith, but subvert it, not to edifie his Church but distract it, and lay all in confusion and blood! Let any one consider how likely this is to be.

This therefore could never be a point, *bonâ fide*, disputable, but to such as were horribly hoodwinkt with prejudice, and blinded with a desire of having a thing concluded by the Church which was of such unspeakable advantage, as they then thought, for the *magnifying* the *Priesthood*, though I believe nothing will turn more to their Disrepute and shame in the conclusion. Now I dare appeal to Monsieur *Maimbourg* himself, whether we are to stand to the Determination of a *fallible* Synod in a *Point*, that, besides what I have

have already hinted, *contradicts* all those *Common Notions*, which I have above recited, and in which all Mankind are agreed. And such is this Point of *Transubstantiation*.

9. Now for the third *Prop*, That whatever Matters of *Opinion* (as they are for the present but such) are decided by such a Synod, pass into *Articles* of *Faith*; this *Prop* is also really a Puller down of this general *Maxim*. For by an *Article* of *Faith*, must be meant such an Article, as after the *Synodical* Decision, is necessary to be believed by all Parties upon pain of Damnation. But to this I answer, first, No *Falshood* can be an *Article of Faith*, nor can what is in it self false, by all the declaring in the World that it is true, become true, by the first *Common Notion*. And secondly, Since the whole Church before, in which arose the Controversie, were in a *salvable* Condition, how Unchristian an act must this be, to put so many thousand Souls in the State of Damnation, by so *unnecessary*, nay *mischievous* a Synodical Decision! And therefore what pretence can there be to the *Assistance* of the *Holy Ghost*, which Christ has promised his Church, when they machinate that, which so manifestly tends, according as the *Synod* acknowledges, to the Damnation of such a multitude of Souls, which before the Decision were in a salvable Condition, and also to most *barbarous Persecutions* of their *Persons*, as it is notoriously known in History, touching *Transubstantiation*?

10. The fourth *Prop* charges those with the guilt of Schism and Heresie that will not close with the above-said *Synodical Decisions*, be they what they will. In which matter we cannot judge whether the charge be right, unless we first understand what is truly and properly *Heresie* and *Schism*. The former whereof I demand

demand what it can be, but a diffent from the *Catholick Church* even in those things in it, that are *Apostolical*. For whatever *National* Church is found to have *all* and *nothing* else in it but what is *Apostolical*, or not *inconsistent* with the Apostolical Doctrine and Practice, is most assuredly one part of that *one Catholick* and *Apostolick* Church, which we profess our Belief of in our *Creed*. And for the latter it can be nothing else but a separation from the *Catholick* Church, or from any Church that is part thereof, even then, when she approves her self to be *Catholick*, that is to say even then, when she is *Apostolick*, or, though she be Apostolick, and offers no opinions or usages but such as are conformable to the usages and Doctrines of Christ and his Apostles, or have no repugnancy thereto. To separate from the Church in such circumstances as these, certainly is that great Crime of *Schism*; but to separate from that part of the Church which imposes opinions and practices plainly *repugnant* to the Precepts of Christ and his Apostles, this is no *Schism* but *Union* with the *truly antient* Catholick and Apostolick Church. And the declaring it *Schism* does not, nor can make it so, by *Common Notion* the first. And if it were *Schism* to separate from such a Church as propounds things repugnant to the Precepts of Christ and his Apostles, the guilt of this *Schism* is not upon them that thus separate, but upon those that impose such *Anti-Apostolical* matters.

11. The fifth *Prop*, That these *decisive Synods* or *Assemblies* are to *decide* according to the *Rule* of the *Word of God*; the strength of this Prop he endeavours more fully to display *pag*. 34. and he calls upon the Brethren of the Reformed Churches to reflect seriously upon these two Propositions he sets down.

K 2 The

The first is, That as the Word of God is *infallible* in it self, so certainly the judgment of him who truly judges according to this *Rule* is also *infallible*: And consequently they are obliged to believe, That the Church when she judges according to *this Rule* or the Word of God, does not only not err, but that she also cannot err.

The second, That they [the Reformed] are bound [as well as we the Romanists] to believe that the Church of God deciding *Controversies* of *Faith*, does judge according to the *true* sense of the *word* of God: Because upon the matter it is concerning this *very sense* that she gives judgment betwixt the Parties, who give it a *different sense*, and who are obliged in Conscience to submit to her judgment, under pain of being *Schismaticks* and *Hereticks*, as their Synod of *Dort* has positively declared.

12. The first of these Propositions may pass for firm and sound, provided that the meaning of *her judging according to this rule* is the *giving the right and genuine sense thereof*: Of which she can neither assure her self nor any one else, but by being assured of that *Holiness, Integrity*, and *singleness* of Heart, in those of the *Synod*, that makes them capable of the *Assistance* of the *Holy Ghost*; and also that their *Decision* clashes not with those *indeleble* Notions in the Humane Soul, that are *previous Requisites* for the understanding the meaning of *not only* the Holy Scriptures, but of any *Writing* whatever. And *unto which* if they find any thing in the *Letter* of the Sacred Writ *repugnant*, they may be sure it is a *Symbolical* or *Figurative* Speech, but in *other Writings*, that it is either a *Figurative Speech* or *Nonsence*. He that has not this *previous* Furniture, or makes *no use* of it, it is impossible he should prove a safe Judge of the sense of Scripture.

pture. And if he runs *counter* to what is *certainly true*, it is evident his Interpretation is *false* by the second *Common Notion*, and that he is not inspired by *Common Notion* the eleventh.

Touching the second Proposition, I demand how any can be bound to stand to the judgment of any *Synod,* if they decline the *previous Requisites,* without which it is *impossible* to understand the right meaning of *any Writing whatsoever*; and whether their pretending to judge *according to a Rule,* does not imply, that there are some *Common Principles,* in which *all Parties* are agreed, according to which, though they cannot discern that the Synod has certainly defined right, yet if the *Synod* run *counter* to them, they may be sure they have defined wrong, touching the *very sense* controverted between the *Parties.* Their professing they judge according to the *Rule,* implies the Rule is in some measure known to all that are concerned. Nor does it at all follow, because the *Object* of their *decision* is the *very sense* controverted between the *Parties,* that the *Synod* may give what judgment she will, break all Laws of *Grammar* and *Syntax* in the expounding the Text, much less contradict those Rules which are *infinitely more Sacred,* and inviolable, the *Common Notions* which God has imprinted *essentially* on the Humane Understanding. If such a violence be used by any Interpreters of Scripture, neither the *Synod* of *Dort,* nor any Reformed Church, has or will declare, That under pain of being *Schismaticks* and *Hereticks,* they are obliged in Conscience to submit to their determination.

CHAP.

CHAP. IX.

1. The examination of the sixth Prop, by demanding whether the Maxim Monsieur Maimbourg proposes is to be understood in the full sense, without any Appeal to any common agreed on Principles of Grammar, Rhetorick, Logick and Morality. 2. Instances of enormous Results from thence, with a demand whether the Protestant Churches would allow of such absurd Synodical Decisions. 3. That the Citations of History, touching the Synod of Dort, prove not, that all Synodical Decisions pass into proper Articles of Faith, with the Author's free judgment touching the Carriage of that Synod, and of the Parties condemned thereby. 4. His judgment countenanced from what is observed by Historians to be the sentiments of King James in the Conference at Hampton Court.

1. AND yet the sixth and last *Prop* of the general *Maxime* implies as much, which affirms, That both the *Protestants* and *Papists* are agreed in *all* the *five* foregoing *Supposals*, or to speak more compendiously, in that his general *Maxime*, That that Church in which are found the two Parties concerned, has ever had the power to determine all differences, and to declare that as *matter of Faith*, which *before* there was *no obligation* to *believe*, and that we are bound to acquiesce in their decisions under the penalty of being *Schismaticks*.

But I demand here of Monsieur *Maimbourg*, whether he will have his *Maxime* understood in a full latitude of sense, and that *immediately* without recourse to *any Principles* in which the *Synod* and the *Parties*

are

are agreed, and Counter to which if any determination be made, it is null, such as *Grammatical Syntax* and *Lexicographical* sense of Words, and (which are Laws infinitely more sacred and inviolable) the *Common Notions* (as I said before) *essentially* imprinted on the Soul of man, either of *Truth* or *Morality*, whether without being bounded by these, the *Protestant* Churches as well as the *Pontifician* are agreed, that we are to stand to the Determination of a *Synod*, under the penalty of being *Schismaticks*?

2. As for example, If a *Synod* should interpret, *Drink ye all of this*, of the Clergy *only*, and declare it does not reach the *Laity*, though the Apostles and Primitive Church understood it did: If notwithstanding St *Paul's* long Exhortation against *Religious* Exercise in an unknown Tongue, 1 *Cor.* 14. they should by some distinction or evasion conclude it lawful. If when as it is said, Thou shalt not make to thy self any graven Image to worship and fall down before it, they should distinguish and restrain it only to the graven Images of the *Heathen Gods*. If when as it is said, Thou shalt have no other Gods but me, they should distinguish Gods into *Supream* and *Subordinate*, and declare, we may have many *Subordinate* Gods, but only *One Supream*. If when as it is said, Honour thy Father and thy Mother, they should restrain it to a *Father* or *Mother of the same Religion* with our selves, whether *Political* Father or *Natural*, otherwise we are free from this Command, and may despise both our *Natural* Parents and our *Prince*, if they be not of the same perswasion with our selves. And whereas it is said, Thou shalt not commit Adultery, if they should understand it only of such an Adultery as is committed for the *mere pleasure* of the Flesh, *not* for the *health* of the Body, or assisting the *Conjugal Impotency* of his Neighbour.

Neighbour. If the Commandment againſt Murther, or Killing an Innocent Perſon, they ſhould reſtrain to Murther that is accompanied with delight in *Cruelty*, not that which is committed to raiſe a *livelyhood*, or ſecure an *Intereſt* the Murtherer has eſpouſed. If the Commandment againſt *Stealing*, they ſhould reſtrain to ſuch Theft as is againſt Men of our Religion and Perſwaſion, but that we may rob and ſteal from others without ſin. And according to the ſame tenour they ſhould interpret, Thou ſhalt not bear falſe witneſs againſt thy Neighbour, *&c.* I demand, I ſay, whether Monſieur *Maimbourg* does conceive, that the *Proteſtants*, nay, or his own Party, are agreed that all ſuch determinations are to be ſubmitted to upon penalty of being *Schiſmaticks*. Let him ask the *Reformed* Churches if they be thus agreed, or rather let him ask his own Conſcience, if he think they are. Wherefore it is plain, that what he produces out of the Hiſtory of the Synod of *Dort*, reaches not the point that he drives at, that is to ſay, That it is acknowledged by them, that after a Synod has decided the Controverſie, or given the ſenſe of places of Scripture controverted, be it what it will be, the Deciſion is to be ſtood to, under penalty of being *Schiſmaticks* and that there are not ſome commonly known Truths, common Notions of Reaſon and Morality, with which if the determination of a *Synod* does claſh, it is *ipſo facto* null, and a demonſtration that the Spirit of God did not aſſiſt.

3. I obſerve farther, That all the Citations that are produced either by Monſieur *Maimbourg* himſelf, or his *Tranſlator*, in his *Preface* and *Appendix*, will not amount to the Proteſtants profeſſing that every Controverſie or controverted Opinion, after the *Deciſion* of the *Synod*, paſſes into an *Article of Faith*, which properly

perly fignifies fuch a Doctrine, as without the Belief of which, when it is propofed, he that mis-believes it forfeits his Salvation ; for hereby the Synod of *Dort* had damned all the *Lutheran* Churches. For my own part I muft confefs, that in points that are fo obfcure, intricate and abftrufe, and which, as touching the main part of them, have exercifed and much baffled humane underftanding through all Ages, it had been a great piece of Chriftian Prudence for that *Synod* to have made Decrees againft all bitternefs of fpeech of the difagreeing Parties one againft another, and to have admonifhed them that they were bound, notwithftanding their difference of Opinion, to live in mutual Love one to another, which is the true Badge of Chrift's genuine Difciples, rather than to have exafperated one Party againft another, by making that Doctrine *Authentick*, which is really in it felf from places of *Scripture*, and *Reafon* fo *intricate* and *difputable*. But it feems to have been the fleight of Satan for the weakning the Reformed Churches that drove them to it. But I muft fay, on the other fide, that when the Synod had determined, they who were determined againft, ought to have fubmitted to her determination in a thing fo *really difputable*, and by this Chriftian Policy to have conferved the peace of the Church, and out-witted the Devil. For if they had had any modefty in them, they might very well in fuch abftrufe, dark and difputable points have compromifed with the *Synod*, and preferred the peace and fafety of the *Reformed* Churches, before the fatisfaction of their own *Opinionativenefs*.

4. And that wife Prince, *King James* the firft of Blefled Memory, feems to come near to what I have faid, in the words delivered by his Embaffadour at the Synod of *Dort*, as they are cited by Monfieur *Maimbourg*

bourg himself in his *Peaceable Method*, pag. 23. That for the allaying those troubles, *There was but that one only means which the Church had ever made use of*, a National Synod, *which was to be judge in the case, and to decide which of the two Opinions was more conformable to the Word of God: or at least how and in what manner the one or the other might be tolerated in the Church of God.* Which latter part is cunningly left out by the *Translator*, in his *Preface, pag.* 3. But in those latter words, King *James* plainly intimates his moderate Sentiments touching the Controversy, and that he would not have the Decision made too rigidly and pinchingly on either side. And suitably to this excellent judgment of his, in the Conference at *Hampton-Court*, when the *Puritans* would have had the nine *Lambeth* Articles, which are more full and express against the points of *Arminianism*, to be embodyed into the Articles of our Church, concluded on in the Convocation holden at *London*, in the Year 1562. the King earnestly refused it. And in his Instructions to his *Divines* he sent over to the Synod of *Dort*, this remarkable one was amongst the rest, That they would advise the Churches that the Ministers do not deliver in Pulpit to the People those things for ordinary Doctrines, which are the highest points of the Schools, and not fit for vulgar Capacities, but *disputable* on both sides. And we may be sure when he was so careful in this for the foreign Churches he would not neglect to infuse the same good Principles into his own: And that he could not easily believe that upon the *Decision* of the *Synod* of *Dort*, that passed into an *Article of Faith*, without which there is no Salvation, which yet he would have hid from the knowledge of the People.

CHAP.

CHAP. X.

1. *What* Synodical *Decisions are capable of passing into proper Articles of Faith, and what not.* 2. *The necessity of distinguishing the* doctrinal *Decisions of* Synods *into* Articles of Faith, *properly so called, and* Articles of Communion. 3. *The meaning of the King's Answer to Mr.* Knewstubs, *in the Conference at* Hampton-Court: *And that* Synods *have* unlimited *Power to put what sense they please on places of Scripture, and make them pass into* Articles of Faith, *not proved to be the Opinion of the Protestant Churches.* 4. *That our* English *Church is against it, largely proved out of her Articles.* 5. *No* Article of Faith *pre-existent in Scripture that cannot be fetched thence but by interpreting against the* Proleptick *Principles of* rightly circumstantiated *Sense and* Common Notions *ingrafted* essentially *in the Humane Understanding.* 6. *Of Decision of Points* necessary *to Salvation, and to the justifying the Christian Worship, and those that are* less necessary, *and* less clear, *and lastly, those that have an* Insuperable Difficulty *on* both sides. 7. *Monsieur* Maimbourg's *general* Maxime, *that it is not agreed in by the Protestant Churches, abundantly demonstrated, with a Note of the* Subtilty *of the* Romanists *in* declining *the Dispute of the particular merits of their Cause, and making it their business to perswade,* first, *that* their Church is Infallible. 8. *A Meeting with Monsieur* Maimbourg *once more in his own Method, and thereby demonstrating that* Transubstantiation *is grosly false, and consequently the Church of* Rome fallible, *with an hint of a true* peaceable Method of reconciling Papists and Protestants.

1. Where-

1. WHerefore it seems needful to take notice of this distinction of the *Doctrinal* Decisions of *Synods*, that some pass into, or rather are of the nature of the *Articles of Faith*, the knowledge of them being *necessary* to keep us from Sin and Damnation. And such were the *Doctrinal* Decisions of those ancient *Primitive* Councils, who out of Scripture plainly declared the truth of the *Divinity* of Christ and *Triunity* of the *Godhead*, without which the Church would be involved in *gross Idolatry*. And therefore the *Decisions* of the Controversies did naturally pass into *professed Articles* of the *Christian Faith*, and such as our Salvation depended on. But to imagine that every *Doctrinal* Decision of a *Synod* passes into a *proper* Article of *Faith*, without which there is no Salvation, and that a *Synod* has power to make that an *Article of Faith*, before which men were safe and sinless as to that point, is to put it into the power of a *Synod* to damn God knows how many Myriads of men which Christ dyed for, and had it not been for these curious, or rather mischievous Decisions, might have been saved; than which what can be more prodigious?

2. Whence we see plainly, it is *most necessary* to make this distinction in *Doctrinal* Decisions of *Synods*, that some may be *Articles of Faith*, others only *Articles of Communion*, that if any oppose or disparage the said Articles, whether they be of the Clergy or Laity, they make themselves obnoxious to *Excommunication*; and if a Clergy-man does not subscribe to them, he makes himself uncapable of *Ecclesiastical* Imployment. This is all that Monsieur *Maimbourg* can squeeze out of all his Citations out of the story of the Synod of *Dort*, so far as I can perceive, or his *Translator*,

flator in his *Preface* and *Appendix*, out of those he produces touching the Church of *England*.

3. And that which his *Translator* in his *Preface* would make such a great business of, *viz.* This wise King's answer to M*r* *Knewstubs*, at the Conference at *Hampton Court*, when he was asked, *How far an Ordinance of the Church was to bind men without impeachment of their Christian Liberty*: to which he said, he would not argue that point with him, but answer therein as Kings are wont to speak in Parliament, *Le Roy s'avisera*. And therefore I charge you never speak more to that point how far you are bound to obey when the Church has once ordained it. I say, nothing more can be collected out of this answer, but that he modestly intimated his Opinion, that he meant not that *all* Synodical *Decisions* passed into *Articles of Faith*, but may be only *Articles of Communion* in the sense I have already explained. And what I have already said, if seriously and considerately applyed to what he produces in his *Appendix*, will easily discover that they prove nothing more touching the Church of *England*, than what we have already allowed to be her Doctrine touching the Authority of Synods.

But that a *Synod* without any limitation or appeal to certain *Principles* in which both the *Synod* and *Parties* contesting are all agreed, may by her bare *immediate* Authority, give what sense she pleases on places of Scripture, alledged in the Controversy, and that her *Decision* passes into an *Article of Faith*, which the Parties cast are bound to assent to, under the pain of becoming *Hereticks* and *Schismaticks*: Nothing can be more contrary than this to the Declarations of the Church of *England*. So far is it from truth, That *all* the *Protestant* Churches are agreed in his grand *Maxime* above mentioned.

4. Let

4. Let the Church of *England* speak for her self, *Artic.* 19. "As the Church of *Jerusalem*, *Alexandria*, "and *Antioch*, so also the Church of *Rome* has erred, "not only in their *Living* and Ceremonies, but also "in *Matters of Faith*. And Article 21. General "Councils may not be gathered together without the "Commandment and Will of Princes. And when "they be gathered together (forasmuch as they be "an Assembly of men, whereof all be not governed "with the Spirit and Word of God) they may err, "and sometimes have erred even in things appertain- "ing to God: wherefore things ordained by them, as "*necessary to Salvation*, have neither Strength nor "Authority, unless it may be declared that they be "taken out of the Holy Scriptures. Here our Church plainly declares, That forasmuch as a Council or Synod consists of *fallible* Persons, they can determine nothing *necessary to Salvation*, but what they can make out that it is clearly, to any unprejudiced Eye, contained in the Scripture, not fetched out by weak and *precarious* Consequences, or *phanciful* Surmises, much less by a *distorted* Interpretation, and *repugnant* to *Common Sense* and *Reason*, which are necessarily supposed in the understanding of any Scripture or Writing whatsoever, as I have intimated above.

And even that Article (20.) which the *Translator* produces in his *Preface*, in the behalf of Monsieur *Maimbourg's* grand *Maxime*, do but produce the whole Article and it is plainly against it. For the words are these: "The Church has power to de- "cree Rites and Ceremonies and Authority in Con- "troversies of Faith; and yet it is not lawful for the "Church to ordain any thing that is contrary to "God's Word written, neither may it so expound "one place of Scripture that it be repugnant to a- "nother.

"nother. Wherefore although the Church be a "Witness and Keeper of Holy Writ, yet as it ought "not to decree any thing *against* the same; so *beside* "the same, ought it not to inforce any thing to be be-"lieved for *Necessity of Salvation.* It is true, the Church is here said to have Authority in *Controversies of Faith.* As certainly if any should raise new Stirs in any National Church, touching such points as the Antient Primitive Synods have concluded for, in the behalf of the *Divinity* of *Christ*, and *Triunity* of the God-head, pretending they have clearer demonstrations than ever yet were proposed against those Decisions or any of like nature, which may concern the *Justifiableness* of our *Christian Worship*, and *indispensable* way of *Salvation*, the Church has Authority as she ever had, in such Controversies, to ratifie such *Articles of Faith*, but she is not said to have Authority to make every *Synodical* Decision an *Article of Faith*, whether the nature thereof will bear it or no. Nay her Authority is excluded from inforcing any thing besides what is clearly enough contained in the Scripture (as assuredly those points are above-mentioned, though with weak or cavilling men they have been made questionable) to be believed for *Necessity of Salvation.* Which is the proper Character of an *Article of Faith*, according as the *Preface* to the *Athanasian* Creed intimates. And Monsieur *Maimbourg* himself is so sensible of this main Truth, that in the Explication of his general *Maxime*, he acknowledges that the Church has no Autority to coin any *New* Articles of Faith, but only to declare she has discovered them *existent-before* in the Scriptures, but not so clearly espy'd or discerned as by an assembled Synod.

5. But certainly no *Article of Faith*, that is to say, no Truth necessary to Salvation can be said to be *pre-existent*

existent in the Scriptures, and having lain hid to be discovered afterwards, that is not discovered but by such forced Interpretations of the Text, that are repugnant to *Common Sense* and *Reason*. Is not this a Reproach to the Wisdom of God, that he should inspire the Holy Penmen to set down Truth *necessary to Salvation* so obscurely, that the meaning cannot be reached without doing violence to *Common Sense* and *Reason*, and running counter to those *previous Principles*, without which it is impossible to make sense of any writing whatever? Or without interpreting one place of Scripture *repugnantly* to the plain sense of another. Which this Article expresly forbids as unlawful. So plain is it that our Church limits the Authority of a Synod to certain Rules agreed of on all hands, against which they have no Authority to define any thing: And *plain places* of Scripture is one Rule, contrary to which it is not lawful to interpret any either *pretendedly* or *really* obscure place. Nor can any place at all be plain without the admittance of those *Proleptick* Principles of *rightly circumstantiated sense* and *common* undeniable *Notions essentially* ingrafted in the mind of man, whether they relate to *Reason* or *Morality*. These, both *Synod* and *Contesters* are supposed to be agreed on, and therefore no *Synodical Decision* repugnant to these according to our Church in interpreting of Scripture (if I rightly understand her) ought to have Autority with it.

6. But as for *doctrinal* Decisions, such as concern the *Justifiableness* of the Christian Worship, and are of *Necessity* to *Salvation*, and such as, although either weak or willful cavilling men may make questionable, yet are clearly enough delivered in Scripture, these, questionless, a Synod has Autority to determine as *Articles of Faith*. And such as have not the like

Clearness

CHAP. X.   *the* Real Presence.   81

Clearness nor *Necessity*, as also innocent and indifferent Rites and Ceremonies, when the one and the other seem *advantagious* to the Church, such *Synodical* Decisions may pass into *Articles* of *Communion*, in that sense I have above explained. And lastly, as in that case of the Synod of *Dort*, when the points controverted have on both sides that *invincible* Obscurity and Intricacy, and there seems to be *forcible* Arguments for either conclusion; What I humbly conceive is to be done in that case, I have fully enough expressed already, and therefore think it needless again to repeat.

7. In the mean time, I hope, I have made it manifoldly apparent that Monsieur *Maimbourg*'s general *Maxime*, *viz*. That the Church, in which are found the two Parties concerned, has ever had the Power to determine all differences, and to declare that as *Matter of Faith*, which before there was no Obligation to believe; And that we are bound to acquiesce in her Decisions under the penalty of being *Schismaticks*, is not, (especially as he would have his *Maxime* understood) agreed on by all Churches, as well *Protestant* as *Pontifician*. And that therefore this *Snare* or *Net*, wherewith he would catch and carry Captive the Protestants into a Profession of the Infallibility of the Church in *Synodical* Decisions, so that the Church must be first allow'd *Infallible*, that we may glibly swallow down whatsoever she decides, even *Transubstantiation* it self, with all other Errours of the Church of *Rome*; this *Net* or *Snare*, I hope, I have sufficiently broken. And I will only note by the bye, how the subtilest *Romanists* declining the *Merits* of the *Cause*, labour Tooth and Nail to establish the *absolute Infallibility* of their Church. But our Saviour tells us, *By the fruit you shall know them.*

M   Wherefore

Wherefore any man or Company of men that profess themselves *infallible*, their *Infallibility* must be examined by their *Doctrines*, which if they be plainly any one of them *false*, their boast of *Infallibility* most certainly is not true.

8. But forasmuch as an *Appeal* to a *Maxime* pretended to be agreed upon by both sides, both *Papists* and *Protestants*, is made use of with so much Wit and Artifice, to ingage the *Protestants* to imbrace *Transubstantiation* and the rest of the *Romish* Errours: I hope Monsieur *Maimbourg* will not take it amiss, if I civilly meet him again in his own Way, and show him by an Appeal, not only to *one* Maxime, but above a *dozen* at least of *Common Notions*, which I did above recite, and in which both *Papists* and *Protestants*, and all mankind are agreed, that it may demonstratively be made evident that the Doctrine of *Transubstantiation* is grosly false.

For that which in it self is false, no *declaring* or saying it is true, though by the vote of an *entire Synod*, can make it true, by the *first* of the Common Notions above mentioned, *Chap.* 8. *Sect.* 4.

Secondly, Whatever is plainly repugnant to what is *true*, is certainly *false*, and consequently can be no *due* Article of a *true Faith* or *Religion*, by the *second* and *third* Common Notions. And therefore *Transubstantiation* cannot pass into an *Article of Faith* by the Authority of any *Synod* whatever.

Thirdly, Now that the Doctrine of *Transubstantiation* is false, is manifest from the assurance of our Senses *rightly circumstantiated*. To which our Saviour Christ appeals, who is wiser than all the Synods that ever were or will be, as was observed in Common Notion the *fourth*. But our *Senses* assure us it is *Bread* still, not the *Body of Christ*.

Fourthly,

Fourthly, If *Transubstantiation* be true, an Essence or Being that is *one* remaining *still one*, may be *divided* or separated *from it self*, which is repugnant to the *fifth* Common Notion.

Fifthly, If Transubstantiation be true, the *whole* is not bigger than the *part*, nor the *part* less than the *whole*, which contradicts the *sixth* Common Notion.

Sixthly, If Transubstantiation be true, the parts in a Division do not only agree with the whole, but agree one with another; and are indeed absolutely the same; for divide a consecrated Wafer into two, *viz. A.* and *B.* this *A.* and *B.* are the *same* intire *Individual* Body of Christ according to this Doctrine, which contradicts the *seventh* Common Notion.

Seventhly, If the said Doctrine be true, one and the same Body may be a *Cube* and a *Globe* at once, have the figure of an *Humane Body* and of a *Pyramid* and *Cylinder* at the same time, according as they shall mould the Consecrated Bread, which is repugnant to the *eighth* Common Notion.

Eighthly, *Transubstantiation*, if it be any truth at all, it is a *Revealed* Truth; but no Revelation the *Revealing* whereof, or the *manner* of Revealing is *repugnant* to the *Divine Attributes*, can be from God, by Common Notion the *ninth*: but if this Doctrine of *Transubstantiation* were a Truth, it seems not to sute with the Wisdom of God to reveal a Truth that seems so palpably to overthrow and thwart *all* the *innate Principles* of humane *Understanding*, and the assurance of the *rightly circumstantiated* Senses, to both which Christ himself appeals, and without which we have no certainty of the Miracles of Christ and his Apostles. And he hence exposes his Church to be befool'd by all the lucriferous fictions of a fallacious Priesthood.

And besides this, the circumstances or *manner* of its first *Revelation* at the Lord's Supper as they would have it, shows it cannot be; for the Consecrated Bread retaining still the shape and all other sensible qualities of Bread without any change, and that by a *miraculous* supporting them, now *not inherent* in their *proper* subject *Bread*, which is transubstantiated into that very Body that holds it in his hands, or seems so to do: I say, as I have also intimated before, to be thus at the expence of so *vast* a *Miracle* here at his last Supper, and to repeat the same Miracle upon all the Consecrations of the Bread by the Priest, which is the most effectual means to make all men Infidels, as to the belief of *Transubstantiation*, and to occasion thence such *cruel* and *bloody Persecutions*, is apparently contrary to the *Divine Wisdom* and *Goodness*; and therefore neither *pretended Tradition* nor *fresh Interpretation* of the inspired Text, can make so gross a falshood true, by the *tenth* and *eleventh* Common Notions.

Ninthly, If *Transubstantiation* be true, one and the same Body may be many thousand times bigger or less than it self at the same time, forasmuch as the *least Atom* or particle of his Body or *Transubstantiated* Bread is his whole Body as well as the *bigger lump* according to this Doctrine, which contradicts the *Twelfth* Common Notion.

Tenthly, If this Doctrine be true, The *same Individual* Body still existing and having existed many Years, may notwithstanding be made whiles it already exists, which contradicts the *Thirteenth* Common Notion.

Eleventhly, If *Transubstantiation* be true, one and the same Body may be present with it self, and many Thousands of Miles absent from it self at once;

once; be shut up in a Box, and free to walk in the Field, and to ascend into Heaven at the same time, contrary to the *Fourteenth* and *Fifteenth* Common Notions.

And lastly, If this Doctrine be true, a man may swallow his own Body *whole*, Head, Feet, Back, Belly, Arms, and Thighs, and Stomach it self through his Mouth, down his Throat into his Stomach, that is to say, every whit of himself into one knows not what of himself, less than a Mathematical Point or nothing. This Christ might have done, and actually did if he did eat the Consecrated Bread with his Disciples, which contradicts the *Sixteenth* Common Notion.

Wherefore since in vertue of *one* single *Maxim*, Monsieur *Maimbourg* supposing the *Protestants* as well as the *Papists* agreeing therein (though in that, as I have show'd, he is mistaken) would draw in the Protestants to imbrace the Doctrine of *Transubstantiation*, and other Errors of the *Roman* Church, I appeal to him how much more reasonable it is, that he and as many as are of his perswasion should *relinquish* that Doctrine, it contradicting so many *Common Notions*, which not only all *Papists* and *Protestants*, but indeed all the whole World are agreed in. And hence clearly discerning the *Infallibility* of the *Roman* Church, upon which this and other erroneous Doctrines are built (such as Invocation of Saints, Worshipping of Images, and the like) plainly to fail, that they should bethink themselves what need there is to reform their Church from such gross errours, and to pray to God to put it into the mind of their Governours so to do; which would be a *peaceable method indeed for the reuniting Protestants and Catholicks in matters of Faith, and principally*

pally in the subject of the Holy Eucharist, as the Title of his *Method* has it.

But to require an *Union*, things standing as they are, is to expect of us that we *cease to be men* to become *Christians* of a *novel Mode* unknown to the Primitive Church, and under pretence of *Faith* to abjure the *indeleble Principles* of *sound Reason*, those immutable *Common Notions* which the Eternal *Logos* has *essentially* ingrafted in our Souls, and without which neither *Certainty* of *Faith* can consist, nor any assured sense of either the *Holy* Scriptures or *any* Writing else be found out or understood.

Soli Deo Gloria.

AN
Advertisement
TO THE
READER.

Reader,

ALthough I had writ some few *Notes*, such as I conceived were fit, either further to confirm, or else to clear the sense of several Passages in my *Discourse* of the *Real Presence*; yet in humble submission to their Judgments, that I easily prefer before my own in such Cases as these, I have willingly omitted the publishing of them *all*, saving *this*, which is upon that Passage in the first Impression of my Discourse, *pag.* 38. *l.* 5. but in this second Edition, *pag.* 35. *l.* 15. The *Passage* is this: *And yet in the same place St.* Augustine *says*, &c. The *Note* this.

In the same place, namely in the same place of *Philippus Mornæus de Eucharistia*, lib. 4. cap. 8. pag. 751. *Docuerat (*says *Mornæus) post* Paulum Augustinus, *indui nos Christum in Baptismo ; in eodem etiam Corporis & sanguinis Christi participes fieri.* Now there are several places in St. *Augustine*, wherein he asserts that *Infants* partake of the *Eucharist*, that they may have *life in them*, alluding to those words of our Saviour in the sixth of St. *John*, v. 53, 54. *Except ye eat the flesh of the son of man, and drink his blood, ye have no life in you. He that eats my flesh and drinks my blood,*

N   *has*

An Advertisement to the Reader.

has eternal life. *Mornæus* therefore though upon a miſtake of his in Hiſtory (for he goes upon this falſe Hypotheſis, that, though the Cuſtome of *Communicating Infants* had obtained ſome time in the Church, ſuppoſe from St. *Cyprian*'s time ſomewhat onwards, yet it had been worn out again, at leaſt for the moſt part, in the times of St. *Auguſtine*:) yet I ſay, his Hypotheſis being given him, he rationally enough collects, and firmly concludes, that St. *Auguſtine*, when he argues from the communicating Infants, underſtood that they received the Fleſh and Blood of Chriſt (*viz*. mentioned *John* 6.) in their very *being Baptized*. For the *Communicating Infants* being worn out, as *Mornæus* ſuppoſes in St. *Auſtin*'s Time, and yet he affirming they partake of the *Eucharist*, where can they partake of it but in their Baptiſm? This reaſoning, I ſay, had been firm, if *Mornæus* had not been miſtaken in his Hypotheſis. For it was an univerſal Cuſtome even in St. *Auſtin*'s time himſelf, to give the *Eucharist* to *Infants* after *Baptiſm*. And *Dallæus* has learnedly made it out, that it was the general Cuſtome of the whole Chriſtian Church thus to do from *Cyprian*'s time, till ſeveral Ages after St. *Auſtin*, the Cuſtome being grounded upon thoſe ſayings of our Saviour in the ſixth of St. *John* above-recited, *v*. 53, 54. See *Dallæus de Cultibus Religioſis Latinorum*, lib. 5. cap. 3 & 4.

But ſo far as I ſee, though for ſureneſs they added the *Eucharist* to the *Baptiſm* of Infants, yet the wiſer ſort of them held, that Life and Salvation by Baptiſm alone is obtainable, provided the other be not omitted out of contempt or wilful neglect. The words of *Fulgentius*, which *Dallæus* cites, *cap*. 4. *pag*. 587. are remarkable as to this point. They are concerning the ſtate of a certain *Æthiopian* Servant, who having

having been *Baptized*, but weak, expired before they could give him the *Eucharist*. Wherefore *Ferrandus Diaconus* proposing his doubt to *Fulgentius*, touching the state of this *Æthiopian* Servant, whether he might be saved or no; freely and judiciously answers him, that he need not to be sollicitous touching that matter: for as much as every one by the very *Baptism* he receives, is made a member of Christ, and so is to be conceived *to eat the Flesh of Christ* according to the *truth* of the *Mystery* (*secundum Mysterii veritatem*) though he does not receive it *secundum veritatis Mysteria*. *Qui enim,* says he, *membrum corporis Christi fit, quomodo non accipit quod ipse fit? Quando utique illius fit verum corporis Membrum, cujus corporis est in sacrificio sacramentum. Hoc ergo fit ille regeneratione sancti Baptismatis, quod est de sacrificio sumpturus Altaris.* This sentence of *Fulgentius*, for the weight and elegancy of it, is worthy to be writ in Letters of Gold. I will adventure to render it in *English*, though it must needs lose of the elegancy it has in the *Latin*. *For he who is made a Member of Christ, how can he but receive what he himself is made? For as much as he is made a true Member of that Body of which the consecrate Sacrament is a sign. Therefore he is made by Regeneration in holy Baptism, that which he is to receive from the Sacrament on the Altar,* that is, he partakes of that *Flesh* and *Blood* of *Christ*, of which he himself pronounces, My Flesh is Meat indeed, and my Blood is Drink indeed; and he that eateth not my Flesh and drinketh not my Blood, has no life in him. Which words was the occasion of *Communicating Infants*. But this free and learned Father of the Church *Fulgentius* shows, how that they that are *Baptized* are possessed of this Flesh and Blood already, in vertue of their very *Baptism*. Which is the point *Mornæus*

An Advertisement to the Reader.

næus would have won out of several Passages in St. *Austin*; but his Hypothesis failing, that attempt has proved frustraneous. But I hope this of *Fulgentius* will compensate that loss.

And further to confirm the truth of this golden Sentence of that venerable Father, I shall offer this brief Demonstration, premising these two things, *viz.* (1.) That which we partake of in our *Baptismal Regeneration* in being born of the Spirit, *John* 3. *v.* 5, 6. is such, as with it we are in the state of Life and Salvation, but without it we are not in the state of Life and Salvation. (2.) That which we partake of in the Celebration of the *Holy Eucharist*, in eating the Flesh of the Son of Man, and drinking his Blood, *John* 6. *v.* 53, 54. is such, as with it we are in the state of Life and Salvation, but without it we are not in the state of Life and Salvation. Or, which is all one, That which is such, as with it we are in the state of Life and Salvation, but without it we are not in the state of Life and Salvation, we partake of in the Celebration of the *Holy Eucharist*, in eating the Flesh of the Son of Man, and drinking his Blood.

But now to proceed. That which is such that with it we are in the state of Life and Salvation, but without it we are not in the state of Life and Salvation, where-ever that is received, it is one and the same thing *realiter*, nor can be conceived two distinct things *really separate* from one another, or not to be in the same Subject. For it plainly implies a contradiction, that they should be two several things, of each whereof *separatim* from one another, it may be said truly, That with it we are in the state of Life and Salvation, but without it we are not in the state of Life and Salvation.

As let these two several things, for Argumentation sake, be *A.* and *B.* and let *C.* be the state of Life and Salvation. If we say, with *A.* we are in *C.* but without *A.* we are not in *C.* we cannot say then, with *B.* we are in *C.* but without *B.* we are not in *C.* For [With *A.* we are in *C.*] is a plain contradiction to [Without *B.* we are not in *C.*] and [Without *A.* we are not in *C.*] is a plain contradiction to [With *B.* we are in *C.*] Whence it is a manifest Repugnancy to conceive otherwise, than that *A.* and *B.* that have been, for Dispute sake, supposed to be *really* different things, must be one and the same thing *realiter*, as the Schools speak, and as we have above explained.

It remains only now that we make good the *two Points* we have premised.

First then, Whenas our Saviour says to *Nicodemus, John* 3. 3. *Except a man be born again, he cannot see the Kingdom of God*; Certainly, *seeing the Kingdom of God*, does imply at least so much, that he that is thus born again is in the state of Life and Salvation: Our Church Catechism also seeming to express this Priviledge touching Baptism, by an *Inheritour of the Kingdom of Heaven*, as if by our Baptismal Regeneration, we become Heirs that have a Right to that Celestial Kingdom. And St. *Paul* says expresly to *Titus, Ch.* 3. We are saved *Lavacro Regenerationis*. And then when he says, *Except a man be born of Water and the Spirit he cannot see the Kingdom of God*, does it not plainly imply, that if he be born of Water and the Spirit, that he shall see the Kingdom of God, and so *be* in the state of Life and Salvation. Which yet he *is not* according to the very Words of our Saviour, unless he be born of Water and the Spirit. And therefore in our Baptismal Regeneration

neration in being born of the Spirit, *v.* 6. we partake of that with which we are in the state of Life and Salvation, and without which we are not in the state of Life and Salvation, according to the *first Point* premised.

The second, *viz.* That which we partake of in the *Holy Eucharist*, in eating the Flesh of Christ and drinking his Blood, is such, as with it we are in the state of Life and Salvation, and without it we are not in the state of Life and Salvation, *this* is *expresly* declared *John* 6. 53, 54. *Except ye eat the flesh of the son of man, and drink his blood, ye have no life in you. Whoso eateth my flesh, and drinketh my blood, hath eternal life,* &c. Wherefore in being *born of the spirit* in our *Baptismal Regeneration,* we then partake of the *Flesh* and *Blood* of Christ, as we do afterwards in the *Holy Communion,* it being repugnant that they should be *two* really *distinct* things, as was demonstrated above. But in being *born of the spirit,* we do not partake of the *natural* Flesh and Blood of Christ, and therefore there is as St. *Jerome* phrases it (for not *Gratian,* but St. *Jerome,* is the first Author of that distinction) a *Divine* or *Spiritual* Flesh and Blood (distinct from his *Natural*) which we partake of both in *Baptism* and the *Lord's Supper.* In the one as the *Seed* and *Element* of our *Regeneration,* in the other as the *Aliment* or *Nutriment* of our *New Birth.*

This is clear enough already, but that the Reader may not suspect any trick put upon him in my using a Geometrical Form in a Theological Argument, I will exhibit the proof of *Fulgentius* his assertion in yet a more close and succinct way, reducing all into one single Syllogism, Thus:

That with which we are in the state of Life and Salvation, and without it we are not in the state of Life

Life and Salvation, is the thing received in the *Holy Eucharist*, in eating the Flesh and drinking the Blood of Christ.

But the thing received in *Baptism* in being born of the Spirit, is that with which we are in the state of Life and Salvation, and without it we are not in the state of Life and Salvation.

Therefore the thing received in *Baptism*, in being *born of the spirit*, is the thing received in the *Holy. Eucharist* in *eating the Flesh* and *drinking the Blood of Christ*; which is the very assertion of that excellent Father of the Church *Fulgentius*, which I undertook to demonstrate to be true, which I have done accordingly in this single Syllogism, the two premised Points having been clearly proved before.

Thus have I finished my *Note* upon this single Passage of my *Discourse* of the *Real Presence*, in which *Mornæus* is found not rightly to have understood St. *Austin*; and being not conscious to my self of any mistake in the management of the said Discourse, but *this*, I thought it necessary, though I omit all the rest, to publish this *Note* upon that Passage out of *Mornæus*, wherein St. *Austin* is concerned, That if any Antagonist appear, he may be prevented from triumphing in the Discovery of a Mistake, which is acknowledged to be such already; and that others in the mean time may be more punctually informed, nor be led into any Errour touching this present Matter by this Passage in my Book.

I will only add this reasonable Request of the Reader, and so conclude, *viz.* That, since it has been thought fit to speak of St. *Jerome*'s Divine or Spiritual Body of Christ (who is the *Logos Incarnate*) only in *general*, he will not be so ill-natured as to conceive any condition of it in *particular*, or fix any

sense,

sense, which he thinks *most absurd*. But if he have several incongruous conceits thereof, that he would be so *humane* as to think the most tolerable to be my sense: But if he will so far strain courtesy with himself, as not to rest in his thoughts till he has found out such a sense as he thinks *congruous* and *unexceptionable*, and will be so *Heroically Candid and Charitable* as to take that to be my meaning, I can assure him he has not much missed the Mark. For the distinct *Idea* which I have thereof, after anxious and impartial scrutiny, is such as clashes with neither Scripture nor sound Reason, nor with any truly Apostolick Doctrine so far as I can judge. And so far as it shall be found clashing with any of these, so far shall I willingly disown it and discard it from being mine.

THE END.

Imprimatur.

Ex Æd. Lamb.
Feb. 14.
1686.
Guil. Needham RR^{mo} *in Christo P. ac D.D. Wilhelmo Archiep. Cant. à Sacris Domest.*

A DISCOURSE OF THE HOLY EUCHARIST,

IN THE TWO GREAT POINTS

OF THE

Real Presence

AND THE

Adoration of the Host.

IN

ANSWER to the TWO DISCOURSES lately Printed at OXFORD on This SUBJECT.

To which is prefixed
A Large HISTORICAL PREFACE relating to the same ARGUMENT.

LONDON,
Printed for Richard Chiswell, at the *Rose* and *Crown* in S. *Paul*'s Church-Yard. MDCLXXXVII.

THE
PREFACE.

THE *nature of the Holy* Eucharist *is a subject that hath been both so frequently insisted upon, and so fully explain'd in our own and other Languages, that it may well be thought a very needless undertaking for any one to trouble the World with any farther Reflections upon it.* For not to mention now those Eminent Men who have heretofore labour'd in this work, nor to run beyond the points that are here designed to be examined ; What can be said more evidently to shew the impossibility of the pretended substantial change *of the* Bread *and* Wine *into the* Body *and* Blood *of Christ in this Holy Sacrament*, than has been done in the late excellent Discourse against Transubstantiation? It is but a very little time since the Adoration of the Host has been shewn not only to be a novel invention, contrary to the practice of all Antiquity, but the danger of it evidently demonstrated, notwithstanding whatever pretences can be made of *a* good intention *to excuse them from the charge and danger of Idolatry*, who continue the practice of it. And both these not only still remain unanswer'd ; but if we may be allow'd to judge either

The Preface.

by their own strength, or by our Adversaries silence, are truly and indeed unanswerable.

It is not therefore out of any the least Opinion that any thing more need be said to confirm our cause, much less that I esteem my self able to undertake it with the same success that those other Champions of our Faith have done it, that I venture these Discourses to a publick view. But since our Adversaries still continue, without taking notice of any of these things, to cry up their Great Diana *no less than if she had never at all been shewn to be but an* Idol, *I thought it might not be amiss to revive our Instances against it: And that we ought not to appear less sollicitous by a frequent repetition of our Reasons, to keep men in the* Truth, *than others are by a continual insisting upon their so often baffled* Sophistry, *to lead them into* Error.

'Twas an ingenious Apology that Seneca *once made, for his often repeating the same things;* 'That he did 'but inculcate over and over the same Counsels, to 'those that over and over committed the same faults: *And I remember an antient* Father *has left it as his Opinion, that it was useful for the same truths to be vindicated by many,* 'because that one Man's Writings 'might possibly chance to come where the others did 'not; and what was less fully or clearly explain'd by 'one, might be supplied and enlarged by the other. *And a greater than either of these, S.* Paul, *has at once left us both an example and a warrant for this sollicitude;* Phil. 3. 1. 'To write the same things to you, 'to me (*says he*) is not grievous, but for you it is 'safe.

Indeed I think if there be any need of an excuse for this undertaking, it ought to be rather to Apologize *for a*

far

far greater absurdity which we all commit in writing at all against those Men, who in these Disputes concerning the Holy Sacrament, have most evidently shewn that to be true of Christians, which was once said of the antient Philosophers, That there can be nothing so absurd which some Men will not adventure to maintain.

In most of our other Controversies with those of the Church of Rome, *we shew them to be* Erroneous; *in this they are* Extravagant; *And as an eminent Pen has very justly express'd it,* ' The business ' of *Transubstantiation* is not a Controversie of *Scri-* ' *pture* against *Scripture,* or of *Reason* against *Rea-* ' *son,* but of downright *Impudence* against the plain ' meaning of *Scripture,* and all the *sense* and *reason* ' of mankind. Discourse against Transubstantiation, Pag. 2.

The truth is, as the same Person goes on, ' It is a ' most self-evident falshood: and there is no Do- ' ctrine or Proposition in the World that is of it ' self more evidently true, than Transubstantiation ' is evidently false. *And if such things as these must be disputed, and this Evidence,* ' That what we ' see and handle, and taste to be Bread is Bread, ' and not the Body of a Man; and what we see and ' taste to be Wine is Wine, and not Blood, may ' not pass for sufficient without any farther Proof. ' I cannot discern why any Man that hath but ' confidence enough to do so, may not deny any ' thing to be what all the World sees it is, or af- ' firm it to be what all the World sees it is not, ' and this without all possibility of being further ' confuted. Ibid.

But

The Preface.

But yet since it has pleased God so far to give over some Men to a spirit of delusion, as not only seriously to believe this themselves, but also rashly to damn all those that cannot believe it with them, we ought as well for the security of those who have not yet abandoned their own sense *and* reason, *in compliance only with others who in this matter profess to have laid aside* theirs; *as in charity to such deluded Persons as are unhappily led away with these Errors, to shew them their unreasonableness:* To convince them *that* Christianity *is a* wise *and* rational Religion: *that 'tis a mistaken Piety to suppose that Men ought to believe* Contradictions; *or that their* Faith *is ever the more perfect, because the* Object *of it is impossible: That our* Senses *ought to be trusted in judging aright of their proper Object; that to deny this is to overthrow the greatest external Evidence we have for our Religion, which is founded upon their judgment; or if that will be more considerable, is to take away all the grounds that even themselves can pretend to, wherefore they should disbelieve them in favour of* Transubstantiation.

And this I perswade my self I have in the following Discourse sufficiently shewn, and I shall not need to repeat it again here. For the words *themselves, which are the grounds of this great Error, I have taken that* Method *which seemed to me the most proper to find out the true meaning of them; and, as far as the nature of the Enquiry would permit, have endeavour'd to render it plain and intelligible even to the meanest* Capacity. *And I have some cause to hope that the most learned will not be dissatisfied with the design, what ever they may be with*
the

The Preface.

the performance; it being from such that I have taken the greatest part of my Reflections, and in which I pretend to little of my own besides the care of putting together here, what I had observed scattered up and down in parts elsewhere.

It was so much the more fit at this time to insist upon this manner of arguing, in that a late disturber of the Fathers, the better to shew the Antiquity of his new Religion, has pretended to search no less than into the secrets of the Jewish Cabala after it, and to have found out Transubstantiation there amongst the rest of the Rabbinical Follies: Now however the very name of Galatinus be sufficient to Learned Men to make them esteem his Judgment in his Jewish to be much the same as in his Christian Antiquity which follows after, in those eminent pieces of S. Peter's and S. Matthew's Liturgies, S. Andrew's work of the Passion of our Lord; Dionysius's Ecclesiast. Hierarch. &c. yet because such stuff as this may serve to amuse those who are not acquainted with the emptiness of it, I was so much the rather inclined to shew what the true notions of the Jewish Rites would furnish us with to overthrow their pretences; and that the Rabbins Visions are of as little moment to confirm this conceit as their own Miracles.

Consensus Veterum p. 21, &c.

Ibid. p. 27.

But whatever those of the other Communion shall please to judge of my Arguments, yet at least the Opinions of those eminent Men of their own Church may certainly deserve to be consider'd by them, who have freely declared that there is not in Scripture any evident proof of Transubstantiation; nay some of whom have thought so little engagement upon them either from that or any other Authority to believe it,

B ..that

The Preface.

that they have lived and died in their Church without ever embracing of it.

And of this the late Author of the * Historical Treatise of Transubstantiation, and which is just now set forth in our own Language, may be an eminent instance, being a Person at this day living in the Communion of the Church of Rome, and in no little Esteem among all that know Him. It is not fit to give any more particular character of Him at this time. They who shall please to peruse his Book, will find enough in it to speak in his Advantage; and if they have but any tolerable disposition to receive the truth, will clearly see, that this point of Transubstantiation was the production of a blind and barbarous Age; unknown in the Church for above one thousand Years, and never own'd by the greatest Men in any Ages since. The truth is, if we enquire precisely into this business of Transubstantiation, we shall find the first foundation of it laid in a Cloyster by an unwary Monk about the beginning of the 7th Century: carried on by a Cabal of Men, assembled under the name of a (a) General Council to introduce the worship of Images into the Church, Ann. 787. (b) formed into a better shape by another (c) Monk Ann. 818. and He too opposed by almost all the Learned Men of his Age; and at last confirmed by a (d) Pope of whom their own Authors have left us but a very indifferent (e) character; and in a (f) Synod of which I shall observe only this, that it gave the Pope the power of unmaking Kings, as well as the Priests that of making their God.

* *Traitté d'un Autheur de la Communion Romaine touchant la Transubstantiation.* Lond. 1686.

About 636 or 640. See *Blondel de l'Eucharistie.* c. 14. p. 365.
(a) 2. Concil. Nic.
(b) *Blondel. l. 6. cap.* 18. *pag.* 426.
(c) *Paschasius Radbertus.*
(d) See the Treatise of Transubstantiation; Hist. of the 9th Age.
(e) *Innocent.* III*h. Super omnes mortales ambitiosus & superbus, pecuniæque sititor insatiabilis, & ad omnia scelera pro præmiis datis vel promissis certus & proclivis.* Matt. Paris.
(f) Concil. Lateran. IV. Can. 3. *de Hæreticis.*

But

The Preface.

But indeed I think we ought not to charge the Council *with either of these Attempts; since, contrary to the manner of proceeding in such* Assemblies, *received in all Ages, nothing was either judged or debated by the* Synod: † *The* Pope *only himself formed the* Articles, *digested them into* Canons, *and so read them to the* Fathers; *some of which, their own* Historian *tells us, approved them, others did not, but however all were forced to be contented with them.*

† *His omnibus congregatis in suo loco præfato, & juxta morem Conciliorum generalium in suis Ordinibus singulis collocatis, facto capitulo* LXX *See this confirmed by Monsieur du Pin. Dissert.* VII. *Parif.* 4° 1686. *pag.* 572, 573.

prius ab ipso Papa exhortationis sermone, recitata sunt in pleno Concilio quæ aliis placabilia, aliis videbantur onerosa. Matt. Paris. *ad Ann.* 1215.

Such was the first rise of this new Doctrine; 1215 *years after* Christ. *But still the most learned Men of that and the following Ages doubted not to dissent from it.* (a) Aquinas *who wrote about* 50 *years after this definition, speaks of some, who thought the substantial form of the Bread still to remain after Consecration:* (b) Durandus *doubted not to assert the continuance of the Matter of the Elements, whatever became of the form; and that 'twas* (c) *rashness to say that* Christ's *Body could be there no otherwise than by Transubstantiation: To which* (d) Scotus *also subscribed, that the truth of the Eucharist might be saved without Transubstantiation,* (e) *and that in plain terms ours was the easier, and to all appearance the truer interpretation of* Christ's *words; in which* (f) Ockam *and* (*) d'Alliaco *concurr'd with him.* (g) Fisher *confess'd that there was*

(a) See 3. q. 75. Art. 6. *Utrum facta consecratione remaneat in Hoc Sacramento forma substantialis Panis?* (b) *In.*4 *d.* 11. *q.*9. *Quid ergo dicendum de conversione substantiæ Panis in Corpus Christi? Salvo meliori judicio, potest æstimari, quod SI in isto Sacramento fiat Conversio substantiæ Panis in Corpus Christi, quod ipsa fit per Hoc quod corrupta formâ Panis materia ejus fit sub formâ Corporis Christi* (c) *Id. in* 4. *dist.* 11. *q.* 4. *Art.* 14. (d) *Scotus in* 4. *dist.* 11. *q.* 3. (e) *Id.* 4. *sent. d.*11.*q.* 3 (f) *Ockam in* 4. *q.*5. (*) *Alliaco in* 4. *q.*6. *art.*2.(g) *Contr. capt. Babyl. cap.* 10.

B 2 nothing

The Preface.

nothing to prove the true presence of Christ's Body and Blood in their Mass: (a) Ferus would not have it inquired into, How Christ's Body is there; and (b) Tonstall thought it were better to leave Men to their Liberty of belief in it. Those who in respect to their Churches definition did accept it, yet freely declared that (c) before this Council it was no matter of Faith, nor but for its decision would have been now; That the Ancients did not believe it; that the Scripture does not express it; *in short*, that the interpretation which we give is altogether as agreeable to the words of Christ, *and in truth* free from infinite inconveniences with which the other abounds. *All which plainly enough shews that not only the late* private 'Heretical Spirit, whose imperious sentiments, and ' private Glosses, and contradictory interpretations ' (*as a late* * *Author has elegantly expressed it*) ' like the victorious Rabble of the Fishermen of ' *Naples* riding in triumph, and trampling under ' foot Ecclesiastical Traditions, Decrees, and Con- ' stitutions, Ancient Fathers, Ancient Liturgies ' the whole Church of Christ, but especially ' those words of his, This is my Body, *has opposed this Doctrine*; *but even those who are to be supposed to have had the greatest reverence for all these, their own* Masters *and* Doctors, *found it difficult to embrace so* Absurd *and* Contradictory *a Belief*.

And here then let me beseech those into whose hands these Papers may chance to fall, seriously to consider this matter, and whether the sole Authority of such a Pope as Innocent III, whose actions towards one of our own Kings, and in favour of that very ill Man Dominick and his Inquisition, were there

(a) *Ferus in Matt. 26. Cum certum sit ibi esse* Corpus Christi, *quid opus est disputare num* Panis substantia maneat, vel non?
(b) *Lib. 1. de Eucharistiâ:* See the Treatise of Transubstantiation, 1. part.
(c) *Vid. Bell-arm. de Euch. l. 3. c. 23. p. 767, 768. Suarez in 3. part. D. Th. tol. 3. disp. 50. p. 593, 594. Cajetan. in 3. D. Th. q. 75. art. 1. Scotus, l. c. 4. Sent. d. 11. q. 3. Vid. etiam Ockam, Alliac. loc. supr. cit.*
* *Consensus Veterum Pag. 27.*

there nothing else remaining of his Life, might be sufficient to render him detestable to all good Men, ought to be of so great an Authority with us, as to engage us to give up our senses and our reason; nay and even Scripture and Antiquity it self, in obedience to his arbitrary and unwarrantable Definition.

It is I suppose sufficiently evident from what has been before observed, how little assurance their own Authors had, for all the definition of the Council of Lateran, of this Doctrine. I shall not need to say what debates arose among the Divines of the Council of Trent about it. And though since its determination there, Men have not dared so openly to speak their Minds concerning it as before, yet we are not to imagine that they are therefore ever the more convinced of its Truth.

I will not deny but that very great numbers in the Roman Communion, by a profound ignorance and a blind obedience, the two great Gospel perfections with some men, disposed to swallow any thing that the Church shall think fit to require of them, may sincerely profess the belief of this Doctrine; because they have either never at all considered it, or it may be are not capable of comprehending the impossibility of it. Nor shall I be so uncharitable as to suppose that all, even of the learned amongst them, do wilfully profess and act in this matter, against what they believe and know to be true. I will rather perswade my self that some motives or prejudices which I am not able to comprehend, do really blind their eyes, and make them stumble in the brightness of a mid-day light. But yet that all those, who nevertheless continue to live in the external Communion of the Church of Rome, are not thus

sincere

sincere in the belief of it, is what I think I may without uncharitableness affirm; and because it will be a matter of great importance to make this appear, especially to those of that Persuasion; I will beg leave to offer such proofs of it as have come to my knowledge, in some of the most eminent Persons of these last Ages, and to which I doubt not but others, better acquainted with these secrets than I can pretend to be, might be able to add many more Examples.

And the first that I shall mention is the famous † Picherellus, of whom the testimonies prefix'd to his Works speak so advantagiously, that I shall not need say any thing of the esteem which the learned World had of him. * I must transcribe his whole Treatise should I insist on all he has delivered repugnant to their Doctrine of Transubstantiation. Suffice it to observe that in his Exposition of the words of Institution, This is my Body, He gives this plain interpretation of them, This Bread is my Body *which is both freely allowed by the Papists themselves to be inconsistent with their belief as to this matter; and which he largely shews not only to be his* own, *but to have been the constant* Doctrine of *the* Primitive Fathers *in this point*.

But in this it may be there is not so much ground for our admiration, that one who was not very fond of any of the Errors of that Church, should openly dissent from her in this: It will more be wondred that a person so eminent amongst them as Cardinal du Perron, and that has written so much in defence

---

† *Petri Picherelli Expositio Verborum institutionis Cænæ Domini.* Lugd. Batav. 1629. 12°.

* Hoc est Corpus meum, i. e. Hic panis fractus est Corpus meum. pag. 10. Hoc est Corpus meum, i. e. Panis quem frangimus est communio cum Corpore Christi. pag. 14.—— and pag. 27. Expounding Gratian. dist. 2. Can. Non Hoc Corpus, Ipsum Corpus invisibiliter, de vero & germano Corpore in Cœlis agente intelligitur : Non ipsum visibiliter de Corpore & sanguine Sacramentalibus, Pane & Vino ; Corporis Christi & sanguinis symbolis: Quæ rei quam significant nomen per supradictam metonymiam mutuantur.

of Transubstantiation, *should neverthelefs all the while Himself believe nothing of it. And yet this we are assured he freely confess'd to some of his Friends not long before his death: That he thought the Doctrine to be* Monstrous; *that He had done his endeavour to colour it over the best He could in his Books; but that in short he had undertaken an* ill cause, *and which was not to be maintain'd. But I will set down the relation as I find it in* Monsieur Drelincourt's * Answer *to the* Landgrave *of* Hesse; *and who would not have presum'd to have offer'd a relation so considerable, and to a person of such* Quality, *had he at all fear'd that he could have been disproved in it.* ' † *Your Highness* ' (*says He*) *may believe me if you please: But I can* ' *assure you with all sincerity and truth that if the late* ' Cardinal du Perron *has convinced you of the Truth* ' *of* Transubstantiation, *he has convinced you of that* ' *of which he could never convince himself, nor did* ' *he ever believe it. For I have been informed by* ' *certain Persons of Honour, and that are in all re-* ' *spects worthy of belief, and who had it from those that* ' *were eye witnesses; That some friends of that* Illu- ' strious *and Learned* Cardinal *who went to see him* ' *as he lay languishing upon his Bed, and ill of that di-* ' *stemper of which he died, desired him to tell them* ' *freely, what he thought of* Transubstantiation: ' *To whom he answer'd,* That 'twas a MONSTER. *And* ' *when they farther ask'd him, How then he had written*

* Reponse à la Lettre de Monsig. le Prince Ernest aus cinq Ministres de Paris, &c. Geneve 1664.

† Votre Alteffe me croira s'il luy plait. Mais je luy puis dire avec toute sincerité & verité, que si le defunt Cardinal du Perron luy a perfuadé la Transubstantiation, il luy a perfuadé ce qu'il n'a pû se perfuader à soy-mème, & qu'il n'a nullement cru. Car je fcay par des Gens d' Honneur & dignes de foy, qui l'avoient apris

de temoins oculaires, que des Amis de cet illustre & fcavant Cardinal, qui l' estoient allé visiter lors qu' il estoit languiffant en son lit, & malade de la maladie dont il est mort, le prierent de leur dire franchement ce qu'il croyoit de la Transubstantiation, & qu'il répondit, qu' il la tenoit pour un Monstre. Et comme ils luy demanderent, comment donc il en avoit écrit si amplement & si doctement; il repliqua, qu'il avoit deployé toutes les Adreffes de son Esprit pour colourer cet abus, & pour le rendre plausibile; & qu' il avoit fait comme ceux qui font tous leurs Efforts pour defendre une mauvaise Cause.

' *so*

'*so copiously and learnedly about it? He replied, That*
'*he had done the utmost that his Wit and Parts had ena-*
'*bled him, to* COLOUR OVER THIS ABUSE *and*
'RENDER IT PLAUSIBLE; *But that he had done like*
'*those who employ all their force to defend an* ILL
CAUSE. *And thus far* Monsieur Drelincourt. *I could to this add some farther circumstances which I have learnt of this matter, but what is here said may suffice to shew what the* real Opinion *of this great* Cardinal, *after all his Voluminous Writings, as to this* Doctrine *was; unless some future Obligations shall perhaps engage me to enter on a more particular account of it.*

To these two great instances of another Nation I will beg leave to subjoyn a third of our own Country: Father Barnes the Benedictine, *who in his Pacifick Discourse of most of the points in Controversie between us and the Papists, expresly declares,* 'That the Assertion of *Transubstantiation,* or of the substantial change of the Bread, though it be indeed the 'more common Opinion, is yet no part of the 'Churches Faith: And that the Scripture and Fathers, when they speak of a μετιωία may be sufficiently Expounded of that admirable and supernatural change of the Bread, by the presence of Christ's Body added to it, without the *departure* of the *substance* of the *Bread* it self.

Catholico-Romano-Pacificus Oxon. 1680. Pag. 60. *Assertio Transubstantiationis seu mutationis substantialis panis, licet sit Opinio communior, non tamen est fides Ecclesiæ. Et Scripturæ & Patres docentes μετουσίαν, sufficienter exponi possunt de admirandi & supernaturali mutatione Panis per Præsentiam Corporis Christi ei accedentem, sine substantialis Panis desitione.* Et. P. 95. Μετουσίαν *illam in Augustissimo Sacramento factam, plerique graves & antiqui Scriptores ita explicant, ut non fiat per desitionem substantiæ panis, sed per receptionem supernaturalem substantiæ Corporis Christi in substantiam Panis.* V. pl

It appears by these words how little this Monk *thought* Transubstantiation *an* Article of Faith. *But a greater than he, and who not only did not esteem it necessary*

The Preface.

necessary for Others, *to receive it, but clearly shews that he did not believe it himself, is the Illustrious* Monsieur de Marca, *late* Archbishop *of* Paris, *and well known to the World for his great Learning and Eminence.* His Treatise *of the* Eucharist *was publish'd with Authority, by one of his near Relations the* Abbé Faget *at* Paris 1668. *with some other little* Tracts *which he had received from the* Archbishops *own hands. In the close of that Treatise he thus delivers his Opinion:* '† The species of the Bread is
' in its Essence and Nature distinct from the Body
' of Christ adjoyn'd to it, although the reason of
' the Eucharist requires that the inward substance
' of the Bread should be converted into that Body
' after a manner that exceeds all Imagination. But
' yet this change hinders not but that the BREAD
' which is seen still RETAINS its own NATURE,
' BEING, and ESSENCE, or SUBSTANCE, toge-
' ther with the proprieties of its true Nature,
' among which one is the faculty of nourishing our
' Bodies, &c. Whence it follows that it was rightly
' observ'd by *Gelasius,* that the Sacrament of the
' *Body* and *Blood* of Christ was a *Divine thing*,
' because the *Bread* and *Wine* being perfected by

Illustriss. atq; Reverend P. de Marca Parisiens. Archiep. Dissertationes posthumæ. De Sanctissimo Eucharistiæ Sacramento dissertatio, in qua
† *Species Panis est Essentiâ & Naturâ distincta à Corpore* Christi *sibi adjuncto, licet ratio Euchariſtiæ id exigat, ut substantia Panis interior conversa fuerit in illud Corpus modo quodam qui omnem cogitationem exsuperat. Cæterum mutatio illa non officit quin* Panis, *qui videtur,* [*id est, Accidentia*] *suam*

Naturam, Extantiam & Essentiam [SIVE SUBSTANTIAM] *retineat, & naturæ veræ Proprietates, inter quas est alendi corporis* humani facultas——. *Unde consequitur rectè observatum à* Gelasio *Sacramenta* Corporis *&* Sanguinis Christi *divinam rem esse, quia* Panis & Vinum *in divinam transeunt substantiam, S. spiritu perficiente, nempe in* Corpus Christi *spiritale: sed ex alia parte non desinere substantiam & naturam* Panis *&* Vini, *sed ea permanere in suæ proprietate* Naturæ. *Quoniam scil. postquam* Panis *in divinam substantiam transivit,* [NON INTERIIT INTEGRA PANIS NATURA QUAM SUBSTANTIAM QUOQUE VOCAT, NEC DESIVIT : SED] *in suæ proprietate Naturæ permansit ad alendum Corpus idonea, quod est præcipuum conficti panis munus.* Note, That in the Paris Edition, they have put in those words printed in the Black Letter (*id est, Accidentia*) and omitted those that I have caused to be set in Capitals : But in the *Original leaf*, which I have left in S. *Martin's* Library to be seen by any that pleases, and which was cut out for the sake of this passage, it stands as I have said : and as it is truly represented in the *Holland Edition.*

C 'the

'the *Holy Spirit* paſs into the *Divine ſubſtance*,
'*viz.* the *ſpiritual Body of Chriſt*; but on the other
'ſide, that the SUBSTACNE and NATURE of the
'BREAD and WINE do not ceaſe to be, but continue
'ſtill in the *propriety* of their own *Nature.*

And here I ſuppoſe any one who reads this paſſage alone of this *Treatiſe* might without the help of * Monſieur Baluze's *Animadverſion* eaſily have concluded, 'That if this be indeed the work of 'Monſieur de Marca, 'twill be impoſſible to hinder 'him from paſſing with many Perſons for a 'HERETICK as to the point of the *Euchariſt.* But before I quit this *Inſtance*, I cannot but obſerve with reference to this Treatiſe, what care the *Romaniſts* take to hinder the ſentiments of learned Men in this Point from coming to a publick knowledge: And which might give us ſome cauſe to ſuſpect, that their great concern is not ſo much whether they do indeed believe Tranſubſtantiation themſelves, as not to let the World know that they do not.

* Baluze 2 Lettre à Monſieur le Préſid. Marca. *S'il eſt vray, ce que j'ay de la peine à croire, que feu Monſigneur ait compoſé les Traittez que M. Faget a fait imprimer ſous ſon nom, dont il ſe vante dans la Preface & dans la Vie d'avoir les Originaux écrits de la main de l'Auteur, nous ne ſçaurions empeſcher que feu Monſigneur ne paſſe dans l'Eſprit de beaucoup de Gens pour* HERETIQUE, *au ſujet de l'Euchariſtie.*

This has been heretofore ſhewn in another Treatiſe with reference to S. Chryſoſtom; whoſe * Epiſtle to Cæſarius ſome of the Sorbonne Doctors cauſed moſt ſhamefully to be cut out of Monſieur Bigot's Edition of Palladius, becauſe it too plainly ſpoke the Doctrine of the Proteſtants as to this point. And the ſame has almoſt happened to this Treatiſe of Monſieur de Marca here mentioned: † Before it came to a publick ſight, the paſſages that ſeemed moſt viſibly to op-

* Defence of the Expoſition of the Doctrine of the Church of Engl. Appendix, p. 127. n. v.

† See the Preface to the Reader before the Edition of the ſame Treatiſes 12° Anno 1669. and *Monſieur Baluze's* Letter to the Biſhop of *Tulle* on this occaſion. *p.* 5.

The Preface.

pose their *Doctrine, were either* changed *or* suppress'd ; * *(of which the passage before cited is one). as appears by the* Paris Edition *now extant of them.* But † *the Providence of God that brought to light the other, has discover'd this cheat too* ; *For before the alarm was given, and that the* Chancellor, (*a*) *the* Sorbonne Doctors, *but especially Monsieur* Baluze *by his Letters to the* President de Marca, *the* Archbishop's Son, *upon this occasion, had awakened the* Abbé Faget *to consider more nearly what he had done ;* (*b*) *several Presents had been made of the intire work as it was in the Authors MS.* ; *and, if we may credit their own relations, the* Printer *who was a* Protestant *and the same that printed* (*c*) *Monsieur* Claude's *Books against the* Perpetuité, *had obliged that learned Person with a Copy* ; *by which means both the genuine sentiments of Monsieur* de Marca *in opposition to* Transubstantiation *are preserved, and their fraudulent endeavours to suppress his opinion discovered.*

* The *Original letters* cut out by them having fallen into my Hands, may be seen by those that desire it in S. Martin's Library.
† See *Monsieur Baluze* 2. *Lettre* pag. 15.
(*a*) *Mais enfin le refus que Mrs. de Sorbonne luy ont fait de luy donner leur approbation------ luy ont fait ouvrir les yeux, s'estant laissé entendre, quoyqu'un peu tard, qu'il a fait une Sottise.* ibid.
(*b*) Et p. 16. *Je dis, un peu tard* ; *parce*

qu'il avoit de ja fait des presentes de son livre, & que le libraire en avoit aussi debité quelques uns.
(*c*) *Baluze Lettre à Monsieur l'Evesque de Tulle*, p. 5.

To this eminent Person *I will beg leave to subjoyn a fifth, and he too no less known to the World both for his Learning and Reputation, nor less a* Heretick *in this point, however not hitherto so openly discovered as the other* : *and that is Father* Sirmond *the* Jesuit. *In his life of* Paschasius Radbertus, ' *he tells us,* That this Monk was the first ' who explained the genuine sense of the Catho' lick Church in this mystery : *and indeed if what* * Blondel *and some others have observed concerning him be true, that it was for* Impanation, *not* Transub-

Sirmond. *Vit.* Pasch. Radbert.
* *Eclaircissement de l'Euch.* c.19. p. 431, &c.

substantiation; *the Jesuit perhaps spoke his real judgment of him, though not in that sense that he is usually understood to have done it.*

But however that be, certain it is that this learned Father *so little believed the Doctrine of the present* Roman Church *as to this* point, *that he freely confess'd he thought it had herein departed from the antient Faith; and at the desire of one of his Friends wrote a short* Treatise *to confirm his Assertion. This though it be not yet made publick, is neverthess in the hands of several Persons of undoubted integrity: I will mention only one, whose learning and worth are sufficiently known to the World, viz.* Monsieur Bigot: *who discoursing with Father* Raynauld *at* Lyons *about this matter, the* Jesuit *confess'd to him that it was true, that he had himself a copy of his* Treatise *which he would communicate to him, and that it was Father* Sirmond *whom upon this account he reflected upon in his Book,* de bonis & malis Libris, *where he observes,* 'That Men of great parts love to innovate, and invent always somewhat of their own in difficult matters.'

<small>Ingenia præclara in rebus difficilibus aliquid semper de suo comminiscuntur. Nam præclara ingenia multa novant circa scientias. Theoph. Raynaudi S. J. Erotemata de malis ac bonis libris: Lugduni 1653. p. 251.</small>

When Monsieur Bigot *return'd to claim the performance of his promise, the* Jesuit *excused himself to him that he could not light upon it; which when he afterwards told to Father* Chiflet *another* Jesuit *of* Dijonois, *he again confirmed to him the truth of the relation, and voluntarily offer'd him a Copy of the* Treatise, *which he told him was transcribed from Father* Sirmonds *Original. This Monsieur fieur* Bigot *has not only acknowledged to some of his Friends of my acquaintance, but promised to communicate to them the very* Treatise ; *and I dare appeal to the candor of that worthy Person for the truth of what I have here related, and whose name I should not have mentioned, but only to remove all reasonable cause of suspicion in a matter of such importance.*

And what I have now said of Father Sirmond, *I might as truly affirm of a fourth* Person *of as great a name, a* Doctor *of the* Sorbonne, *whose Treatise against* Transubstantiation *has been seen by several persons, and is still read in the MS. But because I am not at liberty to make use of their names, I shall not any further insist upon this example.*

My next instance will be more undeniable, and it is of the ingenious Monsieur de Marolles *Abbot of* Ville-loyn, *well known in* France *for his excellent Writings and great Abilities. A little before his death, which happen'd about the beginning of the Year* 1681. *being desirous to free his Conscience as to the point of the* Holy Eucharist, *in which he supposed their Church to have many ways departed from the right Faith, he caused a* Paper *to be* Printed, *in which he declares his thoughts concerning it; and sent it to several of his most learned Acquaintance, the better to undeceive them in this matter. One of these Persons, to whom this Present was made, having been pleased to communicate to me the very* Paper *which by the* Abbot's *order was brought to him, it may not perhaps be amiss to gratifie the* Reader's *curiosity, if I here insert it at its full length.*

* *Permission*

* Permission hoped for to speak freely for the Truth.

<small>* The Abbot means, that now at his death he hoped he might speak freely what he durst not in his Life-time do.</small>

'I Cannot but exceedingly wonder that a certain
' Preacher, who reads the Holy Scriptures,
' and will maintain nothing but by their Autho-
' rity, should nevertheless undertake to defend a-
' gainst all Opposers by the Scriptures, the Real
' Presence in the Eucharist out of the act of re-
' ceiving; and think himself so sure to overcome
' in this Occasion, as to talk of it as a thing cer-
' tain, and in which he knows he cannot be re-
' sisted.

'It would certainly be more safe not to be too much
' prepossessed with any thing. I will not name the
' Person, because I have no mind to displease him;
' But in the mean time, neither Sense, nor Rea-
' son, nor the Word of God have suggested to him
' one word of it; unless the Apostle was mistaken
' when he said, ' *If ye are risen with Christ, seek*
' *those things that are above, where Christ is sate*
' *at the right hand of God. Set your affection on things*
' *above and not on things upon the Earth.* Coloss. 3.
' 1, 2. For how could he speak after this manner,
' if Jesus Christ be still upon Earth by his real
' Presence under the species in the Eucharist?

'When he ascended into Heaven, he said not
' to his Disciples which saw his wonderful Ascen-
' sion;

'fion ; *I shall be with you always by my* Real Presence *under the species of the Eucharist, which shall be publickly exposed to you.* In his Sermon at the Supper which he had just now celebrated, and which immediately preceded his *Passion*, Jesus Christ according to S. *John* says expresly to his Apostles, that he was about to leave them, that he should not be long absent, that he would send to them the *Comforter*; but not one word of his *Real Presence in the Eucharist*, which he had so lately instituted under the *Bread* and *Wine*, to be a Mystery of our Faith for the nourishment of the *Soul* to *life Eternal*, as ordinary *Bread* and *Wine* are for the nourishment of the *Body* to a *temporal Life*, and that too for ALL the faithful, as is clearly signified by those Words, *Drink ye all of this.* Whereupon I have elsewhere remark'd the custom of *Libations* which were in use time out of mind throughout the whole *Roman* Empire, and which custom was establish'd in honour of the gods : As may be seen in the Version of *Athenæus* in 1680; and as I had observed long before upon *Virgil* and *Horace*, though there was but little notice taken of it. Which makes me think it very probable, that our Saviour intended to sanctifie this Profane custom, as he did some others, which I have remarked in the same place.

'When Men undertake to prove too much, they very often prove nothing at all: To maintain that *Jesus Christ* is intire in the *Eucharist* with all his Bodily extension, and all his Dignity, so as he is in Heaven; so that under the *Roundness* of the *Bread* there is nothing that is *Round*;
'under

'under the *Whiteness* there is nothing *White*; this
'is what the Scripture has not said one word of.
'They are indeed meer *Visions*, and which are not
'so easie to maintain as Men may think. The
'Priest who celebrates breaks the *Host* in three
'pieces; One of these he puts into the Cup, of
'the two others he communicates, in memory as
''tis plain of what we read, That *Jesus the night
'in which he was betray'd took Bread, and when
'he had given thanks he brake it, and said, Take,
'Eat, This is my Body which is broken for you, Do
'this in Remembrance of Me.* 1 Cor. 11. 23, 24. In the
'*Mass* there is here no more *Bread*, they are only
'the *appearances of Bread*, that is to say, the *Ac-
'cidents*, and which are not tied to any *Substance*.
'And yet so long as there is but one *Atom* of
'those *Accidents* which they call *Eucharistical species*
'in the *Consecration* that has been made, the *true
'Flesh* of the Lord Jesus is so annex'd to them,
'that it remains there whole and intire, without
'the least confusion, and may be so in diverse places
'at the same time. I doubt not but those who
'teach us this Doctrine have thought of it more
'than once; but have they well consider'd it? for
'there is not one word of it in all the *Sacred
'Writings*.

'Is it nothing that *Jesus Christ* said to his A-
'postles but a little while before his *Passion*, when
'he was now about to celebrate his Holy Supper
'with them, *You shall have the Poor always with
'you, but me ye shall not have always, Matth.* 26.
'11. His *Real Presence* in the *Eucharist*, out of
'the act of communicating, not excepted?

'They

The Preface.

'They say to the People, Behold your Creator
'that made Heaven and Earth: And the People see-
'ing the consecrated Bread in the *Ciboire* wherein 'tis
'carry'd abroad, says, Behold the *good God* going
'in procession to confound the *Hereticks*: and ac-
'cording to their natural inclination, they a-
'dore with all their Hearts they know not what,
'because so they have been instructed; and the
'better to maintain their prejudice intire in this
'matter, they become mad: But alas! they know not
'what they do, and we ought to pity their
'Excess.

'On the other side, who can tell whether the
'Priest has *consecrated*, or indeed whether he be
'capable of *consecrating*? Is it a point of Faith
'to believe, that among so many Priests, not one
'of them is a *Cheat* and an *Impostor*? This cer-
'tainly cannot be of Faith; and if this be not,
'neither is that which exposed with so much Pomp,
'to carry the true Body of the Lord through the
'Streets, of Faith. Thus the belief is at best but
'*Conjecture*; and then whatsoever in such cases is
'not of Faith is sin, according to the Apostle,
Rom. 14. 23.'

'I know not what colour can be sufficient to
'excuse so strong an Objection, unless Men will
'absolutely resist the Holy Scripture, and right
'Reason founded upon it.

''Tis further said, that Jesus Christ is in ma-
'ny places at the same time, in the *Hosts* which
'are carried in very different manners; But neither
'for this is there any Text of Scripture. You will
'say, this may be; I answer, the Question here
'is not of the Infinite power of Jesus Christ, but
'of

'of his Will, and which we must obey when it is
'known to us; and of this as to the present point
'we read nothing in the Holy Scripture. The
'shorter way then would be to say, that the Sa-
'crament of one Parish is not the same with that
'of another, although both the one and the other
'concur in the same design to worship God; as
'the Paschal Lamb of one Family, was not the
'Lamb of another, although both the one and the
'other were to accomplish the same Mystery.
'Thus for instance, on *Corpus Christi-day*, the Sa-
'crament of S. *Germain d' Auxerrois*, where the
'perpetual Vicar consecrates the Host, and *Monsieur*
'the Dean, the first *Curé*, carrys it the Procession
'under a rich Canopy crown'd with Flowers, this
'Host is not the same with that of S. *Paul*'s which
'is carried after another manner, *viz*. the Image
'of that Apostle made of Silver gilt, falling from
'his Horse at his Conversion, under the Sacra-
'ment of Jesus Christ hung up in rays of Gold,
'and carried under the covering of another state-
'ly Canopy; and so of all the other Churches.

'As for the stories of several *Hosts* that have
'been stabb'd with Penknives, and have bled, they
'serve only to bring in some superstition contrary
'to the word of God, which never pretended that
'there was material *Blood* in the consecrated
'*Bread*, because it is the *Body* of Jesus Christ in
'*a mystery of Faith*.

'For what is said of an *Infant* that was seen in
'the stead of the *Host*, and of the figure of Christ
'sitting upon a *Sepulchre* instead of the same
'*Host*, are meer *Fables* suggested by the *Father*
'*of Lies*.

'It

The Preface. xxiii

'It is further reported of certain Robbers that
'carrying away the Veſſel in which the *Hoſt* is
'kept, they have thrown the *Hoſt* it ſelf upon
'the ground, and trampled it under foot, ſome-
'times have caſt it into naſty places, without any
'fear that it ſhould avenge it ſelf; This is a moſt
'horrible thought, and of which we ought not to
'open our mouths, but only to deteſt ſo dreadful
'a profanation.

'The ſame muſt be ſaid of thoſe *Hoſts* which
'have been caſt up, as ſoon as received, whether
'by ſick perſons, or ſometimes by debauched Prieſts,
'diſordered with the laſt nights intemperance; both
'which have ſometimes happened, not to ſay any
'thing of thoſe other terrible inconveniences, re-
'mark'd in the Cautions concerning the *Maſs*. All
'which ſhew that Men have carry'd things too
'far, without any warrant from the Word of
'God.

'It is not therefore ſo eaſie, as ſome imagine,
'to maintain the Doctrine of the *Real Preſence*
'out of the Uſe, againſt the Opinions of any Op-
'poſer.

'In the mean time the Truth is terribly obſcured,
'and few give themſelves the trouble to clear it.
'On the contrary it ſeems that among the many
'Writers of the Age, there are ſome who make it
'their whole buſineſs to hide it, and to keep them-
'ſelves from finding it out, as if they deſired never to
'be wiſer than they are. The vanity of lying flat-
'ters them but too much in all the Humane paſſions
'which ſway them.

'There are neverthelefs ſome faithful Diſciples,
'and Apoſtolick Souls who are exempted, to obey

'God

'God by his Grace, and to give glory to his Name.
'It was not long before his departure that *David*
'said, *Every man is a lyar*: Pſal. 115. 2. and S. *Paul*
'to the *Romans* 3. 4. to ſhow that God only is true,
'adds immediately after from *Pſalm* * 50. 6. *Thou that*
'*mighteſt be juſtified when thou ſpeakeſt, and be clear*
'*when thou judgeſt.*

    * Li. 4.

    Such was the *Opinion of* Monſieur de Marolles as to this point: *I ſhould too much treſpaſs upon the Reader's patience to inſiſt thus particularly upon others of leſſer note.* The Author of the late Hiſtorical Treatiſe of Tranſubſtantiation, *has fully ſhewn not only his* own Opinion, *but the* Tradition *of all the* Ages *of the* Church *againſt it: And though I dare not ſay the ſame of whoever he was that ſet forth the* † Moyens ſurs & Honneſtes, &c. *that he did not believe* Tranſubſtantiation *himſelf, yet this is clear,* 'That he did not deſire any one ſhould be 'forced to believe it; or indeed be encouraged 'to ſearch too nicely into the *manner how Chriſt is* '*Preſent and Eaten in the Holy Sacrament.*

† *Il nous ſuffit que J. C. qui eſt la Verité meme nous ait aſſuré que ce Sacrament eſt veritablement ſon Corps, & qu'il ait ordonné de manger ſa chair & boire ſon ſang: car il faut abſolument qu'il y ſoit, puis q'il il nous ordonne de l'y manger, ſans s'embaraſſer l'Eſprit de quelle maniere & comment cela ſe fait* 2. Part, p. 102.

    Whether Monſieur de Meaux *believes this Doctrine or not, his authority is become of ſo little importance, that I do not think it worth the while to examine. Yet the firſt* French * Anſwer *to his* Expoſition *obſerves, that in the* ſuppreſs'd Edition of

* Advertiſſement n. 14. p. 22. Mr. B.— Speaking of that Edition, *Il n'y avoit en aucun lieu de l'Article, ni le terme de Tranſubſtantiation, ni cette propoſition, que* 'le pain & le vin ſont changez au corps & au ſang de J. C. dans 'la derniere [*Edition*] apres ces mots, le propre Corps & le propre ſang de J. C. il a 'ajouté auſquelles le pain & le vin ſont changez; ceſt ce qu'on appelle Tranſubſtantiation.

The Preface.

it he had not at all mentioned 'that the Bread and
'Wine are *turned* into the *Body* and *Blood* of *Christ*;
*those words in the close of that Paragraph which we
now read*, viz. 'that the Bread and the Wine are
'changed into the proper Body, and proper
'Blood of Jesus Christ, and that this is that
'which is called Transubstantiation, *being put in*;
† for the greater neatness of the Discourse and Stile,
since.

† *Monsieur de Meaux* Letter of his alterations; *Vind.* p. 13. & 117. *pour l'ordre, & pour une plus grande netteté du discours & du stile.*

But now for his Vindicator, 'tis evident, if he
understands his own meaning, that he is not very well
instructed about it. *'It is manifest, *says he*, that
'our dispute with Protestants is not about the
'manner, *How Jesus Christ is Present*, but only about
'the Thing it self, whether the Body and Blood
'of Jesus Christ be truly, really, and substan-
'tially present after the words of Consecration,
'under the species or Appearance of Bread and
'Wine, the substance of Bread and Wine being not
'so present.

* Vindication of the Bishop of Condom's Expos. Pag. 83.

*In which words, if his meaning be to exclude total-
ly the* 'manner, How Jesus Christ becomes pre-
'sent in the Eucharist, *as his expression is*, *from
being a matter of Faith, it might well have been
ranged amongst the rest of their* new Popery 1686.
But *if he designs not to exclude the* manner *of* Christ's
Presence, *but only the* mode *of the* Conversion, *as
he seems by some other of his words to insinuate*, viz.
whether it be by Adduction, &c. *from being a matter of Faith, he ought not then to have deny'd the* manner of Christ's Presence in the Eucharist, *which their
Church has absolutely defined to be* by that wonderful
and singular Conversion so aptly called Transubstantiation; *but more precisely to have explain'd his* School-
nicety

nicety, *and which is altogether as* unintelligible, *as the* Mystery *which 'tis brought to* explain.

I might to the particulars hitherto mentioned, add the whole Sect of their new Philosophers, *who following the* Hypothesis *of their Master* Des-cartes, *that* Accidents *are nothing else but the* Modes *of* Matter, *must here either renounce his Doctrine or their Churches Belief. But I shall close these remarks, which have already run to a greater length than I designed, with one instance more, from a* Prelate *of our own* Church, *but yet whose truly Christian sincerity will I am perswaded justifie him even to those of the* Roman Communion : *and it is the learned Archbishop* Usher, *who having been so happy as to convert several* Roman Priests *from their errors, and inquiring diligently of them, what they who said* Mass *every day, and were not obliged to confess* Venial Sins, *could have to trouble their* Confessors *so continually withal; ingenuously acknowledged to him, that the chiefest part of their constant* Confession *was their* Infidelity *as to the point of* Transubstantiation, *and for which as was most fit, they mutually quitted and absolved one another.*

<small>The same is affirmed by Monsieur du Moulin of several Priests in France : Disp. Sedanens. de Sacr. Euch. par. 4. p. 846. Nec abs re de intentione presbyteri dubitatur, cum plurimi Sacerdotes cacant Missam reluctante Conscientiâ, quales multos vidimus qui ejurato Papismo fatebantur se diu cecinisse Missam animo à Missâ alienissimo.</small>

And now that is thus clear from so many instances of the greatest Men in the Roman Church, *which this last Age has produced; and from whose discovery we may reasonably enough infer the like of many others that have not come to our knowledge, that several Persons who have lived and enjoyed some of the greatest* Honours *and* Dignities *in that* Communion, *have nevertheless been* Hereticks *in this*

this points, may I beseech those who are still mis-led with this great Error, to stop a while, and seriously examine with me two or three plain considerations, and in which I suppose they are not a little concerned.

And the first is, Of their own danger: *but especially upon their* Own Principles.

It is but a very little while since an ingenious Person now living in the French Church, *the* Abbé Petit *publish'd a Book which he* ' calls (a) The truths of the
' Christian Religion proved and
' defended against the antient Here-
' sies by the Truth of the Eucha-
' rist: *And what he means by this*
' *truth, he thus declares in his* Preface,
' *viz.* the change of (b) the Bread
' into the Body of the Son of God,
' and of the Wine into his Blood.
' *He there pretends that this Do-*
' *ctrine however combatted by us*
' *now, was* (c) yet more undoubt-
' ed in the Primitive Church than
' either the divinity of Christ and
' the Holy Ghost, or the certainty
' of our future Resurrection. *And*
' *this he wrote as the Title tells us,*
' *(d)* To confirm the new Converts
' in the Faith of the Catholick Church; *meaning according to their usual figure, the* Roman. *How far this extravagant undertaking may serve to convince them I cannot tell; this I know, that if*

(a) *Les Veritez de la Religion prouveés & defendues contre les anciennes Here-sies, par la verité de l'Eucharistie.* 1686.

(b) *Que du pain divienne le Corps & fils de Dieu, & du Vin son sang. Preface p. 7.*

(c) *Quoiqu'il n'y ait point, presentement de veritez plus incontestables que les trois grands articles de nostre foi, qui sont contenus dans le symbole, c'est à dire, la divinité de J. C. la divinité du S. Esprit, & la Résurrection: Cependant j'ose dire que la presence réelle de J. C. au Saint Sacrament etoit une verité encore plus indubitable dans les premiers siecles de l'Eglise. Pref. p. 5.*

(d) *Traitté pour confirmer les Nouveaux Convertis dans la foi de l'Eglise Catholique.*

we may credit those who have been that Abbot's most intimate acquaintance, he believes but very little of it himself, unless he also be become in this point, a new Convert.

But now if what has before been said of so many eminent Persons of their Church be true, as after a due and diligent examination of every particular there set down, I must beg leave to profess I am fully perswaded that it is; 'twill need no long deduction to shew how dangerous an influence their unbelief must have had, in some of the chiefest instances of their constant Worship.

(e) *Concil. Trid. Sess. vii. Can. 11. si quis dixerit in ministris dum Sacramenta conficiunt, non requiri intentionem, saltem faciendi quod facit Ecclesia, Anathema sit.*
(f) *Vid. de defectibus circa Missam, c. de defectu Intentionis. In Missali. R.*

For 1. It is the Doctrine of the (e) Council of Trent *that to make a* Sacrament, *the* Priest *must have, if not an* Actual, *yet at least a* Virtual Intention *of doing that which the Church does:* And in the (f) Rubricks of their Missal, *the want of such an* Intention *in the* Priest *is one of the defects there set down as sufficient to hinder a* Consecration. *Now if this be true, as every* Roman Catholick *who acknowledges the Authority of that Synod must believe it to be;* 'tis then evident *that in all those* Masses *which any of the Persons I before named have said, there could have been no* Consecration: *It being absurd to suppose that they who believed not* Transubstantiation, *could have an* intention *to make any such* change *of the* Bread *into the* Body *of* Christ, *which they thought it impossible to do.*

Now if there were no Consecration, *but that the* Bread *continued* meer Bread *as it was before;* then Secondly, All those *who attended at their* Masses, *and* Adored *their* Hosts, *pay'd the* supream worship *of* God *to a bare* Wafer, *and no more. How far the modern*

modern plea of their good Intention *to* Adore Chrift *in thofe facred Offices, may excufe them from having committed* Idolatry, *it is not neceffary I fhould here examine. They who defire a fatisfaction in this matter, may pleafe to refur to a late excellent* Treatife *written purpofely on this Subject, and where they will find the weaknefs of this fuppofal fufficiently expofed. But fince* (a) *many of their own greateft Men confefs that if any one by mi-ftake fhould worfhip an* Unconfecrated Hoft, *taking it to have been* Confecrated, *he would be guilty of* Idolatry; *and that fuch an* Error *would not be fufficient to excufe him; may they pleafe to confider with what* Faith *they can pay this* Divine Adoration *to that which all their* Senfes *tell them is but a bit of* Bread; *to the hinderance of whofe Converfion fo many things may interpofe, that were their Doctrine otherwife as* infallible, *as we are certain it is* falfe, *it would yet be a hundred to one that there is no* Confecration: *in a word; how they can worfhip that which they can never be fecure is* changed *into* Chrift's Body, *nay when, as the examples I have before given fhew, they have all the reafon in the World to fear, whether even the* Prieft *himfelf who fays the* Mafs *does indeed believe that he has any* Power, *or by confequence can have any* intention, *to turn it into the* Flefh of Chrift.

A Difcourfe concerning the Adoration of the Hoft. *Lond.* 1685. (a) *Vid. Catharin. in Catlet. pag.* 133. *Ed. Paris.* 1535. Where he quotes *S. Thomas* and *Paludanus* for the fame Opinion: This Book of his was feen and approved by the Pope's order by the Divines at *Paris:* as himfelf tel's us in the review of it. *Lugdun.* 1542.

And the fame confideration will fhew, Thirdly; *How little fecurity their other Plea of* Concomitance, *which they fo much infift upon, to fhew the fufficiency of their* Communicating *only in one kind, viz.* 'that they receive the Blood *in the* 'Body, *can give to the* Laity, *to fatisfie their*

E *Confciences*

Consciences that they ever partake of that Blessed Sacrament as they ought to do. Since whatever is pretended of Christ's Body, 'tis certain there can be none of his Blood *in a meer* Wafer: And if by reason of the Priest's infidelity, the Host should be indeed nothing else, of which we have shewn they can never be sure; neither can they ever know whether what they receive be upon their own Principles, *an* intire Communion.

And then Lastly, for the main thing of all, The Sacrifice of the Mass; *it is clear that if* Christ's Body *be not* truly *and* properly *there, it cannot be* truly *and* properly offer'd; *nor any of those great benefits be derived to them from a* morsel of Bread, *which themselves declare can proceed only from the* Flesh *and* Blood *of their Blessed Lord*.

It is I know an easie matter for those who can believe Transubstantiation, *to believe also that there is no hazard in all these great and apparent dangers. But yet in matters of such moment Men ought to desire to be well assured, and not exposed even to any possible defects.* I do not now insist upon the common remarks, which yet are Authorized by their own Missal, *and may give just grounds to their fears*; 'That 'if the Wafer be not made of 'Wheat but of some other Corn, 'there is then no Consecration: 'If it be mixed not with com- 'mon, but distill'd Water, it is 'doubtful whether it be Conse- 'crated. If the Wine be sowre 'to such a certain degree, that then it becomes 'incapable

De defectibus circa Missam: De defectu panis. Si panis non sit triticeus, vel si triticeus, sit admixtus granis alterius generis in tantâ quantitate, ut non maneat panis triticeus, vel sit alioqui corruptus: non conficitur Sacramentum. Si sit confectus de aquâ rosaceâ vel alterius distillationis, dubium est an conficiatur? Et de defect. vini. Si Vinum sit factum penitus acetum, vel penitus putridum, vel de uvis acerbis seu non maturis expressum, vel admixtum tantum aquæ ut vinum sit corruptum, non conficitur Sacramentum.

'incapable of being changed into the Blood of
'Chrift; *with many more of the like kind, and
*which render it always uncertain to them, whether
there be any change made in the
bleffed* Elements *or no*; * *the Re- lations I have given, are not of counterfeit* Jews *and* Moors, *who to escape the danger of the* Inqui- fition *have fometimes become* Priefts,

* *Du Moulin*, in the place above cited, mentions one that in his time was burnt at *London* for Confecrating a Hoft in the name of the Devil. *Thef. Sedan. Th.* 97. *n.* 10. *p.* 845. *Vol.* 1.

and adminiftred all the Sacraments for many years together, without ever having an intention to Ad- minifter truly any one of them, and of which I could give an eminent inftance in a certain Jew *now living; who for many Years was not only a* Prieft, *but a* Profeffor *of Divinity in* Spain, *and all the while in reality a meer* Jew *as he is now. The* Perfons *here mention'd were Men of undoubted re- putation, of great learning and fingular efteem in their* Church; *and if thefe found the impoffibili- ties of* Tranfubftantiation *fo much greater than ei- ther the pretended* Authority *or* Infallibility *of their* Church; *certainly they may have juft caufe to fear, whether many others of their* Priefts *do not* Live *in the fame infidelity in which thefe have* Died, *and fo expofe them to all the hazards now mentioned, and which are undeniably the confequences of fuch their* Unbelief.

But thefe are not the only dangers *I would defire thofe of that* Communion *to reflect on upon this occafion. Another there is, and of greater confe- quence than any I have hitherto mentioned, and which may perhaps extend not only to this* Holy Eucharift, *but it may be to the invalidating of moft of their other* Sacraments. * *It is the Doctrine of the* Roman

* *Eugenii* IV. decret. in Act. Concil. Flo- rent. Ann. 1439. Concil. Labb. Tom. 13. p. 525. Con- cil. Trident. Seff. VII. Can. 2.

E 2

Roman Church *that to the* Validity *of every* Sacrament, *and therefore of that of* Orders *as well as the rest three things must concur,* 'a due *matter*, a 'right *form*, and the *Person* of *the Minister con-* 'ferring *the* Sacrament, *with an* intention *of doing* 'what *the* Church *does. Where either of these is wanting, the* Sacrament *is not performed. If therefore the* Bishop *in conferring the Holy Order of* Priesthood *has not an* intention *of doing what the Church does,* 'tis plain that the Person to be ordained receives no Priestly Character *of him*; *nor by consequence has any power of* consecrating *the Holy* Eucharist, *or of being hereafter advanced to a* higher degree. *Now the* form *of conferring the* Order *of* Priesthood *they determine to be this*; † The Bishop delivers the Cup with some Wine, and the Paten with Bread into the Hands of the person whom he Ordains, saying, 'Receive the 'Power of offering a Sacrifice *in the Church for the* 'living *and the* dead, *in the name of the* Father, '*and of the* Son, *and of the* Holy Ghost. *By* 'which Ceremony *and* words, *their* Catechism *tells* 'us, *He is constituted an Interpreter and Mediator* 'between God and Man; *which is to be esteemed* '*the chiefest Function of a Priest. So that then the* intention *necessary to the conferring the Order of* Priesthood *is this*; *to give a Power to* consecrate, *i.e. to* Transubstantiate *the* Host *into* Christ's Body, *and so* offer *it as a* Sacrifice *for the* Living *and the* Dead.

If therefore any of their Bishops, for instance Cardinal du Perron, *or* Monsieur de Marca, *did not believe that either the* Church *or themselves as* Bishops *of it, had any* Authority *to confer any such*
Power,

† *Ibid. pag.*
538. *Catech.*
Concil. Trid.
de Sacr. Ord.
n. xxii. *p.* 222.
Item, n. L. *p.*
228.

Power, *they could not certainly have any* Intention of doing *in this case* what the Church *intends to do. Having no such* Intention, *the Persons whom they pretended to* Ordain *were no* Priests. Being *no* Priests *they had no* Power to Consecrate. All *the* Hosts *therefore which were either* offered *or* taken, *or worshipped in any of the* Masses *celebrated by those* Priests *whom these two* Bishops Ordained, *were only* meer Bread, *and not the* Body of Christ; *And as many of them, as being afterwards advanced to a higher dignity, were consecrated* Bishops, *received no* Episcopal Character, *because they were destitute of the* Priestly *before. Thus the danger still encreases: For by this means, the* Priests *whom they also* Ordain *are no* Priests; *and when any of them shall be promoted to a higher degree, are uncapable of being made* Bishops; *And so by the Infidelity of these two Men, there are at this day infinite numbers of* Priests *and* Bishops, *who* say Mass, *and confer* Orders *without any manner of power to do either*; *and in a little time it may be there shall not be a true* Bishop *or* Priest *in the whole* Gallicane Church. *But,*

II. *A second* Consideration *which I would beg leave to offer from the fore-going instances is this: What reliance we can make upon the* Pretended Infallibility *of their* Church; *when 'tis thus plain that so many of the most learned Men of their own* Communion *did not only not believe it to be* Infallible, *but supposed it to have* actually Erred, *and that in those very Doctrines that are at this day esteemed the most considerable* Points *in difference between Us.*

It

It is plain from what has been said in the forego-ing reflection, *that disbelieving* Transubstantiation, *they must also have lookt upon all the other Conse-quences of it,* viz. *the* Adoration of the Host, *the* Sacrifice of the Mass, &c. *as Erroneous too. Now though it be not yet agreed among them, nor ever likely to be, where the* supposed Infallibility *of their* Church *is seated, yet since all manner of Authority has conspired to establish these things;* Popes *have* decreed *them,* Councils defined *them, and both* Popes *and* Councils anathematized *all those that shall pre-sume to doubt of them; 'tis evident either these Men did not believe the* Church *to be* Infallible, *as is pretended; or they did not believe the* Roman, *to be, according to the modern phrase, indeed the* Ca-tholick Church.

III. *And upon the same grounds there will arise a third* Reflection, *which they may please to make with us; and that is, with what Reason they can press us with the* Authority *of their* Church *in these matters; when such eminent persons of their own* Communion, *and who certainly were much more Ob-liged to it than we can be thought to be, yet did not esteem it sufficient to enslave their belief.*

It is a reproach generally cast upon us, that we set up a private Spirit *in opposition to the* Wisdom *and* Authority *of the* Church of God: *and think our selves better able to* judge *in matters of* Faith, *than the most* General Council *that was ever yet as-sembled. This is usually said, but is indeed a foul* Misrepresentation *of our Opinion. All we say is, that every Man ought to* act Rationally *in matters of* Religion, *as well as in other concerns; to em-ploy*

ploy his Understanding with the utmost skill and diligence that he is able, to know God's will, and what it is that he requires of us. We do not set up our own judgments *against* the Authority of the Church; *but having both the* Holy Oracles *of* God, *and the* Definitions of Men *before us, we give to each their proper weight. And therefore if the* one *at any time contradicts the* other, *we resolve, as is most fitting, not that* our own, *but* God's Authority *revealed to us in his* Word, *is to be preferred. And he who without this* examination *servilely gives up himself to follow whatever is required of him*; He *may be in the right, if his* Church *or Guide be so; but according to this method shall never be able to give a* reason *of his* Faith; *nor if he chance to be born in a* False Religion, *ever be in a capacity of being better instructed. For if we must be allowed nothing but to obey only, and not presume to* enquire *why*; He *that is a* Jew *must continue a* Jew *still; he that is a* Turk, *a* Turk; *a* Protestant *must always be a* Protestant: *In short, in whatsoever* profession *any one now is, in that he must continue, whether* true *or* false, *if* reason *and* examination *must be excluded all place in* matters *of* Religion.

* *And indeed after all their clamours against us on this occasion, yet is this no more than what themselves require of us, when 'tis in order to their own advantage. Is a* Proselyte *to be made, they offer to him their* Arguments: *They tell him a long story of their* Church; *the* Succession, Visibility, *and other Notes of it. To what purpose is all this, if we are not to be* Judges, *to examine their pretences whether these are sufficient marks of such a Church as they suppose; and if they are, whether they do indeed agree to theirs, and then upon a full*

* All this is lately granted by the Catholick Representer. Cap. VI.

a full conviction submit to them. Now *if this be their intention,* 'tis *then clear, let them pretend what they will, that they think us both capable of* judging *in these matters, and that we ought to follow that, which all things considered we find to be most* reasonable, *which is all that we desire.*

And *for this we have here the undoubted* Examples *of those Eminent* Persons *of their* own Communion *before named;* who *notwithstanding the* Authority *of their* Church, *and the* decision *of so many* Councils *esteemed by it as* General, *have yet both thought themselves at liberty to* examine their Decrees, *and even to pass sentence too upon them, that they were erroneous in the* Points *here mentioned. And therefore certainly we may modestly desire the same liberty which themselves take ; at least till we can be convinced, (and that by such Arguments as we shall be allow'd to judge of,) that there is such an* infallible Guide *whom we ought in all things to follow without further inquiry, and where we may find him; and when this is done I will for my part promise as freely to give up myself to his Conduct, as I am till then, I think reasonably, resolved to follow what according to the best of my ability in* proving all things, *I shall find indeed to be* Good.

IV. *I might from the same* Principles, *Fourthly, argue the* Reasonableness *of our* Reformation, *at least in the opinion of those great Men of whom we have hitherto been speaking : And who thinking it allow'd to them to dissent themselves from the received* Doctrine *of their* Church, *which they found to be erroneous, could not but in their Consciences justifie us, who, as* a national Church, *no way subjected to their* Authority, *did the same*; *and by the right which every such* Church *has within it self*, reformed *those* Errors, *which like the* Tares *were sprung up with the* Good Seed. *This 'tis evident they must have approved*; *and for one of them, the* Abbot of Ville-loyne, *I have been assured by some of his intimate Acquaintance, that he had always a particular respect for the* Church of England, *and which others of their* Communion *at this day esteem to be neither* Heretical *nor* Schismatical.

V. *But I may not insist on these things, and will therefore finish this* Address *with this only remonstrance to them*; *That since it is thus evident, that for above* 1200 *years this* Doctrine *was never* establish'd *in the* Church, *nor till then, in the opinion of their own most learned Men, any* matter of Faith; *since the Greatest of their Writers in the* past Ages *have declared themselves so freely concerning it as we have seen above, and some of the most eminent of their* Communion *in the* present *have ingenuously acknowledged that they could not believe it*; *since 'tis confess'd that the* Scripture *does not require it*; Sense *and* Reason *undoubtedly oppose it, and the* Primitive Ages *of the* Church, *as one of their own* Authors *has very lately shewn, received it not*; *They will at least suffer all these things to dispose them to an indifferent Examination*, wherefore at last it is that they do believe this great Error? Upon *what* Authority *they have given up their* Senses *to* Delusion; *their* Reason *to embrace* Contradictions; *the* Holy Scripture *and* Antiquity, *to be submitted to the dictates of two* Assemblies, *which many of themselves esteem to have been rather* Cabals *than* Councils:

cils : *And all to support a* Doctrine, *the most injurious that can be to our* Saviour's Honour ; *destructive in its nature not only of the certainty of the* Christian Religion, *but of every thing else in the World ; which if* Transubstantiation *be true, must be all but* Vision *: for that cannot be* true *unless the* Senses *of all* Mankind *are* deceived *in judging of their* proper Objects, *and if this be so, we can then be sure of nothing.*

These Considerations, *if they shall incline them to an impartial view of the following* Discourses, *they may possibly find somewhat in them, to shew the reasonableness of our dissent from them in this matter : However they shall at least I hope engage those of our own* Communion *to stand firm in that* Faith *which is thus strongly supported with all sorts of Arguments* ; *and convince them how dangerous it is for Men to give up themselves to such* prejudices, *as neither* Sense *nor* Reason, *nor the* word *of* God *nor the* Authority *of the* best *and* purest Ages *of the* Church, *are able to overcome.*

A

A TABLE OF THE Principal Matters Contained in this TREATISE.

PREFACE.

THE *occasion of this Discourse.*   Page i
   The method made use of for the explaining the nature of this Holy Eucharist.   iv
No Proof of Transubstantiation in Holy Scripture.   v
The rise and establishment of it.   vi, vii
Several of their greatest Men before the Council of Trent *believed it not.*   vii, viii
And many have even since continued to disbelieve it.   x

A Table of the Principal Matters

So, Picherellus.	x	*F.* SIRMOND.		xv
Cardinal du PERRON.	xi	*Monsieur* L——.		xvii
F. Barnes.	xii	*Monf.* de Marolles.		*ib.*
Monsieur de MARCA.	xiii	Others.		xxiv,&c.

 Confequences *drawn from thefe Examples:*

I. *Of the danger of the* Papifts, *efpecially upon their own* Principles. xxvii
  With reference to this Sacrament: *and therein to the*
   1. *Confecration.* xxvii.
   2. *Adoration.* *ib.*
   3. *Communion in one kind.* xxix
   4. *Mafs.* xxx
  With reference to their entire Priefthood. xxxi
II. *Againft the* Infallibility *of the* Roman *Church.* xxxiii
III. *Againft its* Authority. xxxiv
IV. *As to the Reafonablenefs of our* Reformation. xxxvi
V. *That thefe things ought to difpofe thofe of that* Communion *to an impartial fearch into the grounds of their belief as to this matter.* xxxvii

---

PART I.

The Introduction.

Of the Nature *of this* Holy Sacrament *in the General.*
 Pag. 1

Chrift's defign in the Inftitution of it. 2
That he eftablifh'd it upon the Ceremonies of the Jewifh *Pafsover.*
 3, 4, 5, 6
The method from hence taken to explain the nature of it. 6, 7

CHAP.

contained in this Treatise.

CHAP. I.

Of Transubstantiation; *or the* Real Presence *established by the* Church of Rome.   8

What is the Doctrine of the Church of Rome *in this point.* ib.
--- *This shewn upon the Principle before laid down, to be repugnant,*
     1. *To the design and nature of this* Holy Sacrament. 12
     2. *To the expression it self,* This is my Body.   14
The Papists *themselves sensible of it.*   18
That the Sixth *of* S. John *does not at all favour them.*   20
--- *This Doctrine shewn further to be repugnant,*
     I. *To the best and purest* Tradition *of the Church.* 24
     II. *To the right* Reason.   32
     III. *To the common* Sense *of all Mankind.*   36
Conclusion of this Point, and transition to the next.   37

CHAP. II.

Of the Real Presence *acknowledged by the* Church *of* England.   41

The notion of the Real Presence *falsly imputed, by a late Author to our Church.*   42
   In answer to this Four things proposed to be considered,
I. *What is the true notion of the* Real Presence *as acknowledged by the* Church of England.   43
                                   II. *That*

A Table of the Principal Matters

II. *That this Notion has been constantly maintained by* our *most Learned and Orthodox* Divines.   46
—*So those abroad;*   Calvin.   47
    ———— Beza.   49
    ————Martyr, *&c.*   51
—*For our own Divines; consider the express words of the twenty ninth Article, in* K. Edw. VI. *time.*   52
    ———— *Archbishop* Cranmer.   53
    ———— *Bishop* Ridley.   55
—*That the same continued to be the Opinion of* our Divines *after.*   56

    Shewn

1. *From the History of the Convocations proceeding as to this point in the beginning of* Q. Eliz. *Reign.*   ib.

2. *From the Testimonies of* our Divines.
    ———— *Bp.* Jewell.   59
    ———— *Mr.* Hooker.   60
    ———— *Bp.* Andrews.   62
    ———— *A. B. of* Spalatto.   64
    ———— *Bp.* Montague   *ib.*
    ———— *Bp.* Taylour.   66
    ———— *Mr.* Torndyke.   69

Whose Testimonies are cited at large: Of

1. Reformatio Legum Ecclesiasticarum.
2. *Bp.* Morton.
3. *A. B.* Usher.
4. *Bp.* Cosens.
5. *Dr. Jo.* White.
6. *Dr. Fr.* White.
7. *Dr.* Jackson.
8. *Dr.* Hammond.

Whose Authorities are refer'd to;   71, 72

III. *That* the *alterations which have been made in our* Rubrick, *were not upon the account of* our Divines *changing their Opinions, as is vainly and falsly suggested.*   72

                    IV. *That*

contained in this Treatise.

IV. *That the* Reasons *mentioned in our* Rubrick, *concerning the* Impossibility *of* Christ's Natural Body's *existing in several places at the same time, is no way invalidated by any of this Author's* Exceptions *against it.* 77
  1. *Not by his First Observation.* ib.
  2. *Nor by his Second.* 79
  3. *Nor by his Third.* 80
  4. *Nor by his Fourth.* 81
The Objection, of this Opinion's, being downright Zuinglianism *; Answered.* 82
And the whole concluded. 84

PART II.

CHAP. III

Of the Adoration of the Host *as prescribed and practised in the* Church of Rome.

Two things proposed to be considered;
I. *What the Doctrine of the* Church of England *as to this point is.* 86
  Our Authors exceptions against it, Answered. 87
II. *What is the Doctrine of the* Church of Rome *: and whether what this Author has said in favour of it may be sufficient to warrant their Practice as to this matter.* 91
  Their Doctrine stated. ib.

The

A Table of the Principal Matters, &c.

The Defence *of it*, unsufficient: *shewn in* Answer,
  1. *To his* Protestant Concessions.   93
  2. *To his* Catholick Assertions.

First.	96	Fifth.	102
Second.	99	Sixth.	103
Third.	ib.	Seventh.	104
Fourth.	100	Eighth.	ib.

  3. *To the* Grounds *he offers of their Belief.*   105
The Lutherans *Practice no Apology for theirs.*   106

Ground { First.   }   108
       { Second.   }   109
       { Third. Answer'd. }   113
       { Fourth.   }   114
       { Fifth.   }   115

Some Arguments *proposed, upon their* own Principles, *against* this Adoration.   117
Conclusion.   125

ERRATA.

PAG. xvii. l. 10. fourth r. sixth. p. xviii. l. 10. in r. on. p. xxii. l. 33. r. they are. p. xxiv. l. 5. r. That thou. p. 13. marg. *Hammond*. l. 6. p. 129. p. 64. marg. *Casaubon*. ib. l. 19. Body is of Christ. p. 76. l. 24. *dele*. which. p. 80. l. 15. then that. p. 91. l. 27. r. this Holy. p. 98. l. 16. *for* then r. the. p. 112. l. 18. *Catholica*. l. 20. asks.

A few lesser Faults there are, which the Reader may please to correct.

A DISCOURSE OF THE Holy Eucharist,

With particular Reference To the two GREAT POINTS OF THE REAL PRESENCE, AND The Adoration of the HOST.

INTRODUCTION.

Of the Nature of this HOLY SACRAMENT *in the General.*

TO understand the true design of our Blessed Saviour, in the *Institution* of this *Holy Sacrament*, we cannot, I suppose, take any better course than to consider first of all, what Account the Sacred Writers have left us of the *Time* and *Manner* of the doing of it.

Introduction

Now for this St. *Paul* tells us, 1 Cor. 11. 23. "*That the Lord Jesus the same night in which he was betray'd* (having first eaten the Passover according to the Law, Exod. 12. Matt. xxvi. 20.) *took Bread, and* _{Matt. xxvi.} "*when he had given thanks he brake it,* * *and gave* "*it to the Disciples, and said, Take, Eat, This is my* "*Body which is broken for you, This do in Remembrance* '*of Me. After the same manner also he took the Cup* "*when he had supp'd, saying, This Cup is the* New-Te- "ſtament *in my Blood: This do ye, as oft as ye Drink* "*it in Remembrance of me.*

Such is the Account which St. *Paul* gives us of the *Original* of this *Holy Sacrament*: Nor do the Evangelists diſſent from it; only that St. *Matthew* with reference to the *Cup*, adds, *Drink ye* A L L *of it*, Matt. xxvi. 27. to which St. *Mark* ſubjoins a particular Obſervation, and which ought not here to be paſs'd by, "That *they* A L L *drank of it*, Mark xiv. 23.

It is not to be doubted, but that the deſign of our Bleſſed Saviour in *inſtituting* this *Holy Sacrament*, was to Abolish the *Jewish Paſſover*, and to eſtablish the Memory of another, and a much greater *Deliverance*, than that of the firſt-born, now to be wrought for the whole World in his Death. The *Bread* which he *brake*, and the *Wine* which he *poured out*, being ſuch clear *Types* of his *Body* to be *broken*, his *Blood* to be *shed* for the Redemption of Mankind, that it is impoſſible for us to doubt of the Application.

And as God Almighty under the Law, deſigned that other Memorial of the *Paſchal Lamb*, now changed into a ſo much better and more excellent Remembrance, to continue as long as the Law its ſelf

ſtood

Introduction.

stood in force: So this Blessed *Eucharist*, establish'd by Christ in the room of it, must no doubt have been intended by Him, to be continued in his Church, as long as the *Covenant* seal'd with that *Blood* which it exhibits, stands: And therefore, that since *that* shall never be abolish'd; 'tis evident that *this* also will remain our Duty, and be our perpetual Obligation to the end of the World.

This is the import of our Saviours Addition, *Do this in Remembrance of Me*; and is by St. *Paul* more fully expressed in those Words, which he immediately subjoyns to the History of the Institution before recited, 1 Cor. xi. 26. "*For as often as ye eat this Bread, and drink this Cup, ye do shew*, i.e. in the *Jewish* Phrase, set forth, Commemorate *the Lords Death till his coming*.

And that this Holy *Sacrament* now establish'd in the place of the *Jewish Passover*, might be both the better understood, and the easier received by them; it is a thing much to be remarked for the right explaining of it, how exactly he accommodated all the Notions and Ideas of that Ancient *Ceremony* to this new *Institution*.

I. In that *Paschal Supper*, the Master of the House took *Bread*, and presenting it before them, instead of the usual *Benediction of the Bread*, He brake it, and gave it to them, saying, ‖ *This is the Bread of Affliction which our Fathers ate in Egypt*. In this *Sacred Feast*, our Saviour in like manner takes *Bread*, the very *Loaf*, which the *Jews* were wont to take for the Ceremony before mentioned; breaks it, and gives it to his Disciples, saying,

‖ See Dr. *Hammond* on Mat. xxvi. lit. E. *Casaubon* in Mat. xxvi. 26. *&c.*

Introduction.

saying, *This is my Body which is broken for you;* alluding thereby, not only to their *Ceremony* in his *Action*, but even to their very manner of Speech in his Expression, to the *Passover* before them, which in their Language they constantly called, * the *Body* of the *Paschal Lamb*.

<small>* גופו של פסח
Vid. Buxtorf. Vindic. contr. Capel. p. 14. *Hammond* in Mat. xxvi. 1. e. &c.</small>

II. In that *Ancient Feast*, the Master of the House in like manner after Supper took the *Cup*, and having given thanks, gave it to them, saying, † *This is the Fruit of the Vine, and the Blood of the Grape.* In this *Holy Sacrament* our Blessed Lord in the very same manner takes the *Cup*, he Blesses it, and gives it to his Disciples saying, *This Cup is the* New-Testament *in my Blood;* his *Action* being again the very same with theirs; and for his *Expression*, it is that which *Moses* used, when he ratified the Ancient Covenant between God and the *Jews*; [Exod. xxiv. 8. compared with *Hebr.* ix 20.] saying, *This is the Blood of the Testament.*

<small>† Allix preparat. a la Sainte Cene. cap. 2. pag. 16.</small>

III. In that *Ancient Feast*, after all this was finish'd, they were wont to sing a * *Hymn*, the Psalms yet extant, from the cxiii. to the cxix. thence called by them, *the Great Hallelujah*. In this *Holy Supper*, our Saviour and his Disciples are expresly recorded to have done the like, and very probably in the selfsame words. [See *Matt.* xxvi. 30. *Mark* xiv. 26.] In a word, *Lastly*,

<small>* Dr. *Lightfoot's* Heb & Talmud. Observat.on Mat. xxvi. ver. 26, 27. T. 2. p. 259, 260.</small>

IV. That *ancient Passover* the *Jews* were commanded to keep in memory of their *Deliverance* out of *Egypt*. The bitter Herbs were a * *remembrance* of the bitter servitude they underwent there, *Exod.* i. 14.

<small>* זכר.</small>

The

Introduction.

The red Wine was a † *Memorial* of the Blood of the Children of *Israel* slain by *Pharaoh*: And for this they were expresly commanded by *Moses*, Exod. xiii. 8. to * *SHEW*, i.e. to annunciate or tell forth to their Children what the Lord had done for them. And so in this *Holy Sacrament*, Christ expresly institutes it for the same end, * *Do this*, says he, *in remembrance of me*; which St. *Paul* thus explains, 1 Cor. xi. 26. " *For as often as ye eat this Bread, and drink this Cup, ye do* (or rather, *do ye*) * *SHEW* (the very word before used) " *the Lords death till his* " *coming.*

So clear an Allusion does every part of this *Sacrament* bear to that ancient *Solemnity*; and we must be more blind than the *Jews* themselves, not to see, that as that other *Sacrament* of *Baptism* was instituted by Christ from the Practise and Custom of the ‖ *Jewish* Doctors, who received their Proselytes by the like washing; so was this Holy *Eucharist* establisht upon the Analogy which we have seen to the *Paschal Supper*, whose place it supplies, and whose Ceremonies it so exactly retains, that it seems only to have heightned the design, and changed the Application to a more excellent Remembrance.

I know not how far it may be allow'd to confirm this Analogie, That it was one of the most ancient Traditions among the * *Jews* of old, that the *Messiah* should come and work out their deliverance, *The very same night in which God had brought them out of Egypt, the night of the Paschal Solemnity.* But

† לזכר

* והגדת לבנך

* Ἐις τὼ ἐμὼ ἀνάμνησιν.

* Τὸν θάνατον τῦ κυρίε καταγγέλλετε.

‖ See Dr *Hammonds* Practical Catechism Lib. 6. pag. 115. Oper. fol. Lond. 1684.

* Vid. Fagium. in Annotat. in Exod. xii. 13. where he renders their words thus, " *Et in eadem die viz.* xv. *mensis Nisan, sc. Martii, redimendus est Israel in diebus Messiæ. Vid. Vol.* I. *Critic. M.* p 498.

certain-

Introduction.

certainly confiderable it is, that as God under the Law, the fame night in which he deliver'd them, inftituted the *Paffover* to be a perpetual *Memorial* of it throughout their Generations; fo here our Saviour inftituted his *Communion* not only in the fame Night in which he deliver'd us, but immediately after having eaten His laft *Paffover*; to fhew us, that what that *Solemnity* had hitherto been to the *Jews*, this *Sacrament* fhould from henceforth be to *us*; and that we by this Ceremony fhould commemorate ours, as they by that other had been commanded to do their Deliverance.

This the Holy *Scriptures* themfelves direct us to, by fo often calling our Bleffed Saviour in exprefs terms, " *The Lamb of God, Joh.* i. 29. St. *Peter* fpeaking of our Redemption wrought by Him, tells us, that it was not obtained by " *corruptible things,* " *fuch as filver and gold, but by the precious Blood of* " *Chrift, as of a Lamb without blemifh, and without* " *fpot,* 1 *Pet.* i. 18. And St. *Paul* fo clearly directs us to this allufion, that no poffible doubt can remain of it; " *Chrift,* fays he, *our Paffover is facri-* " *ficed for us, therefore let us keep the Feaft,* 2 Cor. 1. v. 7.

And now after fo many Arguments for this *Application,* as, being joined together, I think I might almoft call a Demonftration of it; I fuppofe I may without fcruple lay down this foundation both for the unfolding of the nature of this Holy *Sacrament* in the General, and for the Examination of thofe two great *points* I am here to confider in particular, *viz.* That our Saviour in this *Inftitution* addreffing himfelf to *Jews*, and fpeaking in the direct

form

Introduction.

form of the *Paschal* Phrases; and in a *Ceremony* which 'tis thus evident he designed to introduce in the stead of that *Solemnity*; The best method we can take for explaining both the *words* and *intent* of this *Communion*, will be to examine what such men to whom he spake must necessarily have conceived to be his meaning, but especially on an occasion wherein it neither became him to be obscure; and the Apostles silence, not one of them demanding any explication of his words, as at other times they were wont to do, clearly shewing that he was not difficult to be understood.

This only *Postulate* being granted, which I think I have so good reason to expect; I shall now go on to examine by it, the first great *Point* proposed to be consider'd, *viz.* Of the *Real Presence* of Christ in this *Holy Sacrament*, and that

1*st*. As established by the Church of *Rome*.

2*dly*. As acknowledged by the Church of *England*.

PART

PART I.

CHAP. I.

Of Transubstantiation, *Or the* Real Presence *Establish'd by the* Church of Rome.

* Concil. Trid. Seff. 13. cap 4. & Can. 2.

TRansubstantiation is defined by the * Council of *Trent*, to be "A WONDERFUL CONVERSION *of the whole Substance of the* Bread, *in this Holy Sacrament, into the whole substance of the* Body of Christ, *and of the whole substance of the* Wine *into his* Blood; *the* Species *or* Accidents *only of the* Bread *and* Wine *remaining*.

† Catechismus ad Parochos. Par. II. cap. de Euch. Sacr. n. 39. 41, 45.

For the better understanding of which *Wonderful Conversion*, because the Church of *Rome*, which is not very liberal in any of her Instructions, has taken † particular care that this should not be too much explain'd to the People, as well knowing it to be a Doctrine so absurd, that even their credulity could hardly be able to digest it; it may not be amiss if, from the very words of their own *Catechism*, we examine a little farther into it.

Now three things there are, which, they tell us, must be consider'd in it:

I. That

Of Transubstantiation.

I. * "That the *true Body* of Christ our Lord, the "very same that was *Born* of the *Virgin*, and now "sits in Heaven at the right hand of the Father, is "contained in this Sacrament.

"Now by the *true Body*, they mean not only "his *Human Body*, and whatsoever belongs to it, "as *Bones*, *Sinews*, &c. to be contain'd in this Sacra- "ment; ‖ But the *intire Christ*, God and Man; so "that the *Eucharistical Elements* are changed in- "to our Saviour, as to *both* his *Substances*, and the "consequences of *both*, his *Blood*, *Soul*, and *Di- "vinity* its self, all which are really present in "this Sacrament; * the *Body* of Christ by the "*Consecration*, the rest by *Concomitance* with the "*Body*.

Again: When 'tis said, "† That the *whole Sub- "stance* of the *Bread* is changed into his *whole Body*, "and the *whole Substance* of the *Wine* into his *whole* "*Blood*; this is not to be so understood, as if the "*Bread* did not contain the *whole Substance* of his "*Blood*, as well as of his *Body*, and so the *Wine*, the "*whole Substance* of his *Body*, as well as of his *Blood*; "(∴) seeing Christ is intire in each part of the Sa- "crament, nay in every the least *Crumb* or *Drop*, of "either part.

II. "The * second thing to be consider'd for "the understanding of this Mystery, is, That not "any part of the *Substance* of the *Bread* and *Wine* "remains; tho *nothing may seem more contrary to the* "*Senses than this*; in which they are certainly in the "right.

* Catech. ibid. n. xxv. Sect. Primum.

‖ Ibid. n. xxxi. Sect. *Totus Christus ut Deus & Homo in Eucharistia continetur.*

* Ibid. n. xxxiii. Sect. *Per Concomitantiam in Euch. quæ sint.*

† Ibid. n. xxxix. Sect. *Conversio quæ sit in Euchar. &c.*

(∴) Ibid. n. xxxv. Sect. *Christus totus in qualibet particula, &* n. xlii. &c.

* Ibid. n. xxv. Sect. Secundum.

H   III. "† That

Of Transubstantiation.

[†] Ibid. n. xxv. Sect. Tertium & n. xliv. Sect. Accid. sine subjecto const. in Euch.

III. "† That the *Accidents* of the *Bread* and *Wine*, "which either our *Eyes see* (as the *Colour*, *Form*, &c.) "or our *other Senses perceive* (as the *Tast*, *Touch*, "*Smell*) all these are in no *Subject*, but exist by them- "selves, after a *wonderful manner*, and which cannot "be explain'd.

‖ Ibid n. xxxvii. Sect. Primo ratione.

For the rest, the *Conversion* its self, "‖ It is very "difficult to be comprehended, How Christs *Bo-* "*dy*, which before Consecration, was not in the "Sacrament, should now come to be there, since "'tis certain that *it changes not its place*, but is "still all the while in Heaven. Nor is it made

* Ibid. n. xxxix. Sect. Conversio quæ sit in Euch. &c.
† Ibid. n. xliii. Quonam modo Christus existat in Euchar.
(**) Ibid. n. xli. Sect. De Transubstant. curiosius non inquirendum.

"present there by *Creation*, * nor by any *other* "*Change*; For it is neither increased nor dimi- "nish'd, but remains whole in its Substance as be- "fore. † Christ is not in the Sacrament *Locally*; "for he has no *Quantity* there, is neither *Great* nor "*Little*. (**) In a word, Men ought not to "inquire too curiously, how this *Change* can be "made, for it is not to be comprehended, seeing "neither in any natural Changes, nor indeed in the "whole Creation, is there any Example of any thing "like it.

Such is the Account which themselves give of this *Mystery*: From all which we may in short conclude the State of the Question before us, to be this; That we do not dispute at all about Christ's *Real Presence*, which after a *Spiritual* and *Heavenly* manner, we acknowledg in this Holy Eucharist, as we shall hereafter shew; nor by consequence of the *Truth* of Christs *Words* which we undoubtedly believe: But only about this *Manner* of his *Presence*, viz. Whether the *Bread* and
the

Of Transubstantiation.

the *Wine* be changed into the very natural *Body* and *Blood* of Christ, so that the *Bread* and *Wine* themselves do no longer remain; But that under the *Appearance* of them is contain'd that same *Body* of Christ, which was *Born* of the Blessed *Virgin*, with his *Soul* and *Divinity*; which same *Body* of Christ, tho *extended* in all its parts in Heaven, is at the same time in the Sacrament without any *Extension*, neither *Great* nor *Small*, comes thither neither by *Generation*, nor by *Creation*, nor by any *local Motion*; forasmuch as it continues still at the right Hand of God in Heaven, at the very same instant that it exists *whole* and *intire* in every consecrated *Host*, or *Chalice*; nay more, is *whole* and *intire*, not only in the *whole Host*, or the *whole Chalice*; but in every the *least Crumb* of the *Host*, and every the *least Drop* of the *Chalice*, here upon Earth.

And here it might well be thought a very needless, indeed an extravagant undertaking, to prove that those Elements, which so many of our Senses tell us, continue after their Consecration the very same, as to what concerns their *natural Substance*, that they were before, are in reality the very same: That what all the World *Sees*, and *Feels*, and *Smells*, and *Tasts*, to be *Bread* and *Wine*, is not changed into the very natural *Flesh* and *Blood* of a Body actually before existent; had it not entred into the Minds of so great a part of the Christian Church to joyn in the maintaining of a *Paradox*, which has nothing to defend it, but that fond Presumption they have certainly done well to take up, That they cannot possibly be in the *wrong*, and without which it would be very difficult for them to perſwade any ſober man that they are here in the *right*.

To ſhew that thoſe *words*, which they tell us, work all this *Miracle*, and are the only reaſon that engages them to maintain ſo many abſurdities as are confeſſedly the unavoidable Conſequences of this Doctrine, have no ſuch force nor interpretation as they pretend; I muſt deſire it may be remembred what I before remark'd, That this Holy *Sacrament* was eſtabliſh'd by our Saviour in the room of the *Jewiſh Paſſover*, and upon the very *Words* and *Ceremonies* of it. So that, if in that all things were *Typical*; the *Feaſt*, the *Cuſtoms*, the *Expreſſions* merely *alluſive* to ſomething that had been done before, and of which this ſacred Ceremony was the *memorial*; we ought in all reaſon to conclude, that both our Saviour muſt have deſigned, and his Apoſtles underſtood this Holy *Sacrament* to have been the ſame too.

Now as to the *Nature* of the *Paſſover*; we have already ſeen that it was appointed by God as a *Remembrance* of his delivery of the *Jews* out of the Land of *Egypt*, when he ſlew all the *firſt-born* of the *Egyptians*, *Exod.* xii. The *Lamb* which they ate every year in this Feaſt, was an Euchariſtical Sacrifice and *Type* of that firſt *Lamb* which was ſlain in the night of their deliverance, and whoſe Blood ſprinkled upon the Poſts of their Doors had preſerved their Fore-fathers from the *deſtroying Angel*, that he ſhould not do them any miſchief. The *Bread* of *Affliction*, which they broke, and of which they said, perhaps in the very * ſame manner that

* Vid. Cameron Annot. in Matt. xxvi. 26. in illa verba, Λάβετε φάγετε, inter critic. pag. 780. l. 24.

Chriſt

Christ did of the very same Loaf, *Take, eat, this is the Bread of affliction which our Fathers ate in Egypt*; they esteem'd a *Type* and *Figure*, of that unleaven'd Bread which their Forefathers so many Ages before had eaten there; and upon that account called it * "*The Memorial of their delivery out of Egypt.* † The *Cup of Blessing* which they blessed, and of which they *ALL drank* in this Feast, they did it at once in memory both of the *Blood* of the Children of *Israel* slain by *Pharaoh*, and of the *Blood* of the *Lamb*, which being *sprinkled* upon their *doors*, preserved their own from being shed with that of the *Egyptians*.

* Allix Serm. pag. 503.
† Hammond Pract. Catechism. lib vi. pag. 129. Ed. fol.

Now all these *Idea's* with which the Apostles had so long been acquainted, could not but presently suggest to them the same design of our Blessed Saviour in the *Institution* of this Holy Sacrament: That when *He*, as the *Master* of the *Feast*, took the *Loaf*, *Blessed*, and *brake* it, and *gave* it to them, and Bid them in like manner henceforward, *Do this in Remembrance of Him*; He certainly designed that by this Ceremony, which hitherto they had used in *memory* of their deliverance out of *Egypt*, they should now continue the *memory* of their Blessed Lord, and of that deliverance which he was about to work for them. That as by calling the *Lamb* in that Feast " The *Body of the Passover*, they understood that it was the *remembrance* of God's mercy in commanding the *destroying Angel* to *pass over* their Houses when he slew their Enemies; the *memorial* of the *Lamb* which was killed for this purpose in *Egypt*; so Christ calling the *Bread* his *Body*, nay, his *Body broken* for them,

them, could certainly mean nothing else but that it was the *Type*, the *Memorial* of his *Body*, which as yet was not, but was now just ready to be given for their redemption.

This is so natural a reflection, and in one Part at least of this Holy Sacrament so necessary too, that 'tis impossible to explain it otherwise. "*This Cup*, "says our Saviour, *is the New Testament in my Blood*; That is, as * *Moses* had before said of the *Old Testament* in the very same Phrase, the *seal*, the *ratification* of it. Now if those words be taken *literally*, then 1*st*. 'Tis the *Cup* that is *Transubstantiated*, not the *Wine*; 2*ly*, It is *changed* not into *Christ's Blood* (as they pretend) but into the *New Testament* in his Blood; which being confessedly absurd and impossible, it must in all reason follow, That the Apostles understood our Saviour alike in both His Expressions; and that by consequence we ought to interpret those words, *This is my Body which is broken for you*, of the *Bread's* being the *Type*, or *Figure* of his *Body*; as we must that of the *Cup*, That it was the *New Testament in his Blood*, i. e. the *sign*, or *seal* of the *New Testament*.

So naturally do all these Notions direct us to a *figurative* interpretation of his Words; the whole *design* of this *Institution*, and all the *Parts* and *Ceremonies* of it being plainly *Typical*, in *Remembrance* (as Christ himself has told us) *of Him*. But now if we go on more particularly to inquire into the Expression its self, *This is my Body which is broken for you*, That will yet more clearly confirm this interpretation.

* See *Exod.* xxiv. 8. *Heb.* ix 20. And this Allusion is applied by S. *Peter*, 1 Ep. i 2. Vid. *Hammond.* Annot. in loc. lit. a.

Of Transubstantiation.

It has before been observed, That these words of our Saviour in this Holy *Sacrament*, were used by him instead of that other Expression of the *Master* in the *Paschal Feast*, when in the very same manner he took the very same *Bread* into his Hands, and *blessed* it, and *brake* it, and *gave* it to those who were at the Table with Him, saying, *This is the Bread of affliction which our Fathers ate in Egypt.* And can any thing in the world be more plain, than that as never any *Jew* yet imagined, that the *Bread* which they thus took every year, was by that saying of the *Master* of their Feast changed into the very *substance* of that *Bread* which their forefathers had so many Ages before consumed in *Egypt*, in the night of their deliverance; but being thus broken and given to them, became a *Type*, a *Figure*, a *Memorial* of it: So neither could those to whom our Saviour Christ now spake, and who as being *Jews* had so long been used to this *Phrase*, ever imagine, that the pieces of that *Loaf* which He *brake*, and *gave* them, saying, " *This is my Body* " *which is broken for you, Do this in Remembrance of* " *me*, became thereupon the *very Body* of that Saviour from whose Hands they received it; and who did not sure with one *member* of his *Body*, give away his *whole Body* from himself to them; but only designed that by this Ceremony they should *remember* Him, and his *Body* broken for them, as by the same they had hitherto *remembred* the Bread of *affliction which their Fathers ate in Egypt.*

I ought not to omit it, because it very much confirms the force of this Argument, That what I have here said of this *Analogy* of the Holy *Eucharist*, to the
Jewish

Jewish Passover, was not the original remark of any *Protestant*, or indeed of any other Christians differing from the *Church* of *Rome* in this point: But was objected to them long before the *Reformation*, by the * *Jews*, themselves to shew that in their literal Interpretation of these Words, they had manifestly departed from the intention of our Blessed Saviour, and advanced a notion in which 'twas impossible for his Apostles, or any other acquainted, as they were, with the *Paschal* forms, ever to have understood him. And if † St. *Augustine*, who I suppose will not be thought a Heretick by either party, may be allow'd to speak for the Christians; he tells us, we are to look upon the Phrase, *This is my Body*, Just, says He, as when in ordinary conversation we are wont to say, This is *Christmas*, or *Good-Friday*, or *Easter-day*; Not that this is the very day on which Christ was *born*, or *suffer'd*, or *rose* from the dead, but the return or remembrance of that day on which Christ was *born*, or *suffer'd*, or *rose* again.

It is wonderful to consider with what confidence our new *Missionaries* produce these words on all occasions; and thereby shew us how fond they would be of the Holy Scripture, and how willingly they would make it their *Guide in Controversie*, did it but ever so little favour their Cause. Can any thing, say they, be more express? *This is my Body*; Is it possible for words to be spoken more clear and positive? And indeed were all the Expressions of Holy Scripture to be taken in their *literal* meaning, I will not deny, but that those words might as evidently

---

* Vid. apud Author Fortalitii Fidei, Lib 4. Conlid. 6. Impof. 10. Those who have not this Book, may find the Quotation at large in the late Edition of *Joan. Parisiensis*, in Præfat. pag. 73, 74.

† Epistol. xxiii. ad *Bonifac*. Vol. 2. pag. 29. Oper. Ed. Lugd. 1664.

evidently prove *Bread* to be Chrifts *Body*, as thofe other in St. *John*, *I am the Bread that came down from Heaven*, argue a contrary *Tranfubftantiation* of Chrift's *Body* into *Bread*, John vi. 48, 51. or thofe more ufual inftances, *I am the true Vine; I am the door of the fheep; That Rock was Chrift*; prove a great many *Tranfubftantiations* more, *viz.* of our Saviour into a *Vine*, a *Door*, and a *Rock*. But now, if for all this plainnefs and pofitivenefs in thefe expreffions, they themfelves tell us, That it would be ridiculous to conclude from hence, that Chrift was indeed turned into all thefe, and many other the like things; they may pleafe to give us leave to fay the fame of this before us, it being neither lefs impoffible, nor lefs unreafonable to fuppofe *Bread* to be changed into Chrift's *Body*, than for Chrift's *Body* to be changed into *Bread*, a *Vine*, a *Door*, a *Rock*, or whatever you pleafe of the like kind.

But I have already fhewn the ground of this miftake to be their want of confidering the *Cuftoms* and *Phrafes* of the *Jewifh Paffover*, and upon which, both the Holy *Euchariff* it felf, and thefe *Expreffions* in it were founded: And I will only add this farther, in confirmation of it; That in the Stile of the *Hebrew* Language in general, there is nothing more ordinary, than for things to be faid to * *Be* that which they *Signifie* or *Reprefent*. Thus *Jofeph* interpreting *Pharaoh*'s Dream,

* Expreffions of this kind are very frequent in Holy Scripture. *The feed is the Word of God*, Luke viii. 11. *The field is the World; the good feed are the children of the kingdom: The tares are the children of the wicked one*, Matt. xiii. 38. *The feven Angels are the Angels of the feven Churches; and the feven Candlefticks are the feven Churches*, Rev. i. 20. With infinite more of the like kind.

I   *Gen.*

Gen. xli. 26. *The seven good Kine,* says he, *are seven years;* and again, *The seven good Ears of Corn are seven years,* i. e. as is plain, they *signify seven years.* And so in like manner in this place; *Christ took Bread, and blessed, and brake it, and gave it to his disciples, saying, Take, Eat, this is my Body which is Broken for you:* That is, this *Bread* thus *Taken,* and *Blessed,* and *Broken,* and *Given* to you; This *Bread,* and this *Action, signifies* and *represents* my *Body* which shall be *Broken* for you.

And indeed, after all this seeming assurance, it is nevertheless plain, That they themselves are not very well satisfied with their own interpretation. † We have shewn before, how little confidence their greatest *Schoolmen* had of this Doctrine; those who have stood the most stifly for it, could never yet * agree how to explain these words, so as to prove it: And Cardinal *Bellarmine* alone, who reckons up the most part of their several ways, and argues the weakness too of every one but his own, may be sufficient to assure us, that they are never likely to be: And might serve to shew what just cause their own great * *Catharinus* had so long since to cry out, upon his Enquiry only into the meaning of the very first word, *This:* " *Consider,* says he, Reader, into what diffi-
" culties they are thrown, who go about to write up-
" on this matter, when the word *THIS* only has
" had so many, and such contradictory *Expositions,*
" that they are enough to make a man lose his *Wits,*
" but barely to consider them all.

† See the Preface.

* See their Opinions collected by Monsieur *Aubertine* de Eucharistiâ, lib. 1. cap. 9. 11, 12, 13, 14.
* Tract. 2. de Verbis quibus Conficitur.

Of Transubstantiation.

'Twas this forced so many of their † greatest and most learned men before *Luther*, ingenuously to profess, That *there was not in Scripture any evident proof of this Doctrine*; and even Cardinal *Cajetan* since to own, That had not the Church determined for the *literal* sense of those words, *This is my Body*, they might have passed in the *Metaphorical*.

† See their Testimonies cited in the late *Historical Treatise of Transubstantiation*; in the *Defence of the Exposition of the Church of England*, p. 63, 64, 65. In the Preface above, &c.

It is the general acknowledgment of their ‖ greatest Writers at this day, That if the *Pronoun* THIS in that Proposition, *This is my Body*, be referr'd to the *Bread*, which our Saviour Christ *held* in his *Hand*, which he *bless'd*, which he *brake* and *gave* to his Disciples, and of which therefore certainly, if of any thing, he said *This is my Body*, the natural repugnancy that there is between the two things affirm'd of one another, *Bread* and *Christs Body*, will force them to be taken in a *figurative* Interpretation: For as much as 'tis impossible that *Bread* should be *Christ's Body* otherwise than in a *figure*. And however, to avoid so dangerous a Consequence, they will rather apply it to *any thing*, nay to *nothing* at all than to the *Bread*; yet they would do well to consider, whether they do not thereby fall into as great a danger on the other side; since if the *Relative* THIS do's not determine those words to the *Bread*, 'tis evident that nothing in that whole *Proposition* do's; And then how those words shall work so great a change in a *Subject* to which they

‖ See *Bellarmin's* words in the *Defence of the Exposition of the Doctrine of the Church of* England, pag. 56, 57. To which may be added, *Salmer.* Tom. 9. Tr. 20. *Suarez.* Disp. 58. Sect. 7. *Vasquez.* Disp. 201. c. 1. &c.

they have no manner of *Relation*, will, I believe, be as difficult to shew, as the change its self is incomprehensible to conceive.

And now after so plain an evidence of the weakness of that foundation which is by all confessed to be the chief, and has by many of the most Learned of that Church been thought the only Pillar of this Cause; I might well dispense with my self from entring on any farther examination of their other pretences to establish it. But because they have taken great pains of late to apply the † sixth Chapter of St. *John* to the Holy *Eucharist*, tho' it might be sufficient in general to say that no good Argument for a matter of such consequence, can be built upon a place which so many of the * most *Eminent* and *Learned* of that *Communion* have judged not to have the least Relation to this matter; yet I will nevertheless beg leave very briefly to shew the Weakness of this *Second* Attempt too; and that 'tis in vain that they rally these scatter'd Forces, whilst their main Body continues so intirely defeated.

† Concil. Trid. Sess. xiii.

* See them thus ranged by *Albertinus* de Euch. lib. 1. cap. 30. pag. 209. Two *Popes*; Innocent III. Pius II. Four *Cardinals*, Bonaventure, D'Alliaco, Cusan. Cajetane. Two *Archbishops*, Richardus Armachannus, & Guererius Granatensis. Five *Bishops*, Stephanus Eduensis, Durandus Mimatensis, Gulielmus Altisiodorensis, Lindanus Ruremondensis, & Jansenius Gandavensis. *Doctors* and *Professors* of *Divinity* in great abundance; Alexander Alensis, Richardus de media villa, Jo. Gerson, Jo. de Ragusio, Gabriel Biel, Thomas Waldensis, Author. tract. contr. perfidiam quorundam Bohemorum, Jo. Maria Verratus, Tilmannus Segebergensis, Astesanus, Conradus, Jo. Ferus, Conradus Safgerus, Jo. Hesselius, Ruardus Tapperus, Palatios, & Rigaltius. Here are 30. of the *Roman* Church, who reject this Application of this Chapter. For the *Fathers*, see the Learned *Paraphrase* lately set forth of this Chapter, in the *Preface*: All which shews how little strength any Argument from this Chapter can have to establish *Transubstantiation*.

Of Transubstantiation.

It is a little surprizing in this matter, that they universally tell us, That neither the beginning nor ending of our Saviours Discourse in that Chapter belongs to this Matter; that both before and after that passage which they refer to, 'tis all *Metaphor*; only just two or three words for their purpose, *Literal*. But that which raises our wonder to the highest pitch, is, that the very fifty first *Verse* its self on which they found their Argument, is two thirds of it *Figure*, and only otherwise in one Clause to serve their *Hypothesis*.

" *I am*, says our Saviour, *the living Bread which came down from Heaven*; This is Figurative: *If any man eat of this Bread, he shall live for ever*: That is, they say, by a Spiritual Eating by Faith: *And the Bread which I will give, is my Flesh, which I will give for the life of the World*. This only must be understood of a *proper* manducation, of a *real* eating of his Flesh in this Holy Sacrament.

It must be confessed, that this is an Arbitrary way of explaining indeed, and becomes the Character of a Church whose dictates are to be *received*, not *examined*; and may therefore pass well enough amongst those, with whom the supposed *Infallibility* of their *Guides*, is thought a sufficient dispensation for their own *private Consideration*. But for us, who can see no reason for this sudden change of our Saviours Discourse;

may

Of Transubstantiation.

nay think that the connexion of that last Clause with the foregoing, is an evident sign that they all keep the same *Character*; and are therefore not a little scandalized at so *Capernaitical* a Comment, as indeed "*Who can bear it?* *V.* 60. They will please to excuse us, if we take our Saviours Interpretation to be at least of as good an Authority, as 'tis much more reasonable than theirs, *V.* 62. "*Do's this*, says he, *Offend you?* Do's my saying that ye must *eat my flesh*, and *drink my Blood* scandalize you? Mistake not my design, I mean not any *carnal eating* of me; that indeed might justly move your Horrour;" *It* "*is the Spirit that quickneth, the flesh profiteth no-* "*thing; the words that I speak unto you they are spi-* "*rit, and they are life.*

He that desires a fuller account of this Chapter, may please to recur to the late excellent † *Paraphrase* set out on purpose to explain it, and which will be abundantly sufficient to shew the reasonableness of that *Interpretation* which we give of it. I shall only add, to close all, that one Remark which * Saint *Augustine* has left us concerning it; and so much the rather in that it is one of the rules which he lays down for the right Interpreting of Holy Scripture, and illustrates with this particular Example: "*If*, says he, *the saying be Preceptive,* " *either forbidding a wicked action, or commanding to* " *do that which is good, it is no Figurative say-* " *ing : But if it seems to command any Villany,* "*or*

† A Paraphrase with Notes, and a Preface upon the Sixth Chapter of Saint *John*, Lond. 1686.

* De Doctrin. Christian. Lib. 3. Cap. 16.

Of Transubstantiation.

" or *Wickedness*, or forbid what is profitable and
" good, it is *Figurative*. This *saying*, Except ye
" eat the Flesh of the Son of Man, and drink his
" Blood, you have no Life in you, *seems to com-*
" *mand a Villanous or Wicked Thing*: It is there-
" fore a *FIGURE*, enjoining us to communicate in
" the Passion of our Lord, and to lay it up in dear and
" profitable Remembrance, that his Flesh was crucifi'd
" and wounded for our sakes.

And now having thus clearly, I perswade my self, shewn the Weakness of those Grounds, on which this Doctrine of the *substantial Change* of the *Bread* and *Wine* into the *Body* and *Blood* of Christ in this Holy Sacrament is establish'd; I shall but very little insist on any other Arguments against it: Only in a Word, to demonstrate, that all manner of *Proofs* fail them in this great *Error*, I will in the close here subjoin two or three short *Considerations* more, to shew this *Doctrine* opposite, not only to *Holy Scripture*, as we have seen, but also,

  1. To the best and purest *Tradition of the Church*.

  2. To the *Right Reason*, and

  3. To the *Common Senses* of all Mankind.

I. *That*

I. *That this Doctrine is opposite to the best and purest* Tradition *of the* Church.

Now to shew this, I shall not heap together a multitude of Quotations out of those Fathers, through whose hands this *Tradition* must have past: He that desires such an Account, may find it fully done by one of the *Roman Communion*, in a little * Treatise just now publish'd in our own Language. I will rather take a method that seems to me less liable to any just Exception, and that is to lay down some *general Remarks* of undoubted Truth, and whose consequence will be as evident, as their certainty is undeniable. And,

* A Treatise of Transubstantiation, by one of the Church of *Rome*, &c. Printed for *Rich. Chiswell*. 1687.

I. For the *Expressions* of the Holy Fathers; It is not deny'd, but that in their popular Discourses they have spared no words (except that of *Transubstantiation*, which not one of them ever used) to set off so great a *Mystery*: And I believe that were the *Sermons* and *Devotional* Treatises of our own Divines alone, since the *Reformation*, searcht into, one might find Expressions among them, as much over-strain'd. * And doubtless

Such are μεταποίησις, μεταβολὴ, μεταρρύθμησις, μετάληψις, μετασοιχείωσις, but never μετουσίωσις. And Note, there is hardly any of these Words, which they have applied to the *Bread* and *Wine* in the *Eucharist*, but they have attributed the same to the *Water* in *Baptism*.

* See Treatise first, of the Adoration, &c Printed lately at *Oxford*; Which would make the World believe that we hold, I know not what imaginary *Real Presence* on this account; just as truly, as the *Fathers* did *Transubstantiation*.

Of Transubstantiation.

doubtless these would be as strong an Argument to prove *Transubstantiation* now the Doctrine of the Church of *England*, as those to argue it to have been the Opinion of those Primitive Ages.

But now let us consult these men in their more exact composures, when they come to teach, not to declaim, and we shall find they will then tell us, That these Elements are for their * *substance* what they were before, *Bread* and *Wine*: That they retain the true *properties* of their nature, to *nourish* and *feed* the *Body*: that they are things *inanimate*, and void of *sense*: That with reference to the Holy Sacrament they are *Images*, *Figures*, *Signes*, *Symbols*, *Memorials*, *Types* and *Antitypes* of the *Body* and *Blood* of Christ. That in their *Use* and *Benefit*, they are indeed the very *Body* and *Blood* of Christ to every faithful Receiver, but in a *Spiritual* and *Heavenly* manner, as we confess: That, in propriety of speech the *Wicked* receive not in this Holy Sacrament the *Body* and *Blood* of Christ, although they do outwardly press with their teeth the Holy Elements; but rather eat and drink the Sacrament of His *Body* and *Blood* to their damnation.

* It is not necessary to transcribe the Particulars here that have been so often and fully alledged. Most of these Expressions may be found in the Treatise of *Transubstantiation* lately published. The rest may be seen in *Blondel, Eclaircissements Familiers de la Controverse de l' Eucharistie*, Cap. iv, vii, viii. *Claude Rep. au 2. Traitté de la Perpetuité*, i. Part. Cap. iv, v. *Forbesius Instructiones Historico-Theolog.* lib. xi. cap. ix, x, xi, xii, xiii, xv. *Larrogue Histoire de l' Eucharistie*, liv. 2. cap. ii.

II. Secondly, For our Saviours *words* which are supposed to work this great Change, 'tis evident from the *Liturgies* of the *Eastern* Church,

K that

This *Arcudius* himself is forced to confess of some of the latter *Greeks*, viz. That they take these Words only *Συγγραματικῶς*, Historically. See his Book *de Concord. Lib.* 3. *Cap.* 27. And indeed all the ancient Liturgies of that Church plainly speak it; However both He and Goar endeavour to shift it off; in which the Prayer of Consecration is after the words of Institution, and distinct from it. So in *Liturg. S. Chrysostom. Edition.* Goar. *pag.* 76. *n.* 130. 132. are pronounced the Words of Institution. Then *pag.* 77. '*numb.* 139. the Deacon bids the Priest, 'Ευλόγησον Δέσποτα τὸν ἄγιον ἄρτον. Who thereupon thus consecrates it; He first signs it three times with the sign of the Cross, and then thus prays ποίησον τὸν μὲν ἄρτον τοῦτον τίμιον Σῶμα τῦ Χρισῦ Σοῦ. And so the Cup afterwards.

* The same seems to have been the custom of the *African* Church, whose Prayers now used, see in *Ludolph. Histor. l.* 3. *cap.* 5. Where is also the Expression mentioned, *n.* 56. Hic Panis est Corpus meum, &c.

that the *Greek* Fathers did not believe them to be words of *Consecration*; but to be the same in this Holy Eucharist that the *Haggadah*, or History of the *Passover* was in that ancient Feast; That is, were read only as an account of the *Occasion* and *design* of the *Institution* of this Blessed Sacrament, not to work any Miracles in the *Consecration*. And for the * *African* Churches, they at this day expound them in this very Sacrament after such a manner, as themselves confess to be inconsistent with *Transubstantiation*, viz. *This Bread is the Body of Christ.*

III. Let it be considered, *Thirdly*, That it was a great debate in the Primitive Church for above a thousand Years, Whether Christs *Glorified Body* had any *Blood* in it or no? Now how those Men could possibly have questioned whether *Christ's Glorified Body* had any *Blood* at all in it, had they then believed the *Cup* of *Eucharist* to have been *truly* and *really* chan-

See this whole matter deduced through the first Ages to St. *Augustine*, whom *Consentius* consulted about this very matter, in a particular Treatise written by Monsieur *Allix de Sanguine Christi*, 8vo. Paris 80.

Of Transubstantiation.

changed, into the *Blood* of his *Glorified Body*, as is now asserted, is what will hardly, I believe, be ever told us.

IV. We will add to this, *Fourthly*, their manner of opposing the *Heathenism* of the World. With what confidence could they have rallied them as they did, for worshipping gods which their own *Hands* had made? That had neither *Voice*, nor *Life*, nor *Motion*; Exposed to *Age*, to *Corruption*, to *Dust*, to *Worms*, to *Fire*, and other *Accidents*. That they adored gods which their Enemies could spoil them of, Thieves and Robbers take from them; which having no power to defend themselves, were forced to be kept under *Locks* and *Bolts* to secure them.

_{So Justin Martyr. Apol. 2. Tertul. Apolog. cap. 12. Arnobius, lib. 1. Minutius Felix. p. 26. Octav. Julius Firmicus, pag. 37. Edit. Lugdunens. 4to, 1652. Hieron. lib. 12. in Esai. St. Augustinus in Psal. 80. & in Psal. 113. Lactantius Iustit. lib. 2. cap. 4. Chrysostom. Homil. 57. in Genes. &c.}

For. is not the Eucharistical *Bread* and *Wine*, in a higher degree than any of their *Idols* were, exposed to the same raillery? Had their *Wafer*, if such then was their *Host*, any *voice*, or *life*, or *motion*? Did not their own Hands form its *substance*, and their *Mouths* speak it into a *God*? Could it defend its self, I do not say from publick Enemies, or private Robbers, but even from the very *Vermine*, the creeping things of the Earth?

Or should we suppose the Christians to have been so impudent, as notwithstanding all this, to expose others for the same follies of which

K 2   them-

Of Transubstantiation.

themselves were 'more notoriously guilty; yet were there no * Heathens, that had wit enough to recriminate? The other † *Articles* of our Faith they sufficiently traduced; That we should worship a *Man*, and He too a Malefactor, crucified by *Pilate*; How would they have triumph'd, could they have added, That they worshipped a bit of *Bread* too; which *Coster* himself thought a more ridiculous *Idolatry* than any the Heathens were guilty of? Since this Doctrine has been started, we have heard of the Reproaches of all sorts of Men, *Jews*, *Heathens*, *Mahometans*, against us on this account. ‖ Were there no *Apostates* that could tell them of this secret before? Not any *Julian* that had malice enough to publish their Confusion? Certainly had the Ancients been the Men they are now endeavour'd to be represented, we had long ere this seen the whole World filled with the Writings that had proclaimed their shame, in one of the greatest instances of Impudence and Inconsideration, to attacque their Enemies for that very Crime, of which themselves were more notoriously guilty.

* And yet that none did, the Learned *Rigaltius* confesses. *Not.ad Tertul.* l. 2. *ad Uxor.* c. 5.
† See *Tertul.* Apol. c. 21. Et de carne Christi, c. 4. 5. *Justin Martyr*, Apol. 2. *Arnob.* l. 2. *Orig. contr. Celf.* l. 1.

‖ See *du Perron de l' Euchar.* l. 3. c. 29. p. 973.

V. Nor does their manner of Disputing against the *Heretical* Christians any less speak their Opinion in this Point, than their way of Opposing the *Idolatry* of the Heathens. It was a great argument amongst them to expose the frenzy of *Eutyches*, who imagined some such kind of *Transubstantiation* of the humane nature of Christ into the Divine, to produce the Example of the *Eucharist*;

See this fully handled in a late treatise called, *The Doctrine of the Trinity and Transubstantiation compared &c.*, 1687.

Of Transubstantiation.

Eucharist; That as there the Bread and the Wine, says *P. Gelasius*, "Being perfected by the Holy Spirit, pass into the Divine Substance, yet so as still to remain in the property of their own Nature, or Substance of Bread and Wine; So here the Humane *Nature* of Christ still remains, though assumed by, and conjoyned to the *Divine*. Which words, as their *Editor* has done well to set a *Cautè* upon in the Margent to signifie their danger, so this is clear from them, that *Gelasius*, and so the other Writers that have made use of the same Argument, as St. *Chrysostome*, *Theodoret*, &c. must have thought the *Bread* and the *Wine* in the *Eucharist* no more to have been *really* changed into the *very Body* and *Blood* of Christ, than they did believe his *Humane* Nature to have been truly *turned* into the *Divine*; For that otherwise the parallel would have stood them in no stead, nay would have afforded a defence of that Heresie which they undertook to oppose by it.

This Argument is managed by St. *Chrysostome Epist. ad Cæsarium Monachum.* By Theodoret *Dial.* 2. *pag.* 85 Ed G. L. *Paris,* 1642. *Tom.* 4. *Gelasius in Opere contra Eutychen & Nestorium.* He thus states the *Eutychian* Heresie, '*Dicunt unam esse naturam* i. e. *Divinam.* Against this he thus disputes, *Certe Sacramenta quæ sumimus corporis & sanguinis Christi divina res est.——— Et tamen non desinit substantia vel Natura Panis & Vini.——— Satis ergo nobis Evidentur Ostenditur, hoc nobis de ipso Christo Domino sentiendum quod in ejus imagine profitemur.———Ut sicut in hanc sc. in divinam transeant S. Spiritu perficiente substantiam, permanentes tamen in sua proprietate naturæ, sic, &c.*

VI. Yet more: Had the Primitive Christians believed this great *Change*; how comes it to pass, that we find none of those *Marks* nor *Signs* of it, that the World has since abounded with? * No talk of *Accidents* existing without *Subjects*, of the *Senses* being liable to

* See the contrary proved, that the Fathers did not believe this, by *Blondel,* de l'Euch. c. 8. *Claude* Rep. au. 2. Traitte de la *Perpetuite.* part. 1. c. 4.

be *deceived* in judging of their proper *Objects*; in short, no *Philosophy* corrupted to maintain this Paradox. No *Adorations, Processions, Vows* paid to it, as to Christ himself. It is but a very little time since the † *Bell* came in play, to give the People notice that they should fall down and Worship this new God. The ‖ *Feast* in honour of it, is an Invention of Yesterday; the *Adoring* of it in the Streets no ∴ older: Had not those first Christians respect sufficient for our Blessed Saviour? Or, did they perhaps do all this? Let them shew it us if they can; But till then, we must beg leave to conclude, That since we find not the least Footsteps of any of these necessary Appendages of this Doctrine among the Primitive Christians, it is not to be imagined that we should find the *Opinion* neither.

† Under Greg. ix. Ann. 1240 vid. Nauclerum ad Ann. cit.

‖ Instituted by *Urban* iv. Ann. 1264.

∴ Indeed, in all Probability, a hundred years later.

VII. But this is not all: We do not only not find any such Proofs as these of this Doctrine, but we find other Instances directly contrary to this belief. In some Churches they ‖ *burnt* what remained of the *Consecrated Elements*; * In others, they gave it to *little Children* to Eat: † In some, they buried it with their *Dead*; In all, they permitted the Communicants to carry home some *Remnants* of them; they sent it abroad by *Sea*, by *Land*, from

‖ So in that of *Jerusalem*. See Hesych. in Levitic. l. 2. c. 8.

* So in that of Constantinople. Evag. Hist. l. 4. c. 35.

† Vid. apud. Autor. Vit. Basilii, c. 8. in Vit. Pat. l. 1. This Custom was condemned in a Council at *Carthage*, Anno 419. Vid. Codic. Eccl. Afric. Just cl. c. 18.

one

one *Church* and *Village* to another, without any Provision of *Bell* or *Taper*, *Canopy* or *Incense*, or any other mark of *Adoration*; they sometimes made ∵ *Poultices* of the *Bread*; they mix'd the ∴ *Wine* with their *Ink*; all which we can never imagine such holy Men would have presumed to do, had they indeed believed them to be the very *Body* and *Blood* of our Blessed Lord.

∵ Vid. St. August. Oper. imp. contr. Julian. lib. 3. c. 164.
∴ See an instance of this in *Baronius*, Ann 648. Sect. 15. The 8th General Council did the same. In Act. Syn.

VIII. Lastly: Since the prevalence of this Doctrine in the Church, what *Opposition* has it met with? What *Schisms* has it caused? What infinite Debates have there risen about it? I shall not need to speak of the Troubles of *Berenger* in the Eleventh: Of the *Waldenses*, *Albigenses*, and others in the Twelfth Century. Of *Wickliff*, *Hus*, &c. who continued the Opposition; and finally, of the great *Reformation* in the beginning of the last *Age*; by all which this Heresy has been opposed ever since it came to any Knowledg in the Church. Now is it possible to be believed, that so many *Centuries* should pass, so many *Heresies* should arise, and a Doctrine so full of Contradictions remain uncontested in the Church for almost a Thousand years? That *Berenger* should be one of the first that should begin to Credit his *Senses*, to Consult his *Reason*, or even to Defend his *Creed*?

These

These are Improbabilities that will need very convincing Arguments indeed to remove them.

<small>This is the Foundation of the Authors of the Treatises, *De la Perpetuite*: Answered by Monf. *Claude.*</small>
But for the little late *French* trick of proving this Doctrine necessary to have been received in the *Primitive Church*, because it is so in the *Present*, and if you will believe them, 'tis impossible a *Change* should have been made; I suppose, we need only turn the terms of the Argument to shew the Weakness of the Proof, *viz*. That from all these, and many other Observations, that might be offer'd of the like kind, 'tis Evident that this *Doctrine* at the beginning, was not believed in the *Church*, and let them from thence see, if they can conclude that neither is it believed now.

Thus contrary is this Doctrine to the Best and Purest *Tradition* of the Church: Nor is it less, Secondly,

II. *To* Right Reason *too*.

It were endless to heap together all the *Contradictions* that might be offer'd to prove this;
<small>See Mr. *Chillingworth* against *Knot*, c. iv. n. 46.</small>
"That there should be *Length*, and no-"thing *Long*; *Breadth*, and nothing "*Broad*; *Thickness*, and nothing *Thick*; "*Whiteness*, and nothing *White*; *Round*-"*ness*, and nothing *Round*; *Weight*, and nothing "*Heavy*; *Sweetness*, and nothing *Sweet*; *Moisture*, "and nothing *Moist*; *Fluidness*, and nothing *Flow*- "*ing*;

Of Transubstantiation.

" ing; many *Actions* and no *Agent*; many *Passi-*
" *ons*, and no *Patient*; i. e. That there should be a
" *Long, Broad, Thick, White, Round, Heavy, Sweet,*
" *Moist, Flowing, Active, Passive* NOTHING.
" That *Bread* should be turned into the *Substance*
" of Christ, and yet not any thing of the *Bread*
" become any thing of *Christ*; neither the *Mat-*
" *ter*, nor the *Form*, nor the *Accidents* of the
" *Bread*, be made either the *Matter*, or the
" *Form*, or the *Accidents* of *Christ*; that *Bread*
" should be turned into *Nothing*, and at the same
" Time with the same Action turned into *Christ*,
" and yet *Christ* should not be *Nothing*; that the
" same Thing at the same Time should have its
" just *Dimensions*, and just *Distance* of its *Parts*
" one from another, and at the same time not
" have it, but all its *Parts* together in one and
" the self-same *Point*; That the same Thing at
" the same time should be wholly *Above* its self,
" and wholly *Below* its self, *Within* its self, and
" *Without* its self, on the *Right-hand*, and on the
" *Left-hand*, and *Round-about* its self: That the
" same thing at the same time should *move to*
" and *from* its self, and yet *lie still*; or that it
" should be *carried* from one place to another
" through the middle space, and yet not *move*.
" That there should be no *Certainty* in our *Sen-*
" *ses*, and yet that we should know something
" *Certainly*, and yet know nothing but by our
" *Senses*; That that which *Is* and *Was* long ago,
" should now *begin to be*; That that is now to
" be made of *Nothing*, which is not *Nothing*, but
" *Something*; That the same thing should be *Be-*
" *fore*

L

"*fore* and *After* its self. These and many o-
"ther of the like nature are the unavoidable,
"and most of them the avow'd Consequences of
"*Transubstantiation*, and I need not say all of
"them Contradictions to *Right Reason*.

But I shall insist rather upon such Instances as the Primitive *Fathers* have judged to be *absurd* and *impossible*; and which will at once shew both the Falseness and Novelty of this monstrous Doctrine; and such are these; * *That a thing already existing should be produced anew: That a finite thing should be in many places at the same time; That a Body should be in a place, and yet take up no room in it; That a Body should penetrate the dimensions of another Body; That a Body should exist after the manner of a Spirit; That a real body should be invisible and impassible: That the same thing should be its self, and the figure of its self: That the same thing should be contained in, and participate of its self;* † *That an Accident should exist by its self without a Subject, after the manner of a Substance.* All these things the primitive *Fathers* have declared to be in their Opinions gross *Absurdities* and *Contradictions*, without making any exception of the *Divine Power* for the sake of the *Eucharist*, as some do now.

* See Examples of every one of these collected by Blondel, *Eclaircissements familiers de la controverse de l'Eucharistie, cap.* 8. *p.* 253.

† Monsieur Claude Rep. au. 2. Traitte de la Perpetuite, part. I. c. 4. n. 11. p. 73. Ed. 4to. Paris 1668.

And indeed it were well if the impossibilities stopp'd here: but alas! the Repugnancies extend to the very *Creed* its ſelf, and deſtroy the chiefeſt *Articles* of our *Faith*, the Fundamentals of Chriſtianity. How can that man profeſs that he believes our Saviour Chriſt to have been *born* xvi. Ages ſince, of the *Virgin Mary*, whoſe very *Body* he ſees the Prieſt about to make now before his Eyes? That he believes him to have *Aſcended into Heaven*, and behold he is yet with us upon *Earth*? There to *Sit at the right hand of God the Father Almighty*, till in the end of the World *He ſhall come again with Glory to judg both the Quick and the Dead*? And behold he is here carried through the Streets; lock'd up in a Box; Adored firſt, and then Eaten by his own Creatures; carried up and down in ſeveral manners, and to ſeveral places, and ſometimes *Loſt out of a Prieſts Pocket*.

Theſe are no far-fetch'd *Conſiderations*; they are the obvious Conſequences of this Belief; and if theſe things are impoſſible, as doubtleſs, if there be any ſuch thing as *Reaſon* in the World, they are; I ſuppoſe it may be very much the concern of every one that profeſſes this Faith, to reflect a little upon them, and think what account muſt one day be given of their perſiſting obſtinately in a point ſo evidently erroneous, that the leaſt degree of an impartial judgment, would preſently have ſhewn them the falſeneſs of it.

But God has not left himſelf without farther witneſs in this matter; but has given us, *Thirdly*,

IIIdly, The

III. *The Conviction of our* Senses *against it.*

An Argument this, which since it cannot be Answered, they seem resolved to run it down; as the *Stoick* in *Lucian*, who began to call names, when he had nothing else to say for himself.

But if the *Senses* are such ill *Informers*, that they may not be trusted in matters of this moment, would these Disputers please to tell us, What *Authority* they have for the truth of the *Christian Religion*? Was not Christianity first founded upon the *Miracles* of our Blessed Saviour and his Apostles? Or were not the *Senses* judges of those *Miracles*? Are not the *Incarnation*, *Death*, *Resurrection* and *Ascension* of our Lord, the most Fundamental *Articles* of our Faith? Have we any other Argument to warrant our belief of these, but what comes to us by the ministry of our *Senses*? *Did not Christ himself appeal to them for the proof of his own *Rising*?

* John xx. 27, 29.

The *Romanist* himself believes *Transubstantiation* because he reads in the Scripture, or rather (to speak more agreeably to the method of their Church) because he has been told there are such Words there, as, *Hoc est Corpus Meum*: Now not to enquire how far those words will serve to warrant this Doctrine, is it not evident that he cannot

Of Transubstantiation.

cannot be sure there are any such words there, if he may not trust his *Senses*: And if he may, is it not as plain, That he must seek for some other meaning than what they give of them?

Let us suppose the change they speak of to be Supernatural; Be it as much a *Miracle* as they desire: The very Character of a *Miracle* is to be known by the *Senses*. Nor God, nor Christ, nor any Prophet or Apostle, ever pretended to any other. And I shall leave it to any one to judge what progress Christianity would have made in the World, if it had had no other *Miracles* but such as *Transubstantation* to confirm it: *i.e.* Great Wonders confidently asserted, but such as every ones *sense* and *reason* would tell him were both falsely asserted, and impossible to be performed.

But now whil'st we thus oppose the Errors of some by asserting the continuance of the Natural Substance of the Elements of *Bread* and *Wine* in this Holy *Eucharist*; let not any one think that we would therefore set up the mistakes of others; as if this Holy *Sacrament* were nothing more than a meer *Rite* and *Ceremony*, a bare *Commemoration* only of Christ's Death and Passion.

Our Church indeed teaches us to believe, That the *Bread* and *Wine* continue still in their True and Natural *Substance*; but it teaches us also

Of Transubstantiation.

<small>See the Church Catechism, and Article Twenty eighth. The Communion-Office, &c.</small>

also that 'tis the *Body* and *Blood* of Christ, which every faithful Soul receives in that Holy Supper: *Spiritually* indeed, and after a *Heavenly manner*, but yet most *truly* and *really* too.

The Primitive Fathers, of whom we have before spoken, sufficiently assure us, that they were strangers to that *Corporeal change* that is now pretended; but for this *Divine* and *Mystical*, they have openly enough declared for it.

Nor are we therefore afraid to confess a *change*, and that a very great one too made in this Holy Sacrament. The *Bread* and the *Wine* which we here Consecrate, ought not to be given or received by any one in this *Mystery*, as *common* ordinary food. Those Holy Elements which the Prayers of the Church have *sanctified*, and the Divine Words of our Blessed Saviour applied to them, though not *Transubstantiated*, yet certainly separated to a Holy use and signification, ought to be regarded with a very just Honour by us: And whilst we Worship Him whose Death we herein Commemorate, and of whose Grace we expect to be made partakers by it, we ought certainly to pay no little regard to the *Types* and *Figures*, by which he has chosen to represent the *one*, and convey to us the *other*.

Thus therefore we think we shall best divide our Piety, if we *Adore* our Redeemer in *Heaven*, yet omit nothing that may testifie our just esteem of
his

Of Transubstantiation.

his Holy *Sacrament* on *Earth*: Nor suffer the most Zealous Votary for this new Opinion, to exceed us in our Care and Reverence of Approaching to his Holy Table.

We acknowledg him to be no less *Really* Present, tho after another *manner* than they; nor do we less expect to Communicate of his *Body* and *Blood* with our *Souls*, than they who think they take Him carnally into their *Mouths*.

Let our *Office* of *Communion* be examined; let the Reverence and Devotion, with which we Celebrate this Sacred Feast, be consider'd; all these will shew how far the Church of *England* is from a light esteem of this great *Mystery*; indeed, that it is impossible for any to set a higher Value and Reverence upon it.

I shall close this with the Declaration of One, who after many Years spent in great Reputation in their *Communion*, was so happy as to finish his Days in our *Church*; upon his first receiving the Blessed *Communion* among us: "* *Tantam magnorum Præsulum de-* "*missionem, tam eximiam Principum & *"*Populi Reverentiam, in Sacra Eucha-* "*ristia administranda & recipienda, nus-* "*quam ego vidi apud Romanenses, qui tamen* "*se unos Sacramenti istius cultores jactant.* That He never saw in the *Church* of *Rome*, so great a Reverence both in *Administring* and *Receiving* this Holy *Eucharist*, as he found among us;

* Andr. Sallii Votum pro pace, c. 23. p. 90. Ed. Oxon. 1678.

† info-

insomuch, that he supposed it would hardly be believed among them, what from his own Experience, he recounted concerning it.

<small>Vid. ibid. pag. 90. cap. xxiv. n. 7.</small>

Porro hæc quæ narravi & trita nimis ac vulgo nota Videbuntur fratribus nostris Reformatæ Ecclesiæ: Nova omnino & fortè incredibilia Apparebunt Romanæ Congregationis Alumnis; quorum scilicet auribus perpetuò suggeritur per suos Instructores, nullam apud Protestantes existere fidem præsentiæ Christi realis in Eucharistiæ Sacramento, nullam Devotionem aut Reverentiam in eo Sumendo.

And this may suffice for the *first* thing proposed; Of the *Doctrine* of *Transubstantiation*, or of the *Real Presence* professed and established in the *Church of Rome*. Our next Business will be to inquire:

II. What that *Real Presence* of Christ in this Holy *Eucharist* is, which is acknowledged by the *Church of England*.

CHAP.

CHAP. II.

Of the Real Presence *acknowledged by the* Church *of* England.

IT may sufficiently appear from what has been said in the foregoing Chapter, what just reason we have to reject that kind of *Presence* which the *Church of Rome* supposes of Christ in this *Holy Eucharist*. But now in Answer to our Reflections upon them on this Occasion, a late Author has thought fit to make the World believe, that we our selves, in our Opinion of the *Real Presence*, are altogether as absurd as they are; and that the same Exceptions lie against our own *Church*, which we urge against *theirs*: All which, if it were true, would but little mend the matter, unless it may be thought sufficient for a man to prove, that he is not mad himself, because most of his Neighbours are in the same condition. Indeed herein he must be allowed to have reason on his side, that if the Case be so as he affirms, we, of all men living, ought not to press them with such *Contradictions*, as our own Opinion stands equally involved in. _{Two Discourses concerning the Adoration of our B. Saviour in the Eucharist. Oxford, 1687.} _{Tract. I. pag. 15, 16.}

'Tis true, he confesses for what concerns the *Church of England*, as it stood in the latter * end of King *Edward* the *6th*'s time, and as it may perhaps be thought to stand now, since the † reviving of the *Old Rubrick* against the *Adoration* of the *Sacrament* at the end of our *Communion-Office*; it seems not to lye open to such a Recrimination: But taking our Opinion of the *Real Presence* from the Expressions of our own *Di-* _{* Tract. I. §. 25.} _{† Ibid. §. 4.}

M *vines,*

vines, and of those abroad, such as *Calvin*, &c. whose
" Doctrine, amongst all the rest, the *Church* of *England*
" seems rather to have embraced and agreed with, es-
" pecially since the beginning of the *Reformation* by
" Q. *Elizabeth*; it plainly implies, " *That the very Sub-*
" *stance of Christ's Body*; *That his Natural Body*,
" *that very Body that was born of the Blessed Virgin*,
" *and crucified on the Cross, is present as in Heaven,*
" *so here in this Holy Sacrament, either to the worthy*
" *Receiver, or to the Symbols:* which not only contradicts the present Declaration of our Church; *viz.*
" That *the Natural Body of Christ is not in this bles-*
" *sed Sacrament*; but will also lay a necessity upon us
to quit our Reason too that we give for it; *viz.* "*That*
" *it is against the Truth of a Natural Body to be in*
" *more places than One at One time*; and on which we
seem to found our Faith in this matter.

This is, I think, the design of the former of those
Discourses lately Printed at *Oxford*, as to what concerns the Real Presence; and in Answer to which,
that I may proceed as distinctly as possible, I shall reduce my Reflections to these Four Generals:

1. What is the true Notion of the *Real Presence*, as
acknowledged by the *Church* of *England*.

2. That this has been the Notion constantly maintain'd by the Generality of our Divines.

3. That the *Alteration* of the *Rubrick*, as to this
matter, was not upon any such difference in their
Opinions, as this *Author* seems to surmise.

4. That the Reason alledged by it, concerning the
Impossibility of Christ's *Natural Body's* existing in
se-

By the Church of England.

several places at the same time, is no way invalidated by any of his Exceptions against it.

But before I enter on these *Reflections*, I cannot but observe the unreasonableness of our Adversaries, in repeating continually the same Arguments against us without either adding of any the least new force to them, or even taking notice of those Replies that have more than once been made against them. The *Publisher* of this *Treatise* has not been so indiligent an Observer of what has past under his Eyes, with reference to these kind of *Controversies*, as not to know, that this very *Objection*, which is the Foundation of his *First Discourse*, was made by his Old Friend T. G. above Nine Years since; and fully answer'd by his Reverend and Learned *Adversary* not long after. And therefore that he certainly ought either quietly to have let alone this Argument already baffled, and not have put the World in Mind where that Debate stopp'd; or, at least, he should have added some new strength to it. But to send it again into the World in the same forlorn State it was before; to take no notice either from whose Store-house he borrow'd it, or what had been returned to it; This is in effect to confess, that they have no more to say for themselves: And 'tis a sad Cause indeed that has nothing to keep it up, but what they know very well we can answer, and that they themselves are unable to defend.

But to return to the *Points* proposed to be consider'd: And,

First, To state the Notion of the *Real Presence*, as acknowledged by the *Church* of *England*.

I must

Of the Real Presence acknowledged

I must observe, 1*st*. That our *Church* utterly denies our Saviour's *Body* to be so *Really Present* in the Blessed *Sacrament*, as either to leave *Heaven*, or to exist in *several places at the same time*. We confess, with this Author, that it would be no less a Contradiction for Christ's *Natural Body*, to be in several places at the same time by any other *Mode* whatsoever, than by that which the *Church* of *Rome* has stated; the repugnancy being in the *thing its self*, and not in the *manner of it*. 2*dly*, That we deny that in the Sacred *Elements* which we receive, there is any other *Substance* than that of *Bread* and *Wine*, distributed to the Communicants; which alone they take into their Mouths, and press with their Teeth. In short, "All which the "Doctrine of our *Church* implies by this Phrase, is "only a *Real Presence* of Christ's Invisible *Power* and "*Grace*, so in and with the *Elements*, as by the faith-"ful receiving of them, to convey *spiritual* and *real* "*Effects* to the Souls of Men. As the *Bodies* assu-"med by Angels, might be called their *Bodies*, while "they assumed them; or rather, as the *Church* is the "*Body* of Christ, because of his Spirit quickening and "enlivening the Souls of Believers, so the *Bread* and "*Wine*, after *Consecration*, are the *Real*, but the *Spiritual* "and *Mystical Body* of Christ.

Thus has that learned Man, to whom *T. G.* first made this Objection, stated the Notion of the *Real Presence* profess'd by us; and that this is indeed the true *Doctrine* of the *Church* of *England* in this matter, is evident not only from the plain words of our *xxviii. Article*, and of our *Church Catechism*; but also from the whole Tenour of that *Office* which we use in the celebration of it. In our *Exhortation* to it, this Blessed Eucharist is expresly called "The Commu-
"nion

"*nion* of the *Body* and *Blood* of our Saviour Christ: We are told, "that if with a true Penitent Heart "and lively Faith we receive this Holy Sacrament; "then we *Spiritually eat* the *Flesh* of Christ, and *drink* "his *Blood.* When the Priest delivers the consecrated *Bread,* he bids the Communicant "Take and eat this "in Remembrance that Christ died for thee, and *feed* "on him in thy *Heart* by Faith with Thanksgiving. In our Prayer after the Receiving, "We thank God, "for that he doth vouchsafe to feed us who have duly "received these Holy *Mysteries,* with the *Spiritual* "food of the most precious *Body* and *Blood* of his "Son our Saviour Jesus Christ, and doth assure us "thereby of his favour and goodness towards us, and "that we are very Members, incorporate in the *Mystical* "*Body* of his Son. All which, and many other the like Expressions, clearly shew, that the *Real Presence* which we confess in this Holy *Eucharist* is no other than in St. *Pauls* Phrase, a *Real Communion* of Christ's *Body* and *Blood*; or as our Church expresses it *Article* xxviii. "That to such as rightly and worthily, and with Faith "receive the same, the *Bread* which we break is a partaking of the *Body* of Christ, and likewise the *Cup of Blessing* is a partaking of the *Blood* of Christ.

Hence it was that in the Prayer of *Consecration* in King *Edward* vi. time, the *Church* of *England* after the Example of the ancient *Liturgies* of the *Greek Church* used that Form, which our Author observes to have been since left out. "And with thy Holy Spirit vouch- Tract. I. 2. "safe to Bless and Sanctifie these thy Gifts and Crea- "tures of *Bread* and *Wine,* that they may be unto us "the *Body* and *Blood* of thy most dearly beloved Son "Jesus Christ — *i.e.* as the Sense plainly implies, may Communicate to our Souls all the Blessings and Graces

ces which Chrift's *Body* and *Blood* has purchafed for us; which is in Effect the very fame we now pray for in the fame Addrefs— " Hear us, O Merciful Fa- " ther we moft humbly befeech thee, and grant that " we receiving thefe thy Creatures of *Bread* and " *Wine,* according to thy Son our Saviour Jefus Chrifts " Holy Inftitution, in remembrance of his Death and " Paffion, may be *partakers* of his moft Bleffed *Body* " and *Blood*. Between which two Petitions there is fo near an Affinity, that had not our Author been very defirous to find out *Myfteries* where there are indeed none; He would hardly have fuffer'd his *Puri-*

Pag. 3.

tan Friend to have lead him to make fo *heavy a complaint*, about fo fmall a Variation.

I will not deny but that fome Men may poffibly have advanced their *private Notions* beyond what is here faid: But this is I am fure all that our *Church* warrants, or that we are therefore concern'd to defend. And if there be indeed any, who as our Author here expreffes it, do believe Chrifts *natural Body* to be as in *Heaven*, fo in the Holy *Sacrament*; they may pleafe to confider how this can be reconciled with the *Rubrick* of our *Church*, " That the natural *Body* and *Blood* of " our Saviour Chrift are in *Heaven* and not *here*, it " being againft the truth of Chrifts *natural Body*, to " be at one time in *more places* than *one*.

In the mean time I pafs on to the next thing I propofs'd,

Secondly, To fhew in Oppofition to the Pretences of our *Adverfary*, that this has been the *Notion* of the *Real Prefence* conftantly maintain'd by our moft Learned and Orthodox Divines.

And

By the Church of England.

And here, because our *Author* has thought fit to appeal not only to our own, but to the forreign Divines for this new Faith which he is pleas'd to impose upon us, *viz.* "That the very Substance of Christs "Body, that his *natural Body*, that that very *Body* that "was born of the Blessed Virgin, and crucified on "the Cross, &c. is present, as in *Heaven*, so *Here* in "this Holy *Sacrament*; *i. e.* in both at the same time: I must be content to follow his Steps, and enquire into the Doctrine first of Mr. *Calvin* and his followers; next of our own Country-men in this Particular.

<small>Tract. I. §. 7.</small>

And first for Mr. *Calvin*, and his followers, I cannot but observe what different charges are brought against them in this matter. On the one hand we are told by *Becanus* the *Jesuit*, that, "*The *Calvinists, says* "*he,* deny the *Body* and *Blood* of Christ to be *truly,* "*really,* and *substantially* present in the *Eucharist* : On the other, Here is one will prove, that they believe his *very Body,* his *natural Body,* now in Heaven, to be nevertheless at the same time in the *Holy Sacrament.* It were to be wish'd that they would let us once know what 'tis they will stick to, and not by such contradictory charges shew to all the World, that both their *Accusations* may be *false*, but that it is utterly impossible they should both be *true*.

<small>* Calviristæ negant corpus & sanguinem Christi, vere, realiter, & substantialiter præsentem esse in Eucharistiâ. Becani manuale. l. 3. c. 9. p. 501. Ed. Luxembergi. 1625.</small>

And indeed in this very instance they are both false; The *Calvinists* hold neither the one or other of these Extreams. In the Edition of his *Institutions* printed at *Basil* 1536. Mr. *Calvin* thus delivers his Opinion, of the *Body* and *Blood* of Christ in the Holy *Eucharist.* "We say, that they are *truly* and *Effica-*

<small>CALVIN.</small>

<small>Dicimus verè & Efficaciter exhiberi non autem naturaliter. Quo scil. significamus non substantiam ipsam corporis, seu verum & natura'e Christi corpus illic dari, sed omnia quæ in suo corpore nobis Beneficia Christus præstirit. EA est corporis PRÆSENTIA quam Sacramenti ratio postulat. Edit. Basil. 8°. 1535.</small>

ciously

Of the Real Presence acknowledged

"*ciously* exhibited to us, but not *naturally*: By which we signifie, not that the *very Substance* of his *Body*, or that the *true* and *natural Body* of Christ are given there, but all the *Benefits* which Christ did for us in his *Body*. This is that Presence of his *Body*, which the nature of the *Sacrament* requires."

But because I do not find these words in the *Editions* of that Book since, least any one should thereupon conclude that he had also changed his Opinion; we may observe the very same delivered by him in *another of his Books, and which will be so much the more considerable, in that it was written purposely for the clearing of this matter. Now in this he affirms, "† That Christs *Body* was not only once given for our Salvation, but is also every day reached out to us for our Sustenance, that so, whilst he dwells in us, we may also enjoy the Fellowship of all his goods.— Then he explains How Christ is our *food*, viz. † because by the incomprehensible Vertue of the *Holy Spirit*, he inspires his Life into us, that he may communicate it to us, no less than the vital juice is diffused from the Root into all the Branches of the Tree, or than Vigour flows from the *Head* into all the members.— He declares Christs *Body* to be *finite*, and en-

closed

---

* Dilucida explicatio &c. Contra Westphalum. Edit. Anno 1561.

† Christi corpus non modò semel fuisse datum in salutem nostram, dum ad expianda peccata immolatum in cruce fuit, sed quotidiè nobis in alimentum porrigi, ut dum ipse habitat in nobis, bonorum etiam ejus omnium societate fruamur.— Apud Hospin. Hist. Sacram. Part 2da Ann. 1561. p. 477.

† Rursum alimentum à nobis vocatur hoc sensu, quia incomprehensibili spiritûs Virtute nobis vitam suam inspirat ut sit nobis communis, non secus atque à radice arboris vitalis succus in ramos se diffundit, vel à capite in singula membra manat Vigor. Ibid.— Imprimis obstaculum de corporis immensitate submovere necesse est. Nisi enim constet finitum esse cæloq; comprehendi nulla erit diffidii conciliandi Ratio— p.478. Christus sicuti in gloriam cœlestem semel est receptus, ita locorum intervallo quoad *carnem*, est à nobis dissitus ; *Divinâ* autem *Essentiâ* & *virtute*, *gratiâ* etiam *spirituali* cælum & terram implere.— Idem ergo Corpus quod semel filius Dei Patri in sacrificium obtulit, quotidie nobis in Cœna offert, ut sit in Spirituale Alimentum. Tantùm de modo tenendum est, non opus esse descendere *carnis Essentiam* è cœlo ut eâ pascamur, sed ad penetranda impedimenta & superandam locorum distantiam sufficere *Spiritûs virtutem*.— Commenta procul facessant ; qualia sunt de Corporis *ubiquitate*, vel de occultâ sub panis symbolo *inclusione*, vel de *substantiali* ejus in terris *præsentiâ*. Hospin. p. 478. Hæc omnia refert ex illo *Calvini* loco.

"closed in *Heaven*; and therefore as to his *Flesh* to
"be distant in place from us.—That it is not necessary
"that the Essence of his *Flesh* should *descend* from
"*Heaven*, that we may be fed with it, but that to re-
"move all such impediments, and overcome the di-
"stance of places, the *Virtue* of the *Spirit* is sufficient—
"In short, that all *inventions* contrary to this are to be
"rejected, such as, The *Ubiquity* of Christs Body,
"the *inclosing* of it under the *Symbol* of *Bread*, and
"his *Substantial presence upon Earth*.

By all which it sufficiently appears, that Mr. *Calvin* was no friend to our Authors Fancy; but evidently explained the *Real Presence* after that *Spiritual manner* we have before laid down.

For *Beza*, and the rest as he calls them, of *the same Sect*; we cannot better learn their Opinion than from the *Acts* of the *Colloquy of Poissy*, and which chiefly lay upon this *Point*. At this *conference* the most eminent Men of the *Calvinian* Party were assembled; the first of them which spoke, was *Beza*: In that part of his Discourse which referr'd to the *Holy Eucharist*, his words were much like those which our Author has quoted out of him. And by his own *Exposition* of them, we shall be better able to judg of his meaning, than by his *Adversaries Gloss*. "* We do not say that

BEZA.
* See Hospin. Hist. Sacram. Part. 2. ad Ann. 1561. p. 515. Edit. Genev. 1681. Comment. de statu Relig. & reipub. in Galliâ ad Ann. 1561. p. 112. *Et postea* pag. 138. ita se exprimit in eundem planè sensum "affirmamus J. C. adesse in usu Cœnæ, in quâ nobis offert, dat & verè exhibet Corpus

suum & sanguinem suum operatione Spiritus Sti. nos verò recipimus, edimus & bibimus spiritualiter & per fidem illud ipsum corpus quod pro nobis mortuum est, eùmq; illum sanguinem pro nobis effusum. Edit. Ann. 1577. 8°. Beze. Hist. Eccles. pag. 595. 595.

For all this see *Beza*'s own History ad Ann. 1561. p. 524. And when in the Conference *D'Espence* pressed them with departing from *Calvin*; *Beza* declared, that they were not at all contrary to him: That for the word *Substance*, which he sometimes used in expressing Christs *Real Presence*, it was only to signifie, that they did not feign any *imaginary Body* of Christ, or *fantastick reception* or *communion* of His *Body* in this Holy Supper; But that for the rest, they all believed, that no one could participate of him otherwise than *Spiritually* and by *Faith*, not in taking Him into the Mouth, or eating him with the Teeth. See pag. 599. Ibid.

N in

"in the Eucharist there is only a *commemoration* of the "death of our Lord Jesus Christ; nor do we say, that "in it we are made *partakers* only of the *fruits* of "his *death* and *passion*; but we joyn the *ground* with "the *fruits*, affirming with St. *Paul*, that the *Bread* "which by Gods appointment we break, is the *parti-* "*cipation of the Body of Christ* crucified for us; the "*Cup* which we drink, the *Communion of the true Blood* "that was shed for us; and that *in the very same Sub-* "*stance which he received in the Womb of the Virgin,* "*and which he carry'd up with him into the Heavens.*—
Then descending to the *Popish* Doctrine of *Transub-stantiation*: "It overthrows, *says he*, the truth of "Christs *Humane nature* and of his Ascension——. So little did he suppose, that Christs *natural Body* could be at the same time both in *Heaven* and in the *Sacrament*. Hereupon he explains himself yet farther;—— "But "now if any one should ask of us, whether we make "Christ *absent* from the *Holy Supper* ? We answer, "By no means. But yet if we respect the *distance* of "*place* (as when we speak of his *Corporal presence*, and "of his *Humanity*, we must) we affirm, *says he*, that "Christs *Body* is as far distant from the *Bread* and "*Wine*, as *Heaven* is from *Earth*— If any one shall "from thence conclude, that we make Christ *absent* "from the *Holy Supper*, he will conclude amiss: For "this Honour we allow to God, that though the *Body* "of Jesus Christ be now in *Heaven* and *not elsewhere*, "and we on *Earth* and *not elsewhere*, yet are we made "*partakers* of his *Body* and *Blood* after a *spiritual man-* "*ner*, and by the means of *Faith*.

Thus do's *Beza* in like manner expound their Doctrine of the *Real Presence*, by a *real communion* of Christs *Body* and *Blood*, and flatly condemns our Authors

thors invention, of his *natural Bodie*'s being either in the *Symbols*, or any where else upon *Earth*. The PETER MARTYR. same is the account which † *Peter Martyr* in the same conference gave of it; and of whom * *Espensius*, one of the *Popish* delegates, confess'd "That no Divine of that time had spoken "so clearly and distinctly concerning this *Sacrament*, as he "did. And however ∴ *Genebrard* safely pretends that the other *Protestants* dissented from him, yet 'tis certain they were so far from it, that they all Subscribed the very same Paper out of which he read his Declaration. But I will close this with the same words with which these *Protestants* did their final resolution in the *Colloquy* as to this matter; "We "affirm that no *distance* of *place* can hinder the *Com-* "*munion* which we have with Chrifts *Body* and *Blood*; "because the Supper of the Lord is a Heavenly thing, "and though upon Earth we receive with our mouths "*Bread* and *Wine*, viz. the true *Symbols* of his *Body* "and *Blood*; yet by *Faith*, and through the Operation of the *Holy Spirit*, our Souls (of which this is

† Respondeo pro meâ parte, Corpus Christi non esse *Verè* et *substantialiter* alibi quàm in Cælo. Non tamen inficior Christi corpus verum,& sanguinem illius Verum quæ pro salute humana tradita sunt in Cruce,fide spiritualiter percipi in Sacrâ Cœnâ. Histoire Eccles. de Beze. liv. 4. p. 606. Anno 1561.
* Vid. Hist. de Beze ib. p. 599. Comment. de stat. rel. p. 140. ad Ann 1561. *Hospin.* pag. 518.
∴ See *Hospin.* of this whole matter pag. 520.

Affirmamus nullam locorum distantiam impedire posse communicationem quam habemus cum Christi corpore & sanguine, quoniam Cœna Domini

est res cœlestis; et quamvis in terrâ recipimus ore panem & vinum, vera scil. Corporis & sanguinis signa; tamen fide & spiritus sancti operatione mentes nostræ (quarum hic est præcipuè cibus) in cælum clatæ perfruuntur corpore & sanguine præsente. Et hoc respectu dicimus, Corpus verè se pani conjungere, & sanguinem vino; non aliter tamen quam *sacramentali ratione*, neque *locali* neque *naturali modo*, sed quoniam Efficaciter significant Deum illa dare fideliter communicantibus, illósque fide verè & certo percipere. *Hospin.* l. c. Comm. ibid. p. 142. *Ubi subjicitur* "Hæc est perspicua de Corporis & sanguinis *J. C.* Præsentia in Sacramento Cænæ Ecclesiarum Reformatarum sententia—— Beze Hist. Eccles. pag. 615. *where he adds,* that they reject not only *Transubstantiation* and *Consubstantiation,* but also toute maniere de presence par laquelle le corps de Christ n'est colloqué maintenant reellement ailleurs qu'au ciel. *And then adds,* why they thus use the word substance in this matter, and what they mean by it. See pag. 515. ad Ann 1561.

"the

"the chief food) being carry'd up into Heaven, en-
"joy the *Body* and *Blood* present. And in this respect
"we say that the *Body* do's truly joyn its self to the
"*Bread*, and the *Blood* to the *Wine*, but yet no other-
"wise than *Sacramentally*, neither after a *local* or *na-*
"*tural manner*. But because they do effectually signi
"fie, that God gives them to the Faithful Communi-
"cants, and that they do by Faith truly and certain-
"ly receive them.

And thus far I have consider'd the forreign Divines produced by our *Author*, and in which we find the very same Explication which our *Church* gives of the *Real presence*. For our own Authors, I shall insist the rather upon them, both to take off any impression which the scraps here put together by those whose business it is to represent their *own Sence*, not their *Authors*, might otherwise be apt to make upon some Men; and also to shew the exact concord there has been ever since the *Reformation* amongst us as to this matter.

Now for what concerns our *Divines* in King *Edward* vi^ths. time, we have our Authors own confession, that towards the latter end of the Reign of that excellent Prince, they seem to have deny'd any such *Real* and *Essential presence* as he would fasten upon those of Queen *Elizabeth's* after. "For as the first
"days of this Prince, *says he*, seem to have been more
"addicted to *Lutheranism*, so the latter days to *Zwin-*
"*glianism*; as appears in several expressions of Bi-
"shop *Ridley* and *Peter Martyr*. And indeed the *Articles* agreed upon in the *Convocation* at *London* 1562. plainly shew it; in the xxixth. of which we find this express Clause; "Since the very being of humane
"*Nature* doth require that the *Body* of one and the
"same

1 Treatise §. xxvi. pag 15.

"same man cannot be at one and the same time in
"*many places*, but of neceſſity muſt be in ſome cer-
"tain and determinate *place*; Therefore the *Body* of
"*Chriſt* cannot be preſent in *many* different *places* at
"the ſame time. And ſince, as the Holy Scriptures te-
"ſtifie, Chriſt hath been taken up into *Heaven*, and
"there is to abide till the end of the World, it be-
"cometh not any of the faithful to believe or profeſs,
"that there is a *Real* or *Corporal* Preſence, as they
"phraſe it, of the *Body* and *Blood* of Chriſt in the
"*Holy Euchariſt*. I ſhall therefore produce only a
Witneſs or two of this *King*'s Reign; and ſo paſs on to
thoſe that follow.

  And 1ſt, A. B. *Cranmer* in his Anſwer to *Gardi-*   A.B. CRAN-
ner, Biſhop of *Wincheſter*, objecting to him, That he   MER.
deny'd the *Preſence* of Chriſt in this Holy *Euchariſt*,
replies, That it was "a thing he never ſaid nor thought.
"——My book in divers places ſaith clean contrary,   Anſwer to
"That Chriſt is with us *ſpiritually preſent*; is eaten and   Gardiner, Bi-
"drunken of us, and dwelleth within us, although   ſhop of *Win-*
"*Corporally* he be departed out of this World, and   *cheſter*. Fol.
"gone into *Heaven*, pag. 5.——As he giveth *Bread*   London, 1551.
"to be *eaten* with our *Mouths*, ſo giveth he his very   Pag. 5.
"*Body* to be *eaten* with our *Faith*. And therefore I
"ſay, that Chriſt giveth himſelf *truly* to be *eaten*,
"*chawed* and *digeſted*; but all is *ſpiritually* with *Faith*,
"not with *Mouth*, pag. 9.——As the waſhing out-   Pag. 5.
"wardly in Water is not a vain Token, but teacheth
"ſuch a waſhing as God worketh inwardly in them
"that duly receive the ſame; ſo likewiſe is not the
"*Bread* a vain Token, but ſheweth and preacheth to
"the godly Receiver, what God worketh in him by
"his Almighty Power ſecretly and inviſibly. And
                    "there-

"therefore as the *Bread* is outwardly *eaten indeed* in
"the Lord's Supper, so is the *very Body* of Christ *in-*
"*wardly* by *Faith eaten indeed* of all them that come
"thereto in such sort as they ought to do; which
"eating nourisheth them unto Everlasting Life. And

<small>Assertio veræ & Catholicæ Doctrinæ de Sacramento Corporis & Sanguinis, J. Christi Servatoris nostri. *Lich.*, 8vo. 1601.</small>

in his Treatise of the *Holy Sacrament*, Lib. 3. where
he sets himself particularly to state this very Question,
How Christ is present in this Holy Sacrament, He declares, Cap. 2. "That whereas the *Papists* suppose
"Christ to be under the *Species* of Bread and *Wine*;
"we believe him to be in those who worthily receive these Holy *Elements*: They think him to be
"received by the *Mouth*, and to enter with the *Bread*
"and *Wine*; We assert, that he is received only by
"the *Soul*, and enters there by *Faith*. That Christ is
"present only *sacramentally* and *spiritually* in this sacred *Mystery*, p. 116. That since his *Ascension* into
"*Heaven*, he is *there*, and not on *Earth*, p. 118. and
"that he cannot be in both together, 128.——In
"short, he gives us this Rule for interpreting the Expressions of *the Fathers*, where it is said, That we
"eat the *flesh*, and *drink the blood* of *Christ*; That
"we receive in the Holy Sacrament, the *very body*
"that hung on the *Cross*, &c. cap. 14. p. 180. These,
"*says he*, and other Expressions of the like kind (which
"speak Christ to be upon *Earth*, and to be received
"of Christians by *eating* or *drinking*), are either to be
"understood of his *Divine Nature* (which is every
"where); or else must be taken *figuratively* or *spiritually*. For he is *figuratively* only in the *Bread* and
"*Wine*; and *spiritually* in those that receive this *Bread*
"and *Wine worthily*. But *truly*, and as to his *Body*
"and *Flesh*, he is in *Heaven only*; from whence he shall
"come to judge the quick and the dead.

Thus

Thus did this Learned and Holy *Martyr* understand **Bp. *RIDLEY*.**
our Doctrine of the *Real Presence*; and the same was
the *Idea* which his Companion both in *Doctrine* and
Suffering, Bishop *Ridley*, has left us of it. In his Discourse of the *Lord's Supper*, pag. 33. he tells us, " That *Ridlei de Cæ-*
" the *Substance* of the *Bread* continues as the Matter of *nā Dominicā*
" this Sacrament; but so, that by reason of its change, *neve apud J.*
" as to *Use, Office* and *Dignity*, it is turned *Sacramen-* *Crispinum.*
" *tally* into the *Body* of Christ; as in *Baptism*, the *Wa-* 1555.
" *ter* is turned into the *Laver* of *Regeneration*——That
" the *Humane Nature* of Christ is in *Heaven*, and can-
" not in *any manner* lye hid under the form of *Bread*,
" p. 34.——Then he enquires, whether therefore we
" take away the *Presence* of Christ's *Body* from the *Sa-*
" *crament?* p. 35. And utterly denies, that this is ei-
" ther said or thought by him. The *Substance* of the
" true *Body* and *Blood* of Christ, *says he*, is always in
" *Heaven*, nor shall it depart thence before the end of
" the World. Now this *Substance* of his *Body* and
" *Blood* being conjoyned to his Divine Nature, has
" not only Life in it self, but can, and is wont to be-
" stow it upon all those who partake of it, and believe
" in his Name.——Nor is it any hindrance to this, that
" Christ *still* remains in *Heaven*, and that we are upon
" *Earth*. For by *Grace*, that is, *Life* (as S. *John* in-
" terprets it, *c.* 6) and the Properties of it, as far as
" may be profitable to us in this our Pilgrimage here
" below, he is with us to the end of the World. As
" the *Sun*, who though he never leaves his *Orb*, yet
" by his *Life*, *Heat*, and *Influence*, is *present* to us: *pag.*
36, 37.

Hitherto then there can be no doubt, but that
both the *Church* and the *Divines* knew no other *Real*
Presence than what has been before acknowledged to
be

be still our *Doctrine*. We must now go on to the times of tryal, the days of Q. *Elizabeth*, and her Successors, when our Author supposes, "that Men of different Judgments had the Power. Now for proof of this, besides the Expressions of particular Men, which we shall presently consider, we have Two General Presumptions offer'd to us; One, "That Dr. *Heylin*, and "others, have observed, *he says*, of this Queen, that "she was a *zealous propugner* of the *Real Presence*; which may be very true, and yet but little to the purpose, if she *propugned* it in the same sense that her Brother King *Edward* the 6th, and the *Church of England* had done before, and not in the new Notion imposed upon her by this Author, but without any manner of proof to warrant his suggestion. The other, "That " upon the Re-view made by her Divines of the *Common-Prayer* and *Articles*, they struck out of the One " the *Rubrick* against the *Adoration* of the *Sacrament*, " and the Passage before mention'd (being of the same " temper as the Declaration in the *Liturgy*), out of the " *xxixth Article*; and which has accordingly been o- " mitted ever since.

And here I cannot but again take notice of the disingenuousness of this Author, in dissembling the true Account that has so largely been given by our late accurate Compiler of the *History* of our *Reformation* of this whole matter, only for the advancing so pitiful an Insinuation of what I dare appeal to his own Conscience whether he did not know to be otherwise. I will beg leave to transcribe the whole Passage; and shall then leave it to the indifferent *Reader* to judge whether a man so well acquainted with Books, and so interested in this matter, could have lived so long in the world without hearing

ing of so eminent a matter in our *Church-History* as this.

The Author is treating about the difference between the *Article* establish'd in King *Edward* the six's time, and those in Q. *Elizabeth*'s.

"In the *Article* of the Lord's Supper there is a great
" deal left out; For instead of that large Refutation
" of the *Corporal Presence*, from the Impossibility of a
" *Bodies* being in more places at once; from whence it
" follows, That since Christ's *Body* is in *Heaven*, the
" Faithful ought not to believe or profess a *Real* or *Cor-*
" *poral Presence* of it in the Sacrament. In the new
" Article it is said, [*That the Body of Christ is given*
" *and received after a spiritual manner; and the means*
" *by which it is received, is Faith.*] But in the Original
" Copy of these *Articles*, which I have seen subscribed
" by the Hands of *All* that sate in either House of *Con-*
" *vocation*, there is a further *Addition* made. The *Ar-*
" *ticles* were subscribed with that precaution which was
" requisite in a matter of such consequence: For be-
" fore the *Subscriptions* there is set down the Number
" of the *Pages*, and of the *Lines* in every *Page* of the
" *Book* to which they set their Hands.

Dr. *Burnet*'s Hist. of the Reformation, Vol 2. Pag. 405. Ann. 1559. Edit. 2. 1683.

MSS. C. Cor. Christ. Cant.

In that *Article* of the *Eucharist* these words are added; " Christ when he ascended into *Heaven* made his
" *Body* Immortal, but took not from it the *Nature* of a
" *Body*: For still it retains, according to the Scriptures,
" the *Verity* of a *Humane Body*; which must be always
" in *One definite place*, and cannot be spread into ma-
" ny, or all places at Once. Since then Christ being
" carry'd up to *Heaven*, is to remain there to the end of
" the World, and is to come from thence, and from
" no place else (as says S. *Austin*) to judge the Quick
" and the Dead: None of the Faithful ought to *be-*
" *lieve*

An Explanati-on of Christ's Presence in the Sacrament.

"lieve or *profess* the *Real*, or (as they call it) the *Cor-*
"*poral* Presence of his. *Flesh* and *Blood* in the *Eucha-*
"*rist*.

"But this in the *Original* is dash't over with *minium*;
" yet so that it is still legible. The Secret of it was this;
" The *Queen* and her *Council* studied (as hath been al-
" ready shewn) to unite all into the *Communion* of
" the *Church*: And it was alledged, that such an ex-
" press *Definition* against a *Real Presence*, might drive
" from the *Church* many who were *still* of that *Perswa-*
" *sion*; and therefore it was thought to be enough
" to condemn *Transubstantiation*, and to say, that
" *Christ* was *present* after a *spiritual manner*, and re-
" ceived by *Faith*. To say more, as it was judged su-
" perflous, so it might occasion division. Upon this
" these words were by common consent left out. And
" in the next *Convocation* the *Articles* were subscribed
" without them; of which I have also seen the *Origi-*
" *nal*.

" This shews, that the *Doctrine* of the *Church* subscri-
" bed by the whole *Convocation*, was at that time con-
" trary to the belief of a *Real* or *Corporal Presence* in
" the *Sacrament*; only it was not thought necessary or
" expedient to publish it. Though from this silence,
" which flowed not from their *Opinion*, but the *Wis-*
" *dom* of that time, in leaving a Liberty for different
" *Speculations*, as to the *manner* of the *Presence*; S<small>OME</small>
" have since inferr'd, that the chief Pastors of this
" *Church* did then disapprove of the *definition* made in
" King *Edwards* time; and that they were for a *Real*
" *Presence*.

Thus that Learned *Historian*. And here let our *Adversary* consider what he thinks of this Account; and whether after so evident a Confutation from plain *matter of Fact* of his Objection before it appear'd, we may not reasonably complain both of his Weakness and In-sincerity; neither to take any notice of such a plain History of this whole Transaction, or to imagine that so vain a Surmise of Q. *Elizabeth's* being a great *propugner of the Real Presence*, would be sufficient to obviate so clear and particular an Account of this matter.

But though this might suffice to shew the continuance of the same *Doctrine* of the *Real Presence* in this *Queen's*, that was before profess'd in her Brother's Reign; yet it may not be amiss to discover a little further the truth of this matter, and how falsly this Author has alledged those great Names he has produced. I will therefore beg leave to continue my Proof, with an Induction of the most Eminent of our *Divines* that I have at this time the Opportunity to consult, to our own days.

And first for Bishop *Jewel*; though the part he had in the *Convocation* before mention'd, may sufficiently assure us of his Opinion; yet it may not be improper to repeat the very words of a Person of his Learning and Eminence in our *Church*. In his Reply to *Harding* thus he expresses the *Doctrine* of the *Church* of *England*, as to the *Real Presence* : " Whereas Mr.
" *Harding* thus unjustly reporteth of us, that we main-
" tain a *naked Figure*, and a *bare Sign* or *Token only*,
" and nothing else ——— He knoweth well, we feed
" not the People of God with *bare Signs* and *Figures*,
" but teach them, that the *Sacraments* of Christ be Ho-
" ly *Mysteries*; and that in the Ministration thereof
" Christ is set before us even as he was crucified upon
" the Cross. ——— We teach the People, not that a
" *naked Sign* or *Token*, but that Christ's *Body and Blood*
" indeed

Bp. *JEWEL*.

Vth Article of the *Real Presence* against *Harding*, pag. 237. *Lond.* 1611.
See also his Defence of the Apology of the Church of *England*, pag. 215, &c.

"*indeed and verily* is given unto us; that we *verily eat*
"it; that we *verily drink* it; that we verily be relie-
"ved and live by it: that we are Bones of his Bones,
"and Flesh of his Flesh; that Christ dwelleth in us, and
"we in him:——Yet we say not, either that the *Sub-*
"*stance* of the *Bread* and *Wine* is done away, or that
"Christ's *Body* is let down from *Heaven*, or made *Re-*
"*ally* or *Fleshly present* in the *Sacrament*. We are
"taught according to the *Doctrine* of the Old Fathers,
"to *lift* up our Hearts to *Heaven*, and *there* to feed
"upon the Lamb of God——Thus *spiritually* and
"with the Mouth of our *Faith*, we eat the *Body* of
"Christ, and *drink* his *Blood*; even as *verily* as his *Bo-*
"*dy* was *verily broken*, and his *Blood verily shed* upon
"the *Cross*—— Indeed the *Bread* that we receive with
"our *Bodily Mouths*, is an *earthly* thing; and therefore
"a *Figure*; as the *Water* in *Baptism* is likewise also a
"*Figure*. But the *Body* of Christ that thereby is *repre-*
"*sented*, and there is *offer'd* unto our *Faith*, is the *thing*
"*it self*, and not *Figure*. To conclude, Three things
"herein we must consider: 1*st*, That we put a diffe-
"rence between the *Sign* and the *thing* it self that is
"*signified*: 2. That we seek Christ above in *Heaven*,
"and imagine not him to be *present Bodily* upon the
"Earth: 3. That the *Body* of Christ is to be *eaten* by
"*Faith only*, and none *otherwise*.

I shall not trouble the Reader with any more of our

Mr. *HOOKER*. Divines who lived in the beginning of this *Queen's* Reign, and subscribed the *Article* before-recited; but pass on directly to him whom our Author first mentions, the Venerable Mr. *Hooker*, and whose Judgment

Tr. I. cap. 2 §
10. Pag. 6. having been so deservedly esteemed by all sorts of men, ought not to be lightly accounted of by us.

And

And here I must observe, that this Learned Person is drawn in only by a Consequence, and that no very clear one neither, to favour his Opinion. The truth is, he has dealt with Mr. *Hooker* just as himself, or one of his Friends has been observed to have done on the like occasion with the incomparable *Chillingworth*; has pick'd up a Passage or two that seemed for his purpose; but dissembled whole Pages in the same place that were evidently against him. For thus Mr. *Hooker* in the Chapter cited by him, interprets the words of *Institution:* "If we doubt, *says he,* what those admirable "words may import, let him be our Teacher for the "meaning of Christ, to whom Christ was himself a "School-master. Let our Lord's Apostle be his Inter- "preter; content we our selves with his Explication; "*My Body, the Communion of my Body; My Blood,* "the *Communion of my Blood.* Is there any thing "more expedite, clear and easie, than that as Christ "is termed our Life, because through him we obtain "Life: So the *parts* of this *Sacrament* are his *Body* and "*Blood,* because they are *Causes* instrumental, upon "the receit whereof the *participation* of his *Body* and "*Blood* ensueth? ——The *Real Presence* of Christ's "most blessed *Body* and *Blood* is not therefore to be "sought for in the *Sacrament,* but in the *worthy Recei-* "*ver* of the *Sacrament*——And again, *p.* 310. he thus "interprets the same words; This Hallow'd Food "through the concurrence of Divine Power, is in "verity and truth unto faithful Receivers instrumen- "tally a Cause of that *mystical participation,* whereby "as I make my self wholly *theirs,* so I give them in hand "an actual possession of all such saving *Grace* as my sa- "crificed *Body* can yeild, and as their *Souls* do present- "ly need. *This is* to them and in them *my Body.*

Difference between the Protestant and Socinian Methods, in answer to the Protestants Plea for a *Socinian,* pag. 54.

And

And this may suffice in Vindication of Mr. *Hooker.* Those who desire a fuller Account, may find several Pages to the same purpose in the Chapter which I have quoted. The next our Author mentions, is the Learned Bishop *Andrews*, in that much noted passage, as he calls it, in the Answer to *Bellarmine.*

Bishop
ANDREWS.
1 Tract. pag.
7. §. xi. n. 1.

And indeed we need desire no other Passage to judge of his Opinion in this matter; in which 1st. He utterly excludes all defining any thing as to the *manner* of Christs *Presence* in the *Eucharist.* 2. He professes that a *Presence* we believe, and that no less a *True* one than the *Papists.* 3. He plainly insinuates that the *presence* of Christ in the *Eucharist*, was much the same as in *Baptism*; the very allusion which the Holy † Fathers were wont to make, to express his *Presence* by in this Holy Sacrament; which since our Adversaries can neither deny, nor yet say is so *real*, as to be *Essential* or *Corporeal*; they must of necessity allow that there may be a *true Presence* (which is all the Bishop affirms,) without such a *Substantial* one as this Author here contends for.

† Habemus Christum præsentem ad Baptismatis Sacramentum, habemus eum præsentem ad Altaris Cibum & Potum. *Augustin.* Stola, quæ est Ecclesia Christi, lavatur in ipsius sanguine vivo *i. e.* in lavacro regenerationis. *Origen.* Statim baptizatus in sanguine agni Vir meruit appellari. *Hieron.* Christi sanguine lavaris, quando in ejus mortem Baptizaris. Leo. P. &c.

See Sermon vii. on the Resurect. pag. 454. Serm. Lond. 1641.

But to shew that whatever this Bishop understood by the *Real presence*, it could not be that Christs *glorified Body* is now actually *present* in this Sacred *Mystery*, will appear demonstratively from this, that he declares it is not this *Body* which we either *Represent* or *partake* of there; insomuch that he doubts not to say, that could there be a *Transubstantiation*, such as the *Church* of *Rome* supposes, it would not serve our turn, nor answer the design of this *Sacrament.* 'Tis in his Sermon on 1 Cor. v. 7, 8. "We will mark, "*saith he*, something more: That *Epulemur* doth here "refer to *Immolatus*: To Christ not *every way consi-* "*der'd*, but *As* when he was *Offer'd.* Christs *Body*
"*That*

" *that now is, true* ; But not Chrifts *Body as now it is*, but
" *as then it was*, when it was *offer'd, rent*, and *flain*,
" and *facrificed* for us. Not as now he is *glorified* ;
" for fo he is not, he cannot be *Immolatus* ; For as he
" is, he is immortal and impaffible ; But as then he was
" when he *fuffer'd death*, that is *paffible* and *mortal*.
" Then in his paffible State, he did inftitute this of
" ours, to be *a memorial* of his *Paffible* and *Paffion* both.
" And we are in this Action not only *carry'd up to*
" *Chrift (furfum Corda)* [*fo that Chrift it feems is not
" brought down to us*] but we are alfo *carry'd back* to
" Chrift, as he was at the *very inftant*, and in the
" *very Act* of his *offering*. So, and no *otherwife*, doth
' this Text teach ; So, and no *otherwife* do we *Repre-*
" *fent* him. By the incomprehenfible power of his E-
" ternal Spirit, not *He alone*, but *He as at the very*
" *act of his offering is made prefent to us*, and we in-
" corporate into his *death*, and invefted in the *Benefits*
" of it. If an *Hoft* could be turned into him now
" *glorified* as he is, it would not ferve ; *Chrift offer'd* is
" it. Thither muft we look ; to the *Serpent lift up* :
" thither we muft repair ; even *ad Cadaver* : We muft
" *Hoc facere*, do that is then done. So and no other-
" wife is this *Epulare* to be conceived. And fo I think
" none will fay they *do* or *can turn* him.

Whatfoever *Real prefence* then this Bifhop believed,
it muft be of his *crucified Body*, and as in the State of
his *death* ; and that I think cannot be otherwife *prefent*
than in one of thofe two ways mentioned above by
Arch-Bifhop *Cranmer*, and both of which we willingly
acknowledge ; either *Figuratively*, in the *Elements* ;
or *Spiritually*, in the Souls of thofe who worthily
receive them.

And from this Account of Bifhop *Andrew's* Opinion

Of the Real Presence acknowledged

<small>CASAUBON, KING JAMES, A. Bishop of Spalato.</small>

on, we may conclude what it was that *Casaubon* and King *James* understood by the *Real Presence*, who insist upon that Bishops words to express their own Notion and meaning of it. Nor can we make any other judgment of the Arch Bishop of *Spalato*; who

<small>See the 1. Tra. §. xi. note 2. pag. 7.
* Vol. 3. de Rep. Eccles. lib. 7. cap. 11. pag. 200. 201.</small>

in the next § * to that cited by our Adversary is very earnest against those who receive *unworthily* this Holy Sacrament, and by consequence ties not Christs *natural Body* to the *Bread*; and declares it to be after a *Spiritual imperceptible* and *miraculous* manner. As for the term *Corporaliter*, which he there uses, and which *Melancthon* and some others had used before him, that may be well enough understood in the same Sence, as *verè* or *realiter*; and is often so used both in

<small>Coloss. ii. 9, 17.</small>

Scripture and in the Holy *Fathers*. As when St. *Paul* says of Christ, that in "*Him dwelleth the fulness of the Godhead Bodily*; that is *really*, in opposition to the *Shechinah* or *Presence* of God in the *Tabernacle*. And again, *The Body of Christ*; that is the

<small>See Hammond in Coloss. 1. Annot. d.</small>

substance, the *reality*, opposed to the *types* and *figures* of the Law. And so in the *Hebrew* Exposition עצם is often used for *Essence* as well as *Body*, and applied

<small>Arch-Bishop LAWD.</small>

to *Spiritual* as well as *Corporal* things.

Nor can I see any more reason to understand Arch-Bishop *Lawd* in any other Sence. He asserts the *true*

<small>1 Tract. §. xiv. pag. 8.
† Bishop HALL.
* MONTAGUE Origenes Eccles. Tom. prior. par. poster. p. 247. 249. 250. &c</small>

and *real Presence* of Christ in this Sacred Feast; but he do's not say, that Christ's *natural Body* which is now in *Heaven*, is also in this *Holy Sacrament*, or in the *worthy receiver*; nor have we any reason to believe that he understood it so to be. * And the same must be said of † Bishop *Hall*, Bishop *Montague*, and Bishop Panis in *Synaxi* sit corpus Christi;— Sed et *Corpus* Christi CREDENTES sunt. Ad *eundem* utrumque *modum* & mensuram; sed non *Naturaliter*;— Itaque nec *Panis* ITA est *Corpus* Christi; *Mystice* tantum, non *Physice*. vid. plur.

Bilson

Bilson; in whose expressions as they are quoted by our Author, I find nothing that proves the Sence he would impose upon them; and whose works had I now by me, I might possibly be able to give some better account of them. Though after all, should one of these in his violence against his Adversaries, or the others in their *pacifick design* of reconciling all Parties as to this Point, have said more than they ought to do, I do not see but that it ought to have been imputed to the circumstances they were in and the designs they pursued, rather than be set up for the measure either of their own, or our *Churches* Opinion. *MONTAGUE BILSON.*

And now I am mentioning these things, I ought not pass over one other eminent instance of such a charitable undertaking, and which has given occasion to our Author of a Quotation he might otherwise have wanted, in that excellent Bishop of St. *Andrews* Bishop *Forbes*; concerning whose Authority in this matter I shall offer only the censure of one, than whom none could have given a more worthy Character of a person, who so well deserved it as that good Bishop did; "I do not deny, but his earnest desire of a ge-"neral *Peace* and *Union* among all Christians, has "made him too favourable to many of the Corrupti-"ons in the Church of *Rome*: But though a *Charity* "that is not well ballanced, may carry one to very "indiscreet things; yet the principle from whence "they flow'd in him, was so truly good, that the *Er-*"*rors* to which it carry'd him, ought to be either ex-"cused, or at least to be very gently censured." Bishop *FORBES.* Author of the Life of Bishop *BEDEL*; in the Preface.

There remain now but two of all the Divines he has produced to prove his new fancy, which he would set up for the *Doctrine* of the *Church of England*; and those as little for his purpose as any he has hitherto mentioned;

Bishop TAYLOR.

Polemical discourses. p. 182. London. 1674.

mentioned; Bishop *Taylor* and Mr. *Thorndyke*. For Bishop *Taylor*, I cannot acquit our *Author* of a wilful prevarication; since it is evident that he has so plainly opposed his Notion, and that in the very Book he quotes, and which he wrote on purpose to shew our meaning of the *Real Presence*, that he could not but have known that he *misrepresented* him. I shall set down the state of the Question as it is in the beginning of that *Treatise*. "The *Doctrine* of the *Church* of *England*, and generally of the *Protestants* in this *Article* is; That after the Minister of the Holy Mysteries hath rightly pray'd and blessed or consecrated the *Bread* and the *Wine*; the *Symbols* become changed into the *Body* and *Blood* of Christ after a *Sacramental*, *i.e.* in a *Spiritual Real* manner. So that all that worthily communicate, do by *Faith receive* Christ *Really*, *Effectually*, to all the purposes of his Passion — It is *Bread* and it is *Christs Body*: It is *Bread* in in *Substance*, Christ in the *Sacrament*; and Christ is as *really* given to all that are truly dispos'd, as the *Symbols* are p. 183. — It is here as in the other Sacrament; for as there *natural Water* becomes the *laver of Regeneration*; so here *Bread* and *Wine* become the *Body* and *Blood* of Christ: but there and here too the first *Substance* is changed by *Grace*, but remains the *same* in *nature*— We say that Christs *Body* is in the Sacrament *really*, but *Spiritually*. They (the *Papists*) say it is there *really*, but *Spiritually*. For so *Bellarmin* is bold to say that the word may be allowed in this Question. Where now is the difference? Here; By *Spiritually* they mean present after the manner of a *Spirit*; by *Spiritually* we mean present to our *Spirits only*; that is, so as Christ is not present to any other Sence but that of *faith* or *spiritual* susception —

"They

"They say that Chrifts *Body* is *truly* prefent there, as
"it was upon the *Crofs*, but not after the *manner* of all,
"or any *Body* — But we by the *real Spiritual Prefence* of
"Chrift, do underftand Chrift to be prefent, as the Spi-
"rit of God is prefent in the Hearts of the faithful, by
"*Bleffing* and *Grace*; and this is *ALL we mean* befides
"the *tropical* and *figurative* prefence.

Such is the Account which that Excellent Bifhop here gives not only of his own, but, as he exprefly terms, it of the *Church of* England's, *and the Generality of the Proteftants Belief in this Matter.* Our Author's diffimulation of it is fo much the more inexcufable, by how much the more zealous an Advocate he makes him of his Caufe, when all this that I have tranfcribed, was in the very fame Section, and almoft in the fame Page with what he has cited. For his little Remark upon the Title of the Bifhops Book, where he calls it of the *Real Prefence* and *Spiritual*, whence he would infer a difference between the two Terms, and find fomething *Real* that is not *Spiritual* in this *Sacrament*; it is evident that the Defign of that Diftinction was this: There be feveral forts of *Real Prefences*; the *Papifts*, the *Lutherans*, the *Church of England*, all allow a *Real Prefence* in the *Sacrament*, but after different *Manners*; it was therefore neceffary to add fomewhat more, to fhew what kind of *Real Prefence* he undertook to maintain, and he knew no word more proper to exprefs it by than *Spiritual*, which does not therefore imply a Diftinction from, but Limitation of the other Term *Real.* And thus he explains it, *N.* 6. and 7. of that Section, where he fhews that the *Spiritual* is alfo a *Real Prefence*, and indeed more properly fo than any other. In fhort, thus he concludes the State of the Queftion, in the fame Section,

Treatife 1ft. p. 20th.

Pag. 183.

Pag. 186.

on, between us and the *Church* of *Rome*, so that now, *says he*, The Question is not, "Whether the *Symbols* be *changed* into Christ's *Body* and *Blood* or no? For it is granted on all sides: But whether this *Conversi-on* be *Sacramental* and *Figurative*? Or whether it be *Natural* and *Bodily*? Nor is it whether Christ be taken *Really*, but whether he be taken in a *Spiritual* or in a *Natural Manner*? We say the Conversion is *Figurative, Mysterious*, and *Sacramental*; they say, it is *Proper, Natural*, and *Corporal*. We affirm that Christ is *really taken* by *Faith*, by the *Spirit*, to all *real Effects* of his Passion (this is an Explication a little different from our Authors) "They say he is taken by the *Mouth*, and that the *Spiritual* and the *Virtual* taking him in *Virtue* or *Effect*, is not sufficient, tho' done also in the Sacrament. *Hic Rhodus, hic Saltus.*

If this does not yet satisfie him that he has injur'd this Learned Man in the Representation of his Opinion, directly contrary to his Sense, I will offer him yet one Passage more, taken from another part of his Works, and which, I hope, will throughly convince him. It is in the 5*th*. Letter, to a Gentleman that was tempted to the Communion of the *Church* of *Rome*. He had proposed to the Bishop this Question. "Whether, without all danger of *Superstition* or *Idolatry*, we may not render Divine *Worship* to our Blessed Saviour, as present in the Blessed *Sacrament* or *Host*, according to his *Humane Nature*, in that *Host*? The Question is certainly every way pertinent to our present Purpose; let us see what the Answer is that he makes to it. "We may not render Divine *Worship* to him as *present* in the Blessed *Sacrament* according to his *Humane Nature*, without danger of *Idolatry*, because he is not there according to his *Humane Na-ture*,

See *Polemic. Disc. Append. Pag.* 69. 70.

"*ture*, and therefore you give Divine Worship to a
"*Non-Ens*, which must needs be *Idolatry*. Well, but   Treat. 1st.
still it may be the Bishop does not intend to exclude Pag. 10.
the *Corpus Domini*, but only the *Corporal* or *Natural
Manner* of that *Body*: Let us therefore hear how he
goes on. "For *Idolum nihil est in mundo*, Saith
"St. *Paul*, and Christ as *Present* by his *Humane Nature*
"in the *Sacrament* is a *Non-ens*. For it is not true;
"there is no suchthing. What, not as Christ there, no
way as to his Humane nature?— No, he is *saith the*
"*Bishop*, present there by his Divine power, and his
"Divine Blessing, and the *Fruits* of his *Body*, the *real
"effective Consequents* of his *Passion*; but for *any other*
"*Presence*, it is *Idolum*; it is nothing in the World. A-
"dore Christ in Heaven; for the Heaven must contain
"him till the time of restitution of all things. This then
is Bishop *Taylor*'s Notion of the *Real Presence*: and
now I am confident our Author himself will remit him
to the Company of those Old *Zuinglian* Bishops, *Cranmer*, *Ridley*, and the rest, who lived before that Q.
Elizabeth had *propugned* the *Real Presence* of his new
Model into the Heads of the *Governours* of the *Church
of England*.

And now I am afraid his Cause will be desperate
unless Mr. *Thorndyke* can support it. And how Mr. *THORN-*
unlikely he is to do it, he might have learnt from *DYKE*.
what has been answered to *T. G.* on the same Occasion.
∵ *T. G.* Had in his first *Dialogue* quoted the same place ∵ *T. G.* Dia-
which our Author has done since, to prove his belief logue 1st.
of the *Real Presence*: His * *Adversary* confesses this, but Pag. 21.
produces another that explains his meaning; "† if * Answer to
"it can any way be shew'd, *says he*, that the *Church* Pag. 92.
"did ever pray that the *Flesh* and *Blood* might be substi- † *THORN-
"tuted instead of the Elements under the Accidents of DYKE* Laws
                                          "them of the Church.
                                                  Ch. 4. Pag. 30.

"them, then I am content that this be accounted
"henceforth the *Sacramental presence* of them in the
"*Eucharist*. But if the *Church* only prays that the Spi-
"rit of God coming down upon the *Elements*— may
"make them the *Body* and *Blood* of Christ, so that
"they which receive them may be *filled* with the *Grace*
"of his *Spirit*, then is it not the Sence of the *Catholick*
"*Church* that can oblige any many to believe the abo-
"lishing of the *Elements* in their *bodily substance*, be-
"cause supposing that they remain, they may never-
"theless come to be the instruments of Gods Spirit
"to convey the operation thereof to them that are di-
"spos'd to receive it, no otherwise than his *Flesh* and
"*Blood* convey'd the *Efficacy* thereof upon Earth. And
"that I suppose is reason enough to call it the *Body*
"and *Blood* of Christ *Sacramentally*, that is to say, as in
"the *Sacrament* of the *Eucharist*.

Thus Mr. *Thorndyke* expresses himself as to the *Real Presence*: But yet after all, I will not deny but that this Learned Person seems to have had a particular Notion in this matter, and which is far enough from what our *Author* would fix upon him. He thought that the *Elements* by *Consecration* were united to the Godhead of Christ, much after the same manner as his *Natural Body* was by *Incarnation*; and that so the very *Elements* became after a sort his *Body*. "The Church

See his Just Weights and Measures, 4*to*. *Lond*.1662.— Pag. 54.

"from the beginning did not pretend to consecrate by
"these bare words, *This is my Body, this is my Blood,*
"as operatory in changing the Elements into the *Body*
"and *Blood* of Christ; but by that Word of God
"whereby he hath declared the Institution of this Sa-
"crament, and commanded the use of it; and by the
"Execution of this Command. Now it is executed,
"and hath always been executed by the Act of the
"Church

"*Church* upon God's Word of *Institution*, praying
"that the Holy Ghost coming down upon the present
"*Elements*, may make them the *Body* and *Blood* of
"*Christ*. Not by *changing* them into the *Nature* of
"*Flesh* and *Blood*; as the *Bread* and *Wine* that nou-
"rished our Lord Christ on Earth, became the *Flesh*
"and *Blood* of the Son of God, by becoming the *Flesh*
"and *Blood* of his Manhood, *Hypostatically* united to
"his *Godhead*, saith *Gregory Nyssene*. But immediate-
"ly and *ipso. facto*, by being united to the *Spirit* of
"*Christ*; *i. e.* his *Godhead*. For the *Flesh* and *Blood*
"of Christ by *Incarnation*, the *Elements* by *Consecra-
"tion* being united to the *Spirit* ; *i. e.* the *Godhead* of
"Christ, become both one *Sacramentally*, by being both
"one with the *Spirit* or *Godhead* of Christ, to the con-
"veying of God's *Spirit* to a Christian.

And thus have I consider'd the several *Divines* produced for this new Conceit concerning the *Real Presence*; and shewn the greatest part of his Authors to be evidently against it; some not to have spoken so clearly that we can determine any thing concerning them; but not one that favours what they were alledged for; *viz.* to shew that they believed Christ's *Natural Body* to be both in *Heaven* and in the *Sacrament* ; only after another *manner* than the *Papists*. It were an easie matter to shew how constant our *Church* has been to the *Doctrine* of the *true, real, spiritual Presence* which it still asserts, and which it derived from its first Reformers, whose words have been before set down by a *cloud* of other Witnesses; as may be seen by the short *Specimen* I have put together in the * *Margent*. But I have insisted too long already on this matter; and shall therefore pass on to the *Third* thing I proposed to consider ; *viz.*

* Reformatio legum Eccles. ex Authorit. Henr. 8. & Edw. 6. Lond. 1641. Tit. de Sacram. cap. 4. pag. 29. ——*Morton de Euch.* part. 2. Class. 4. cap. 1. §. 2. pag. 224. *Lat.* 1640. 4to.——— *Fr. White* against *Fisher*, pag. 407. *Lond.* 1624. Fol.—A. B. *Usher*'s.

B. *Usher*'s Answer to a Challenge, c of the *Real Presence*, p. 44, 45. *Lond.* 1525.——— Id. Serm before the House of Commons, pag. 16, 19, &c ———Dr. *Hammond* Pract. Catech. part. ult. Answer to this Question; the Importance of these words, *That the Body and Blood of Christ are verily and indeed taken and received*, p. 130. Edit. *Lond.* Fol. 1584.——— Dr. *Jackson*'s Works, Tom. 3. pag. 300, 302. *Lond.* 1573. Dr. *Jo. White*'s Way to the True Church. *Lond.* 1624. §. 51. N. 10 pag. 209. *Cosens* Hist. Transubst. p. 3, 4, 12, &c. Edit. *London*, 1675. 8vo.

Thirdly, That the *Alterations* which have been made in our *Rubrick*, were not upon the account of our Divines changing their Opinions, as is vainly and falsly suggested.

To give a rational Account of this Affair, we must carefully consider the Circumstances of the Times, the Tempers and Dispositions of the Persons that lived in them; and what the Designs of the *Governing* Parties were with reference to them; and then we shall presently see both a great deal of Wisdom and Piety in the making of these *Alterations*; allowing the Opinions of those who did it, to have continued, as we have seen, in all of them the same.

When first this *Rubrick* was put into King *Edward*'s Liturgy, the *Church* of *England* was but just rising up out of the Errors and Superstitions with which it had been over-run by the prevalency of *Popery* upon it. It had the happiness to be *reformed*, not as most others were, by private persons, and in many places contrary to the desires of the *Civil Power*; but by a Unanimous Concurrence of the Highest *Authority* both *Civil* and *Ecclesiastical*, of *Church* and *State*. Hence it came to pass, that *Convocations* being assembled, *Deliberations* had of the greatest and wisest Persons for the proceeding in it, nothing was done out of a Spirit of Peevishness or Opposition; the *Holy Scriptures* and *Antiquity* were carefully consulted; and all things examined according to the exactest measures that could be taken from them; and a diligent distinction made of what

was

was *Popery*, and what *true* and *Catholick Christianity*, that so the One only might be rejected, the other duly retained.

Now by this means it was that the Ancient *Government* of the *Church* became preserved amongst us; a just and wise *Liturgy* collected out of the *Publick Rituals*: Whatever *Ceremonies* were requisite for *Order* or *Decency*, were retain'd; and among the rest, that of receiving the *Communion kneeling* for One, which has accordingly ever since been the manner establish'd amongst us. But that no Occasion of Scandal might hereby be given, whether to our *Neighbour-Churches* abroad, or to any particular Members of our own at home: That those who were yet weak in the Faith, might not either continue or fall back into Error, and by our retaining the same *Ceremony* in the *Communion* that they had been used to in the *Mass*, fancy that they were to *adore* the *Bread* as they did before: For all these great Ends this Caution was inserted; that the true Intent of this *Ceremony* was only for *Decency* and *Order*; not that any *Adoration* was thereby *intended*, or ought to be done unto any Real or Essential *Presence of Christ's Natural Flesh and Blood, which were not there, but in Heaven, it being against the Truth of Christ's Natural Body to be at One time in more places than One.*

And this is sufficiently intimated in the words of the *Rubrick* to have been the first Cause and Design of it. Thus it continued the remainder of King *Edward's* time: But now Queen *Elizabeth* being come to the Crown, there were other Circumstances to be consider'd. Those of the *Reformed* Religion abroad were sufficiently satisfied, both by this *publick Declaration*, which had stood so many years in the *Liturgy* of our Church;

Church; and by the Conversation and Acquaintance of our Divines, forced by the dispersion in the foregoing Reign, to seek for refuge among their Brethren in other Countries, of our Orthodox Faith, as to this Point. Our own Members at home had heard too much of this matter in the publick Writings and Disputations, and in the constant Sufferings of their *Martyrs*, not to know that the *Popish Real Presence* was a meer Figment, an *Idolum*, as Bishop *Taylor* justly stiles it; and their *Mass* to be *abhorred* rather than *adored*. There was then no longer need of this *Rubrick* upon any of those Accounts for which it was first establish'd; and there was a very just reason now to lay it aside. That great *Queen* desired, if possible, to compose the Minds of her Subjects, and make up those Divisions which the differences of *Religion*, and the late unhappy Consequences of them had occasion'd. For this, she made it her business to render the publick Acts of the *Church of England* as agreeable to all Parties as Truth would permit. The Clause of the *Real Presence* inserted in the *Articles* of her first *Convocation*, and *subscribed* by all the *Members* of it (to shew that their belief was still the same it had ever been as to this matter) was nevertheless, as we have seen, struck out for this end their next Session. The Title of *Head* of the *Church*, which her Father had first taken, her Brother continued, and was from both derived to her, so qualified and explained, as might prevent any Occasion of quarrelling at it by the most captious persons. That Petition in the *Litany* inserted by King *Henry* viii. "*From the Tyranny of the Bishop of* "Rome, *and all his detestable Enormities, Good Lord*, &c. struck out: And in conformity to what was done in the *Articles* as to this Point, this *Rubrick* also was omitted, lest it should give *Offence* to those who were still

zea-

By the Church of England.

zealous for their mistaken Principles and Worship. This was the Wise and Christian Design of that Excellent *Princess*; and how happy an Effect this Moderation might have had, if the Bishop of *Rome* had not by his Artifice and Authority with some of her Subjects, prevented it, the first Years of her Reign sufficiently shew.

Thus was the Occasion and Reason of its omission in Q. *Elizabeth*'s time, as great as the necessity of its first Insertion in King *Edward*'s. And in this state it continued all the Reign of that *Queen*, and of her two Successors, King *James* and King *Charles.* 1*st*, I shall not need to say by what means it was, that new Occasion was given for the reviving of it. We have all of us heard, and many of us seen too much of it. How Order became Superstitious, and Decency termed Idolatry: The *Church* of *England* traduced as but another Name for *Popery*; and this *Custom* of *kneeling at the Communion*, one of the strongest Arguments offer'd for the Proof of it. And now when Panick Fears had found such prevalence over the Minds of Men, as to destroy a King, and embroil a Kingdom into a *Civil War*, of almost Twenty Years continuance; and tho by the good hand of God our King and our Peace were again restored, yet the minds of the People were still unsetled, and in danger of being again blown up upon the least Occasion; what could be more advisable to justifie our selves from all suspicion of *Popery* in this matter, and induce them to a *Conformity* with us in a *Ceremony* they had entertain'd such a dread of, than to revive that ancient *Rubrick*; and so quiet the Minds of the People now, by the same means by which they had been setled and secured before?

This I am perswaded is so *rational* an Account, as will both justifie the proceedings of our Governours in these

these Changes, and shew the dis-ingenuity of those, who not only knowing, but having been told these things, will still rather impute it to an imaginary wavering, or uncertainty of Opinion, than to a necessary and Christian Accommodation to the Times. For the change in the Prayer of *Consecration*, I have already said, that 'tis in the Words, not the Sense: And if our Governours thought the present Expressions less liable to exception than the former, they had certainly reason for the Alteration. For the other Exceptions there is very little in them, whether the Minister lay his Hand on the Sacred Elements, when he repeats the words of *Institution*, as at this time, or only consecrates them by the Prayers of the *Church*, and the Words of Christ, without any other *Ceremony*, as heretofore: Whether with the *Church* of *Rome* we use only the words of Christ in the distribution; or with most of the Reformed Churches, the other Expression, " *Take* " *and eat this*, &c. or (as we chuse rather) joyn them both together: Whether we sing the *Gloria in Excelsis Deo*—before or after the receiving; but because the chiefest Mystery he thinks lies in this, That whereas in King *Edward*'s days the *Rubrick* called it an *Essential Presence*, which we have now turned into *Corporeal*; I must confess I will not undertake to say what the Occasion of it was; if they thought this latter manner more free from giving Offence than the other would have been, I think they did well to prefer it. Let every one entertain what Notion he pleases of these things; this I have shewn is the Doctrine of the *Church* which we all subscribe, " That the *Natural Body* and " *Blood* of our Saviour Christ are in *Heaven*, and not *here*; *i. e.* in the Sacrament; and if there can be any other *Real Presence* than such as I have shewn to have been the

con-

constant belief of our Divines consistent with this *Rubrick*, I shall no more desire to debar any one the belief of it, than I shall be willing to be obliged to believe it with him.

And now after so clear an Account as I have here given of the several changes that have been made in our *Rubrick*, were I minded to recriminate, and tell the World what Alterations have been made in their Mass, & those in Points infinitely more material than any thing that can be alledged against us, I much question whether they would be able to give us so good an account of it. And something of this I may perhaps offer as a *Specimen* of the wisdom of this Author in the choice of his Accusation before we part; In the mean time I go on to the last thing proposed to be here consider'd.

4thly. that the *Reason* mention'd in our *Rubrick* concerning the *Impossibility* of Chrlsts *natural Body*'s existing in *several places* at the *same time*, is no way invalidated by any of this *Authors* exceptions against it.

Now these being most of them founded upon the former mistaken Notion of the *Real presence* falsely imputed to us, will admit of a very short and plain consideration.

1st. He *observes* "That *Protestants*, but especially our "*English Divines* generally confess the *presence* of our "*Saviour* in the Eucharist to be an *ineffable Mystery*. Well, be it so; what will he hence infer? Why "this "he conceives is said to be so in respect of something in "it *opposite* and *contradictory* to, and therefore in-"comprehensible and ineffable by *Humane Reason*. But supposing they should not think it so from being *Opposite* and *Contradictory* to, but because the manner how Christ herein communicates himself to us is *hid from*, and

Treatise 1st.
§. xx. n. 1.
pag. 13.

Of the Real Presence acknowledged

and *above* our Humane Reason; might not this be sufficient to make it still be called an *ineffable*, and *incomprehensible Mystery*? Whereas the other would make it rather plain and *comprehensible Nonsence*. 'Tis a strange Affection that some Men have got of late for *Contradictions*; they are so in love with them, that they have almost brought it to be the definition of a *Mystery*, to be the *Revelation* of something to be believ'd in *Opposition to Sense and Reason*. And what by their *Notions* and *Parallels*, have advanced no very commendable Character of Christianity; as if it were a *Religion* full of *Absurdities*; and as *Fisher* the Jesuit once told King *James* 1ˢᵗ· with reference to this very Subject, *the rather to be believed because it is contrary to Reason*. But if this be indeed our Authors Notion of *Mysteries* (and the truth is *Transubstantiation* can be no other *Mystery*) we desire he will be pleased to confine it to his own *Church*, and not send it abroad into the World as ours too. We are perswaded, not only that our *Worship* must be a *reasonable Service*, but our *Faith* a *Reasonable Assent*. He who opposes the Authority of Holy Scriptures, "says Bishop *Taylor*, against manifest and cer-"tain *Reason*, do's neither understand himself nor "them. *Reason* is the voice of God as well as *Revelation*, and what is opposit to the one, can no more be agreeable to the other, than God can be contrary to himself. And though, if the *Revelation* be *clear* and *evident*, we submit to it, because we are then sure it cannot be *contrary* to *Reason*, whatever it may appear to us; yet when the *contradiction* is *manifest*, as that a *natural Body should be in more places than one at the same time*, we are sure that interpretation of Holy *Scripture* can never be the right which would infer this, but especially when there is another, and much more reasonable,

---

Bishop *TAYLOURS* Polem. Disco. of the *Real presence*. Sect. ii. pag. 231.

Ibid.

nable, that do's not. And in this we are after all justified by one whose Authority I hope our *Author* will not question, even his own self; " If, *says he*, we are " certain there is a *contradiction*, then we are certain " there neither *is* nor *can be a contrary Revelation*; and " when any *Revelation*, tho' *never so plain*, is brought; " *we are bound to interpret it so, as not to affirm a cer-* " *tainly known impossibility.* And let him that sticks to this rule, interpret Chrifts words for *Transubstantiation* if he can. Treatife 1ft. §. 29. pag. 21.

" But do not our own Authors sometimes say, that " notwithstanding all the difficulties brought against " *Transubstantiation*, yet if it can be shewn that God " has revealed it, they are ready to believe it? Perhaps some may have said this, because for that very Reason that there are so many *contradictions* in it, they are sure it cannot be shewn that God has *revealed* it. But if he means, as he seems to insinuate, that notwithstanding such *plain contradictions* as they charge it with, they thought it possible nevertheless, that God might have revealed it, and upon that supposition, they were ready to believe it; I answer from his own words, that their supposal then was *Absurd* and *impossible*; since he himself assure us, that " None can be- " lieve a thing true, upon *what motive soever*, which " he first knows to be certainly *false*, or which is all " one, *certainly* to *contradict*. For these we say *are* " *not verifyable by a divine Power*; and *Ergo*, here I " may say, should a divine power declare a truth, it " would transcend its self. Which last words if they signifie any thing and do not *transcend Sense*, must suppose it impossible for such a thing as implies a *certain Contradiction*, to be revealed. Treatife 1ft. § xx. n. 3. pag. 14.

II. *Observation*, But our Author goes on, "I con- " ceive that any one thing that seemeth to us to include
" a

" a Perfect *Contradiction*, can no more be effected by
" divine Power than another, or than many others the
" like may. Seeing then we admit that some seeming
" *Contradictions* to Reason may be verified by the Di-
" vine power in this *Sacrament*, there is no reason to
" deny but that this may be also as well as any other.

Now not to contend with him about words; whoever told our Author, that we allow'd that there was any thing in this Sacrament, as received by us, that *seemed* to us to include a *Perfect Contradiction* ? *Perfect Contradictions* we confess are all of them *equally verifyable by a divine Power*, that is, are all of them *impossible*. And for this we have his own word before. Now if there be any *such* things as *perfect contradictions* to be known by us, that which *seems to us* to be a *perfect contradiction*, must *really be a perfect contradiction*; unless *contradictions* are to be discover'd some other way than by seeming to our *Reason* to be so. And such it not only *seems*, but undoubtedly *is*, for the same *One, natural, finite* Body, to be in more *places* than *one* at the *same time*; if *to be* and not *to be*, be still the measure of *Contradictions*. He that says of such a *Body*, that it is in *Heaven* and on *Earth*, at *London* and *Rome*, at the *same time*, says in Effect that 'tis *one* and *not one*; *finite* and *not finite*; *in one place* and *not in one place*, &c. All which are such *seemingly perfect contradictions*, that I fear 'twill be a hard matter to find out any *Power* by which they *can be verify'd*.

Treatise 1st. §. xxii. p. 15.

III. *Observation*. He observes Thirdly ; "That those
" who affirm a *Real* and *Substantial presence* of the *very*
" *Body* of Christ to the worthy communicant, contra-
" distinct to any such other *Real presence* of Chrifts Bo-
" dy, as implies only a *presence* of it in *Virtue*, and *Spiri-*
" *tual Effects*, &c. must hold this particular *seeming Con-*
" *tradiction* to be *True*, or some other equivalent to it.

If

If by the *Real Presence* of the *very Body of Christ*, he means, as he before explains it, That Christ's *Natural Body*, that *very Body which is now in Heaven*, *should be also at the same time here upon Earth*; it is, I think, necessary for those who will affirm this, to hold some such kind of *Contradiction*, as he says: And 'tis for that very *Reason*, I am perswaded, he will find but few such Persons in the *Church* of *England*; which so expresly declares, that Christ's *Natural Body* is in *Heaven*, and *not here*, upon this very account, "*That it is contrary to the truth of a Natural* "*Body to be in more places than one at the same time.* However, if any such there be, as they herein depart from the *Doctrine* of their *Church*, so it is not our concern to answer for their *Contradictions*.

IV. He observes, lastly: "It seems to me that "some of the more judicious amongst them (the "Divines he means of the *Church* of *England*) have "not laid so great a weight on this Philosophical Po- "sition, as *wholly* to support and regulate their Faith "in this matter by it; as it stands in opposition not "only to *Nature's*, but the *Divine Power*: because "they pretend not any such certainty thereof, but "that if any Divine *Revelation* of the contrary can "be shewed, they profess a readiness to believe it.

Tract. 1. §. xxviii. p. 20.

I shall not now trouble my self with what some of our Divines may seem to him to have done in this matter; 'tis evident our *Church* has laid stress enough upon this *Contradiction*. Indeed where so many gross Repugnancies both to *Sense* and *Reason* are crowded together, as we have seen before there are in this *Point*, it ought not to be wondered if our *Divines* have not supported and regulated their

R   Faith

Faith *wholly* upon this one alone. We do not any of Us think it either safe or pious to be too nice in determining what God *can*, or *cannot* do; we leave that to the bold Inquisitiveness of their *Schools*. But this we think we may say, that if there are any unalterable Laws of Nature, by which we are to judg of these things; then God can no more make *one Body* to exist in *ten thousand places* at the *same time*, than he can make *one*, continuing *one*, to be *ten thousand*, than he can *divide* the same thing from *its self*, and yet continue it still *undivided*. And if any of our Divines have said, that they cannot admit that one Body can be in several places at once, "till the Papists can demonstrate the possibility "thereof by Testimony of Holy Scripture, or the "ancient Tradition of the Primitive Church, or "by apparent Reason. We need not suppose that they said this, doubting whether it implied a *Contradiction*, but because the certainty of the *Contradiction* secured them against the possibility of any such Proof. *

* *This is evident in B. Taylor, who thought that God could not do this, because it implied a Contradiction: Real Presence,* §. xi. n. 1. p. 230. *and* Ibid. n. 27. *He saith 'tis utterly impossible. So also Dr.* White *professes, that according to the Order which God has fixed by his Word and Will, this cannot be done:* Confer. *pag.* 446, 447. *and before, pag.* 181. *to this Objection, That tho in Nature it be impossible, for one and the same Body to be in many places at once, yet because God is Omnipotent, he is able to effect it: We answer, says he, It implieth a* Contradiction, *that God should destroy the nature of a thing, the nature of the same thing remaining safe: See more,* p. 180, 181. White's *Works,* Lond. 1624.

And now I know but one Objection more that is, or can be offered against what I have said, and which having answered, I shall close this Point: "For if "this be all the *Church* of *England* understands, when it speakes of a *Real Presence*, viz. *A Real Sa-*

cramental Presence of Christ's Body and Blood in the Holy Signs, and a real Spiritual Presence in the inward Communion of them to the Soul of every worthy Receiver; will not this *precipitate us* into downright ‖ *Zuinglianism*, and render us after all our pretences as very *Sacramentaries* as they? Indeed, I am not able directly to say whether it will or no, because I find the Opinion of *Zuinglius* very variously represented as to this matter. But yet, First, If by *Zuinglianism* he means that which is more properly * *Socinianism*, viz. *a meer Commemoration of Christ's Death*, and a *Thanksgiving to God for it*; 'tis evident it does not, forasmuch as we positively confess, that in this *Holy Sacrament*, there is a *Real and Spiritual Grace* communicated to us, even all the benefits of that *Death* and *Passion* which we there *set forth*. And this, or somewhat very like it, I find sometimes to have been maintained by † *Zuinglius*. But now, Secondly, If by *Zuinglianism* he understands such a *Real Presence*, as denies only the Co-existence of Christ's *Natural Body* now in *Heaven*, at the same time in this *Holy Sacrament*, but denies nothing of that *Real* and *Spiritual * Communion*, of it we have before mentioned; this is indeed our *Doctrine*, nor shall we be ashamed to own it for any *ill Names* he is able to put upon it. But yet I wonder why he should call this *Zuinglianism*; since if the common name of *Catholick*, or *Christian Doctrine*, be not sufficient, he might have found out a more ancient Abettor of this *Real Presence*, than *Zuinglius*, and the truth is, one of the most dangerous Opposers both of their

‖ See 1. Treatise, pag. 23. §. xxxii. p.24. §. xxxii. p.25. §. xxxvi. xxxvii, &c.

* Smalcius de Cœn. Dom. p. 347. Id Disp. 9. de Hypocr. p. 289. Volkelius lib. iv. cap. 12. p. 304, 315, &c. Socinus in Parænesi, c. iv. Schlichtingius disp. de Cœn. Dom. p. 701.
† Zuingl. See de Provid. Dei, cap. 6, &c.

* *And this our Author seems to insinuate: See the places above cited: And indeed others have alledged this as the true Opinion of* Zuinglius: *See* Calvin. Tract. de Cœn. Dom. Defens. Sacram. Admonit. ad Westphal. & Passim. alibi. Vid. insuper h[...]r. de Cr[...]d. Confess. c. 7. *And [e]specially*, H[...]p[...]. p. 42, 55, 177, &c. Hist. Sacr. part 2.

Head

Head and their *Faith* that ever was; I mean St. *Paul*, who has not only clearly express'd himself against them, as to this Point of the *Eucharist*, 1 Cor. x. 16. but in most of their other Errors left such pernicious Sayings to the World, as all their *Authority* and *Infallibility*, let me add, nor all their *Anathema*'s neither, will not be able to overcome.

I shall close up this Discourse of the *Real Presence* acknowledged by us in this Holy *Sacrament*, with a plain familiar Example, and which may serve at once both to illustrate, and confirm the Propriety of it. A Father makes his last *Will*, and by it bequeaths his *Estate* and all the Profits of it to his *Child*. He delivers it into the Hands of his *Son*, and bids him *take* there his *House* and *Lands*, which by this his *last Will* he delivers to him. The *Son* in this case receives nothing but a *Roll of Parchment*, with a *Seal* tied to it from his *Father*; but yet by virtue of this *Parchment* he is intituled to his *Estate*, performing the Conditions of his *Will*, and to all the Benefits and Advantages of it: And in that *Deed* he *truly* and *effectually* received *the very House* and *Lands* that were thereby conveyed to him. Our Saviour Christ in like manner, being now about to leave the World, gives this *Holy Sacrament*, as his final *Bequest* to us; in it he conveys to us a right to *his Body* and *Blood*, and to all the *Spiritual Blessings* and *Graces* that proceed from them. So that as often as we receive this Holy *Eucharist*, as we ought to do, we receive indeed nothing but a little *Bread* and *Wine* into our *Hands*; but by the *Blessing* and *Promise* of Christ, we by that *Bread* and *Wine*, as *really* and *truly* become *Partakers* of Christ's *Body* and *Blood*, as the *Son* by the *Will* of his

Vid. Cosens Hist. Transubstantionis, cap. v. §. 5. p. 57.

by the Church of England.

his *Father* was made *Inheritor* of his *Estate*: Nor is it any more necessary for this, that *Christ's Body* should come down from *Heaven*, or the outward Elements which we receive, be *substantially turned* into it, than it is necessary in that other case, that the very *Houses* and *Lands* should be given into the Hands of the *Son* to make a *real delivery* or *conveyance* of them; or the *Will* of the *Father* be *truly* and *properly changed* into the very *Nature* and *Substance* of them.

PART.

PART II.

CHAPTER III.

Of the Adoration of the Host, *as prescribed and practised in the* Church *of* Rome.

WE are now arrived at the last Part of this *Discourse*; in which I must thus far change the *Method* I pursued in the Other Subject, as to consider,

First, What the *Doctrine* of the *Church* of *England* as to this Point is; and what our *Adversaries* Exceptions against it are.

Secondly, What is the *Doctrine* of the *Church* of *Rome*; and whether what this *Author* has said in favour of it, may be sufficient to warrant their *Practice* as to this Matter.

For the former of these, The Doctrine *of the* Church *of* England, we shall need go no farther than the *Rubrick* we have before-mention'd; wherein it is expresly declared, with reference to this Holy Sacrament, "That no *Adoration* is intended, or "ought to be done, either to the Sacramental *Bread* "and *Wine* there *bodily* received, or to any *Corporal* "*Presence* of Christ's *Body* and *Blood:* For that the "Sacra-

Rubr. at the end of the Communion.

"Sacramental *Bread* and *Wine* remain still in their
" very *Natural Substances*, and therefore may not be
" *adored*, (for that were *Idolatry* to be abhorred of
" all Faithful Christians) and the *natural Body* and
" *Blood* of our Saviour Christ, are in *Heaven* and
" not *here*; it being against the truth of Christ's
" *natural Body*, to be *at One time* in *more places* than
" *One*.

This then being sufficiently cleared, let us see what this *Author* has to *observe* against it.

1. "He supposes that we will grant, that if there Treatise 1.
" were a *Corporal Presence* of Christ's *Natural Body* Ch. 4. §. 39.
" in this Holy *Sacrament*, then *Kneeling* and *Adoration* p. 27.
" would be here also due upon such an Account.
He means, that were Christ himself here in his *Body* actually present, He ought to be *adored*; and this he need not doubt of our readiness to grant.

2. "Tho the *Corporeal Presence* of Christ's *Body*, Ib. §. xl.
" *i. e.* of its being there *ad modum Corporis*, or clo-
" thed with the ordinary Properties of a Body, be de-
" ny'd; as it is, not only by the *English* Divines,
" but by the *Lutheran* and *Roman*: Yet let there be
" any other manner of *Presence* (known from Di-
" vine Revelation) of the very same *Body* and
" *Blood*; and this as *Real* and *Essential*, as if *Corpo-*
" *real*; and then I do not see but that *Adoration* will
" be no less due to it *thus*, than *so*, Present.

Now to this I shall at present only say, That the *Supposition* being *absurd*, do's not admit of a *rational* Consideration. Those who deny a *bodily Presence* of Christ's *Body* in the Eucharist, and ask whether *Adoration* may not be paid to his *Body*, which is confess'd not to be *bodily present* there, supposing it to be there some other way; ought to have no other

Of the Adoration of the Host,

satisfaction than this, that they suppose an Impossibility, a thing which cannot be; and therefore concerning which no reasonable Answer can be given. Some I know have been more free, and allowing for the unreasonableness of the *Supposal,* have resolved contrary to our Author: But I think it very needless to dispute of the Affections of a *Chimera*; and wrangle about Notions that have neither Use nor Existence.

Treatise 1. p. 28. §. xli. 3. He *observes,* lastly, "That the *Church* of *England* hath believed and affirmed such a *Presence* (*he means of Chrift's* Body *in the* Eucharist) to which they thought *Adoration* due. I presume it was then in the Times of *Popery*; for since the *Reformation,* I have shewn before, that she has always held the contrary. But our Author will prove it, *Ibid.* and that since the *Reformation*; "For, *he says,* he has in his time met with no less than five of our Writers, and those of no mean Account neither, that have been of this Opinion. This indeed is a very notable way of proving the *Doctrine* of our *Church:* But what now if I should bring him *fifteen Others* that have deny'd it; then I hope the *Doctrine* of the *Church* of *England* may be as fair for the contrary. But we will examine his Evidence.

Treatise 1. §. xlii. p. 28. First; "Bishop *Andrews,* he says, declares, that "tho we *adore* not the *Sacrament,* yet we adore *Christ* "in and with the *Sacrament,* besides and without the "*Sacrament*: and assures the World, that K. *James* "looked upon Christ to be *truly present,* and *truly* "to be *adored* in it. How this *Bishop* thought Christ *truly present* in the *Sacrament* we have seen before; and may from thence easily conclude how he supposed he might be *adored* there: *viz.* As in all other
Holy

Holy Offices, in which we confess Him by his *Divine Power* to be *present* with us, but especially in this *Sacred Mystery*. And thus we all *adore* him, both in and with, and without the *Sacrament*; we confess him to be *truly present*, and therefore *truly* to be *adored* by us. But now for Christ's *Natural Body*, (of which, and not of Christ himself, our Dispute is) if that be any otherwise *truly present* than as we before shew'd, let it be remembred, that according to this *Bishop*, it must not be his *Glorified Body*, his *Body* as it now is; but his *Body Crucified*, his *Body* as *offer'd for us*, and in the *State of his Death*; so He expresly affirms; and this I believe our *Author* himself will confess in his sense to be impossible. See above.

His next Witness is Bishop *Taylor*: " We *worship*, " He means, says this Author, the *Body*, or the *Flesh* " of Christ [in the Eucharist]. But is he sure the Bishop meant so? If he be, I am sure the Bishop thought we all of us committed *Idolatry* in so doing. For being consulted, as we have seen above, " whe- " ther without all danger of *Idolatry* we may not " render *Divine Worship* to our Blessed *Saviour* as " present in the Blessed *Sacrament* or *Host*, accord- " ing to his *Humane Nature* in that *Host*? He expresly declares, " We may not render Divine Wor- " ship to Him as present in the Blessed *Sacrament*, " according to his *Humane Nature*, without danger " of *Idolatry*, because he is not there according to his " *Humane Nature*; and therefore you give *Divine* " *Worship* to a *Non Ens*, which must needs be *Ido-* " *try*. And indeed this our Author knew very well was his Opinion, who himself in his next Treatise, cites the xiii*th* Section of his *Real Presence*, which was written on purpose to prove the unlaw- Treatise 1. S. xliii. p. 28.

See Polemical Discourses 5. Letter, at the end, p.

Treatise 2. p. 9. S. vi. n. 2.

fulness

fulness of worshipping Christ's *Body* in this *Sacrament*. But *dissimulation* of other Mens Opinions in matter of Religion, is perhaps as lawful on some Occasions, as if it were their *own*: And why may not an *Author* prevaricate the *Doctrine* of his *Adversary* in defence of the *Catholick Faith*, since I have read of a * *Protestant* Minister, who in the Troubles of *France* being brought over to the King's Interest, was secretly reconciled to the *Church* of *Rome*, and permitted so far to dissemble his own Opinion, as not only to continue in the outward profession of the *Protestant Religion*, but even to exercise the Functions of his *Ministry* as before; and that by the express leave of his *Holiness*, for three whole Years, the better to carry on the *Catholick Cause* in betraying the Secrets, and managing the Debates of his Brethren.

* The Story was publish'd in the *Memoirs of Monsieur* D'eageant, *printed with permission at* Grenoble, 1658. pag. 245 *I will set it down in his own words.*
Il'y avoit deja quelque tems que D'eageant avoit gagné l' un des Ministres de la Province de Languedoc, qui etoit des plus employez aux Affaires & meneés de ceux de la R. P. R. & en l' Estime particuliere de Monsieur de Lesdiguiers. Il avoit meme secrettement moyenné sa Conversion; & obtenu un Bref de Rome, portant qu' en core qu' il eut eté receu au giron de l' Eglise, il luy etoit permis de continuer son Ministere durant 3 Ans, pourveu qu'en ses preches il ne dit rien de contraire à la creance de la vraye Eglise, & qu' il ne celebrât poinct la cene. Le Bref fût obtenu, afinque le Ministre pût estre continué dans les Emplois qu'il avoit, & decouvrir les meneés qui se faisoient dans le Royaume.

As for Bishop *Forbes*, and the Arch-bishop of *Spalatto*, it is not to be wondred if Men that had entertained the Design of *reconciling all Parties*, were forced to strain sometimes a little farther than was fit for the doing of it. And for Mr. *Thorndyke*, we have seen that his Notion of the *Real Presence* was particular, and widely different both from theirs and ours; and therefore that we are not to answer for the Consequences of it. But however, to quit these

these just Exceptions against them: Will he himself allow every thing to be the *Doctrine* or not of the *Church* of *Rome*, which I shall bring him three of their *Authors* to affirm or deny? If he will, then *Transubstantiation* is not their *Doctrine*, for I have already quoted above twice three of their most Learned Men against it. To *adore* an *Unconsecrated Host* by mistake, is *Idolatry*; for so S. *Thomas*, *Paludanus*, *Catharine*, and others, assure us: To worship the *Host*, supposing their Doctrine of *Transubstantiation* false, a worser *Idolatry* than any Heathens were ever guilty of; so several of their Writers confess. But now if our Author will not allow this to be good *arguing* against them, with what reason do's he go about to urge it against us?

Secondly; We must in the next place consider what the *Doctrine* of the *Church* of *Rome* as to this *Point* is; and whether what this *Author* has advanced in favour of it, may be sufficient to warrant their *practice* of this *Adoration*.

For the Doctrine of the *Church* of *Rome*, I find it thus clearly set down by the *Council of Trent*: "There can be no doubt, but that all the Faithful of "Christ, after the manner that has ever been re-"ceived in the *Catholick Church*, ought to give that "*Supreme Worship* which is due to the *true God*, to "this *Holy Sacrament*. For it is nevertheless to be "*adored*, because it was instituted by our Lord

Concil. Trid. Sess.xiii.cap.5. p. 57. Nullus itaq; dubitandi locus relinquitur, quin omnes Christi fideles pro more in Catholicâ Ecclesiâ semper recepto Latriæ cultum, qui Vero deo Debetur, huic Sanctissimo Sacramento in veneratione exhibeant. Neq; enim ideò minùs est Adorandum quòd fuerit à Christo D. ut sumatur institutum: Nam illum eundem Deum præsentem *IN EO* adesse Credimus, quem Pater æternus introducens in Orbem Terrarum, dicit; *Et adorent eum omnes Angeli Dei.* Hebr. I.

"Christ that it might be *received*; Forasmuch as we believe the *same God* to be present *in it,* of whom the Eternal Father when he brought him into the World, said, *And let all the Angels of God worship him.* That therefore, according to this *Council* is to be *worshipped,* which Christ *instituted* to be *received*; and *in which* they believe *Christ* to be *present* : But 'tis no other than the *Holy Sacrament,* as these *Trent*-Fathers here expresly and properly stile it; which we all confess Christ *instituted* to be *received,* and *in which* they suppose *Christ* to be *present* : And therefore 'tis the *Sacrament* which is to be *adored.* Which reasoning I find Card. *Pallavicini* thus improving in his History of this *Council* : " It is well known, *says he,* that to make a *Whole Adorable* with the *Supreme Adoration,* it is sufficient that *One part* of that Whole merits such a *Worship.* This he illustrates in the Example of Christs *Humanity*; and thence concludes, " How then ought we not in like manner to *adore* this *Sacrament* which is a *Whole,* that contains as its principal part *the Body of Christ* ?

Card. Pallavicino Istoria del Concilio di Trento: parte seconda, l. 12. c.7. pag. 298. Ora è notissimo, che, acciòche un Tutto s'adori con adorazione di Latria, basta che una parte di quel tutto meriti questo culto.——Come dunque non douremo parimente adorare questo Sacramento, il quale è un Tutto che contiene come parte principale il Corpo di Christo.

It is therefore, as I conceive, the undoubted *Doctrine* of the *Church* of *Rome*, that the Holy *Sacrament* of the *Eucharist*, for the Reason here given, is to be *adored*, with that *Supreme Adoration that is due to the true God.*

Now to warrant their *Practice* in this Matter, our Author thus proceeds in proof of it:

I. He

I. He premises some Propositions, which he calls, *Protestant Concessions*. <small>Answer to his second Discourse.</small>

II. Some others, which he stiles, *Catholick Assertions*. And then,

III. Goes on to shew what warrant they have for that Belief on which this *Adoration* is founded.

I shall distinctly follow him in every one of these.

In his first Part, which he calls, *Protestant Concessions*, I will go on with him thus far: <small>I. Part, Protestant Concessions.</small>

1*st*. * " That Supreme and Divine *Adoration* is <small>* §. I. pag. 1.</small>
" due to our Lord and Saviour *Jesus Christ*.

2*dly*, † " That where-ever the *Body* of our *Lord* <small>† Ibid. §. II.</small>
" now is, there must also his *whole Person* be.

" And therefore, 3*dly*, ‖ That where-ever *Christ's* <small>‖Ibid. §. III.</small>
" *Body* is *truly* and *really present*, there his *Divine*
" *Person* is *supremely adorable*.

But now for his next Assertion; * " That it is af- <small>* §.V.n.1.p.2.</small>
" firmed by many *Protestants*, especially those of
" the *Church* of *England*, that this *Body* and *Blood* of
" our Lord is *really present*, not only in *Virtue*, but
" in *Substance* in the *Eucharist*. † If he means, as in <small>† See Treatise 1. p. 5. §. 7.</small>
his former *Treatise* he explain'd himself, that the *very natural Body* of Christ, that *Body* that was *born of the Virgin*, and *crucified on the Cross*, and is *now* in *Heaven*, is also as to *its Substance* truly and really present on *Earth* in the Holy *Eucharist*, or to the *worthy Receiver*: I have in the foregoing *Chapter* fully shewn this *new Fancy* to be neither the *Doctrine* of
the

Of the Adoration of the Host,

the *Church* of *England,* nor the Opinion of those very *Writers* whom he produces for proof of it. And as to the ‖ *adoration* of it upon any such account, I have just now declared his Mistake of them in that Point too. And I shall not follow our Author's ill Example in repeating it all over again.

‖ Disc. 2. p. 8.
§. vi. n. 1.

For his * fifth Remark, "That the *Lutherans* affirm that *Christ's Body* and *Blood* are *present,* not only to the worthy *Communicants,* but to the *Consecrated Symbols,* and whilst so present, which is during the *Action* of the Lord's Supper (*i. e.* says he, as I conceive them from the *Consecration,* till the end of the *Communion*) are to be *Adored.* I answer; First, As to the former part, it is confess'd that the *Lutherans* do indeed suppose Christ to be present, not only to the *worthy Communicants,* but also to the *Consecrated Symbols.* But now, secondly, for the other part, that during the *Action of the Lord's Supper, He is to be Adored there*; this is not so certain. For, 1. I do not find any thing establish'd amongst them as to this matter, neither in the *Confession* of *Auxpourg,* nor in any other *publick Acts* of their *Church.* 2. I find several of their Divines utterly denying, that *Christ's Body* is to be *Adored* in the *Holy Sacrament*; and our * *Author* himself confesses it. Tho now, 3. † I will not deny but that some others of them do allow, if not that *Christ's Body,* yet that *Christ* himself is to be *Adored* after a peculiar manner in the *Action* of the *Lord's Supper*; and as far as I conceive, do by the Action mean, as our Author here represents it, from the *Consecration* to the end of the *Communion.* So that then, with this Limitation, his Proposition I presume may be admitted; "That the *Lutherans* do acknowledg, "that

* §. vii. p. 10.

* See below, Disc. 2. p. 15.
† Conrad. Schlusselburgius, Catal. Hæret. l. 3. arg. 45. p. 205. Item Arg. 103. p. 280. It. arg. 174. p. 327. Francof. 1605. And Hospinian quotes it of Luther himself, that it was his Opinion, Concord. discor. p. 358. n. 16. Genev. 1678.

"that Christ is present during the Action of the
"Lord's Supper; and therefore it is by several of
"them supposed, that he ought to be *adored* in it.

As to the sixth and last *Concession*, which he draws §. vi. p.10,11.
from Monsieur *Daille's Apologie*, "That tho we do
"not our selves belive the *Real Presence* of Christ's
"*Body* in the *Signs*, yet neither do we esteem the
"belief of it so criminal, as to oblige us to break off
"*Communion* with all those that hold it; and there-
"fore, that had the *Roman Church* no other Error
"but this, that it would not have given us any suffi-
"cient cause of separation from it; we are ready
to admit it; always supposing that the belief of it
had not been press'd upon us neither, as a necessary
Article of Communion; nor any *Anathema* pronounced against us for not receiving it. And for the o-
ther part of it which he subjoyns, "That a Disciple Ibid. pag. 11.
"giving Divine Honour, upon mistake, to another
"Person, much resembling our Saviour Christ,
"would have been no *Idolater*; from whence he
would infer, "That therefore allowing a *Consecra-
"ted Host* to be truly *Adorable*, a Person that should
"by mistake adore an *unconsecrated One*, would not
"be guilty of *Idolatry*. We are content to allow it;
tho what use he can make of it in this *Controversy*,
unless against his own Brethren, S. *Thomas*, *Paludanus*, and others, I do not understand; since he knows
we utterly deny any *Host,consecrated* or *not*, to be fit to
be *worshipped*. And this may serve for his first Foundation of *Protestant Concessions*,; which were they
every one as certain as his first is, that *Christ is to be
adored*, I cannot see what his Cause would gain by it;
and he has not by any *Application* of them in this
Treatise, given us the least reason to think that they
are

are of any moment in it. But some Men have a peculiar faculty of amusing the World with nothing: and I remember, I once heard a judicious and modest Man give this *Character* of an Author much resembling ours, with reference to his *Guide in Controversy*, that for a *Book* which carried a great appearance of *Reasoning*, it had the least in it of any he ever met with. But I go on,

<small>2. Part. Catholick Assertions.</small>

II. To his *Catholick Assertions*.

<small>Pag. 13. §. ix.</small>
And first: "*Catholicks* (as he calls them) affirm "in the *Eucharist* after the *Consecration*, a *Sign*, or "*Symbol* to remain still distinct, and having a divers "*Existence* from that of the *thing signified*, or from "*Christ's Body* contained in or under it. This 'tis true the *Papists*, or if you please, the *Catholicks* do affirm; because that otherwise they could not call it a *Sacrament*. But now, if we enquire what that which they *call a Sign*, or a *Symbol* in this Holy *Sacrament* is, we shall find it to be neither such as our Blessed Saviour establish'd, nor indeed any thing that can in propriety of Speech be so termed.

For our Saviour Christ, 'tis evident that the *Symbols* instituted by him, were *Bread* and *Wine*: They were these that he *took* and *blessed*, and *gave* to his *Disciples*; and commanded them also in like manner to *take*, and *bless*, and *give to others* in *remembrance of him*; and as the *Symbols* of his *Body* and *Blood* in this *Holy Eucharist*. But now for the *Papists*; they destroy the *Bread* and the *Wine*; they leave only a few aiery, empty *Species*, that is, appearances of something, but which are really nothing, have no *substance* to support them.

The

as practised in the Church of Rome.

The *Symbols* establish'd by Christ were *Festival Symbols*, a matter apt for our *Corporal Nourishment*; so signify to us, that as by them, *viz.* by *Bread* and *Wine*, our *Bodies* are nourished to a *Corporal Life*; so by the *Body* and *Blood* of Christ, which they both *represent* and *communicate to us*, our Souls are fed to *Life Everlasting*. But for that which hath no *Substance, i. e.* nothing which can be converted into our *Bodily Nourishment*; how that can be a *Symbol* of this *Spiritual Food*, I do not very well understand. Indeed our Author tells us, "That tho after Conse- [Pag. 14. §. x.] "cration, the *Substance* of the *Bread* and *Wine* is de- "ny'd to remain, yet is *Substance* here taken in such "a sense, as that neither the *hardness*, nor the *soft- "ness*, nor the *frangibility*, nor the *savour*, nor the "odour, nor the *nutritive virtue* of the *Bread*, nor no- "thing *visible* or *tangible*, or otherwise *perceptible* by "any *Sense*, is involved in it: That is to say, that the *Symbol* or *external Sign* then in this Eucharist, is according to them, a *hard, soft, frangible, gustible, odoriferous, nutritive, visible, tangible, perceptible nothing.* Verily a fit *external Species* indeed to contain, a *one, manifold; visible, invisible; extended, unextended; local, illocal; absent, present; natural, supernatural; corporal, spiritual* Body.

Secondly; Concerning the *Adoration* of the *Sacrament*, he tells us, "That this word *Sacrament*, is [Pag. 14. §. xi.] "not to be taken always in the same sense; but "sometimes to be used to signify only the *external* "*Sign*, or *Symbols*; sometimes only the *Res Sacra- "menti*, or the thing contain'd under them, which "is the more principal part thereof. This indeed is a sort of new Divinity. I always thought hitherto, that when we talked of a *Sacrament*, properly so called,

T

called, we had meant an *outward and visible Sign of an inward and spiritual Grace*: and that this particular *Sacrament* had been a whole composed of the *External Species*, (whatever they are) as the *Sign*; and the *Body* and *Blood* of Christ as the *inward part*, or *thing signified*. Thus I am sure the *Catechism* of the *Council* of *Trent* instructs us. First, for the name; it tells us, that "*The Latin Doctors have thought* "*that certain Signs, subjected to the Senses, which de-* "*clare, and as it were set before the Eyes, the Grace* "*which they effect, may fitly be called Sacraments*. And for the *nature* of them, thus it defines a *Sacrament* from S. *Austin*, "It is the *sign* of a *holy thing*; or more fully, as I before said; *a visible sign of an in-* "*visible Grace, instituted for our Justification*. So that neither the *Symbols* alone, nor the *invisible part*, or *Grace alone*, can with any manner of *propriety* be called a *Sacrament*; but the *Sign* referr'd to the *Grace*; and as it is the *Symbol* instituted by Christ for the *conferring* of it.

Catech. ad Parach. part 2. de Sacram. n. iii. & v. p. 92.

This therefore can with no good reason be called a *Catholick Assertion*; being neither *general* nor *true*: But however, since he seems content to allow it to be an *impropriety of Speech*, and that, I confess, the * *Catechism* of the *Council* of *Trent* does lead him into it; let us see what use he can make of it. † "And "as Protestants much press, so *Catholicks* (*Roman* "*Catholicks*) willingly acknowledg a great diffe- "rence between these two, 'The worshipping of the "*Sacrament*, as this word is taken for the *Symbols*; "and the worshipping of *Christ's Body* in the *Sacra-* "*ment*. There is, no doubt, a *great difference* between *these two*: but then, they who tell us, the *Sacrament* is to be *Adored*, if they will speak *rationally*, must

* Catec. Conc. Trid. part 2. de Euch.§.viii. nota p. 144.
† Pag.15.§.xi.

must mean neither the *one* nor *other* of these, but the *Host*; that is, as Card. *Pallavicini* expounds it, The *whole*, of which *Christ's Body is a part*; in the language of the *Council of Trent*; the *Sacrament* IN WHICH they believe *Christ* to be *present*, and for that *Cause adore* it; as the Cardinal again argues; *that, To make a *Whole Adorable*, it *is sufficient that one part be so*; *and therefore since the Body of Christ is adorable, the Sacrament for its sake is to be worshipped*. It is therefore a meer shift to tell us that the *Sacrament* is to be *adored*; *i. e. Christ's Body* in the *Sacrament*. Nor will the remark of our Author help us out, that tho the *Chapter* indeed calls it the *Sacrament* IN WHICH *is Christ's Body*, yet the *Canon* speaks more *precisely*, and calls it *Christ in the Sacrament*; unless he supposes the *Council* to have been *infallible* in the *Canons* only, and not in the *Chapters*; as some have thought, that they may be out in their *Proofs*, but cannot be in their *Conclusions*. But however, since he so much desires it, for my part I shall be content to allow them this too; for I should be glad by any means to see them sensible of their Errors. But yet so as that it be esteem'd only a *private Opinion this*, not a *Catholick Assertion*.

 Thirdly; *Catholicks*, he means the *Papists* still, "ground their *Adoration*, not upon *Transubstantiati-* "*on*; as if *Transubstantiation* defeated, *Adoration* is "so too; but on a *Real Presence* with the *Symbols*, "which in general is agreed on by the *Lutherans* to- "gether with them. By which Assertion, if he means only to make this Discovery, That *Christ's Real Presence*, together with the *Substance* of the *Bread* and *Wine*, is in his Opinion as good a ground for *Adoration*, as if he were there only with the

* *See above,* pag. 91, 92.

Pag. 16. §. xiii.

P. 21. §. xvii.

Species of the *Bread*, the *Substance* being changed into his *Body*; I have no more to say to it. But if he would hereby make us believe, that 'tis all one whether Christ be *adored*, as supposed here by the *Lutherans* in this Holy *Eucharist*, and as imagined there by the *Papists*; I must then deny his *Assertion*; and desire him to keep home to his own *manner of Real Presence*, and which I shall presently convince him, will leave them in a much worse condition than their Neighbours, whom he would draw into the same Snare with them. And therefore, whereas he concludes,

P. 22. §. xviii.   Fourthly; "That supposing *Transubstantiation* "to be an *Error*, yet if the Tenent of *Corporal* or *Real* "*Presence* (as held by the *Lutherans*, or others) be "true; *Catholicks* (he would say *Papists*) pléad "their *Adoration*, is no way frustrated, but still "warrantable: I must tell him, that the *Adoration* of those among the *Lutherans*, who worship Christ in this Sacrament upon the account of his *Real Presence* in, or with the *Bread*, tho it be an Error, yet is infinitely more excusable than theirs, who suppose the *Bread* to be turned into Christ's *Body*; and because it may not be thought that I speak this out of any prejudice against them, I will here offer my Reasons for it.

1*st*, They that *adore Christ* as *really present*, together with the *Bread*, do no violence to their *Senses*: They confess, that what they *see*, and *taste*, and *feel*, and *smell*, is *really Bread* and *Wine*. Whilst the *Papist* in denying the *Bread* and *Wine* to remain; or that what he *sees*, and *feels*, and *smells*, and *tastes*, is what all the World perceives and knows it is, contradicts his *Senses*, and in them the *Law* of *Nature*,

that

that Means which God has given us to *direct* and *lead* us into the search of *Truth*; and by Consequence errs against infinitely greater Means of *Conviction*, and so is more inexcusable than the Other.

2dly; They who worship Christ, as supposing Him to be together with the *Bread* in this *Holy Eucharist*, are erroneous indeed in this, that they take Christ's *Body* to be where really it is not; but yet their Object is undoubtedly right, and in that they are not mistaken. But now for the *Papist*; he *adores*, 'tis confess'd, what he thinks to be Christ's *Body*; and would not otherwise *adore* it: But yet still 'tis the *Host* that he *adores*, the Substance that is under those *Species* which he sees; and which if it be not Christ, but meer *Substance* of *Bread*, the Case is vastly alter'd between the *Lutheran* and *Him*. The former *adores Christ*, only as in a place where he is not; the latter not only do's this, but moreover *adores* a *Substance* for Christ which is not his *Body* and *Blood*, but a meer *Creature* of *Bread* and *Wine*.

Monsieur *Daille* therefore might rightly enough say of a *Lutheran*, "that his *Adoration* is mistaken, "not in this—that it addresseth it self to an *Object* "not *adorable*, but only that by Error it seeks and "thinks to enjoy it in a place where it is not; and so "becomes only *vain* and *unprofitable:* And yet our Author has no manner of Reason from thence to pretend, that a *Papist* who terminates his *Adoration* upon a *Substance* which *really* is not Christ's *Body*, but only mistaken by him to be so, shall be in the same Condition: there being an apparently vast difference between worshipping Christ in a place where he is not, and worshipping that for Christ which really

P.23. §.xix.

really is not Chrift, but only a created *Sub-ftance*.

And this in truth our Author feems to have been fenfible of, and therefore thinks to evade it, by faying, Ibid p. 23. " That they do not worfhip the *Subftance* that is in " that *place*, under fuch *Accidents* whatever it be, " (which if *Bread* fhould happen to be there, he " confeffes would make them *Bread-worfhippers*) but " they worfhip it only upon *fuppofition* that it is " Chrift's *Body*, and not *Bread*.

Well, be this fo: But what now if they are miftaken in their *Suppofition*: They worfhip, he confeffes, the *Subftance* that is under thofe *Accidents*, fuppofing it to be Chrift's *Body*; but ftill, miftaken or not, that *Subftance* which is under thofe Species, whatever it be, they do worfhip: And if they have, as he thinks, a *rational ground* for this *Suppofition*, which we fhall fee by and by, yet this will only excufe them from being *formal Idolaters*; but will not hinder but that their Worfhip is ftill directed to an *undue Object*, if that which is under the *Species* be indeed but *Bread*, and not Chrift's *Body* as they imagine. And this then may ferve to argue the falfenefs of what he lays down as his

P. 22. §. xix. Fifth, *Catholick Affertion*: " That fuppofing both " the *Lutherans* and *Papifts* miftaken in their Opi- " nion, yet there can be no pretence why the One " fhould not be as excufable as the others. Since as I have faid; 1*ft*, They err more grofly in abandoning the conviction of their *Senfes*, which the *Lutherans* do not; 2*dly*, They worfhip a *Subftance* for *Chrift*, which really is not: To which if this be not enough, I will add yet two other Reafons: 3*dly*, That they make the *Confecration*, without which

which Chrift is not prefent upon their own Principles, to depend on fuch uncertainties (as I fhall more fully fhew anon) that they can never be fure that Chrift is there, which the *Lutherans* are free from: And laftly; They *Anathematize* thofe who diffent from them as to this *Point*, and fo make a *Schifm* in dividing the *Unity of the Church*, which the *Lutherans* are fo far from doing, that they neither eftablifh any Doctrine of *Adoration* at all, nay many of them do not believe it; and upon occafion, freely *communicate* with thofe who diffent from them in their belief, both of their way of the *Real Prefence*, and of the *Adoration*. And for the fame reafon I cannot totally affent to his

Sixth Affertion: "That fuppofing there be no "fuch *Real Prefence* as either of them believes, yet "that their *adoration* of Chrift, who is a true *Object* "of *Supreme Adoration*, and only by them miftaken "to be in fome *place* where He is not, cannot be "termed any fuch *Idolatry*, as is the *worfhipping* of "an *Object* not at all *adorable*.

P. 25. §. xxi.

This as to what concerns thofe of the *Lutherans* who adore Chrift in the Sacrament, is true: But for the *Papift* it is not. He intends, I allow it, to worfhip Chrift, but he miftakes an *Object* for *Chrift*, which is only a piece of *Bread*. He worfhips his *Hoft*, fuppofing it to be our *Saviour's Body*, but his Error is grofs, and he not only miftakes Chrift to be in a place where he is not, but he miftakes that to be Chrift which indeed is not, but only a *fimple Wafer*. His Worfhip therefore is not like the *Manichees* worfhipping of Chrift in the *Sun*; but rather as if the *Manichee* fhould, from fome miftaken grounds, have fancy'd the *Sun* it felf to be turned

into

into Christ's *Body*; and then in defiance of all *Scripture, Sense,* and *Reason,* should have fallen down before it; but with a *good Intention* not to *adore* the *Sun,* but the *Body* of our Blessed Lord under the *Species* or *Accidents* of the *Sun*. This is the true *Parallel*; only that herein still the *Manichee* would have been the more excusable of the two, by how much the *Sun* is a more likely Object to be mistaken for Christ's *glorified Body* than *a Morsel of Bread*; and less capable of being discovered by our *Senses* and *Examination* not to be so.

It remains then, that these *Lutherans* only *adore* Christ where he is not; the *Papists* not only do this, but more-over they *adore* that for *Christ* which *really is not*, but a meer *created Substance*. Both the One and the Other are Erroneous; but the Papist's Mistake, renders him at the least guilty of *material Idolatry*, whereas the *Lutherans* is only an undue Application of his Worship as to the *Place,* but right as to the *Person*. Let us see,

Seventhly; How far their Mistake will excuse them, in answer to his *seventh Assertion:* "That how-
"ever a *Manichæan* may be guilty of *Idolatry* for
"worshipping Christ in the Sun; and an *Israelite*
"for worshipping God as specially resident in the
"*Calves* of *Dan* and *Bethel,* because it is *adoring* a
"Fancy of their own, without any *rational Ground*
"or *Pretence* thereof; and however meerly a *good*
"*Intention,* grounded upon a *culpable Ignorance,* can
"excuse none from *Idolatry,* or any other Fault; yet
"if *Catholicks, (i.e.* the pretended Roman Catho-
"licks) can produce a *rational Ground* of their ap-
"prehending Christ *present* in the *Eucharist,* tho
"possibly mistaken in it, they are to be ex-
"cused

P.26. §.xxii.

as practised in the Church of **Rome.**

"excused from *Idolatry*. Which Proposal is so just, that I am very willing to allow it; and shall be heartily glad that the *Grounds* of their *Mistake* may in the End prove to have been so *reasonable* as to excuse them. But then it must be remembred too, that he confesses if these *Grounds* be not *reasonable*, but as he says of the *Manichees*, their *adoring of the Host* be indeed an *adoring* a *Fancy* of their own without any *rational Ground*; So that their ignorance in this Matter is culpable, then by their own allowance they are *Idolaters*.

   This therefore brings me to the last Thing to be enquired into.

   III. What *Grounds* they have for this *Adoration*? and whether they be such as, should they be mistaken in it, will be sufficient to excuse them?

And thus after a great deal of *Preamble*, but very little to the purpose, we are at last come to the main *Question*. I have already so largely shewn our Reasons against *Transubstantiation*, or that *Real Presence* on which this *Adoration* is built, that I shall not need to insist here. Yet because the stress of this *Controversy* depends principally on this last Part, I will,

   1*st*, Examine the strength of those *Grounds* which this *Author* has offer'd, to warrant their *Adoration*.

   2*dly*, I will propose an Argument or two upon their own allowed *Principles* against it.

But before we proceed to these Points, we must yet have one touch more upon the old String: "For the *Lutherans, he says,* being allow'd to have such a plausible *Ground* or Motive for their *Adoration,* whereby they become Absolved by other Protestants from *Idolatry,* in *adoring* our Lord as present there, I see not why the *Grounds* of *Roman Catholicks* should be any whit less valued than theirs."

In Answer to which, the *Reader* may please to remember, that I have before said, that we do not excuse those *Lutherans* who do this so much upon this Principle, that they have a more *plausible Ground* or *Motive* for their *Adoration*; but for this rather, that confessing the *Substance* of the *Bread* to remain, they do not mistake their *Object,* but pay their *Adoration* indeed to *Christ,* only supposing him to be there where in Truth he is not. But, 2*dly,* this Author is very much mistaken if he thinks the *Lutherans* have no better a Foundation for their *Real Presence* than the *Papists.* Indeed, were the difference no greater than between a *Con* and a *Trans,* it would, I confess, be hardly worth the while to contend about it. But when we come to the Point it self, we may observe these four Advantages, among many others of the *Lutherans* side. 1. They confess for the outward *Elements,* that they are *really* what they appear to be, *Bread* and *Wine*; and so they do no *Violence* to their *Senses*; which, as I have said, is a great *aggravation* against the *Papists.* 2. By this means they are at no defiance with all those Texts of Scripture where they are so often called *Bread* and *Wine* after *Consecration*: All which the *Papist* contradicts, but the *Lutheran* does not. 3. From the words of Christ,

Christ, *This is my Body*; we all of us confess may be inferr'd, that *Christ's Body* is in this Holy *Sacrament*: But whence do's the *Papist* infer the destruction of the *Substance* of the *Bread*; so that what is *taken*, and *blessed*, and *given*, is not *Bread*, but *Christ's Body* under the appearance of *Bread*? This is an Error which I am sure the Text gives no manner of colour to; and therefore our Author cannot with any reason pretend, as he do's, whether we consult the Text of Holy *Scripture*, or our own *Senses*, that they have as good *grounds* for their *Real Presence*, as the *Lutherans* have for theirs. To all which let me add, 4*thly*, that by *Transubstantiation* they destroy the very Nature of a *Sacrament*, by leaving no true external *Sign* or *Symbol*, and which is another unanswerable Argument against them, whilst the *Lutherans* acknowledging the *Substance* of the *Bread* to remain, do not destroy at all the Nature of this *Sacrament*, but retain the same *Sign* which our Blessed Lord established, and so have no Objection on this side neither to convict them.

But yet notwithstanding all this, " Do not some "of our Writers confess, that the *Papists* Interpre-"tation is more rational than the *Lutherans*? I Answer; What certain *Protestants* may have said in Zeal for their own Opinions, and in particular *Hospinian* upon the account of his Master *Zuinglius*, I cannot tell: But sure I am, we are not bound to answer for all that any *Protestant* Author has said. And if these Reasons I have here given for the contrary are valid, they ought to be more regarded, than the ungrounded Assertions of a *Sacramentary* Historian.

Pag. 26, 27.

Pag. 27.

Well, but still the "*Papist* do's not ground his "*Adoration* upon *Transubstantiation*, but on *Corporal* "*Presence*; and so they must *both* be excused, or "neither.

This is a fetch to very little purpose: For let me ask this Author; He confesses he founds his *Adoration* upon the *Corporal Presence*: Do's he believe the *Corporal Presence* in the way of *Transubstantiation* exclusive to all others, or no? If he do's, then 'tis evident that the *Corporal Presence* and *Transubstantiation*, must with him stand or fall together; and so if he *adores* on the account of the *Corporal Presence*, he do's it upon the account of *Transubstantiation*. If he do's not believe this, 'tis plain he is no *Papist*, nor submits to the *Authority* of the *Church of Rome*, which has defined the *Corporal Presence* to be after this particular manner, exclusive to all Others, and *Anathematized* all that dare to deny it.

Laying aside therefore this Comparison, *and which in truth will do them but very little kindness*:

Pag. 27. §. xxiv. "Let us view more particularly what rational "Grounds they have to exhibit for this their belief "of their *Corporal Presence* of Christ in the *Eu-* "*charist*, and of the *Adoration* of him upon that "account.

Ibid.

I. *Ground*: And the first is *Divine Revelation*: For which our Author offers the two usual Instances, of the *words of Institution*, and the *6th Chapter of S. John*; both which therefore I have at large discoursed on above, and I believe sufficiently shewn how false a Foundation these are of this belief.

* Pag. 27, 28.

But yet since our Author reminds us; * "*That a-* "*gainst these no Argument taken from our Senses or* "*Reason*

"*Reason is valid*: I will beg leave to remind him of his own Assertion too, * "That none can believe a "thing true upon *what Motive soever*, that he knows "certainly to be *false*, or which is all one, certain- "ly to *contradict*——So that if our *Reason* then "makes us *certain* of such a *contradiction*, we may "be certain that there neither is nor can be a *contrary* "*Revelation*; and when any *Revelation*, tho *NE-* "*VER SO PLAIN*, is brought, *we are bound* "*to interpret it so, as not to affirm a certainly known* "*impossibility*.

[*] See Treatise 1. p. 14.

P. 21. Treat. 1.

From which Principle it seems to me to follow, that were *Hoc est Corpus meum*, as evident a proof of *Transubstantiation*, as their own Authors confess it is not; yet if our *Sense* and *Reason* tell us that there are certain *Contradictions* against the common *Principles* of *Nature*, and the *universal Sentiments* of all Mankind, no otherwise to be avoided but by taking those words in the *sense* in which we do; we are then *BOUND* to interpret them so, as to avoid these *Impossibilities*. And this I am confident I have at large shewn above to be the Case, and thither I refer the *Reader*.

II. **Ground.** Their second Ground is founded up- on the *Authority* of those *Councils* that have deter- mined this Matter; "The Declaration, *as he calls* "*it*, of the most *Supreme* and *Universal Church-* "*Authority* that hath been assembled in former "Times for the decision of this *Controversy*, long "before the birth of *Protestantism*.

P. 28. §. xxv.

These are great Words indeed; but I wonder who ever heard before that a few miserable * *Synods* of particular Prelats, such as are all those to which he refers us, assembled against *Berengarius*, were the most

* These are his Synods; at *Rome, Vircelles, Tours; Rome* a- gain, *An.* 1059. and again, *An.* 1078.

most supream and universal Church-Authority. For his little Reflection, that they were assembled long before the birth of *Protestantism*, I must tell him, I doubt he is mistaken. The Religion of *Protestants*, like that of *Papists*, is compos'd of two great parts; *Catholick Christianity*, common in some measure to us all; and *Protestations against Popery.* Now 'tis true, for what concerns the latter of these, we allow *Popery* to have the advantage of us, as to the Point of *Antiquity*, nor are we ashamed to own it: It being necessary that they should have fallen into *Errors*, before we could *protest* against *them*; but as to the present matter, our Author in his * *Guide*, to which he refers us, confesses that *Berengarius*, against whom these little *Synods* were called, proceeded upon *Protestant Grounds, i. e.* in effect was a *Protestant* as to this Point: And therefore 'tis false in him now to say, that these Councils were *assembled long before the birth of Protestantism.*

* Disc. 1. p. 55. §. lvii.

But I return to his Church Authority; and answer; 1. If this Doctrine be certainly contrary to *Sense* and *Reason*, as was before said, then he has told us before, that " *no Motive whatever, no Revela-* " *tion, tho never so plain, can be sufficient to engage us* " *to believe it.* 2. For his *Councils*, the eldest of them was above a thousand Years after Christ, when by our own Confession, the Error, tho not of *Transubstantiation*, yet of the *Corporal Presence*, was creeping into the Church. 3. These *Councils* were themselves a *Party* against *Berengarius*, and therefore no wonder if they condemned him. 4. They were neither *universal* of the whole Church, or even of the *Western Patriachate* in which they assembled; and therefore we can have no security that they did not err,

as practised in the Church of Rome.   111

err, tho we should grant this Priviledg to a truly *General Council* that it could not. 5. 'Tis evident that some of them did err; forasmuch as the very * *Formularies* of Recantation prescribed to *Berengarius*, do not agree the one with the other; and one of them was such, that their own † Authors tell us it must be *very favourably interpreted, or it will lead us into a worser Error than that which it condemn'd.* 6. Were they never so infallible, yet they none of them defined *Transubstantiation*, but only a *Corporal Presence*; and so whatever *Authority* they have, it is for the *Lutherans*, not the *Papists*. 7. And this their own Writers seem to own; forasmuch as none of them pretend to any *definition* of *Transubstantiation* before the *Council* of *Lateran*; and till which time they freely confess it was no *Article of Faith.*

* *In the first Formulary prescribed him by P. Nicholas 2. in the Synod of Rome, 1059. He thus declares,* Panem & Vinum quæ in altari ponuntur post consecrationem non solum Sacramentum sed etiam verum Corpus & Sanguinem, D. N. J. Christi esse; & sensualiter non solùm SA-CRAMENTO, sed in Veritate manibus Sacerdotum, tractari, frangi, & fidelium dentibus atteri. *The former Part of which Confession is* Lutheran; *the latter utterly deny'd by the C. of R. at this day. In the second Formulary prescribed him by* Gregory viith, 1078. Confiteor Panem & Vinum —— converti in veram ac propriam Carnem & Sanguinem J. C. D. N. Et post consecrationem esse verum Corpus Christi —— non tantùm per signum & virtutem Sacramenti, sed in proprietate naturæ, & veritate substantiæ. *This speaks of a Conversion, but of what kind it says not; and* Lombard *and the other Schoolmen, to the very time of the Council of* Lateran, *were not agreed about it: and P.* Gregory *himself in his MS. Work upon St. Mat. knew not what to think of it.* † Jo. Semeca ad Can. Ego Berengar. not. ad Jus Canon. "Nisi sunè "intelligas verba Berengarii in majorem incides Hæresim quam ipse habuit; & ideò omnia referas ad species ipsas; nam de Christi Corpore partes non facimus. *So* Hervæus *in* 4. dist. qu. 1. art. 1. *says, that to speake the more expresly against the Hereticks, he declined a little too much to the opposite side. So* Ricardus de Media Villa *in* 4. dist. princip. 1. qu. 1. Berengarius fuerat infamatus quòd non credebat Corpus Christi realiter contineri sub pane, ideò ad sui purgationem, per verba excessiva contrarium *Asseruit.*

Such is the Church Authority which this *Discourser* would put upon us. But now that I have mentioned the *Council* of *Lateran*, as I have before observed, that it was the same Council which established Pag. 28.

blish'd this Error, that also gave power to the *Pope* to *depose Princes,* and *absolve their Subjects from their Obedience*; so I cannot but remak further in this place, the *Zeal* of our *Author* in the *defence* of its *Authority*. It is but a very little while since another of their *Church,* ‖ Father *Walsh,* in his Letter to the Bishop of *Lincoln,* did not think that the * Learned Person of our Church, to whom he refers us, had so clearly proved these *Canons* to have been the genuine † *Acts* either of the *Council,* or even of the *Papist* himself, but that a Man might still have reason to doubt of both: But indeed, tho that *Father* be of another mould, yet there are still some in the World, and I believe of this *Author*'s acquaintance, who like this *Council,* never the worse for such a *decision*; but think the third *Canon* as necessary to keep *Princes* in a due *Obedience* to the *Church,* as the first, de Fide Catholiâ, to help out the obscurity of the Text in favour of *Transubstantiation*.

‖ Lond. 1616. Pag. 352, &c.
* *Mr.* Dodwel *Consid. of present Concernment,* §. 31.
† *Monsieur du* Pin *utterly denies these Canons to have been the Decrees of the Council. Dissert.* vii. c. iii. §. 4.

But he goes on; and upon these Premises, "Asks "us, What more *reasonable* or *secure* course in "matters of Religion can a private and truly hum- "ble Christian take, than where the sense of a *Di- "vine Revelation* is disputed, to submit to that In- "terpretation thereof, which *the Supreamest Authority "in the Church,* that hath heretofore been convened "about such matters hath so *often,* and *always in "the same manner* decided to him, and so to act ac- "cording to its Injunction?

Pag. 28, 29. §. xxv.

Now, not to say any more as to his Expression of the *Supremest Church Authority,* which it may be he will interpret not *absolutely,* but with this *Reserve, that hath been convened about such matters;* I answer from himself, 1. It is a more *reasonable* and *secure* course

course to follow that *Interpretation* which is agreeable to the *common Sense* and *Reason* of Mankind, and against which he tells us, not only the *Authority* of a *Synod*, but even a *Divine Revelation* is not sufficient to secure us. 2. These *Synods*, as I have shewed, besides that they were *particular*, were moreover *Parties* in the case. And then, 3. It is false to say that they always decided the *same*, or, that that which they decided is the *same* which the Church of Rome now holds in this matter. All which our * Authors have fully proved, and this *Discourser* therefore ought to have answered.

* *Particularly* Blondel, *to whom this Author refers us,* Eclairciss. de l'Euch. c. 20, &c. Albertinus de Euch. lib. 3. p. 947.

III. Ground. "But now, *he says*, if these Coun-
"cils be declined, as not being so ancient as some
"may expect; *i. e.* not held before some Contro-
"versy happen'd in the Church touching the Point
"they decided: They have yet another *very rational*
"*Ground* of their belief, and that is, the evident Te-
"stimony of the more Primitive Times. It would
have been more to the purpose, if he could honestly
have said of the *most Primitive Times.* But however
his Modesty is the greater now, tho his Argument
be not so strong. As to the Point of *Antiquity*, I
have already fully discussed it above; and we are but
very lately assured by one of their own *Authors*,
that *Antiquity* is of our side in this Point. For the
six or seven Fathers he has mentioned, ‖ some of
them are *spurious*; others have been † expresly answered by us; and all of them at large by Monsieur
Aubertine, Larrogue, and others. If this does not

P. 29. §. xxvi.

Treatise of Transubstantiation, by an Author of the C. of R.

‖ S. Ambrose de Sacramentis. Euseb. Emyssen. de Paschate.
† Cyril Hierosol. *in the Relat. of the Conference at my Lady* T. 1676. *in the Paper sent my Lady* T. p. 50, 51, 52. *And for* S. Ambrose de Sacr. *allowing the Book, yet see the Explication of what is there said, given by himself,* l. 5. c. 4. *See a late Treatise of the Doct. of the Trinity and Transubst. compared, Part* 1. p. 45, 47.

Of the Adoration of the Host,

satisfy him, he may shortly expect a fuller account in our own Language; * a *Specimen* of which has already been given to the World in Earnest of what is suddenly to follow.

* Transubstantiation no Doctrine of the Primitive Fathers. Cyrill's Authority examined, p. 13, 14. Ambrose's, p. 18, 19. Chrysostom's, p. 40. Greg. Nyssen's, p. 48.

IV. *Ground*. His next *Ground* is taken " from " the universal Doctrine and Practice of the later " both *Eastern* and *Western* Churches till *Luther*'s " Time, and at present also excepting his Followers. To which I answer; That this *Ground* is not *certainly true*, and if it were, yet *certainly 'tis nothing to the purpose*. 1. *It is not certainly true*: Indeed, that the latter Ages of the *Western Churches* before *Luther*, that is, from the time of the Council of *Laterane*, did profess the belief of *Transubstantiation* is confess'd: And that a great part of the *Greek Church* at this day do's the same, since their new *Colledge* at *Rome*, and their *Money* and *Missionaries* sent among them have corrupted their Faith, I do not deny: But that this was so before *Luther* is not so certain; and whosoever shall impartially read over the long debate between the late Monsieur *Claude*, and Monsieur *Arnaud* concerning this matter, will, I believe, confess that this can be no *rational Ground* for their belief. *Ludolphus* tells us of the *Ethiopian* Church, that at this day, it neither believes *Transubstantiation*, nor *Adores the Host*: and *Tellezius* confesses it, because they consecrate with these words, " *This Bread is my Body* : For the * *Greeks*, the *Muscovites*, the *Armenians*, the *Nestorians*, *Maronites*, &c.

Hist Ethiop. l. 3. c. 5. n. 48.

Ibid.

* De Ecclef. Græc. Stat. Hodiern. D. Smith, p. 116.

Lond. 1678. Claude Reponse au 2. Traitte; liv. 3. c. 8. p. 434, &c. Charenton. 1668. Id. ult. resp. à Quevilly 1670. lib. 5. c. 1, 2, 3, 4, 5, 6. Histoire Critique de la creance & des Coutumes, des Nations, du Levant. — Voyage du Mont Liban. Remarques, p. 302, 303, &c. Larrogue Hist. de l'Eucharistie, liv. 2. c. 19. pag. 781. Edit. Anist. 12°. Albertinus de Eucharistiâ, p. 988, 989. fol. Daventriæ 1554.

those

those who please to interest their Curiosity in a matter of so little moment as to their Faith, may satisfy themselves in the Authors, to which I refer them. Tho now, 2. To allow the matter of Fact to be true, I pray, what force is there at last in this Argument, "The Church both Eastern & Western, "in these last Ages have believed *Transubstantiation*; "therefore the *Papists* have a *rational Ground* to be- "lieve it. That is to say, you *Protestants* charge us for believing *Transubstantiation*, as Men that act contrary to the design of Christ in this *Holy Eucharist*, that have forsaken the *Tradition* of the *Primitive Ages* of the *Church*; that destroy the nature of this *Holy Sacrament*, and do violence to the common *Sense* and *Reason* of Mankind: Be it so; yet at least we have this *rational Ground* for our belief, tho it should be false, *viz.* That we did all of us peaceably and quietly believe it, till you came with your *Scripture*, and *Antiquity*, and *Sense*, and *Reason*, to raise Doubts and Difficulties about it; nay more, we all of us still do believe it, except those that you have perswaded not to do so.

Spectatum admissi risum teneatis Amici?

V. *Ground.* Of no greater strength is his last *Ground* for their belief, *viz,* "That since *Luther's* "Time no small number of *Protestants*, even all the "*Genuine Sons* of the *Church* of *England*, have pro- "ceeded thus far, as to confess a *Real Presence* of "our Lord's *Body* and *Blood* in the *Eucharist*, and "*Adoration* of it, as present there. For, 1. If we did *acknowledg* this, yet it seems we are mistaken in it; and then what grounds can it be for a *Papist* to believe

P.31. §.xxviii.

believe *Transubstantiation*, that we *Hereticks* by a Mistake do not believe it, but only a *real spiritual Presence,* and as such are *Anathematized* by them for our Error? 2. I have before shewn, that were this a *rational Ground,* yet it fails them too; for neither do the *Genuine Sons* of the *Church* of *England,* nor any other that I know of, either believe Christ's *natural Body* to be substantially present in the Holy *Eucharist,* or to be *adored* there: I am sure if there be any such, they cannot be the *Genuine Sons* of the *Church* of *England* in this Matter, who believe so expresly contrary to her formal Declaration, as this Author has himself observed.

Ibid. Pag. 32.

And then for the *Lutherans,* to whom he again returns; it is hard to conceive what *rational ground* of Security they can derive from their practice; that because they commit no *Idolatry* in worshipping what they know certainly to be Christ, the *Papist* commits none for worshipping what he do's not know certainly is Christ; in truth what, if he pleased, he might know certainly is not Christ.

And now after a serious and impartial Consideration of the Grounds produced in Vindication of this *Worship;* tho I could have wish'd I might have found them as *rational* as our Author pretends them to be, and shall be glad, as they are, that they may hereafter prove sufficient to excuse them from the Guilt of *formal Idolatry* in this *Adoration;* yet I must needs say, I do in my Conscience think 'tis more

P. 33. §. xxx.

"an excess of *Charity,* than any necessity of Argu-
"ment, if our *Writers* do sometimes, either not
"at all, or but faintly, charge them with *Idolatry.*
And the Testimonies he produces, argue rather the candor of our Affections towards them, even such

as

as to hope, almoft againft Hope for their fakes; than give any fecurity to them in their Errors. And becaufe I would willingly, if poffible, convince them of it, I will very briefly fubjoin a Reafon or two.

2dly; Why even upon their own *Principles* I am not fatisfied that they have fuch a *rational Ground* for this *Adoration*, as may be fufficient to excufe them.

For, *1ſt*, It is granted by this Author, " That a *P.26. §.xxii.* " meerly *good Intention* grounded upon a *culpable Ig-* " *norance*, cannot excufe them from *Idolatry*. So that if their *ignorance* then be really *culpable*, their *good Intention* will not be fufficient to excufe them. Now the *ignorance* upon which this practice is founded, is their miftaken interpretation of thofe words, *This is my Body*; and whether that be a *rational* or *culpable* Miftake, we fhall beft be able to judg by two or three Obfervations.

1. It is confefs'd by the greateft Men of their Church, that there is *no neceſſity* to interpret thofe words in that manner that they do; fo that had not the Authority of their Church interpofed, they might have been *equally verified* in our Interpretation. And this muft be allow'd, unlefs we fhall fay, that all places of Holy Scripture muft be underftood in a *literal fenfe*, whatever the Confequence be of fo doing.

2. Our Author himfelf confeffes, that if the taking of them in the *literal fenfe* do's involve a *certain Contradiction*, then it cannot be right; but we are *bound* to feek out fome other Expofition to avoid a *certain Contradiction*.

3. It is undeniable, that their Interpretation of these words destroys the certainty of *Sense*, and in that of the Truth of the *Christian Religion*, which was confirmed by *Miracles*, known only by the *evidence* of *Sense*; and by Consequence of this particular Point, that *Transubstantiation* is revealed to us by God, or can be rely'd upon as coming from him.

Now from these Principles I thus argue: If that *sense* of these words, *This is my Body*, upon which they ground their *Adoration*, do's necessarily imply many plain and certain *Contradictions*, then by their own Confession that cannot be the right *sense* of them. But that it do's so, and that without gross and culpable *Ignorance* they cannot doubt of but know it, I thus shew. He that believes these words in the sense of *Transubstantiation*, must believe the same *natural Body*, at the same time, to be in tenthousand several places upon Earth, and yet still to be but *one Body*, and that all the while in Heaven: He must believe that the same *natural Body* is at the same time *extended* in all its Parts, and yet continuing still the *same Body* without any change, to be *unextended*, and have no distinct Parts, nor be capable of being divided into any: He must believe the same *Body* at the same time, to move, and to lie still: to be the Object of our Senses, and yet not to be perceptible by any: With infinite others of the like kind * as I have more fully shewn before. But now all these are gross *Contradictions*, contrary to the *Nature* of a *Body*, and to the common *Principles* of *Reason* in all Mankind; and no Man can, without *culpable Ignorance* pretend not to know them to be so: And therefore, notwithstanding any such supposed *Divine Revelation* as may be pretended from those words,

* See above, Ch. 2. of *Transubstantiation*. Pag. 32, 33.

words, *This is my Body*, they cannot, by our Author's own *Rule*, without *culpable Ignorance*, not know that they are mistaken in this Matter.

Again: No *Papist* can have any reason to believe *Transubstantiation* to be true, but because he reads those words of Holy Scripture, *This is my Body*. That these words are in Scripture, he can know only by his *Senses*: If his *Senses* therefore are not to be trusted, he is not sure there are any such words in Scripture. If they are to be trusted, he is then sure that the *Interpretation* which he puts upon them must be *false*.

Since then it is confess'd, that there is *no necessity* to understand those words in a *literal sense*; and that both upon the account of the *Contradictions* that such an Exposition involves to the *common Principles of Reason*, and to the certain *Evidence of the Senses of all Mankind*, it is necessary to take them in some other meaning, it remains that without gross and *culpable Ignorance* they cannot pretend not to know, that this could never have been the intention of our Blessed Saviour in those *words*; and that such *Ignorance* will not *excuse* them, our Author himself has freely confess'd.

But, 2*dly*, let us quit this Reflection, and for once suppose the possibility of *Transubstantiation*. Yet still it is confess'd by them: 1. That there is no Command nor Example in holy Scripture for *adoring* Christ in the *Eucharist*. 2. That infinite Defects may happen to hinder him from being there; and then what they *worship* is only a piece of *Bread*. 3. That they can never be sure that some of these *Defects* have not happened; and by consequence, that what they suppose to be *Christ's Body*, is indeed any more than a *meer Wafer*. From

From whence I argue ;

He that without any Command or Warrant of God, pays a *Divine Adoration* to that which he can never be sure is more than a *meer Creature*, can never be sure that he do's not commit *Idolatry :* But whosoever worships the *Host,* worships that which he can never be sure is more than a *meer Creature* ; and therefore he can never be sure that in so doing he do's not commit *Idolatry.*

Now concerning the former of these, how dangerous it is for any one to give *Divine Worship* to what he can never be sure is any more than a *meer Creature,* be it considered, what *jealousy* God has at all times express'd of his *Honour* as to this Matter; how strict he has been in the peculiar vindication of his Supreme *Prerogative* in such Cases. How therefore he that will come to him, must be very well assured that it is God to whom he approaches ; and therefore if he has but the least reason to *doubt* of it, ought not to worship with a *doubting Mind* ; because he ought not to do that the *omitting* whereof can be no *fault,* but the *doing* of which may, for ought he knows, be a very great *Sin.*

And for the second ; Whether every *Roman Catholick,* who *adores* the *Host,* has not even upon his own *Principles,* very great cause to doubt, whether he *adores* Christ's *Body,* or only a bit of *Bread,* will appear from those infinite Defects which they themselves allow as sufficient to hinder a *Consecration* ; and which make it great odds, were their Doctrine otherwise never so true, whether yet one *Host* in twenty, it may be in five hundred, be consecrated.

1. With reference to the Holy *Elements* to be consecrated : If the *Bread* be not all, or at least the greater

as practised in the Church of Rome.

ter part, of *Wheat-flower*; if it be not *mix'd* with pure *Water*; if the *Bread* be corrupted, or the *Wine* sour; if the *Grapes* of which the *Wine* was made were not *ripe*; if any thing be *mingled* with the *Wine* but *Water*; or if there be so much *Water* mix'd with it, that that becomes the prevailing Ingredient; in all these Cases, and many others which I omit, there is no *Consecration*. And of all this, he who *adores* either the *Bread* or *Wine*, can have no security. But, ^{See all this in the beginning of the Missal, *de defectibus circa Missam.*}

2. Be the Elements right, yet if the Priest, being either ignorant, or in haste, or unmindful of what he is about, should by mistake, or otherwise, err in pronouncing of *the words of Consecration*; whether by *Addition*, or by *Diminution*, or by any other *Alteration*, there is no *Consecration*: The *Bread* and *Wine* continue what they were; and of this too he that worships them can never be certain.

3. Let the words be never so rightly pronounced, yet if the Priest had *no intention to consecrate*; if he be a secret *Atheist*, or *Jew*, or *Moor*: If he be a careless negligent Man; it may be do's not believe he has any Power to make such a Change, (as I have shewn that several of their greatest Men in this very *Age* have doubted of it.): If he consecrate a number of *Wafers* for a *Communion*, and in his telling Mistakes, intending to consecrate but *twenty*, and there are *one and twenty* before him; in all these Cases, for want of a *due intention* in the *Priest*, there it no *Consecration*; but that which is *adored*, is only a little *Bread* and *Wine*.

4. Let the Priest have a good *Intention*, yet if he be *no Priest*; if he were not rightly Baptized, or Ordained; if he were a *Simoniac*, or *Irregular*, or ^{See above in the Preface.}

Y a

a Bastard, &c. Or if there were no defect in his *Ordination*, yet if there was any in his who *ordained* him; or in the *Bishops* that *ordained* that *Bishop* that *ordained* him; and so back to the very Time of the *Apostles*, if in the whole Succession of Priests to this day, there has been but any *one Invalidity*, whether by Error or Wilfulness, or for want of a due Intention, or by Ignorance, or by any other means; then he that *consecrates* is no true *Priest*, and by consequence has no Power to *consecrate*; and so all is spoiled, and whosoever *worships* in any of his *Masses*, adores only a piece of *Bread* instead of our Saviour's Body.

When therefore so many *Defects* may interpose upon their own Principles to hinder this *Conversion*, that 'tis exceeding probable, nay 'tis really great odds, that not one *Host* in twenty is consecrated; it must certainly be very hazardous to worship that for God, which upon their own *Principles* they can never be sure is so; nay, which 'tis twenty to one is not *God*, but a meer inanimate Creature of *Bread* and *Wine*.

* See Bellarm. de Justif. c. 8.

Pag. 23.

Adv. VI. quodlibet. Sect. 10. Suppos. 2.

See Grison, Tract. de Exam. doctr. consid. 6.

'Tis this has forced their most Learned Men to confess, that they can never be *sure* of a *Consecration*; and our Author himself to declare, "That they "do not worship the Substance that is under the Ac-"cidents of *Bread* and *Wine*, WHATEVER IT BE, "but UPON SUPPOSITION that it is CHRIST'S "BODY; Which is what Pope *Adrian* 6th, following herein the Authority of the Council of *Constance*, prescribed; that they ought always to *adore* the Host with such a reserve: "The Council of *Constance*, "*says he*, excuses those who in their simplicity *adore* "an *unconsecrated Host*, because this condition is tacitly

as practised by the Church of Rome.

"citly implied, *if it be rightly consecrated:* And there-
"fore he advises, let them so adore the Host, *I ADORE*
"*THEE IF THOU ART CHRIST.* But now if, as
the Apostle tells us in another case, *Whatsoever is not of
Faith, is Sin*; and, *He that doubts, is damned if he eats:*
I shall leave it to any sober Christian to say what security there can be in such a *Worship,* which is neither advised, encouraged, or commanded in Holy Scripture;
and which they themselves confess they can never be
certain is addressed to a right *Object*; and therefore are
forced to such Shifts and Reserves, as were they once
admitted, might make any other Creature in the World
as warrantably *adorable* as their *Host*.

How much better were it for them to *adore* their
Blessed Saviour in *Heaven,* where his *glorified Body*
most certainly is: Where there can therefore be no
danger to *lift up our Hearts* unto him. Were his Sacred
Body indeed *substantially present* in this Blessed *Sacrament,* yet still it would be in a manner to us imperceptible, in the state of his Death, and by consequence of
his Humiliation; and we might therefore have some
cause to doubt whether, since we have received no Command concerning it, it were our Saviour's Pleasure that
his *Body* should be *adored* by us in that State: So that
there could be no Sin in the not doing of it. But
now amidst so many Doubts, not only upon Ours, but e-
ven upon their own Principles, that they dare not themselves *worship at a venture,* that which yet they do *worship*; tho I shall leave them to their own Master to
stand or fall at the Great Day, yet I must needs profess
I think there is very much hazard in it. A great Sincerity, and great Ignorance, may excuse a poor untaught,
and therefore *blindly obedient* Multitude: but for their
Guides, who lead them into Error, for those to whom

Of the Adoration of the Host,

God has given Capacities and Opportunities (as to those now among us he has done, of being better informed) I can only say, *Lord, lay not this Sin to their Charge!*

And this may suffice to have been said to the third Thing proposed, of their *Rational Grounds* for this Worship. For what our Author finally adds; "That to adore that which the Adorer believes not to be our Lord, but Bread, would be unlawful to be done by any, so long as the Person continues so perswaded—But then if we suppose the Church *justly* requiring such Adoration upon such a true Presence of our Lord, neither will the same Person be free from sinning greatly in his following such his Conscience, and in his not adoring.

Pag. 37. §. xxxiii.

I Answer: It will then be time enough to consider this, when either the *Church* to which we owe an *Obedience*, shall require it of us, or they be able to prove that in such a Case the *Church* would not *sin* in *Commanding*, and not *we* in *refusing* to *obey* her. But, blessed be God, there is no great danger of either of these: Our *Church* is too well perswaded of the unlawfulness of such a *Worship*, ever to require it of us. And for that Church which has so uncharitably undertaken to *Anathematize* all those who will not own her *Authority*, and receive her Errors, tho never so gross, as Articles of Faith: We are so fully convinced of the unreasonableness of her Pretences, and of our own Liberty, that we shall hardly be brought to submit our selves to the Conduct of such a *blind Guide*, lest we fall into the same *Ditch*, into which she her self is tumbled. And it would certainly much better become our Author, and his Brethren, to consider how they can justify their *Disobedience* to their own *Mother*, than to
en-

endeavour at this rate to lead us into the same *Apostacy*, both to our *Religion* and our *Church* with them.

The Conclusion.

AND thus by the Blessing of God, and the Advantage of a good Cause, have I very briefly passed through this Author's *Reflections*, and I am perswaded sufficiently shewn the weakness and falsity of the most of them. If any one shall think that I ought to have insisted more largely upon some Points, he may please to know, that since by the importunate Provocations of those of the *other Communion*, we have been forced too often to interrupt those Duties of our *Ministry*, in which we could rather have wish'd to have employ'd our Time, for these kind of Controversies which serve so very little to any purposes, either of true Piety, or true Charity among us: We have resolved thus far at least to gratify both our selves and others, as to make our *Disputes* as *short* as is possible; and loose no more time in them, than the necessary Defence of our selves and the Truth do require.

I have indeed pass'd by much of our Author's *Discourses*, because they are almost intirely made up of tedious and endless *Repetitions* of the same things, and very often in the same words. But for any thing that is Argumentative, or otherwise material to the main *Cause*, I do not know that I have either let the Observation of it slip, or dissembled at all the Force of it.

It was once in my thoughts to have made some Reflections in the Close upon the *Changes* of their *Rituals*, in requital for our Author's Observations on the *Alterations* of our *Liturgie*; but I have insisted longer
than

than I designed already, and shall therefore content my my self to have given the Hint of what might have been done, and shall still be done, if our Author, or any in his behalf desire it of me.

In the mean time I cannot but observe the unreasonableness of that *Method* which is here taken; from the Expressions of some of our Divines, and the Concessions of others, whose profess'd Business it was to reconcile, if possible, all Parties, and therefore were forced sometimes to condescend more than was fit for the doing it; and even these too miserably *mangled* and *misrepresented*, to pretend to prove the *Doctrine* of our *Church* contrary to the *express Declarations* of the *Publick Acts* and *Records* of it. This has been the endeavour of several of our late Writers, but of this *Discourser* above any. Had those worthy Persons, whose Memory they thus abuse, been yet living, they might have had an ample Confutation from their own Pens; as, in the very Instance before us, has been given them for the like ill use made by some among them, of the pious *Meditations* of a most Excellent and Learned *Father* of our *Church*; and who might otherwise in the next Age have been improved into a new Witness against us. I do not think that Bp *Taylour* ever thought he should have been set up as a favourer of *Popery*, who had written so expresly and warmly against it. Yet I cannot but observe a kind of Prophetick Expression in his Book of the *Real Presence*, which being so often quoted by these Men, I somewhat wonder it should have slipp'd their Remark: Where speaking of their Shifts to make any One they please of their side, he has these words; "And——I know no reason, *says he*, but it may be possible, but a WITTY MAN may pretend, when I am dead, that in this

Real Presence, §. ii. n. 28. pag. 291.

"Dis-

The Conclusion.

"*Discourse* I have pleaded for the *Doctrine* of the Ro-
"man *Church*.

We have now lived to see some of those WITTY
MEN that have done but little less than this; tho
how *Honest* they are in the mean time, I will not determine. But I hope this Design too shall be from
henceforth in good measure frustrated: And therefore,
since neither their *New Religion*, nor their *New Advo-
cates* will do their Business; since it is in vain that they
either *misrepresent* their own *Doctrine*, or our *Authors*
in favour of it; may they once please either honestly
to avow and defend their Faith, or honestly to confess
that they cannot do it. Such shuffling as this, do's but
more convince us of the *weakness* of their *Cause*; and
instead of defending their *Religion* by these Practices,
they only encrease in us our *ill Opinion* of that, and les-
sen that *good One* which we willingly would, but shall
not always be able to conserve of *those*, who by such
indirect means as these, endeavour to support it.

FINIS.

Books lately printed for Richard Chiswell.

A Dissertation concerning the Government of the Antient Church: more particularly of the Encroachments of the Bishops of Rome upon other Sees. By WILLIAM CAVE, D.D. Octavo.

An Answer to Mr. Serjeant's [Sure Footing in Christianity] concerning the Rule of Faith: With some other Discourses. By WILLIAM FALKNER, D.D. 4o.

A Vindication of the Ordinations of the Church of England; in Answer to a Paper written by one of the Church of Rome, to prove the Nullity of our Orders. By GILBERT BURNET, D.D. Octavo.

An Abridgment of the History of the Reformation of the Church of England. By GILB. BURNET, D.D. Octavo.

The APOLOGY of the Church of England; and an Epistle to one Signior Scipio, a Venetian Gentleman, concerning the Council of Trent. Written both in Latin, by the Right Reverend Father in God, JOHN JEWEL Lord Bishop of Salisbury: Made English by a Person of Quality. To which is added, The Life of the said Bishop: Collected and written by the same Hand. Octavo.

The Life of WILLIAM BEDEL, D.D. Bishop of Kilmore in Ireland. Together with Certain Letters which passed betwixt him and James Waddesworth, a late Pensioner of the Holy Inquisition of Sevil, in Matter of Religion; concerning the General Motives to the Roman Obedience. Octavo.

The Decree made at ROME the Second of March, 1679. condemning some Opinions of the Jesuits, and other Casuists. Quarto.

A Discourse concerning the Necessity of Reformation, with respect to the Errors and Corruptions of the Church of Rome. Quarto, First and Second Parts.

A Discourse concerning the Celebration of Divine Service in an Unknown Tongue. Quarto.

A Papist not Misrepresented by Protestants. Being a Reply to the Reflections upon the Answer to [A Papist Misrepresented and Represented]. Quarto.

An Exposition of the Doctrine of the Church of England, in the several Articles proposed by the late BISHOP of CONDOM, [in his Exposition of the Doctrine of the Catholick Church]. Quarto.

A Defence of the Exposition of the Doctrine of the Church of England; against the Exceptions of Monsieur de Meaux, late Bishop of Condom, and his Vindicator. 4o.

A CATECHISM explaining the Doctrine and Practices of the Church of Rome. With an Answer thereunto. By a Protestant of the Church of England. 8o.

A Papist Represented and not Misrepresented, being an Answer to the First, Second, Fifth and Sixth Sheets of the Second Part of the [Papist Misrepresented and Represented]; and for a further Vindication of the CATECHISM, truly representing the Doctrines and Practices of the Church of Rome. Quarto.

The Lay-Christian's Obligation to read the Holy Scriptures. Quarto.

The Plain Man's Reply to the Catholick Missionaries. 24o.

An Answer to THREE PAPERS lately printed, concerning the Authority of the Catholick Church in Matters of Faith, and the Reformation of the Church of England. Quarto.

A Vindication of the Answer to THREE PAPERS concerning the Unity and Authority of the Catholick Church, and the Reformation of the Church of England. Quarto.

A FULL VIEW OF THE Eucharist.

Imprimatur,

Liber cui titulus [A Full View of the Doctrines and Practices of the Ancient Church, relating to the Eucharist, &c.]

Octob. 6.
1687.
H. Maurice, *Reverendissimo in Christo* P. D. Wilhelmo *Archiepiscopo Cant. à Sacris.*

A FULL VIEW

OF THE

Doctrines and Practices

OF THE

Ancient Church

Relating to the

EUCHARIST.

Wholly different from those of
The Present *ROMAN* Church,
And inconsistent with the Belief of

TRANSUBSTANTIATION.

BEING

A sufficient Confutation of *Consensus Veterum*, *Nubes Testium*, and other *Late Collections* of the *Fathers*, pretending the contrary.

Rectum est Index sui & Obliqui.

LONDON,

Printed for **Richard Chiswell** at the *Rose and Crown* in St. *Paul*'s Church-yard. MDCLXXXVIII.

A PREFACE to the READER.

THAT which is here offered to thy Perusal, was occasioned by some late Pamphlets *, that appeared, much about the same time, in Print, pretending by a Heap of Testimonies from the Fathers to prove, as in some other Doctrines, so particularly in that of the *Corporal Presence* and *Transubstantiation*, That the *Ancient Church*, and the *present Roman*, are at a good Agreement.

<small>* *Succession of Church and Sacraments. Consensus Veterum. Nubes Testium.*</small>

It is very hard for *Us* to believe this, and scarce credible that *they themselves* did so, when we see so much Unsincerity in their Allegations; such Deceit and contrived disguising the Sense of the *Fathers*, in their Translations; such late, uncertain, and supposititious Writings cited by them, under the Venerable Names of *Ancient Authors*: When the way that *Procrustes* took, of stretching Limbs, or chopping them off, to make all agree to his Bed who were to be laid in it, is used to make the *Ancient* and the *Present Church* to agree, a *Consent* thus procured can occasion but a short and a sorry Triumph. Yet

PREFACE.

Yet those Performances have been cry'd up, and they are look'd upon as *Storehouses* and *Repositories*, whence any Champion of theirs who enters the Lists, may be furnish'd from the *Fathers*, either with what is necessary for his own Defence, or the assailing of an Adversary. The *Representer*, since that, made great use of them, in a brisk Attaque he made upon the *Dublin Letter*, tho' the Success, I believe, did not answer his Expectation. The *Convert of Putney*'s Performance (who in his *Consensus Veterum* made the largest Shew of Fathers on behalf of Transubstantiation) has had a particular Consideration given it, by his worthy Answerer * : And so all the other Testimonies in the rest of them, that are of any seeming strength and moment, have received Answers to them from other Hands; particularly from the Learned Author of *The Doctrine of the Trinity and Transubstantiation compared*, Part 1.

If any thing, after all, seems to be wanting on our Part, it is this ; That as our Adversaries have made a *Shew of Fathers* (for I can give it no better name) pretended to countenance their Doctrines of the *Corporal Presence* and *Transubstantiation*; so we also ought to have *our Collection of Testimonies* from the *Ancients*, made faithfully and impartially, wherein their true Sense in these

* *Veteres Vindicati.*

PREFACE.

these Matters may be clearly seen and viewed, and thereby their Dissent from this Church appear plainly, in those things that either *constitute* this Doctrine, or are necessary *Consequents* of it. And this is that which I have undertaken in the following Papers; wherein as the Usefulness of the Design has encourag'd me to take some Pains, so I shall think them well bestowed, if the Reader will bring an honest and unprejudic'd Mind to the Perusal of them, and suffer himself to be determin'd in his Opinions concerning this Controversie, according to the Evidence of Truth here offered for his Conviction. If the Differences (which the annexed Contents of the Chapters give an Account of) are of such a Nature, and stand at such a wide Distance, that it's impossible ever to bring Transubstantiation to shake Hands with them as Friends; and if the two Churches, the *Ancient* and the *Present Roman*, are really divided and disagreeing, as I pretend to have demonstrated, in those Points, it will then I hope hereafter be ridiculous, to talk confidently of a *Consent of Fathers*, and of a *Cloud of Witnesses* on their Side.

But if I am herein mistaken, I am so little tender of my Reputation, compared with Truth, that I heartily desire to be confuted and made a Convert; for I am conscious to my
self

PREFACE.

self of no false Fathers I have cited for true ones; of no disguising or perverting their Sense, by an Ill Translation of their Words; (which I have therefore set down in their own Language) of no imposing upon the Reader a Sense of my own making, contrary to what I believe that they intended.

I have but one Request more to make to the unknown Author of a Book intituled, *Reason and Authority, &c.* who mentioning the *Defence of the Dublin Letter* * (for which I have some reason to be concern'd) says, That *the Authorities of the Fathers there urged are; as he conceives, in the Sense of them, either mistaken or misapplied, and that he shall endeavour to reconcile them to other Expressions of the Fathers,* and to (that which he calls) *the Catholick Doctrine of Transubstantiation.* I humbly desire, when he is about this *Reconciling Work*, and his Hand is in, that he would go on to reconcile also the *Differences* urged in the following Papers. Which if he shall do to any purpose, I promise to return the Complements he has pass'd upon *that Defender* with Interest, and to alter my present Opinion of him, upon his Performances in that Book.

Farewell.

* Pag. 119.

THE

THE CONTENTS OF THE CHAPTERS.

BEING

A Summary of the DIFFERENCES betwixt the *FAITH* and *PRACTICES* of the *Two Churches*.

CHAP. I. The First Difference. *The Roman Church asserts perpetual Miracles in the Eucharist: The Ancient Church owns none but those of God's Grace, working Changes in us, not in the Substance of the Elements.* Page 1

CHAP. II. The Second Difference. *They differ in determining what that Thing is which Christ calls* My Body; *which the Ancient Church says is Bread, but the Roman Church denies it.* 7

CHAP. III. The Third Difference. *The Roman Church believes, That Accidents subsist in the Eucharist without any Subject: This the Fathers deny.* 12

CHAP. IV. The Fourth Difference. *The Roman Church uses the Word* Species, *to signifie those self-subsisting Accidents: the Fathers never take* Species *in this Sense.* 16

CHAP. V. The Fifth Difference. *The Fathers differ from this Church about the Properties of Bodies*; as,
   1. *They assert, That every organiz'd Body, even that of Christ, is visible and palpable.* 21
   2. *That every Body possesses a Place, and is commensurate to it, and cannot be in more Places than one, nor be entire in one Part, nor exist after the manner of a Spirit.* All which

a *Transub-*

The Contents.

Transubstantiation denies. Page 22
3. That it is impossible for one to dwell in himself, or partake of ones self; this inferring Penetration of Dimensions, and that a greater Body may be contained in a lesser; which the Fathers deny. 29

CHAP. VI. The Sixth Difference. *The Roman Church teaches us to disbelieve the Report of our Senses, which tell us, That Bread and Wine remain in the Eucharist: The Fathers urge this Evidence, even with relation to Christ's true Body.* 31
  Object. The Fathers call upon us not to believe our Senses in the Case of the Eucharist.
  Answ. 1. The Fathers appeal to our Senses in this Case. 39
    2. They call upon Men not to regard their Information, in Matters wherein none question the Truth of their Information. ibid.
    3. The true Reason why the Fathers call us off from listning to our Senses, is, to make us regard and attend to things beyond their Information. 40
  A Place of S. Cyril of Jerusalem, and another of S. Chrysostome, explain'd. 42

CHAP. VII. The Seventh Difference. *When the Fathers call the Eucharist Christ's Body and Blood, the Roman Church understands it of Christs Natural Body; but the Fathers mean it commonly of the Bread and Wine. Several Observables from the Fathers, to explain and prove this; as,*
  1 Obs. They tell us of their studiously concealing the Mysteries from some Persons. 44
  2 Obs. The Fathers, in their manner of speaking concerning Christ's Body, point at another thing than his Natural Body. 46
  3 Obs. They speak of Christ's Body with Terms of Restriction and Diminution. 48
  4 Obs. They give as Reasons why it is call'd Christ's Body, (which none do for calling things by their Proper Names) from its Resemblance and Representation. 49
  5 Obs. What they call Christ's Body, they say is without Life or Sense. 51
  6 Obs. They speak of Divisions and Parts of it, not to be affirmed of his Natural Body. 52
  7 Obs. They speak of making Christ's Body, differently from

The Contents.

from the Sense of the Roman Church. 54
They affirm, 1. *That whatsoever is made, was not before it was made.* 55
2. *That* Bread *is made his* Body, *and that it is made of* Bread and Wine 55, 56
They call it sometimes Mystical Bread, sometimes Christ's Mystical Body. 57
8 Obs. *They speak of Christ's Body as sanctified and sacrificed in the Eucharist, which is only true of his Typical Body.* 58
The Natural Body of Christ cannot be sanctified nor sacrificed properly. 59

CHAP. VIII. The Eighth Difference. *When the Fathers mention a Change and Conversion in the Eucharist, the Roman Church understands such a Change as abolishes the Substance of Bread and Wine: The Fathers never understand it so.* 62
Several Assertions of the Fathers to explain this.
1 Assert. *They distinguish between the Conversion of a thing, and its abolishing.* ibid.
2 Assert. *When they speak of a Conversion into what was before, they suppose an Accession and Augmentation of that into which the Change is made.* 63
3 Assert. *The Fathers use the same Terms of* Conversion, Passing into, Becoming another thing, *&c. in other Cases besides that of the Eucharist, wherein all confess no Change of Substances is made.* 65
Some Axioms of the Fathers to this purpose. ibid.
Their Instances of such Changes given, in Nature, *in* Regeneration, *in* Christ's Incarnation, *our* Resurrection, *in* Baptism, *wherein the Change, however exprest, can be only in Qualities.* 65, 66, 67
4 Assert. *The Fathers, by a Change in the Eucharist, mean either a Change into a Sacrament, or that of Efficacy and Virtue, by infusing and adding Grace.* 69, 70
5 Assert. *They express as fully, and in the same manner, our substantial Change into Christ's Body, as of the Bread into Christ's Body.* 72

CHAP. IX. The Ninth Difference. *The Roman Church asserts a substantial Presence of Christ's Natural Body in the Eucharist, which the Fathers deny.* 74

The Contents.

Several Positions of the Fathers to this purpose.
1 Pos. *The Fathers look upon Christ's Body as absent from Earth since his Ascension; tho' in another sense he is present still.* ibid.
2 Pos. *They distinguish the presence of Christs Body from the Sacrament of it, which they make to be a memorial of him as gone away.* 77, 78
3 Pos. *Whatsoever presence of Christ the Fathers speak of in the Eucharist, they acknowledge the same in Baptism, and as fully.* 79, 80
They speak of those Waters as turned into Blood, of our being Baptized in Blood, and yet neither they, nor any else, dream'd of Transubstantiation. 82
4 Pos. *They so consider the presence of Christs Body in the Eucharist, as can no way agree to his glorified Body.* 83
5 Pos. *According to them, the Presence of Christs Body to us now, is a presence to our Faith, a presence of Union, Efficacy and Grace.* 85
What foul play the Romanists have used with an Author that deny'd this. 90
An Account of a late Learned Dissertation concerning Christs Body and Blood, occasion'd by a doubt proposed to S. Austin. 91

CHAP. X. The Tenth Difference. *The Fathers assert positively, that the substance of Bread and Wine remain after Consecration, which the R. Church denies.* 93
Proved by their asserting, that Christ offered the same oblation with Melchisedek. 101
Fraction in the Eucharist can only agree to the Bread. 103

CHAP. XI. The Eleventh Difference. *The Fathers make the Bread and Wine to be the Sacrament, Sign, Figure, Type, Antitype, Image, &c. of Christs Body and Blood, which Transubstantiation contradicts.* 105
Instances of the particulars. Their calling it a Sacrament. ibid.
Signs. 106. Types. 107. Antitypes. ibid. A Figure. 108. Image. 110.
Further Remarks of the Fathers confirming the Argument, as
1 Remark. *They say an Image, Figure, &c. cannot be the thing it self.* 111
2 Rem. *That an Image, Type, &c. must visibly demonstrate*

The Contents.

strate that, of which it is an Image, Type, &c. 112
3 *Rem. They make the Elements to be the Signs, Symbols,* &c. *of Christ as absent.* 113
Some Passages out of the old Liturgy in Bertram's *time.* 114
The Doctrine of the Christians of St. Thomas *in the East-Indies, confirming the same.* 115

CHAP. XII. The Twelfth Difference. *The Fathers assert that Christs Body is not eaten Corporally and Carnally, but only spiritually. Whereas the Rom. Church teaches a Corporal Eating of Christs Body.* 116

Berengarius's *Recantation supposes this in the most literal sense.* ibid.
Tho' this sense was opposed afterwards. 117. *Yet all Rom. agree that Christs Natural Body is taken into ours.* 118. *How long they assert it makes its stay there.* ibid. *Horrid Cases how resolved.* 119. *What the Fathers call understanding things Carnally.* 120. *That they opposed the literal and carnal eating of Christ's Body.* 121, 122, 123. *Considerations proving they did not so understand it.*
1 Consid. *They say we partake of Christs Body in Baptism, which can be only spiritually.* 125
2 Consid. *They distinguish eating Christs true Body from the Sacramental.* 126
3 Consid. *They assert, that the Fathers under the Old Test. did eat the same spiritual meat with us, because they ate it by Faith.* 127
4 Consid. *They represent Christs Body as dead, and that so it must be taken: Ergo spiritually.* 128
Two remarkable sayings of S. Austin *to prove all this.* 130

CHAP. XIII. The Thirteenth Difference. *The Fathers assert, that the Faithful only eat Christs Body and drink his Blood, not the wicked: the Ro. Church extends it to both.* 131
The Church of Rome *will have not only the wicked but bruit Creatures to eat it.* 132
The Cautions of the Mass suppose this. ibid.
The Fathers will not allow the wicked to partake of Christs Body. 133
Two remarkable Testimonies of St. Austin. 136

CHAP. XIV. The Fourteenth Difference. *The different practices and usages of the two Churches, argue their different opinions*

The Contents.

opinions about the Eucharist. 137
  Eight Instances of their differing practices given.
1 Instance. *The Ancient Church excluded Catechumens Penitents, &c. from being present at the Mysteries, enjoining all present to communicate.* ibid.
In the Ro. Ch. any may be Spectators, tho' none receive but the Priest. 139
2 Inst. *The old practice was to give the Communion in both kinds.* 140
Transubstantiation made this practice cease. 141. *New devices for security against profaning Christs Blood.* 142 *No reason why the Fathers have not been as cautious in this as the Ro. Church, but their different belief.* 143
3 Inst. *The Elevation of the Host that all may adore it, the Roman practice.* 145
This not used in the first Ages at all; when used afterwards, not for Adoration. 145, 146
4. Inst. *The Rom. Church allows not the people to receive the Sacrament with their Hands, but all is put by the Priest into their Mouths, contrary to the Ancient Practice.* 147
5 Inst. *The Anc. Church used Glass Cups for the Wine; which would be criminal now.* 148
6 Inst. *They mixed of old the Consecr. Wine with Ink, which would now be abhorr'd.* 149
7 Inst. *In the Reservation of the Eucharist: Three differences herein consider'd.*
  1 Difference. *The Anc. Church took no care to reserve what was not received in the Eucharist: but the Ro. Church reserves all.* 151, *&c.* 2 Differ. *What had been publickly received, the Anc. Church allowed liberty to reserve privately.* 156. *The present Ch. in no case allows such private reservation.* 157. 3. Differ. *They put what was so reserved to such uses of old, as the Ro. Church would think profane.* 157, 158, *&c.*
8 Inst. *The infinite sollicitous caution to prevent accidents in the administration of the Sacrament; their frights and strange expiations when they happen, all unknown, and strangers to the Ancient Church.* 160, *&c. Which is proved positively, from the continued practice of Communicating Infants, till Transubstantiation abolished it.* 165

This

The Contents.

This still a practice in the Eastern Churches; that submit not to the Roman Church. 167

CHAP. XV. The Fifteenth Difference. *About their Prayers in two particulars.* 1. *That the old Prayers in the* Canon *of the Mass, agree not with the Faith of the now Ro. Church.* 168
2. *That their New Prayers to the Sacrament have no Example in the Anc. Church.* 175

CHAP. XVI. The Sixteenth Difference. *That our ancient Saxon Church differ'd from the present Rom. Church in the Article of the corporal presence.* 182, &c.
The Saxon Easter-Sermon produc'd as a Testimony against them. 183, 184, &c.
Two Epistles of Elfric *the Abbot, declare against that Doctrine.* 187, 188.
A Remarkable Testimony also of Rabanus *Archbishop of* Mentz *alledged.* 189

CHAP. XVII. The Conclusion of the whole. *Shewing, that Heathens and Jews reproached not the Ancient Christians about the Eucharist.* 191. *Transubstantiation occasion'd new Calumnies from both.* 194. *The Jew's Conversion seems to be hopeless, whilst this is believed by them to be the common Faith of Christians.* 195. *That the Jews have better explained Christs words of Institution; agreed better with the Ancient Church in understanding the Sacrament in a figurative sense; and have confuted Transubstantiation by unanswerable Arguments, proved by Instances, from* p. 196. *to the end.*

Faults Escaped.

Page 5. line 16. marg. r. Serm. 5. p. 10. l. 7. marg. r. τετίμηκεν, p. 39. l. 11. r. supposes, p. 53. l. 2. marg. r. μελέτα, p. 68. l. 26. marg. r. Serm. 5, p. 69. l. 10. r. thou art wholly changed in the inward Man, Ibid. l. 12. marg. r. totus in interiore homine mutatus es, p. 73. l. 6. marg. r. qui, p. 98. l. 5. à fine r. ἀναζόμθυον, p. 149. l. 26. r. Paten, p. 152. l. 10. r. Evagrius, p. 171. l. 23. r. that of Abel.

CHAP.

CHAP. I.

The First Difference.

The Church of Rome *is forced to assert a continued Series of Miracles to justifie her Doctrine of Transubstantiation. But the Fathers never mention any Miracles in the Eucharist, save only the Effects of God's powerful Grace, working great Changes in us, and advancing the Elements in the use of them thereunto, without changing their Nature and Substance.*

TO give the Reader a View of what Wonders are to be believed, according to what the *Trent Council* has decreed concerning *Transubstantiation*, we need go no further than to the *Trent Catechism* [*], which tells us, there are *three most wonderful things, which the Catholick Faith without any doubting, believes and confesses are effected in this Sacrament, by the Words of Consecration.*

[*] Ad Parochos, part. 2. num. 25.

1. *That the true Body of Christ, that same Body which was born of the Virgin, and sits at the Right-hand of the Father, is contained in this Sacrament.*

2. *That no Substance of the Elements remains in it, tho' nothing may seem more strange and remote from our Senses.*

3. *What is easily collected from both, That the Accidents, which are seen with our Eyes, or are perceived by our other Senses, are without any Subject* (in which they subsist) *in a strange manner, not to be explained. So that all the Accidents of Bread and Wine may be seen, which yet inhere in no Substance, but subsist by themselves, since the Substance of the Bread and Wine are so changed into the very Body and Blood of our Lord, that the Substance of Bread and Wine cease wholly to be.*

B   But

A full View of the Doctrines and Practices

But others of the Romish Writers have made a larger and more particular Enumeration of the Miracles wrought in the Eucharist, which no Created Power can effect, but God's Omnipotency alone. I'le give them in the Words of the Jesuite *Pererius* *, who reckons these Nine distinct Miracles.

* In Joan. c. 6. Disp. 16. num. 48.

1. *The same Christ remaining in Heaven, not departing thence, and without any local mutation, is really and corporally in the Sacrament of the Eucharist.*

2. *Nor is he thus there only in one consecrated Host, but is together in all Hosts consecrated throughout the whole Earth.*

3. *Tho' the Body of Christ in the Sacrament has all its Quantity and Colour, and other sensible Qualities; yet as it is in the Sacrament, it is neither there visibly nor quantitatively* * *as to its situs, and extension unto Place.*

* Quantum ad situm, & extensionem ejus ad locum.

4. *Tho' the Body of Christ be in it self greater than a Consecrated Host, yet according to the* (Esse) *Being it has there, it is whole in that Host; nor only whole in the whole consecrated Host, but also whole in every part thereof.*

5. *If those Accidents of the Consecrated Host be corrupted, and it should happen that of them Worms or any other Animal be generated, there is a great Miracle in their Generation: For either the* Materia prima *is created anew, out of which the substantial Form of those Animals is produced, as many Divines now think; or, according to S.* Thomas, *which seems to be a greater Miracle, The Quantity that was of the Consecrated Host, supplies the place of the* Materia prima, *and in it is produced the substantial Form of those Animals which are generated from thence.*

6. *The very Conversion of Bread and Wine into the Body and Blood of Christ, which is properly called by Divines* Transubstantiation, *is a great Miracle; for such a Transmutation is found in no other thing, and is besides all the Order and Course of Nature, and can be made by no Created Power, but by God's Omnipotency alone.*

7. *The Manner by which such Transubstantiation is made, is not without a Miracle; for it is made by the Words of Consecration, pronounced rightly, and, as it ought, by a Priest. Therefore, as naturally supposing the last disposition in Matter to produce the Form of Fire, the Form of Fire is infallibly*

of the Ancient Church, relating to the Eucharist.

bly *produced in that Matter: So the Words of Consecration being pronounced by the Priest, Christ himself is infallibly in that Consecrated Host.*

8. *After Consecration, the whole Substance of Bread and Wine ceasing to be, yet their Accidents do not cease, but remain: Neither do they remain inhering in any other Subject, but* (per se existunt) *exist by themselves, which is truly besides and above the Nature of Accidents, whose* esse (*as the Schools say*) *is* inesse, *because they can neither be produced nor remain naturally without a Subject.*

9. *Lastly, Those Accidents of the Consecrated Host, tho' without the Substance of Bread and Wine, yet have the same natural Virtue which Bread and Wine had before Consecration; viz. the Virtue of nourishing, encreasing, and strengthning the Body of the Person that receives it; when yet Nutrition is made by conversion of the Substance of the Food into the Substance of the Living Creature.*

By reason of which Miracles (he says) *the Church sings thus in the Hymn for* Corpus-Christi *day.*

    Quod non capis, Quod non vides,
Animosa firmat fides, præter rerum ordinem:
      Etsi sensus deficit,
    Ad firmandum cor sincerum
      Solà fides sufficit:
Præstat fides supplementum sensuum defectui.

      That is,

What never yet was understood,
Nor ever seen by any Creature,
A confident Belief makes good,
Tho' cross to all the Laws of Nature.

Tho' Sense will not be brought t'allow it,
  A Heart sincere may be secure,
  And, waving all its Scruples, sure,
Since Faith alone's enough to do it;
  For Faith supplies the Senses want,
  And makes good Measure, where that's scant.

A full View of the Doctrines and Practices

As for the *Fathers*, they are so far from consenting to this *heap of Miracles* in the Eucharist, that we have reason to think, as to some of them, they never entred into their thoughts, nor never troubled themselves about them; and, for the most of them, tho' they are direct Consequences of Transubstantiation, yet they are opposed and contradicted by the *Fathers*, as shall be shewn in Particulars afterwards: Here it shall suffice to say in general, That the Fathers give us this as a Character of the old Hereticks, to urge God's Omnipotency to countenance and give a colour to their Figments and absurd Opinions. Thus *Gr. Nazianzen* says of the *Apollinarians*, * *That being pressed with these Reasonings, they fly to this, That to God it is possible.* And *Tertullian*, when *Praxeas* also urged God's Omnipotency, gives this excellent † Answer to him. *If we may so abruptly use this Sentence, (viz. That to God all things are easie) in our Presumptions, we may then feign any thing we please of God; as if he had done a thing, because he was able to do it. But because (God) can do all things, we are not to believe he has done that which he has not done; but we are to inquire, whether he has done it or no.*

* Ὑπὸ τούτων ἐξειργόμενοι τῶν λογισμῶν, καταφεύγουσιν ἐπὶ τὸ, Δυνατὸν εἶναι Θεῷ. Orat. 51.
† *Contr. Praxeam*, c. 10. *Si tam abruptè in præsumptionibus nostris hâc sententiâ utamur, quidvis de Deo confingere poterimus; quasi fecerit, quia facere potuerit. Non autem quia omnia potest facere, ideo credendum est illum fecisse, etiam quod non fecerit; sed an fecerit, requirendum.*

Thus *Gr. Nyssen* * asserts, *That the Will of God is the Measure of his Power.* And *Clemens of Alexandria* †, *That God who is Omnipotent, will effect nothing that is absurd.* And *Origen* ‖, *When we say, That God can do all things, we know how to understand all things, not of such things as cannot exist, and are unintelligible.*

* *Gr. Nyssen in Hexaemeron.* Μέτρον τῆς δυνάμεως τῦ Θεῦ τὸ θέλημα γίνε〈ται〉.
† *Stromat. l. 4. prope finem.* Ἄτοπα γὰρ ἃ συντελέσει ὁ Παντοκράτωρ.
‖ *L. 5. contr. Cels.* Οἴδαμεν ἀκούειν τὸ Πᾶν, οὐκ ὅτι τῶν ἀνυπάρκτων, οὐδ' ὅτι τῶν ἀδιανοήτων.

Obj. If any object, That the *Fathers* often bring in Instances of Gods miraculous Power (as St. *Ambrose* does in the *Red Sea* and the River *Jordan*, and in the miraculous Conception of our Saviour, &c.) to create Faith in Men as to the great Change that is wrought in the Eucharist.

Ans. I

of the Ancient Church, relating to the Eucharist.

Ans. I answer, True indeed: But then it is to be remembred, (what shall hereafter be more fully declared) that the Change there is not terminated upon the Substance of the Elements, nor is God's Power shewn upon them, to alter their Nature from what they were before, so as to destroy them; but it is an addition of Grace to their Nature, and an advancement of them to produce wonderful Effects upon us in the use of them. So that now the Element of Water *in Baptism* is no more a common thing, but is employed by God to wash away our Sins, to cleanse our Souls, and to regenerate and renew us: And in the *Eucharist* the Bread and Wine, which in themselves are the Food of our Bodies, are advanced to be a Means to communicate the Body and Blood of Christ to us, for the nourishing and refreshing our Souls, and to make us Partakers of the saving Effects of his Death and Passion; which are only Miracles of God's Grace. And the *Fathers* urge the forementioned Miracles *in Nature,* to assure us of these Wonders of *Divine Grace*. And this they do not only in the case of the *Eucharist*, but of *Baptism* also; where yet none assert any Conversion of the Substance of Water into any other thing. Thus S. *Ambrose* [*] : Mary *conceived by the Holy Ghost, without the intervention of any Man, as* S. *Matthew tells us*; She was found with Child of the Holy Ghost. *If then the Holy Spirit coming upon the Virgin made her to conceive, &c. we need not question but that the same Spirit coming upon the Water of Baptism, or on him that is baptized, do's produce true Regeneration.* And P. *Leo Mag.* [†] *Christ gave to the Water, what he gave to his Mother; for the Power of the most High, and the Overshadowing of the H. Spirit; which caused* Mary *to bring forth our Saviour, the same causes the Water to regenerate a Believer.* Excepting therefore these Wonders of God's Grace, the *Fathers* knew no other Miracles in the Sacraments; and these Wonders are common to both the Sacraments, and not peculiar to one of them only.

[*] *De iis qui initiantur, c. 9. ad finem.* Si ergo superveniens Spiritus S. in Virginem conceptionem operatus est, & generationis munus implevit: Non utique dubitandum est, quod superveniens in fontem, vel super eum qui baptismum consequitur, veritatem regenerationis operetur.

[†] *De Nativit. Dom. Ser.* 4. Christus dedit aquæ, quod dedit Matri: Virtus enim Altissimi & obumbratio Spiritus S quæ fecit ut Maria pareret Salvatorem, eadem facit ut regeneret unda credentem.

This

This even *Card. Cajetan* [*] was so sensible of, that he tells us, *We must not dispute concerning God's Power when we treat of Sacraments.* And again, *It is a foolish thing to assert in this Argument, whatsoever God can do.*

[* *In 3. part. q. 75. art. 1.* Non est disputandum de divina potentia, ubi de Sacramentis tractatur. *Ibid. art. 2.* Stultum est ponere in hoc argumento, quicquid Deus potest facere.]

He was not ignorant of what S. *Austin* had said long before [†], who speaking of Signs taken to signifie other things, and instancing in the Bread taken and consumed in the Sacrament, adds, *But because these things are known to men, as being made by men, they may have Honour given them for their relation to Religion; but cannot raise Astonishment, as Miracles or Wonders.* Which he could never have said, if he had believed the Wonders and Miracles of *Transubstantiation*.

[† *Lib. 3. de Trin. c. 10.* Quia hæc hominibus nota sunt, quia per homines fiunt, honorem tanquam religiosa possunt habere, stuporem tanquam mira non possunt.]

I'le conclude this Head with another Saying of his [*], which may be as well applied to the absurd Paradoxes and Miracles which the *Roman Church* advances in this Case of the *Eucharist*, as ever it was to those he there confutes about *Baptism*. *These are the Prodigies of your Opinions; these are the uncouth Mysteries of New Dogma's; these are the Paradoxes of Pelagian Hereticks, more wonderful than those of the Stoick Philosophers.——The things you say are Wonderful, the things you say are New, the things you say are False. We are amazed at your Wonders, we are cautious against your Novelties, and we confute your Falsities.*

[* *Lib. 3. cont. Julian. c. 3.* Hæc sunt sententiarum portenta vestrarum, hæc inopinata mysteria Dogmatum novorum, hæc paradoxa Pelagianorum hæreticorum mirabiliora quàm Stoicorum Philosophorum.—— Mira sunt quæ dicitis, nova sunt quæ dicitis, falsa sunt quæ dicitis. Mira stupemus, nova cavemus, falsa convincimus.]

But this Difference being more *general*, we go on to more *particular* ones.

CHAP.

CHAP. II.

The Second Difference.

The Church of Rome *differs from the Fathers, in determining what that thing is which Christ calls* MY BODY.

THE *Trent Catechism* (a), tho' it do's not determine what the word [THIS] refers to, (only telling us, that it must demonstrate the whole Substance of the thing present) yet it expresly denies, that it refers to the *Substance of Bread*; for it adds, *If the Substance of Bread remained, it seems no way possible to be said that,* THIS IS MY BODY. So *Bellarmine* confesses (b), that this Proposition, *This Bread is my Body*, must be taken figuratively, that the Bread is the Body of Christ by way of signification, or else it is plainly absurd and impossible. And he acknowledges (c), that this Proposition, *The Wine is the Lord's Blood*, teaches, that Wine is Blood by similitude and likeness. And elsewhere (d), *It cannot be a true Proposition, in which the Subject is supposed to be Bread, and the Predicate the Body of Christ; for Bread and Christ's Body are* res diversissimæ, *things most different*. And a little after, *If we might affirm* disparata de disparatis, *different things of one another, you might as well affirm and say, that something is nothing, and nothing something; that Light is Darkness, and Darkness Light; that Christ is Belial, and Belial Christ; neither do's our Faith oblige us to defend those things that evidently imply a Contradiction*.

So also *Vasquez* (e), *If the Pronoun* [THIS] *in Christ's Words pointed at the Bread, then we confess it would follow, that no Conversion could be made by virtue of these Words, because the Bread, of which it is affirmed* (sc. that it is Christ's Body) *ought to remain*.

(a) *Ad Paroch part.* 2. *n.* 37. §. *Hæc vero.* Si panis substantia remaneret, nullo modo dici videretur, Hoc est Corpus meum.
(b) *De Euchar. l.* 1. c. 1. sec. Nonus.
(c) *Ib. lib.* 2. *cap.* 9. §. *Observandum.*
(d) *Lib.* 3. *cap.* 19.
(e) *Disp.* 180. *cap.* 9. n. 9¹. Si pronomen Hoc in illis verbis demonstraret panem, fatemur etiam vere, ut nulla conversio virtute illorum fieri possit, quia panis, de quo enunciatur, manere debet.

Now that which the present *Roman Church* dare not affirm, because if it be taken properly, it is untrue, absurd,

surd, impossible, as implying a Contradiction, we shall now shew that the *Fathers* plainly affirm it, who yet could not be ignorant of this Absurdity. From whence it necessarily follows, that they took the whole words [*THIS IS MY BODY*] figuratively, as the *Protestants* do, since they cannot be taken otherwise, if Bread be affirmed to be Christ's Body, as the Romanists confess. Now that the Fathers affirmed that *Bread is Christ's Body*, is certain by these following Testimonies.

(f) *Adv. Hæres. l. 5. c. 2.* Τὸ ἀπὸ τ͂ κτίσεως ποτήριον αἷμα ἴδιον ὡμολόγησε, κ̀ τὸν ἀπὸ κτίσεως ἄρτον ἴδιον σῶμα διαβεβαιώσατο.

S. *Irenæus* (f). *Our Lord confessed the Cup which is of the Creature to be his Blood; and the Bread which is of the Creature, he confirmed it to be his Body.*

(g) *Pædag. lib. 2. c. 2.* Εὐλόγησέν γε τὸν οἶνον, εἰπὼν, Λάβετε, πίετε, τοῦτό μέ ἐςι τὸ αἷμα, αἷμα τ͂ ἀμπέλου· τὸν λόγον τὸν περὶ πολλῶν ἐκχεόμενον εἰς ἄφεσιν ἁμαρτιῶν, εὐφροσύνης ἅγιον ἠλλεγορεῖ νᾶμα.

Clement of Alexandria (g). *Our Lord blessed the Wine, saying, Take, drink, this is my Blood, the Blood of the Grape. For the Holy River of Gladness* (so he calls the Wine) *do's allegorically signifie the Word* (i. e. *the Blood of the Word*) *shed for many for the remission of Sins.*

(h) *Adv. Judæos, c. 21.* Panem corpus suum appellans.
(i) *Idem adv. Marcion. lib. 3. cap. 19.* Panem corpus suum appellans, ut & hinc eum intelligas corporis sui figuram pani dedisse, &c.

Tertullian (h). *Calling Bread his Body.* Speaking of Christ.
And against *Marcion* (i) he says the same; *Calling Bread his Body, that thou mayst know that he gave to Bread the Figure of his Body, &c.*

(k) *Lib. 4. adverf. Marc. c. 40.* Acceptum panem & distributum Discipulis, corpus suum illum fecit, Hoc est corpus meum dicendo, id est, figura corporis mei.

And in the next Book (k). *The Bread that he took and distributed to his Disciples, he made it his Body, saying, This is my Body, that is, the Figure of my Body.*

(l) *Epist. 76. ad Magnum.* Quando Dominus corpus suum panem vocat de multorum granorum adunatione congestum, &c.

S. *Cyprian* (l), *When our Lord called the Bread, which is made up of many united Grains, his Body, &c.*

(m) *Harmon. in Bibl. Patrum,* 1624. *Tom.* 7. Accepto pane, deinde vini calice, corpus esse suum ac sanguinem testatus, &c.

Tatianus Syrus (m). *Christ taking the Bread, and after that the Cup of Wine, testified that they were his Body and Blood, &c.*

Origen

Origen (n). *That Bread which our Lord confessed to be his Body.*

Eusebius (o). *Christ appointed them* (or delivered to them) *to make use of Bread for a Symbol of his Body.*

Cyril of *Jerusalem* (p). *When Christ affirms, and says of the Bread,* This is my Body, *who will dare to doubt further of it?*

S. *Jerome* (q). *Let us hear, that the Bread which our Lord brake and gave to his Disciples, is the Body of our Saviour.* Which he explains further elsewhere (r), *That as Melchisedek prefiguring him had done, when he offered Bread and Wine, so he also represented the Truth of his Body and Blood.*

(n) *Hom* 35. *in Matth*. Panis iste quem Dominus corpus suum esse fatetur.
(o) *Demonstr. Evang. lib.* 8. Ἄρτῳ δὲ χρῆσθαι συμβόλῳ τ̄ ἰδίε σώματ[ος] παρεδίδυ.
(p) *Catech. Myst̄ag.* 4. Αὐτῦ ἀποφηναμένυ κ̣ εἰπο.]θ· περὶ τ̄ ἄρ]υ, Τετό μυ ὁςὶ τὸ σῶμα, τίς τολμήσει ἀμφιβάλλειν λοιπόν;
(q) *Epist. ad Hedibiam*. Nos audiamus panem quem fregit Dominus, deditque discipulis suis, esse corpus Salvatoris, &c.
(r *Comm. in* 26. *Matt.* Quomodo in præfiguratione ejus Melchisedek ---- panem & vinum offerens fecerat, ipse quoque veritatem sui corporis & sanguinis repræsentaret.

S. *Chrysostom* (s). *What is the Bread? The Body of Christ. What do they become that receive it? The Body of Christ. Not many Bodies, but one Body.*

(s) *In* 1 *Cor. Hom.* 24. Τί γάρ ἐςιν ὁ ἄρ]Ộ ; Σῶμα Χριςῦ. Τί ϳ γίνον]αι οἱ μεταλαμβάνον]ες; Σῶμα Χριςῦ. Οὐχὶ σώμα]α πολλά, ἀλλὰ σῶμα ἕν.

S. *Austin* (t.) *What your Faith is to be instructed in, is, That the Bread is the Body of Christ, and the Cup the Blood of Christ.*

And elsewhere (u.) *Our Lord doubted not to affirm,* This is my Body, *when he gave the Sign of his Body.*

Gaudentius (x). *When our Lord reached the Consecrated Bread and Wine to his Disciples, he said thus,* This is my Body.

(t) *Serm. ad recens. baptizat.* apud Fulgentium, Bedam, &c. Quod fides vestra postulat instruenda, Panis est corpus Christi, Calix sanguis Christi.
(u) *Contr. Adimantum*, c. 12. Non dubitavit Dominus dicere, Hoc est corpus meum, cum daret signum corporis sui.
(x) *In Exod. tract.* 2. Cùm panem consecratum & vinum discipulis suis porrigeret Dominus, sic ait, Hoc est corpus meum.

Cyril of *Alexandria* (y). *Christ, when he had broken the Bread, as it is written, distributed it, saying,* This is my Body.

Theophilus Antioch. (z), or the Author under his Name upon the Gospels, speaks just S. *Cyprian's* Language. When *Jesus* said, This is my Body, *he called the Bread his Body, which is made up of many Grains,*

(y) *In Joan.* 20. 26, 27. Διαπλάσας τὸν ἄρτον, χ[α]ὶ γέγρα[π]), διεδίδυ, λέγων, Τυτο ὁςὶ τὸ σῶμα μυ, &c.
(z) *Com. in Matth.* 26.

A full View of the Doctrines and Practices

Grains, by which he would represent the People, &c.

Theodoret (a). *In the delivery of the Mysteries, he called the Bread his Body, and that which is mixed (Wine and Water in the Cup) Blood.*——And afterwards, *He honoured the visible Symbols with the appellation of his Body and Blood, &c.*

Facundus Hermian. (b). *Our Lord himself called the Blessed Bread and Cup which he delivered to the Disciples, his Body and Blood.*

Maxentius (c) speaking of the Church, that is called Christ's Body, adds, *Also the Bread which the whole Church partakes of, in memory of the Lord's Passion, is his Body.*

Isidore of Sevil (d) says, *We call this, by his Command, the Body and Blood of Christ, which being made of the Fruits of the Earth, is sanctified and made a Sacrament, by the invisible Operation of the Spirit of God.*

Bede (e). *Christ said to his Disciples,* This is my Body, &c. *because Bread strengthens the Body, and Wine produces Blood in the Flesh; This relates mystically to Christ's Body, and That to his Blood.*

The Seventh General Council at Constantinople (f), after reciting the Words of the Institution, *This is my Body,* after his taking, and blessing, and breaking it, adds, *Behold the Image of his Life-giving Body made preciously and honourably.* And afterwards, *It pleased him that the Bread of the Sacrament, being the true Figure of his natural Flesh, should be made a Divine Body, being sanctified by the coming of the Holy Ghost upon it, &c.*

Druthmarus (g). This is my Body, *that is to say, in a Sacrament*——*Because among all things that are the Food of Life, Bread and Wine serve to strengthen and refresh our Weaknesses, it is with great Reason that he would in these two things establish the Mystery of his Sacrament. For Wine both chears us and increases Blood, and therefore very fitly the Blood*

of

(a) In Dialog. 1. Ἐν δὲ γε τῷ μυστηρίῳ προσφορᾶς, σῶμα τ᾿ ἀρτον ἐκάλεσε, κὶ αἷμα τὸ κρᾶμα. Τὰ ὁρώμενα σύμβολα τῇ τοῦ σώματ[ος] κὶ αἵματ[ος] προσηγορίᾳ τιμήσας, &c.

(b) In Defens. 3. capit. lib. 9. c. ult. Ipse Dominus benedictum panem & calicem quem discipulis tradidit, corpus & sanguinem suum vocavit.

(c) Dialog. 2. c. 13. Sed & panis ille quem universa Ecclesia in memoriam Dominicæ passionis participat, corpus ejus.

(d) Originum lib. 6. cap. 19. Hoc, eo jubente, corpus Christi & sanguinem dicimus, quod dum fit ex fructibus terræ, sanctificatur & fit Sacramentum, operante invisibiliter Spiritu Dei.

(e) Comm. in Marc. 14. ——Quia panis corpus confirmat, vinum vero sanguinem operatur in carne, hic ad corpus Christi mysticè, illud refertur ad sanguinem.

(f) Extat in Conc. Nicen. 2. Art. 6. Ἰδοὺ ἂν ἡ εἰκὼν τοῦ ζωοποιοῦ σώματ[ος] αὐτῆ ἡ ἐντίμως, κὶ τιμιωδῶς προσκαλουμένη. Τὸν τῆς εὐχαριστίας ἄρτον, ὡς ἀψευδῆ εἰκόνα τῆς φυσικῆς σαρκὸς, διὰ τοῦ ἁγίου πνεύματ[ος] ὁπηροιήσεως ἁγιαζόμενον, θεῖον σῶμα εὐδόκησε γενέσθαι.

(g) Comm. in Matth. 25. Hoc est corpus meum; id est, in Sacramento——Quia inter omnes vitæ alimonias cibus panis & vinum valent ad confirmandam & recreandam nostram infirmitatem,

of the Ancient Church, relating to the Eucharist.

of Christ is figured by it; because whatsoever comes to us from him, chears us with true Joy, and increaseth all Good in us.

recte per hæc duo mysterium sui Sacramenti confirmare placuit. Vinum namque & lætificat & sanguinem auget; & idcirco non inconvenienter sanguis Christi per hoc figuratur, quoniam quicquid nobis ab ipso venit lætificat lætitiâ verâ, & auget omne bonum nostrum.

Rabanus Maurus (h) explaining the Words of Institution, says, *Because Bread strengthens the Body, therefore it is fitly called the Body of Christ; and Wine, because it produces Blood in our Flesh, is therefore referred to the Blood of Christ.*

In the *Æthiopick* Churches (i) they use this Phrase, (which the Church of *Rome* is so shy of) *This Bread is my Body.*

Bertram (k). *I am confident, no Christian doubts, but that Bread was made the Body of Christ, which he gave to his Disciples, saying,* This is my Body, &c. And he there shews, that this is made by the same change, whereby the Manna and the Water of the Rock in the Wilderness were turned into his Body and Blood.

To conclude this Head; It is plain, that there is a general Consent of Fathers on the Protestant Side in this Particular, *That the Bread and Wine are Christ's Body and Blood.* And it is the more remarkable, because they give us this Sense, when they are explaining Christ's Words, and in their Commentaries upon the Gospels where the Words of Institution are recorded.

(h) *Comm. in Matth.* 26. Quia panis confirmat corpus, ideo corpus ille Christi congruenter nuncupatur, vinum autem quia sanguinem operatur in carne, ideo ad sanguinem Christi refertur.

(i) *Ludolphi Æthiop. Hist. l. 3. c. 5 n. 56.*

(k) *De Corp & Sang. Dom. pag. 40. late Eng. & Lat. Translation.* Non putamus ullum fidelium dubitare, panem illum fuisse corpus Christi effectum, quod Discipulis donans dicit, *Hic est corpus meum, &c.*

C 2   CHAP.

CHAP. III.

The Third Difference.

The Church of Rome *believes, That Accidents in the Eucharist subsist without a Subject; but the Fathers say the contrary, That Accidents cannot subsist without a Subject, and yet never except the Eucharist.*

THe *Catechism* of the *Trent Council* * says, *That the Accidents which are either seen with our Eyes, or perceived by our other Senses, are without any Subject, by a wonderful manner, and such as cannot be explained.* They grant that we may see all the Accidents of Bread and Wine, but *that they inhere in no Substance, but sustain themselves.*——And afterwards † discourse thus: *The Species of Bread and Wine subsist in this Sacrament, without any Subject in which they are: For since the Body and Blood of Christ is truly in this Sacrament, so that no Substance of Bread and Wine remains, because those Accidents cannot be inherent in the Body and Blood of Christ, it remains, that the Accidents sustain themselves, above all Order of Nature, being upheld by nothing else besides. And this* (they say) *was the perpetual constant Doctrine of the Catholick Church.*

* *Ad Parochos, part.* 2. *de Euchar.* n. 25.

† *Ibid.* n. 44. §. *Tertium restat.*

How false this Assertion is, we shall now shew from the Testimonies of the *Fathers.*

Irenæus (a). *We cannot understand Water without Moisture, nor Fire without Heat, nor a Stone without Hardness: For these are united one to another, one cannot be separated from the other, but must always co-exist.*

Athanasius (b), (or the Author against the *Arians* in his Works) asserts, That *every Quality is in a Substance.*

Isidore Pelusiota (c) says, That *Quality cannot be without Substance.*

(a) *Lib.* 2. c. 14. Non potest intelligi aqua sine humectatione, neque ignis sine calore, neque lapis sine duritia. Unita enim sunt invicem hæc; alterum ab altero separari non potest, sed semper coexistere.
(b) *Orat.* 5 *contra Arianos.* Πᾶσα ποιότης ἐν οὐσίᾳ ἐστί.
(c) *Lib.* 2. *Epist* 72. Ποιότης (οὐσίας) μὴ ὑπαρχούσης, ἀνυπαρκτον εἶ ἡ ποιότης.

Methodius

of the Ancient Church, relating to the Eucharist.

Methodius (d). *Quality cannot be separated, as to its Subsistence, from Matter.* And a little before he says, *This is the most impossible of all things.*

S. *Basil* *. *if by your reasoning you can distinguish Figure from a Body, yet Nature admits no such Difference, but one must be understood in conjunction with the other.*

Greg. *Nazianzen* (e) proves the Holy Ghost not to be a Quality, because then it must be in a Subject. *For*, says he, *either it do's subsist by it self, or is of the same kind with those which are called Accidents, which are in another.*

This would be ill reasoning, if Transubstantiation were true; for the Holy Ghost might be a Quality, yet be in no Subject, as well as the Colour and Taste of Bread may be in the Eucharist, without Bread or any other Substance in which it is.

Gr. *Nyssen* (f) affirms, *That as that is not a Body to which Colour, and Figure, and Solidness, and Space, and Heaviness, and other Properties are wanting; so,* as he adds, *where those aforesaid do concur, they produce a Bodily Subsistence.*

S. *Austin* (g). *It is monstrous, and at the furthest distance from Truth, that what would not be at all unless it were in a Subject, yet should be able to exist when the Subject ceases to be.* This is a Saying with a witness to confute Transubstantiation, where there is the Appearance and Figure, Taste and Weight of Bread, and yet no Substance of Bread is there. Again he says (h), *Every thing that is in a Subject, and always remains, it is necessary that the Subject also should always remain.*

Again * elsewhere. *When the Subject is changed, every thing that is in the Subject is necessarily changed.* And again: *That which exists not by it self, if it be forsaken of that by which it exists, undoubtedly will not be at all.*

(d) *Apud Photium Codic.* 232. Μὴ δυνατὸν χωρίζεσθαι καθ' ὑπόστασιν ἀπὸ τῆς ὕλης ἡ ποιότης. —— Ἐστὶν ἁπάντων ἀδυνατώτ.

* *Epist.* 43. Ἀλλὰ κἂν λόγῳ διακρίνῃς τὸ σχῆμα τ σώματος, ἡ φύσις ε παραδέχεται τ διακρισιν, ἀλλὰ συνημμένως νοεῖσθαι ἕτερα τὸ ἕτερον.

(e) *Orat.* 37. Ἢ ἀφ' ἑαυτὸ ὑφεστηκότων παῖλος ἐπιδέξει, ἢ τῶν ἐν ἑτέρῳ θεωρουμένων· ὃν τὸ μὲν οὐσίαν καλοῦσιν — τὸ δὲ συμβεβηκός.

(f) *De Opificio Homin.* c. 24. Ὅτε δ' ἂν συνδράμῃ τὰ εἰρημένα, ἡ σωματικὴν ὑπόστασιν ἀπεργάζεται.

(g) *Soliloq. lib.* 2. c. 12. Monstruosum enim & à veritate alienissimum est, ut id quod non esset, nisi in ipso (sc. *subjecto*) esset, etiam, cùm ipsum non fuerit, posse esse.

(h) *Ibid. cap.* 13. Omne quod in subjecto est, si semper manet, ipsum etiam subjectum maneat semper necesse est.

* *De Immortal. Anim. cap.* 5. Mutato subjecto, omne quod in subjecto est necessariò mutari. *Et cap.* 8. Quod per se non est, si deseratur ab eo per quod est, profectò non erit.

13

Also in another place (i). *Take away Bodies from their Qualities, and there will nothing remain where (those Qualities) should be; and therefore it follows necessarily, that they will not be at all.*

Cyril of *Alexandria* (k) teaches the same copiously. He calls it Madness to affirm, That the Essence of the Son consists in Subjection to the Father. For, says he, *how can Subjection be conceived to subsist by it self, without existing in any thing else?* And afterwards: *If there be no Subject, and nothing præexists in which those things are wont to be done, how can they exist by themselves, which are understood and defined in the Order of Accidents?*

And elsewhere he says (l), *To* the *Unbegotten, is predicated of the Divine Essence, as inseparable from it; just as* Colour *is always predicated of every Body.*

And in another place (m) disputing about the Eternity of the Son, and how proceeding from the Father he is not separated from him, he instances in Accidents that are inseparable from their Subjects. *We see*, says he, *Heat inseparably proceeding from Fire; but it is the Fruit of the very Essence of Fire, proceeding inseparably from it; as also Splendor is the Fruit of Light. For Light cannot subsist without Splendor, nor Fire without Heat; For what is begotten of them, do's always adhere to such Substances.*

Again, in his Dialogues (n) of the Trinity, he asks, *Whether Black and White, if they be not in their Subjects, can subsist of themselves?* And the Answer is, *They cannot.*

Claud. Mamertus (o). *In corporeal things, the Body is the Subject, and the Colour of the Body in the Subject: In incorporeal matters, the Soul and Discipline are Instances; which are so connected, that the Body cannot be without Colour, nor the Rational Soul without Discipline—— Can we ever prove, that what is in the Subject abides, when the Subject it self perishes?* *Isidore*

(i) Epist. 57. ad Dardanum. Tolle ipsa corpora qualitatibus corporum, non erit ubi sint, & ideo necesse est ut non sint.

(k) In Joan. lib 4 cap. 1. Ὑπολαγὴ ἡ ἐν αὐτὴ καθ᾽ ἑαυτὴν πῶς ἂν ὑφιςάναι νοοῖτο, μὴ ἐνυπάρχουσα τῷ ὄντων τινί. Πῶς ἂν εἴεν αὐτὰ καθ᾽ ἑαυτὰ, κᾴτοι κτ τ τῶν συμβεβηκότων τάξιν νοεῖται τε καὶ ὁρίζεται.

(l) Thesaur. assert. 31. Τῆς οὐσίας τ Θεῦ τὸ ἀγέννητον ὡς ἀχώριςον κατηγορηθήσεται, ὥσπερ ἀεὶ κ τ παντὸς σώματος χρῶμα.

(m) Ibid. assert. 16. Ἀπὸ δὲ γε τ πυρὸς κ μεμειωμένως ὁρῶμεν τ θερμασίαν ἐκπορέχεσαι, ἀλλ᾽ ὅτι τ τε πυρὸς οὐσίας καρπὸς, &c.

Ἀεὶ γὰρ ἐξαπ... τ τοιαύτας οὐσίας τὰ ἐξ αὐτῶν πληρώματα.

(n) De Trinitate, Dial. 2. p. 451. Τω λευκότητα π χρὺ ἡ τω μελανίαν αὐταῖς τε καθ᾽ ἑαυτὰς ἀφ᾽ ὑπάρχειν οἵητ᾽ ς διδάξ; Οὐδαμῶς.

(o) De Statu Animæ, l. 3. c. 3. In rebus corporeis subjectum est corpus, & color corporis in subjecto: in incorporeis animus & disciplina, quæ ita sibi nexa sunt, ut nec sine colore corpus, nec sine disciplina rationalis sit animus—— Utrum nam probare valeamus manere quod in subjecto est, ipso intereunte subjecto?

Isidore Hispal. (p). *Quantity, Quality, and Situation, can none of 'em be without a Subject.*

Bertram (q) proves against the *Greeks*, That the Holy Ghost was not in Jesus Christ as in *his Subject*; because, says he, the Holy Ghost is not an Accident that cannot subsist without its Subject.

These Testimonies of the Fathers may suffice to shew how they differ from the *Church of Rome*, in this Point, *of Accidents being without a Subject*, which to them is so necessary a Doctrine, that Transubstantiation cannot be believed without it; and if the Fathers had believed Transubstantiation, it is incredible that they should deny this Doctrine, without so much as once excepting the Case of the Eucharist: None can imagine how their Memory and Reflection should be so short, especially when (as we have heard) they form their Arguments to prove the Eternity of the Son of God, and the Personality of the Holy Ghost, from the inseparability of Accidents from their Subject. Nay, one of them says (r), *That if God himself had Accidents, they would exist in his Substance.*

When therefore P. *Innocent* (s) asserts, That in the Eucharist *there is Colour and Taste, and Quantity and Quality, and yet nothing coloured or tasteful, nothing of which Quantity or Quality are Affections*: This is plainly to confound the Nature of all things, and to turn Accidents into Substances. So that if, for instance, the Host should fall into the Mire, and contract Dirt and Filth, this Filth sticks in nothing, or else Accidents are the Subject of it; for it is confessed on all hands, That Christ's Body cannot be soiled or made filthy. Not to insist upon the Nonsense of his Assertion, which is just as if one should talk of an Eclipse without either Sun or Moon, or of an Horses Lameness without a Leg, concerning which only Lameness can be affirmed.

(p) *Originum lib.* 2. *cap.* 26. Quantitas, qualitas, & situs, sine subjecto esse non possunt.
(q) *Contra Græc. l.* 2. *c.* 7. in *Tom.* 2. *Spicilegii D. Acherii.*

(r) *Orat.* 5. *contra Arianos, inter Athanasii Opera.*

(s) *De Myst. Missæ, l.* 4. *c.* 11. Est enim hic color & sapor & quantitas & qualitas, cùm nihil alterutro sit coloratum aut sapidum, quantum aut quale.

CHAP.

CHAP. IV.

The Fourth Difference.

The Church of Rome *has brought in the Word* SPECIES, *to signifie those* Accidents without any Subject: *But the* Fathers *never take it in this Sense.*

I Need only refer the Reader, for the first part of this Assertion, to the Thirteenth Session of the *Council of Trent, Canon* 2. *&* 3. where the Word *Species* is so used: And to what we heard before out of their *Catechism*, of *the Species of Bread and Wine subsisting without any Subject in which they are*. Every one knows this is their *Customary Word*, to express Appearances of things by, when nothing real is under them to support them.

But now we shall see this to be a strange and foreign usage of this Word, which the *Fathers* know nothing of in *their Sense* ; but instead of denoting Accidents (by the Word *Species*) which are in no Subject, they use it commonly for the *Substance*, the *Nature*, the *Matter* of a thing, the *Subject* it self that appears: Not for *Appearances without a Subject*.

S. *Ambrose* often uses this Word *Species*, but never in the Sense of the *Romanists:* For which take these Instances.

S. *Ambrose* says (*a*), *That at the Marriage* (of Cana) *our Lord being requested, did change the Substance of Water into the Species of Wine.* That is, not into the Appearance of Wine, but into real Wine that he changed it.

And in another place*, *He provided for the Marriage a more necessary Species: i. e. Wine*, more agreeable to a Marriage-Feast than *Water*.

(*a*) *Serm.* 21. Dominum rogatum ad Nuptias aquæ substantiam in vini speciem commutasse.

* *Serm.* 22. Speciem magis necessariam Nuptiis præstitit.

In

of the Ancient Church, relating to the Eucharist. 17

In another Book *(b)*, speaking of Holy Vessels which he broke for the Redemption of Captives, he says, *This Number and Order of Captives far excels the Species of Cups. i. e.* all sorts of them.

Again elsewhere *(c)*. *The Species of Iron is heavier than the Liquor of Water*: *i. e.* the Substance of Iron.

S. *Austin (d)*. *They were all baptized into Moses in the Cloud and in the Sea. If therefore the Figure of the Sea availed so much, how much will the Species of Baptism avail?*

In another place *(e)*. *To make the visible Species of Bread, many Grains are mixed together into one.*

Again *(f)*, speaking of the Bread in the Sacrament, he says, *When by Mens Hands it is brought to that visible Species* (i. e. to the Substance of Bread) *it is not sanctified so as to become so great a Sacrament, without the invisible Operation of the Spirit of God.*

So elsewhere *(g)*. *They all drank of the same spiritual Drink; they one thing, and we another; but tho' another as to the visible Species, yet as to the Spiritual Virtue signifying this same thing.* Where the *Visible Species*, it's plain, denotes *Water* to the Jews, and *Wine* to us, not the Accidents only.

And in another Tractate *(h)* to the same sense, speaking of the Jews. *Behold the Signs are varied, Faith remaining the same. To them the Rock was Christ; to us, that which is placed on the Altar is Christ: They drank the Water flowing from the Rock, for a great Sacrament of the same Christ; what we drink, the Faithful know. If you regard the* Visible Species, *it is another thing; but if the intelligible Signification, they drank the same spiritual Drink.*

And so in another Book *(i)*, speaking of things assumed to signifie matters to us, he says, *When it is assumed, sometimes it is shewn in an Angel, sometimes in that* Species *which is not what an Angel!*

(b) Officior. lib. 2. cap. 28. Hic numerus captivorum, hic ordo præstantior est quam *species poculorum.*

(c) De iis qui initiant. cap. 9. Gravior est ferri *species* quam aquarum liquor.

(d) In Joan. tract. 11. Omnes in Moyse baptizati sunt in nube & in mari Si ergo figura maris tantum valuit, *species baptismi* quantum valebit?

(e) Serm. ad Infantes. Ut sit *species visibilis* panis, multa grana in unum conspergentur.

(f) Lib. 3. de Trinit. cap. 4. Quod cùm per manus hominum ad illam *visibilem speciem* perducitur, non sanctificatur ut sit tam magnum Sacramentum, nisi operante invisibiliter Spiritu Dei, &c.

(g) In Joan. tract. 26. Omnes eundem spiritualem potum biberunt; aliud illi, aliud nos; sed *specie visibili* quidem, tamen hoc idem significante virtute spirituali.

(h) Tract. 45. in Joan. Videte, fide manente, signa variata. Ibi petra Christus, nobis Christus quod in altari Dei ponitur; & illi pro magno Sacramento ejusdem Christi biberunt aquam profluentem de petra, nos quid bibamus norunt fideles: si *speciem visibilem* intendas, aliud est, si intelligibilem significationem, eundem potum spiritualem biberunt.

(i) Lib. 3. de Trinit. cap. 10. Cùm autem suscipitur, aliquando in Angelo demonstratur, aliquando in ea *Specie*

D

quæ non est quod Angelus, quamvis per Angelum disposita ministretur.

(k) *In Exod. tract. 2.* Rectè etiam vini *specie* tum sanguis ejus exprimitur, quia cùm ipse in Evangelio dicit, *Ego sum Vitis vera*, satis declarat sanguinem suum esse omne vinum quod in figura passionis ejus offertur.

(l) *In Psal.* 104. Succurrit, non solum eis *speciem* frumenti, sed & vini & olei administrans.

(m) *Lib. 2. Operis Paschal.*

gel is, tho' *it is ordered and disposed by an Angel's Ministry*. And his next Instance of such things is, *ipsum Corpus*, a Body it self.

So Gaudentius (k). *Also by the Species of Wine his Blood is then rightly expressed; for when he says in the Gospel,* I am the true Vine, *he fully declares, That all the Wine that is offered for a Figure of his Passion, is his Blood.*

Arnobius jun. (l) *Our Lord succours them, not only by affording them the* Species *of Corn, but also of Wine and Oyl.* Where the Word *Species*, to be sure, relates to the Substance and the thing it self, not to the Accidents of Corn, and Wine, and Oyl.

Sedulius (m) speaking of the Offerings of the Wise Men that came to Christ, says,

Ipsæ etiam ut possent Species *ostendere Christum;*
Aurea nascenti fuderunt munera Regi,
Thura dedere Deo, Myrrham tribuere Sepulchro.

That is,

They point to Christ even by the Gifts they bring;
Gold they present unto him as a King,
Incense as God, Myrrh for his Burying.

The things they present are, you see, his *Species*.

(n) *Lib. 1. de Gub. Dei. p.21. Edit. Baluz.* Adde medicatas aquas vel datas vel immutatas, *Speciem* servantes, *Naturam* relinquentes.

(o) *De Rebus Eccles. cap. 16.* Corporis & sanguinis sui Sacramenta panis & vini substantia Discipulis tradidit—— Nihil ergo congruentiùs *his Speciebus* ad significandam capitis & membrorum unitatem, potuit inveniri.

Salvian's words are plain (n). *Add,* says he, *those healed Waters either given or changed, which preserved their* Species, *and relinquish'd their* Nature. Here *Species* is taken for the Substance remaining, and *Nature* for the Qualities of the Water that were changed.

Walafridus Strabo (o) shewing how Christ in the Last Supper delivered to his Disciples *the Sacraments of his Body and Blood in the Substance of Bread and Wine*, adds, *Nothing more agreeable than these Species could be found, to signifie the Unity of the Head and Members.* Rupertus

of the Ancient Church, relating to the Eucharist.

Rupertus Abbas (p). *Nothing of the Sacrifice enters into him that has no Faith; besides the* visible Species *of Bread and Wine.* No one ever thought, but that the Wicked partak'd as much of the outward Elements as the Faithful; but he says a little before, That when the Priest distributes the Sacrifice to be eaten by the Faithful, *the Bread and Wine is consumed and passes away.* Therefore by the *visible Species* he means the *Bread and Wine,* which the Wicked only partake of.

(p) *De Offic. lib.* 2. *cap.* 9. In illum in quo fides non est, præter visibiles Species panis & vini, nihil de Sacrificio pervenit.

It has been largely proved by *Salmasius* (q), That in the Civil Law and the *Theodosian Code,* the word *Species* is used for *things* there spoke of; as, *Species annonariæ,* for all sorts of Corn; *Species publicæ,* for Goods brought to the several Ports; *Species vini, frumenti, olei,* for Wine, Corn, and Oyl; and not the Accidents of them.

(q) *Simplicius Verinus de Transubst.* p. 230, &c.

It is not to be expected that any thing should be cited out of Greek Authors, whose this Word is not; and yet it is observable, That even among them the Word εἶδος, that answers to the Latin Word *Species,* is taken in the Sense of the *Latin Fathers,* and not in that of the present Church of Rome. To give only two Instances.

The Author under the Name of *Dionysius* the *Areopagite* (r), speaking of Christ's Incarnation, uses the Phrase of *Assuming our Species*; which his *Scoliast, Maximus,* thus explains; εἰδοποιούμενον, that is, *When he had assumed our Species or Nature*; not meerly an Appearance of our Nature.

(r) *Eccles. Hierarch. cap.* 3. Ἐξ ἡμῶν εἰδοποιούμενον.

Τοῦτ᾽ ἐστὶ τὸ καθ᾽ ἡμᾶς εἶδος, ἤγουν τὴν φύσιν λαβόντα.

Theophylact (s). *Because,* says he, *Bread and Wine are things familiar to us, and we could not endure, but should abhor to see Flesh and Blood set before us; therefore Christ, the Lover of Men, condescending to us, preserves the* Species *of Bread and Wine,* (that is, the Elements themselves) *but he changes them into the Virtue of his Flesh and Blood.*

(s) *In Marc.* 14. Τὸ μὲν εἶδος ἄρτου καὶ οἴνου φυλάττει, εἰς δύναμιν δὲ σαρκὸς καὶ αἵματος μεταστοιχειοῖ.

To conclude this Head, *Bertram* (t), following the Sense of the Ancients, uses these Phrases indifferently; *according to the visible Species,* and *according to the visible Creature,* or *according to the Substance of the Creatures.* Which are Modes of

(t) *Lib. de Corp. & Sang. Christi.* Secundùm Speciem visibilem, secundùm visibilem Creaturam, & secundùm creaturarum substantiam.

Speech which the present *Roman Church* will not allow of in the Eucharist: For they tell us their plain Belief, what *Species* are, in a *Sequence* on *Corpus-Christi* day, which explains it thus:

> Sub diversis Speciebus,
> Signis tantum, & non rebus,
> Latent res eximiæ.

Admirable things lie hid under the different *Species, which are only Signs, and not Things.*

CHAP. V.

The Fifth Difference.

The Fathers differ from the Roman Church, in their Assertions about the Nature and Properties of Bodies.

EVery one knows what the Sentiments of the *Roman Church* are herein, and what they must necessarily assert believing Transubstantiation: That a Body that is Organical, as Christ's is, may be invisible and impalpable; commensurate to no Space: That it may possess one Place, so as to be in more at the same time: That it may be entire in one Part and in one Point, and may exist after the manner of a Spirit.

See *Bellarmine de Eucharist. lib.* 1. *cap.* 2. *reg.* 3. *& lib.* 3. *c.* 7.

(a) *Sess.* 13. *cap.* 3. Totus Christus & integer sub specie panis, & sub qualibet ejus speciei parte existit.

The *Council of Trent* says (a), *Whole and entire Christ is in the Eucharist, under the Species of Bread, and under every part of the Species of Bread.*

I shall now show, That the Fathers assert quite contrary to all these Maxims of the *Roman Church*, giving us a different Account of the Nature and Properties of Bodies; and in the Particulars forenamed, make no difference betwixt Christ's Body and ours.

I *Assertion.*

1 *Assertion.* They assert, That every Organiz'd Body, not excepting the Body of Christ, is visible and palpable.

Tertullian (b). I *understand nothing by the Body of a Man, &c. but what is seen and felt.*
Methodius (c). God is Incorporeal, and therefore Invisible.
Eustathius Antioch. (d). If he was Invisible, without doubt he was Incorporeal. Speaking of *Samuel* raised at *Endor.*
Didymus (e). If a thing be Invisible, it presently follows, that it is Incorporeal.
Greg. Nazianzen (f). If God be a Body, what kind of Body, and how?——an impalpable and invisible one?——This is not the Nature of Bodies. And he cries out, (Τῆς ἐξουσίας;) *O strange Licence!* to imagine thus.
Greg. Nyssen (g) says, *That is not a Body, that wants Colour, Figure, Solidness, Space, Weight, and the rest of its Attributes.*
S. *Austin (h)*, speaking of our Lord, says, *He is always with us by his Divinity; but if he were not corporally absent from us, we should always carnally see his Body.*
Ephrem Antioch. (i). No Man of any sense can say, That the Nature of that which is palpable and impalpable, of that which is visible and that which is invisible, is the same. Altho' the *Valentinians* in *Eulogius (k)* say, *That the Nature of that which is visible, and that which is invisible, is the same.* And so did the *Manichees.* Ibid.
Vigilius (l), speaking of the Lord's Body, says, *It is necessary the Flesh, as well as the Word, if they be of one Nature, be uncreated and invisible—— But it is impossible that Flesh should be the Subject of such Conditions.*
Titus Bostrensis (m). Every thing that falls under our Sight, seeing it is a Body, is in Nature opposite

(b) *De Resurrect. c.* 35. Corpus hominis non aliud intelligam quam— quod videtur, quod tenetur.
(c) *Apud Photium Cod.* 234. Ἀσώματ⊙ ὢν, διὸ κὶ ἀόρατ⊙.
(d) *De Engastrimytho.* Εἰ ωδὴ ἀόρατ⊙ ἰιῶ, ἀναμφιλόγως ἀσώματ⊙ ἰιῶ.
(e) *Caten. in Joan.* 4. 24. Ἀκολυθεῖ ἢ εὐθέως τῷ ἀοράτῳ τὸ ἀσώματον.
(f) *Orat.* 34. Πότερον σῶμα, κὶ πῶς; — τὸ ἀναφὲς κὶ ἀόρατον; — ἢ γδ αὐτὴ φύσις σωμάτων.
(g) *De Opific. hom. cap.* 24. Οὐκ ὅτι σῶμα, ᾧ τὸ χρῶμα, κὶ τὸ σχῆμα, κὶ ἡ ἀντιτυπία, κὶ ἡ διάςασις, τὸ βάρ⊙, κὶ τὰ λειπὰ τ̃ ἰδιωμάτων ἐ πάρεςιν.ὅλον.
(h) *De Verb. Domini, Ser.* 60. Semper quidem Divinitate nobiscum est, sed nisi corporaliter abiret à nobis, semper ejus corpus carnaliter videremus.
(i) *Apud Photium, Cod.* 229. Οὐδεὶς ἂν εἰπεῖν δῶτα) ἰεν ἔχων, ὡς ἡ αὐτὴ φύσις ψηλαφητῆ κὶ ἀψηλαφητῆτε, κὶ ὁρατῆ κὶ ἀοράτε.
(k) Ibid. Cod. 230. Ἡμεῖς τ̃ ὁρατὰ κὶ ἀόρατα μίαν ἒ τ̃ φύσιν ςὰ ὃν.
(l) *Lib.* 4. *contr. Eutych.* Necesse erit ut caro, sicut & verbum, si unius cum eo est naturæ, increata sit & invisibilis, *&c.* Sed carnem his conditionibus subjacere impossibile est.
(m) *Contr. Manich. l.* 2. Omne quod sub aspectum cadit, cum

A full View of the Doctrines and Practices

fit corpus, natura oppofitum eft inafpectabili & incorporeo, &c.

(*n*) *De Fide Orth. lib.* 1. *c.* 4. Πῶς σῶμα—ἀναφὲς καὶ ἀόρατον;

(*o*) *Moral. lib.* 14. *c.* 33. Erit itaque fubtilis, quia & incorruptibilis; erit palpabilis, quia non amittet effentiam veracis naturæ.

(*p*) *Tom.* 3. *Concil. Labbe. p.* 817. Οὐ γὰρ ἐν ἀλλότριον αὐτῷ τὸ ἑνωθὲν αὐτῷ σῶμα, ὃ καὶ ἁπτὸν ἡ φαμὲν, καὶ ὁρατόν.

pofite to that which is invifible and incorporeal.

Damafcen (*n*). How can that be a Body, &c, which is impalpable and invifible?

Gregory the Great (*o*), fpeaking of a glorified Body, fays, *It will therefore be a fubtile Body, becaufe it will be incorruptible; and it will be palpable, becaufe it fhall not lofe the Effence of its true Nature.*

Cyril of *Alex.* in his Explication of the third *Anathema* of the *Eph. fme Council* (*p*). *He is not a Stranger to that Body which he has united to himfelf, which we fay is capable to be felt, and to be feen.*

In fine, The Church of *Rome* makes Chrift's Body invifible tho' it be prefent; the Fathers never make it fo, but becaufe it is abfent.

(*q*) *Caten. in Joan.* 16. 10. Ἀναληφθεῖσα εἰς οὐρανὸς, καὶ ἀφανὴ γεγονότα τοῖς ἀνθρώποις.

(*r*) *Homil.* 53. Si fit præfens, non creditur, fed videtur; cùm autem abfens fuerit, non videtur, fed creditur, dum timetur.

So *Ammonius* (*q*). *He was taken up into Heaven, and became invifible unto Men.*

And the *Author imperfecti Operis in Matthæum* (*r*). *When he is prefent, he is not believed, but feen; but when he is abfent, he is not feen, but believed, whilft he is feared.*

2 *Affertion.* The *Fathers* affert, That every Body is *quantum*, and as it has Quantity, poffeffes a Place or Space, and is commenfurate to it: That a Body cannot be in more than one Place, nor be intire in one Part, nor exift after the manner of a Spirit. All which are falfe, if Tranfubftantiation be true.

(*s*) *Contr. Eunom. l.* 2. Οὐσίαν τριχῇ διαστατήν.

(*t*) *De Opific. Hom. c.* 24. Ἐξαιρεῖ δὲ τέτων εἰ ὑφαιρεθείη τὸ ὑποκείμενον, πᾶς ὁ τῷ σώματος συνδιαλύει λόγος.

(*u*) *Lib.* 4. *de Orig. Anim. c.* 11. Corpus eft quicquid majori-

S. *Bafil* (*s*) makes that to be *incorporeal*, whofe Effence cannot be divided three ways (or has not three Dimenfions).

Greg. Nyffen (*t*) fays, That if you *take Quantity, Solidnefs, and other Properties from the Subject, the whole Nature of the Body is diffolved,* &c.

S. *Auftin* fays fo much upon this Argument, that I muft only mention fome few Teftimonies out of a great Heap that might be collected.

He fays (*u*), *A Body is that which confifts of greater*

of the Ancient Church, relating to the Eucharist. 23

greater and lesser Parts, containing greater and lesser Spaces of Place.

Again (x), distinguishing Bodies into gross and subtile ones, he says, Both are Bodies, *none of which can be every where whole and entire, because by reason of its innumerable Parts, it must have another Place elsewhere; and how great or little soever a Body is, it possesses a Space of Place, and so fills that Place, that it is not whole in any part of it.* And a little after: *God is not thus said to fill the World, in the same manner as Water or Air do's, so that by a lesser part of himself he fills a lesser part of the World, and by a greater part a greater.* So that, according to him, none but God and Spirits can have such an Existence.

So in his Epistle to *Euodius* (y). *There is no Body so little, which after its manner do's not possess a local Space; neither is it whole every where in that Space it possesses, but less in a part of that Space than in the whole.*

eo quod occupat ubique sit totum, sed minus

And again (z). *There can be no Body, either Celestial or Terrestrial, Aereal or Aqueous, that is not less in a part than in the whole; nor can it any ways have another part in the place of this part, but must have one here, another elsewhere, throughout the several distant and divided Spaces of Place, &c.*

aliud alibi per spatia quælibet locorum

But the Nature of the Soul is not found to be extended to the Spaces of Place by any Bulkiness.

He says the same in another Epistle (a), and adds, *Take away local Extent from Bodies, and they will be no where; and if they are no where, they will not be at all.*

In the same Epistle, speaking of the Divine Persons, that nothing hinders why they may not be every where *simul*, argues thus:

bus & minoribus suis partibus, majora & minora spatia locorum continentibus, constat.

(x) *Epist.* 3. *ad Volusian.* Quorum nullum potest esse ubique totum, quoniam per innumerabiles partes aliud alibi habeat necesse est: & quantumcumque sit corpus seu quantulumcunque corpusculum loci occupet spatium, eundemque locum sic impleat, ut in nulla ejus parte sit totum.—— Non sic Deus dicitur implere mundum, velut aqua, velut aer, ut minore sui parte minorem mundi impleat partem, & majore majorem. Novit ubique totus esse, & nullo contineri loco.

(y) *Epist.* 101. Nullum esse quantulumcunque corpusculum, quod non pro suo modo loci occupet spatium; nec in sit in parte quàm in toto.

(z) *Contra Epist. Manichæi, cap.* 16. Nec omnino potest esse aliquod corpus sive cœleste, sive terrestre, sive aereum, sive humidum, quod non minus sit in parte quàm in toto, neque ullo modo possit in loco hujus partis habere aliam partem, sed aliud hic, distantia & dividua, &c.

Animæ vero natura nullo modo invenitur locorum spatiis aliquâ mole distendi.

(a) *Ad Dardanum Epist.* 57. Spatia locorum tolle corporibus, nusquam erunt; & quia nusquam erunt, nec erunt.

For

Non enim corpora funt, quorum amplior fit in tribus quam in fingulis magnitudo, nec loca fuis molibus tenent, ut diftantibus fpatiis fimul effe non poffint.

Ubique totum præfentem effe non dubites tanquam Deum, & in eodem Templo Dei effe tanquam inhabitantem Deum, & in loco aliquo cœli, propter veri corporis modum.

(b) *De Civit. Dei, l. 22. c. 29.* Deus totus in cœlo eft, totus in terra, non alternis temporibus fed utrumque fimul, quod nulla natura corporalis poteft.

(c) *Epift. 6. ad Italicam.* Omne quod oculis corporeis confpici poteft, in loco aliquo fit neceffe eft, neque ubique fit totum, fed minore fui parte minorem locum occupet, & majore majorem.

(d) *Cont. Epift. Manichæi, c. 16.* Aeris partes fuos quoque implent locos, nec fieri poteft ut aer quo impletur hæc domus, fimul fecum in eadem domo habere poffit etiam illum aerem quem vicini habent.

(e) *De Immort. Animæ, c. 16.* Moles omnis quæ occupat locum, non eft in fingulis fuis partibus tota, fed in omnibus, quare aliqua pars ejus alibi eft, & alibi alia.

(f) *Tract. 31. in Joan.* Homo fecundùm corpus in loco eft, & de loco migrat, & cum ad alium locum venerit, in eo loco unde venit non eft: Deus autem implet omnia & ubique totus eft, non fecundùm fpatia tenetur locis. Erat tamen Chriftus fecundùm vifibilem carnem in terra, fecundùm invifibilem Majeftatem in cœlo & in terra.

For they are not Bodies, whofe Magnitude is larger in Three than in One; nor do they poffefs Places by their Bulk, fo as not to be able to be in diftant Spaces at once, (which is the Nature, he acknowledges, of Bodies).

He fays alfo of Chrift, *We are not to doubt that whole Chrift is every where prefent as God, and is in the fame Temple of God, as an inhabiting Deity, and in one certain place of Heaven, by reafon of the Nature of his true Body.*

Elfewhere (b). *God is whole in Heaven, and whole on Earth; not at different times fucceffively, but both together; which no Corporeal Nature is capable of.*

Again (c). *Every thing that may be feen with Bodily Eyes, muft of neceffity be in fome Place; nor can it be whole every where, but muft poffefs a leffer Place by a leffer Part of it felf, and a greater Place by a greater Part.*

He repeats almoft the fame, in his Twenty eighth Epiftle.

And in another Book (d). *The Parts of Air alfo fill their Places; nor is it poffible that the Air that fills this Houfe, fhould together with it have the Air that is in a Neighbour's Houfe.*

Again elfewhere (e). *Every thing of Bulk that poffeffes a Place, is not whole in its fingle Parts, but whole in all its Parts; therefore one Part of it is in this Place, and another in another.*

In another Tract (f). *Man, as to his Body, is in a Place, and paffes from one Place to another; and when he comes to another Place, he is no longer in that Place from whence he came. But God fills all things, and is every where whole, not confined to Places according to Spaces. Chrift, according to his vifible Flefh, was on Earth; according to his invifible Majefty, in Heaven and Earth.*

To

of the Ancient Church, relating to the Eucharist.

To name but two or three more out of S. *Austin*, who seems to speak Prophetically (g). *Having said thus, he ascended into Heaven, and would precaution us against those that he foretold would arise in succeeding Ages, and say, Lo here is Christ, or lo there ; whom he warned us not to believe: And we shall have no Excuse if we shall believe them against this so clear, open, and manifest* Voice *of our Pastor, &c.*

(g) *De Unit. Eccles. c.* 10. His dictis mox ascendit in cœlum, præmunire voluit aures nostras adversus eos, qui procedentibus temporibus exsurrecturos esse prædixerat, & dicturos, Ecce hic Christus, ecce illic. Quibus nec crederemus admonuit. Nec ulla nobis excusatio est, si crediderimus

contra vocem Pastoris nostri tam claram, tam apertam, tam manifestam, &c.

And in his Book against *Faustus*(h), he says, That Christ, *according to his Corporal Presence, cannot be at the same time in the Sun, and in the Moon, and on the Cross.*

(h) *Lib.* 20. *cap.* 11. Secundùm præsentiam corporalem simul & in Sole, & in Luna, & in Cruce esse non posset.

Lastly, in another Tract (i). *Our Lord is above, yet also Truth the Lord is here: For the Body of our Lord in which he arose, must be in one Place ; his Truth is diffused every where.*

(i) *Tract.* 30. *in Joan.* Sursum est Dominus, sed etiam hic est veritas Dominus. Corpus enim Domini in quo resurrexit uno loco esse oportet

(the Printed Copies absurdly read potest) veritas ejus ubique diffusa est.

Neither do the rest of the *Fathers* differ from his Doctrine, but give their full Consent to it.

Anastasius Nicænus (k). *It is impossible to imagine a Body without a Place, and other things without which it cannot be, &c.*

(k) *In Collect. adv. Severianos in Bibl. Patr. Tom.* 4. Impossibile est cogitare corpus sine loco, & sine aliis extra quæ esse non potest, &c.

Didymus Alexandr. (l) proves the Holy Ghost to be God, because he is in more Places than one. *The Holy Ghost himself, if he were one of the Creatures, would at least have a circumscribed* (or bounded) *Substance, as all things have that are made------ But the Holy Spirit, seeing he is in more than one, has not a bounded Substance.* And afterwards he says, That the Holy Ghost was present with the Apostles, tho' dispersed to the ends of the Earth; and adds, *The Power of Angels is altogether a Stranger to this.*

(l) *De Spiritu S. lib.* 1. Ipse Spiritus S. si unus de creaturis esset, saltem circumscriptam haberet substantiam, sicut universæ quæ factæ sunt— Spiritus autem, cùm in pluribus sit, non habet substantiam circumscriptam.

Angelica virtus ab hoc prorsus aliena.

Theodoret (m) makes this a Consequence from Angels being of a determinate Substance, *That then they require a Place to be in : For only the Divinity,*

(m) *In Genes.* qu. 3. Τόπῳ ἄρα περιστόν ꞏ μόνον γὰρ τὸ Θεῖον, ὡς ἀσώματον ἔφαμεν οὐκ ἐν τόπῳ.

vinity, says he, *as being undetermined, is not in a Place.* And elsewhere (n), speaking of Christ's Body after the Resurrection, he says, *Still it is a Body, having its former Circumscription.*

Cyril of Alexandria (o), disputing against those that thought the *Son* was begotten of the Substance of the *Father,* by a division of his Substance, says, *If the Divine Nature did admit of Section and Division, then you conceive of it as a Body ; and if so, then it must be in a Place and in Magnitude and Quantity ; and if endued with Quantity, it could not avoid being circumscribed.*

Fulgentius (p) also. *That which is circumscribed by any End (or Bound), must be contained in a Place, or in Time.*

And again (q), speaking of Christ's Body: *If the Body of Christ be a true one, it must be contained in a Place.*

S. Greg. Nazianzen (r) makes it *impossible for one Body to be in divers.*

So do's Damascen (s) make it impossible that one Body should pass thro' another, unless there be τέμνον καὶ τεμνόμενον, *that which divides, and that which is divided.*

Claud. Mamertus (t). *Nothing illocal is corporeal: every thing illocal is also incorporeal.*

And again (u). *It is plain, that no Body can be touched wholly together, nor can the least Whole you can imagine, be in one Place,* (that is, in one Point.) And he instances in a Grain of Poppy, or the least part of it, *That it has not its lower Parts there where it has its upper Parts, nor its right-hand Parts there where its left-hand Parts are, nor its Parts before there where it has its Parts behind.*

S. Hilary (x) speaking of Christ as God, says, *He is a Spirit penetrating and containing all things. For according to us he is not corporeal, so that when he is present in one Place, he should be absent from another, &c.*

(n) Dialog. 2. Σῶμα ἢ ὅμως ὅτι, ἣ περιγραφὴν ἔχων σεσαρκωμένον.

(o) De S. Trinit. Dial. 2.

Εἰ ἢ τοῦτο, καὶ ἐν τόπῳ πάντως που, καὶ ἐν μεγέθει, καὶ ποσῷ, καὶ ἐτειδὴ πέπωται, μὴ φυγεῖν περιγραφήν.

(p) Ad Trasimund. lib. 2. c. 7. Quod aliquo circumscribitur fine, necesse est ut loco teneatur aut tempore.

(q) Ib. c. 18. Si verum est corpus Christi, loco utique oportet contineri. (*The printed Copies read* potest contineri, *without Sense.*)

(r) Σῶμα ἐν σώμασιν ὅτι, ὅπερ ἀδύνατον. Orat. 34.

(s) De Fide Orth. l. 1. c. 4.

(t) De Statu Animæ, l. 2. c. 3. Nihil illocale corporeum: omne illocale incorporeum quoque est.

(u) Ibid. lib. 1. c. 18. Hinc patet omne corpus totum simul tangi non posse, nec in uno loco esse quamlibet minimum totum posse. —— Illic non habet interiora sua ubi habet superiora sua, nec illic dextra ubi sinistra, nec anteriora illic ubi posteriora.

(x) In Psal. 124. Spiritus namque est omnia penetrans & continens. Non enim secundum nos corporalis est, ut cum alicubi adsit, absit aliunde, &c.

of the Ancient Church, relating to the Eucharist.   27

And elsewhere (*y*). *A Man, or any thing like him, when he is in a Place any where, cannot then be elsewhere; because that which is there, is contained where it is; and he that is placed any where, his Nature is uncapable to be every where.*

So also *Nazianzen* (*z*). *A Vessel of the capacity of one Measure, will not contain two Measures; nor the Place that will hold one Body, can receive two or more Bodies into it.*

Again (*a*) a little after. *This is the Nature of Intellectual Beings, that incorporeally and indivisibly they mingle with one another, and with Bodies.*

And elsewhere (*b*) he proves the Deity of the Holy Ghost, because *he penetrates all intellectual, pure, and most subtile Spirits* (as the Angels, and also Apostles and Prophets) *at the same time, when they are not in the same places, but dispersed severally*; which shews, that the Holy Spirit is uncircumscribed.

S. *Basil* uses the same Argument (*c*) to prove the same. *Every one of the other Powers we believe to be in a circumscribed Place; for the Angel that was present to* Cornelius, *was not in the same place that he was in when he was present to* Philip; *nor the Angel that talked with* Zacharias *at the Atar, did at the same time fulfil his Station in Heaven. But the Spirit, we believe, could at the same time act both in* Abaccuk, *and in* Daniel *when he was in* Babylon, *&c. For the Spirit of the Lord filled the Universe.* Which is an ill Argument, if Christ's Body could be in more Places at the same time.

Arnobius (*d*) disputing against the Heathens, who said that their Gods did inhabit their Statues, whom yet they believed to be finite and bounded, urges them thus. *The Gods that inhabit in Statues, are they single Gods that are in single Statues whole, or divided into several parts? For one God* (finite as theirs were) *cannot be in many Statues at the same time, nor again exist divided into Parts, by being cut asunder. For let us suppose that*

(*y*) Lib. 8 de Trinitate. Homo, aut aliquid ei simile, cùm alicubi erit, tum alibi non erit; quia illud quod est illic continetur ubi fuerit, infirma ad id natura ejus, ut ubique sit, qui insistens alicubi sit.

(*z*) Orat. 51. Ἀγγεῖον μεδίμναῖον ἀ χωρήσει διμέδιμνον, οὐδὲ σώμαῖΘ ἑνὸς τόπΘ δύο ἢ πλείω σώματα.

(*a*) Paulo post. Τοιαύτη ẞ ἡ τῶν νοητῶν φύσις, ἀσωμάτως κỳ ἀχωρίςως κỳ ἀλλήλοις, κỳ σώμασι μίγνυται.

(*b*) Orat. 37. Διὰ πάντων χωρῶν πνευμάτων νοερῶν, καθαρῶν, λεπτοτάτων — κτ ταυτὸν κỳ ἐκ ἐν τοῖς αὐτοῖς τόποις, ἄλλων ẞ ἀλλαχῆ νενεμημένων, ᾧ δηλοῦται τὸ ἀπεείγραπ]ον.

(*c*) De Spir. S. cap. 14. Ἄλλων ἑκάςη δυνάμεων ἐν περιγραπῷ τόπῳ τυγχάνειν πεπιςευ), &c.

Πνεῦμα ẞ Κυρίκ πεπλήρωκε τ̀ οἰκουμλύω.

(*d*) Lib. 6. contra Gentes. In simulachris Dii habitant, singulini in singulis toti, an partiliter atque in membra divisi? Nam neque unus Deus in compluribus potis est uno tempore inesse simulachris, neque rursus in partes sectione interveniente divisus. Constituamus enim decem millia simulachrorum to-

E 2

that there are ten thousand Statues of Vulcan *all the World over : can one at one time be in all those ten thousand Statues ? I think not. If you ask, Why so ? Even because those things that are of a particular and singular Nature, cannot be made many, retaining the entireness of their simplicity.*

Again : ———*If this be supposed, that one Deity can dwell in them all at one time, then you must either say of every God, that he can divide himself from himself, so as to be the same, and another too, not separated by any difference, but that he shall be the very same, and yet another ; which because Nature refuses and rejects, you must say and confess, That there are innumerable* Vulcans, *if we will suppose him to be and to dwell in all his Statues ; or else that he is in none of them, because Nature prohibits his division among many.* All this would be very ill Reasoning, if he believed that which the *Church of Rome* does, That all this which he disputes against, is done in the Eucharist.

S. Ambrose (*e*). *Since every Creature is bounded within certain Limits of its Nature, &c. how dare any one call the Holy Ghost a Creature, who has not a limited and determined Virtue ? For he is always in all things, and in all places, which is the Property of the Divinity, and of Supreme Rule.*

And afterwards mentioning that place of the Psalmist, *Whither shall I go from thy Spirit ?* he adds, *Of what Angel do's the Scripture say thus ? of what Principality ? of what Power ? What Angel's Virtue do we find diffused among many ?*——— *Who can doubt then that to be Divine, that is at once infused into more, and is not seen ; and that to be Corporeal, which is seen of every one, and held by them ?*

Tertullian (*f*) also proves the Deity of Christ, by his Presence in every place. *If Christ be only Man, how is he every where present with those that call upon him ? seeing this is not the Nature of Man, but of God, to be present in every place.*

Author.

---

to esse in orbe *Vulcani :* nunquid esse ut dixi, decem omnibus in millibus potis est unus uno in tempore? Non opinor. Quâ causâ? Quia quæ sunt privata singulariaque naturâ multa fieri nequeunt, simplicitatis suæ integritate servata — Si hoc fuerit sumptum, posse unum in omnibus eodem tempore permanere, aut Deorum unusquisque dicendus ita ipsum semet ab ipso se dividere, ut & ipse sit & alter, non aliquo discrimine separatus, sed & ipse idem & alius; quod quoniam recusat & respuit aspernaturque natura, aut innumeros dicendum est confitendumq; esse *Vulcanos,* si in cunctis volumus eum degere atque inesse simulachris, aut erit in nullo, quia esse divisus natura prohibetur in plurimis.

(*e*) *Lib. de Spir. S. c.* 7. Cùm omnis creatura certis suæ naturæ sit circumscripta limitibus, &c. quomodo quis audeat creaturam appellare Spiritum S. qui non habeat circumscriptam determinatamq; virtutem? quia & in omnibus & ubique semper est, quod utique Divinitatis & Dominationis est proprium.

———De quo hoc Angelo Scriptura dicit? de qua Dominatione? de qua Potestate? Cujus invenimus Angeli virtutem per plurimos esse diffusam?——— Quis ergo dubitet quin divinum sit, quod infunditur simul pluribus nec videtur; corporeum autem quod videtur à singulis & tenetur?

(*f*) *Lib. de Trinitate.* Si homo tantummodo Christus, quomodo adest ubique invocaturis? cùm hæc non hominis natura est sed Dei, ut adesse in omni loco possit.

of the Ancient Church, relating to the Eucharist.

Author Quæst. ad Antioch. *(g)* denies that Angels can be present in many places at once, and adds, *That it's God's Property only to be found in two places, and in the whole World at the same moment of time.*

(g) Quæst. 26. Μόνε τ̃ Θεῖ ὅξιν ἐν δυσὶ τόποις, κὴ ἐν ὅλῳ τῷ κόσμῳ ἐν αὐτῇ τῇ ῥοπῇ ἐνεῖσκως.

In consequence of this Doctrine of theirs about Bodies, the Fathers in the last place assert,

3 *Assertion.* That is it impossible for one to dwell in himself, or to partake of, and have ones own Body in himself; because whatsoever contains, must be greater than that which is contained in it; and there would be a Penetration of Dimensions, which they deny.

Cyril of Alex. (h) lays it down as a Rule, that *Nothing can partake of it self.*

And elsewhere (i). *Seeing nothing can partake of it self, but this is with relation to another, it is altogether necessary to affirm, That that which partakes should be different in nature from that which is partaked of.*

And again (k) he says, *That to partake of ones self, is absurd so much as to imagine it.*

S. *Chrysostom* (l) says, *He that dwells in the Tabernacle, and the Tabernacle it self, are not the same; but one thing dwells in another thing; for nothing dwells in it self.*

Gelasius Cæsarien. (m). *The Word was made Flesh, not being it self changed, but dwelling in us. The Tabernacle is one thing, and the Word is another; the Temple is one thing, and God that dwells in it another.*

See also the like Saying in *Methodius*, cited by *Photius* his *Bibliotheca. Cod.* 234. *pag.* 920. *ult. Edit.*

In a word, the Fathers oppose all Penetration of Dimensions in Bodies, and say (n), *That it is impossible for one Body to penetrate another Body.*

(h) De Trin. Dialog. 6. Μέτοχον ἑαυτῶ παντελῶς ἐδέν.

(i) Ibid. Dial. 5. & 7. Ἐπειδὴ ἑαυτῶ μὲν ἐκ ἄν τι μετάλχοι ποτὲ, πᾶσι δ' ἄν αὐτὸ τῇ πρὸς ἕτερον χέσι, τὸ μέτοχον τ̃ μετεχομένε, πάντα πῶς ἀνάγκη κὴ ἑτεροφυὲς ἐπ̃ λέγειν.

(k) Idem in Joan. lib. 2. c. 1. Μόνον ἐννοεῖν ἀπίθανον.

(l) Hom. 10. in Joan. citat. à Theodoret. Dial. 2. Ἀλλ' ἕτερον ἐν ἑτέρῳ σκηνοῖ —— ἐδὲν γὸ ἐν ἑαυτῷ κατοικεῖ.

(m) Citat. à Theodoret. Dial. 1. Ἐν ἡμῖν σκηνώσας· ἕτερον σκηνὴ, κὴ ἕτερον ὁ λόγος· ἕτερον ὁ ναὸς, κὴ ἕτερον ὁ ἐνοικῶν αὐτῷ Θεὸς.

(n) Author. Libr. cui tit. Celebres Opiniones de Anima, c. 10. Σῶμα γὸ διὰ σώματος χωρῆσαι ἀδύνατον.

And

30   *A full View of the Doctrines and Practices*

(o) *Ibid. cap. ult.* Sic dici poſſet in milii grano cœlum contineri.

And the same Author says (o), That if this were possible, *you might then say, That Heaven it self might be contained in a Grain of Millet.*

The Fathers argue against *Marcion*, upon this Rule, That *whatsoever contains another thing, is greater than that which is contained in it.*

(p) *Hæref.* 42. *fec.* 7. Τὸ περιεκτικὸν μεῖζον τε περιεχομένε.
(q) *Contr. Marcion. l.* 1. c. 15.
(r) *Adv. Hær. l.* 2. c. 1.
(s) *De Vita Mosis.*

So do's *Epiphanius* (p). So do's *Tertullian* (q). *Irenæus* (r) has the same Rule, and laughs at *Marcion*'s God upon that account.

Greg. Nyſſen (s) proves that the Deity has no Bounds, by this Argument, *That otherwise what contains would be greater than the Deity contained therein.*

(t) *Ad Autolycum, l.* 2. Μεῖζον γὰρ δεῖ τὸ χωροῦν τῶ χωρυμένω.

Theophylus Antioch. (t) says, *This is the Property of the Almighty and True God, not only to be every where, but to inspect and hear all things. Neither is he contained in a Place, for else the containing Place would be greater than himself; for that which contains, is greater than that which is contained in it.*

(u) *De Fide ad Petr. c.* 3. Unaquæque res ita permanet, ficut à Deo accepit ut effet, alia quidem fic, alia autem fic. Neque enim fic datum eſt corporibus ut fint, ficut fpiritus acceperunt, &c.

I will conclude this Chapter with the remarkable Words of *Fulgentius* (u). *Every thing so remains, as it has received of God that it should be, one in this manner, and another on that. For it is not given to Bodies to exist after such a manner as is granted unto Spirits,* &c.

CHAP.

CHAP. VI.

The Sixth Difference.

The Church of Rome *(suitably to the strange Doctrine it teaches about Christ's Body and Blood) teaches us not to believe the Report our Senses make, That the Substance of Bread and Wine remain in the Sacrament; but to pass a contrary Judgment to what they inform us herein. But the Fathers teach the contrary, That we may securely relie upon the Evidence of our Senses, as to any Body, even as to the true Body of Christ.*

THat the *Church of Rome* would not have us in this Matter to attend to the Evidence of Sense, is needless to prove, since nothing is more common than to hear them call upon us to distrust them, and to believe against their Report. Thus the *Trent Catechism* * teaches us to believe, *That no Substance of the Elements remains in the Eucharist,* tho' nothing seems more strange and remote from our Senses than this. And again †, *We so receive the Body and Blood of Christ, that yet we cannot perceive by our Senses that it is truly so.*

As for the *Fathers,* they are Strangers to this Doctrine, nor did they betray the Christian Cause in this manner, by taking away all Certainty from the Testimony of our Senses. They, on the contrary, proved the Truth of Christ's Body against the *Valentinians,* the *Marcionites,* and other Hereticks, by this Argument, which the Church of *Rome* rejects; they made their Appeals frequently (as S. *John* had done before them) to what had been seen with Mens Eyes, to what their Ears had heard, and their Hands had handled, without any suspicion of their being deceived.

Thus *Irenæus* (a). *This meets with them who say, That Christ suffered only seemingly. For if he did not truly suffer, no Thanks are due to him, when there was no Passion. And when he shall begin truly to suffer, he will seem a Seducer, when he exhorts*

* *Ad Paroch. de Euchar. part.* 2. num. 25. ——Nullam Elementorum substantiam remanere, quamvis nihil magis à sensibus alienum & remotum videri possit.
† *Ib.* n. 46. Corpus & sanguinem Domini ita sumimus, ut tamen quod verè sit, sensibus percipi non potest.

(a) Lib. 3. adv. Heref. c. 20. Hoc autem & illis occurrit, qui dicunt eum putativè passum: Si enim non verè passus est, nulla gratia ei, cùm nulla fuerit passio. Et nos cùm incipiemus verè pati, seducens videbitur, adhortans nos vapulare & alteram præbere maxillam, si ipse illud non prior in veritate passus est. Et quemadmodum illos seduxit, ut videretur ipse hoc quod non erat, & nos seducit adhortans perferre ea quæ ipse non pertulit.

exhorts us to suffer Stripes, and to turn the other Cheek, if he first did not suffer this in truth. And as he seduced them, in seeming to be that which he was not; so he seduces us, whilst he exhorts us to suffer the things which he did not suffer.

(b) Id. lib. 5. cap. 1. citante Theodoreto, Dial. 2. Οὐ γὰ δοκήσει ταῦτα, ἀλλ' ἐν ὑποςάσει ἀληθείας ἐγένετο· εἰ ἢ μὴ ὢν ἄνθρωπ@ ἐφαίνετο ἄνθρωπ@, ἔτε ὁ κ͞ς ἐπ' ἀληθείας ἔμεινε πνεῦμα Θεῦ, ἐπεὶ ἀόρατον τὸ πνεῦμα, ἔτε ἀλήθεια τις κ͞υ ἐν αὐτῷ· ἃ γὰ κ͞υ ἐκεῖνα ἄφ' ἐφαίνετο.

Again (b). These things were not done seemingly only, but in reality of truth; for if he appeared to be a Man when he was not so, he neither did remain the Spirit of God, which he truly was, since a Spirit is invisible, nor was there any Truth in him; for he was not that which he appeared to be. He thought it, you see, absurdity enough to say, That Christ appeared what he was not. But what absurdity can this be to them that say, it is constantly so in the Sacrament, where that appears so and so, which is not so, as the Bread and Wine, according to them, do's?

Again (c). As Christ therefore rose again in the Substance of our Flesh, and shewed to his Disciples the Print of the Nails and the Opening of his Side, and these are Indications of his Flesh which arose from the Dead; so also, he says, he will raise us up by his Power.

(c) Id. lib. 5. cap. 7. Quomodo igitur Christus in carnis substantia resurrexit & ostendit discipulis figuram clavorum & apertionem lateris; hæc autem sunt indicia carnis ejus quæ surrexit à mortuis; sic & nos, inquit, suscitabit per virtutem suam.

(d) De carne Christi, c. 5. Maluit, crede, nasci, quam aliqua ex parte mentiri, & quidem in semetipsum; ut carnem gestaret sine ossibus duram, sine musculis solidam, sine sanguine cruentam, sine tunica vestitam, sine fame esurientem, sine dentibus edentem, sine lingua loquentem, ut phantasma auribus fuerit sermo ejus per imaginem vocis.

Ecce fallit & decipit & circumvenit omnium oculos, omnium

Tertullian also argues thus against Marcion (d). Believe it, he chose rather to be born (which Marcion thought absurd) than in any respect to lie, and that against himself; so as to carry Flesh about him hard without Bones, solid without Muscles, bloody without Blood, cloathed without a Garment, craving Food without Hunger, eating without Teeth, speaking without a Tongue, so that his Speech was a Phantasm to Mens Ears by the Image only of a Voice. Then he instances in Christ's shewing his Hands and Feet to his Disciples after his Resurrection: Behold, says he, it is I my self; for a Spirit has not Flesh and Bones. But, as he goes on, according to Marcion's Interpretation, Behold, he cozens, and deceives, and circumvents

all

of the Ancient Church, relating to the Eucharist.

all Mens Eyes, all Mens Senses, all their Approaches and Touches. Thou therefore shouldst not have brought down Christ from Heaven, but from some Society of Juglers, &c.

Again (e). *Now when the Flesh of Christ is found to be a Falsity, it follows also, That all the things done by the Flesh of Christ, are falsly acted; such as his meeting Persons, his touching them, his Conversation, and even his Miracles themselves, &c.* que virtutes. Ibid. *An credam ei de interiore substantiæ, qui sit de exteriore frustratus? Quomodo verax habebitur in occulto, qui fallax repertus in aperto?*

And when *Marcion* had instanced in the Appearances of Angels to *Abraham* and to *Lot*, like Men, meeting with them, and eating, and doing that they were commanded, *Tertullian* answers (f), *Know that this is not granted neither, that those Angels had only seeming Flesh, but of a true, solid, humane Substance.*

He adds afterwards (g), *It suffices me to define that, which is agreeable to God, viz. the truth of that thing, which he has made the Object of three Senses that testifie it, viz. Sight, Touch, and Hearing.*

And again (h), *Thou now honourest thy God with the Title of Fallaciousness, if he knew himself to be another thing, than what he made Men to believe he was.*

And in his next Book against *Marcion* (i). *The Argument of the Woman that was a Sinner belongs to this, to prove that when she kissed our Lord's Feet, watred them with her Tears, wiped them with her Hairs, and anointed them, she then handled the Truth of a solid Body, and not an empty Phantôme.*

Again, in the last Chapter (k). *Why do's he offer to their inspection his Hands and his Feet, which are Members consisting of Bones, if he had no Bones? Why did he add,* and know that it is I my self, *to wit, whom they had known before to have had a Body?*

(e) Idem. adv. Marcion. l. 3. c. 8. Jam nunc cùm mendacium deprehenditur Christi caro; sequitur ut & omnia quæ per carnem Christi gesta sunt, mendacio gesta sunt, congressus, contactus, convictus, ipsæ quoque virtutes.

sensus, omnium accessus & contactus. Ergo jam Christum non de cœlo deferre debueras, sed de aliquo circulatorio cœtu, &c.

(f) Ibid. c 9. Scito, nec illud concedi tibi, ut putativa fuerit in Angelis caro, sed veræ & solidæ substantiæ humanæ.

(g) Ibid. c. 10. Sufficit mihi hoc definire, quod Deo congruit, veritatem scilicet illius rei, quam tribus testibus sensibus objecit, visui, tactui, auditui.

(h) Ibid. c.11. Jam Deum tuum honoras fallaciæ titulo, si aliud se esse sciebat, quam quod homines fecerat opinari.

(i) Lib. 4. c. 18. Illius peccatricis feminæ argumentum eò pertinebit, ut cùm pedes Domini osculis figeret, lacrymis inundaret, crinibus detergeret, unguento perduceret, solidi corporis veritatem, non phantasma inane tractaverit.

(k) Ibid. c. 43. Cur autem inspectui eorum manus & pedes suos offert, quæ membra ex ossibus constant, si ossa non habebat? Cur adjecit, & scitote quod ego sum, quem scilicet corporeum retro noverant?

F   May

May not we ask, agreeably to this Reasoning of *Tertullian*, Why do's Chrift offer to our fight the Accidents of Bread and Wine, if there be no Bread and Wine remaining in the Euchariſt; eſpecially when what we ſee, we knew to be Bread and Wine before?

But the moſt remarkable Teſtimony of *Tertullian*'s is in his Book *de Anima* (*l*), where on ſet purpoſe he oppoſes the *Academicks*, that would not have Men give credit to their Senſes. He urges againſt them, *That there is no Abuſe of the Senſes but has a Cauſe of it; and if thoſe Cauſes deceive the Senſes, and our Opinions by them, the Fallacy is not to be charged upon our Senſes, that follow thoſe Cauſes; nor upon our Opinions, that are directed by our Senſes, which follow thoſe Cauſes.*

—— And afterwards he cries out, O *thou malapert Academy, what doſt thou do?* (in charging Deceit upon the Senſes) *Thou overturneſt the whole State of Life, thou diſturbeſt all the Order of Nature, thou blindeſt the Providence of God himſelf, who* (according to thee) *has ſet lying and deceitful Senſes as Lords over all his Works, for to underſtand, inhabit, diſpenſe, and enjoy them, &c.*

—— *It is no ways lawful and fit to call thoſe Senſes in queſtion, leſt we ſhould doubt of their Credit even in Chriſt himſelf; leſt it ſhould be ſaid, that he falſly ſaw Satan thrown down from Heaven, or falſly heard his Fathers Voice teſtifying concerning him, or was deceived when he touched* Peter's *Wives Mother, or perceived afterwards a different Scent of the Ointment which he accepted for his Burial, and afterwards a different Taſte of the Wine which he conſecrated in memory of his Blood.*

—— *Neither was Nature abuſed in his Apoſtles. Faithful was their Sight and Hearing in the Mount; faithful and true was the Taſte of that Wine which was Water before, at the Marriage in* Galilee; *faithful was* Thomas's *Touch, who thereupon believed.*

(*l*) *De Anima, cap.* 17.

Nulla ſenſuum fruſtratio cauſâ caret, quod ſi cauſæ fallunt ſenſus, & per ſenſus opiniones, jam nec in ſenſibus conſtituenda fallacia eſt, qui cauſas ſequuntur, nec in opinionibus qui ſenſibus diriguntur ſequentibus cauſas.—— Quid agis, Academia procaciſſima? Totum vitæ ſtatum evertis, omnem naturæ ordinem turbas, ipſius Dei providentiam excœcas, qui cunctis operibus ſuis intelligendis, incolendis, diſpenſandis, fruendiſque fallaces & mendaces Dominos præfecerit ſenſus, &c.

—— Non licet, non licet nobis in dubium ſenſus iſtos devocare, ne & in Chriſto de fide eorum deliberetur; nè fortè dicatur, quod falſo Satanam proſpectarit de cœlo præcipitatum; aut falſo vocem Patris audierit de ipſo teſtificatam; aut deceptus ſit cùm Petri ſocrum tetigit, aut alium poſteà unguenti ſpiritum ſenſerit, quod in ſepulturam ſuam accepravit; alium poſteà vini ſaporem, quod in ſanguinis ſui memoriam conſecravit. —— Atqui nè in Apoſtolis quidem ejus ludificata natura eſt. Fidelis fuit & viſus & auditus in monte; fidelis & guſtus vini illius, licet aquæ ante, in nuptiis Galilææ; fidelis & tactus exinde creduli Thomæ.

Recite

Recite John's *Testimony*: *That which we have seen*, says he, *which we have heard, which we have seen with our Eyes, and our Hands have handled of the Word of Life. This is all a false Testification, if the Nature of the Sense of our Eyes, and Ears, and Hands is a Lie and a Cheat.*

And in the next Chapter (m). *The Understanding seems to use Sense as a Leader, an Author, and principal Foundation; neither can Truths be laid hold of without it.*

S. *Austin* teaches the same (n) Doctrine. *Our Eyes do not deceive us, for they can only report to the Mind how they are affected.*——*If one thinks that an Oar is broken in the Water, and when it is taken out of the Water made whole again, he has not a Bad Reporter, but he is an ill Judge. For the Eye, according to its Nature, neither could nor ought to perceive it otherwise while in the Water; For if the Air is a different* Medium *from Water, it must perceive it one ways in the Air, and another ways in Water. Therefore the Eye sees rightly; for it was made only to see: But the Mind judges amiss, &c.*

So also S. *Hillary* (o). *He takes away their foolish Rashness, who contend that our Lord was seen in the Flesh in a deceitful and false Body; that the Father feigning Truth, shewed him in the habit of false Flesh,* (as the Romanists make Christ's Body to be shewn *in habitu falsi panis*) *not remembring what was said after his Resurrection to the Apostles that thought they saw a Spirit;* Why are ye troubled, &c. Behold my Hands and my Feet, that it is I my self; for a Spirit has not Flesh and Bones, as ye see me have.

(m) Cap. 18. Videtur intellectus duce uti sensu, & auctore & principali fundamento, nec sine illo veritates posse contingi.

(n) *De vera Relig.* cap. 33. Ne ipsi quidem oculi fallunt; non enim renunciare possunt animo nisi affectionem suam.——Si quis remum frangi in aqua opinatur, & cum inde aufertur integrari, non habet malum internuncium, sed malus est judex. Nam ille pro natura sua non potuit aliter in aqua sentire, nec aliter debuit. Si enim aliud est aer, aliud aqua, justum est ut aliter in aere, aliter in aqua sentiatur. Quare oculus recte videt; ad hoc enim factus est ut tantum videat: sed animus perverse judicat, &c.

(o) *In Psal.* 137. Tollit stultissimam eorum temeritatem, qui frustrato falsoque corpore Dominum in carne visum esse contendunt; ut eum Pater ementita veritate in habitu falsae carnis ostenderit; non recordantes post resurrectionem corporis spiritum se videre credentibus Apostolis dictum esse, *Quid conturbati, &c. videte manus & pedes meos, quoniam ipse ego sum, palpate & videte, quoniam spiritus carnem & ossa non habet, sicut me videtis habere.*

Epiphanius (p) is very large in arguing the Truth of Christ's Body, from what was sensibly done to his Body; and if he argues truly, then what is sensibly done to the Bread in the Eucharist, proves the Truth of Bread remaining, and not only the Appearance of it.

(p) *Haeres.* 42.

He asks *Marcion* (q), *How could he be taken and crucified, if, according to thy saying, he could not be handled?* ——*For thou canst not define him to be a Phantôme, whom thou confesseft to fall under the Touch.*

Again (r) he argues, That Chrift had a true Body, becaufe he went into the Pharifee's Houfe and fat down. *That which fits down, is a bulky Body.*

And when the Woman wafhed his Feet with her Tears, he adds, *Not the Feet of a Phantôme.* And kiffed them, *perceiving his Body by her Touch.* And, *What Feet did fhe kifs, but the Feet made up of Flefh and Bones, and other Parts?*

So again (s), the Woman that touched Chrift and was healed, *fhe did not touch Air, but fomething Humane that might be touched.*

Again (t). *An Imaginary thing, or Wind, or a Spirit or Phantôme, admits neither of Burial nor a Refurrection.* But why may not a Phantôme as well be buried and raifed, as Accidents be broken and diftributed, when no Bread remains?

Again, he obferves (u) from that of his kneeling down and praying, That all this was done ἐν ἀληθείᾳ, becaufe his Difciples faw him, *and he was found to his Difciples under their Touch.*

So alfo concerning Chrift's Crucifixion, he obferves (s), That the piercing his Hands and Feet with Nails, and handling of them to do it, could not be δόκησις καὶ φάντασμα, *an imagination or fhew.* But if the *Church of Rome* fay true, he is out; for it is only δόκησις and a Phantôme, when I chew and faften my Teeth in the Hoft, there being no Subftance that I bite.

He afterwards (y) challenges *Marcion* from that Expreffion, *He was known in breaking of Bread. How,* fays he, *was this breaking of Bread performed? was it by a Phantôme, or from a Body* (z) *bulky, and really acting it?*

Here

of the Ancient Church, relating to the Eucharist.   37

Here I may well observe, That if the very breaking of Bread, argues a true Body that did perform that thing; how much more forcible is our Question to the *Romanists*, What means the mention of Bread broken in the Eucharist, (as Christ is said to break Bread) if nothing be broken at all but only in shew and appearance?

Epiphanius also elsewhere (*a*) says, when Christ shewed to them *Moses* and *Elias* in the Mount, *He did not present an Image or a Phantôme, as intending to deceive his Apostles; but shew'd what they were really.*

(*a*) *Hæres.* 64. *sec.* 36. Οὐκ εἰδωλον ἢ φαντασμα τοῖς Ἀποστολοις ἐνδολομεν[ο]ς ἀπαθαν, ἀλλ' ὁ ἦσαν ἀψευδῶς.

Athanasius (*b*) says, *Christ did both eat Meat, and permitted his Body to be touched by his Disciples, that not only their Eyes, but also their Fingers might be brought in for Witnesses of the Truth; so removing all suspicion of a Phantôme or Ghostly Appearance.*

(*b*) *Orat.* 2. *de Ascen. Christi.*

Λύσας τ̄ φαντασίας τ̄ ὑποψίαν.

S. *Chrysostome* (*c*) brings in Christ saying thus. *It is not my way to mock or abuse mine with a false appearance. If the Sight is afraid of a vain Image, the Hands and Fingers may find out the Truth of my Body. Perhaps some Mist may deceive the Eyes; but a corporal Touch owns a Body.*

(*c*) *De Resurrect. Hom.* 9. *Lat. Paris.* 1588. *Tom.* 3. *pag.* 775. Non est meum meos ludificare phantasmate; vanam imaginem visus si timet, veritatem corporis manus & digitus exploret. Potest fortasse aliqua oculos caligo decipere, palpatio corporalis verum corpus agnoscat.

Also elsewhere (*d*), speaking of Seeing and Hearing, he says, *By these Senses we learn all things exactly, and seem Teachers worthy of credit, concerning such things which we receive by our Sight or Hearing, seeing we neither feign, nor speak falsly.*

(*d*) *Hom.* 29. *in Joan.* Διὰ τῆς αἰσθήσεων τούτων ἡμεῖς πάντα μανθάνομεν ἀκριβῶς, ἢ ἀξιόπιστοι δοκῶμεν εἶ διδάσκαλοι, ὑπὲρ τῶν ἢ ὄψει προλαβουμεν, ἢ ἀκοῇ ἐξάμεθον.

But lest any one should pretend, that the Eucharist is a Mystery, and that in such things our Senses may impose on us, and deceive us, it is very remarkable how this Father distinguishes betwixt them.

He tells us (*e*) wherein *Deception* do's consist, viz. *when a thing do's not appear to be what it is, but appears to be what it is not.* But he makes a Mystery to be another thing (*f*), viz. *when we see not what we believe, but see one thing, and believe another thing: For this,* says he, *is the Nature of our Mysteries.*

S. *Austin*

(*e*) *Hom.* 13. *in Ep. ad Ephes.* Ὅταν τι δεῖ μὴ φαίνηται, ἀλλ' ὅπερ μὴ δεῖ δείκνυται.

(*f*) *Hom.* 7. *in* 1 *ad Cor.* Μυστήριον καλεῖται, ὅτι οὐχ ἅπερ ὁρῶμεν πιστεύομεν, ἀλλ' ἕτερα ὁρῶμεν ᾗ ἕτερα πιστεύομεν· τοιαύτη γὰρ ἡ τῶν μυστηρίων ἡμῶν φύσις, &c.

S. *Auſtin* (g) makes the concurrent Teſtimony of Senſe, eſpecially that of Feeling, to give ſufficient aſſurance to us. Thus he ſays. *There is no cauſe to doubt of Chriſt's Reſurrection, whoſe preſence the Eye do's own, the Hand handles, and the Fingers examine.* ——*If we perhaps ſhould ſay, That* Thomas *his Eyes were deceived, yet we cannot ſay ſo of his Hands; for in clearing the Reſurrection, doubt may be made of the Sight, but no doubt can be made of Feeling.*

Again elſewhere (h). *Who but Devils, that are Friends to Cozenage, could perſuade them, that Chriſt deceived Men, when he ſuffered, when he died, and when he ſhewed his Scars?*

Again (i). *This, which is like Magick, ye are ſaid to aſſert, That Chriſt's Paſſion and Death was only in appearance, and in a deceitful Shadow; ſo that he ſeemed to die, when he did not die. Whence it follows, that you muſt aſſert alſo his Reſurrection to be in ſhew, imaginary, and fallacious. For he cannot be truly raiſed, who did not truly die: And if ſo, then he ſhewed falſe Scars to his doubting Diſciples; neither did* Thomas *cry out,* My Lord and my God, *becauſe he was confirmed in the Truth, but becauſe he was deceived by a Cheat.*

Suitably to which, he aſſerts in another place (k), *If the Body of Chriſt was a Phantôme, Chriſt deceived us; and if he deceive us, he is not the Truth. But Chriſt is the Truth; therefore the Body of Chriſt was not a Phantaſtical Body.*

(g) *Serm. de Temp.* 161. Cujus præſentiam agnoſcat oculus, attrectet manus, digitus perſcrutetur. ——Si fortè diceremus Thomæ oculos fuiſſe deceptos, at non poſſemus dicere manus fruſtratas; in reſurrectionis enim manifeſtatione de aſpectu ambigi poteſt, de tactu non poteſt dubitari.

(h) *Contra Fauſtum*, l. 14. c. 10. Qui niſi Dæmones, quibus amica fallacia eſt, iſtis perſuaderent, Quod Chriſtus fallaciter paſſus, fallaciter mortuus ſit, fallaciter cicatrices oſtenderit?

(i) *Ibid. l.* 29. *c.* 2. Illud eſt quod Magiæ ſimile dicimini aſſerere, quod paſſionem mortemque ejus ſpecie tenus factam & fallaciter dicitis adumbratam, ut mori videretur, qui non moriebatur. Ex quo fit, ut ejus quoque reſurrectionem umbraticam, imaginariam fallacemque dicatis: Neque enim ejus, qui non verè mortuus eſt, vera eſſe reſurrectio poteſt: ita fit, ut & cicatrices diſcipulis dubitantibus falſas oſtenderit, nec Thomas veritate confirmatus, ſed fallacia deceptus clamaret, *Dominus meus, & Deus meus, &c.*

(k) Lib. 83. *Quæſtion. Quæſt.* 14. Si phantaſma fuit corpus Chriſti, fefellit Chriſtus: & ſi fallit, veritas non eſt. Eſt autem veritas Chriſtus; non igitur phantaſma fuit corpus ejus.

Now againſt all theſe plain Teſtimonies, I know only one Objection can be made, which we are to conſider, *viz.*

Objection. *That ſome of the Fathers call upon us not to believe our Senſes, nor to regard their Information; and that particularly they do ſo in the Caſe of the Euchariſt.*

To this Objection, I ſhall give theſe ſatisfactory Anſwers.

Anſ. 1.

of the Ancient Church, relating to the Eucharist.

Ans. 1. *It is certain, that the Fathers appeal to our Senses even in the matter of the Eucharist.* We have seen Instances before, particularly in *Tertullian*; to which let me add one remarkable Testimony out of S. *Austin* (*l*). *This which you see upon God's Altar, you were shewn last night; but you have not yet heard what it is, what it meaneth, and of how great a Thing it is a Sacrament. That which you see, is Bread and the Cup; thus much your own Eyes inform you, &c.* He appeals to their Eyes, you see, as to the Elements before them, and suppose, that when they tell them there is Bread and a Cup, they were not deceived. But then he informs them of that which their Senses could not be judge of, because not an Object of them, which was understood by the Bread and the Cup, as we shall hear afterwards.

(*l*) *Serm. ad recen. Baptizat. apud Fulgentium, Bedam, &c.* Hoc quod videtis in altari Dei etiam transacta nocte vidistis: sed quid esset, quid sibi vellet, quam magnæ rei Sacramentum contineret nondum audistis. Quod ergo videtis, panis est & calix, quod vobis etiam oculi vestri renunciant, &c.

Ans. 2. *The Fathers call upon Men not to regard the Information of their Senses, in matters wherein yet none questions the truth and certainty of their Information.* Therefore this is no Argument to question the Truth of what our Senses inform us of in the Eucharist, because they would not have us to regard them.

Thus *Cyril* of *Jerusalem* (*m*), speaking of holy Chrism. *Take heed you do not think,* says he, *this to be meer simple Ointment.* Sense indeed reaches no further than that; but then comparing Chrism with the Eucharist, (which is not to be look'd upon as common Bread after Consecration) he adds, *We are to look upon this* Holy Ointment *not as bare and common Ointment, after Consecration; but as the Grace of Christ, &c.*

(*m*) *Catech. Mystag.* 3. Ὅρα μὴ ὑπονοήσῃς ἐκεῖνο τὸ μύρον ψιλὸν εἶ).

Καὶ τὸ ἅγιον τοῦτο μύρον ὐκ ἔτι ψιλόν, ὐδὲ κοινὸν μεθ᾽ ἐπίκλησιν, ἀλλὰ Χριστοῦ χάρισμα, &c.

So also he says of Baptism (*n*), *Come not to the Font as to simple and meer Water, but to the Spiritual Grace that is given together with the Water.* And a litle after, *Being,* says he, *about to descend into the Water, do not attend to the simpleness of the Water.* And yet, for all this, he never intended to deny it to be true Water.

(*n*) *Idem Catech. Illum.* 3. Μὴ ὡς ὕδατι λιτῷ πρόσελθε τῷ λύτρῳ, ἀλλὰ τῇ μετὰ τοῦ ὕδατος διδομένῃ πνευματικῇ χάριτι. Μὴ τῷ ψιλῷ τοῦ ὕδατος πρόσεχε, &c.

Gelasius Cyzic. (*o*). *We are not to consider our Baptism with sensitive, but with Intellectual Eyes.* Or,

(*o*) *Diatypos.* c. 4. Τὸ βάπτισμα ἡμῶν ὐ τοῖς αἰσθητοῖς ὀφθαλμοῖς καταονοητέον, ἀλλὰ τοῖς νοεροῖς.

(p) Serm. 2. in Append. Sermon. 40. à Sirmondo Editor. Non debetis aquas illas oculis æstimare, sed mente.

(q) De his qui initiantur, c. 3. Quod vidisti aquas utique, sed non solas, Levitas illic ministrantes, summum Sacerdotem interrogantem & consecrantem. Primo omnium docuit te Apostolus, *non ea contemplanda nobis quæ videntur, sed quæ non videntur, &c.* Non ergo solis corporis tui oculis credas. Magis videtur quod non videtur, quia istud temporale, illud æternum aspicitur, quod oculis non comprehenditur, animo autem & mente cernitur.

(r) In Joan. Hom. 24. Πειθώμεθα τοίνυν τῇ ἀποφάσει τ̑ Θεῦ· ὄψεως γδ ὄψις πολλαχῦ κỳ σφάλλεδ, ἐκείνω δ̓ ἀμηχανὸν διαπεσεῖν.

(s) Hom. 89. in Matth. Τὰ ῥήματα αὐτῦ τ̑ ὄψεως ἡμῶν πιςότερα. Ἐι γδ κỳ τὸ φαινόμβμον ἐκ ὅςι Χρις⊖, ἀλλ' ἐν τύτῳ τῷ σχήματι αὐτὸς λαμβάνεὶ κỳ προσαιτεῖ.

(t) De Doctr. Christ. l. 2. c. 1. De signis differens, hoc dico, ne quis in eis attendat quod sunt,

Or, as S. *Austin* says (*p*), *You ought not to make an Estimate of those Waters with your Eyes, but with your Mind.*

Thus also S. *Ambrose* (*q*), speaking of Baptism. *As to what thou hast seen, to wit, the Waters, and not those alone, but Levites there ministring, and the Bishop asking Questions and Consecrating: First of all, the Apostle has taught thee, That we are not to look upon the things that are seen, but on the things that are not seen, &c. Do not therefore only believe thy bodily Eyes: That is rather seen, which is not seen; because that is Temporal, this is Eternal, which is not comprehended by our Eyes, but is seen by our Mind and Understanding.*

S. *Chrysostom* (*r*), speaking also of Baptism, thus breaks out. *Let us believe God's Affirmation, for this is more faithful than our Sight; for our Sight often is deceived, that is impossible to fall to the Ground.*

It is so frequent an Expression of S. *Chrysostome, That God's Word is more to be credited than our Eyes,* that he applies it not only to the Sacraments, but even to the Case of Alms-giving: For thus he says(*s*); *Let us be so affected when we give Alms to the Poor, as if we gave them to Christ himself: For his Words are more sure than our Sight. Therefore when thou seest a poor Man, remember the Words whereby Christ signified, that he himself is fed. For tho' what is seen is not Christ, yet under this shape he receives thy Alms, and asks it.*

Ans. 3. *The Fathers in the matter of Signs and Sacraments therefore call upon us not to listen to our Senses, and credit them, because, in such Cases, they would have us to consider things beyond and above their information; such as relate to their Use and Efficacy; these being spiritual things signified by what is visible, wherein they place the Mystery, and which Sense can neither discover nor judge of.*

S. *Austin* has a Rule (*t*) in this Case. *I say this, treating of Signs; in which none ought to attend to what they are, but rather that they are Signs,*

of the Ancient Church, relating to the Eucharist. 41

Signs, that is, that they signifie. For a Sign *is a thing, which, besides what appears affecting the Senses, do's of it self make somewhat else to come into our thoughts.* sed potius quod signa sunt, id est, quod significant. Signum est enim res, præter speciem quam ingerit sensibus, aliud aliquid ex se faciens in cogitationem venire.

So also *Origen* (*u*) describes a Sign to be *a Note of another thing besides that which the Sense gives testimony to.*

(*u*) In *Joan.* tom. 18. ad finem. Σύμβολον ἕτερόν, ϖὲρὰ τὸ αἰϑἠτῶς γεγνημβρον.

But none has so fully declared this Matter, and answered the former Objection, as S. *Chrysostome*, in the place forecited, whose Words deserve to be set down at large (*x*). Where treating of Baptism, the Eucharist, and other Mysteries, after he has told us (as we heard before) what a Mystery is, *viz.* When we do not meerly believe what we see, *but see one thing and believe another*, he goes on thus.

(*x*) In 1 Cor. *Hom.* 7. Edit. *Savil. Tom.* 3. p. 280. Ἕτερα ὁρῶμβρ κ̓ ἕτερα πιϛεύομβρ.

I and an Infidel are diversly affected with them. I hear that Christ was crucified, I presently admire his Benignity: He hears *the same, and he counts it Infirmity. I hear that he was made a Servant, and I admire his Care:* He, *when he hears the same, counts it Infamy.* And so he goes on with his Death and Resurrection, and the different Judgment is made of them, and proceeds to speak of the Sacraments. *The Infidel hearing of the Laver* (of Baptism) *esteems it simply Water; but I do not look meerly upon what I see, but regard the cleansing of the Soul by the Spirit. He thinks that my Body only is washed; but I believe that my Soul is made clean and holy; I reckon the Burial, Resurrection, Sanctification, Righteousness, Redemption, Adoption of Sons, the Inheritance, the Kingdom of Heaven, the Supply of the Spirit. For, I do not judge of the things that appear by my Sight, but by the Eyes of my Mind. I hear of the Body of Christ. I understand what is said, one way; an Infidel, another.* Which he further illustrates admirably thus. *As Children looking upon Books, know not the Power of Letters, understand not what they look upon; nay, even to a grown Man that is unlearned, it will be the same, when a Man of Skill will find out much hidden Virtue, Lives, and Histories contained therein. And if one of no skill receive a Letter, he will judge it only to be Paper and Ink; but he that has*

Ἀκύων λᾳβὼν ἐκεῖνΘ̓, ἁπλῶς ὕδωρ νομίζει· ἐγὼ δ̓ ᾰ τὸ ὁρώμ̓ον ἁπλῶς βλέπω, ἀλλὰ τὸν τ̒ ψυχῆς καθαρμὸν τὸν διὰ τ̒ πνδ̒μαθ̓Θ̓, &c.

Οὐ ϳ̓ τῇ ὄψει κρίνω τὰ φαινόμβρα ἀλλὰ τοῖς ὀφθαλμοῖς τ̒ διανοίας· ἀκύω σῶμα Χειϛᾶ. ἑτέρως ἐγὼ νοῶ τὸ εἰρημβρον, ἑτέρως ὁ ἀπιϛΘ̓.

G Skill.

Skill hears an absent Person speak, and discourses with him, and speaks what he pleases to him again by his Letters. Just thus it is in a Mystery; Unbelievers hearing, seem not to hear; but the Believers, being taught Skill by the Spirit, perceive the Power of the hidden things.

This Discourse of S. *Chrysostome*'s explains a Place of S. *Cyril* of *Jerusalem* (y), and teaches us how to understand it; where speaking of the Eucharist, he says, *Do not consider it as bare Bread and Wine; for it is the Body and Blood of Christ, according to our Lord's Affirmation. And altho Sense suggests this to thee, let Faith confirm thee. Do not judge of the Matter by thy Taste; but by Faith be undoubtedly persuaded, that thou art honoured with the Body and Blood of Christ.*

And afterwards: *Being fully persuaded, that the visible Bread is not Bread, tho' the Taste perceive it such, but the Body of Christ; and the visible Wine is not Wine, tho' the Taste would have it so, but the Blood of Christ.*

All which must be only understood of the Sacramental Relation that the *Bread* and *Wine* have to the *Body* and *Blood* of *Christ*, which the Sense of Tasting acquaints us nothing at all with, and therefore is not a fit Judge of this; but we are to believe, and not doubt of its Truth.

It will also help us to understand another Place of S. *Chrysostome*, (Homil. 83. in Mattb.) where he bids us, *Believe God every where, without contradicting him, tho' what he says seems contrary to our Reasonings, and to our Eyes; but let his Word prevail above our Reasonings and our Eyes. Let us do the same in the Mysteries, not fixing our Eyes only upon the things set before us, but let us hold fast his Words: For his Word cannot deceive us; but our Sense easily may: That can never fall to the ground; but this often fails. Since therefore the Word says,* This is my Body, *let us be persuaded of it and believe it, and look upon it with intellectual Eyes: For Christ has given us nothing sensible,*

of the Ancient Church, relating to the Eucharist. 43

ſible, but in ſenſible things all things intelligible. Thus in Baptiſm, by what is ſenſibly done, there is the Gift of Water; but what is perfected, is intelligible, viz. *our Regeneration and Renovation.*

If the Reader do's but remember that Baptiſm is as much concerned in this Diſcourſe of S. *Chryſoſtome*, as the Euchariſt; and that we are as much required not to truſt our Eyes, that may deceive us, but to truſt the Word of God in the one caſe as well as the other; it will not give the leaſt countenance to the Abſurdities of Tranſubſtantiation.

And as for thoſe Words of his, *That Chriſt delivered nothing ſenſible to us,* they muſt be underſtood with an abatement, That we are not to be intent and to fix our Thoughts meerly upon what we ſee; for elſe it is certain, that there is ſomething ſenſible delivered in the Euchariſt, elſe there would be no Sign nor no Sacrament; and that *Father* would contradict himſelf, who in the very next Words tells us, That *by ſenſible things he has delivered intelligible* (that is, ſpiritual) *things to us*; for which he brings what is beſtowed upon us in Baptiſm as a Proof.

G 2 CHAP.

CHAP. VII.

The Seventh Difference.

When the Fathers call the Eucharist Christ's Body and Blood, the Roman Church understands it of Christs natural Body given there. But the Fathers do not so; but understand it most commonly of the Elements of Bread and Wine, even when they call them the Body of Christ, and give us the reasons why they so call them.

I Need not tell you, how the Romish Writers catch at every place of the Fathers, where they meet with the mention of *Christs Body and Blood*: all their Citations are full of little else but Testimonies of this kind.

But if they had a mind to understand their sense, and did not meerly listen to the sound of their words, they would quickly see them interpret themselves, so that there could be no mistake, nor countenance given hereby to Transubstantiation, or any presence of Christ but what is spiritual. Which by a few Observations out of them will appear.

I. Observ. *The Fathers give us warning of it, and tell us, That they studiously conceal and hide the Mysteries from some persons, both out of the Church, and in it.* Therefore their meer expressions concerning it, are not sufficient to inform us of their meaning.

Thus *Cyril of Jerusalem* (a) tells us, *That we do not speak openly of the mysteries among the Catechumens, but often speak many things covertly, that the faithful that are acquainted with the matter, may understand it, and they that are unacquainted may not be hurt.*

S. *Austin* (b) in like manner. *What is it that is hidden and not publick in the Church? The Sacrament of Baptism, and the Sacrament of the Eucharist. The very Pagans see our good w.rks, but the Sacraments are h.d from them.*

(a) Catech. Illum. 6. pag. 149. Edit. 4. Parif. 1608. Ἀλλὰ πολλὰ πολλάκις λέγομεν ἐπικεκαλυμμένας, &c.

(b) In Pfal. 103. Quid est quod occultum est, & non publicum in Ecclesia? Sacramentum Baptismi, Sacramentum Eucharistiæ. Opera nostra bona vident & Pagani, Sacramenta vero occultantur illis.

S.

of the Ancient Church, relating to the Eucharist.

S. *Chrysostome* (c) (upon those words, *why are they then Baptized for the dead*) says, *I have a mind to speak it openly, but I dare not, because of them that are not initiated. For they make our Exposition more difficult, compelling us either not to speak plainly, or to declare to them things that ought to be conceal'd.*

(c) *In* 1 *Cor.* 15. *Hom.* 40.

Οὐ τολμῶ δὲ διὰ τοὺς ἀμυήτους.

Ἡ μὴ λέγειν σαφῶς, ἢ εἰς αὐτοὺς ἐκφέρειν τὰ ἀπόῤῥητα.

Upon this account they concealed what was apt to be despised (whether they did well or no in this I shall not here question) scarce vouchsafing to name the visible Elements, but mentioning them with more glorious Titles, such as could not be disregarded. Thus they called *Baptism* by the name of φώτισμος, *illumination*; and they called the *Eucharist*, the *Sacrifice*, quod norunt fideles, *which the faithful know*, (thus concealing it) or *the Sacrifice of the Body and Blood of Christ*. They call the Lords *Table* an *Altar*, and the *Ministers Priests*, tho' all these are to be understood in a figurative and improper sense.

Thus S. *Austin* says (d), *Almost all call the Sacrament the Body of Christ*. Which very phrase shews, that the *Sacrament* is not in substance Christs *natural Body*. For who would phrase it so, *almost all call it*, in giving a proper name to a thing? ex. gr. would any say, that almost all call a House a House, or a Man a Man? but to say, that almost all call Kings Gods, tells you, that however for certain Reasons, *Kings* are called *Gods*, yet they are not really and properly so.

(d) *De verb. Dom. Serm* 53. Penè quidem Sacramentum omnes corpus ejus dicunt.

The same Father (e) speaking of several things, whereby Christ may be signified and set forth, either by words written, or spoken, &c. he says, *We do not call these the Body and Blood of Christ, but that only, which being taken from the fruits of the earth, is rightly received by us to our spiritual health*, &c.

(e) *De Trinit.* l. 3. c. 4.
— Sed illud tantum quod ex fructibus terræ acceptum & prece mystica consecratum, ritè sumimus ad salutem spiritualem, &c.

If the other things had been called so, any one would have understood it must be improperly so called, and so must this too, as his following words tell us, that *even this is not sanctified to become so great a Sacrament, but by the invisible operation of the Spirit of God.*

Non sanctificatur ut sit tam magnum Sacramentum, nisi operante invisibiliter Spiritu Dei.

So

(f) Orig. Lib. 6. cap. 19. Eo (sc. *Christo*) jubente, corpus Christi & sanguinem dicimus, quod dum fit ex fructibus terræ, sanctificatur,& fit Sacramentum, operante invisibiliter Spiritu Dei.

So *Isidore* of *Sevil* *(f)* gives the same account, *By the command of Christ, we call the Body and Blood of Christ, that which being made of the fruits of the earth, is sanctified and made a Sacrament by the invisible operation of the spirit of God.*

2. *Observ. The Fathers oft-times in their very manner of speaking concerning the Body and Blood of Christ, point at another thing than his Natural Body; so that we need no Commentary upon their words to explain them, for they carry at first hearing our sense and meaning in them, and not that of the Romanists.* To give a few instances.

(g) Epist. 63. ad Cæcilium. Cùm dicat Christus, *ego sum vitis vera*, sanguis Christi non aqua est utiq; sed vinum — Quomodo nec Corpus Domini potest esse farina sola, aut aqua sola, nisi utrumq; adunatum fuerit & copulatum, & panis unius compagine solidatum.

S. *Cyprian (g)* discoursing against those that Consecrated and drank only Water in the Sacrament, says, *When Christ says,* I am the true Vine, *the Blood of Christ it's plain is not Water but Wine.* —— *So neither can the Lords Body be flour alone, or water alone, unless both of them be united, and coupled and kneaded together into one Loaf.*

Where no Body can doubt of S. *Cyprian's* meaning, that by *Christs Body* he understands not his *natural Body*, but the *Sacrament* of it.

(h) Pandect. Canon. p. 565. Μηδέν πλέον τῶ σώμα[τι] κỳ τῶ αἵμα[τι] τῶ κυρία προσενεχθήσεται, ὡς κỳ αὐτὸς ὁ κύριος παρέδωκεν· τῦτ' ὅτι ἄρτος κỳ οἶνος ὕδατι μεμιγμένοι.

And so the *Council of Carthage, (h)* decreed against the *Armenians* (who made use of Wine only in the Eucharist) *That nothing shall be offered, but the Body and Blood of Christ, as the Lord himself delivered it,* (the phrase carries its sense in the face of it, if they had said no more, but they add) *that is,* Bread and Wine mixed with Water.

(i) Dialog. 1. Τῷ μὲν σώματι τὸ τῶ συμβόλυ τέθεικεν ὄνυμα· τῇ δὲ συμβόλῳ τὸ τῶ σώμα[τος], &c.

What can be more plain than that of *Theodoret (i),* when he says, *That our Saviour changed the names, and on his Body he put the name of the sign* (or symbol) *and on the sign the name of his Body?* A little before he shows how. *You know,* says he, *that God called his Body Bread, and elsewhere he called his flesh Wheat* (σῖτον), *except a Corn of Wheat fall to the Earth and die,* Matth. 12. *But in the delivery of the mysteries, he called Bread his Body, and that which is mixed* (κρᾶμα) *Blood.* Is it not clear, that neither in one case, nor the other, these sayings

sayings are to be understood properly, but figuratively? Especially when *Theodoret*, before all I now have cited, makes this comparison. *As after Consecration, we call the mystical fruit of the Vine the Lords blood ; so he (Jacob) called the Blood of the true Vine, the Blood of the Grape.* Both the one and the other must be figuratively understood.

Ib. Ὥσπερ ον μυστικὸν τ̅ ἀμπέλυ καρπὸν μ{]α̅ τ̅ ἀγιασμὸν αἷμα δεσποτικὸν ὀνομάζομ{μ, ὕτω τ̅ ἀληθινῦς ἀμπέλυ τὸ αἷμα σαφυλῆς ὠνόμασεν αἷμα.

When S. *Cyprian* in the forecited Epistle (*k*) says, that some might make it an Objection, that by partaking of the Communion early in the Morning, they might be discovered to the Heathen Persecutors by the smell of the Wine, he expresses it thus, *One fears this, lest by tasting Wine he should smell of Christ's Blood.*

(*k*) Epist. 63. Hoc quis vereretur, ne per saporem vini redoleat sanguinem Christi.

S. *Jerome* has such another saying, which cannot well be mistaken to express any other sense but ours, when speaking of Virgins (*l*) that were reproved for drinking Wine to excess, he says, *they made this excuse, (joining sacrilege to their drunkenness) and said God forbid that I should abstain from the Blood of Christ.*

(*l*) Epist. ad Eustochium. Ebrietati sacrilegium copulantes aiunt, absit ut ego me abstineam à sanguine Christi.

Either they said nothing to the purpose, or they took that which they called *the Blood of Christ*, for Wine properly.

Thus also S. *Chrysostome* (*m*) speaking of the rudeness of the Souldiers in the Church, says, that in the tumult, *the most holy Blood of Christ was shed upon the Souldiers Cloths.* Which could be nothing but Sacramental Wine.

(*m*) Epist. 1. ad Innocent. Τὸ ἀγιώτατον αἷμα χειεῖ εἰς τὰ τ̅ σρατιωτῶν ἱμάτια ἐξεχέτω.

Leo the Great, speaking of the *Manichees*, that for fear of the Laws came to the Communion of the *Catholicks*, and directing how to discover them, he says (*n*), *They so behave themselves in the Communion of the Sacraments, that they may sometime be more safely concealed ; with an unworthy mouth they take the Body of Christ, but altogether decline drinking the Blood of our redemption.*

(*n*) Serm. 4. de Quadrages. Ita in Sacramentorum communione se temperant, ut interdum tutiùs lateant ; Ore indigno Christi Corpus accipiunt, sanguinem autem redemptionis nostræ haurire omninò declinant.

In the sense both of *Leo* and the *Manichees*, the *Body* and *Blood* here must be taken figuratively ; for such bad men as they, in the sense of the Antients, could not eat, or any way receive *Christ's Body* in a

proper

48   *A full View of the Doctrines and Practices*

proper sense, but being understood of the Type of it, *viz.* of the Sacramental Bread, that they would receive; but not the Type of his Blood; *viz.* the Wine, because, as S. *Austin* (*o*) observes, *they drink no Wine, saying, it is the Gall of the Prince of darkness.* They had no more prejudice against the Blood than the Body of Christ, only they took it to be Wine, which they abhorred.

(*o*) *De Heref.* 46. Vinum non bibunt, dicentes fel esse principum tenebrarum.

3. Observ. *The Fathers speak of Christ's Body and Blood in the Eucharist, with such terms of restriction and diminution, which plainly tell us, that they understood it not of his substantial and natural Body, but in a figurative sense.* Thus Origen (*p*) says, That Bread in the Eucharist *is made by Prayer a certain holy Body.*

And S. *Austin* (*q*), *Christ took in his hands what the faithful understand, and* after a sort, *carried himself when he said,* This is my Body.

Bede (*r*) upon the same Psalm, has the same term of restriction, *Christ* after a sort, *was carried in his own hands.*

S. *Austin* elsewhere (*s*), *In a certain sense, the Sacrament of the Body of Christ is Christ's Body; and the Sacrament of the Blood of Christ, is Christ's Blood.* Just as at *Easter* we say, this day Christ rose, because it is a memorial of it.

S. *Chrysostome* (*t*) says of the Consecrated Bread, *That it has no longer the name of Bread* (tho' the nature of it remains) *but is counted worthy to be called the Lord's Body.*

Theodoret in like manner (*u*), *He honoured the visible Symbols with the appellation of his Body and Blood.*

Facundus Hermian. (*x*) is most express. *We call,* says he, *the Sacrament of his Body and Blood, which is in the Consecrated Bread and Cup, his Body and Blood; not that properly the Bread is his Body, and the Cup his Blood,* &c.

So also is S. *Chrysostome* (*y*) in another place; where he shows, that the word *Flesh*, is not always taken for the φύσις σώματος, the nature and

(*p*) *Contr. Celsum* l 8. p. 399. *Edit. Cantabr.* Σῶμα ἅγιόν τι.
(*q*) *In Psal.* 33. *conc.* 2. Accepit in manus quod norunt fideles & ipse se portabat quodammodo, cùm diceret hoc est Corpus meum.
(*r*) *In Psal.* 33. Christus quodammodo ferebatur in manibus suis.
(*s*) *Epist.* 23. *ad Bonifac.* Secundum quendam modum Sacramentum Corporis Christi, Corpus Christi est; Sacramentum sanguinis Christi, sanguis Christi est.
(*t*) *Epist. ad Cæsarium.* Dignus habitus est Dominici Corporis appellatione.
(*u*) *Dialog.* 1. Τὰ ὁρώμενα σύμβολα τῇ τοῦ σώματ[ος] κ̀ αἵματ[ος] προσηγορίᾳ τετίμηκεν.
(*x*) *In defens.* 3. *capit. l.* 9. — Non quod propriè Corpus ejus sit panis, & poculum sanguis, &c.
(*y*) *In Gal.* 5. 17. *Vol.* 3. *Savil. p.* 755.

of the Ancient Church, relating to the Eucharist. 49

and substance of the Body (which is the only proper sense) and he gives other instances which are improper; as that *flesh* signifies *a depraved will*. And adds two other improper senses, in these words. *By the name of Flesh, the Scripture is wont also to call the mysteries*; he adds also, that it calls the *Church* so, when it calls it *the Body of Christ*.

Τὴν πονηρὰν ϖροαίρεσιν.

Καὶ τὰ μυσήρια καλεῖν εἰώθη ἡ γραφή.

The very phrase of being *wont to call*, shows, that of which it is affirmed to be improperly so called, as the phrase of *being thought worthy of the name* (as we heard before) argues the name not properly to agree to it.

4. Observ. *The Fathers, knowing, that the Eucharist was not in a proper sense Christ's Body, give us several reasons why it is called his Body.* But no body uses to give a reason why he calls a thing by its proper name. I shall not name all the reasons here, but reserve some to another place; when we consider the Sacrament, as a Sign, Figure, Type, Memorial, &c.

1. One reason they give is *from its likeness and resemblance*, either in respect of what it consists of, or from the likeness of its effects.

S. *Austin*'s saying is remarkable (z), *If the Sacraments had not a resemblance of those things of which they are Sacraments, they would not be Sacraments at all: But from this resemblance they take commonly the name even of the things themselves which they resemble.*

(z) *Epist.* 23. Si Sacramenta quandam similitudinem earum rerum non haberent quarum Sacramenta sunt, omninò Sacramenta non essent. Ex hac autem similitudine plerunq; etiam ipsarum rerum nomina accipiunt.

Bede also gives (a) the same reason in his Commentary on the *Romans*.

(a) *In Cap.* 5. *Epist. ad Roman. Lib.* 4. *cap.* 4.

The Author of the Book of Sacraments under S. *Ambrose* his name, speaks thus. *Thou mayst say perhaps., I do not see the substance of Blood. Well, but it has its likeness. For as thou hast received the likeness of his death, so thou drinkest the likeness of his pretious Blood.*

Fortè dicis, speciem sanguinis non video. Sed habet similitudinem. Sicut enim mortis similitudinem sumpsisti, ita etiam similitudinem pretiosi sanguinis bibis, &c.

S. *Cyprian* (b). *When Christ called Bread, made up of many united grains of Corn, his Body, he shewed the unity of Christian people whom he bore; and when he call'd Wine pressed out of many Grapes,*

(b) *Epist.* 76. ad *Magnum*. Quando Dominus Corpus suum panem vocat, de multorum granorum adunatione congestum, populum nostrum quem

H and

portabat indicat adunatum: & quando fanguinem fuum vinum appellat de botris atq; acinis plurimis expreſſum atq; in unum coactum, gregem item copulatam.

(c) De Inſtit. Cleric. c. 31. Propterea Dominus noſter Corpus & fanguinem fuum in eis rebus commendavit, quæ ad unum aliquid rediguntur ex multis five granis five acinis, & Sanctorum Charitatis unitatem fignificaret.

(d) De Offic. Eccleſ. l. 1. cap. 18. Panis quia confirmat Corpus, ideo Corpus Chriſti nuncupatur; vinum autem quia fanguinem operatur in carne, ideo ad fanguinem Chriſti refertur.

and put together his Blood, he fignified alfo the uniting of a multitude of the Chriſtian flock together.

noſtrum fignificat commixtione adunatæ multitudinis copulatam.

So *Rabanus Maurus* (c). *Therefore our Lord commended his Body and Blood in thoſe things, which confiſting of many Grains or Grapes, are brought together into one, whereby he might fignify the unity of the Charity of Saints.*

Others again from the likeneſs of its effects.

Thus *Iſidore* of *Sevil* (d). *Bread, becauſe it ſtrengthens the Body, is therefore called the Body of Chriſt; and Wine, becauſe it produces Blood in the Fleſh, is therefore referred to the Blood of Chriſt.*

The fame reafon is alfo given by *Rabanus Maurus*, in his Commentary upon the 26 Chap. of S. *Matthew*.

2 *Reaſon.* Another reafon, why they call the Euchariſt Chriſts Body, is, *becauſe it fupplies the place, is inſtead of it, is its repreſentative, its pledge and pawn.*

(e) Lib. 6. de Orat. Corpus ejus in pane cenfetur, *Hoc eſt corpus meum.*

(f) Tract. 45. in Joan. Videte, fide manente, ſigna variata. Ibi Petra Chriſtus, nobis Chriſtus quod in altari Dei ponitur.

(g) De Civit. Dei, l. 18. c. 48. Quodammodo omnia ſignificantia videntur rerum quas ſignificant fuſtinere perſonas, ſicut dictum eſt ab Apoſtolo, Petra erat Chriſtus, quoniam Petra illa de qua hoc dictum eſt, fignificabat utiq; Chriſtum.

(h) Catech. Myſtag. 4. — Ὡς σώματος καὶ αἵματος μεταλαμβάνωμεν Χριστοῦ· ἐν τύπῳ γὰρ ἄρτυ, &c.

(i) Orat. 18. — Ἀντὶ τῆ βρέφης πεπιλυξώμεθα τὸν διὰ τοῦ βρέφους εὐλογούμενον ἄρτον.

Tertullian (e). *His Body is reputed to be in the Bread,* This is my Body.

S. *Auſtin* (f). *See how the ſigns are varied, Faith remaining the fame. There* (in the Wilderneſs) *the rock was Chriſt, to us that which is placed on Gods Altar is Chriſt.*

Again elfewhere more fully (g). *All things intended to fignify, ſeem in a ſort to ſuſtain the perſons of thoſe things which they fignify, as the Apoſtle ſays,* The Rock was Chriſt, *becauſe that Rock of which this is ſpoken, did fignify Chriſt.*

Cyril of *Jeruſalem* (h) ſays, *Wherefore with all aſſurance, let us receive it* (viz. The Bread and Wine) *as the Body and Blood of Chriſt; for in the type of Bread his Body is given thee, and in the type of Wine his Blood.*

Proclus of *Conſtantinople* (i). *Inſtead of the Manger let us venerate the Altar; inſtead of the Infant*

let

of the Ancient Church, relating to the Eucharist.

let us embrace the Bread that is blessed by the Infant, (viz. Christ.)

Victor Antiochen. (k) *When the Lord said this is my Body, this is my Blood, it was fit that they who set forth the Bread, should, after giving of thanks, reckon it to be his Body, and partake of it; and account the Cup to be instead of his Blood.*

The Author of the Commentaries attributed to S. *Jerome* (l). *Christ left to us his last remembrance, just as if a person taking a Journey from home, should leave some pledge to one whom he loves, that as oft as he look'd upon it, he might call to mind his kindnesses and friendships.*

So also *Amalarius* (m). *Christ bowing his head gave up the Ghost. The Priest bows himself, and commends to God the Father this which is offered as a Sacrifice in the place of Christ.*

inclinato capite, emisit spiritum. Sacerdos inclinat se, & hoc quod *vice Christi* immolatum est, deo Patri commendat.

(k) *In Marc.* 14. *Citante Bulingero adv. Casaub.*
Αὐτῶ σῶμα νομίζειν.
Τὸ δὲ ποτήριον ἐν τάξει αἵματος ἡγεῖσθαι.

(l) *In* 1 *Cor.* 11. Ultimam nobis commemorationem sive memoriam dereliquit, quemadmodum si quis peregrè proficiscens, aliquod pignus ei quem diligit derelinquat, ut quotiescunq; illud viderit, possit ejus beneficia & amicitias memorare.
(m) *De Offic. Eccles.l.*3.c.25. *Edit. Hittorpii,* p.425. Christus,

5. Obſerv. *That altho', for the Reasons given, the Fathers call the Sacrament Christ's Body, yet they plainly say, that what is distributed in the Eucharist is without any life or sense, which cannot be said of Christ's natural Body.*

Epiphanius (n). *We see what our Saviour took in his hands* (viz. Bread) *and having given thanks said,* This is mine, *and that; and yet we see, that it is not equal to it nor like it, not to the incarnate Image, not to the invisible Deity, not to the Lineaments of members; for this* (the Bread) *is of a round form, and insensible as to any power.*

Theophilus of *Alexandria* (o), discoursing against *Origen*, who did not believe that the H. Ghost did operate upon things inanimate, says, He (Origen) *do's not remember, that the mystical waters in Baptism are consecrated by the coming of the H. Ghost, and that the Lords Bread, whereby the Body of our Saviour is shown, and which we break for our sanctification, and the H. Cup, which are all placed upon the Table of the Church, and are indeed*

(n) *In Anchorat.*
Τοῦτο μὲν ἐστι τόδε. —— οὐκ ἴσον ἐστὶν, οὐδὲ ὅμοιον, οὐ τῇ ἐνσάρκῳ εἰκόνι, οὐ τῇ ἀοράτῳ θεότητι, &c.
—— Στρογγυλοειδὲς κ᾽ ἀναίσθητον ὡς πρὸς τὴν δύναμιν.

(o) *Epiſt. Paschal.* 2. Non recogitat aquas in Baptismate mysticis adventu Sp. Sancti consecrari, panemq; Dominicum, quo Salvatoris Corpus ostenditur, & quem frangimus in Sanctificationem nostri, & S. calicem, qui in mensa Ecclesiæ collocantur, & utique inanima sunt, per invocationem & adventum Spiritûs S. sanctificari.

A full View of the Doctrines and Practices

indeed without life, yet are Sanctified by the Invocation and advent of the H. Ghost.

S. *Jerome* (p) commending the foresaid work, and admiring at the profit the Churches would reap thereby, says, *That they who are ignorant, being instructed by Scripture-Testimonies, may learn, with what veneration they ought to meddle with holy things, and serve at the Altar; and that the H. Chalices and H. Veils, and the rest of the things that appertain to the Celebration of our Lord's Passion, are not to be look'd upon as having no sanctity, as being without life and sense, but by reason that they accompany the Body and Blood of our Lord, are to be venerated with the same majestick regard, that his Body and Blood is.*

(p) *Epist. ad Theoph. Alex.* Ut discant qui ignorant eruditi testimoniis Scripturarum, qua debeant veneratione Sancta suscipere & Altaris servitio deservire; sacrosq; calices & sancta velamina, & cætera quæ ad cultum pertinent Dominicæ Passionis, non quasi inanima & sensu carentia Sanctimoniam non habere, sed ex consortio *corporis & sanguinis Domini,* eadem qua Corpus ejus & Sanguis Majestate veneranda.

6. Observ. *That the Fathers speak of Divisions and parts of the Eucharist, which cannot be truly said of the natural Body of Christ, which the Rom. Church confesses to be impassible, but only of the Sacramental Bread and Wine.*

Cyprian (q). *Another who was also defiled, the Sacrifice being Celebrated by the Priest, was so bold, as privily to take a part of it with others, but he could not eat and handle the Holy* (Body) *of the Lord.*

Clemens Alexandr. (r). *When the Bishop, according to custom had divided the Eucharist, they suffered every one of the people to take a portion of it.*

Origen (s) (if they be his genuine words) says, *When ye receive the Lords Body, ye keep it with all caution and veneration, lest any little portion of it should fall down, lest any thing of the consecrated gift should slip down to the ground,* &c.

S. Basil (t) showing, that they that have received the Communion in the Church may reserve it, and Communicate themselves at home with their own hand, and that the practice was thus in *Alexandria* and *Egypt*; adds, that *when the Priest has distributed the Sacrifice, he that re-*

(q) *Lib. de Lapsis.* Quidam alius & ipse maculatus, sacrificio à Sacerdote celebrato, partem cum cæteris ausus est latenter accipere, sanctum Domini edere & contrectare non potuit.

(r) *Strom. l.* 1. —Ἔχασον τῷ λαῷ λαβεῖν τὴν μοῖραν ἐπιτρέπουσιν.

(s) *Hom.* 13. *in Exodum.* Cùm suscipitis Corpus Domini, cum omni cautela & veneratione servatis, ne ex eo parum quid decidat, ne consecrati muneris aliquid dilabatur, &c.

(t) *Epist.* 289. *ad Cæsariam.*

ceives

of the Ancient Church, relating to the Eucharist. 53

ceives it whole, and takes daily a part of that which was so given him, ought to believe that he rightly receives it.——— *It is the same in virtue, whether a person receive a single part from the Priest, or many parts together.*

S. *Ambrose* agrees with it, (*u*) speaking of the Blood of Christ. *Whether thou takest,* says he, *a little, or drinkest a larger draught, there is the same perfect measure of redemption to all.*

So also S. *Austin* (*x*) speaking of that upon the Lord's Table which is blessed and sanctified, (which is Bread) he says of it, *that it is broken into little parts to be distributed.* Which cannot be said of Christ's proper Body.

And elswhere (*y*) his phrase concerning communicating is, *to take a part from the body of the immaculate Lamb.*

Also in another place, he says (*z*), *In receiving we know what we think. We receive a little portion, and are fatted at heart.*

Cyril of *Alexandria* (*a*) says, *The least part of the Consecrated Bread* (which he calls the Eulogy) *mingles the whole Body into it self, and fills it with its own energy, and thus both Christ is in us, and we again are in him.*

Eusebius (*b*) tells the story of the Presbyter, that when *Serapion* was a dying, *sent him,* by a Boy, *a little bit of the Eucharist.*

And *Prosper* (*c*) has a like story of a possessed Woman, *that received a short and small portion of our Lords Body.*

And P. *Pius* I, in an Epistle attributed to him (and made use of by *Bellarmine* (*d*)) speaks of *some of the Blood of Christ dropping and distilling on the ground,* and directs what is to be done in that case.

Ταύτὸν τίνυν ἐςι τῇ δυνάμει εἴτε μίαν μερίδα δέξαταί τις παρὰ τοῦ ἱερέως, εἴτε πολλὰς μερίδας ὁμοῦ.

(*u*) *Epist.* 1. *ad Justum.* Etsi parum sumas, etsi plurimum haurias, eadem perfecta est omnibus mensura redemptionis.

(*x*) *Epist.* 59. *ad Paulin.* —— Ad distribuendum comminuitur.

(*y*) *Epist.* 86. *ad Casulanum.* De agni immaculati corpore partem sumere.

(*z*) *De Verb. dom. serm.* 33. In accipiendo novimus quid cogitemus. Modicum accipimus & in corde saginamur.

(*a*) *In Joan.* 6. 57. Ὀλιγίςη εὐλογία σύμπαν ἡμῶν εἰς ἑαυτὴν ἀναφέρει τὸ σῶμα, καὶ τῆ ἰδίας ἐνεργείας ἀναπληροῖ, ὅτω τε ἐν ἡμῖν γίνεται Χριςὸς, καὶ ἡμεῖς αὖ πάλιν ἐν αὐτῷ.

(*b*) *Eccles. Hist.* l. 6. c. 36. —— Βραχὺ τῆς εὐχαριςίας.

(*c*) *Dimidium temporis.* c. 6. —— Brevem portiunculam Corporis Dominici.

(*d*) *De Euchar.* l. 2. cap. 5. Si quid de sanguine Domini stillaverit in terram.

7. Ob-

7. Obſerv. *The Fathers ſpeak of making the Body of Chriſt in the Euchariſt, in a ſenſe quite different from that of the Romaniſts.*

S. *Jerome* frequently uſes the phraſe of *making Chriſts Body*, and ſpeaking of the Presbyters that ſucceeded to the Apoſtles, in one Epiſtle (e) he ſays, *they make the Body of Chriſt with their Holy Mouth.*

(e) Epiſt. 1. ad Heliodor. Qui Chriſti Corpus Sacro ore conficiunt.

And in another Epiſtle (f) ſays of them, *That upon their Prayers the Body and Blood of Chriſt is made.*

(f) Ad Evagrium. Ad quorum preces Chriſti Corpus ſanguiſq; conficitur.

Alſo in a third Epiſtle (g) he deſcribes a Prieſt to be *one that mediates betwixt God and Men, and one that makes the fleſh of the Lamb with his holy mouth.*

(g) Ad Fabiolam. Sequeſter Dei & hominum, & carnes agni ſacro ore conficiens.

Here now they of the Church of *Rome* take care to advance the Prieſthood, tho' even with words of Blaſphemy. One crys out (h), *He that created me without me, is created by my means.*

(h) Stella Clericorum. Qui creavit me ſine me, creatur mediante me.

So alſo *Biel* (i). *He that created me (if I may be bold to ſay it) has given me power to create himſelf, and he that created me without me, is created by my means.*

(i) In Canon. Miſſæ, Lect. 4. Qui creavit me (ſi fas eſt dicere) dedit mihi creare ſe, & qui creavit me ſine me, creatur mediante me.

Biel alſo (in the ſame Lecture) makes a compariſon between the Prieſts and the Bl. Virgin, and makes them to carry it from her in this matter.

Illa prolatis octo verbulis, Ecce Ancilla Domini, fiat mihi ſecundùm Verbum tuum, ſemel concepit Dei filium & mundi Redemptorem. Iſti à Domino conſecrati, quinq; Verbis eundem Dei Virginiſq; filium advocant quotidie corporaliter. Attendite, O Sacerdotes, in quo gradu & dignitate ſitis conſtituti.

She by pronouncing eight words, Behold the Handmaid of the Lord, &c. *Conceived once the Son of God and the Redeemer of the World. They* (viz. the Prieſts) *being conſecrated by the Lord, by ſpeaking five words, do call the ſame Son of God, and the Virgin, bodily before them every day. And then crys out. Conſider, O Prieſts, in what high degree and dignity you are placed.*

But

of the Ancient Church, relating to the Eucharist.   55

But now the Fathers they sufficiently explain themselves, that this of *making Christs Body*, cannot be understood of the *natural* and *proper Body* of Christ. For

First, They lay it down as a Rule, that *whatsoever is made, was not before it was made.*

Thus *Athenagoras* (*k*) says, *That which is already is not made, but that which is not.*

Tertullian in like manner says (*l*,) *Nothing that has a* fieri, *is without a beginning, but it begins to be while it begins to be made.*

Athanasius (*m*). *It is the property of Creatures and works, that they are said to exist out of non-entities, and not to be before they are made.*

Greg. Nyssen (*n*). *If he made it, he made that which was not at all.*

S. *Hilary* (*o*). *Every thing that is made, was not before it was made.*

S. *Ambrose* (*p*). *That which is made begins to be.*

S. *Austin* (*q*). *To make is true of that which was not at all.*

Cyril Alexand. (*r*). *It cannot be, that what already exists, should be brought into being, but what does not exist.*

Vigilius also (*s*). *To be made, is the usual property of him, who never subsisted before.*

Cassianus also (*t*). *Things already sprung up, cannot return into that state; that they should be generated by a new creation.*

These sayings do very ill accord with the Doctrine of the Roman Church (*u*), which teaches, that the Conversion in the Eucharist is made, *without any change in our Lord; for neither is Christ generated, or is changed, or increased.*

(*k*) De resurrect. Τὸ ὂν ἐ γίνε), ἀλλὰ τὸ μὴ ὄν.
(*l*) Lib. contr. Hermog. cap. 19. Nihil quod fieri habet sine initio est, quin initium sit illi dum incipit fieri.
(*m*) Contr. Arian. Orat. 3. Κτισμάτων κỳ ποιημάτων ἴδιον, τὸ λέγεῶς ἐξ ὐκ ὄντων, κỳ ὐκ ἦν πρὶν γυννηθῆ.
(*n*) Contr. Eunom. l. 9. Εἰ ἐποίησε, τὸ μὴ ὂν πάντως ἐποίησε.
(*o*) De Trin. l. 12. Omne quod fit, antequam fiat non fuit.
(*p*) De Incarn. l. 3. Quod fit incipit.
(*q*) De moribus Manich. c. 7. Facere enim est quod omninò non erat.
(*r*) Thesaur. Assert. 20. Οὐ γὰρ ἂν δή ποτε τὸ ἤδη ὂν εἰς τὸ ᾗ φέρεῖο, ἀλλὰ τὸ μὴ ὄν.
(*s*) Lib. 3. cont. Eutychen. Fieri, ejus soleat esse proprium, qui nunquam ante substiterat.
(*t*) Lib. 7. de incarn. c. 2. Quæ orta jam fuerint, redire in id rursum non queant ut novâ creatione generentur.
(*u*) Catechis. ad Paroch. de Eucharist. n. 39. Sine ulla Domini nostri mutatione; neq; enim Christus aut generatur, aut mutatur, aut augescit.

Secondly, They so speak of *making Christs Body*, that it cannot be understood of any other than his typical and mystical Body. For the Fathers say, *That* Bread *is made his* Body.

Tertullian.

Tertullian (x). *Christ when he had taken Bread, and distributed it to his Disciples, made it his Body, saying,* This is my Body.

Eusebius (y). *Christ commanded his Disciples* (speaking of the Symbols of the Divine Oeconomy delivered to them, i. e. Bread and Wine) *to make the image of his Body.*

Cyril of Jerus. (z). *When the Invocation is over, the Bread is made the Body of Christ, and the Wine the Blood of Christ.*

Greg. Nyssen (a) says, *At first the Bread is common Bread, but after the mystery has consecrated it, it is called and is made the Body of Christ.*

S. Austin (b). *Not all Bread, but only that which receives Christ's blessing, is made the Body of Christ.*

Canon of the Mass. Which Oblation, O Almighty God, we beseech thee vouchsafe to make blessed, allowable, firm, rational, and acceptable, that it may be made to us the Body and Blood of thy most dear Son our Lord Jesus Christ, &c.

Also the Fathers say still more expresly, that the Body and Blood of Christ, *is made of Bread and Wine.*

Thus the Author of the Book of Sacraments under S. Ambrose's name (c). *Perhaps thou wilt say, My Bread is usual Bread: but tho' that Bread be Bread before the Sacramental words, yet upon Consecration, of Bread is made the Flesh of Christ.*

Gaudentius (d). *The Creator and Lord of nature himself, who produces Bread out of the Earth, of Bread again (seeing he is able, and has promised it) he makes his own Body; and he that of Water made Wine, made also of Wine his Blood.*

Now all this can be meant of nothing else, but what we heard out of *Eusebius* before, of the *Image of his Body,* which he commanded his Disciples to make.

S. Je-

(x) *Cont. Marc. l. 4. c. 40.* Acceptum panem & distributum discipulis, Corpus suum illum fecit, *hoc est Corpus meum* dicendo.

(y) *Demonst. Evang. lib. 8.* Τὴν εἰκόνα τοῦ ἰδίου σώματος ποιεῖσθαι.

(z) *Catech. Mystag. I.* Ἐπικλήσεως γενομένης, ὁ μὲν ἄρτος γίνεται σῶμα Χριστοῦ, ὁ δὲ οἶνος αἷμα Χριστοῦ.

(a) *Orat. in Christi Baptisma.* Σῶμα Χριστοῦ λέγεται τε καὶ γίνεται.

(b) *Serm. de diversis,* 87. Non omnis panis, sed accipiens benedictionem Christi, fit Corpus Christi.

Canon Missæ. Quam oblationem tu Deus in omnibus, quæsumus, benedictam, adscriptam, ratam, rationabilem, acceptamq; facere digneris, ut nobis Corpus & sanguis fiat dilectissimi tui filii Domini nostri J. Christi, &c.

(c) *Lib. 4. de Sacram. c. 4.* Tu fortè dicis, meus panis est usitatus: sed panis iste panis est ante verba Sacramentorum, ubi accesserit consecratio *de pane fit caro Christi.*

(d) *In Exod. trac. 2.* Ipse naturarum Creator & Dominus, qui producit de terra panem, de pane rursus, qui potest & promisit, efficit proprium corpus, & qui de aqua vinum fecit, & de vino sanguinem suum.

S. *Jerome* also explains it of the Sacramental Bread and Wine, upon those words of the Prophet (e), *They shall flow together to the goodness of the Lord, for Wheat, and for Wine and Oil.* He adds, *Of which the Lords Bread is made, and the type of his Blood is fulfilled, and the blessing of sanctification is shown.*

And in another place (f). *Of this Wheat the Bread that descended from Heaven is made, and which strengthens the heart of man.* Which must be understood of the Bread received in the Eucharist.

So *Tertullian* (g) explains himself. *He made Bread his Body,* saying, This is my Body, *That is, the Figure of my Body.*

And *Leo Magn.* (h). *Neither may the Presbyters, without the Bishops Command, make the Sacrament of the Body and Blood of Christ.*

S. *Chrysostom* (i) speaking of Wine, says, *By this the matter of the good things for our Salvation is perfected.* Where by those *good things*, he plainly means the Wine in the Eucharist.

It is also very observable, that the Fathers sometimes call this the *mystical Bread and Wine*, and sometimes the *mystical Body and Blood of Christ*.

Thus S. *Austin* (k) says, *Our Bread and Cup is made mystical to us, by a certain consecration, and does not grow so.*

S. *Chrysostom* (l) thus. *The mystical Body and Blood is not made without the grace of the spirit.*

When S. *Ambrose* (m) had said, *This Body which we make is of the Virgin.* He explains this phrase by another before it, *viz. That Sacrament which thou receivest is made by the Word of Christ.* And also by another saying of his that follows. *It was true Flesh of Christ that was Crucified and buried ; it is therefore truly the Sacrament of his Flesh.* Where you see he distinguishes these two, the Flesh of Christ Crucified, and that in the Sacrament, which is only mystically so.

(e) *In Jerem.*31.12. De quo conficitur panis Domini, & sanguinis ejus impletur typus, & benedictio Sanctificationis ostenditur.

(f) In cap.9. Zachar. De hoc tritico efficitur ille panis qui de Cœlo descendit & confortat cor hominis.

(g) Antea citat. Corpus suum illum (sc. panem) fecit, hoc est Corpus meum dicendo, id est, Figura Corporis mei.

(h) Epist. 88. Nec licet Presbyteris nisi eo (sc. Episcopo) jubente, Sacramentum Corporis & sanguinis Christi conficere.

(i) Hom. 29. in Genes. Ἡ ὑπόθεσις τῶν σωτηρίας ἡμῶν ἀγαθῶν διὰ τούτο τελεῖται.

(k) Contr. Faust. l. 20. c. 13. Noster panis & calix certa consecratione, mysticus fit nobis, non nascitur.

(l) De resurrect. mort. Hom. 33. Σῶμα καὶ αἷμα μυστικὸν οὐκ ἄν τοῖς μετ' οὗ τοῦ πνεύματος χάριτ[ος] γίνεται.

(m) Lib de iis qui initiant. c. 9. Hoc quod conficimus Corpus ex Virgine est.

Sacramentum illud quod accipis sermone Christi conficitur.

Vera utiq; caro Christi quæ crucifixa est, quæ sepulta est. Vere ergo carnis illius Sacramentum est.

I   *Hesychius*

Hesychius (n) speaking of Jews, Pagans, and Hereticks, says, that *the Soul in Society, with them may not eat of the myſtical Body*, that is, of the Euchariſt.

And elſewhere (o) ſpeaking of the Cup in the Sacrament, uſes this phraſe, *Chriſt drinking himſelf and giving to the Apoſtles the intelligible Blood to drink.* Where *intelligible Blood* is the *myſtical Blood* in the Euchariſt, according to his conſtant uſe of that word.

Procopius of *Gaza* (p) upon thoſe words of the Prophet, of Gods *taking away the Staff of Bread* and *ſtay of Water* ; and telling us, that Chriſts Fleſh is meat indeed, and his Blood drink indeed, which they that have not, have not *the ſtrength of Bread and Water* ; he adds, *there is another enlivening Bread alſo taken from the Jews*, &c. where he means *the Euchariſt*, diſtinguiſhing it from Chriſts proper Fleſh and Blood.

S. *Ambroſe* (q) makes the ſame diſtinction, where ſpeaking of the Benediction of *Aſſer*, that *his Bread was fat*, &c. and that *Aſſer* ſignifies *riches* ; he adds, *Jeſus gave this Bread to the Apoſtles, that they ſhould divide it among believing people, and he now gives it to us, being that which the Prieſt daily Conſecrates with his words. This Bread is made the food of Saints. We may alſo underſtand thereby the Lord himſelf, who gave his Fleſh to us, as he ſays,* I am the Bread of Life. What can be more clear, than that he diſtinguiſhes here between the Euchariſtical Bread (which he calls the Saints food) and Chriſt himſelf the Bread of Life?

8. Obſerv. *The Fathers ſpeak of Chriſt's Body ſanctified and ſacrificed in the Euchariſt ; which cannot be underſtood of any thing, but his repreſentative and Typical Body.*

S. *Auſtin* (r) ſpeaking of that *which is upon the Lords Table* (which the Church of *Rome* will have to be Chriſt's Natural Body) ſays, that *it is bleſſed and ſanctified.* And

---

(n) *In Levit. lib. 6.* — Corpore myſtico non veſcetur.

(o) *Id. ibid. lib. 2.* Chriſtus bibens ipſe, & Apoſtolis biberedans ſanguinem intelligibilem.

(p) *In Eſa. cap. 3.*

Καὶ ἄλλος δὲ τῶν Ἰουδαίων ἀφῃρῆ ὁ ζωοποιὸς ἄρτος.

(q) *De benedict. Patriarch. c. 9.* Hunc panem dedit (*Jeſus*) Apoſtolis, ut dividerent populo credentium, hodieq; dat nobis eum, quem ipſe quotidie ſacerdos conſecrat ſuis verbis. Hic panis factus eſt eſca Sanctorum. Poſſumus & ipſum Dominum accipere, qui carnem ſuam nobis dedit, ſicut ipſe ait, Ego ſum panis vita.

(r) *Epiſt.* 59. Quod in Domini menſa eſt — — beneficitur & ſanctificatur.

of the Ancient Church, relating to the Eucharist.

And *Gaudentius* (s), speaking of Christ, whom he compares to the Paschal Lamb, says, *Through all the Houses of the Churches, in the mystery of Bread and Wine, being sacrificed he refreshes, being believed on he quickens, being consecrated he sanctifies them that consecrate.*

This can be only true in *representation*, which is said of Christ's being *sacrificed* and *sanctified* (or consecrated) by us; for the *proper* and *natural* Body of Christ can neither be *sanctified* in a proper sense, nor *sacrificed* by us, as I shall now show.

1. *Not sanctified properly.*

For this in the sense of the Fathers, is *Dedication to God*; and tho' we may dedicate *our selves* to God, yet not the *Son of God* to him.

Origen (t). *To sanctify a thing, that is, to vow it to God.*

Cyril Alexandr. (u). *That which is said to be sanctified do's not partake of all holiness, but it rather signifies that which is devoted to God in honour of him.* Now Christ is certainly partaker of all Holiness.

Jobius. (*). *We say a place, or Bread, or Wine is sanctified, which are set apart for God, and are not put to any common use.*

Hesychius (x). *That which is sanctified and offered, because it is offered it begins to be sanctified, therefore that it was not holy before.* This cannot be affirmed of Christ's proper Body, which was never other than holy, but may of the *Typical Bread* which was common before.

2. *Not sacrificed properly.*

Therefore *Gaudentius* (y) in the forecited Tract, says, *We offer the Labours*, &c. *Of the Passion, in the Figure of the Body and Blood.*

S. Austin (z). *Was not Christ offered once in himself, and yet every day in the Sacrament he is offered for the people?*

(s) *In Exod. tract.* 19. Per singulas Ecclesiarum domos in mysterio panis & vini reficit immolatus, vivificat creditus, consecrantes sanctificat consecratus.

(t) *In Levit. hom.* 11. Sanctificare aliquid, hoc est, vovere Deo.

(u) *Com. in Esaiam. Edit. gr. lat.* p. 178. Τὸ ἁγιαζόμενον λεγόμενον, οὐχὶ παντὸς ἁγιασμοῦ μέτοχόν ἐστι, σημαίνει δὲ μᾶλλον ᾗ τὸ εἰς δόξαν ἀνατεθειμένον τῷ Θεῷ.

* *Apud Photium, cod.* 222. Ἁγιάζεσθαι τὸν τόπον, ἢ τὸν ἄρτον, ἢ τὸν οἶνον, ἅ τῷ Θεῷ φαμὲν ἀφορίζεσθαι ᾗ πρὸς μηδεμίαν κοινὴν ὑποπίπτειν χρῆσιν.

(x) *In Levit. l.* 7. Quod sanctificatur & offertur, eo quod offertur Sanctificari incipit, ergo prius non erat sanctum.

(y) *In Exod. tract.* 19. Labores Passionis, &c. in figura corporis & sanguinis offerimus.

(z) *Epist.* 23. *ad Bonifac.* Nonne semel immolatus est Christus in seipso, & tamen in Sacramento omni die populis immolatur?

He opposes, you see these two, to be Sacrificed in himself, (and that is but once) and to be offered in the Sacrament, and that may be every day.

Also elsewhere (*a*). *Does Christ die so often as Easter is celebrated? Yet this Anniversary remembrance, do's as it were represent what was done of old, and so admonishes us as if we saw our Lord hanging on the Cross.*

And in the second Exposition it self, he says (*b*). *He gave us his Supper, and he gave us his Passion, viz. By representation.*

S. *Chrysostom* (*c*) says the same; *The mystery* (*viz.* the Eucharist) *is the Passion and the Cross.*

Which he explains thus elsewhere (*d*). *We always offer the same Sacrifice, or rather make a remembrance of* (his) *Sacrifice.*

So *Eulogius* of *Alexandria* (*e*), speaking of the tremendous mystery of Christs Body, says, *It is not the offering of different Sacrifices, but the remembrance of that one Sacrifice once offered.*

Theodoret also fully (*f*) tells us, That it is manifest to those that are skill'd in divine matters, that *we do not offer any other Sacrifice, but make a remembrance of that one saving one.*

S. *Austin*'s words are also remarkable (*g*.) To eat Bread in *the N. Testament is the Sacrifice of Christians.*

Eusebius (*h*) speaking of Christ's Sacrifice offered for our Salvation, adds. *He commanded us to offer to God continually the remembrance instead of the Sacrifice.* What can be more plain?

S. *Ambrose* says (*i*) that Christ is offered here, but it is (in imagine) *in an image*, and he opposes this to his offering himself (in veritate) *in truth.*

S. *Austin* (*k*) says, *Our Priest who offered himself an holocaust for our sins, also commended the similitude of his Sacrifice to be celebrated in memory of his passion.*

And

(*a*) *In Psal.* 21. *Præfat. in secundam expos.* Quotiens Pascha celebratur, nunquid toties Christus moritur? Sed tamen anniversaria recordatio, quasi repræsentat quod olim factum est, & sic nos facit moneri tanquam videamus in cruce pendentem Dominum.

(*b*) *In secunda expos. Psal.* 21. Cœnam suam dedit, Passionem suam dedit.

(*c*) *Hom.* 83. *in Matth.* Μυστήριον ἐστὶ τὸ πάθ⊙ καὶ ὁ σταυρός.

(*d*) *Hom.* 17. *in Epist. ad Hebr.* Τὴν αὐτὴν (θυσίαν) ἀεὶ ποιοῦμεν, μᾶλλον δὲ ἀνάμνησιν ἐργαζόμεθα θυσίας.

(*e*) *Apud Photium cod.* 280. Οὐ θυσιῶν ἔστι διαφόρων προσαγωγή, ἀλλὰ τῆς ἅπαξ προσενηνεγμένης θυσίας ἀνάμνησις.

(*f*) *In Epist. ad Hebr.* 8. 4. Ὡς οὐκ ἄλλω τινὰ θυσίαν προσφέρομεν, ἀλλὰ τῆς μιᾶς ἐκείνης καὶ σωτηρίας τὴν μνήμην ἐπιτελεῖν.

(*g*) *De civit. Dei, l.* 17. *cap.* 5. *in fine.* Manducare panem in N. Testamento est Sacrificium Christianorum.

(*h*) *Demonstr. Evan. l.* 1. *c.* 10. Μνήμην δὲ ἡμῶν παραδοὺς ἀντὶ θυσίας τῷ Θεῷ διενεγκεῖν προσφέρειν.

(*i*) *De Offic. l.* 1. *cap.* 48.

(*k*) *Quæstion* 83. *quæst.* 61 Ipse etiam Sacerdos noster qui seipsum obtulit holocaustum pro peccatis nostris, & ejus Sacrificii similitudinem celebrandam in suæ Passionis memoriam commendavit.

And elsewhere (*l*). *The Flesh and Blood of this Sacrifice --- after Christ's Ascension, is celebrated by the Sacrament of remembrance.*

Lastly, *Fulgentius* (*m*) calls the Sacrifice, which the H. Catholick Church ceases not to offer through the whole World, *the Sacrifice of Bread and Wine*; and says, that in this Sacrifice, *there is a thanksgiving and a commemoration of the Flesh of Christ which he offered for us.*

For want of apprehending things thus, they of the Church of *Rome* are tempted to utter words bordering upon Blasphemy; and with *Corn. à Lapide,* * to make their *Sacrificing Priest* greater than Christ the *Sacrifice.* dam modo majorem esse Christo ipso sacrificato. In omni enim Sacrificio sacerdos major est sua victima quam offert.

(*l*) *Contr. Faustum,* l. 20. c. 21. Hujus Sacrificii caro & sanguis — Post ascensum Christi per *Sacramentum memoriæ* celebratur.

(*m*) *De fide ad Petrum,* c. 16. Sacrificium panis & vini.

—— Gratiarum actio atq; commemoratio est carnis Christi quam pro nobis obtulit.

* *Comm. in Heb.* 7. *v.* 7. Adde Sacerdotem quatenus gerit personam Christi Sacrificantis, quo-

CHAP.

CHAP. VIII.

The Eighth Difference.

The Church of Rome *in all Sayings of the Fathers that mention a Change and Conversion in the Eucharist, understand it of such a Change as abolishes the Substance of Bread and Wine, the Accidents only remaining: But the Fathers never use these Phrases in this Sense.*

IT is acknowledged by us, That the Fathers speak frequently of a Change of the Bread and Wine, and their passing into, and being converted into Christ's Body and Blood. It is needless therefore to cite their Testimonies to this purpose; but I shall evidently prove, that they do not understand this *Change* and *Conversion* in the Sense of Transubstantiation.

To give some Order to their Testimonies, I shall not cite them in a heap, but as Proofs of several Assertions of theirs, which overthrow the Change by Transubstantiation.

I *Assertion.* *The Fathers make a difference betwixt the Change or Conversion of a Thing, and its Abolition.* When they *affirm* the one, they at the same time *deny* the other. But Transubstantiation supposes the Elements, as to the Matter and Substance of them, to perish and to be destroyed, when they are said to be changed.

You cannot well imagine that the *Fathers*, if they thought of Miracles wrought in the Sacrament, yet should ever dream of any such as had no agreement with all the Miracles that God ever wrought before. They well knew, (and our Adversaries do not deny it) that in all other Supernatural Changes, there was only the introducing of a new Form, the *Materia substrata* (the common Matter) remaining. So it was when *Moses*'s Rod was turned into a Serpent, when the Waters were turned into Blood, *Lot*'s Wife into a Pillar of Salt, the Wine in *Cana* of *Galilee* changed into Water; in all these, neither the old Matter was lost, nor new Matter created. The *Fathers* therefore laugh at any such Change where the Things changed utterly perish.

Tertullian

Tertullian (n) charges it as a great Absurdity against the *Marcionites*, that, according to them, *To be changed, was to perish wholly, and as to what they were before.*

(n) *De Resurrect. Carn. c. 55.* Quasi demutari, sit in totum & de pristino perire.

He has many smart Sayings against them, for denying the same Bodies to appear and rise at the Resurrection; and urges that of 1 *Cor.* 15. shewing that there will be a Change, not a Destruction of our Flesh. For, says he, *A Change is one thing, and Destruction is another. But it will perish in the Change, if that Flesh do not remain in the Change which shall be exhibited at the Resurrection.*

Aliud est demutatio, aliud perditio. Peribit autem demutata, si non ipsa permanserit in demutatione quæ exhibita fuerit in resurrectione.

―― *As therefore that which is destroyed, is not changed; so that which is changed, is not destroyed. For, to perish, is wholly not to be what it had been; but to be changed, is to be otherwise than it was. Moreover, by being otherwise, the thing may still be; for it has a Being which perishes not; for it only suffered a Change, not a Destruction.*

―Quomodo ergo quod perditum est, mutatum non est, ita quod mutatum est perditum non est. Perisse enim, est in totum non esse quod fuerit; mutatum esse, aliter esse est. Sed porrò dum aliter est, id ipsum potest esse; habet enim esse quod non perit; mutationem enim passum est, non perditionem.

Gelasius (o) also disputing against the *Eutychians*, who thought that the Humanity was converted into the Divinity, so that nothing remained, (just as with them the Bread is converted into Christ's Body, nothing of its Substance remaining) says thus: *Neither do's our Condition by the Union of the Deity seem to be glorified, but rather to be consumed, if it do's not subsist the same in Glory, but the Deity existing alone, the Humanity now ceases to be there, &c.*

(o) *De duabus Naturis.*

Nec videatur glorificata nostra conditio unione Deitatis, sed potius esse consumpta, si non eadem subsistit in gloria, sed solâ existente Deitate, humanitas illic esse jam destitit, &c.

――*By this way, it will not be found to be sublimated, but abolish'd.*

―Per hoc non sublimata, sed abolita potius invenitur.

The thing is so clear against Transubstantiation, that *Scotus* (p) confesses it. *I say, properly speaking, That Transubstantiation is not a Change.*

(p) *In 4. dist. 11. art. 1. sec. ad propositum.* Dico propriè loquendo, quod transubstantiatio non est mutatio.

2 *Assertion.* When the Fathers speak of converting a thing into another thing that was before, they suppose an *Accession* and an *Augmentation* made to that, into which the *Conversion* is made. Just as it is in Nourishment of our Bodies, the Food converted into them, makes an Increase of them.

Cyril

A full View of the Doctrines and Practices

(q) *Epist.* 1. *ad Succensum.*

Καϊηγορεύομϰν τ̃ Θεότητ[Θ-] ὡς μινητῆς κ̔ ὡς προσλαβούσης τι ἐν ἑαυτῇ, ὃ μὴ δεῖ κτ̀ φύσιν ἴδιον αὐτῆς.
Ἀμήχανον.

(r) *De duabus Naturis.*—— Accesserit, accreveritque Deitati.
—— transfusione humanitatis adjectæ velut aucta videatur.

(s) *Epist. ad Zachariam, & in Hom. de Corp. & Sang. Domini.*

——Πολλῷ μᾶλλον διὰ τ̀ ἐπιφοιτήσεως τ̃ ἁγίε πνεύματ[Θ-], ὁ ἄρτ[Θ-] κ̔ ὁ οἶν[Θ-] εἰς ἐπαύξησιν τ̃ σώματ[Θ-] τ̃ Χριστῦ, ἠδ ἐν σῶμα, κ̔ ὐ δύο.

(t) *In cap. 6. Joan.*

Ἐμποιήσεως τ̃ ἁγίε πνεύματ[Θ-].

Συνεξομοιοῦτο κ̔ εἰς αὐξησιν κ̔ σύςασιν συνεβάλλετο κτ̀ τὸ ἀνθρώπινον· κ̔ νῦν ἂν ὁ ἄρτ[Θ-] εἰς σάρκα τ̃ κυρίε μεταβάλλεται.

Cyril. of *Alexandr.* (q) arguing against those Hereticks who thought the glorified Body of Christ was converted into his Divinity, he says, *Thus we derogate from the Divinity, as if it were made, and as receiving something into it self, which is not proper to its Nature.* And he makes this Conversion to be *impossible* upon this account.

Gelasius (r) uses the same Phrases, of *Accession* and *Increase to the Deity*, and that *by the transfusion of the Humanity added to it, the Divinity would seem to be increased.*

Thus the later *Greeks* thought it was in *Christ's* Body, into which the Bread was changed.

Damascen (s), speaking of the Body of Christ which we partake of: *I declare*, says he, *it cannot be said, there are two Bodies of Jesus Christ, there being but one alone. For, as the Child, as soon as it is born, is compleat, but receives his growth from eating and drinking; and tho' he grows thereby, yet cannot be said to have two Bodies, but only one; so, by greater reason, the Bread and Wine, by the Descent of the Holy Spirit, are made one only Body, and not two, by the Augmentation of the Body of Christ.*

Theophylact (t) expresses it thus: *The Bread is changed* (μεταποιεῖθ) *into the Flesh of Christ by the ineffable Words, the mystical Benediction, and coming of the Holy Spirit upon it. No Man ought to be troubled in being obliged to believe that Bread becomes Flesh: For when our Lord was conversant in Flesh, and received his Nourishment from Bread, this Bread he did eat was changed into his Body, being made like to his holy Flesh, and contributed to augment and sustain it after a humane manner: And thus now is the Bread changed into our Lord's Flesh.*

See more Testimonies of the following *Greeks* in Monsieur *Claude*'s *Catholick Doctrine of the* Eucharist, in answer to Monsieur *Arnaud*, Lib. 3. *cap.* 13. *pag.* 228, 229. *in Fol.*

3 *Assertion,*

3. *Assertion*, (and the most remarkable) is this. *The Fathers use the same Terms of passing into, being changed, converted, becoming another thing, &c. in other Cases besides the Eucharist, wherein all agree there is no Change of Substances made.* Therefore there is no Argument can be drawn from such Expressions in favour of Transubstantiation, no not when the Word *Nature* or *Substance* is exprest in the Change.

Tertullian (*u*) has dashed this out of countenance, when he says to *Marcion*, *If thou defendest a Transfiguration and Conversion as far as the passing of the Substance of a thing into another, then Saul, who was turned into another Man, went out of his Body, &c.*

(u) De Resur. Carn. c. 55. Si transfigurationem & conversionem in transitum substantiæ cujusque defendis, ergo & Saul in alium virum conversus de corpore suo excessit, &c.

——Again, *It's possible to be changed*, says he, *to be converted and reformed into what shall happen at the Resurrection, and yet the Substance be preserved.*

Ibid. Ita & in resurrectionis eventum mutari, converti, reformari licebit, cum salute substantiæ.

But this will more fully appear, by the Axioms the Fathers lay down, and by the Instances they give.

Their Axioms are such as these.
Cyril. of Alexandr. (*x*). *For a thing to be made, do's not always signifie a change of Nature.*
Cyril. of Jerus. (*y*). *Whatsoever the Holy Spirit touches, that is always sanctified and changed.*
S. Jerome (*z*). *By the Fire of the Holy Spirit, all that we think, speak, and act, are changed into a Spiritual Substance.*

(x) Thesaur. Assert. 20. Τὸ γίνεσθαι ὁ πάντως φύσεως σημαίνει μεταβολὴν.
(y) Catech. Mystag. 5. Πάντως γὰρ ὧν ἐὰν ἐφάψηται τὸ ἅγιον πνεῦμα τοῦτο ἡγίασαι, ϰ̀ μεταβέβληται.
(z) In cap. 43. Ezekiel. Per ignem Spiritus sancti omnia quæ cogitamus, loquimur ac facimus in spiritualem substantiam convertuntur.

If these Sayings be strictly scann'd, they will amount to no more than a producing new Vertues and Qualities, which were not before.

Their Instances also shew the same.

1. *Of Miraculous Changes in Nature.*
S. Ambrose (*a*). *Let them learn, that Nature may be converted, when the Rock flowed out Waters, and Iron swam above Water.*

(a) In Hexem. l. 3. c. 2. Discant naturam posse converti, quando petra aquas fluxit, & ferrum aquæ supernatavit.

K   Again,

Again (b), speaking of Changes in the *Red Sea* and *Jordan*, when the Waters stood on an heap; *Is it not clear*, says he, *that the Nature of the Sea-waves and the Rivers Current was changed?*——Moses *threw Wood into the Water, and the Nature of the Waters lost its Bitterness.*——Elisha *also threw Wood into the Water, and Iron swam; and this we know was done besides Nature.*

Epiphanius (c) says, *The Hand of* Moses *was changed into Snow.*

S. *Chrysostome* (d) (speaking of the *Babylonian* Furnace) says, *The Elements forgetting their proper Nature, were changed to become profitable to them; and the very Beasts were no longer Beasts, nor the Furnace a Furnace.*

2. *Of the Change by the Fall.*

S. *Austin* says (e), *By Sin Man fell from the Substance in which he was made.*

3. *Of the Change by Regeneration.*

Gr. *Nyssen* (f) says, That by the Discipline of Christ *Men are changed into a Nature that is more Divine.*

And again (g). *Having divested themselves of Flesh and Blood, and being changed into a Spiritual Nature.*

Macarius (h) says, *Our Souls must be altered and changed from their present Condition, into another Condition, and into a Divine Nature.*

Cyril of Alexandria (i) speaks of Regeneration as that which *transmutes and changes us into the Son of God.*

4. *Of the Change in the Incarnation of Christ, and the Resurrection.*

Gr. *Nyssen* (k), speaking of Christ, whom he calls our First-fruits, says, That *by his mixing with God, he is changed into a Divine Nature.*

And

(b) *Lib. de iis qui initiant.* c. 9. Nonne claret naturam vel maritimorum fluctuum vel fluvialis cursus esse mutatam?—— Misit Moyses lignum in aquam & amaritudinem suam aquarum natura deposuit.——Misit etiam Elisæus lignum in aquam, & ferrum natavit; utique & hoc præter naturam factum esse cognoscimus.

(c) *Hæres.* 64. Εἰς χιόνα μεταβάλλει.

(d) *In Psal.* 10. Τὰ στοιχεῖα τ̅ οἰκείαν ἀγνοήσαντα φύσιν πρὸς τὸ χρήσιμον ἐκείνοις μεταβάλλουσιο, κ̅ τὰ θηρία ἐκ ἔτι θηρία ἦν, ὐδὲ ἡ κάμινος κάμινος.

(e) *In Psal.* 68. Conc. 1. Per iniquitatem homo lapsus est à substantiâ in qua factus est.

(f) *In Cantic.* Hom. 1. Μεταποιηθῆναι τῇ φύσει πρὸς τὸ θειότερον.

(g) *In Cantic.* Hom. 9. Ἔξω γενόντες σαρκὸς κ̅ αἵματΘ, εἰς ὃ ἢ πνευματικὴν μεταστοιχειωθέντες φύσιν.

(h) Hom. 44. Δεῖ ἀλλαγῆναι κ̅ μεταβληθῆναι τὰς ψυχὰς ἡμῶν ἀπὸ τ̅ νῦν καταστάσεως εἰς ἑτέραν κατάστασιν κ̅ φύσιν θείαν.

(i) *De S. Trin. Dial.* 3. Μεταστοιχειοῦσα πρὸς τ̅ υἱόν.

(k) *Contr. Eunom.* l. 2. Διὰ τ̅ πρὸς τ̅ Θεὸν ἀνακράσεως εἰς θείαν φύσιν μεταποιηθείσης.

of the Ancient Church, relating to the Eucharist. 67

And again (*l*) he uses this Phrase of Christ's Flesh, That *this is also changed into the Deity.*

Chrysologus (*m*) of the Incarnation; *God is changed into Man.*

The Author under the Name of *Eusebius Emissenus* (*n*) asks, *What is the Rod turned into a Serpent?* He answers, *God changed into Man.*

Tertullian (*o*), speaking of the Resurrection; *We shall be changed in a moment into an Angelical Substance.*

S. *Hilary*'s (*p*) Phrase of it is, *A Change of Earthly Bodies into a Spiritual and Ethereal Nature.*

Macarius (*q*) speaking of the Saints; *They are all changed into a Divine Nature.*

Chrysologus (*r*), speaking of Christ; *Let him come, let him come, to repair our Flesh, make our Souls new, change our Nature into a Celestial Substance.*

Cyril of Alexand. says (*s*) *At the Resurrection there will be another kind of Life, and a Change of our very Nature.*

S. *Austin* (*t*) says, *Our mortal Flesh is converted into the Body of an Angel.* —— *He that could change Water into Wine, is able to change Hay* (so he calls our Bodies that are Grass) *into Gold, and of Flesh make an Angel. If he made of Filth a Man, can he not make of Man an Angel?*

And elsewhere (*u*), speaking of our Bodies; *When it shall put on Incorruption and Immortality, now it will be no longer Flesh and Blood, but be changed into a celestial Body.*

Cassian. (*x*) (speaking of Christ's Flesh after the Resurrection;) *The Nature of his Flesh is changed into a spiritual Substance.*

5. Of the Change in Baptism.

S. *Chrysostome* (*y*). *Verily the Power of Baptism is great,* &c. *it do's not suffer Men to be* any longer *Men.*

(*l*) *Ibid. l.* 5. Μεταποιηθῆναι ᾗ ταύτην πρὸς τ̄ Θεότητα.

(*m*) *Serm.* 45. Deus in hominem convertitur.

(*n*) *Hom. de Pasch.* 3. Quid est Virga in Serpentem? Deus in hominem commutatus.

(*o*) Demutati in atomo erimus in Angelicam substantiam. *Contr. Marc. l.* 3. *c. ult.*

(*p*) *In Psal.* 138. Demutatio terrenorum corporum in spiritualem æthereamque naturam.

(*q*) *Hom.* 34. Εἰς θείαν φύσιν ἅπαντες μεταβάλλουσ̄.

(*r*) *Serm.* 45. Veniat, veniat ut carnem reparet, animam innovet, ipsam naturam in cœlestem commutet substantiam.

(*s*) *Orat. in Resurr. Christi.* Ἀλλὰ ζωῆς εἶδος αὐτῆς τ̄ φύσεως ἡμῶν μεταροίχεωσις.

(*t*) *Serm.* 12. de 40. à *Sirmond.* Edit. Caro mortalis convertitur in corpus Angeli. —— Ille qui potens fuit mutare aquam in vinum, potens est mutare fœnum in aurum, & de carne facere Angelum. Si de sordibus fecit hominem, de homine non faciet Angelum?

(*u*) *Cont. Adimant.* c. 12. Cùm induerit incorruptionem & immortalitatem, jam non caro & sanguis erit, sed in corpus cœleste mutabitur.

(*x*) *De Incarn. l.* 3. c. 3. Natura carnis in spiritualem est translata substantiam.

(*y*) *In Acta, Hom.* 23. Οὕτως μεγάλη τ̄ βαπτίσματος ἡ δύναμις, &c. οὐκ ἀφίησιν ἀνθρώπους ἔτι ἀνθρώπους.

Nazianzen.

68 *A full View of the Doctrines and Practices*

(z) *Orat. 40.* Χριστὸν μεταπεποίημαι τῷ βαπτίσματι.

(a) *In Joan. 3. 5.* Διὰ τῆς ἐνζύμου ἐνεργείας τοῦ ἁγίου ὕδατος περὶ θείαν τινὰ καὶ ἀφθίνον ἀναστοιχείωσιν διαμείβει.

(b) *Idem Epist. ad Letorum.* Ἐκ μεταληψίας μεταστοιχειούμεθα διὰ τῆς λύσεως χάριτος.

(c) *Cont. Crescon. lib. 4. c. 54.* Uno die tria, alio quinque millia credentium in suum corpus conversa suscepit.

(d) *In Joan. tract. 11.* Unde rubet Baptismus nisi sanguine Christi consecratus?

(e) *Serm. 14. de Passione.* Susceptus à Christo, & Christum suscipiens, non idem est post Lavacrum qui ante baptismum fuit, sed corpus regenerati sit caro crucifixi; hæc commutatio dextræ est excelsi, &c.

(f) *De Nativ. Dom. Serm. 4.* Christus dedit aquæ quod dedit matri: virtus enim altissimi & obumbratio Spiritus S. quæ fecit ut Maria pareret Salvatorem, eadem facit ut regeneret unda credentem.

Nazianzen (z). *I am changed into Christ in Baptism.*

Cyril of Alexandr. (a). *By the energy of the Spirit the sensible Water is changed into a kind of divine and unspeakable Power.*

Again (b), *That they are transelemented by Regeneration, through the Grace of the Laver of Baptism.*

S. Austin (c), speaking of Baptized Converts to Christianity. *It received on one day Three, on another Five thousand Believers converted into his Body.*

Again (d) elsewhere he asks, *How comes Baptism to be red, but by being consecrated with the Blood of Christ?*

Leo the Great (e). *He that is received by Christ, and receives Christ, is not the same Man after as before Baptism; but the Body of the Regenerate Person becomes the Flesh of Christ crucified; this is a Change by the Right Hand of the most High, &c.*

And again (f). *Christ gave to the Water, what he gave to his Mother: For the Virtue of the most High, and the Overshadowing of the Holy Ghost, which made Mary to bring forth a Saviour, the same makes the Water to regenerate a Believer.*

[Where we may also note by the way, That the mention of God's Omnipotence in the Case of Sacraments, do's not infer a substantial Change made there, since it do's not do it in *Baptism*; and yet the Omnipotency of God is seen in working Changes there.]

(g) *Ad Neoph. post Baptism. Serm. 2.* Aqua nostra suscipit mortuos & evomit vivos, ex animalibus veros homines factos, ex hominibus in Angelos transituros.

Zeno Veronens. (g). *Our Water receives the Dead and vomits forth the Living, being made true Men of meer Animals, such as are to pass from being Men into Angels, &c.* He says this of *Baptism*, which is not like common Water, which receives the Living to the bottom, and vomits forth the Dead.

Author

of the Ancient Church, relating to the Eucharist.

Author sub nomine Eusebii Emisseni (h). The Waters are suddenly changed, which are afterwards to change Men, viz. that are baptized in them.

Again (i). *A Man by the Water of Baptism, tho' outwardly he seems the same, yet inwardly he is made another Man.——The Person is not touched, and Nature is changed.*

Again (k). *Nothing is added to what is outward, and he is wholly changed in what is inward ——He is changed by a native Whiteness into the Dignity of his first Original; and by the Water of Baptism, or by the Fire of the Holy Spirit, is made the Body of that eternal Bread.*

(h) *Hom.* 2. *de Epiphan.* Mutantur subitò aquæ, homines postmodum mutaturæ.
(i) *Id. Hom.* 3. *de Epiph.* Homo per aquam baptismi, licet à foris idem esse videatur intus tamen alter efficitur —— persona non contingitur, & natura mutatur.
(k) *Idem Hom.* 5. *de Pasch.* In exteriore nihil additum est, & totum in interiore mutatum est —— In illam primæ originis dignitatem nativo candore mutatur, ac per aquam Baptismi, vel per ignem Spiritus S. æterni illius panis corpus efficitur.

4 *Assertion.* **The Change in the Eucharist which the Fathers so often mention, is either a Change into a Sacrament, or a Change of Efficacy and Virtue, by infusion and addition of Grace.**

What can be plainer (as to the first) than that of *Isidore of Sevil* (l)? Speaking of the Bread and Wine, he says, *These two are visible; but being sanctified by the Holy Spirit, they pass into a Sacrament of his divine Body.*

As for the Change of *Virtue and Efficacy,* take the following Testimonies, among many others.

Theodotus (m). *The Bread and Oil are sanctified by the Power of the Name, not being the same they were according to appearance when taken, but are changed powerfully into a Spiritual Virtue.* The like he says of the Water in Baptism, That it not only retains the less (that is, the Substance of Water) but also has Sanctification added to it.

Epiphanius also (n) speaks the same. *Here in Christ the virtue of Bread and force of Water are strengthned; not that the Bread is thus powerful to us, but the Virtue of the Bread* (which Christ puts into it). *For Bread is indeed an Aliment, but there is in it a Virtue to enliven us.*

(l) *De Offic. Ecclef.* l.1.c.18. Hæc duo sunt visibilia, sanctificata autem per Spiritum S. in Sacramentum divini corporis transeunt.

(m) *Epitom. ad fin. Operum Clem. Alex.* Καὶ ὁ ἄρτος καὶ τὸ ἔλαιον ἁγιάζεϑ τῇ δυνάμει τ͂ ὀνόματος, ὐ τὰ αὐτὰ ὄντα κ͂ τὸ φαινόμενον οἷα ἐλήφϑη, ἀλλὰ δυνάμει εἰς δύναμιν πνδματικὴν μεταβέβληται.—— Οὐ μόνον χωρεῖ τὸ χεῖρον, ἀλλὰ καὶ ἁγιασμὸν προσλαμβάνει.

(n) *In Compendio de Fide Ecclef.* Ἐνταῦϑα ἢ ἐν Χριστῷ ἰσχυροποιουμένων τ͂ δυνάμεως τ͂ ἄρτε, καὶ τ͂ ὕδατος ἰσχύος. ἵνα ἐκ ἄρτος ἡμῖν γένηϑ δύναμις, ἀλλὰ δύναμις ἄρτε, καὶ βρῶσις μ͂ ὁ ἄρτος, ἡ ϑ δύναμις ἐν αὐτῷ εἰς ζωογόνησιν.

Cyril

Cyril of Alexandr. (o). *God condescending to our Infirmities, indues the Oblations set before us with a Virtue of Life, and changes them into the Efficacy of his Flesh.*

And in the fore-cited place of his Comment upon *John* (p) he says, *The least particle of the Eucharist mixing it self with our whole Body, fills it with its own Efficacy, &c.*

Theodoret (q) tells those that partake of the Divine Mysteries, That they must not consider the Nature of the Things seen, but upon the change of Names, *believe the change made by Grace.* And he adds, That Christ honoured the visible Symbols with the Name of his Body and Blood, *not changing the Nature* (or Substance) *of them, but adding Grace to Nature.*

Theophylact (r) also says the same; *Our Lord preserves the Substance* (εἶδος, the same with φύσις in *Theodoret*) *of Bread and Wine, but changes them into the Virtue of his Flesh and Blood.*

Greg. Nyssen (s), speaking of the Privileges which *Consecration* advances things to, instances first in the Water of Baptism, and the great and marvellous Efficacy thereof; and proceeds to that of an Altar, which is at first but a common Stone, but after Dedication becomes an Holy Altar, which the Priests only touch with Veneration: And then adds the Instance of the Eucharist, *which at first is common Bread, but after the Mystery has consecrated it, it is called and becomes the Body of Christ. So the mystical Oil, and so the Wine before the Benediction, are things of little worth; but after the Sanctification of the Spirit, each of them operates excellently.*

So *Ammonius* (t) says, *The sensible Water is transelemented into a Divine Virtue* (for the Fathers make Changes in Baptism as well as the Eucharist) *and sanctifies those in whom it is.* Nay, he affirms, That *the Water differs only from the Spirit in our manner of Conception, for it is the same in Energy.*

Cyril

of the Ancient Church, relating to the Eucharist. 71

Cyril of *Jerusalem* (*u*) calling the *Flesh* and *Bread* in the Feast of Idols *defiled*, by the Invocation of impure Devils, he illustrates it thus. *As the Bread and Wine of the Eucharist, before the Invocation of the adored Trinity, is bare* Bread and Wine; *but after Invocation, the Bread is made the Body of Christ, and the Wine the Blood of Christ; so also in the same manner those Meats of the Pomp of Satan, in their own Nature being simple things, yet by the Invocation of Devils they become impure.*

(*u*) Catech. Mystag. 1. Μιαθέντα.

Ἄρτος ὢν καὶ οἶνος λιτός.

Τὸν αὐτὸν ἢ τρόπον τὰ τοιαῦτα βρώματα τῆς πομπῆς τῦ Σατανᾶ, τῇ ἰδίᾳ φύσει λιθά ὄντα, τῇ ἐπικλήσει τῶν δαιμόνων βέβηλα γίνε).

That's the Change here, That those Meats are in Quality (not in Substance) made impure; and so (if the Comparison hold) the Change in the other is, That they are *Hallowed Bread and Wine*, in Use and Efficacy different from what they were before.

The Author under *Cyprian*'s Name (*x*), speaking of Chrysm, says, *Truth is in the Sign, and the Spirit in the Sacrament.*

(*x*) De Unct. Chrysmat. Inest Veritas signo, & Spiritus Sacramento.

Thus S. *Ambrose* (*y*) understands the *Body of Christ* for that *Divine Substance and Presence of the Spirit* (which is the δύναμις & ἐνέργεια of Christ's Body). *Christ is in that Sacrament, because it is the Body of Christ. It is not therefore Corporeal but Spiritual Food: For the Body of God is a Spiritual Body. The Body of Christ is the Body of the Divine Spirit* (not his natural Body) *because it is the Spirit of Christ.*

(*y*) De iis qui init. c. 9. in fine

In illo Sacramento Christus est, quia corpus est Christi. Non ergo corporalis esca, sed spiritalis est. Corpus enim Dei corpus est Spiritale. Corpus Christi, corpus est divini Spiritus, quia Spiritus Christi (sc. est.)

Here *Corpus Dei* is *Corpus Spirituale*, that is, *Substantia Spiritualis, & Spiritus*.

The Author under his Name. (*z*). *How can that which is Bread be the Body of Christ? By Consecration.*——*To answer thee therefore, It was not the Body of Christ before Consecration; but after Consecration, I tell thee, it is the Body of Christ.* He said it, and it was done; he commanded, and it was created. *Thou thy self wast an old Creature; but after thou wast consecrated, thou beganst to be a new Creature,* &c.

(*z*) De Sacram. lib. 4. cap. 4. Quomodo potest qui panis est, corpus esse Christi? Consecratione.—— Ergo ut tibi respondeam, Non erat corpus Christi ante consecrationem; sed post consecrationem, dico tibi, quod corpus est Christi. Ipse dixit, & factum est; ipse mandavit, & creatum est. Tu ipse eras vetus creatura; posteaquam consecratus es nova creatura esse cœpisti, &c.

A full View of the Doctrines and Practices.

So that, according to this Author, as in Regeneration by Baptism Man changes his Nature, so do's the Consecrated Bread in the Eucharist change its Nature. Therefore it is no substantial Change, because the other confessedly is not so.

(a) Comm. in Matth. 26.

—Ita Deus præcipit agi à nobis, transferens spiritualiter panem in corpus, vinum in sanguinem, ut per hæc duo memoremus quæ fecit pro nobis de corpore suo, &c.

Druthmarus (a), speaking of a Person taking a long Journey, and leaving a Pledge behind him to remember him by, he adds, *Thus also God has commanded us to do, spiritually changing the Bread into his Body, and the Wine into his Blood, that by these two things we may remember what he hath done for us with his Body and Blood,* &c.

§ *Assertion.* The Fathers express in the same manner, and as fully, our *substantial* Change into *Christ's* Body, as of the Bread into *Christ's* Body. Yet none will from such Expressions assert the former; and there is the same reason not to do the latter.

(b) Orat. Catech. cap. 37.
Οὕτως τὸ ἀθανάτισθὲν ὑπὸ τῦ Θεῦ σῶμα ἐν τῷ ἡμετέρῳ γενόμενον ὅλον πρὸς ἑαυτὸ μεταποιεῖ καὶ μεταλλοιοῖ.

—Τὸ ἀθάνατον σῶμα ἐν τῷ ἀναλαβόντι αὐτὸ γενόμενον, πρὸς τὴν ἑαυτῆς φύσιν τὸ πᾶν μεταποίησεν.

(c) In Joan. lib. 4. *cap.* 3.

—Ἐν ἑαυτῷ ζήσει, πάντως ὅλος εἰς ἐμὲ μετασυχευμένος.

(d) De Nat. Dom. Serm. 10.
Christi caro de utero virginis sumpta, nos sumus.

(e) Id. de Passion. Serm. 14.
Non aliud agit Participatio corporis & sanguinis Christi, quàm ut in id quod sumimus transeamus.—Ipsum per omnia spiritu & carne gestemus.

Gr. *Nyssen (b)*. As a little Leaven, according to the Apostle, likens the whole Mass to it self; *so the Body (of* Christ*) put to death by God, coming into our Body, do's change and convert the whole into it self.*

And again, a little after. *His immortal Body being in him that receives it, changes the whole into its own Nature.*

Cyril of *Alexandria (c)* says, He that receives me by a participation of my Flesh, shall have Life in himself, being wholly transelemented into me.

P. *Leo Magn. (d). We are the Flesh of* Christ, *taken from the Womb of the Virgin.*

And elsewhere *(e). The Participation of the Body and Blood of* Christ *intends nothing else but that we should pass into that which we receive.* —— *That we may carry him in all things both in Spirit and Flesh.* (Not as *Bellarmine* and others pervert the Sense, reading *gustemus.*)

Again,

Again, in another place (*f*). *In that mystical Distribution of Spiritual Food, this is bestowed on us, this is taken, that receiving the Virtue of the Celestial Meat, we should pass into his Flesh, who was made our Flesh.*

(*f*) *Epist.* 23. In illa mysticâ distributione spiritualis alimoniæ, hoc impertitur, hoc sumitur, ut accipientes virtutem cœlestis cibi in carnem ipsius, quia caro nostra factus est, transeamus.

See more Testimonies to this sense in the Chapter following, Position 3.

CHAP. IX.

The Ninth Difference.

The Fathers *differ from the Church of* Rome, *in their Belief of Christ's Presence in the Eucharist. The Church of* Rome *asserts the substantial Presence of Christ's Natural Body there; but the* Fathers *deny it.*

THe former is the Assertion of the *Roman Church* in the *Trent Council*, in which an *Anathema* is pronounced (*g*) against such as deny, *That in the Holy Sacrament of the Eucharist is contained truly, really, and Substantially the Body and Blood of Christ,*——*but shall say, That he is in it only as in a Sign, or Figure, or Virtue.* And the Catechism ad Parochos (*h*) says, That *the True Body of our Lord Christ, the same that was born of the Virgin, and sits in the Heavens at the Right-hand of the Father, is contained in this Sacrament.*

I will now shew, that the Fathers advance such Positions as plainly contradict this Doctrine.

1 Position. *The Fathers ever since Christ's departure and Ascension into Heaven, look upon his Body as absent from Earth, tho' in another sense he is still present.*

All those Testimonies before produced under the Fifth Difference, concerning Bodies being commensurate to Space, and not being in more places than one, and saying this of *Christ's Body* as well as of other Bodies, are a Proof of this Position; but besides those, I will here add some further direct Proofs of it.

S. *Ambrose* thus (*i*). *Ascend* (speaking to Christ) *that we may follow thee with our Minds, whom we cannot see with our Eyes.* S. Paul *has taught us how we should follow thee, and where we may find thee. Seek those things that are above, where Christ sits, &c.*——*Therefore we ought not to seek thee upon Earth, nor in the Earth, nor according to the Flesh, if we would find thee.*
——Mary

(*g*) *Conc. Trid. Sess.* 13. *cap.*6. *Can.* 1.

(*h*) *Part.*2. *de Eucharist.n.*25.

(*i*) *Com. in Luc.* 24. Ascende nobis, ut te sequamur mentibus, quem oculis videre non possumus, &c.
——Ergo non supra terram, nec in terra, nec secundùm carnem quærere te debemus, si volumus invenire. Nunc enim secundùm carnem non novimus Christum.

of the Ancient Church, relating to the Eucharist.

—— *Mary could not touch him, because she sought him on Earth:* Stephen *touched him, because he sought him in Heaven.* Stephen *among the Jews saw him absent.*

S. *Austin* is so copious in this Argument, and his Testimonies so many, that a good Choice of them is only necessary. Thus he says (k). *Therefore our Lord absented himself from every Church, and ascended into Heaven, that our Faith may be edified; for if thou knowest nothing but what thou seest, where is Faith?*

Again (l). *Christ is always with us by his Divinity; but unless he were corporally absent from us, we should always carnally see his Body, and should never spiritually believe.*

This is a clear Testimony, that Christ is absent as to his Natural Body; and that if it were not so, he would be visible to us still.

Again (m), expounding those words, *The Poor ye have always with you, but me ye have not always;* He spake this, says he, *concerning the Presence of his Body: For according to his Majesty, according to his Providence, according to his unspeakable and invisible Grace, that is fulfilled which he said,* Behold I am always with you, &c. *But according to the Flesh which he assumed, according to what was born of the Virgin,* &c. (directly contrary to the *Trent* Catechism) *ye shall not have me always with you.*

And in another place (n). *According to the beautiful Presence of his Divinity, he is always with the Father; according to his corporal Presence he is now above the Heavens, at the right hand of the Father* (he forgot to add, and in the Holy Sacrament) *but according to the Presence of Faith, so he is in all Christians.*

What can be more plain than another Saying of his (o)? *We believe on him who sits now at the right hand of the Father; but yet whilst we are in the Body, we are absent as in a strange Country*

—— *Maria quia quærebat in terra, tangere non potuit;* Stephanus *tetigit, quia quæsivit in cœlo.* Stephanus *inter Judæos vidit absentem.*

(k) *Serm.* 140. *de Tempore.* Ideo Dominus noster absentavit se corpore ab omni Ecclesia, & ascendit in cœlum, ut fides ædificetur: si enim non nosti nisi quod vides, ubi est fides?

(l) *Serm.* 60. *de Verb. Dom.* Semper quidem Divinitate nobiscum est, sed nisi corporaliter abiret à nobis, semper ejus corpus carnaliter videremus, & nunquam spiritualiter crederemus.

(m) *Tract.* 50. *in Joannem.* Loquebatur de præsentia corporis sui: nam secundùm Majestatem suam, secundùm Providentiam, secundùm ineffabilem & invisibilem Gratiam, impletur quod ab eo dictum est, *Ecce ego vobiscum omnibus diebus,* &c. Secundùm carnem vero quam assumpsit, secundùm id quod de Virgine natus est, &c. non semper habebitis me vobiscum.

(n) *Serm.* 120. *de diversis.* Secundùm præsentiam pulchritudinis & divinitatis suæ semper cum patre est; secundùm præsentiam corporalem jam supra cœlos ad dextram patris est; secundùm præsentiam vero fidei in omnibus Christianis est.

(o) *Serm.* 74. *de diversis.* Credimus in eum jam sedentem ad dextram patris; sed tamen quamdiu sumus in corpore peregrinamur ab eo; nec eum dubitantibus, vel negantibus & dicentibus, *Ubi est Deus tuus*, valemus ostendere.

Country from him; nor can we shew him to those that doubt, to those that deny him, and say, Where is thy God?

If S. *Austin* had believed, as the *Roman* Church do's, the Corporal Presence of Christ in the Eucharist, he could have pointed to him upon the Altar, if any had asked, *Where is thy God?*

(p) In *Joan.* 9. 5. Κἂν ἐκ τ́ κόσμε χωνῇ διὰ τ́ σάρκα, πάρεςι πάλιν ἐδὲν ἧπον τοῖς ἐν αὐτῷ, ἡ ὁπησδήποτε τοῖς ὅλοις ἡ θεία τε κὶ ἀρρητ⊙ αὐτῦ φύσις, ἐδενὸς ἀποδημέσα τ́ ὄντων, ἡ ἀπολιμπανέμίνη τινὸς παντἀχῇ δ̀ τοῖς πᾶσι παρεῦσα κὶ πληρύσα μ̇ τό ϯ τὸ συμπάν.

(q) In *Joan.* 17. 12.

Cyril of *Alexandria* (p) says, *Tho' Christ be absent from the World as to his Flesh, yet he is present to those that are in him, and to the whole Universe, by his Divine and Ineffable Nature; neither is he absent from any Creature, nor distant from any, but is every where present to all, and fills the whole Universe.*

And elsewhere (q), speaking of the Disciples, who thought it a great loss to them, that being taken up to Heaven, he would now be absent according to his Flesh, he says, They ought not only to have respected and looked *to his Fleshly Presence*, but to have understood, *that tho' he was separated from their Society according to the Flesh, nor could be seen by their bodily Eyes, yet that he was present and assistant always by the Power of his Divinity.*

Εἰς τ́ ἔνσαρκον παρεσίαν.
— Εἰ τ́ πρὸς αὐτῶ συνεσίας ἀπινοσφίζοιτο χ́τ σάρκα——ἀλλὰ γε παρόντα κὶ συνόντα διὰ παντὸς τῇ τ́ θεότητ⊙ ἐξεσία.

Fulgentius (r). *One and the same* (Christ) *according to his Humane Substance, was absent from Heaven when he was upon Earth, and left Earth when he ascended up to Heaven; but according to his Divine and Immense Substance, neither left Heaven when he descended from Heaven, nor forsook Earth when he ascended into Heaven.*

(r) Ad Trasimund. l. 2. c. 17. Unus idemque secundùm humanam substantiam, absens coelo cùm esset in terra, & derelinquens terram cum ascendisset in coelum. Secundùm Divinam vero immensamque substantiam nec coelum dimittens, cùm de coelo descendit, nec terram deserens cùm ad coelum ascendit.

(s) Id. ibid. c. 18. Quomodo corporaliter ascendit in coelum, & in suis fidelibus prædicatur esse in terra, si non est in illo divinitatis immensitas quæ coelum implere possit & terram?

Again (s). *How did he corporally ascend into Heaven, and yet is said to be in the Faithful on Earth, unless the Immensity of the Divinity be in him, which can fill Heaven and Earth?* Yes, a *Romanist* would have told him of another way, That even his Body could be present in Heaven and Earth, *after the manner of a Spirit.*

(t) Contr. Eutych. l. 1. Hoc erat ire ad patrem & recedere

Vigilius Tapf. (t). *This was to go to the Father and recede from us, to take from the World the Nature*

Nature that he had taken from us.—— *For see the Miracle, see the Mystery of both* (Natures) *distinct* (not a Word of the Mystery of a Body being in more places than one); *The Son of God according to his Humanity departed from us; according to his Divinity he says to us,* Behold I am with you always, &c.—— *Those whom he left and departed from by his Humanity, he did not leave nor forsake by his Divinity.*

Again (u). *When Christ was on Earth, he was not in Heaven; and now because he is in Heaven, he surely is not on Earth,* &c.—— *Because the* Word *is every where, but his Flesh is not every where, it appears plainly, that one and the same Christ is of both Natures, and that he is every where according to the Nature of his Divinity, and contained in a Place according to the Nature of his Humanity* (which would be a bad Argument, if his Body were in Heaven and in the Eucharist at the same time). And then he concludes, *This is the Catholick Faith and Confession, which the Apostles delivered, the Martyrs confirmed, and the Faithful now still keep and preserve.*

Leo Magn. (x). *Christ being raised up to Heaven in sight of his Disciples, he put an end to his bodily Presence.* (So he explains it, that he was to remain at the Right-hand of his Father, till he should come again to judge the Quick and Dead.)

Bede (y). *Christ ascending after his Resurrection into Heaven as a Conqueror, left the Church as to his bodily Presence, which yet he never left destitute of the security of his Divine Presence, remaining in the Church always to the end of the World.*

This may abundantly suffice to prove the First Position.

à nobis, auferre de mundo naturam quam susceperat à nobis.
—— Nam vide miraculum, vide utriusque proprietatis mysterium, Dei filius secundùm humanitatem suam recessit à nobis, secundùm divinitatem suam ait nobis, *Ecce vobiscum sum omnibus diebus,* &c.—— Quos reliquit & à quibus decessit humanitate sua, non reliquit nec deseruit divinitate sua.

(u) Id. ibid. l. 4. Quando in terra fuit, non erat utique in coelo, & nunc quia in coelo est non est utique in terra, &c.—— Quia verbum ubique est, caro autem ejus ubique non est, apparet unum eundemque Christum utriusque esse naturæ, & esse quidem ubique secundùm naturam divinitatis suæ, & loco contineri secundùm naturam humanitatis suæ.
—— Hæc est Fides & Confessio Catholica, quam Apostoli tradiderunt, Martyres roborarunt, & Fideles nunc usque custodiunt.

(x) Serm. 2. de Ascens. Dom. Christus coram Discipulis elevatus in coelum, corporalis præsentiæ modum fecit.

(y) Com. in Marc. 13. Christus ad Patrem post resurrectionem victor ascendens, Ecclesiam corpcraliter reliquit, quam tamen nunquam divinæ præsidio præsentiæ destituit, manens in illa omnibus diebus usque ad consummationem seculi.

2 Position. *The Fathers distinguish the Presence of Christ's Body from the Sacrament of it, which they make to be*

be a Memorial and Pledge of Christ, as gone away and absent.

(z) *In* 1 *Cor.* 11. 29.

Ζωῆς βρύουσα βάπιζα.

"Ωσπερ γδ ἡ παρκσία ἀυτῶ, ἡ τὰ μεγάλα ἐκεῖνα κ᾿ ἀπόῤῥηία κομίζασα ἡμῖν ἀγαθὰ τοὺς μὴ δεξαμρύς ἀυτω μᾶλλον κατέκρινεν, ὅτω κ᾿ τὰ μυσήεια μείζον۞ ἐφόδια κολάσεως γίνη]αι τοῖς ἀναξίως μετέχυσι.

S. *Chrysostome* (z), expounding those words, *He that eateth and drinketh unworthily, eateth and drinketh judgment*; and asking how that Table, which is the Cause of so many good things, *and flows with Life*, should be made Condemnation to any, resolves it thus; That this happens not from its own Nature, but from the Purpose of him that approaches this Table. For, says he, *as Christ's Presence, which brought those great and unspeakable Blessings to us, did condemn those the more that did not receive it; so also the Mysteries make way for greater Punishments to those that unworthily partake of them.* A remarkable Testimony, because we see he distinguishes the Presence of Christ, from the Sacrament of it; compares the one with the other, and because of the Relation that the Mysteries have to Christ, and that both are intended to convey great Blessings, therefore they both, when unworthily treated, occasion greater Punishments.

(a) *Contr. Faust. l.* 20. *c.* 21. Hujus sacrificii caro & sanguis ante adventum Christi per victimas similitudinum promittebatur, in passione Christi per ipsam veritatem reddebatur, post ascensum Christi per Sacramentum memoriæ celebratur.

(b) *In* 1 *Cor.* 11. Hoc est, benedicens etiam passurus, ultimam nobis commemorationem sive memoriam dereliquit. Quemadmodum si quis peregre proficiscens, aliquod pignus ei quem diligit derelinquat, ut quotiescunque illud viderit, possit ejus beneficia & amicitias memorari; quod ille si perfecte dilexit, sine ingenti desiderio non possit videre, vel fletu.

S. *Austin* (a). *The Flesh and Blood of this Sacrifice, before Christ's coming, was promised by Victims of Resemblance, in the Passion of Christ it was exhibited in the Truth it self; after Christ's Ascension it is celebrated by the Sacrament of Remembrance.* Where you see, the *Sacrament of Remembrance* is opposed to the *Exhibition of the Truth.*

Author Comm. in Epistolas Pauli (inter Hieronymi Opera) (b), upon those words, *He took Bread, and after he had given thanks, he brake it: That is*, says he, *blessing us even when he was about to suffer, he left his last Memorial with us. Just as if one travelling into another Country, should leave a Pledge with him whom he loved, that whensoever he look'd upon it, he might call to mind his Favours and Friendship; which such a Person, if he perfectly lov'd him, could not behold without a great passion or weeping.*

It

It will be very hard to reconcile this *Pledge of Absence* with such a *constant Presence* of his Body as the Church of *Rome* teaches, even there where we are required to look upon that Pledge, and remember our absent Friend. *Sedulius* has the same Exposition of the Place, almost in the same words.

Primasius also confirms it (c), upon those words, *The same night that our Lord was betrayed, he took Bread.* He left, says he, *to us his last Memorial.*——— *God our Saviour gave us an Example, that as often as we do this, we may call to mind that Christ has died for us all. Therefore we call it* Christ's Body, *that when we remember this, we may not be unthankful for his Grace. As if one that was a dying should leave some Pledge to one whom he loved, which he, after his death, when ever he look'd upon, could not contain his Tears, if he perfectly loved him.*

(c) *In* 1 *Cor.* 11.

Ultimam nobis commemorationem reliquit.— Salvator Deus exemplum dedit, ut quotiescunque hoc facimus, in mente habeamus, quod Christus pro nobis omnibus mortuus est. Ideo nobis dicitur *Corpus Christi*, ut cùm hoc recordati fuerimus, non simus ingrati gratiæ ejus: quemadmodum si quis moriens relinquat ei quem diligit aliquod pignus, quod ille post mortem ejus, quandocunque

viderit, nunquid potest lacrymas continere, si eum perfectè dilexerit?

Bede (d) has also given us the same Account. *As*, says he, Moses *witnesses that the Tree of Life was placed in the midst of Paradise, so by the Wisdom of God, to wit, of Christ, the Church has Life given it, in whose Sacraments of his Flesh and Blood she now receives* the Pledge of Life, *and hereafter shall be made happy in a* present Sight of him. Where you see he distinguishes this Pledge from his *present Aspect* hereafter.

(d) *In Proverb. lib.* 1. *c.* 3. Sicut in medio Paradisi, lignum vitæ positum testatur Moses, ita per Sapientiam Dei, viz. Christi, vivificatur Ecclesia, cujus & nunc Sacramentis carnis & sanguinis *pignus vitæ* accipit, & in futuro *præsenti* beatificabitur *aspectu*.

Gaudentius (e) calls the Eucharist *that hereditary Gift of his New Testament, which on the night that he was delivered to be crucified, he left with us as a Pledge of his Presence. This is the Provision of our Journey, by which we are fed and nourished in this way of Life, till removing from this World, we go to him.*

(e) *In Exod. tract.* 2. Vere illud est hæreditarium munus Testamenti ejus novi, quod quod nobis ea nocte qua tradebatur crucifigendus, tanquam pignus suæ præsentiæ dereliquit. Hoc illud est viaticum nostri itineris, quo in hac via vitæ alimur ac nutrimur, donec ad ipsum pergamus de hoc seculo recedentes.

Still we see it is a *Pledge of Absence.*

3 Position. *Whatsoever Presence of Christ the Fathers speak of in the Eucharist, they acknowledge the same in Baptism,*

tism, and in as full Expressions. So that if we will follow the *Fathers*, we may as well assert a Substantial Presence of Christ's Body in *Baptism*, as in the *Eucharist*. But this on all hands is denied.

Gaudentius (*f*) in the Place last cited, speaking of our Lord Jesus, says, *We believe him to be in his Sacraments*. He had spoke of both Sacraments before, and his words may well be understood of both. I am sure *other Fathers* give their full consent to it.

S. *Basil* (*g*) speaking of the Excellency of Christ's Baptism, and the supereminent Glory of it, says, That Christ the Son of God has determined it, *That one greater than the Temple, and greater than Solomon is here*.

So Gr. *Nazianzen* (*h*). *Behold, one greater than the Temple is here, to them that perfectly consider.*

S. *Ambrose* (*i*), speaking of Baptism, says, *O Christ, I find thee in thy Sacraments.*

And again (*k*). *Believe that there is the Presence of the Divinity.*

So afterwards (*l*). *Believe that the Lord Jesus is present, being invoked by the Prayers of the Priests.*

S. *Austin* (*m*), upon those words, *The poor ye have always with you, but me ye have not always*; discourses thus concerning *having Christ now*. *Now thou hast Christ by Faith, now thou hast him by the Sign of Christ, now by the Sacrament of Baptism, now by the Meat and Drink of the Altar.*

Here you see he makes no difference of having Christ at present these several ways he mentions.

S. *Chrysostome* (*n*). *As when thou art baptized, it is not he* (viz. the Priest) *that baptizes thee, but it is God that holds thy Head by his invisible Power, and neither Angel, nor Archangel, nor any other, dare approach and touch thee, &c.*

The same Father * thus speaks of one to be baptized, *Thou shalt presently embrace our Lord himself,*

(*f*) Tract. 2 in Exod. in fine. — Quem Sacramentis suis inesse credimus.

(*g*) De Baptism. lib. 1. cap. 2. Μεῖζον τ̄ ἱερὸν ὧδε, καὶ μεῖζον τ̄ Σολομῶντ® ὧδε.

(*h*) Orat. 40. Ἰδοὺ πλεῖον τ̄ ἱεροῦ ὧδε, πρὸς τοῖς τελείως λογιζομένοις.

(*i*) Apol. David. c. 12. Christe, in tuis te invenio Sacramentis.

(*k*) De his qui initiant. c. 2. Crede illic esse Divinitatis præsentiam.

(*l*) Ibid. cap. 5. Crede adesse Dominum Jesum invocatum precibus Sacerdotum.

(*m*) In Joan. tract. 50. Habes Christum in præsenti per fidem, in præsenti per signum Christi, in præsenti per baptismatis Sacramentum, in præsenti per altaris cibum & potum.

(*n*) Hom. 51. in Matth. Lat. Græc. Savil. Hom. 50. pag. 322. Ὥσπερ γὰρ ὅταν βαπτίζῃ, οὐκ αὐτός σε βαπτίζει, ἀλλ' ὁ Θεὸς ἐστιν ὁ κατέχων σε τ̄ κεφαλὴν ἀοράτῳ δυνάμει, καὶ οὔτε ἄγγελ®, οὔτε ἀρχάγγελ®, οὔτε ἄλλ® τις τολμᾷ προσελθεῖν καὶ ἅψασθαι, &c.
* Id. Epist. ad Colos. Hom. 6.

himself, *be mingled with his Body, be incorporated into that Body which is seated above, whither the Devil cannot approach.*

So the Author of the Commentaries upon S. *Mark* (o) speaks to those that are to be baptized, as if Christ were present. *You that are to receive Baptism, first lay fast hold on the Feet of your Saviour, wash them with your Tears, wipe them with your Hair,* &c.

Marcus the *Hermite* (p) speaking of a baptized Person, says, *Upon his Baptism he has Christ lying hid in him.*

S. *Chrysostome* again (q). *If Christ be the Son of God, and thou hast put him on (*viz.* in Baptism) having the Son in thy self, and being made like to him, thou art brought into one Kindred and Nature.*

Again elsewhere (r), speaking of Christ's partaking of our Flesh and Blood, he says, *He communicated with us, not we with him: How then are we of his Flesh and of his Bones? He means this; That as he was begotten by the Holy Ghost without the concurrence of Man, so are we regenerate in Baptism.*——*As therefore the Son of God was of our Nature, so are we also of his Substance; and as he had us in himself, so also we have him in our selves.* And all this is by Baptism.

Cyril of *Alexandr.* (s) says of the Soul, That *it is conjoined perfectly to Christ by holy Baptism.* And tho' every one knows that Union supposes Presence and Nearness, yet this is never made an Argument that Christ is present corporally in *Baptism.* No more can such like Phrases, used by him concerning the *Eucharist*, be urged as a Proof of it.

S. *Hilary* (t) speaks many things of our real Union with Christ in the Sacrament of the Eucharist. *We truly receive the Word in the Lord's Food; how is he not then to be thought naturally to dwell in us?*——*We under the Mystery*

(o) Inter Opera Chrysost. Hom. 14. Vos qui accepturi estis Baptismum, primum tenete pedes Salvatoris, lavate lachrymis, crine tergite, &c.

(p) De Baptism. Ἀπὸ τ͂ βαπτίσματ[Θ] τὸν Χριςὸν ἐν ἑαυτῷ κεκρυμμένον ἔχει.

(q) In Gal. 3. v. 27. Εἰ ὁ Χριςὸς υἱὸς τ͂ Θεῦ, σὺ ἢ αὐτὸν ἐνδέδυσαι, τὸν υἱὸν ἔχων ἐν ἑαυτῷ ἢ πρὸς αὐτὸν ἀφωμοιωθεὶς, εἰς μίαν συγγένειαν ἢ μίαν ἰδέαν ἤχθης.

(r) In Ephes. 5. v. 30. Ὅτι ὥσπερ ἄνευ συνουσίας ἐκεῖν[Θ] γεγόν[η] ἐν πνεύματ[Θ] ἁγίῳ, ὕτω ἢ ἡμεῖς γινώμεθα ἐν τῷ λυτῷ.

——Ὡς ἂν ὁ υἱὸς τ͂ Θεῦ τῆ ἡμετέρας φύσεως. ὕτω ἢ ἡμεῖς τῆς οὐσίας αὐτῶ· ἢ ὡς ἡμᾶς ἐκεῖν[Θ] ἔχει ἐν ἑαυτῷ, ὕτω ἢ ἡμεῖς αὐτὸν ἔχομεν ἐν ἡμῖν.

(s) Tom. 6. in Collectan. Συναφθεῖσα τελείως τῷ Χριςῷ διὰ τ͂ ἁγίου βαπτίσματ[Θ].

(t) Lib. 8. de Trinit. Nos vere Verbum cibo Dominico sumimus, quomodo non naturaliter manere in nobis existimandus est? &c.——Nos sub Mysterio vere carnem corporis

do truly take the *Flesh of his Body, and thereby shall be one, because the Father is in him, and he in us.* ——— *So that since he was in the Father by the Nature of the Divinity, we on the contrary in him by Corporal Nativity, and he might be believed again to be in us by the Mystery of the Sacraments.*

But then it is observable, that he do's not say these great things only of the *Eucharist*, that by partaking of it we have a natural Union with Christ; but he says we have the same by *Faith*, by *Regeneration*, and by *Baptism* (*u*). *How dost thou not understand a natural Unity in those, who are one by the nature of one Faith?* ——— Again, *The Unity of Consent has no place in those, who are one in the Regeneration of the same Nature.* ——— Again, *What should Agreement of Wills do here, when they are one by this, that they are cloathed with one Christ, by the Nature of one Baptism?*

I'le add but one Testimony more, out of *Fulgentius* (*x*); but it is very home. *Neither need any one at all doubt, that then every Believer is made Partaker of our Lord's Body and Blood, when he is made a Member of Christ in Baptism.*

And yet even this do's not infer a Substantial Presence of Christ in Baptism.

To make this Position still more full and cogent, let me add, *That the Father's so speak of the Waters of Baptism, as if they were turned into Blood, and we dyed in that Blood, and baptized in Blood; and yet all these neither prove the Presence of Christ's natural Body, nor Transubstantiation there.*

To name a few Testimonies.

S. *Jerom* (*y*) upon those words, *Wash ye, make ye clean,* says, *Be ye baptized in my Blood by the Laver of Regeneration.*

Again (*z*) he says of the Eunuch, *He was baptized in the Blood of the Lamb whom he read of in the Prophet.*

---

sui sumimus, & per hoc unum erimus, quia Pater in illo est & ille in nobis.——— Ut cùm ille in Patre per naturam Divinitatis esset, nos contra in eo per corporalem Nativitatem, & ille rursum in nobis per Sacramentorum inesse mysterium crederetur.

(*u*) *Ibid.* Quomodo non naturalem in his intelligis unitatem, qui per naturam unius fidei unum sunt? ——— Cessat in his assensûs unitas, qui unum sunt in ejusdem regenerationis naturæ. ——— Quid hic animorum concordia faciet cum per id unum sint, quod uno Christo per naturam unius Baptismi induantur?

(*x*) *De Bapt. Æthiop cap. ult.* Nec cuiquam aliquatenus ambigendum est, tunc unumquemque fidelium corporis sanguinisque Dominici participem fieri quando in Baptismate membrum Christi efficitur.

(*y*) *In Esa.* 1. Baptizemini in sanguine meo per lavacrum regenerationis.

(*z*) Baptizatus est in sanguine agni quem legebat. *In Esa.* 43.

So

of the Ancient Church, relating to the Eucharist.

So S. *Austin* (a). *Whence comes Baptism to be red, but because it is consecrated with Christ's Blood?*

Prosper (b). *They are dyed in the Blood of Christ in Baptism.*

S. *Chrysostome* (c) speaking to those that were to receive Baptism. *You shall be cloathed with the Purple Garment dyed in the Lord's Blood.*

Julius Firmicus (d). *Seek for the Noble Fountains, enquire for the pure Waters, that there, after thy many Stains, the Blood of Christ with the Holy Spirit may make thee White.*

Cæsarius (e), or the *Author* of the *Paschal Homily. The Soul enters the Waters of Life, that are red as it were, being consecrated by the Blood of Christ.*

Isidore of Sevil (f). *What is the Red Sea, but Baptism consecrated by the Blood of Christ?*

And again (g). *The true Israel enters the Red Sea, to wit, Baptism, signed with the Blood of Christ.*

And *Primasius* (h). *The Red Sea signifies Baptism, graced with the Blood of Christ.*

(a) *In Joan. tract.* 11. Unde rubet Baptismus, nisi sanguine Christi consecratus?

(b) *De Promiss. part.* 2. Baptismo sanguine Christi tinguntur.

(c) *Catech. ad illuminand.* Τῆ πορφύραν περιβάλλων τῷ αἵματι βεφάσων δεσποτικῷ.

(d) *De Error. Prof. Relig.* c. 28. Quare fontes ingenuos, quare puros liquores, ut illic te post multas maculas cum Spiritu S. Christi sanguis incandidet.

(e) *Hom.* 5. *Paschal.* Ingreditur anima vitales undas, velut rubras sanguine Christi consecratas.

(f) *In Exod.* c. 19. Quid Mare rubrum, nisi Baptismum Christi sanguine consecratum?

(g) *De vocat. Gent.* c. 23 Verus Israel ingreditur Mare rubrum, baptismum scilicet Christi cruore signatum.

(h) *In* 1 *Cor.* 10. Mare rubrum significat Baptismum Christi sanguine decoratum.

4 Position. *The Fathers so consider the Presence of Christ's Body in the Eucharist, as can no way agree to the Presence of his natural and glorified Body there.*

The Fathers (as I have before proved, see *Chap.* 7. *Observ.* 4. *Reason* 2.) look upon the *Bread and Wine* in the Eucharist as the *Representative Body* of Christ ; and thus Christ's Body is indeed present by that which is its *Proxy* or *Pledge*: But this Presence in a proper sense is Absence, and does suppose it.

I shall therefore here only insist upon one Consideration of Christ's Body there, which can only agree to his *Representative Body*, but not to the *Natural* and *Glorified Body of Christ.* Viz.

The Presence of Christ's Body in the Eucharist, which the Fathers speak of, is of his Body as crucified, and slain, and dead. Now this cannot agree to his *Natural Body*, which, by our

A full View of the Doctrines and Practices

Adversaries Confession is impassible and invulnerable now it is glorified, and cannot admit any separation of Parts, which Crucifixion do's suppose, nor die any more. It is plain by the words of Institution, that the Body of Christ there spoken of, is his *broken Body*, such as Crucifixon caused, and his *Blood* is considered as *shed* and *poured out* of his Veins, and *separated* from his Body, which our Adversaries that speak of his Presence in the Sacrament do not believe.

But the Fathers did believe this, and say so; for which at the present, in stead of all, I need cite only S. Chrysostome (i), whose Phrase for the Eucharist is, *While this Death is perfected, this tremendous Sacrifice, these ineffable Mysteries.*

Again (k). *Christ lies before us slain.*

In another place (l). *While the Sacrifice is brought forth, and Christ the Lord's Sheep is slain.*

And elsewhere (m). *What dost thou, O Man? Thou swearest upon the Holy Table, and there thou killest thy Brother, where Christ lies slain.*

Again (n) he expresses it thus rhetorically: *When thou seest the Lord slain and lying, and the Priest standing by the Sacrifice and praying, and all the People purple-dyed in that precious Blood, &c.*

Again in another place (o), speaking of the Priest standing before the Holy Table, &c. he adds, *When thou seest the Sheep* (viz. Christ) *slain and divided*, &c.

So also elsewhere (p). *O wonderful! The Mystical Table being prepared, the Lamb of God slain for thee, &c. his Blood emptied into the Cup out of his immaculate Side, for thy Purification, dost thou not fear?*

This slaying and dividing the Body of Christ, this emptying the Blood out of his Veins, he speaks of, cannot be understood of any thing, but of his *Representative Body*.

Neither can another Saying of his have any other sense (q); where telling us how *Christ has given us leave to be filled with his holy Flesh*, he adds, *He has proposed himself before us slain.*

So

(i) Hom. 21. in Act. Τῦ θανάτυ ἐπ]ελεμβὼν ἐκείνυ,ἢ φεικ-]ῆς θυσίας, τῶν ἀφάν]ων μυσηείων.

(k) Homil. de Prodit. Judæ. Ἐσφαγμῦὸς πρόκει] ὁ Χεισός.

(l) In Epist. ad Ephes. Hom. 3. Ἐκφερομένης τ θυσίας, καὶ τ̂ Χεισῦ τεθυμένε τ̂ προβάτε τ̂ δεσποτικῦ.

(m) Ad Popul. Antioch. hom. 15. —Ἔνθα ὁ Χεισὸς κεῖ] τεθυμέν(Θ.

(n) Lib. 3. de Sacerdotio. "Οταν ἴδης τὸν κύειον τεθυμένον καὶ κείμενον, καὶ τὸν ἱερέα ἐφεστῶτα τῷ θύματι καὶ ἐπευχόμενον, καὶ πάντας ἐκείνῳ τῷ τιμίῳ φοινισσομένες αἵματι, &c.

(o) In Cœmeter. appel. "Οταν ἴδης τὸ πρόβαιον ἐσφαγιασμένον καὶ ἀπηρτισμένον, &c.

(p) De Pænit. in Encæn. Τῦ ἀμνῦ τ̂ Θεῦ ὑπὲρ σῦ σφαγια-ζομένε, &c. Τὸ αἵμα] ἐν τῷ κρατῆρι εἰς σὴν κάθαρσιν ἐκ τ̂ ἀκεράτυ πλευρᾶς κενουμένε, ἒ φοβῇ;

(q) Hom. 51. in Matth. Τῶν ἁγίων σαρκῶν αὐτῦ ἐμπλησθῆναι ἔδωκεν ἡμῖν.—ἑαυ]ὸν παρέθηκε τεθυμένον.

of the Ancient Church, relating to the Eucharist. 85

So that if we eat his Flesh, it must be his dead Body; for so he is set before us to be eaten: But that's impossible.

But all this is easily understood in our way, or rather as he himself has explained it, when he says (r), *The Mystery is the Passion and Cross of Christ.*

(r) *Hom.* 83. *in Matth.* Μυϛηϵιον ϵϛὶ τὸ πάθϴ κϳ ὁ ϛαυϵὸς.

With which agrees that of S. *Austin* (s). *He gave his Supper, he gave his Passion.*

(s) *In Psal.* 21. Cœnam suam dedit, passionem suam dedit.

Or, as he says in another place (t), comparing the Gentiles to those Dogs that lick'd *Lazarus*'s Sores; *Yet*, says he, *they lick the Passions of our Lord in the Sacraments of his Body and Blood with a devout Sweetness.*

(t) *Super Evang. lib.* 2. qu. 38. ——Tamen passiones Domini in Sacramentis corporis & sanguinis ejus suavitate lambunt devotissimâ.

The Reader will meet with further Testimonies to this purpose afterwards, under the Head of *Eating Christ's Body* and *drinking his Blood*, which, according to the *Fathers*, is to be done *mystically* and *spiritually* (considered as slain), and therefore his Presence must be such too: For his Body is *present* just as it is *eaten.*

The Sum of all is this, That according to the *Fathers*, Christ is considered in the Sacrament as *dead and slain*, and therefore can be only present there *typically* and *by representation*: For so *Card. Perron* himself confesses (u), *The Sacrament is not really the Body of Christ, put in the actual state of one slain, dead, and without Life; nor do's it contain it so, but in that respect do's only represent it.*

(u) *De locis Augustin. cap.* 3. Sacramentum non est realiter corpus Christi in actuali occisi, mortui & inanimati statu constitutum, nec eâ ratione illud continet, sed eatenus tantum repræsentat, &c.

5 Position. *That according to the Fathers, the Presence of Christ's Body to us now, is a Presence to our Faith and Minds, a Presence of Union, of Efficacy and Grace.*

This is S. *Austin*'s constant Doctrine. I have cited a place out of him before, where reckoning up the several Presences of Christ (x), the *Presence of his Divinity*, so he is with his Father; his *Corporal Presence*, so, he says, he is *now above the Heavens, at the Right Hand of the Father*; and he knows but one more, which is the *Presence of Faith, by which he is in all Christians.*

(x) *Serm.* 120. *de diversis.*
——Secundùm præsentiam corporalem jam supra cœlos ad dextram patris est.
——Secundùm vero præsentiam fidei in omnibus Christianis est.

Thus

Thus also elsewhere (y). *Christ is in Heaven, but he is also in the Hearts of Believers.*

And again (z), exhorting the Jews *to hear and take hold on Christ*, he brings one in asking, *Whom shall I lay hold of? one that is absent? &c.* He answers, *Send forth thy Faith, and thou hast hold of him. Thy Fathers laid hold of him in his Flesh, do thou hold him in thy Heart, because Christ who is absent, is also present, for if he were not present, he could not be held by us.* But still all is to be done by Faith, for the Reason he gives; *He brought his Body into Heaven, but his Majesty (i. e. his Divinity) was not withdrawn from the World.*

And afterwards (a). *According to the Presence of his Majesty, we always have Christ; according to the Presence of his Flesh, it was rightly said to his Disciples,* Me ye have not always. *The Church had him a few days according to his Fleshly Presence; now it holds him by Faith, and sees him not.*

So again (b), speaking of those *whom he kept when he was with them*, he says, *These Words can be rightly understood of none but those who believing in him, were begun to be kept by him by his Corporal Presence, and whom he was about to leave by his Bodily Absence, that he might keep them, together with his Father, by his Spiritual Presence.*

Lastly, S. *Austin* says (c), *Our Lord comforting us, who now that he sits in Heaven cannot handle him, but only touch him by Faith, says to* Thomas, Because *thou hast seen, thou hast believed; blessed are they that have not seen and believe.*

S. *Cyril of Alexandria* agrees perfectly with this Doctrine (d), and knows no other Presence of Christ now, but what is Spiritual and Divine, since he ascended to the Father, and left the World. *For they that judge aright, and are of a confirmed Faith, must be persuaded, that tho' Christ*

(y) Serm. 12. de diversis. In cœlo quidem Christus est, sed etiam in corde credentium.

(z) In Evang. Joan tract 50. —— Audeant & teneant. Responder, Quem tenebo? absentem? Quomodo in cœlum manum mittam, ut ibi sedentem teneam? Fidem mitte, & tenuisti: parentes tui tenuerunt carnem, tu tene corde, quoniam Christus absens etiam præsens est, nisi præsens esset à nobis teneri non posset, &c.
—— Corpus enim suum intulit cœlo, majestatem non abstulit mundo.

(a) Ibid. propè finem. Secundùm præsentiam majestatis semper habemus Christum: secundùm præsentiam carnis rectè dictum est discipulis, *Me autem non semper habebitis.* Habuit illum Ecclesia secundùm præsentiam carnis paucis diebus. modo fide tenet, oculis non videt.

(b) In Ev. Joan. tract. 106. Non rectè intelliguntur ——nisi hi quos in se credentes servare jam cœperat præsentia corporali, & quos relicturus fuerat absentia corporali, ut eos cum patre servaret præsentia spirituali.

(c) Expos. in Epist. Joan. tract. 1. Dominus consolans nos qui ipsum jam in cœlo sedentem manu contrectare non possumus, sed fide contingere, ait illi, *Quia vidisti & credidisti, beati qui non viderunt & credunt.*

(d) In Joan. 13. 33. Διακείσθω ἢ δεῖν ἀναγκαῖον ἐῖ φημὶ, τοῦ οἴγε φρονοῦσιν ὀρθῶς, ᾗ ἰδρυμένην ἔχουσι τ᾽ πίστιν, ὡς εἰ κ᾽ ἄπεστιν ἡμῶν τῇ σαρκὶ, τ᾽

of the Ancient Church, relating to the Eucharist. 87

Christ be absent from us in the Flesh, having undertaken a long Journey to God and the Father, that yet he compasses all things by his Divine Power, and is present to them that love him, &c.

And again (*e*). *It seemed to them intolerable, to be separated from Christ, tho' he was always present with them by the Power and Efficacy of the Spirit.*

Elsewhere (*f*) he lays it down as a Rule, *That Christ's Spirit dwelling in the Saints, supplies the Presence and Power of Christ in his absence.*

And many more Places I might name out of him.

Their Sense is well exprest in that short Saying of the *Author* under S. *Cyprian's* (*g*) Name, which I'le again repeat. *Truth is in the Sign, and the Spirit in the Sacrament.*

S. *Ambrose* (*h*) knows of no other Presence of Christ now, but what makes the Father to be present with him too, and that is the Presence of the Spirit and of Grace. His Words are very remarkable. *The Spirit then so comes, as the Father comes: For the Son said,* I and my Father will come, and make our abode with him. *What? do's the Father come corporally?* (And the same may be ask'd too of the Son, by what follows.) *The Spirit so comes, as that in him when he comes is the full Presence of the Father and the Son.*—— A little after, *We have therefore proved, that there is one Presence, and that there is one Grace* (which explains what the Presence is) *of the Father, Son, and Holy Ghost, which is so Celestial and Divine, that the Son gives thanks to the Father for it,* &c.

Bede (*i*) observing how many times Christ appeared to his Disciples after his Resurrection, says, *He designed to shew by these frequent Appearances, that he would be spiritually or divinely present in all Places at the Desire of the Faithful.*

(*c*) Ibid. in v. 35. Οὐ φορητὸν ἐδιεφαίρετο τὸ χωρίζεσθαι Χριστῷ, καίτοι συνόντος αὐτοῖς διὰ παντὸς τῇ τ̅ πνεύματος δυνάμει τ̅ κ̅ συνεργείᾳ.

(*f*) In Joan. 14. 27. Τὴν αὐτὴ τ̅ Χριστοῦ παρουσίαν τ̅ κ̅ δύναμιν ἀναπληροῖ τὸ πνεῦμα αὐτῷ τοῖς ἁγίοις ἐνοικῶν.

(*g*) *De Unct. Chrysmat.* Inest veritas signo, & Spiritus Sacramento.

(*h*) *De Spir. Sanct. l.* 1. *c.* 10. *propè finem.*

Sic ergo venit Spiritus, quemadmodum venit Pater: dixit enim Filius, *Ego & Pater veniemus & mansionem apud eum faciemus.* Nunquid corporaliter Pater venit? Sic ergo Spiritus venit, in quo cum venit, & Patris & Filii plena præsentia est.—— *Paulo post,* Probavimus igitur unam præsentiam esse, unam gratiam esse, Patris, Filii, & Spiritus Sancti, quæ tam cœlestis & divina est, ut pro ea gratias agat Patri Filius, &c.

(*i*) *Hom. æst. de temp. feria* 6. *Pasch.*

Hac ergo frequentia corporalis suæ manifestationis ostendere voluit Dominus, ut diximus, in omni loco, se bonorum desideriis divinitùs esse præsentem. Apparuit namque ad monumentum lugentibus, aderit & nobis absentiæ ejus recordatione salubriter contristatis. Apparuit in fractione panis his, qui se peregrinum esse putantes ad hospitium vocaverunt, aderit & nobis cùm peregrinis & pauperibus quæcunque possumus bona libenter impendimus. Aderit & nobis in fractione panis, cùm *Sacramenta corporis ejus*, videlicet panis vivi, casta & simplici conscientia sumimus.

(k) In *Joan. lib. 6. cap.* 35. Et idem ipse Christus & homo & Deus. Ergo ibat per id quod homo erat, & manebat per id quod Deus erat. Ibat per id quod in uno loco erat, & manebat per id quod ubique Deus erat.

(l) *De bono Persev. l.* 2. c. 13. Quod ergo in Sacramentis fidelium dicitur, ut *sursum corda habeamus ad Dominum*, munus est Domini —— ut ascendat & quæ sursum sunt sapiat, ubi Christus est in dextra Dei sedens, non quæ super terram, &c.

(m) *Ad Hedybiam* qu. 2. Ascendamus cum Domino cœnaculum magnum stratum & mundatum, & accipiamus ab eo *sursum* calicem N. Testamenti, ibique cum eo Pascha celebrantes inebriemur ab eo vino sobrietatis.

(n) *Hom.* 24. *in* 1 *Cor.* 10.

Faithful. He appear'd to the Women that wept at the Sepulcher; he will be likewise present with us, when we grieve at the remembrance of his absence. He appear'd, whilst they broke Bread, to those who, taking him for a Stranger, gave him entertainment; he will be likewise with us whilst we liberally receive the Poor and Strangers: He will be likewise with us in the Fraction of Bread, when we receive the Sacraments of his Body, which is the Living Bread, with a pure and chaste Heart.

All this speaks only the Presence of his Divinity, and no other.

For, as *Alcuinus* (k) says, *The same Christ who is Man, is likewise God; he left them as to his Manhood, but remained with them as to his Godhead. He went away, with reference to that, by which he is but in one place,* (N. B.) *yet tarried with them by his Divinity, which is every where.*

All *Liturgies*, when the Eucharist is celebrated, call aloud, Ἄνω τὰς καρδίας, *Sursum corda,* Lift up your Hearts. The meaning of which we are told by S. *Austin* (l). What therefore is said in the Sacraments of the Faithful, that we should lift up our Hearts to the Lord, *it is a Gift of the Lord.* And he explains it, *That by the Divine Aid the Soul is helped to ascend, and set it's Affections upon things above, where Christ is sitting at God's right Hand, and not upon things on the Earth.*

S. *Jerom*'s Words (m) are very emphatical. *Let us, with our Lord, ascend the great upper Room prepared and made clean, and receive from him* above *the Cup of the New Testament, and there celebrating the Passover with him, be inebriated by him with the Wine of Sobriety.*

All you see is *above*, and our Presence too with him there.

S. *Chrysostome* (n) speaking how we ought to approach to the tremendous Sacrifice with Concord

Concord and ardent Charity, says, *From thence we become Eagles, and so fly to Heaven it self: For,* where the Carcase is, thither will the Eagles come. He calls his Body the Carcase, because of his Death; and he calls them Eagles, shewing, that he who comes to this Body ought to be sublime, and have nothing common with Earth, nor be drawn downward and creep, but continually fly upward, and look to the Sun of Righteousness, and to have the Eye of his Mind quick-sighted: *For this is a Table for Eagles, not for Jackdaws.*

Gr. *Nazianzen* (o) speaking of his Adversaries, says, *Will they drive me from the Altars? I know another Altar, whose Types the things now seen are, upon which no Ax has been lift up, no Iron Tool or other Instrument has been heard; but is wholly a Work of the Mind, and an Ascent by Contemplation. Before this will I present my self, on this will I offer acceptable things, Sacrifice, Oblation, and Holocausts, so much more excellent than the things now offered, as Truth excels a Shadow.*

If Christ's Body were corporally present, it is not conceivable, what better Oblation than that we could present, no more than of what other Oblation this should be only a Type and Shadow.

Oecumenius (p) upon those words, *Let us draw near with a true heart, in full assurance of Faith,* says thus: *Seeing there remains nothing visible, neither the Temple, that is Heaven, nor the High Priest, that is Christ, nor the Sacrifice, that is his Body; it remains that we have need of Faith.*

I shewed before, that the *Fathers* never make Christ's Body *invisible,* but only from its *distance* and *absence*: And so it must be understood here, that he and his Body, the Priest and the Sacrifice are *invisible,* being both in Heaven, at that distance which makes Heaven it self and its Inhabitants *invisible* to us; and therefore he recommends *Faith,* which can only make them present to us.

Author imperfecti Operis in Matthæum (q), (among the Works of *Chrysostome* in Latin) has this Saying: *If therefore it*

(o) *Orat.* 28. *contr. Maxim.*

(p) *In Heb.* 10. v. 22.

(q) *Hom.* 11. *Si ergo vala*

sanctificata, ad privatos usus transferre sic periculosum est, in quibus non est verum corpus Christi, sed mysterium corporis ejus continetur; quanto magis vasa corporis nostri, quæ sibi Deus ad habitaculum præparavit, non debemus locum dare Diabolo agendi in eis quod vult.

it be so dangerous a thing, to turn the Sanctified Vessels to private Uses, in which is not the true Body of Christ, but only the Mystery of his Body is contained therein; *how much more as to the Vessels of our Body, which God has prepared for himself to dwell in, we ought not to give place to the Devil to act in them what he pleases.*

One may trust an Adversary as to his Opinion of what makes against him; These Words were look'd upon as so considerable an Objection, that an Attempt to corrupt them was practised long ago. The Learned Archbishop *Usher* (in the Preface of his Answer to the Jesuit's Challenge) has observ'd, That those words [*in quibus non est verum corpus Christi, sed mysterium corporis ejus continetur*] were left out wholly, in an Edition at *Antwerp*, 1537. and at *Paris*, 1543. and in another at *Paris, apud Audoenum Parvum*, 1557. Dr. *James* (in his Corruption of True Fathers, *p.* 53.) says, Those words are found in all the ancient Copies at *Oxford*, as Archbishop *Usher* says they were extant in the ancienter Editions, as in 1487. And I my self have seen one *Paris Edition*, even in the Year 1536. (*apud Claud. Chevallonium*) where those words are extant. So that I conclude, That the *Antwerp* Edition first mentioned (*apud Joan. Steelsium*, 1537.) was the first that made the Alteration. But then I further observe, That in the large *Paris Edition* in Latin of S. *Chrysostome*, 1588. which I have by me, those words are inserted indeed in the Text, but inclosed within two Brakets, with this Note in the Margin, [*Hæc in quibusdam exemplaribus desunt,*] which is very fine work, when they themselves had omitted them in the forenamed Prints.

They have plaid the same Prank with the same Author, in another of his Homilies, (*viz.* Hom. 19.) whose Words were not favourable to the Real Presence of Christ's Body in the Eucharist. The words are these.

Sed forte dices, quomodo dicere illum possum, non esse Christianum, quem video Christum confitentem, altare habentem, Sacrificium panis & vini offerentem, baptizantem, &c.

Perhaps thou wilt object, How can I say that he is not a Christian, whom I see confessing Christ, having an Altar, offering the Sacrifice of Bread and Wine, *baptizing,* &c.

In the *Paris Edition apud Audoenum Parvum, An.*

of the Ancient Church, relating to the Eucharist.

An. 1557. as Dr. *James* Notes, those words, [*Sacrificium panis & vini*] are changed into these, [*Sacrificium corporis & sanguinis Christi.*] The *Paris* Edition of 1588. (before mentioned) tho' it had more Conscience than to insert this Change into the Text, yet so far complied with the Cheat, as to put in the Margin [alias, *Sacrificium corporis & sanguinis Christi.*]

If this Trade had gone on successfully, they might have had in time a *Consent of Fathers* on their side; but it can never be without it.

I will conclude this Particular with one Observation more, of what the Reader may find at large discoursed of, in a late Learned Dissertation of Monsieur *Allix* (r), upon occasion of an Epistle of S. *Austin* to *Consentius*, who enquired of him, *Whether now the Body of Christ has Bones and Blood?* The very reading of that 146th Epistle of S. *Austin*, wherein he plainly, in his Answer to that Question, betrays his doubting of it, as well as in other of his Works; his distinguishing betwixt Christ's having a true Body after his Resurrection, and his having Flesh and Blood; the Testimonies there of other of the *Ancients*, especially of *Origen* and his Followers, that seem plainly to make both the glorified Body of Christ, and also of Believers, to be of another Composition than that of proper Flesh and Blood; these, I say, are a Demonstration, that the *Ancient Fathers* did not believe any Presence of true Flesh and Blood to be now in the Eucharist.

(r) *Dissert. de Sanguine D. N. Jesu Christi ad Epist.* 146. *S. Augustini. Utrum nunc corpus Domini ossa & sanguinem habeat.*

Neither do I think the Answer given to this Dissertation by *Monsieur Boileau*, Dean of *Sens* (s), to be a satisfactory one in this Particular. For tho' I should grant (which yet I see not sufficiently cleared by him) that generally the *Fathers*, and S. *Austin* also, did believe, that Christ had a Body, after the Resurrection, of the same Substance, tho' differing in Qualities, from what he had before; yet there are Three things that he has by no means said any thing material to, in his Answer.

(s) *Disquisit. Theolog. de Sangu. Corporis Christi post resurrectionem.*

1. That he has given no Account of S. *Austin*'s studious declining to determine any thing in particular about the

Blood

Blood of Christ, when he had never so fair an occasion to do it; but waves this always, even where he seems, as he do's in his *Retractations*, to determine for his having palpable Flesh and Bones.

2. Why S. *Austin* should ever at all doubt or hesitate about this Matter of Christ's Blood after his Resurrection, is unconceivable, if he, with the rest of the *Fathers*, had such a constant Belief of its Presence in the Eucharist, as the *Romanists* affirm.

3. That tho' the *Fathers* use the Argument of the Eucharist to prove the Truth of Christ's Body, yet none ever urged *Origen* or his *Followers* with an Argument from thence, to confute their Opinions, differing from the pretended common Sentiments about the Body and Blood of Christ, by what lay so plainly before them, of his Body and Blood being in the Eucharist, if they had believed it. But I refer the Reader to *Monsieur Allix* his Dissertation, before-named, wherein he may find abundant Satisfaction in these Matters; and also will see how sadly the *Romanists* are put to it, to answer the Difficulties about the Blood of Christ, which they pretend to shew in so many Churches, and is produced in such Quantities, that may well cause a new Doubt, Whether if his Resurrection-Body have any Blood in it, we must not suppose it to be of a *new Creation*, since what was in his Body when he died, cannot suffice to furnish more Blood, if so much, as their Vials and Glasses are filled withal.

CHAP.

CHAP. X.

The Tenth Difference.

The Fathers assert positively, that the substance of the Elements remain after Consecration; that Bread and Wine are taken, eaten and drunk in the Sacrament: which all that believe Transubstantiation must deny.

WE have seen before that the *Fathers* say plainly, that it was Bread which Christ called his Body, when he blessed it. Now we shall see, that the Fathers are as positive, that after Consecration, and the change made by it, yet still the Bread and Wine remains.

I begin with that famous Testimony of S. *Chrysostome* against the *Apollinarians*; produced first by P. *Martyr*; by some of our Adversaries charged upon him as his Forgery, because it was so full against them; by others shifted off to another *John of Constantinople*, and denied to be S. *Chrysostome*'s; but vindicated for his, by the Learned *Bigotius*, who had transcribed it out of the Florentine Library of S. *Mark*'s Monastery, and prepared it for the Press, in his Edition of *Palladius*; then suppressed by some Doctors of the *Sorbonne*, and the printed leaves taken out of the Book; but now lately recovered and published to their shame. A passage of which (the subject of this great contest) I shall here set down.

See *Append. to the Defence of the Exposition of the Doctrine of the Church of* England, *p.* 142, 143, &c.

Christ is both God and Man: God, for that he is impassible, Man for that he suffered. One Son, one Lord, he the same without doubt, having one Dominion, one power of two united natures: not that these (natures) are consubstantial, seeing each of them do's retain without confusion its own properties, and being two are inconfused in him. *For as* (in the Eucharist) *before the Bread is consecrated, we call it Bread, but when the grace of God by the Priest has consecrated it, it has no longer the name of Bread,*

Deus & homo Christus: Deus propter impassibilitatem, Homo propter Passionem. Unus Filius, unus Dominus, idem ipse proculdubus unitarum naturarum unam dominationem, unam potestatem possidens, etiamsi non consubstantiales existunt, & unaquæq; in commixtam proprietatis conservat agnitionem, propter hoc quod inconfusa sunt, [duo] dico. Sicut enim antequam sanctificetur Panis, Panem nominamus, divinæ *autem illum Sanctificante gratiâ, mediante sacerdote, liberatus est quidem appellatione panis, dignus autem habitus est dominici corporis appellatione, etiamsi natura panis in ipso permansit, & non duo corpora, sed unum corpus filii prædicatur. Sic & hic Divinâ ἐνιδρυσάσης, id est, inundante corporis naturâ, unum filium, unam personam, utraq; hæc fecerunt. Agnoscendum tamen natura, sed in duabus perfectis.*

Bread, but is counted worthy to be called the Lords Body, altho' the *nature of Bread remains in it, and we do not say there are two Bodies, but one Body of the Son.* So here, the divine nature being joined to the (*humane*) Body, they both together make one Son, one Person; but yet they must be acknowledged to remain without confusion, and after an indivisible manner, not in one nature only, but in two perfect natures. *inconfusam & indivisibilem rationem, non in unâ solùm.*

Another remarkable Testimony, is in *Theodoret's Dialogues*; some part of which I hope the Reader will not think it tedious to be inserted here, since by observing the thread of his Discourse, he will see his undoubted sense to be, that the substance of the Bread and Wine remain in the Eucharist, and the change is by *addition* not *annihilation*; and I will add his Greek where it is needful.

Dial. I.   *Orthodoxus*. Do you not know that God called his Body Bread? *Erannistes*. I know it. *Orth*. Elsewhere also he calleth his Flesh Wheat. *Eran*. I know that also. *Unless a Corn of Wheat fall into the ground and die*, &c. *Orth*. But in the delivery of the mysteries, he called the Bread his Body, and that which is mixed (viz. *Wine and Water in the Cup*) Blood. *Eran*. He did so call them. *Orth*. But that which is his Body by nature (κτ᾽ φύσιν τὸ σῶμα) is also to be called his Body, and his Blood (viz. *by nature*) Blood. *Eran*. It is confess'd.

Τῷ μὲν σώμα]τι τὸ τῆς συμβόλε τέθεικεν ὄνομα, τῷ δὲ συμβόλῳ τὸ τῆ σώμα]Θ.

Orth. But our Saviour changed the names, *and on his Body he imposed the name of the symbol (or sign) and on the symbol he put the name of his body*; And so having called himself a Vine, he called the Symbol Blood. *Eran*. Very right. But I have a mind to know the reason of this change of names. *Orth*. The scope is manifest to those that are initiated in

Μὴ τῇ φύσει τῶν βλεπομένων προσέχειν, ἀλλὰ διὰ τῆς ὀνομάτων ἀναλλαγῆς, πιστεύειν τῇ ἐκ τῆ χάριτ[Θ] γεγενημένῃ μεταβολῇ.

Divine things. For he would have those that participate the divine mysteries, *not to attend to the nature of those things that are seen, but upon the changing of the names, to believe the change that is made by grace.* For he that called his Body, that is so

by

by nature, Wheat and Bread, and again termed himself a Vine, *he honoured the visible Symbols with the appellation of his Body and Blood, not altering nature, but to nature adding grace.*

Οὕτω τὰ ὁρώμϟα σύμβολα τῇ τε σώματ[ος] κ) ἅιματ[ος] προσηγορία τετίμηκεν, ἐ τλὼ φύσιν μεταβαλὼν, ἀλλὰ τλὼ χάριν τῇ φύσει προστεθεικώς.

Proceed we now to the next Dialogue.

Orth. The mystical Symbols offered to God by the Priests, pray tell me what are they signs of? *Eran.* Of the Lords Body and Blood. *Orth.* Of his Body truly or not truly such? *Era.* Of that which is truly (*his Body*). *Orth.* Very right. For there must be an original of an Image (τ᾿ εἰκόν[ος] ἀρχέτυπον) for Painters imitate nature, and draw the Images of visible things. *Era.* True. *Orth.* If then the divine mysteries are *Antitypes of a true Body*, then the Lords Body is a true Body still, not changed into the nature of the Deity, but filled with Divine Glory. *Era.* You have seasonably brought in the Discourse of the Divine Mysteries; for thereby I will shew that the Lords Body is changed into another Nature. Answer therefore my Question. *Orth.* I will. *Era.* What call you the Gift that is offered before the Priests Invocation? *Orth.* I may not openly declare it, for perhaps some here present may not be initiated. *Era.* Answer then Ænigmatically. *Orth.* I call it the food that is made of a certain grain. *Era.* How call you the other Symbol? *Orth.* By a common name that signifies a kind of drink. *Era.* But how do you call it after Consecration? *Orth.* The Body of Christ, and the Blood of Christ. *Era.* And do you believe you partake the Body and Blood of Christ? *Orth.* Yes, I believe it. *Era.* As then the Symbols of Christs Body and Blood are one thing before the Priests Invocation, but after the Invocation, are changed and become another thing; so the Lords Body, after his Assumption, is changed into a Divine Essence. *Orth.* You are caught in a Net of your own weaving. *For after sanctification, the mystical Symbols do not depart from their own nature; for they remain still in their former substance, and figure and form, and may be seen and touched just as before. But they are understood to be that which they are made, and are believed and venerated, as being those things they are believed to be.*

Dial. 2.

Τῦ ὄντ[ος] σώ. ματ[ος] ἀντίτυπα.

Οὐδὲ γὰρ μϟ τ᾿ ἁγιασμὸν τὰ μυστικὰ σύμβολα τ῀ οἰκείας ἐξίστη φύσεως· Μένει γὰρ ὅτι τ῀ προτέρας ουσίας, κ) τ῀ σχήματ[ος] κ) τ῀ εἴδυς, κ) ὁρατά ἐστι, κ) ἁπτά, οἷα κ) πρότερον ἦν. Νοεῖ) δὲ ἅπερ ἐγένετο, κ) πιστεύε) κ) προσκυνεῖ), ὡς ἐκεῖνα ὄντα ἅπερ πιστεύε).

How

How shamefully Mr. *Sclater* has attempted to pervert these last words of *Theodoret*, he has been told sufficiently by his Answerer.

The next Testimony is of *Gelasius* (t) Bishop of *Rome*. *The Sacraments of the Body and Blood of Christ which we take, are surely a divine thing ; for which reason we become by them partakers of the Divine nature ; and yet the substance or nature of Bread and Wine do's not cease to be ; and indeed the Image and likeness of the Body and Blood of Christ are celebrated in the action of the mysteries: therefore it appears plainly enough to us, that we ought to think that of our Lord, which we profess and celebrate and receive in his image ; that as they* (viz. the Elements) *pass into that Divine substance, the H. Spirit effecting it, their nature still remaining in its own property ; so that principal mystery whose efficiency and virtue these* (the Elements) *truly represent to us, remains one entire and true Christ ; those things of which he is compounded* (viz. the two natures) *remaining in their properties.*

Ephrem Antiochenus (u) treating of the two Natures (which he calls palpable and impalpable, visible and invisible) united in Christ, adds, *Thus the Body of Christ which is received by the faithful, do's not depart from its sensible substance, and yet remains unseparated from the intellectual grace. So Baptism becoming wholly spiritual and one, it preserves its own sensible substance, I mean Water, and do's not lose what it is made to be.*

(t) *De duabus naturis in Christo.* Certè Sacramenta quæ sumimus, corporis & sanguinis Christi, divina res est, propter quod & per eadem divinæ efficimur consortes naturæ; & tamen esse non desinit substantia vel natura panis & vini ; & certè Imago & similitudo corporis & sanguinis Christi in actione mysteriorum celebrantur. Satis ergo nobis evidenter ostenditur, hoc nobis in ipso Christo Domino sentiendum, quod in ejus imagine profitemur, celebramus & sumimus ; ut sicut in hanc, sc. in Divinam transeunt Spiritu S. perficiente substantiam, permanente tamen in suæ proprietate naturæ, sic illud ipsum mysterium principale, cujus nobis efficientiam Virtutemq; veraciter repræsentant, ex quibus constat propriè permanentibus, unum Christum, quia integrum verumq; permanere.

(u) *Apud Photii Biblioth. cod.* 229. Οὔτε [Greek text] λαμβανόμενον σῶμα Χριστοῦ, [Greek text] τῆς αἰσθητῆς οὐσίας ἐκ ἐξίσταται, [Greek text] τῆς νοητῆς ἀδιαιρέτου μένει χάριτος· [Greek text] τὸ βάπτισμα [Greek text] πνευματικὸν ὅλον γενόμενον [Greek text] ἐν παντὶ γένει, [Greek text] τὸ ἴδιον τῆς αἰσθητῆς οὐσίας, τὸ ὕδωρ λέγω, διαφυλάττει, [Greek text] ὃ γέγονεν οὐκ ἀπόλεσιν.

Our Adversaries, to testify the respect they have for the Fathers, when they do not speak as they would have them, they try to make them speak so as no Body shall understand their true sense. And as the *Putney Convert* did by *Theodoret*, so the Jesuit *Andr. Schottus* (not for want of skill, but honesty) has dealt with this of *Ephrem*, making it, by his translation, obscure, or rather unintelligible nonsense. For the

of the Ancient Church, relating to the Eucharist. 97

first words [τῆς αἰσθητῆς ουσίας ἐκ τἔίςα] he translates [sensibilis essentiæ non cognoscitur, *it is not known of a sensible nature,*] and the other expression about Baptism [κỳ τὸ ἴδιον τῆς αἰσθητῆς ουσίας, τῷ ὕδατι λέγω, διασώζει] he turns it thus. [Hocq; substantiæ sensibilis proprium est per aquam, inquam, servat. *And this is the property of sensible substance, it keeps, I say, by Water.*] A good Man cannot take more pains to find out Truth than this Man do's that it may be lost.

The next Testimony, is of *Facundus*, (x) the African Bishop. Christ vouchsafed to receive the Sacrament of Adoption, both when he was Circumcised and when he was Baptized: and the Sacrament of Adoption may be called Adoption, just as we call the Sacrament of the Body and Blood of Christ, *which is in the Consecrated Bread and Cup*, his Body and Blood. Not that properly Bread is his Body, and the Cup his Blood, but because they contain in them the mystery of his Body and Blood. *Hence it is, that our Lord himself called the Bread and Cup he blessed, and gave to his Disciples, his Body and Blood.*

(x) Lib. 9. defens. 3. capit. cap. 5. Sacramentum adoptionis suscipere dignatus est Christus, & quando circumcisus est & quando baptizatus est: & potest Sacramentum adoptionis adoptio nuncupari, sicut Sacramentum corporis & sanguinis ejus *quod est in pane & poculo consecrato*, corpus ejus & sanguinem dicimus; non quod proprie corpus ejus sit panis, & poculum sanguis, sed quod in se mysterium corporis sanguinisq; contineant. *Hinc & ipse Dominus benedictum panem & calicem, quem discipulis tradidit, corpus & sanguinem suum vocavit.*

Nothing can be more positive than these five Testimonies, that the Bread and Wine remain in their substance after Consecration. And I cannot but here add the remarkable Confession of an Adversary, concerning two of them.

For thus *Card. Alan* (y) says, *Concerning these two*, Gelasius *and* Theodoret, *I readily perswade my self, that they are the only persons in all Antiquity* (tho' I have already produced three more *of their mind*) *who inclined to that, which was afterwards a common errour, so to defend the true Conversion of Bread, that they granted the matter of the Element to remain, as they saw it did in all other natural transmutations.*

(y) De Euchar. Sacram. l. 1. c. 35. De duobus, Gelasio & Theodoreto, facile mihi persuadeo, eos solos esse ex omni Antiquitate, qui inclinaverunt in communem postea multorum errorem, ut ita defenderent veram conversionem panis, ut materiam Elementi, sicut in cæteris naturalibus transmutationibus fieri videbant, relictam esse concederent, &c.

But

A full View of the Doctrines and Practices

But we will try whether the rest of the Fathers did not also speak the same thing.

Justin Martyr (z) speaking of the oblation of fine Flour for those that were cleansed from Leprosy, says, *It was a type of the Bread of the Eucharist, which our Lord J. Christ commanded us to make in memory of his passion.* What we make (as was show'd, cap. 8. observ. 7.) can be only Bread, not Christs Body in a proper sense.

Again (a) telling us of the Bishops praying and giving thanks over the Elements, he adds, *that the Deacons give to every one present leave to take of the Bread and Wine of the Eucharist.*

That this was his sense appears further, by another Character he gives of it in the same place, when he calls it *Food by which our Flesh and Blood by a change are nourished.*

What he says in another place (b) of Christians remembring their Lords Passion *by their dry and wet food*, can agree only to Bread and Wine, which therefore must be supposed to remain.

S. *Irenæus* (c) asserts with *Justin*, that the Bread and Cup of the Eucharist is that, *by which the substance of our Flesh is nourished and consists.*

In another place (d) he not only says, *that our Flesh is nourished by the Body and Blood of our Lord*, but adds, *As the Bread that is from the Earth, perceiving the Lords Invocation, is not now common Bread, but the Eucharist, consisting of two things, an Earthly and an Heavenly,* &c. Tho' not common Bread, yet Bread still, because else it would consist only of one thing, *viz.* Christs Body, and no *earthly thing* besides.

Origen (e). *If every thing that enters into the mouth goes into the Belly and is cast into the draught, then also the food that is sanctified by the word of God and Prayer, as to the material part of it* (which can be nothing but Bread) *goes into the Belly,*

(z) Dial. cum Tryph. Τύπος ἦν τοῦ ἄρτου τῆς εὐχαριστίας ὃν εἰς ἀνάμνησιν τοῦ πάθους Ἰησοῦς Χριστὸς ὁ κύριος ἡμῶν παρέδωκε ποιεῖν.

(a) Apol. 2. Οἱ διάκονοι διδόασιν ἑκάστῳ τῶν παρόντων μεταλαβεῖν ἀπὸ τοῦ εὐχαριστηθέντος ἄρτου, καὶ οἴνου, καὶ ὕδατος —

Τροφὴ ἐξ ἧς αἷμα καὶ σάρκες κατὰ μεταβολὴν τρέφονται ἡμῶν.

(b) Dial. cum Tryph. p. 345. Edit. Parif. 1615. Τροφῆς αὐτῶν ξηρᾶς τε καὶ ὑγρᾶς.

(c) L. 5. adv. hæref. c. 2. Ex quibus augetur & consistit carnis nostræ substantia.

(d) Ibid. l. 4. c. 34. Carnem quæ à corpore Domini & sanguine alitur.

Quemadmodum qui est à terra panis, percipiens invocationem Domini, jam non communis panis est, sed Eucharistia ex duabus rebus constans, terrena & coelesti, &c.

(e) Comm. in Matth. 15. v. 15. p. 254. Edit. Huet. —Καὶ τὸ ἁγιαζόμενον βρῶμα διὰ λόγου Θεοῦ καὶ ἐντεύξεως, κατ' αὐτὸ μὲν τὸ ὑλικὸν εἰς τὴν κοιλίαν χωρεῖ, καὶ εἰς ἀφεδρῶνα ἐκβάλλει.

of the Ancient Church, relating to the Eucharist.

Belly, &c. *but in respect of the Prayer that is superadded --- it becomes profitable*, &c. *Nor is it the matter of the Bread, but the word that is said over it that profits him that eats it not unworthily of the Lord.*

Cyprian (f). *We have found that it was a mixed Cup which our Lord offered, and that it was Wine which he called his Blood.*

Macarius (g). *In the Church is offered Bread and Wine, the Antitype of his Flesh and Blood, and they that are partakers of the visible Bread, do spiritually eat the Flesh of the Lord.*

Epiphanius (h) in a place I before cited, speaking of the Eucharist, says, *that the Bread is food, but the virtue that is in it, is for begetting Life. It do's not cease to be food, tho' the quickening power is all from the grace and spirit of God in it.*

S *Ambrose* (i) speaking of the Benediction of *Assur, Her Bread is fat,* &c. says, *Christ gave this Bread to the Apostles, to divide it among believing people, and now he gives it to us, whenas the Priest daily Consecrates with his words. This Bread is made to be the food of Saints.*

S. *Austin* (k). *We only call that the Body and Blood of Christ, which being taken from the fruits of the Earth, and Consecrated by mystical Prayer, we rightly receive to our spiritual health in memory of our Lords Passion. Which, when it is by the hands of men brought to that visible substance, is not sanctified to become so great a Sacrament, unless the spirit of God invisibly operate.*

Again (*l*). *Bread made for this purpose is consumed in receiving the Sacrament.* But it is neither received nor consumed till it be Consecrated, nor then but when eaten.

And again elsewhere (*m*). *The Eucharist is our daily Bread; but let us so receive it, that we may not only have refreshment for our bellies, but for our minds.*

(f) *Epist. ad Cæcilium, l.* 2. *Ep.* 3. *alias* 63. Invenimus calicem mixtum fuisse quem Dominus obtulit, & vinum fuisse quod sanguinem suum dixit.

(g) *Homil.* 27. Ἐν τῇ ἐκκλησίᾳ προσφέρεται ἄρτος καὶ οἶνος, ἀντίτυπον τῆς σαρκὸς αὐτοῦ καὶ τοῦ αἵματος, καὶ οἱ μεταλαμβάνοντες ἐκ τοῦ φαινομένου ἄρτου, πνευματικῶς τὴν σάρκα τοῦ κυρίου ἐσθίουσι.

(h) *In Compend. fidei.* Καὶ βρῶσις μὲν ὁ ἄρτος, ἡ δὲ δύναμις ἐν αὐτῷ εἰς ζωογόνησιν.

(i) *De Benedict. Patriarch. c.* 9. Hunc panem dedit Apostolis, ut dividerent populo credentium, hodiéq; dat nobis eum, quum ipse quotidiè sacerdos consecrat suis verbis. Hic panis factus est esca Sanctorum.

(k) *L.* 3. *de Trin. c.* 4. Corpus Christi & sanguinem dicimus illud tantum, quod ex frugibus terræ acceptum & prece mysticâ consecratum, ritè sumimus ad salutem spiritualem in memoriam pro nobis Dominicæ Passionis; quod cùm per manus hominum ad illam visibilem speciem perducitur, non sanctificatur ut fit tam magnum Sacramentum nisi operante invisibiliter Spiritu Dei.

(l) *Idem Ibid. c.* 10. Panis ad hoc factus in accipiendo Sacramento consumitur.

(m) *Serm.* 9. *de divers. cap.* 7. Eucharistia panis noster quotidianus est; sed sic accipiamus illum, ut non solum ventre sed & mente reficiamur.

Upon this account it is, that looking upon the Sacrament as a refreshing food to our Bodies (as S. *Austin* here speaks) the *Ancients* believed, that by partaking of the Eucharist, they *Broke their Fasts*; this appears beyond all question in what *Tertullian* (n) says; who in resolving a doubt that troubled some minds, what they should do, when it happened that by a private vow they undertook a strict Fast (which obliged them not to take any refreshment till Evening) and this fell out upon a station day (which was usually *Wednesdays* and *Fridays*) when the Fast was ended at three a Clock by receiving the Communion. *Most think*, says he, *that on the station days they ought not to be present at the Prayers of the Sacrifices* (when the Eucharist was administred) *because the Fast was broken upon receiving the Lords Body.* *Tertullian* excepts not against this reason, but grants it, and finds out such an expedient as would be counted ridiculous in the *Roman* Church (where this of the Sacraments breaking the Fast is not believed) which is, to be present, and to take the Sacrament, and *reserve it* to be eaten at night.

(n) *Lib. de Orat. c. 14. ad finem.* Stationum diebus non putant pleriq; sacrificiorum orationibus interveniendum, quod statio solvenda sit accepto corpore Dominico.

By receiving the Lords Body, says he, *and reserving it, both is salved, both the partaking of the Sacrifice (i.e. of the Eucharist given at three a Clock) and the execution of their duty* (he means of fasting till Evening, according to their Vow, and eating the Sacrament then, and not before.) But to proceed with our Testimonies.

Accepto corpore Dominico & reservato, utrumq; salvum est, & participatio Sacrificii & executio officii.

Hesychius (o). *God therefore commanded Flesh to be eaten with Bread, that we might understand, that that mystery (viz. the Eucharist) was spoken of by him, which is both Bread and Flesh, as the Body of Christ the living Bread that descended from Heaven.* It can be only Bread and Flesh in *our* way, for in that of Transubstantiation it is only Flesh and no Bread.

(o) *In Levit. l. 2. c. 8.* Propterea carnes cum panibus comedi præcipiens, ut nos intelligeremus illud ab eo mysterium dici, quod simul panis & caro est, sicut Corpus Christi panis vivi qui de Cœlo descendit.

S. Austin (p). *Of the very Bread Judas and Peter both took a part, and yet what Society, what agreement, what part has Peter with Judas?*

(p) *Lib. cont. Donatist. c. 6.* De ipso pane & de ipsa Dominica manu, & *Judas* Partem & *Petrus* accepit; & tamen quæ Societas, quæ consonantia, quæ pars *Petri* cum *Juda*?

Again

of the Ancient Church, relating to the Eucharist. 101

Again (*q*). *The Fathers did eat the same spiritual meat with us, but the corporal was different, they did eat Manna, we another thing* (he means Bread) —— *and they all drank the same spiritual drink, they one thing, we another, another as to the visible substance, but in spiritual virtue signifying the same thing.*

And again elsewhere (*r*). *Behold while Faith remains the same, the signs are varied. There* (in the Wilderness) *the Rock was Christ, to us that which is placed on the Altar* (viz. Bread) *is Christ ; And they drank the Water that flowed from the Rock for a great Sacrament of the same Christ, what we drink the faithful know*, (viz. Wine) *if you regard the visible substance it is another thing, if the spiritual signification they drank the same spiritual drink.*

Again in another place (*s*). *We have received to day the visible food ; but the Sacrament is one thing, and the virtue of the Sacrament is another.*

(*q*) *Id Tract. in Joan.* 26. Patres manducaverunt spiritualem utiq; eandem (*escam*) nam corporalem alteram, quia illi Manna, nos aliud —— & omnes eundem potum spiritualem biberunt, aliud illi, aliud nos, sed specie visibili quidem, tamen hoc idem significante virtute spirituali.

(*r*) *Id. Tract.* 45. *in Joan.* Videte ergo, fide manente, signa variata. Ibi Petra Christus, nobis Christus quod in Altari ponitur ; & illi pro magno Sacramento ejusdem Christi biberunt aquam profluentem de Petra, nos quid bibamus norunt fideles. Si speciem visibilem intendas aliud est, si intelligibilem significationem eundem potum spiritualem biberunt.

(*s*) *Tract.* 26. *in Joan.* Nam & nos hodie accepimus visibilem cibum ; sed aliud est Sacramentum, aliud est virtus Sacramenti.

That which he calls here *cibus visibilis* (the visible food) a little after S. *Austin* calls it *visibile Sacramentum* (a visible Sacrament) where he distinguishes this again from the *Virtus Sacramenti* (the Virtue of the Sacrament) so that the *visible food*, and the *visible Sacrament*, with him are the same.

I have already produced the Testimonies (*vid. chap.* 8. *Observ.* 5.) where the Fathers make what is distributed in the Eucharist to be without Life or sense ; which can be true of nothing else but of the Bread and Wine. So that unless we make them distribute what they had not consecrated, the Bread and Wine must remain after Consecration.

The same is also evidently proved from another common assertion of the Fathers, *that Christ offered the same oblation with Melchisedek.*

S. Cyprian (*t*). *Who was more a Priest of the most High God, than our Lord Jesus Christ, who offered a Sacrifice to God the Father, and offered this same that Melchisedeck had offered, that is Bread*

(*t*) *Lib.*2. *Epist.* 3. Quis magis sacerdos Dei summi, quam Dominus noster Jesus Christus, qui Sacrificium Deo Patri obtulit & obtulit hoc idem quod Mechisedec

A full View of the Doctrines and Practices

obtulerat, id est panem & vinum, suum scilicet corpus & sanguinem? Bread and Wine, to wit his Body and Blood? Which indeed the Wine and Bread was by *representation*, but if you understand this of *proper Flesh and Blood* offered in the Eucharist, then it is not the same oblation with that of *Melchisedeck*.

Isidore Pelusiota (*u*). Melchisedeck performed his sacred Office in Bread and Wine, by which he foresignified the type of the divine mysteries.

Eusebius (*x*). For as he (Melchisedeck) being a Priest of the Gentiles never seems to have made use of Bodily Sacrifices, but blessed Abraham only in Bread and Wine. After the same manner also, first our Lord and Saviour himself, then all the Priests that derive from him, performing in all Nations their spiritual function according to the Ecclesiastical Sanctions, by Bread and Wine do express the mysteries of his Body and saving Blood, Melchisedeck having foreseen these things by a divine spirit, and having used before these images of future things.

S. *Jerome* (*y*). Melchisedeck by Bread and Wine, which is a simple and a pure Sacrifice, did dedicate Christs Sacrament.

S. *Austin* (*z*). Melchisedeck, bringing forth the Sacrament of the Lords Supper (i. e. *Bread and Wine*) knew how to figure Christs Eternal Priesthood.

Again (*a*) upon those words, *Thou art a Priest for ever*, &c. He adds, *Since now there is no where any Priesthood or Sacrifice, according to the Order of* Aaron; *and that is every where offered under Christ the Priest*, which Melchisedeck brought forth when he blessed Abraham.

In many other places S. *Austin* says the same.

Arnobius (*b*). *Christ by the mystery of Bread and Wine, is made a Priest for ever.*

S. *Chrysostom* (*c*). *Why did he say*, a Priest after the Order of Melchisedeck? *Even because of the mysteries, because he also brought out Bread and Wine to* Abraham. *Isidore*

(*u*) Lib. 1. Epist. 431. ad Paulad. Μελχισεδεκ ἄρτῳ καὶ οἴνῳ ἱερατεύων, δι᾽ ὧν τῆς θείων μυστικῶν προεσήμαινε τύπον.

(*x*) Lib. 5. Dem. Evang. c. 3. Ὥσπερ ἐκεῖνος (Melchisedeck) ἱερεὺς ἐθνῶν τυγχάνων, οὐδαμοῦ φαίνεται θυσίαις σωματικαῖς κεχρημένος, οἴνῳ δὲ μόνῳ καὶ ἄρτῳ τ᾽ Ἀβραὰμ εὐλογῶν, ἢ αὐτὸν δὲ τρόπον, &c.

— οἴνῳ καὶ ἄρτῳ, τότε σώματος αὐτοῦ καὶ τοῦ σωτηρίου αἵματος αἰνίττον τὰ μυστήρια, τοῦ Μελχισεδὲκ ταῦτα πνεύματι θείῳ προεωρακότος, καὶ ταῖς μελλόντων ταῖς εἰκόσι προκεχρημένε.

(*y*) Epist. ad Evagrium. Melchisedec pane & vino simplici puroq; sacrificio, Christi dedicaverit Sacramentum.

(*z*) Epist. 95. Melchisedec prolato Sacramento coenæ Dominicæ novit æternum ejus sacerdotium figurare.

(*a*) L. 17. de civit. Dei, c. 17. — Ex eo quod jam nusquam est Sacerdotium & Sacrificium secundum ordinem Aaron, & ubiq; offertur sub sacerdote Christo, quod protulit Melchisedec quando benedixit Abraham.

(*b*) In Psal. 109. Christus per mysterium panis & vini factus est sacerdos in æternum.

(*c*) Comment. in Psal. 110. vel 109. — καὶ διὰ τὰ μυστήρια, ὅτι κἀκεῖνος ἄρτον καὶ οἶνον προσήνεγκε τῷ Ἀβραάμ.

Isidore of Sevil (d). *Let us not offer the Victims of Beasts according to* Aaron, *but let us offer in Sacrifice the oblation of Bread and Wine, that is the Sacrament of Christ's Body and Blood.*

Bede (e). *Our Redeemer is therefore called a Priest, after the Order of Melchisedeck, because taking away the legal Sacrifices, he instituted the same kind of Sacrifice (viz.* Bread and Wine*) should be offered under the N. Testament, for the mystery of his Body and Blood.*

(d) *In Genesin cap.* 12. Non secundùm Aaron pecudum Victimas, sed oblationem panis & vini, id est, corporis & sanguinis ejus Sacramentum in Sacrificium offeramus.

(e) *Hom. de* 55. *in Vigil. S. Jo. Bapt.* Redemptor noster ideo sacerdos esse dicitur secundùm Ordinem Melchisedec, quia, ablatis victimis legalibus, idem sacrificii genus in mysterium sui corporis & sanguinis in N. Testaménto offerendum instituit.

What the Scriptures acquaint us with, that after the Blessing of the Bread, Christ brake it and gave it to his Disciples, is also insisted on by the *Fathers* as done in the Eucharist, in order to the distributing of it to the receivers.

But *Bellarmine* says expresly (f). *That our breaking is not made for distribution, but to signify a certain mystery.* Therefore in the *Roman Church*, that which they give in the Sacrament to the people is *whole*, and not *broken off* from any other thing. Wherein they differ from the *Fathers*, for their Eucharist was what the Apostles call *breaking of Bread, Act.* 2. 46. and the Jesuit *Lorinus* upon that place observes, that it was the manner of the Primitive Church, *to make one Loaf, and when they had consecrated it, to break it into so many parts as there were Communicants, as Christ also did in his Supper.* And thus as it is 1 Cor. 10. 17. *There is one Bread,* &c. *and we being many are one Body,* for we all partake of one Bread.

(f) *L.* 1. *de Missa, c.* 27. Nostra fractio non fit ad distribuendum, sed ad certum mysterium significandum.

Lorinus in Act. 2. *v.* 45. Panem unum conficere, atq; illum consecratum in tot partes frangere, quot erant communicantes, sicut & Christus in coena fecit.

This Fraction, tho' the *Fathers* express it as if it were done to the *proper Body of Christ*, yet they mean it only of the *Bread* that *represents it:* and therefore that must remain, for there is nothing else to be broken.

When therefore S. *Chrysostome* (g) says, that upon the Cross a Bone of him was not broken, *but what Christ did not suffer upon the Cross, that he suffers in the oblation for thy sake, and suffers himself to be broken, that he may fill us all.*

(g) *Hom.* 24. *in* 1 *Cor. Tom.* 3. *Edit. Savil.* p. 397. --- Ἀλλ' ὅπερ οὐκ ἔπαθεν ἐπὶ τοῦ σταυρῦ, τῦτο πάχει ἐπὶ τῆς προσφορᾶς διὰ σὲ, καὶ ἀνέχε) διακλώμ(Θ) ἵνα πάντας ἐμπλήσῃ.

This

This cannot be meant of any thing but what reprefents his Body torn and rent, *viz.* Bread.

(b) *Epift.* 59. ——— Et ad diftribuendum comminuitur.

So S. *Auftin* (b) fpeaks of that upon the Lords Table, which is bleffed and fanctified, *and broke in fmall pieces to be diftributed.* Which can be only Bread.

(i) *Epift.* 86. --- Sicut frangitur in Sacramento Corporis Chrifti.

And this elfewhere (i) he expreffes more plainly. *Paul*, fays he, *broke Bread that night, as it is broken in the Sacrament of the Body of Chrift.*

(k) *Auguft. apud Bedam in* 1 *Cor.* 11. Manducemus Chriftum; vivit manducatus, quia furrexit occifus: nec quando manducamus, partes de illo facimus, & quidem in Sacramento id fit; & norunt fideles quemadmodum manducent carnem Chrifti, unufquifq; accipit partem, &c.

Again (k) S. *Auftin* thus exhorts. *Let us eat Chrift; he lives tho' eaten, for he arofe tho' flain. Neither when we eat him, do we make parts of him; fo indeed we do in the Sacrament, and the faithful know how they eat the Flefh of Chrift* (there.) *Every one takes a part*, &c.

This is a very remarkable Teftimony, becaufe of the diftinction he makes between Chrift's *proper Body*, and *that* in the *Eucharift*, affirming quite different things of them, as this of taking and eating a part, which is only true of the Bread. For as for the true Body of Chrift, we are informed by another,

(l) *Serm.* 159. Non poteft Chriftus edi & dividi. Integer à credentibus fumitur, integer in ore cordis recipitur.

Chryfologus (l). *Chrift cannot be eaten and divided. He is taken whole of Believers, he is received whole in the mouth of the heart.*

I will conclude this Chapter with the fayings of three great perfons among the *Fathers*, who pofitively affert what I have been proving, that the Bread and Wine remain in the Eucharift.

(m) *Hom.* 83. *in Matth.* Ἡνίκα τὰ μυστήρια παρέδωκεν, οἶνον παρέδωκε.

S. *Chryfoftom* (m). Who fays exprefly, *When our Lord delivered the myfteries, he delivered Wine.*

(n) *De Civ. Dei, lib.* 17. *cap.* 5. Manducare panem, eft in N. Teftamento facrificium Chriftianorum.

S. *Auftin* (n). *To eat Bread, is the Sacrifice of Chriftians in the N. Teftament.*

(o) *De fide ad Petrum, cap.* 19. Chrifto nunc, id eft, tempore N. Teftamenti, cum Patre & Spiritu Sancto, cum quibus una eft illi Divinitas, Sacrificium panis & vini in fide & charitate non ceffat.

Fulgentius (o). *Now; that is, in the time of the N. Teftament, the Holy Catholick Church, throughout the whole Earth, do's not ceafe to offer in Faith and Charity, the Sacrifice of Bread and Wine to Chrift, with the Father and H. Spirit, who have one Divinity together with him.* Sancta Ecclefia Catholica per univerfum orbem terræ offerre

CHAP.

C H A P. XI.

The Eleventh Difference.

The Fathers make the Bread and Wine to be the Sacrament, Sign, Figure, Type, Antitype, Image, &c. of Christ's Body and Blood. They of the Church of Rome, *make either the Accidents subsisting without a Subject, or the Body of Christ latent under those Accidents, to be the Sacrament, Sign, Figure, &c. and not the substance of Bread and Wine, which they say is abolished.* Therefore they have no Sacrament such as the *Fathers* assert.

I Might give in here a very large Collection out of the Fathers, calling the Bread and Wine by all those names above mention'd; but to avoid tediousness, I shall only select some few of them (enow to prove the Truth of what I have asserted) under the several heads.

S. *Ambrose* (p). *It is the true Flesh of Christ that was buried; therefore it* (viz. the Eucharist) *is truly the Sacrament of his flesh.*

S. *Austin* (q). *How is the Bread his Body, and the Cup, or what the Cup contains, his Blood? These, Brethren, are therefore called Sacraments, because in them we see one thing, and understand another.*

Again (r). *When the Lord came to the Supper, wherein he commended the Sacrament of his Body and Blood.*

Facundus (s). *Christs faithful ones, receiving the Sacrament of his Body and Blood, are rightly said to receive his Body and Blood.* And he had said before, *Not that the Bread is properly his Body, and the Cup his Blood, but because they contain in them the mystery of his Body and Blood.*

Isidore (t) speaking of the Bread and Wine, says, *These two are visible, but being sanctified by the Holy Spirit they pass into a Sacrament of his Divine Body.*

(p) *De iis qui initiant.* c. 9. Vera utiq; caro Christi, quæ crucifixa est, quæ sepulta est, verè ergo carnis illius est Sacramentum.

(q) *Serm. ad recen. Batif.* Quomodo est panis corpus ejus, & calix, vel quod habet calix, sanguis ejus? Ista, fratres, ideo dicuntur Sacramenta, quia in iis aliud videtur, aliud intelligitur.

(r) *In Psal.* 68. conc. 1. Cùm veniret Dominus ad cœnam, qua commendavit Sacramentum corporis & sanguinis sui.

(s) *Defens* 3. capit. l. 9. Christi fideles Sacramentum corporis & sanguinis ejus accipientes, corpus & sanguinem Christi rectè dicuntur accipere. — non quod proprie corpus ejus sit panis & poculum sanguis, sed quod in se mysterium corporis sanguinisq; contineant.

(t) *De Offic. Eccles.* l. 1. c. 18. Hæc duo sunt visibilia, sanctificata autem per Spiritum Sanctum in Sacramentum Divini Corporis transeunt.

Origen

They call them also Symbols.

Origen (u). Having discoursed (as we heard before) of the Eucharist, concludes thus. *Thus much may suffice concerning the Typical and symbolical Body.* And distinguishes it from the word that was made Flesh, which he calls *true food.*

Eusebius (x). *Having received a command to celebrate the memory of this Sacrifice upon the Table, by the Symbols of his Body and saving Blood, according to the Ordinances of the N. Testament.*

Theodoret (y), not only in the large Testimony produced out of him in the last Chapter, calls the Bread and Wine the Symbols of Christs Body and Blood, but says thus elsewhere. *In the most H. Baptism we see a type of the resurrection, then we shall see the resurrection it self. Now we see the Symbols of the Lords Body, there we shall see the Lord himself.*

They call them Signs.

S. Austin (z). *Our Lord did not doubt to say,* This is my Body, *when he gave the sign of his Body.*

S. Ambrose (a) of the Bread. *Before the Benediction of the Heavenly words, another species is named, after the Consecration the Body of Christ is signified.*

S. Cyprian (b). *Neither can the Blood of Christ, whereby we are redeemed and quickned, be seen to be in the Cup, when Wine is wanting in the Cup, whereby the Blood of Christ is shown.* Speaking against those that used only *Water.*

Tertullian (c). *Neither did he reject Bread, whereby he represents his own Body.*

S. Jerome (d). Christ, says he, took Bread that comforts mans heart, and proceeded to the true Sacrament of the Passover, *That like as Melchisedeck the Priest of the High God had done, when he offered Bread and Wine, so he also might represent the truth of his Body and Blood.*

It's.

(u) *Comm. in Matth.* 15. Καὶ ταῦτα μὲν περὶ τυπικοῦ καὶ συμβολικοῦ σώματος.

(x) *Dem. Evang. l.* 1. *cap.* 10. Τοῦ σώματος τὴν μνήμην ἐπὶ τραπέζης ποιεῖσθαι διὰ συμβόλων τοῦ τε σώματος αὐτοῦ, καὶ τοῦ σωτηρίου αἵματος κατὰ θεσμοὺς τῆς καινῆς διαθήκης παρειληφότες, &c.

(y) *Comm. in* 1 *Cor.* 13. Ἐν τῷ παναγίῳ βαπτίσματι τύπον δὲ αὐτοῦ ὁρῶμεν τῆς ἀναστάσεως, τότε δὲ αὐτὴν ὀψόμεθα τὴν ἀνάστασιν. Ἐνταῦθα τὰ σύμβολα τοῦ δεσποτικοῦ θεώμεθα σώματος, ἐκεῖ δὲ αὐτὸν ὀψόμεθα τὸν δεσπότην.

(z) *Contr. Adimant. c.* 12. Non dubitavit Dominus dicere hoc est corpus meum, cùm daret signum corporis sui.

(a) *De iis qui init. c.* 9. Ante benedictionem verborum Cœlestium alia species nominatur, post Consecrationem Corpus Christi significatur.

(b) Nec potest videri sanguis ejus quo redempti & vivificati sumus, esse in calice; quùm vinum desit calici, quo Christi sanguis ostenditur. *Epist. ad Cæcilium.*

— (c) *L.* 1. *adv. Marcion.* Nec panem reprobavit, quo ipsum Corpus suum repræsentat.

(d) *In Matth.* 26. — Ut quomodo in præfiguratione ejus Melchisedec summi Dei sacerdos panem & vinum offerens fecerat, ipse quoq; veritatem sui corporis & sanguinis repræsentaret.

It's a very trifling objection that our Adversaries make both to this and the former Testimony in *Tertullian*, that the word *repræsentare* (to represent) signifies very often to *exhibit a thing*, and make it *present*; for tho' it should be granted, it would not help their cause, since they both say, that it is Bread that represents his Body, which therefore must remain, since that which is not cannot act any thing: but then I add, that tho' in some Cases to *represent* is to *exhibit*, yet never in the Case of *Sacraments* and *Signs*, for their Essence consists in signification, therefore their representation as Signs, must be to denote and show rather something absent which they represent, than to make it present.

They call them also Types.

Cyril of Jerus. (e). He bids us receive the Bread and Wine with all certainty, *as the Body and Blood of Christ: for in the Type of the Bread his Body is given to thee, and in the type of Wine his Blood.*

(e) *Catech. Mystag.* 4.
— Ὡς σώματ(Θ) κὶ αἵματ(Θ) Χειςῦ· ἐν τύπῳ γὰ ἄςμ δίδο-ται σοι σῶμα, κὶ ἐν τύπῳ οἴνω δίδοῦ τὸ αἷμα.

Greg. Nazianzen (f). *We shall receive the Pass-over now in a Type still, tho' more clear than that of the old Law (for the legal Passover, I am bold to say it, was an obscure Type of a Type) but within a while we shall receive it more perfect and more pure.*

(f) *In Pasch. Orat.* 43. Ed. Basil. Gr. Μεταληψόμεθα ἢ τ̈ πάρα νῦν μὲν τυπικῶς ἔτι, κὶ εἰ τ̈ παλαιᾶ γυμνότερον (τὸ γὰ νομικὸν Πάρα, τολμῶ ἢ λέγω, τύπε τύπ(Θ) ἦν ἀμυδρότερ(Θ)) μι-κρὸν ἢ ὕσερον τελεώτερον κὶ καθαρώτερον.

S. Jerome (g) upon those words of Jerem. 31. *They shall flow unto the goodness of the Lord, for Wheat, and Wine and Oyl,* adds, *Of which is made the Lords Bread, and the Type of his Blood is filled, and the Blessing of Sanctification is shown.*

(g) *In Jerem.* 31.
— De quo conficitur panis Domini, & sanguinis ejus im-pletur typus, & benedictio san-ctificationis ostenditur.

Theodoret (h) calls the Eucharist, *The venerable and saving Type of Christs Body.*

(h) *Dialog.* 3.
— Τέτε τύπον σεπτὸν κὶ σωτή-ειον.

Another name is Antitypes, signifying the same with the former.

Author Constitutionum (i) under the name of Clemens Roman. *Christ delivered to us the mysteries which are antitypes of his precious Body and Blood.*

(i) *Lib.* 5. *cap.* 13.
— Παρέδωδκεν ἡμῖν τὰ ἀντί-τυπα μυσήεια τ̈ τιμίε σώματ(Θ) κὶ αἵματ(Θ).

Again

108   *A full View of the Doctrines and Practices*

(k) Lib. 7. c. 26.

—— κỳ τ̃ τιμίε αἵματ۞ ἒ κỳ ἀνlίτυπα ταῦτα ὀπlελξμᾖ.

(l) *In Proverb.* 9. *citat. in Conc. Nic.* 2. *All.* 6. Τὰ ἢ ῥντὰ διὰ τ̃ οἴνυ κỳ τ̃ ἄρlυ τὰ ἀνlίτυπα τῶ σωμαlικῶν τ̃ Χρισῦ κηρύτlει μελῶν.

(m) *Homil.* 27. Ἐν τῆ Ἐκκλησία προσφέρεlαι ἄρl۞ κỳ οἶν۞, ἀνlίτυπον τ̃ σαρκὸς αὐτῦ κỳ τ̃ αἵμαl۞.

(n) *Orat.* 11.

Εἶπε τί τῶ ἀνlιτύπων τ̃ τιμίυ σώμαl۞ ἢ τ̃ αἵμαl۞ ἢ χείρ ἐθησαύρισεν, &c.

(o) *Catech. Myſtag.* 5. Γλυκόμβοι γὸ, ἐκ ἄρτε κỳ οἴνυ κελεύειν᾿ γλύσεως, ἀλλὰ ἀνlιτύπυ σώμαl۞ κỳ αἵμαl۞ τῦ Χρισῦ.

(p) *Dialog.* 2. Τῦ ὄνlως σώμαl۞ ἀνlίτυπα.

(q) *Recapit. in fine Dialog.* 3.
—— Τῦ δὴ χάριν μεlαλαμβάνυσι τῶ ἀνlιτύπων τῦ σώμαl۞, περιloς γὸ ὁ τύπ۞ ἀνηρημένης τ̃ ἀληθείας.

(r) *Citante Bulingero adv. Caſaub.* p. 166.

—— Οὐδὲ δύο σώμαlα, αὐτὸ τὸ Χρισῦ σῶμα ἐνυπισάlαν ἐν ἐρανοῖς ἕν, κỳ ὁ τότε ἀνlίτυπ۞ ἄρl۞ ἐν ἐκκλησίαις πρὸς τῶ ἱερέων διαδιδόμεν۞ τοῖς πιστοῖς.

(s) *Lib.* 3. *adv. Maricion.* Panem corpus suum appellans, ut hinc etiam intelligas corporis sui figuram pani dedisse.

Again (k). O our Father, we give thee thanks for the precious Blood of Jesus Christ ſhed for us, *and for his precious Body of which we celebrate theſe Antitypes.*

Euſtathius of Antioch (l), expounding thoſe words, *Eat my Bread, and Drink the Wine that I have mingled,* ſays, *He ſpeaks theſe things, by Bread and Wine preaching the Antitypes of Chriſts Bodily Members.*

Macarius (m). *In the Church is offered Bread and Wine, the Antitype of Chriſts Fleſh and Blood.*

Greg. Nazianzen (n) telling the ſtory how his Siſter *Gorgonia* was Cured of a deſperate Malady, by applying the Sacrament mixed with tears to her Body, he expreſſes it thus. *Whatſoever of the Antitypes of the precious Body and Blood of Chriſt her hand had treaſured up,* &c.

Cyril of Jeruſ. (o). *When they taſt, they are not required to taſt Bread and Wine* (i. e. not theſe alone) *but the Antitype of Chriſts Body and Blood.*

Theodoret (as we heard before (p)) calls the Divine Myſteries, *the Antitypes of the True Body of Chriſt.*

And in another place (q) he ſays, *If the Lords Fleſh be changed into the Nature of the Divinity, wherefore do they receive the Antitypes of his Body, for the Type is ſuperfluous* (you ſee Type and Antitype ſignify the ſame) *when the Truth is taken away.*

Theodotus of Antioch (r) ſays, *As the King himſelf and his Image are not two Kings, neither are theſe two Bodies,* viz. *The Body of Chriſt perſonally exiſting in the Heavens, and the Bread, the Antitype of it, which is delivered in the Church by the Prieſts to the Faithful.*

They call it a Figure.

Tertullian (s). *Calling Bread his Body, that thou mayſt thence underſtand, that he gave to the Bread the Figure of his Body.*

Again

of the Ancient Church, relating to the Eucharist. 109

Again (t). The Bread which he took and distributed to his Disciples, he made it his Body, saying, This is my Body, that is, the Figure of my Body.

Ephrem Syrus (u). Diligently consider, how Christ taking Bread in his hands, blessed and brake it, for a figure of his immaculate Body, and also blessed and gave the Cup to his Disciples, for a figure of his precious Blood.

S. Austin (x). He admitted Judas *to the Banquet, in which he commended and delivered to his Disciples the figure of his Body and Blood.*

Bede (y) also says the same, Neither did Christ exclude Judas *from the most holy Supper, in which he delivered to his Disciples the figure of his most holy Body and Blood.*

And elsewhere (z), Christ instead of the Flesh or Blood of a Lamb, substituting the Sacrament in the Figure of Bread and Wine, showed that it was he, to whom the Lord sware, Thou art a Priest for ever after the Order of *Melchisedeck.*

(t) Lib. 4. adv. Marcion. c. 40. Acceptum panem & distributum discipulis, corpus suum illum fecit, hoc est corpus meum, dicendo, id est, figura corporis mei.

(u) Tract. de nat. dei curiose non scrutanda. Diligenter intuere, quomodo in manibus panem accipiens, benedixit & fregit in figuram immaculati corporis sui, calicemq; in figuram pretiosi sanguinis sui benedixit deditq; discipulis suis.

(x) In Psal. 3. Adhibuit (Judam) ad convivium, in quo corporis & sanguinis sui figuram discipulis commendavit & tradidit.

(y) In Psal. 3. Nec à Sacratissimâ coena, in quâ figuram Sacrosancti corporis sanguinisq; suis discipulis tradidit, ipsum (sc. Judam) exclusit.

(z) In Luc. 22. Pro agni carne vel sanguine suae carnis sanguinisq; Sacramentum in panis & vini figurâ subst.tuens, ipsum se esse monstraret, cui juravit Dominus, Tu es sacerdos in aeternum secundum Ordinem Melchisedec.

The words of the *Ambrosian* Office are very remarkable, as they are set down by the Author of the Book of Sacraments under his name, where he asks this Question.

(a) Wouldst thou know that the Eucharist is Consecrated by Heavenly words? Hear then what the words are. The Priest says, Make this oblation to us allowable, rational, acceptable, which is *the Figure of the Body and Blood of our Lord Jesus Christ,* &c.

(a) Lib. 4. de Sacram. c. 5. in initio. Vis scire quia verbis coelestibus consecratur? Accipe quae sint verba. Dicit sacerdos, Fac nobis, inquit, hanc oblationem ascriptam, rationabilem, acceptabilem, quod est Figura corporis & sanguinis Domini nostri Jesu Christi, &c.

This Prayer thus expressed in this Office, signifies more than all that can be cited against us out of these Books; and indeed they were too plain to be continued, when Transubstantiation was believed in the *Roman Church*, and therefore in the present Canon of the Mass they are changed, and instead of *Figura Corporis*, they now read, *Fiat nobis Corpus*, &c.

Lastly,

A full View of the Doctrines and Practices

Lastly, *The Fathers call the Bread and Wine in the Eucharist, the Image of Christ's Body.*

(b) Lib. 8. Demon. Evang.

—— Τὴν εἰκόνα τοῦ ἰδίου σώματος παρακελευόμενος.

(c) Tract. de duabus Naturis.
Certe Imago & Similitudo corporis & sanguinis Christi in actione mysteriorum celebrantur. Satis ergo nobis evidenter ostenditur, hoc nobis in ipso Christo Domino sentiendum, quod in ejus imagine profitemur, celebramus & sumimus, &c.

Eusebius (b). Christ, says he, delivered to his Disciples the Symbols of his Divine Oeconomy, *requiring them to make an Image of his Body.*

Gelasius (c). *Surely the Image and similitude of the Body and Blood of Christ are celebrated in the action of the mysteries. It is evidently therefore shown to us, that we must think of our Lord Christ the same, which we profess, celebrate and take in his Image,* &c.

(d) Comm. in 49 Genes.

Παρέδωκε εἰκόνα τοῦ ἰδίου σώματος μαθηταῖς, μηκέτι τὰς νομικὰς καὶ δι' αἱμάτων θυσίας προσίεμενος. Τὸ πίνον ἄρτι τὸ καθαρὸν τῆς τροφῆς διὰ τῶν λευκῶν ὀδόντων ἐδήλωσε.

(e) Dialog. 3.
—— Ποίας σαρκὸς, ἢ τίνος σώματος, ἢ ποίου αἵματος εἰκόνας δίδως, ἐντέλλετο τοῖς μαθηταῖς τὴν ἀνάμνησιν αὐτοῦ ποιεῖσθαι.

(f) In Concil. Nicen.2.Act.6.
—— Τὴν ἀληθῆ τοῦ Χριστοῦ εἰκόνα.

—— Οὕτω καὶ τὴν εἰκόνα ὕλην ἐξαίρετον, ἤγουν ἄρτου οὐσίαν, προσέταξεν προσφέρειν, μὴ σχηματίζουσαν ἀνθρώπου μορφὴν, ἵνα μὴ εἰδωλολατρεία παρεισαχθῇ.
—— Τὸν τῆς εὐχαριστίας ἄρτον ἀψευδῆ εἰκόνα τῆς φυσικῆς σαρ-

Procopius of Gaza (d) expounding these words spoken of *Juda, His Eyes shall be red with Wine, and his Teeth white with Milk* (Gen. 49. 12.) he applies it to the Eucharist, and that gladness which is obtain'd by the mystical Wine which Christ first tasted, and bad his Disciples take and drink; and the Milk may signify the purity of the mystical food, *for he gave the Image of his own Body to his Disciples; no longer requiring the bloody Sacrifices of the Law, and by the white teeth he denoted the purity of the Bread by which we are nourished.*

Author Dialog. adv. Marcionitas inter opera Originis (e). If Christ, as the *Marcionists* say, was without Flesh and without Blood, *of what Flesh, or of what Body or Blood did he give the Images, and commanded his Disciples to make a remembrance of him by?*

Synodus Constantinop. an. 754. (f). The Fathers there call the Eucharist, the *true Image of Christ,* and say afterwards —— *Christ commanded us to offer an Image, a chosen matter, to wit, the substance of Bread, not having an humane Figure, lest Idolatry should be introduced.*

And again. *It pleased him, that the Bread of the Eucharist, being the true Image of his natural Flesh*

of the Ancient Church, relating to the Eucharist.

Flesh should be made a Divine Body, being sanctified by the coming of the Holy Ghost, the Priest which makes the oblation intervening to make it holy, which before was common.

κὸς, διὰ τῇ τῇ ἁγίῳ πνεύματος ἐπιφοιτήσεως ἁγιαζόμενον, θεῖον σῶμα ἠυδόκησε γίνεδς, μεσιδιοντ τῇ ἐν μεταλήψει ἐκ τῇ κοινῇ περὸς τὸ ἅγιον τἠν ἀναφοραν ποιμένε ἱερέως.

He that would have more Testimonies of this kind, may consult Monsieur *Blondel*, in his *Esclaircissements sur l' Eucharistie*, cap. 4. prop. 8.

The Fathers also make two or three Remarks, which add further strength to this Argument.

First Remark. *They not only make Bread and Wine to be the Image, Type, Figure, &c. of Christs Body Crucified; but they also assert, that an Image, Figure, &c. cannot be the thing it self, of which it is an Image and Figure.*

Tertullian (g). *The Image cannot be every ways adequate to the Truth; for it is one thing to be according to Truth, another to be the Truth it self.*

Athanasius (h). *That which is like to another is not that thing it self to which it is like.*

Hilary (i). *Neither is any one an Image of himself.*

S. Ambrose (k). *None can ever have been an Image of himself.*

Gr. Nyssen (l). *An Image would be no longer such if it were altogether the same with that of which it is an Image.*

S. Austin (m). *What can be more absurd, than to be called an Image with respect to ones self.*

Gaudentius (n). *A Figure is not the Truth, but an imitation of the Truth.*

Theodoret (o). *An Image has the Figures and lines, not the things themselves.*

Cyril of Alexand. (p). *A Type is not the Truth, but rather imports the similitude of the Truth.*

Bertram (q). *A pledge and an Image are of another thing; that is, they do not look to themselves, but to something else.*

(g) *Cont. Marcion.* l. 2. c. 9. Imago veritati non usquequaq; adæquabitur, aliud enim est secundum veritatem esse, aliud ipsam veritatem esse.

(h) *Contr. Hypocr. Milet.* Τὸ ὅμοιόν τινι, ὐκ ἐςιν αυτὸ ἐκεῖνο ᾧ ὅμοιῳ.

(i) *De Synodis.* Neq; enim sibi ipsi quisquam imago est.

(k) *De fide* l. 1. cap. 4. Nemo potest sibi ipsi imago fuisse.

(l) *De anima & resurrect.* Ουκ ἔτι γὰρ ἂν εἰκων, εἰ δ' ἀπάντων ἔτι ταυτὸν ἐκείνῳ.

(m) *De Trinit.* l. 7. c. 1. Quid absurdius quàm Imaginem ad se dici?

(n) *In Exod. tract.* 2. Figura non est veritas, sed imitatio veritatis.

(o) *In Dan.* l. 2. c. 2. Ἡ εἰκὼν χήματα, ὐ πράγματα ἔχει.

(p) *In Amos.* cap. 6. Ὁ δὲ τύπος ὐκ ἀλήθεια, μόρφωσιν δὲ μᾶλλον τῆς ἀληθείας εἰσφέρει.

(q) *De corp. & sang. Domini.* Pignus & Imago alterius rei sunt, id est, non ad se, sed ad aliud aspiciunt.

This

A full View of the Doctrines and Practices

(r) *In Concil. Nic.* 2. *Act.* 6.

Ἐι εἰκὼν τῦ σώματ[ος] ἐςιν, ἐκ ἐνδέχ[εται] τῇ αὐτὸ τὸ θεῖον σῶμα.

(s) *De Orth. fide* l. 4. c. 14.

This *Epiphanius* the Deacon (r) in the second Council of *Nice* confesses, and therefore is fain to deny, that the Eucharist is the *Image* or *Antitype* of Christs Body; For, says he, *If* (the Eucharist) *be an Image of his Body, it cannot be the Divine Body it self.*

Damascen also (s) who was one of the first Innovators in the matter of the Eucharist, denies, that the Bread and Wine are a Type or Figure of Christs Body and Blood, but the very Body and Blood it self; and that when the Antients call them ἀντίτυπα Antitypes, they mean it is so before Consecration of the Elements not after, which I have abundantly showed, by foregoing Testimonies in this Chapter, to be false, and it is confessed by some of the *Roman Authors* themselves.

In a word, the *Fathers* make a sign to be inferiour, and to fall short of the thing signified; thus

(t) *Hom.* 8. *in Epist. ad Roman.* Σφόδρα αὐτῆς καταδεέςερα, ᾗ τοσῦτον, ὅσον σημεῖον τῦ πράγματ[ος] ὑπέρ ἐςι σημεῖον.

S. *Chrysostom* (t) says, *It is inferiour to it, and so much the more, as a sign is below the thing of which it is a sign.*

So also S. *Jerome* (as we heard before) puts *the Body and Blood of Christ* in the Eucharist, in the same rank as to veneration with holy *Chalices, Veils,* and other things that relate to the Passion of our Lord

2 Remark. *The Fathers assert, that an Image and Type must visibly demonstrate that of which it is an Image.*

(u) *Hom.* 1. *in Genes.* Qui viderit imaginem alicujus, videt eum cujus imago est.

Origen (u). *He that sees the Image of a person, sees him of whom it is an Image.*

(x) *Lib.* 1. *cont. Marcel.* c. 4. Αἱ εἰκόνες τῦτων ὧν εἰσίν εἰκόνες ᾗ ἀπόντων δεικτικαί εἰσιν, ὥςε ᾗ τὰ ἀπόντα δι' αὐτῶν φαίνεςθαι δοκεῖν.

Marcellus Anchyr. apud Eusebium (x). *Images are demonstrative of those of whom they are Images, so that by them he that is absent seems to appear.*

(y) *In Cant. Hom.* 15. Τὸ ἀρχέτυπον ἐναργῶς ἐν τῷ μιμήματι καθορᾶςθαι.

Greg. Nyssen (y). *The Original is plainly seen in the likeness of it.*

Hilary (z). *It is necessary that an Image should demonstrate him of whom it is an Image.*

(z) *De Synodis.* Eum cujus Imago est, necesse est ut imago demonstret.

Which

of the Ancient Church, relating to the Eucharist.   113

Which plainly confutes those mens fancies in the Church of *Rome* (a), who make Christ *invisibly present* in the Eucharist, to be the sign of himself *visibly suffering* upon the Cross.

For as *Greg. Nyssen* (b) says, *How can a man form an Idea of a visible thing from an Invisible?*

And *Tertullian* laughs at it as ridiculous, when he says, (c) *No one that intends to show a man, brings in a Helmet, or a Vizard.* Which, we know, hide him from our sight.

Irenæus (d) says, *A Type is often different from the Truth, according to the matter and substance of the Type, but according to the habit and lineaments, it ought to keep likeness, and likewise by things present, show those things that are not present.*

(a) Bellarm. de Euchar. l. 2. cap. 15.

(b) Lib. 1. cont. Eunom. Πῶς ἐκ τῦ ἀορατῦ τὸ ὁρατὸν ποιήσει κατανόησιν;

(c) Lib. de carne Christi c. 11. Nemo ostendere volens hominem, cassidem aut personam introducit.

(d) L. 2. adv. hæres. c. 40. Typus secundùm materiam & substantiam aliquoties à veritate diversus est. Secundùm autem habitum & lineamentum debet servare similitudinem, & similiter ostendere per præsentia, ea quæ non sunt præsentia.

3. Remark. *The Fathers plainly make the Bread and Wine in the Eucharist, to be Signs and Symbols of Christ as absent.*

S. *Ambrose* (e). *Here is the shadow, here the Image, there* (viz. *in Heaven*) *is the Truth. The shadow is in the Law, the Image in the Gospel, the Truth in Heaven.*

Again (f). *Ascend, O Man, into Heaven, and thou shalt see those things, of which there was here only a shadow or Image.*

Maximus (g) the Interpreter of the Spurious *Dionysius*, speaking of the Bread and Wine which he calls *Holy Gifts*, says, *They are Symbols of things above that are more true.*

So again (h) elsewhere he says, *The things of the Old Law were a shadow, those of the New Testament were an Image, but the state of the World to come is the Truth.*

Theodoret (i). *After his coming there will be no more need of Symbols (or Signs) when the Body it self appears.*

(e) L. 1. de Offic. cap. 48. Hic umbra, hic Imago, illic veritas. Umbra in Lege, imago in Evangelio, veritas in Cœlestibus.

(f) In Psalm 38. Ascende ergo, homo, in cœlum, & videbis illa quorum umbra hic erat vel Imago.

(g) In cap. 1. Hierarch. Ecclef. "Αγια δ̄ωρα. Σύμβολα τῶν ἄνω κ̀ ἀληθινωτέρων.

(h) In Cap. 3. Σκιὰ ἢν τὰ τῆ παλαιᾶς, εἰκὼν ἢ τὰ τ κινῆς διαθήκης, ἀλήθεια ἢ ἡ τῆς μελλόντων κατάστασις.

(i) In 1 Cor. 11. 26. Μετὰ ἢν δὴ τὴν αὐτῦ παρουσίαν, ἐκ ἔτι χρεία τῆς συμβόλων τῦ σώματος, αὐτῦ φαινομένε τῦ σώματος.

I refer the Reader to the Testimonies produced before (*Chap.* 10. *Position* 2.) out of S. *Austin, Sedulius, Primasius, Bede,* &c.

Q   I will

I will conclude this Chapter with a passage or two out of the Prayers after the Sacrament in the Old Liturgy, used in Bertram's time (k).

(k) V. Bertram de corp. & sang. Christi prope finem. p. 112. Edit. ult. Lat. Engl.

We who have now received the Pledge of Eternal Life, most humbly beseech thee to grant, (l) *That we may be manifestly made partakers of that which we here receive in the Image of the Sacrament.*

(l) Ut quod in imagine contingimus Sacramenti, manifesta participatione sumamus.

And thus afterwards (m) in another Prayer. *Let thy Sacraments work in us, O Lord, we beseech thee, those things which they contain, that we may really be partakers of those things which now we celebrate in a Figure.*

(m) Ibid. p. 114. Perficiant in nobis quæsumus, Domine, tua Sacramenta quod continent; ut quæ nunc specie gerimus, rerum veritate capiamus.

Bertram Comments upon these Prayers, in such passages as these. " *Whence it appears,* says he, *that this Body and Blood* " *of Christ are the Pledge and Image of something to come, which* " *is now only represented, but shall hereafter be plainly exhibited.* " —— *therefore it is one thing which is now celebrated, and ano-* " *ther which shall hereafter be manifested.* And afterwards "(p. 115.) *The Prayer says, that these things are celebrated in* " *a Figure, not in Truth, that is, by way of similitude (or repre-* " *sentation) not the manifestation of the thing it self.* Now the " *Figure and the Truth are very different things: Therefore the* " *Body and Blood of Christ, which is celebrated in the Church, dif-* " *fers from the Body and Blood of Christ which is glorified since the* " *Resurrection,* &c.

P. 117.

" *We see how vast a difference there is between the mystery of* " *Christ's Body and Blood which the faithful now receive in the* " *Church, and that Body which was born of the Virgin* Mary, " *which suffered, rose again, ascended into Heaven, and sitteth at* " *the right hand of the Father. For this Body which we celebrate* " *in our way (to happiness) must be spiritually received; for Faith* " *believes somewhat that it sees not; and it spiritually feeds the* " *Soul, makes glad the heart, and confers Eternal Life and In-* " *corruption, if we attend not to that which feeds the Body, which* " *is chew'd with our teeth, and ground in pieces, but to that which* " *is spiritually received by Faith. But now that Body in which* " *Christ suffered and rose again, was his own proper Body which* " *he assumed of the Virgin, which might be seen and felt after his* " *Resurrection,* &c..

of the Ancient Church, relating to the Eucharist.

It is very observable, and a great confirmation of what has been said in this Chapter, That the Ancient Christians of S. *Thomas*, inhabiting the Mountains of *Malabar* in the *East Indies*, agree with the *Ancient Church* in denying our Saviours *Corporal Presence* in the Sacrament of the Eucharist; as appears from their *Publick Offices*, and other Books, mentioned in a *Synod* which was celebrated amongst them by *Dom Aleixo de Menezes* Archbishop of *Goa*, in the Year 1599.

In the fourteenth Decree of the third Action of the said Synod, in which most of their *Church Offices* and other Books are Condemned, for containing Doctrines contrary to the Roman Faith, there is particular notice taken of their contradicting the Roman Faith in the point of Transubstantiation.

1. The Book of *Timothy* the *Patriarch* is condemned, for asserting through three Chapters, that the true Body of Christ our Lord is not in the Sacrament of the Altar, but only the Figure of his Body.

2. The *Book of Homilies* is condemned, which teacheth, that the *H. Eucharist* is only the *Image of Christ*, as the Image of a Man is distinguished from a real Man; and that the Body of Christ is not there, but in Heaven.

3. The Book of the *Exposition of the Gospels* is condemn'd, which teacheth, that the *Eucharist* is only the Image of the Body of Christ, and that his Body is in Heaven at the right Hand of the Father, and not upon Earth.

4. Their *Breviary*, which they call *Iludre* and *Gaza*, is condemn'd; which teaches, that the most H. Sacrament of the Eucharist is not the true Body of Christ.

Lastly, The *Office* of the *Burial of Priests* is condemn'd, where it is said, that the most H. Sacrament of the Altar, is no more but the virtue of Christ, and not his true Body and Blood.

This Synod was Printed in the University of *Conimbra*, with the Licences of the Inquisition and Ordinary in the Year 1606. and is in the Possession of a Learned Person, who gave me this account out of it.

CHAP. XII.

The Twelfth Difference.

The Fathers assert, That Christ's Body is not eaten corporally and carnally, but only spiritually. But the Church of Rome teaches a Corporal Eating, a Descent of Christ's Natural Body into ours; and understands the Eating of Christ's Body literally and carnally.

IF the Church of *Rome* declares its own Faith, when it imposes the Profession of it upon another, and makes one abjure the contrary under pain of *Anathema*; then I am sure it was once with a witness for the eating of Christ's Body in the most *literal and proper Sense*; when *An. Dom.* 1059. Pope *Nicholas* II. and the General Council of *Lateran*, prescribed a Profession of it to *Berengarius*, made him swear it, and anathematize the contrary, as it is set down by *Lanfrank* (n); which because the *Nubes Testium* (tho' it has set down two other Forms) durst not give us, I will therefore here transcribe out of him.

(n) *De Eucharist. Sacram. adv. Berengar.*

I Berengarius, *unworthy Deacon, &c. knowing the true Catholick and Apostolick Faith, do anathematize all Heresie, especially that for which I have hitherto been defamed; which endeavours to maintain, that the Bread and Wine placed on the Altar, after Consecration, are only a Sacrament (or Sign), and not the true Body and Blood of our Lord Jesus Christ; and cannot, save only in the Sign, be handled or broken by the Priest's Hands, or be ground by the Teeth of the Faithful. But I agree with the Holy Roman Church, and the Apostolick Seat, and do with my Mouth, and from my Heart profess, That I hold the same Faith concerning the Sacraments of the Lords Table, which our Lord and Venerable Pope* Nicholas *and this Holy Synod, by Evangelical and Apostolical Authority, has delivered to me to hold, and confirmed to me,*

viz.

Ego Berengarius indignus Diaconus Ecclesiæ S. Mauritii Andegavensis, cognoscens veram Catholicam & Apostolicam Fidem, anathematizo omnem Hæresin, præcipue eam de quâ hactenus infamatus sum; quæ astruere conatur panem & vinum quæ in altari ponuntur, post consecrationem solummodo Sacramentum, & non verum corpus & sanguinem Dom. nostri Jesu Christi esse; nec posse sensualiter, nisi in solo Sacramento, manibus Sacerdotum tractari, vel frangi, aut. fidelium dentibus atteri. Consentio autem S. Romanæ Ecclesiæ & Apostolicæ sedi, & ore & corde profiteor de Sacramentis Dominicæ mensæ,

of the Ancient Church, relating to the Eucharist.

viz. *That the Bread and Wine which are placed on the Altar, after Consecration, are not only a Sacrament, but also the true Body of our Lord Jesus Christ, and is sensibly, not only in the Sign and Sacrament, but in truth, handled and broken by the Priests Hands, and ground by the Teeth of the Faithful: Swearing this by the Holy and Co-essential Trinity, and by the most Holy Gospels of Christ. And as for those that oppose this Faith, I judge them, with their Opinions and Followers, worthy of an eternal Anathema*, &c.

eam fidem tenere, quam Dominus & Venerabilis Papa Nicholaus & hæc S. Synodus authoritate Evangelica & Apostolica tenendam tradidit, mihique firmavit: scilicet, Panem & vinum quæ in altari ponuntur post consecrationem, non solum Sacramentum, sed etiam verum corpus D. N. J. Christi esse, & sensualiter non solum Sacramento, sed in veritate manibus Sacerdotum tractari, frangi & fidelium dentibus atteri, jurans per S. & homousion Trinitatem, & per hæc sacrosancta Christi Evangelia. Eos veru qui contra hanc fidem venerint cum dogmatibus & sectatoribus suis æterno anathemate dignos esse pronuncio, &c.

This we may look upon as the Belief of that Church then, and this to be the manner of eating the Body of Christ: since, as *Bellarmine* well observes (*o*), *None are compelled to abjure and anathematize dubious Opinions, but only such as are condemned by the Church as known Heresies.*

(*o*) *De Sacr. Euchar.* l. 3 c. 21. Nec coguntur ulli abjurare &. anathematizare sententias dubias, sed eas tantùm quæ damnantur ab Ecclesia, tanquam hæreses exploratæ.

But however Infallible this *Pope* and that *General Council* were, this way of eating Christ's Body, by *tearing it with the Teeth*, was quickly opposed, (as a late Learned Preface to the Determination of *Joh. Parisiensis* shews at large.)

Peter Lombard could not digest it (*p*): For tho' the *Pope* and *Council* defined, That both the *handling*, and also the *breaking and tearing with the Teeth* of Christ's Body, were not only in the Sign and Sacrament, but in Truth performed; he makes a distinction, and in express words (cited in the Margin) says, That Christ's Body is handled indeed, not only *in Sacrament*, but *in Truth*; but that it is *broken and torn with the Teeth* truly indeed, but yet only *in Sacrament*. That is, in the *visible Species*, as he before explains that Phrase. Directly contrary to *Berengarius*'s Recantation.

(*p*) *Sentent. lib.* 4. *dist.* 12. Fractio & partes quæ ibi videntur fieri, in Sacramento fiunt, i. e. in visibili specie. Ideoque illa Berengarii verba ita distinguenda sunt, ut sensualiter, non modo in Sacramento, sed in veritate dicatur corpus Christi *tractari manibus Sacerdotum: Frangi verò & atteri dentibus, verè quidem* sed in Sacramento tantum.

The

The words also of *Joh. Semeca*, the Author of the Gloss upon the Canon-Law (*q*), are very bold against it. *Unless you understand the words of Berengarius in a sound sense*, (and there can be no other, the words are so plain, but what must contradict it) *you will fall into a greater Heresie than he was guilty of; and therefore you must refer all to the Species*, (that's directly contrary to the Pope and Council) *for we do not make Parts of Christ's Body.*

(*q*) *Gloss. apud Gratian. de Consecr. Dist. 2. c Ego Berengarius. Nisi sanè intelligas verba Berengarii in majorem incides Hæresin quam ipse habuit; & ideo omnia referas ad species ipsas; nam de Christi corpore partes non facimus.*

In fine, all the great Writers, especially the *Jesuits*, have forsaken this Definition, as not to be maintained, and this Eating in the most proper sense is wholly discarded; and we are told (*r*) by *Bellarmine*, That *grinding with the Teeth is not necessarily required to Eating; but it suffices that it be taken in, and transmitted from the Mouth into the Stomach by humane and natural Instruments*, viz. *the Tongue and Palate.*

(*r*) *De Sacr. Euchar. l. 1. c. 11. Ad rationem manducationis, non est necessaria attritio, sed satis est sumptio, & transmissio ab ore ad stomachum per instrumenta humana & naturalia, i. e. linguam & palatum.*

This way, in plainer terms, is *swallowing the Body of Christ without chewing.* And indeed without *this Descent of it into the Body*, there could no Account be given of that Prayer in the *Roman Missal* (*s*): *Lord, let thy Body which I have taken, and thy Blood which I have drunk, cleave unto my Entrals.*

(*s*) *Corpus tuum, Domine, quod sumpsi, & sanguis quem potavi, adhæreat visceribus meis.*

They have also determined how long this Sacred Body makes its stay there. *Aquinas* (whom they all now follow) says (*t*), *The Body of Christ remains in this Sacrament, so long as the Sacramental Species remain: When they cease to be, the Body of Christ ceases to be under them.*

(*t*) *In 3. part. quæst. 76. art. 6. ad 3. Corpus Christi remanet in hoc Sacramento, quousque species sacramentales manent. Quibus cessantibus definit esse corpus Christi sub eis.*

Thus also *Domin. Soto* (*u*). *We ought undoubtedly to hold, That Christ's Body descends into the Stomach.* ——— *Since Digestion is made in the Stomach, there the Species cease to be, and so also Christ's Body, and therefore will not descend into the Draught.*

(*u*) *In 4. dist. 12. qu. 1. art. 3. Est indubiè tenendum quod corpus (sc. Christi) descendit in stomachum.* ——— *Cùm digestio fiat in stomacho illic desinunt esse species, atque adeo corpus, quare non descendit in ventrem.*

But

of the Ancient Church, relating to the Eucharist.   119

But now comes a scurvy Case, that will force out the whole Truth. Suppose, by reason of any Disease, the *Species* should descend further than the Stomach; as in a Flux, when there is no Digestion of the *Species*, nor time to do it in the Stomach, but they are presently carried downward whole, or else brought up immediately, as in case of sudden Vomiting. This also is resolved by the same Principles. So the last-named *Author* (x). *If by reason of any Disease the Species should descend,* (into the Draught, he means) *the Body also it self would descend and be sent forth. For Shame ought not to be a Reason for denying the Truth.*

(x) *Soto ibid. Sed si ob aliquem morbum species descenderent, consequenter & ipsum corpus descenderet & emitteretur. Pudor enim non debet esse in causa negandi veritatem.*

To which S. *Antoninus* (y) agrees, (citing *Paludanus* in the case.) *Therefore the Body and Blood of Christ remains so long in the Belly and Stomach, or Vomit, or any where else, as the Species remain, just as the converted Substance* (viz. Bread and Wine) *would have remained. And if the Species are vomited up whole, or go forth* (downwards) *there is truly the Body of Christ.*

(y) *Part.* 3. *tit.* 13. *cap.* 6. *sect.* 3. *Igitur corpus Christi & sanguis tamdiu manet in ventre & stomacho vel vomitu & quecunque alibi, quamdiu species manent, sicut substantia conversa mansisset. Et si species incorruptæ evomuntur, vel egrediuntur, est ibi vere corpus Christi.*

And he tells us of S. *Hugo Cluniac.* how he commended one *Goderanus*, who (by a strange fervor) swallowed down the Particles of an Host, which a Leper had vomited up with vile Spittle, saying, That S. *Laurence* his Gridiron was more tolerable.

If these Consequences seem horrid and detestable to the Reader, the Doctrine, from which they necessarily flow, ought to be look'd upon much more so.

But now, to return to the Fathers, and their Sense of *Eating the Body of Christ.*

It is evident to any that will impartially consult their Writings, that they were perfect Strangers to all these Cases that are thus currently resolved in the *Roman Church*.

That Christ's Natural Body should enter into ours, is too gross and carnal a Thought, to be attributed to them; and fits only the Imaginations of a *Carnal Church*, and of those *Capernaites*, who in the Sixth of S. *John* ask, *How can this Man give us his Flesh to eat?*

Christ tells them, That the Words he spoke to them were *Spirit* and *Life*. And so the *Fathers* always understood the

Eating

eating of *Christ's Body* and drinking *his Blood*, not in a *literal* and *proper*, but in a *figurative* and *spiritual Sense*; as I shall now prove from their Writings. Wherein it may not be amiss to take notice, first, What their Sense is about understanding things *carnally* and *spiritually*.

S. *Chrysostome* (z) asking this Question, *What is it to think (or understand) carnally?* He answers, *Simply to look upon the things proposed, and to think of no more.* —— *But we ought to view all Mysteries with our inward Eyes: for this is spiritually to view them.*

S. *Austin* (a) gives the same account. *We have a carnal Taste, when we take that which is figuratively spoken, as if it were properly spoken.*

And elsewhere (b). *Every figurative and allegorical Reading or Speech, seems to sound one thing carnally, and to insinuate another thing spiritually.*

S. *Austin* (c) further gives a Rule when to understand a thing literally, and when to understand it figuratively and spiritually. *If the Speech be by way of command, either forbidding a Crime or heinous Wickedness, or bidding a beneficial or good thing to be done, it is not figurative: But if it seems to command a Crime or heinous Wickedness, or forbid an useful and beneficial thing, it is figurative.* And then he gives the Example of his Rule, in those words of Christ, *Except ye eat the Flesh and drink the Blood of the Son of Man, ye have no Life in you.* Now this, says he, *seems to command a Crime or horrid thing; therefore it is a Figure, commanding us to communicate in the Passion of our Lord, and sweetly and profitably to treasure up in our Memory, that his Flesh was crucified and wounded for us.*

Origen said the very same before him (d), and gives the same Instance. *Not only in the Old Testament is found the killing Letter: there is also in the New Testament a Letter that kills him who do's not spiritually consider what is said.* For
if

(z) Hom. 46. in Joan. Τὶ δέ ἐστι τὸ σαρκικῶς νοῆσαι; —— Τὸ ἁπλῶς εἰς τὰ προκείμενα ὁρᾶν, ᾗ μὴ πλέον φαντάζεσθαι. —— Χρὴ δὲ πάντα μυστήρια τοῖς ἔνδον ὀφθαλμοῖς κατοπτεύειν, τοῦτο γάρ ἐστι πνευματικῶς.

(a) De Doctr. Christ. l. 3. c. 5. Cùm figuratè dictum sic accipitur, tanquam propriè dictum sit, carnaliter sapitur.

(b) Serm. 44. de diversis. Omnis figurata & allegorica lectio vel locutio, aliud videtur sonare carnaliter, aliud insinuare spiritualiter.

(c) De Doctr. Christ l. 3. c. 16. Si præceptiva est locutio, aut flagitium aut facinus vetans, aut beneficentiam jubens, non est figurata. Si autem flagitium aut facinus videtur jubere, aut utilitatem aut beneficentiam vetare, figurata est. Nisi manducaveritis carnem filii hominis, &c. facinus vel flagitium videtur jubere: Figura ergo est, præcipiens passioni Domini esse communicandum, & suaviter atque utiliter in memoria condendum, quod caro ejus pro nobis crucifixa & vulnerata est.

(d) Hom. 7. in Levitic. Non solùm in Veteri Testamento occidens Litera deprehenditur, est & in N. Testamento Litera quæ occidit eum qui non spi-

if thou follow this according to the Letter which was said, Unless ye eat my Flesh and drink my Blood, *this Letter kills.*

carnem meam, & biberitis sanguinem meum, occidit hæc litera.

rituaiiter quæ dicuntur adverterit. Si enim secundùm literam sequaris hoc ipsum quod dictum est, *Nisi manducaveritis*

And in another place (e). *We are not to eat the Flesh of the Lamb, as the Slaves of the Letter do, &c.* To which he opposes those *who receive the Spirituals of the Word.*

Such as those whom S. *Austin* mentions (f), who pleased God and died not (*i. e.* eternally). *Because they understood the visible Food* (Manna) *spiritually, they hungred spiritually, they tasted spiritually, that they might spiritually be satisfied.*

Or, as he expresses it a little after (g), *He that eats inwardly, not outwardly; that eats in his Heart, not he that presseth it with his Teeth.* And therefore elsewhere * exhorts them, *Do not prepare your Jaws, but your Heart.*

This is what *Clemens Alexandr.* (h) requires, when he says, *That Christ, when he broke the Bread, set it before them, that we may eat it rationally, i. e.* spiritually.

So S. *Austin* again (i). *The Body and Blood of Christ will then be Life to every one, if what is visibly taken in the Sacrament, be in truth spiritually eaten and spiritually drunk.* Where he makes this to be *eating in Truth*, and the other but *Sacramental.*

So *Macarius* (k) having called the Bread and Wine the *Antitype* of Christ's Flesh and Blood, he adds, *They which are Partakers of the visible Bread, do spiritually eat the Flesh of the Lord.* He should rather have said *orally*, according to the Doctrine of our Adversaries.

S. *Athanasius* (l) expounding those words, *What if ye see the Son of Man ascending where he was before? It is the Spirit that quickneth, the Flesh profiteth nothing*, &c. adds, *He affirmed both of himself, the Flesh and Spirit, and made a difference*

(e) *In Joan. Tom.* 10. Οὐχ ἡμῖν ἐν βρωτέον ἡ σάρκα τῦ ἀμνῦ ὥσπερ ποιῦσιν οἱ ἡ λέξεως δῦλοι, &c.
—Τὰ πνευματικὰ λόγε μέλα λαμβάνοντες.

(f) *In Joan. tract.* 26. Quia visibilem cibum spiritaliter intellexerunt, spiritaliter esurierunt, spiritaliter gustaverunt, ut spiritaliter satiarentur.

(g) *Ibid.* Qui manducat intus non foris, qui manducat in corde, non qui premit dente.

* *Serm.* 33. *de Verb. Dom.* Nolite parare fauces, sed cor.

(h) *Strom. l.* 1. Κλάσας τὸν ἄρτον προέθηκεν ἵνα δὴ φάγωμεν λογικῶς.

(i) *De Verb. Apost. Serm.* 2. Tunc vita unicuique erit corpus & sanguis Christi, si quod in sacramento visibiliter sumitur, in ipsa veritate spiritualiter manducetur, spiritualiter bibatur.

(k) *Homil.* 27.

—Καὶ οἱ μεταλαμβάνοντες ἐκ τῦ φαινομένε ἄρτε, πνευματικῶς ἡ σάρκα τῦ κυρίε ἐσθίει.

(l) *Tract. in illud Evang.* Quicunque dixerit verbum contra filium hominis.

—Ἵνα μὴ μόνον τὸ φαινόμενον, ἀλλὰ ἡ τὸ ἀόρατον αὐτῦ πιστεύοντες.

R *rence*

rence betwixt the Spirit and the Flesh, that not only believing that of him which was visible, but what was invisible, they might learn, that those things which he spake were not carnal, but spiritual. For to how many could his Body have sufficed for Meat, that it should be made the Food of the whole World? But therefore he mentions the Son of Man's Ascension into Heaven, that he might draw them from this corporal Conceit, and hereafter might learn, that the Flesh he spake of was celestial Meat from above, and spiritual Nourishment to be given by him, &c.

It will suffice all the World, if we follow Tertullian's (*m*) Advice. *Since the Word was made Flesh, he is to be long'd for that we may live, to be devoured by Hearing, to be chewed by Understanding, and digested by Faith.*

It is an excellent Comment on this, which Eusebius gives us (*n*) upon those words of *John* 6. *The Flesh profits nothing,* &c. *Do not imagine that I speak of that Flesh I am encompassed withal, as if you must eat that; nor think that I command you to drink sensible and corporeal Blood: But know, that the very Words that I have spoken to you are Spirit and Life. So that these very Words and Speeches of his, are his Flesh and Blood; whereof whoso is always Partaker, being nourished as it were with heavenly Bread, shall be a Partaker of heavenly Life.*——*Let not the hasty hearing of those things by me, of Flesh and Blood, trouble you; for things sensibly heard profit nothing, but it is the Spirit that quickneth them that can spiritually bear them.*

S. *Basil* (*o*) says the same. *There is an intellectual Mouth of the inward Man, whereby he is nourished who receives the Word of Life, which is the Bread that descended from Heaven.*

Facundus Hermian. (*p*) takes this of eating Christ's Flesh to be a Mystery, and that S. *Peter* when he answered, *Lord, whither should we go? thou hast the Words of Eternal Life,* did not then

---

—— Πίστις γὸ ἥρκει τὸ σῶμα πρὸς βρῶσιν, ἵνα κ̀ τῷ κόσμῳ παντὶ τῦτο ζοφὴ γίνη;

—— Ἵνα ἡ σωματικῆς ἐννοίας αὐτοὺς ἀφελκύση.

(*m*) De Resurr. c. 37. Quia & sermo caro erat factus, proinde in causam vitæ appetendus, & devorandus auditu, & ruminandus intellectu, & fide digerendus.

(*n*) Lib. 3. Eccl. Theol. c. 12. Μὴ γὸ τ̀ σάρκα, ἣν περίκειμαι, νομίσητέ με λέγειν, ὡς δέον αὐτὴν ἐσθίειν, μηδὲ τὸ αἰσθητὸν κ̀ σωματικὸν αἷμα πίνειν, ὑπολαμβάνετέ με προστάττειν. —— Ὥστε αὐτὰ εἶ τὰ ῥήματα κ̀ ἡ λόγοι αὐτοῦ ἡ σάρξ κ̀ τὸ αἷμα.

—— Ταῦτα γὸ ὑδὲν ὠφελεῖ αἰσθητῶς ἀκουόμενα, τὸ ἢ πνεῦμα ὅτι τὸ ζωοποιοῦν τῶν πνευματικῶς ἀκούειν δυναμένους.

(*o*) In Psal. 33. Ἔστι μέν τι κ̀ νοητὸν στόμα τῷ ἔνδον ἀνθρώπου, ᾧ τρέφεται μεταλαμβάνων τῷ λόγῳ τῆς ζωῆς, ὅς ἐστιν ἄρτος ἐκ τῷ οὐρανῷ καταβάς.

(*p*) Lib. 12. Defens. 3. capit. c. 1.

of the Ancient Church, relating to the Eucharist.

then understand it. *For*, says he, *if he had understood the Mystery, he should rather have said, Lord, there is no reason we should go away, since we believe we shall be saved by Faith in thy Body and Blood.* He means his Death and Passion, which is his Sense of eating Christ's Body and Blood.

Theodorus Heracleot. (*q*) refers this eating Christ's Flesh to the *sincere embracing the Oeconomy of his Incarnation. These*, says he, *upon the reasoning of their Minds, by assenting to it, as it were tasting the Doctrine, do rationally* (or spiritually) *eat his Flesh, and by Faith partake of his Blood.*

S. *Chrysostom* (*r*) upon those words, *It is the Spirit that quickneth, the Flesh profiteth nothing*, reckons up some of those carnal Doubts that profit nothing; as, *It is a carnal thing*, says he, *to doubt how Christ descended from Heaven, and to imagine him to be the Son of* Joseph, *and how he can give us his Flesh to eat. All these are carnal; which ought to be mystically and spiritually understood.*

Cyril of *Jerusalem* (*s*) says, That the Jews, for want of understanding spiritually Christ's words, *imagined that Christ exhorted them to devour his Flesh*; which is hard to be distinguish'd from the Roman Churches *Oral Manducation.*

This carnal Fancy might well make them shrink, and cry out, *This is a hard Saying, who can bear it?* For, as S. *Austin* (*t*) well observes, *It seems more horrible to eat Humane Flesh, than to kill it*; *and to drink Mans Blood, than to shed it.*

Origen's (*u*) words (for I see no good reason to question they are his) are enough to convince effectually all such *carnal Jews and Christians. There is a Meat and Drink for this material and outward Man, as we call him, agreeable to his Nature, viz. this corporeal and earthly Food. There is likewise a proper Food for the spiritual,*

Quod si mysterium intellexisset, ———— potius diceret, Domine, cur ———amus non est, cùm credamus nos corporis & sanguinis tui fide salvandos.

(*q*) *Catena in Joan.* 6. 54, 55.

—— Τῷ τ̃ ψυχῆς λογισμῷ διὰ τ̃ συγκαταθέσεως ὥσπερ ἀπογευόμενοι τὸ δόγματ(Θ-), λογικῶς ἐσθίοσι τ̃ σάρκα κỳ μεταλαμβάνοσι τὸ αἷματ(Θ-).

(*r*) *Hom.* 45. *in Joan.* Σαρκικὸν ᾗ ὄυ τὸ ἀμφισβηλεῖν πῶς ἐκ τῶ οὐρανῶ καταβέβηκε, κỳ τὸ νομίζειν ἔτι υἱὸς ἑἶν Ἰωσὴφ, κỳ τὸ πῶς δύναται ἡμῖν τ̃ σάρκα δῦναι φαγεῖν· ταῦτα πάντα σαρκικὰ, ἃπερ ἔδει μυστικῶς νοεῖν κỳ πνδυμαλικῶς, &c.

(*s*) *Catech. Mystag.* 4.

Νομίζοντες ὅτι ἐπὶ σαρκοφαγίαν αὐτοὺς περισπᾷ.

(*t*) *Cont. adverf. Legis l.* 2. *c.* 9. Horribilius videatur humanam carnem manducare quam perimere, & humanum sanguinem potare quam fundere.

(*u*) *Prolog. in Cantic.*

Est materialis hujus hominis, qui & exterior appellatur, cibus potusque naturæ suæ cognatus, corporeus iste, sc. & terrenus. Similiter autem & spiritualis hominis ipsius, qui & interior dicitur, est proprium [...], ut panis ille vivus qui de cœlo descendit, &c. —— Rerum vero proprietas unicuique discreta servatur, & corruptibili corruptibilia præbentur, incorruptibili vero incorruptibilia proponuntur.

(*x*) *Hom.* 1. *in Cantic.* Ἀναλογία τις ὅτι τῆς ψυχικοῖς κινήμασι καὶ ἐνεργήμασι πρὸς τὰ τῶ σώματ(Θ) αἰσθήεια, &c. —— Ὁ γδ οἶν(Θ) τε κ᾿ γάλα τῆ γδύσει κεῖτ(α)· νοητῶ ἢ ὄντων ἐκείνων, νοητὴ παντῶς κ᾿ ἡ ἀντίληπλιη τούτων ἡ ψυχῆς ὅτι δύναμις.

(*y*) *Homil.* 26. *in Matth.* —— Ἑαυτὸν δίδωσι ἡμῖν εἰς ἑστίασιν κ᾿ συνευωχίαν πνευματικὴν.

(*z*) *Comment. in Exod.* Cœlestis seu divinus Agnus animarum solet esse cibus.

(*a*) *Tract.* 1. *in Epist. Joan.* —— Ipsum jam in cœlo sedentem manu contrectare non possumus, sed fide contingere.

(*b*) *Tract.* 26. *in Evang. Joan.* Non ad Christum ambulando currimus, sed credendo: nec motu corporis, sed voluntate cordis accedimus. —— Sic se tangi voluit, sic tangitur ab eis à quibus benè tangitur, ascendens ad patrem, manens cum patre, æqualis patri.

(*c*) *Idem Tract.* 27. *in Joan.* Quid est hoc? Hinc solvit illud quod non noverant —— Illi enim putabant eum erogaturum corpus suum, ille autem dixit, se ascensurum in cœlum, utique integrum. Cùm videritis filium hominis ascendentem ubi erat priùs, certè vel tunc videbitis quia non eo modo quo putatis erogat corpus suum, cer-

spiritual, *or, as we call it, inward Man, as that living Bread that came down from Heaven,* &c. —— *But the Property of things is reserved to each distinct, and corruptible things are given to that which is corruptible, and incorruptible things are proposed to that which is incorruptible.*

Greg. Nyssen (*x*) also well expresses it thus. *There is an Analogy betwixt the Motions and Operations of the Soul and the Senses of the Body,* &c.

——*Wine and Milk are judged of by the Taste; but these being intellectual, the Power of the Soul that apprehends them must be altogether intellectual.*

S. *Chrysostom* (*y*) said well, *That Christ gave himself to us for a spiritual Feast and Banquet.*

And *Procopius Gazæus* (*z*). *The Celestial and Divine Lamb is wont to be the Food of Souls.*

S. *Austin* (*a*) indeed tells us, *We cannot handle him who now sits in Heaven; yet,* says he, *we may touch him by our Faith.*

For, as he says elsewhere (*b*), *We run to Christ, not by walking, but by believing; nor do we approach him by the Motion of our Bodies, but by the Will of our Hearts.*

And afterwards.——*Thus he would be touched, and thus he is touched by all that rightly touch him, ascending to the Father, remaining with the Father, equal to the Father.*

And in the next Tractate (*c*) upon those words, *What if ye see the Son of Man ascend,* &c. What do's this mean? He hence resolves that which they did not know ——*For they imagined, that he would bestow his Body upon them; and he told them, that he would ascend into Heaven entire and whole. When you shall see the Son of Man ascending where he was before, then surely you will see, that he do's not bestow his Body after*
that

that manner you think he do's: Surely you will then at least understand, that his Grace is not consumed by bites (of the Teeth)

Gelasius (d) therefore said well: *To believe on the Son of God, this is to see him, this is to hear him, this is to smell, this is to taste him, and this is to handle him.*

These Testimonies, one would think, are sufficient to tell us the Sense of the Fathers in this Matter; yet, with the Reader's leave, I will add a few Considerations more, to put it out of all doubt.

> 1 Consideration. *It appears there is no necessity to understand eating and drinking Christ's Body in the Eucharist, of his natural Body received into ours; because the Fathers say, We eat and drink, and partake of Christ's Body and Blood in Baptism, which, by the confession of all, can be done only spiritually there.*

Thus Cyril of Alexandria (e) says, *The Gentiles could not have shaken off their Blindness, and contemplated the Divine and H. Light, that is, attained the Knowledge of the Holy and Consubstantial Trinity, unless by Holy Baptism they had been made Partakers of his Holy Flesh, and washed away the blackness of their Sin, and shak'd off the Devil's Power.*

And elsewhere (f) speaking of the Eunuch. *He by his Question, says he, shewed, that he was Partaker of the Spiritual Lamb; for he was presently thought worthy of Baptism.*

Fulgentius (g). *Unless ye eat the Flesh of the Son of Man, and drink his Blood, ye shall have no Life in you. Which whosoever can consider, not only according to the Mystery of Truth* (viz. in the Sacraments) *but according to the Truth of the Mystery, will see that this is done in the Laver of Holy Regeneration.*

And again (h). *Neither need any one in the least doubt, that every Believer is then made Partaker*

(d) *Contr. Eutych.* l. 4. Credere in filium Dei, hoc est videre, hoc est audire, hoc est odorari, hoc est gustare, hoc est contrectare eum.

(e) *In Joan.* 9. 6.

—Εἰ μὴ χρόνε μέτοχα τ̂ ἁγίας αὐτῶ σαρκὸς, &c. διὰ τ̂ ἁγίε διαχρόνε βαπίσμα[Θ-.

(f) *Glaphyr. in Exod.* lib. 2. Μέτοχος ἤδη τ̂ νοητῶ πϱοβάτε διὰ τ̂ ἐρωτήσεως ἀπεδείχνυετο, ἠξίε γδ εὐθὺς καὶ βαπτίσε.

(g) *De Bapt. Æthiop. in fine.* Nisi manducaveritis carnem filii hominis, & biberitis ejus sanguinem, non habebitis vitam in vobis. Quod quisquis non solum secundùm veritatis mysteria, sed secundùm mysterii veritatem, considerare poterit, in ipso Lavacro S. Regenerationis hoc fieri providebit.

(h) *Ibid.* Nec cuiquam esse aliquatenus ambigendum, tunc

tè vel tunc intelligetis, quia gratia ejus non consumitur morsibus.

unumquemque fidelium corporis sanguinisque participem fieri, quando in baptismate membrum corporis Christi efficitur.
(i) In Esa. 3.
—Τὸ σῶμα καταπατέντων, ϰ̀ τὸ αἷμα τ̃ διαθήκης κοινὸν ἡγησαμένων.

taker of *Christ's Body and Blood, when he is made in Baptism a Member of Christ's Body.*

Therefore S. *Basil (i)* says, That *the Lord takes away Christ from those who having put him on by Baptism, by sinning afterwards trample upon his Body, and count the Blood of the Covenant an unholy thing.*

2 Consideration. *The Fathers, with reference to Eating and Drinking, distinguish Christ's True Body from his Sacramental one; which they could not do, if Christ's True and Natural Body and Blood were eat and drunk in a proper sense in the Sacrament.*

(k) In 1 Cor. c. 11. v. 29.
Ὥσπερ γὰρ ἡ παρουσία αὐτοῦ, &c. Τοῖς μὴ δεξαμένοις αὐτὴν μᾶλλον κατέκρινεν, ὕτω κ̀ τὰ μυσήρια μείζονΘ ἐφόδια κολάσεως γίνη() τοῖς ἀναξίως μετέχουσι.

(l) Contr. Faustum l. 20. c. 21.
Hujus sacrificii caro & sanguis, &c. — in passione Christi *per ipsam veritatem* reddebatur, post ascensum Christi *per Sacramentum memoriæ celebratur.*

(m) In Psal. 21:
—Intelligent in pane & vino visibiliter sibi proposito aliud invisibile, scilicet corpus & sanguinem verum Domini, qui verus cibus & potus sunt, quo non venter distenditur, sed mens saginatur.

(n) In Esdram lib. 2. cap. 8.
Immolatio Paschæ gloriam insinuet resurrectionis, cùm omnes electi carne agni immaculati, id est, Dei & Domini nostri, non amplius in Sacramento credentes, sed in reipsa ac veritate videntes, reficiuntur.

S. *Chrysostome (k)* expounding those words, *He that eateth and drinketh unworthily,* &c. says, *As Christs Presence, which brought those great and unspeakable Blessings to us, did condemn those the more that did not receive it ; so also the Mysteries make way for greater Punishments to those that unworthily partake of them.*

S. *Austin (l)* (whose words I have given Chap. 10. Posit. 2.) makes the Flesh and Blood of Christ to be *exhibited in the Truth* at his Passion, and *in the Sacrament only the Memory of it* to be celebrated.

Bede (m) upon those words, *The Poor shall eat and be satisfied,* says, *By this Bread and Wine, which are visibly offered to them, they will understand another invisible thing,* viz. *the true Body and Blood of our Lord, which are really Meat and Drink, not such as fills the Belly, but which nourishes the Mind.*

And in another place *(n)* speaking of the Passover. *The Immolation of this Passover represents the Glory of our Resurrection, when all the Elect shall eat together the Flesh of the Immaculate Lamb, I mean of him who is our God and Lord, no more in Sacrament as Believers, but in the thing it self, and in Truth, as Spectators.*

Neither

of the Ancient Church, relating to the Eucharist. 127

Neither is that of *Isidore* of *Sevil* (*o*) to be passed over, who mentions this Prayer in the Liturgy of his Time; *That the Oblation which is offered to God, being sanctified by the Holy Spirit, may be conformed to the Body and Blood of Christ.* Which very Phrase shews a difference betwixt what we receive in the Eucharist, and the true Body and Blood of Christ: Else it would not be *Conformity*, but *Identity*, as Monsieur *Claude* has well observed.

(*o*) *De Officiis Ecclef. l.* 1 *c.* 15.
—Ut oblatio quæ Domino offertur sanctificata per spiritum sanctum, corpori & sanguini Christi *conformetur* (not *confirmetur*, *as the last* Colen *Edition absurdly has printed it*, An. 1617.)

3 Consideration. *They say, That the Fathers under the Old Testament did eat the same spiritual Meat with us; and give this as the Reason why it is spiritual Meat, Because it is not eaten corporally, but by Faith. Therefore both they and we must eat the same Meat only spiritually, not corporally.*

S. *Austin* has said so much in this Argument, that I need go no further. And I might insist upon many Passages I have upon other occasions named before; as that in his Treatise upon S. *John's Gospel* (*p*), where explaining that of *the same spiritual Drink the Fathers drank*, he has such Expressions as these. *See the Signs are varied, Faith remaining the same. There the Rock was Christ* (in Sign); *to us, that which is laid on the Altar is Christ*; *and they drank of the Water that flowed from the Rock, for a great Sacrament of the same Christ*; *what we drink, the Faithful know. If you regard the visible Species or Nature, it is another thing; if the spiritual or intelligible Signification, they drank the same spiritual Drink.*

In another place (*q*). *Their Meat and Drink was the same with ours in Mystery; not in Substance* (or Species) *the same; but in Signification. Because the same Christ who was figured to them in the Rock, is manifested to us in the Flesh.*

To add but one place more, which fully comprehends the whole sense of the Argument (*r*): Where S. *Austin* explaining the same words, of *our Fathers eating the same spiritual Meat,* &c. he discourses thus.

(*p*) *Tract.* 45. *in Ev. Joan.* Videte, fide manente, signa variata. Ibi petra Christus, nobis Christus quod in altari Dei ponitur. Et illi pro magno Sacramento ejusdem Christi biberunt aquam profluentem de petra, nos quid bibamus norunt fideles. Si speciem visibilem intendas aliud est ; si intelligibilem significationem eundem potum spiritualem biberunt.

(*q*) *Idem in Pfal.* 77. Idem in mysterio cibus & potus illorum qui noster, sed significatione idem non specie. Quia idem ipse Christus illis in petra figuratus, nobis in carne manifestatus est.

(*r*) *De Utilit. Pœnitentiæ, cap.* 1.

The

Apostolus dicit, Patres nostros, non patres infidelium, non patres impiorum manducantes & morientes, sed patres nostros, patres fidelium, spiritalem cibum manducasse, & ideo eundem.—— Erant enim ibi quibus plus Christus in corde quam Manna in ore sapiebat. Quicunque in Manna Christum intellexerunt, eundem quem nos cibum spiritalem manducaverunt.——Sic etiam eundem potum, *Petra enim erat Christus.* Eundem ergo potum quem nos, sed spiritalem, id est, qui fide capiebatur, non qui corpore hauriebatur.——Eundem ergo cibum sed intelligentibus & credentibus ; non intelligentibus autem, illud solum Manna, illa sola aqua, &c.	*The Apostle says, That our Fathers, not the Fathers of Unbelievers, not the Fathers of the Wicked, that did eat and die ; but our Fathers, the Fathers of the Faithful, did eat spiritual Meat, and therefore the same.—— For there were such there, to whom Christ was more tasteful in their Heart, than Manna in their Mouth.—— Whosoever understood Christ in the Manna, did eat the same spiritual Meat we do.—— So also the same Drink,* For the Rock was Christ. *Therefore they drank the same Drink we do, but spiritual Drink, that is, Drink which was received by Faith, not what was swallowed down by the Body.——They ate therefore the same Meat, the same to those that understand and believe ; but to them that do not understand, it was only that Manna, only that Water, &c.* Here you see, S. *Austin* calls that Spiritual Drink *which Faith receives, not which the Body takes down.*

And thus whether *Christ be come,* or *be to come,* it's all one (as he says a little after, *Venturus & venit diversa verba sunt sed idem Christus*) because Faith can apprehend *what shall be,* as well as *what is.* But if our Eating be Christ's natural Body swallowed down our Bodies, then their Meat and ours were not the same. For Christ could not be thus their Meat, because then he had not taken Flesh upon him ; therefore those old Fathers could not take it down in the *oral Sense.*

    4 Consideration. *The Body and Blood are to be eaten and drunk, and to be received, as they are represented and set before us in the Sacrament. But there the Body of Christ (according to the Fathers as well as the Scriptures) is set before us as broken and dead, and his Blood as poured out of his Veins. Therefore it can be eaten and drunk by us only figuratively and spiritually.*

If the Reader look back to *Chap.* 10. *Posit.* 4. he will find a great many Testimonies, especially out of S. *Chrysostome,* to prove that the Fathers considered Christ's Body in the Sacrament as slain and dead, and his Blood poured out of his Veins, and separated from his Body: And how S. *Chrysostome,* at the same time when he tells us that Christ has *given us leave to be filled with his Holy Flesh* (s), *he has proposed and set himself before us as slain.*

This I shall now give a further account of, seeing the Fathers speak nothing more plainly and fully than this.   S. *Austin*

(i) Hom. 51. in Matth.
——Τῶν ἁγίων σαρκῶν αὐτὸ ἐμπλησθῆναι ἔδωκεν ἡμῖν——ἑαυτὸν παρέθηκε τεθυμένον.

of the Ancient Church, relating to the Eucharist. 129

S. *Austin* (*t*) not only tells us in general, That we are fed from our Lord's Cross, because we eat his Body; but more expresly says (*u*), That *Christ offered himself a Sacrifice for us to God the Father, on the Table of the Cross, giving to his Catholick Church a vital Banquet,* viz. *by satiating us with his Body, and inebriating us with his Blood.* But all this, by looking upon him on the Table of the Cross, sacrificed and slain.

This made *Gr. Nyssen* (*x*) say, That *the Body of the Victim* (speaking of Christ) *is not fit for eating, if it be alive.*

And S. *Cyprian* (*y*). *Neither should we be able to drink the Blood of Christ, unless it were first trodden and pressed.* Alluding to Grapes in a Wine-press; and that Christ's Blood must be out of his Veins when we drink it, and so considered by us.

But none of the *Ancients* has given a fuller Account of this than *Hesychius* (*z*), who says, That *Christ made his Flesh fit to be eaten after his Passion, which was not fit to be eaten before his Passion: For if he had not been crucified, we could by no means eat the Sacrifice of his Body. But now we eat Food, receiving the Memory of his Passion.*

And again (*a*), he compares the Cross to a *Gridiron, which when our Lord's Flesh is put upon it, makes it fit to be Food of Men: For unless it had been laid thus upon the Cross, we could in no wise mystically have received Christ's Body.*

And because this Food, which is thus *mystically to be eaten,* could not be fit Food for us, unless Christ was crucified and slain; therefore in several places he speaks of Christ as slaying himself in the Eucharist (which cannot be understood properly) before he was slain upon the Cross. Thus he says (*b*), *Christ, by way of anticipation, slew* (or sacrificed) *himself in the Supper of the Apostles, which they know that perceive the Virtue of the Mysteries.*

Again (*c*). *Our Lord first supping upon the figurative Lamb with the Apostles, did afterwards offer his Sacrifice, and a second time, as a Lamb, slew himself.*

S

(*t*) *In Psal.* 100. Nos de cruce Domini pascimur; quia corpus ipsius manducamus.

(*u*) *Serm.* 9. *de* 40. *edit. à Sirmondo.* — Qui se pro nobis in mensa crucis obtulit sacrificium Deo Patri, donans Ecclesiæ suæ Catholicæ vitale convivium, corpore suo nos videlicet satians, & inebrians sanguine.

(*x*) *Orat.* 1. *in Resurr. Dom.* Οὐ γὰρ ἐστι τὸ σῶμα ἱερεῖον πρὸς ἐδωδὴν ἐπιτήδειον εἴπερ ἔμψυχον ἦν.

(*y*) *Lib.* 2. *Ep.* 3. Nec nos sanguinem Christi possemus bibere, nisi prius calcatus fuisset & pressus.

(*z*) *Com. in Lev. l.* 1. — Carnem ejus, quæ ad comedendum inepta erat ante passionem — aptam cibo post passionem fecit. Si enim non fuisset crucifixus, sacrificium corporis ejus minimè comederemus. Comedimus autem nunc cibum, sumentes ejus memoriam passionis.

(*a*) *Ib. l.* 2. Sartaginem, Domini crucem, — accipi oportet, quæ etiam superimpositam Dominicam carnem, esibilem hominibus reddidit. Nisi enim superimposita fuisset cruci, nos corpus Christi nequaquàm mysticè percepissemus.

(*b*) *Ib. l.* 1. Præveniens, seipsum in cæna Apostolorum immolavit, quod sciunt qui mysteriorum virtutem percipiunt.

(*c*) *Ib. l.* 2. Prius figuratam ovem cum Apostolis cænans Dominus posteà suum obtulit sacrificium, & secundò sicut ovem seipsum occidit.

And

And now after all these Testimonies and Considerations, which, put together, demonstratively conclude against any eating of Christ's Body, or drinking his Blood, but what is *spiritual and figurative*; I'll put an end to this Chapter with two remarkable Sayings of S. *Austin*.

(*d*) *In Pſ*. 98.

The first is upon the 98 *Psalm* (*d*), where he confutes those who, when our Saviour spake of *eating his Flesh, and drinking his Blood*, were offended at this, as an hard Saying; and then expounding that which Christ added, *The words I speak are Spirit and Life*, he makes our Lord speak thus to them: *Understand spiritually what I have spoken. You are not to eat this Body which you see, nor to drink that Blood which they shall shed that will crucifie me. I have commended a certain Sacrament to you, which if spiritually understood, will give Life to you; and if it be necessary this Sacrament should be visibly celebrated, yet it must be invisibly* (i. e. spiritually) *understood by you*. No Protestant could chuse Words to express his Mind more fully by, in this Matter.

Spiritualiter intelligite quod locutus ſum. Non hoc corpus quod videtis manducaturi eſtis & bibituri illum ſanguinem quem fuſuri ſunt qui me crucifigent. Sacramentum aliquod vobis commendavi, ſpiritualiter intellectum vivificabit vos; & ſi neceſſe eſt illud viſibiliter celebrari, oportet tamen inviſibiliter intelligi.

His other Saying is against the *Manichees*, who fansied a *latent Christ* in the Fruits of Trees, and Ears of Corn, and professed to eat him that was *passible* with their Mouths. S. *Austin* thus sarcastically derides them (*e*): *Ye expect with open Mouth, who should bring in Christ into your Jaws, as the best Sepulcher for him.*

(*e*) *Contr. Fauſtum l.* 20.*c*. 11. Ore aperto expectatis quis inferat Chriſtum, tanquam optimæ ſepulturæ, faucibus veſtris.

If S. *Austin* had been for *Oral Manducation* of Christ's Body in the Eucharist, he could not have had the confidence to have objected this, as a Reproach to the *Manichees*, which might ſo eaſily have been returned with ſhame upon himſelf.

I conclude therefore, that the *Trent-Fathers*, when they called the *Sacramental* and *Oral Manducation*, real eating, to diſtinguiſh it from the *ſpiritual eating*; and made that Canon (*f*), *If any shall say, That Christ exhibited in the Eucharist, is only* spiritually *eaten, and not also sacramentally and* really, *let him be Anathema:* that herein they were ſo far from deſigning to teſtifie their *Conſent* with the Fathers (who, as you have heard, generally ſay the contrary) that they ſeem rather to have had a *Conspiracy* againſt them.

(*f*) *Conc. Trid. Seſſ.* 13. *Can* 8. Si quis dixerit Chriſtum in Euchariſtia exhibitum, ſpiritualiter tantùm manducari, & non etiam ſacramentaliter ac realiter, anathema ſit.

CHAP.

CHAP. XIII.

The Thirteenth Difference.

The Fathers assert, That the Faithful only eat Christs Body, and drink his Blood in the Eucharist, not the wicked. Whereas they of the present Roman Church extend it to both.

THIS Assertion, being a necessary consequence of the foregoing one, will make my work the shorter for its proof.

What the Church of *Rome* holds in this matter, cannot be questioned. The *Trent Catechism* speaking of such a Person that makes no distinction betwixt the Sacrament and other common food, expresses it thus (g). —— *Who impurely taking the Body of the Lord, which lies hid in the Eucharist* —— there it is hid, they mean, under the species, and the wicked take it.

Therefore *Dom. Soto* (who was one of the Council of *Trent*) says (h); *We must undoubtedly hold, that the Body of Christ descends into the stomach, tho' a wicked man takes it.*

So *Aquinas* (i). *Seeing the Body of Christ always remains in the Sacrament, till the Sacramental Species are corrupted, it follows, that even wicked men do eat the Body of Christ.*

Alensis (k) taking notice of the opinion of some that thought that as soon as the Body of Christ was touched by a Sinners lips, it withdrew it self, says, *This is an errour, and manifestly against the Saints; and therefore it is held commonly, that in this there is no difference betwixt the just and unjust, for both of them receive the very Body of Christ in the Sacrament.*

And a little after. *It must be granted, that the wicked receive the thing which the Sacrament is a sign of, which is Christs true Body, born of the Virgin,* &c.

(g) *Catechis. ad Paroch. Part.* 2. *n.* 27. —— Qui impurè sumens corpus Domini, quod in Eucharistia occultè latet ——

(h) *In* 4. *dist.* 12. *qu.* 1. *art.* 3. —— Est indubiè tenendum quòd corpus (sc. Christi) descendit in Stomachum, etiamsi ab iniquo sumatur.

(i) *Part.* 3. *quæst.* 80. *art.* 3. *conclus.* Cùm corpus Christi in Sacramento semper permaneat, donec species Sacramentales corrumpantur, etiam injustos homines Christi corpus manducare consequitur.

(k) *Part.* 4. *Qu.* 11. *memb.* 2. *art.* 2. *sec.* 2. —— Illud sentire erroneum est & manifestè contra sanctos: & ideo communiter tenetur quod in hoc non est differentia inter justum & injustum, quia uterq; ipsum verum corpus Christi sumit in Sacramento, &c.

—— Unde concedendum, quod mali sumunt *rem Sacramenti*, quod est corpus Christi verum, quod natum est de Virgine, &c.

This ought not to seem a strange Doctrine to be held by those, who say that brute Creatures may devour Chrifts Body. Which is the current opinion.

So *Aquinas* (*l*). *We muſt ſay, that altho' a Mouſe or a Dog ſhould eat a conſecated Hoſt, yet the ſubſtance of Chriſts Body do's not ceaſe to be under the ſpecies, ſo long as the ſpecies remain.*

Alenſis (*m*) is as poſitive and more plain. *If a Dog or a Hog ſhould ſwallow a whole conſecrated Hoſt, I ſee not why nor how the Body of our Lord would not, together with the Species, be conveyed into the Belly of that Dog or Hog.*

It is alſo remarkable, that among three Articles which P. *Gregory* XI. *an.* 1371. prohibited to be taught (*n*) under pain of Excommunication (which was alſo repeated by P. *Clement* VI.) one of them was this. *If a Conſecrated Hoſt ſhould be gnawed by a Mouſe, or taken by a Brute, that then the ſpecies remaining, the Body of Chriſt ceaſes to be under them, and the ſubſtance of the Bread returns.*

This he would not let paſs for good Divinity.

Nor can it at this Day, when this is one of the *Cautions* to be obſerved in the Celebrating of the Maſs.

(*o*) *That if a Fly, or any ſuch animal fall into the Chalice after Conſecration, if the Prieſt nauſeats it, then he muſt take it out and waſh it with Wine, and burn it when Maſs is ended; and the aſhes and the waſh be thrown into the H. Repoſitory. But if he do not nauſeate to ſwallow it, nor fears any danger, let him take it down with the Blood.*

What is all this for, but to tell us, that they look upon it ſtill to be *Chriſts Blood*, and that its better it ſhould be in the Belly of a *Prieſt* than of a *Brute*?

So alſo they give us another Caſe. (*p*) *If a Prieſt ſhould vomit up the Euchariſt, and the ſpecies appear entire, they muſt be taken down reverently, unleſs nauſeated; but in that caſe the Conſecrated Species*

(*l*) Loc. citat. ad Tertium. Dicendum, quod etiamſi mus vel canis hoſtiam conſecratam manducet, ſubſtantia corporis Chriſti non deſinit eſſe ſub ſpeciebus, quamdiu ſpecies illæ manent.

(*m*) Ibid. ſec. 1. loco citat. Si canis vel porcus deglutiret hoſtiam conſecratam integram, non video quare vel quomodo Corpus Domini non ſimul cum ſpecie trajiceretur in ventrem canis vel porci.

(*n*) See Pref. to the determ. of *Jo. Pariſ.* p. 32. Si hoſtia conſecrata à mure corrodatur, ſeu à bruto ſumitur, quod remanentibus ſpeciebus, ſub iis deſinit eſſe Corpus Chriſti, & redit ſubſtantia Panis.

(*o*) De Defect. Miſſæ, ſec. 10. n. 5. ante Miſſal. Roman. Si poſt conſecrationem ceciderit muſca, aut aliquid ejuſmodi, & fiat nauſea Sacerdoti, extrahat eam & lavet cum vino, finitâ Miſſa comburat, & combuſtio ac lotio hujuſmodi in Sacrarium projiciatur. Si autem non fuerit nauſea, nec ullum periculum timeat, ſumat cum ſanguine.

(*p*) Ibid. n. 14. Si Sacerdos evomat Euchariſtiam, ſi ſpecies integræ appareant, reverenter ſumantur, niſi nauſea fiat: tunc

Species must be cautiously separated, and put in some H. Place, till they are corrupted, &c.

enim species consecratæ cautè separentur, & in aliquo loco sacro reponantur, donec corrumpantur, &c.

But I beg the Readers Pardon for presenting him with such nauseous stuff; God grant that they who thus unworthily represent their Saviour, may have grace to repent, that the *thoughts of their hearts may be forgiven them.*

As for the *Fathers,* if by their plain words we can understand their sense, they assert, that only the Faithful, and not the wicked, eat the Body of Christ, and drink his Blood in a *proper sense*

S. *Jerome* (*q*) calls the Flesh of Christ the *food of Believers.*

And *Isidore of Sevil* (*r*) that it is the *meat of the Saints.* And he adds (which makes it their food, and of none else) *which if any one eat, he shall not die eternally.* They therefore often call it the *Bread of Life,* and *Life it self.*

S. *Ambrose* (*s*). *This is the Bread of Life: he that eateth Life cannot die; for how should he die whose Food is Life?*

S. *Austin* says the same (*t*). *When Christ is eaten, Life is eaten. --- When he is eaten he refreshes.*

Again in another place (*u*) distinguishing the Portion of Saints and Sinners, he makes the true *Sons of the Church to partake both of the Dew of Heaven, and the fatness of the Earth.* This fatness of the Earth he explains to be *all visible Sacraments, for they pertain to the Earth. All these,* he says, *the good and bad in the Church have in common. For the bad have and partake of the Sacraments, and what the Faithful know made of Bread-Corn, and Wine.*

If then the visible Sacrament, and that which has its original from Earth, be all that evil men partake of, to be sure they have nothing to do with Christ, the Heavenly Bread, or his Body, which (to' use his Phrase) do's not *pertain to Earth at all,* but is a *Divine Food.*

Which none has more admirably and fully spoke to than
Origen.

(*q*) *In Oseam c.* 8. ——— *Cujus caro cibus credentium est.*

(*r*) *In Genes. c.* 31. ——— Caro ejus qui est *esca Sanctorum.* Quam si quis manducaverit, non morietur in æternum.

(*s*) *In Psal.* 118. *Serm.* 18. Hic est panis vitæ: qui manducat vitam mori non potest; quomodo enim morietur, cui cibus vita est?

(*t*) *Serm. de verb. Evangel. apud Bedam in* 1 *Cor.* 10. Quando Christus manducatur; vita manducatur. — quando manducatur reficit.

(*u*) *Serm.* 44; *de Diversis.* Filli Ecclesiæ habent à rore cœli & fertilitate terræ, &c.

——— à fertilitate terræ omnia visibilia Sacramenta. Visibile enim Sacramentum ad terram pertinet. Hæc omnia communia habent in Ecclesia boni & mali. Nam & ipsi habent, & participant Sacramentis, & quod norunt fideles à tritico & vino.

A full View of the Doctrines and Practices

(x) *In Matth. c.* 15. *v.* 15. *p.* 253. *Ed. Huet.* Καὶ ταῦτα μὲν περὶ τοῦ τυπικοῦ κȷ συμβολικοῦ σώματ[Ꝍ]. Πολλὰ δ᾽ ἂν κȷ περὶ αὐτοῦ λέγοιτο τȣ λόγȣ ὡς γέγονε σὰρξ κȷ ἀληθινὴ βρῶσις, ἥν τις ὁ φαγὼν πάντως ζήσε[ȷ] εἰς τὸν αἰῶνα, ὐδενὸς δυναμένȣ φαύλȣ ἐσθίειν αὐτήν. Εἰ γὰρ οἷόν τε ἦν ἔτι φαῦλον μένοντα ἐσθίειν τὸν γινόμωυον σάρκα, λόγον ὄντα κȷ ἄρτον ζῶντα, ἐκ ἂν ἐγέγραπτο ὅτι πᾶς ὁ φαγὼν τὸν ἄρτον τȣτον ζήσε[ȷ] εἰς τὸν αἰῶνα.

(y) *Homil.* 14.

—— Ἀλλίω τροφὴν δίδωσι τοῖς δέλοις, κȷ ἄλλἰω τοῖς ἰδίοις τέκνοις —— Ἐπειδὴ τὰ τέκνα κληρονομȣ̃σι τὸν πατέρα, κȷ μὴ αὐτȣ̃ ἐσθίωσι ——

—— Ἰδίαν ἀνάπαυσιν κȷ τροφὴν κȷ βρῶσιν κȷ πόσιν, παρὰ τὰς λοιπὰς ἀνθρώπȣς ἐπιρέχει, κȷ δίδωσιν ἑαυτὸν αὐτοῖς, &c.

(z) *In c.* 66. *Esaie.* Dum non sunt sancti corpore & spiritu, nec comedunt carnem Jesu, neqȝ bibunt sanguinem ejus, de quo ipse loquitur; Qui comedit carnem meam & bibit sanguinem meum, habet vitam æternam.

(a) *Contra Donatist. post collat. c.* 6. De ipso pane & de ipsa Dominica manu, & *Judas* partem & *Petrus* accepit.

(b) *Tract.* 59. *in Joan. Evang.* Illi manducabant *Panem Dominum,* ille *PanemDomini* contra Dominum, illi vitam, ille pœnam.

Origen (x). Who having said a great deal about Christs *Typical* and *Symbolical Body* (which S. *Austin* called before the *visible Sacrament*) he goes on thus. *Many things also might be said concerning that word which was made Flesh, and the true Food, which whosoever eats shall surely live for ever, no wicked Men being capable of eating it. For if it were possible, that a wicked man, continuing such, should eat him that was made Flesh, seeing he is the Word, and the living Bread, it would not have been written,* That whosoever eats this Bread shall live for ever.

This is that which *Macarius* (y) discourses of so largely and piously. Telling us, that as a great rich Man, having both Servants and Sons, *gives one sort of meat to the Servants, and another to the Sons that he begot, who being Heirs to their Father, do eat with him.*—— So, says he, *Christ the true Lord, himself created all, and nourishes the evil and unthankful; but the Children begotten by him, who are partakers of his grace, and in whom the Lord is formed; he feeds them with a peculiar refection, and Food, and Meat and Drink, above and besides other men, and gives himself to them that have Conversation with their Father, as the Lord says,* He that eateth my Flesh, and drinketh my Blood, abides in me, and I in him, and shall not see death.

With whom S. *Jerome* (z) agrees, speaking of voluptuous men; *Not being holy in Body and Spirit, they neither eat the Flesh of Jesus, nor drink his Blood; concerning which he says;* He that eateth my Flesh, and drinketh my Blood, hath Eternal Life.

S. *Austin* also (a) says. *Of that Bread, and from our Lords own Hand, both* Judas *and* Peter *took a part.*

But then he (b) makes the distinction himself, that *Judas* received only the *Bread of the Lord,* when the other Disciples receiv'd the
Bread

Bread that was the Lord. Which is directly contrary to Transubstantiation; for according to that, even such a one as *Judas*, must eat the *Lord*, and no *Bread*, when this Father says, that he ate the *Bread* and no *Lord*.

Neither is S. *Austin* singular in this Phrase of the *Bread of the Lord*, to signifie the *real substance* of that *Element* that is eaten in the Sacrament, and not the *proper Body of Christ*.

For so S. *Jerome* uses it (*c*). When he speaks of *Corn*, of which the *Bread of the Lord is made*.

(*c*) *In Jerem. c.* 31. Confluent ad bona Domini super frumento, de quo conficitur *Panis Domini*.

It is also very observable, that as the *Council of Trent* (as we heard before) makes eating Christ *Sacramentally and really* to be the same, and *spiritual eating* to be of another sort, not *real*, but one would think, rather *imaginary*. On the quite contrary, the Fathers distinguish the *sacramental eating* from the *real*, and make the *spiritual and real* eating to be the same; and they will grant that a bad Man may eat Christ *Sacramentally* (that is, in sign) but not *really*; for so none but the faithful can do it.

For thus S. *Austin* (*d*). *Then will this be, that is, the Body and Blood of Christ will be Life to every one, if that which is visibly taken in the Sacrament, be in the Truth it self spiritually eaten, and spiritually drank.*

Which in another place (*e*) he expresses by the *visible Sacrament*, and the *virtue of the Sacrament*.

Again most expresly (*f*). *Christ saying*, He that eateth my Flesh and drinketh my Blood, dwelleth in me, and I in him, *shows what it is*, not sacramentally, *but* really and in truth, *to eat Christs Body, and drink his Blood*.

And therefore in the same Chapter (*g*) speaking of wicked men, he says. *Neither can they be said to eat the Body of Christ, since they are not to be accounted Christs Members*.

S. *Austin* again distinguishes the *Sacramentum rei* (the Sacrament of the thing) from the *res Sacramenti*, the thing of which it is a Sacrament.

(*d*) *Serm.* 2. *de verb. Apost.* Tunc autem hoc erit, id est, Visa unicuiq; erit Corpus & sanguis Christi, si, quod in Sacramento visibiliter sumitur, in ipsa veritate spiritualiter manducetur, spiritualiter bibatur.

(*e*) *Tract.* 26. *in Joan.* Quod pertinet ad virtutem Sacramenti, non quod pertinet ad visibile Sacramentum.

(*f*) *De Civit. Dei l.* 21. *c.* 25. Ipse dicens, qui manducat carnem meam & bibit sanguinem meum in me manet & ego in eo, ostendit quid sit, non *Sacramento tenus*, sed revera Corpus Christi manducare & sanguinem ejus bibere.

(*g*) *Ibid.* Neq; enim isti dicendi sunt manducare Corpus Christi, quoniam nec in membris computandi sunt Christi.

(*h*). *The*

(b) *The Sacrament of this thing ―― is prepared on the Lords Table, and received from the Lords Table, to* some *to Life, and to others to destruction. But the thing it self of which it is a Sacrament, is for Life to every one that partakes of it, and to none for destruction.*

For as S. *Chrysostom* (i) phrases it, *He that receives this Bread, will be above dying?*

I will conclude this Chapter with two remarkable places of St. *Austin*.

The first is cited by *Prosper* (k) who has gathered S. *Austin*'s Sentences. *He receives the food of life, and drinks the Cup of Eternity, who abides in Christ, and in whom Christ inhabits. For he that disagrees with Christ, neither eats his Flesh nor drinks his Blood; altho' he takes indifferently every day the Sacrament of so great a thing to the Condemnation of his presumption.*

The other place is, upon the sixth Chapter of S. *John* (l). *Christ*, says he, *expounded the manner of his assignment and gift, how he gave his Flesh to eat, saying,* He that eateth my Flesh and drinketh my Blood, dwelleth in me and I in him. *The sign that he eateth and drinketh is this, if he abides in* Christ *and* Christ *in him, if he dwells in him and is inhabited by him, if he cleaves to him so as not to be forsaken by him.*

And he concludes with this Exhortation (m). *Let all that has been said, Beloved, prevail thus far with us, that we may not eat Christs Flesh and Blood in Sacrament* (or *sign*) *only, but may eat and drink as far as to the participation of the Spirit, that we may remain as Members in our Lords Body, that we may be enlivened by his spirit,* &c.

(h) *Tract.* 26. *in Joan.* Hujus rei Sacramentum ―― in Dominica Mensa præparatur & de Dominica Mensa sumitur, quibusdam ad vitam; quibusdam ad exitium. *Res vero ipsa cujus* & Sacramentum est, omni homini ad vitam, nulli ad exitium quicunq; ejus particeps fuerit.

(i) *Catena in Joh.* 6. 49. Ταύτης μὲν γὰρ τοῖ τ̄ τροφῆς μεταλαβὼν, ἀνώτερος ἔσται τοῦ θανάτου.

(k) *Lib. Sentent. ex August. sententia* (mihi) 341. vel 339. Escam vitæ accipit & æternitatis poculum bibit, qui in Christo manet & cujus Christus habitator est. Nam qui discordat à Christo, nec carnem ejus manducat, nec sanguinem bibit; etiamsi tantæ rei Sacramentum ad judicium suæ præsumptionis quotidiè indifferenter accipiat.

(l) *Tract.* 27. *in Joan. in initio.* Exposuit (*Christus*) modum attributionis hujus & doni sui, quomodo daret carnem suam manducare, dicens, *Qui manducat carnem meam, & bibit sanguinem meum, in me manet & ego in illo.* Signum quia manducat & bibit, hoc est, si manet & manetur, si habitat & inhabitatur, si hæret ut non deseratur.

(m) *Ibid. propè finem.* Hoc ergo totum ad hoc nobis valeat dilectissimi, ut carnem Christi & sanguinem Christi non edamus tantum in Sacramento, quod & multi mali; sed usq; ad Spiritus participationem manducemus & bibamus, ut in Domini corpore tanquam membra maneamus, ut ejus spiritu vegetemur, *&c.*

CHAP.

CHAP. XIV.

The Fourteenth Difference.

Several Usages and Practices of the Fathers relating to the Eucharist, declare, That they did not believe Transubstantiation, or the Presence of Christ's Natural Body there; whose contrary practices or forbearance of them, in the Roman Church, are the Consequences of that belief. As also some things the present Roman Church practises, because they believe Transubstantiation, and the Corporal Presence, and dare not neglect to practise, so believing; which yet the Ancient Church did forbear the practice of, not knowing any obligation thereto; which plainly argues their different Sentiments about the Eucharist in those Points.

IT is possible this Argument may have as good an effect to open Mens Eyes, as any I have urged before, tho', I think, I have urged very cogent ones. For tho' some Men have a Faculty eternally to wrangle about the Words and Sayings of others, and to shift off an Argument of that kind, yet they cannot so easily get rid of an Objection from Matter of Fact, and a plain Practice. I shall therefore try, by several Instances of Usages and Forbearances, in the cases above-named, whether we may not see as clearly as if we had a Window into their Breasts, that the Ancient Church, and the present Church of *Rome*, were of different Minds and Opinions in this Matter.

1. Instance.

It was a part of the Discipline of the Ancient Church, to exclude the uninitiated, (Catechumens) *the Energumeni,* (acted by evil Spirits) *and Penitents, from being present at the Mysteries, and to enjoin all that were present to communicate.*

It is so known a Case, that the *Deacons* in the Churches cried aloud to bid such depart, as I before named, when they went to the Prayers of the Mass, (which was so called from this dismission of Catechumens, Penitents, *&c.*) that I shall

A full View of the Doctrines and Practices

shall not stay to prove it. (See the Constitutions attributed to *Clemens*, l. 8. cap. 6, 7, 9, 12. and S. *Chrysostom*, Hom. 3. in Ep. ad Ephes.)

By the same Laws of the Church, those that remained, after the exclusion of the rest, were all to communicate; whom the Author of the *Ecclesiastical Hierarchy*, under the name of *Dionysius the Areopagite* (n) calls, *Persons worthy to behold the Divine Mysteries, and to communicate.*

For this (because it is not so universally acknowledged as the former) I shall refer the Reader to the *Second Canon* of the *Council of Antioch* (o), which says, That *they which enter into the Church of God, and hear the Holy Scriptures, and do not communicate in Prayers with the People, or turn away from receiving the Eucharist through any disorderliness, are to be cast out of the Church, till they confess their Sin and repent,* &c.

Which is the same in sense with that *Canon* (p) which is very ancient, (tho' not *Apostolical*, as it pretends) *That all the Faithful that enter, and hear the Scriptures, and do not continue at Prayer, and also at the Holy Communion, are to be separated, as those that bring disorder into the Church.*

S. *Chrysostom* discharges a great deal of his Zeal as well as *Eloquence*, against those Persons that were *present* at the Eucharist, and did *not* communicate (q). *In vain*, he tells them, *do's the Priest stand at the Altar when none participates; in vain is the daily Sacrifice.*—— He minds them, that the *Cryer* had said indeed, That *those that were in penitence* (or penance) *should depart:* but thou, says he, *art not of that number, but of those that may participate* (i.e. not being hindred by any Church-Censures as Penitents were) *and regardest it not.* He says, That the King at the Marriage-Supper, *did not ask, Why didst thou sit down? but why didst thou enter?* And adds, *That whosoever* (being present) *does not receive the Mysteries, stands there too boldly and impudently.*

(n) *Hierarch. Ecclis.* c. 3. Μένωσι δὲ οἱ τῇ τῶν θείων ἐποψίας ἢ κοινωνίας ἄξιοι.

(o) Can. 2. Concil. Antioch. —— ἢ ἀποστρεφομένες τὴν μετάληψιν τ᾽ εὐχαριστίας κατά τινα ἀταξίαν, τύτες ἀποβλήτες γίνεσθαι τ᾽ ἐκκλησίας, &c.

(p) Canon. Apostol. 9. Πάντας τὰς εἰσιόντας πιστὰς ἢ τ᾽ γραφῶν ἀκέοντας, μὴ προσμένοντας κὴ τῇ προσευχῇ, κὴ τῇ ἁγία μεταλήψει ὡς ἀταξίαν ἐμποιόντας τῇ ἐκκλησίᾳ, ἀφορίζεσθαι χρή.

(q) Chrysost. Hom. 3. in Ep. ad Ephes. Εἰκῆ θυσία καθημερινή· εἰκῆ παρεστήκαμεν τῷ θυσιαστηρίῳ.——

——ὅτι ἐν μετανοίᾳ ἀπελθέτω πάντες.

——τῶν δυναμένων μετέχειν κὴ ὁ φροντίζεις——

—— ὁ γὰρ εἶπε, διὰ τί κατεκλίθης; ἀλλά, τί εἰσῆλθες; —— πᾶς ὁ μὴ μετέχων μυστηρίων, ἀναισχύντως κὴ ἰταμῶς ἕστηκας.

dently. The rest is well worthy the reading in that Homily.

Gregory the Great also tells us, (r) it was the custom in his Time, for a *Deacon* to cry aloud, *If any do not Communicate, let him depart.* There must be no *Spectators,* that is, unless they were Communicants. For as *Justin Martyr* (s) acquaints us, it was the usage of his Time, That *the the Deacons reach to every one present of the consecrated Bread, and Wine, and Water, that they may communicate.*

(r) *Dialog. l.* 2. *cap.* 23. Si quis non communicat, det locum.

(s) *Apolog.* 2. Οἱ διάκονοι διδόασιν ἑκάστῳ τῶν παρόντων μεταλαβεῖν ἀπὸ τοῦ εὐχαριστηθέντος ἄρτε, κ) οἴνε, κ) ὕδατ[ος].

If we now look upon the practice of the *Roman Church,* we shall find all quite contrary. There they may have as *many Spectators* as please to come, when there is but *one alone* that *receives* the Eucharist, I mean the *Priest.* Any one that knew nothing of the Matter, would conclude, when he saw their Masses, that they came thither about another Business ordinarily, than to *eat* and *drink,* in remembrance of their *Saviour;* which was the only use that the *Ancients* understood of it. *They* considered it as a *Sacrament,* by Institution designed to represent *Christ's Passion and Crucifixion; these* consider the presence of his Glorified Body and his Divinity there, and are taken up with *adoration* more than any thing else. *That* they will not abate, *every day* you are present, when the Host is shown for that end: But as for the other, the *receiving* of the Eucharist, they are satisfied if it be done but *once a Year.* The *Ancients* look'd upon it as an Invitation to *a Table,* where the Sacrament was to be their *Meal;* but here you are called to look upon the King *present,* and *sitting in state;* and chiefly to take care that, upon the Sign given, all may *fall down* together and *worship him.*

S. *Chrysostom* (t) calls it, a contumely against him that invites one to Feast, to be present and not to partake of it; and asks, *Whether it had not been better for such a one to have been absent?*

(t) *Loc. citat.* Οὐ βέλτιον ἢ τοῦτον μηδὲ παρεγένεται;

But the *Council of Trent* was of another mind, and their Opinion is (u), That *those Masses in which the Priest communicates sacramentally alone, are not to be condemned as private and unlawful, but to be approved and commended.*

(u) *Conc. Trid. Sess.* 22. *c.* 6. Non propterea Missas illas in quibus solus sacerdos Sacramentaliter communicat, ut privatas & illicitas damnare, sed probare, atq; adeo commendare.

And not content with this, they thunder out an *Anathema* (x) against those that say, (and let S. *Chrysostom* look to himself) *that such Masses are unlawful and to be abrogated.*

(x) *Ibid. Can.* 8. *Si quis dixerit Missas, in quibus solus sacerdos Sacramentaliter communicat, illicitas esse adeoq; abrogandas, anathema sit.*

At these Masses the *Novices* and *Catechumens* may be present, and no *Deacon* cries out to them to withdraw; for tho' indeed they may not *eat*, yet they may *worship:* And the *Penitents* that were excluded, while their Penance lasted, from so much as seeing the Sacrament in the *Ancient Church*; in this Church, the oftner they come for this purpose, the more welcome; and by direction, when *publick Penance* has been enjoined, the Holy Altar has been the place chosen before which to perform it; as their Annals (y) tells us of one *Sangunus*, a noted Courtier in *Japan*, that for the expiation of a Crime, came and fell down at the Altar, in the Church of the Royal City, and there *before the Holy Sacrament*, claw'd his Back with Scourges so long, as one of the Seven *Penitential Psalms* was recited.

(y) *Annal. Japon. ad An.* 1579.

These Practices, tho' so contrary to one another, are yet natural enough, and well-suited to the Principles of each Church; but then, it is plain, their Principles and Opinions concerning *the Sacrament*, were widely different; and that such things were never practised of old, was not because Christians then wanted *their Devotion*, but *their Faith*.

2. Instance.

A second practice of the Christian Church of old, was, *giving the Communion in both kinds*; the *Cup*, that is, as well as the *Bread*; tho' now, by a Law of the Roman Church, (in the Council of *Constance* and *Trent*) abolished.

That the *ancient Practice* was to deliver it in both Kinds, has been often proved by *Learned Men* on our side, and particularly by an excellent *late Discourse* against the Bishop of *Meaux* (x) upon this Subject; and has been also acknowledg'd by the Learned Men of the *Roman Communion*, such as *Cassander, Wicelius, Petavius*, &c. Which makes it needless to insist further upon the proof of it.

(x) *Discourse of the Communion in one kind, in Answer to the Bishop of* Meaux's *Treatise.*

We are sure it continued thus even to the Age when Transubstantiation was established by the *Lateran Council*, since we find

find a whole Army of *Charles* King of *Sicily*, (as the Historian (*a*) tells us) just before they went to the Fight against *Manfred, Ann.* 1265. (or 1266, as other Historians will have it) *all received the Body and Blood of Christ.* *Aquinas* agrees, That *it was the ancient Custom of the Church, That all that communicated of the Body, communicated also of the Blood* (*b*). *But for to prevent spilling the Blood,* he says, *in some Churches the practice is, that the Priest alone communicates in the Blood, and the rest in the Body of Christ.*

We see then about what time this *grand Sacrilege*, as *P. Gelasius* calls it (*c*) of dividing one and the same Mystery, made a more publick entry into the Church; it was, when *Transubstantiation* had been newly made an *Article of Faith*; and it was very natural, that *this practice* should, within a while, by easy steps, be a Consequent of *that*. For Transubstantiation makes Christ's Flesh and Blood (the same which he took of the Virgin, and which he had when he was crucified) to be actually and corporally present in the Eucharist, and that in a glorified State, to which Divine Adoration is due; this is apt to beget a profound Veneration, and a mighty Concern, lest any thing contumelious should happen to that which Men justly account so very precious. Now it being certain, that the *Blood* which is under the *Species of Wine*, is subject to those Casualties, by reason of its fluidity, which the *other Species* is not so liable to; and that in the glorified State, the Body and Blood are inseparable; and therefore that *one Species* (*viz.* that of the Bread) contains under it both the Body and Blood together; what could be more agreeable to such Sentiments as these, than that Men should willingly part with their Right, in a Matter wherein they seem not to be much wrong'd (being only deprived of a few Accidents of Wine, when the Blood was secured to them) to secure the Honour of their Saviour. It is true indeed, that the Stream of the contrary Custom, made it difficult to remove that at once, notwithstanding this danger of effusion of the Blood, which they had been wont in all preceding

(*a*) Apud Du Chesn. Tom. 5. Hist. Franc. p. 840. citante Dallæo, de cultib. Latin. lib. 5. c. 12. Cum exercitus esset in procinctu, Decanum Meldensem, associatis sibi Monachis, corpus & sanguinem Christi regiis militibus dedisse.
(*b*) In Joan. 6. Propter periculum effusionis.

(*c*) *Speaking of some Persons that taking the Body, abstained from the Cup of the Holy Blood,* says, Aut integra Sacramenta percipiant, aut ab integris arceantur, quia divisio unius ejusdemq; mysterii sine grandi Sacrilegio non potest pervenire. Apud Gratian. decret. 3. part. 2. dist.

preceding Ages to receive; therefore the Wits of Men being set on work by a new Transubstantiating Doctrine, found out some new Devices, practised first in the Cells of the Monks; but afterwards, about the time of *Berengarius*, brought into the Churches to secure that dreadful Danger, and yet not deprive the People of communicating in the Blood of Christ.

One was the Device of *Intinction*, or steeping the Bread in the Wine, and thus receiving both at once, which as Card. *Cusanus* informs us *(d)* tho' it went not down without great contention at the first change from the old Practice, yet the Universal Church, complying with the Times, permitted it.

But it was not long it was thus suffered, for by a Decree of Pope *Urban* 2. in the Council of *Clermont*, and by an enforcement of it by his Successor P. *Paschal* 2. (whose Epistle to *Pontius* Abbot of *Cluny* concerning this Matter, *Baronius* has given us *(e)*) this practice was abrogated.

A second Device also, about the same time, was brought into play, *Of sucking the Consecrated Wine through little Pipes or Canes* (called *Pugillares*) like *Quills*; concerning which *Cassander* (de communione sub utraq;) gives us an account, and that some of them were to be seen in his Time. And indeed, this seems to be a sufficient security to the danger of Effusion, and also prevents that great Offence of any drops of Blood sticking to the Beards of People when they drank out of the Cup: and yet even this would not satisfy, nor any thing else be a sufficient Caution against the prophanation of the Blood, but only debarring the People wholly of it. Yet this way is still used by the Pope himself, (and I think he has the sole privilege to do it) who in that which is called the *Missa Papalis*, when he himself celebrates and communicates, *he sucks part of the Blood through a golden Quill* *.

(*d*) Epist. 3. ad Bohem. Non parva altercatio in principio mutationis illius prioris ——— tamen universalis Ecclesia, quia ita tempori congruebat, populum cum intincto pane communicare permisit.

(*e*) Baronius Append. ad Tom. 12. ad An. 1118.

* Cum pontifex Corpus Christi sumpserit, Episcopus Cardinalis porrigit ei calamum, quem Papa ponit in Calice in manibus Diaconi existente, & Sanguinis partim sugit. Sacrarum Cerimon. lib. 2. cap. de Missa Majori, Papa personaliter celebrante.

But

But neither do's he always thus communicate, for their Book of *Sacred Ceremonies* acquaints us, (* *) That when He celebrates perfonally on the Night of the *Nativity of our Lord*, that all things are observed, that are defcribed in the *Papal Mass*, except that he communicates at the Altar alone, and not in his eminent and high Seat, and do's not *fuck the Blood with a Quill*, but takes it after the common manner.

* * Ibid. cap. Si Papa in nocte Nativitatis perfonaliter celebrat, *Non fugit fanguinem cum calamo, fed more communi.*

But now, after all, what account can we give of the *Ancient Fathers?* they apprehended it neceffary to receive in both Kinds in all their *Publick Communions*, and fo they practifed. Muft we not then accufe them, either of great *Dulnefs*, or *Indevotion?* either that they wanted *Sagacity*, in not apprehending the imminent danger they in their way expofed the Blood of Chrift to; or that they were guilty of a ftrange *carelefnefs* and *indifferency*, in not preventing it by any of thofe Methods which the Roman Church hath found out to do it? Truly, for my part, I am inclined to have as great, if not a greater opinion of them, in both refpects, (efpecially for their *Devotion*) than I can have of the *Roman Church*; and I am the more perfwaded hereto, becaufe the Apoftles themfelves muft come in to the fide of the *Ancient Church*, their practice being the fame: not to infift upon the *Deference* that ought to be paid to that *Holy Spirit* that we are fure acted *them*; who if there had been any fuch real danger of prophanation, by receiving in both kinds, or ever was likely to be any fuch, would not have failed to have given directions *to them* how they fhould avoid it; and we cannot think the Apoftles would not have fet down thofe Directions *to us* in fome of their Writings. But they have not done it; no not the Zealous St. *Paul*, who yet fays fo much to the carelefs *Corinthians* about this Argument, and tells them, that *they came together, not for the better, but the worfe*; charges them with unworthy receiving, and being *thereby guilty of the Body and Blood of the Lord*, (1 Cor. 11.) and that *for this caufe many were weak and fick among them*, and were *judged of the Lord* for their prophanations, *&c.* But this is none of the Charges againft them, nor does he direct them to any of the wife Methods of the Roman Church for preventing this Danger;
tho'

tho' he says, What he received of the Lord he delivered to them.

There is nothing then remains, but that we assign the true Cause of this different Practice; which can be none other, but the Roman Churches *innovating in their Faith* about the Sacrament, and altering so their Opinions about the Body and Blood of Christ in the Eucharist, that they require a different Conduct for their Devotion; so that neither the Practice of the *Primitive Fathers*, nor the Rules of the *Apostles*, will suit and agree with their Perswasions and Apprehensions. But now the Faith of the *Ancient Church* in this Matter was such, as neither requires nor can admit of any Alteration like what the Church of *Rome* has made in communicating the People only in one Kind. For, as I have before proved, they look'd upon this Sacrament, not as an actual Exhibition and Presentation of the Natural and Glorified Body of our Saviour, which they believed to be absent and contained in the Heavens, but as a Representation of his Crucified Body, where his Blood was separated from his Body, and poured out of his Veins; and that not only the *Elements*, but the *Sacramental Actions* of breaking the Bread, and pouring out the Wine, and our eating and drinking were instituted to shew forth this painful Death of our Lord, and the shedding of his most precious Blood for the Remission of Sins.

By the presence of his *glorified Body* there, (as the Roman Church believes) this cannot be done, no breaking, nor no parts to be made of that, nor no separation of Blood, as out of the Body. But all can be done in the *Representative Body* of Christ, which is the Eucharist, all the Ends of the Institution can be there fully effected, and the Sacrifice on the Cross, in this Image of it, made present to our Faith, and to our Minds, and set livelily before us; and by the Effects of this upon our Hearts, while we partake of the Elements, through the powerful Grace of God's Holy Spirit, we may be prepared to receive all the Blessed Fruits and Benefits of his Passion.

According to these Perswasions, it's plain, there can be no abatement of communicating in the Cup; because, without that, there is no representation of a Crucified Body; for the

distinct

distinct partaking of the Blood, (not as supposed to be contained and received in the other Species) is that which alone shows (as I said before) the separation that was then made of his Body and Blood.

3. Instance.

Another Practice of the *Roman Church* differing from the *Ancient*, is, *The Elevation of the Eucharist, that all present may at once adore it.* For thus the Missal (*) directs, That when the Priest comes to the words of Consecration, and has said, *This is my Body;* then holding the Host, (as he is directed) *he kneels down and adores it.* Then *raising himself as high as he is able, he lifts up the Host on high, and fixing his Eyes upon it,* (which he do's also in the Elevation of the Cup) *he shows the Host reverently to the People to be adored.*

* Ritus celebr. Missam cap. 8. Dicit, hoc est enim Corpus meum, Quibus prolatis, celebrans Hostiam tenens inter pollices & indices——genuflexus eam adorat. Tunc se erigens, quantum commodè potest, elevat in altum Hostiam, & intentis in eam oculis (quod in Elevatione Calicis facit) populo reverenter ostendit adorandam.

This is the present Practice; which the Council of Trent (*f*) endeavours to countenance, by telling us, *That there is no doubt but that all Christians, according to the Custom always received in the Catholick Church, ought to give the Worship of Latria* (which is supreme Worship) *to the most Holy Sacrament in their worship of it.*

(*f*) Sess. 13. c. 5. Nullus dubitandi locus relinquitur, quin omnes Christi fideles pro more in Ecclesia Catholica semper recepto, latriæ cultum qui vero Deo debetur, huic sanctissimo Sacramento in veneratione adhibeant.

By which *Sacrament* (as their best Interpreters explain it) is meant, *Totum visibile Sacramentum,* all that is *visible there,* (together with Christ) and is one entire Object, consisting of *Christ* and the *Species,* and must be together adored. But whatsoever, besides Christ who is invisible, is visible there, call it what you please, is *a Creature*; and I am sure the *Ancient Church* never practised the adoration of any such; and it is strange impudence to talk of the Custom of the *Catholick Church* in this Matter. Neither can it be shown, by any good Testimonies of the *Ancients,* that this *their Elevation,* in order to *Adoration,* was ever used by them: No not so much as *any Elevation* for any purpose, is mentioned by those Fathers, who on set purpose have given an account of the Rites of communicating in the *first Ages* of the Church, neither by *Justin Martyr,* nor the *Author* of the *Constitutions* called *Apostolical;* nor *Cyril* of *Jerusalem,* nor the pretended

V *Denis*

Denis the *Areopagite,* or any other before the *Sixth Century.*

(g) Dallæus de relig. cult. object. l. 2. c. 5.

A diligent Searcher of Antiquity, tells us (g), That he cannot find, among all the Interpreters of Ecclesiastical Offices in the *Latin Church,* the mention of *any sort of Elevation* before the Eleventh Century, (that is, the Age of *Innovation in the Faith* about the Eucharist).

As for the *Greeks* of later date, in them we may meet indeed with *an Elevation* of the Eucharist, but for quite other purposes than *Adoration.* One of the Ends of their *Elevation,* is mentioned by *Germanus* Patriarch of *Constantinople* (h), *which was,* to represent *Christ lifted up upon the Cross, and his Death upon it, and the Resurrection it self.*

(h) *In Tom. 2. Bibl. Pat. Gr. Lat.* —Τὼ ἐπὶ τῇ ςαυρῷ ὕψωσιν, ἡ τ ἐν αὐτῷ θάνατον, ἡ αὐτὼ τὼ ἀνάςασιν.

Another reason they give is, by the showing of this Food of the Saints, to invite and call them to partake of it. Which *Nic. Cabasilas* gives a full account of (i), saying, *That after the Priest has been partaker of the sanctified Things, he turns to the People, and showing them the Holy Things,* (i. e. the Bread and Wine) *calls those that are willing to communicate.* Or, as he still more fully explains it, *The Life-giving Bread being received* (by the Priest) *and shown, he calls those that are likely to receive it worthily, saying, Holy Things are for the Holy* *. *Behold the Bread of Life which ye see. Run therefore you that are to partake of it ; but it is not for all, but for him that is Holy,* &c.

(i) *In Expos. Liturg. apud Bibl. Pat. Gr. Lat. Tom. 2.* Ὁ δ᾽ ἱερεὺς μεταςρὸν τῆς ἀγμάτων, πρὸς τὸ πλῆθος ὀπιςρέφεται, ἡ δείξας τὰ ἅγμα καλεῖ τὸς μεταςεῖν βελομένες.

* Τὰ ἅγια τοῖς ἁγίοις.

It is certain then, that the Roman Practice (when for Adoration they elevate and show the Host) is an Innovation; and that it proceeded from the Novel Doctrines then set on foot in the church, is higly probable ; not only because they commenced about the same time ; but also because their practice suits so exactly with, and springs so freely from those Doctrines, it being so natural when such a glorious Body as our Saviour's is believed to be made present where it was not before, to be wholly taken up with thoughts of Adoration and Worship above any thing else ; as it is notoriously true in this Church, where the main End of the Eucharist, *viz :* communicating

municating in the Body and Blood of Christ is strangely neglected; and they are more concerned, in carrying the Sacrament in Processions, in praying to it before their Altars, in preparing splendid Tabernacles where it may repose, decking and adorning the places of its Residence, and the like, than in engaging Men to *receive it*; which was the main thing the *Ancient Church* designed, that they might worthily partake of it; and when this was not designed, their way was wholly to conceal it.

4. Instance.

Another Practice of the *Roman Church*, different from that of the *Ancient Church*, is, that *now the Communicants Hands are unimployed in receiving the Eucharist; and all is put by the Priest into their mouths.*

Their Hands indeed may bear a part in their Adoration and showing some Signs of that, but otherwise they are useless. For now since Christ's Body is believed to lie hid under the Species of Bread and Wine, that is thought too sacred to be touched by the Hands of any, but the Priests. We may therefore conclude fairly, that if the Fathers had not *this care* to forbid this touching by the Peoples Hands, they had not *this Faith* of the *Roman Church*, that the Natural Body of Christ is in the Eucharist: since if this had been their Opinion, in all probability their practice would have been the same, Since that they had an equal concern for their Saviour's Honour, cannot well be doubted of.

Now that *they* gave the Sacrament into the Peoples Hands, for the space of eight hundred Years or more, is clear by their Testimonies. Of which I'll mention only three or four out of an hundred that might be given.

Clemens of *Alexandria* (*k*) says, That when the Priests have divided the Eucharist, *they permit every one of the People to take a portion of it.*

Tertullian (*l*) reproaches the Christian Statuaries, That *they reached those hands to the Lord's Body, which had made Bodies for Devils.*

(*k*) *Stromat. lib.* 1. "Ἕκαστον τοῦ λαοῦ λαβεῖν τὴν μοῖραν ἐπιτρέπουσι.

(*l*) *Lib. de Idol. Cap.* 7. —Eas manus admovere Corpori Domini, quæ Dæmoniis corpora conferunt.

St. *Ambrose* (*m*) Story is a known one, how he repelled *Theodosius* from the Holy Table, after the slaughter he had made at *Thessalonica*, with these words; *How wilt thou extend thy hands, yet dropping with the Blood of an unjust slaughter? How with those hands wilt thou receive the Lord's most Holy Body?*

He that will consult *Cyril* of *Jerusalem*'s 5th *Mystagogical Catechism*, will find him there directing the Communicant how to order his Hands and Fingers in taking the Sacrament into them. Which a Roman Master of the Ceremonies would not have said a word about, being only concerned about the Mouth.

That this manner of receiving was used in the 9*th* Century, appears by the Capitulary of *Carolus Mag.* (*n*) who ordered, *That all that received the Eucharist (acceperint*, that is, into their Hands) *and did not take it (sumpserint*, that is, into their Mouths) *should be kept back as sacrilegious Persons.* If they had received it by their Mouths only, this distinction could not have been made.

5. Instance.

Another Practice, very unagreeable with the belief of Transubstantiation, is this, That *the Ancient Church was not afraid to administer the Eucharistical Wine in Glass Vessels and Cups:* tho' now it would be a great Crime in the Church of *Rome* to do so.

For that *Ancient Practice*, I might urge that of *Tertullian* (*o*), who reflecting upon the Church's Indulgence to Sinners, mentions the Picture of the Shepherd carrying the Lost Sheep on his Back, drawn on the Chalices, which might be seen by all, being pellucid.

To which he opposes, afterwards, the *Scriptures of that Shepherd that could not be broken*.

As also that of St. *Jerom* (*p*), where speaking of S. *Exuperius*, he says, *Nothing is richer than he who carries the Lord's Body in a wicker Basket, and his Blood in a Glass.* But

---

(*m*) Apud Theodoret. Hist. Ecclesiast. Lib. 5. c. 19. —πῶς ἢ τοιούταις ὑποδέξῃ χερσὶ τὸ δεσπότου τὸ πανάγιον σῶμα;

(*n*) *Capit. Car. M. Lib.* 7. Placuit ut omnes qui Sacram acceperint Euchariſtam, & non ſumpſerint, ut ſacrilegi repellantur.

(*o*) *Lib. de pudicit. c.* 7, & 10. Procedant ipſæ picturæ calicum veſtrorum, ſi vel in illis perlucebit interpretatio pecudis illius, utrumne Chriſtiano an Ethnico peccatori de reſtitutione conſuliet.

Cap. 10.—At ego ejus Paſtoris Scripturas haurio, qui non poteſt frangi.

(*p*) *Epiſt.* 4. *ad Ruſticum*. Nihil illo ditius, qui Corpus Domini caniſtro vimineo, ſanguinem portat in vitro.

But it is needless to add more Testimonies, because the thing is confessed by *Baronius* (*q*), in his Notes upon the Acts of S. *Donatus*, who confesses, That *Glass Chalices seem to have been in use from the Times of the Apostles*. And says a great deal more than I have mentioned, to confirm it.

(*q*) *Notis ad Martyrol. Rom. in August.* 7. A temporibus Apostolorum vitreus Calix in usu fuisse videtur.

And that this Custom continued long in the Church, may be concluded from hence, That *Baronius* can find no earlier prohibition of it, than that of the *Council of Rhemes*, which he says was held in the Days of *Charles the Great*. I have nothing to do with the Commendation he adds of this Prohibition, (being concerned only in the Matter of Fact) saying, That it was very *laudable* ; but I do not think it was so meerly for his Reason, [*ob periculum quod immineret materiæ fragili*] because of *the imminent danger in such brittle Matter*. For if the Custom was as ancient as the Apostles, how came they to want that quick Sense the *Roman Church* now has to prevent that Danger? But we may be certain, that they, and the Church after them, that used such Glasses, had not the present Perswasions of this Church, about a *hidden Deity*, and the *latent glorified Flesh and Blood of Christ* in the Eucharist; else they would have had both the *Discretion* and *Devotion* to have provided him a better place of reception.

Now they have done it in the *Canon Law* (*r*), enjoining, that the *Cup* and *Patent* be, if not of Gold, at least of Silver, (allowing only Pewter in case of great Poverty) but *in no wise the Cup must be of Brass or Copper, the virtue of the Wine causing a rust that procures Vomiting*, (which yet one would think the Blood of Christ, where there is no Wine, should not cause) *but over a Wooden or a Glass Cup, none may presume to say Mass*. All is very agreeable to their several Perswasions.

(*r*) *Can. ut Calix. dist.* 1. *de Consecrat.*
—De ære aut aurichalco non fiat Calix, quia ob vini virtutem æruginem parit, quæ vomitum provocat. Nullus autem de ligneo, aut vitreo calice præsumat missam cantare.

6. Instance.

To this let me add another Instance, more difficult still to be reconciled with the belief of Transubstantiation, *viz. The mixing the Blood of Christ with Ink, for writing things of moment*. So I call the *consecrated Wine*, according to the usual

150 *A full View of the Doctrines and Practices*

Language of the Fathers, giving it the name of *Christ's Blood*; but it's not possible to believe that they who thus used it, thought it to be so, any otherwise than by representation: since you can hardly think of a higher profanation, by any mixture, than this, of blending the true Blood of Christ with Ink, unless I except the case of mixing it with Poison, for the destruction of Persons; and thus *P. Victor* 2. and *P. Victor* 3. and *Henry* 7. Emperor, all died by receiving Poison in the Sacrament, as is attested by numerous and credible Historians.

Taking it therefore for granted, that no Body will have the confidence to assert, that they who thus mixed it with Ink, did believe Transubstantiation, I shall now set down three remarkable Instances of a Pope, a General Council, and a King, that thus used it.

(s) *Ad an. D. 648. Sec. 14.*

The first is of Pope *Theodorus*, who as *Theophanes* (whose words *Baronius* (s) has given us) relates, when *Pyrrhus* the *Monothelite* departed from *Rome*, and was come to *Ravenna*, and returned like a Dog to his Vomit; *and when this was found out, P. Theodorus Calling a full Congregation of the Church, came to the Sepulchre of the Head of the Apostles, and asking for the Divine Cup, he dropped some of the Life-giving Blood into the Ink; and so, with his own hand, made the deposition of excommunicated Pyrrhus.* Thus *Theophanes.*

The next Instance, is, the doing of the same in the Condemnation and Deposition of *Photius* Patriarch of *Constantinople*, by the Fathers of the 4*th Council of Constantinople* (which the Romanists call the 8*th General Council*) which is thus related by *Nicetas* in the Life of *Ignatius* (t).

(t) Apud Concil. Labbe. Tom. 8. pag. 1231.
Ὀυ ψιλῷ τῷ μέλανι τὰ χειρόγραφα ποιέμενοι, ἀλλὰ τὸ φρικωδέςατον, ὡς τῶν εἰδότων ἀκήκοα διαβεβαιωμένων, κỳ ἐν αὐτῷ τῷ σωτηρίῳ τῷ αἵματι βάπλοντες τ̃ κάλαμον, ὅπως ἐξεκήρυξαν Φώτιον, ὅπως αὐτὸν κατεδίκασαν, κỳ πάντας τοὺς κεχειροτονημένους ὑπ' αὐτῦ.

The Bishops *subscribed his Deposition, not with bare Ink, but, which may make one tremble* (*as I have heard it attested by those that knew it*) *dipping the Pen in the very Blood of our Saviour; thus they condemned and exauthoriz'd Photius, and with him, all that had been ordained by him.* All this was *Anno Dom.* 869.

The last Example is, of a Peace or Agreement struck up between *Charles the Bald*, and *Bernard* count of *Barcelona*, in in the same Age, related by *Odo Aribert*; (whose Fragment

Baluzius

Baluzius has given us) *(u)* who tells us, That Agreement at *Tholouse*, was confirmed and signed between the *King* and the *Count*, Sanguine Euchariſtico, *with the Blood of the Eucharist.* Tho' notwithſtanding this *Charles* ſtabb'd *Bernard* with his own hand.

(u) Notis ad Agobardum, p. 129.

7. Inſtance.

The next Inſtance ſhall be, The different Practices of the *Ancient Church* and the *Preſent Roman*, with reference to the *Reſervation* of the Eucharist, after the Communion was ended, and what they did with the *Remains* not received.

Concerning which, for methods ſake, I ſhall refer all to three remarkable differences.

1. Difference.] *What was not received in the Eucharist by the Communicants, the Ancient Church took no care to reſerve it; But the new Roman Church reſerves all publickly that is unreceived, and puts little of it to any uſes that are Sacramental.*

I will not ſay that there was no reſervation of the Remains, after the Eucharist was over, of what had been conſecrated, and not received, even before the Innovations took place, which were introduced by the Roman Church, becauſe there may perhaps be ſome Inſtances given of communicating the Sick out of ſuch Remains; and among the *Greeks* there was alſo communicating, *ex præſanctificatis*, of what had been conſecrated before; but theſe, I ſay, were but later Cuſtoms of the *6th* and *7th* Centuries, and both before and after the contrary Cuſtom did prevail; and where theſe Reſervations were, they employed them to the ends of the Sacrament, for to be *eaten* and not to be *adored*.

But as to the moſt Ancient Cuſtom of the Church, it is truly given by the *Author of the Commentary* upon S. *Paul*'s *Epiſtles*, among S. *Jerom*'s Works *(x)*. Who on thoſe words of S. *Paul* (1 *Cor.* 11.) *This is not to eat the Lord's Supper*, &c. ſays thus, *Meeting in the Church, they ſeparately made their Oblations, and after the Communion, whatſoever remained of the Sacrifices there in the Church, eating a common Supper, they conſumed them together.*

(x) Tom. 9. Edit. Froben. in 1 *Cor.* 11. In Eccleſia convenientes ſuas ſeparatim offerebant, & poſt communionem quæcunq; eis de ſacrificiis ſuperfuiſſent, illic in Eccleſia communem cœnam comedentes pariter conſumebant.

But

But when these *common Meals* ceased, and this way of consumption with them; The *Ancient Church* had other ways to do it. Witness the Practice mentioned by *Hesychius* (y), who explaining that place of the Law, which required, That *whatsoever of the Flesh and Bread remained, should be burnt with Fire*; adds, *which we see also now sensibly done in the Church; that whatsoever happens to remain (of the Eucharist) unconsumed, is burnt.*

Evagerius (z) mentions another different usage, but with the same effect, at *Constantinople*, where, he says, *It was an old Custom, that when a great deal of the Holy Parts of the Immaculate Body of Christ our God remained, they sent for some Youths that went to School, of an unripe Age, who eat them up.*

Nicephorus Callistus says, That this continued so to his Time, and that he himself had been one of those Youths that ate up those Particles (*a*).

Neither was this a Practice of the *Eastern Church* only, but also of the *Western*, as appears by a *Canon* of a Synod of *Mascon* (b), *An.* 585. *Whatsoever Reliques of the Sacrifices shall remain in the Repository after Mass is ended, on Wednesdays and Fridays the Officer shall bring little Children to Church, and appointing them to Fast, they shall receive the said Remains sprinkled with a little Wine.*

If *Transubstantiation* had been their Belief, these had been lewd Prophanations of the Lord's Body.

The Roman Church therefore having this Belief, have ordered Matters quite otherwise, all is reserved that remains; the Pretence I know is, that they may have the Sacrament always in readiness to communicate the Sick withal; but they have been often told, that this is altogether needless, when the Priests with their *portable Altars*, have leave, upon less Occasions, to celebrate Mass privately; and when so many hundred Masses in the great Churches are daily celebrated, how easily may the Sacrament immediately (without being reserved)

(y) *Lib. 2. in Levit. cap. 8.* Quod nunc videmus in Ecclesia sensibiliter fieri, igniq; tradi quacunque remanere contigerit inconsumpta.

(z) Histor. Lib. 4. c. 36. Ἔθ۞ παλαιὸν —— ὅτ᾽ ἄν πλιῆπ χρῆμα τῶ ἁγίων μερίδων τῶ ἀχράντε σώματ۞ Χριςῦ τῷ Θεῦ ἡμῶν ἐναπεμείναι, παῖδας ἀφθόρες —— ταῦ]α ἐοθίειν.

(a) *Lib. 17. Hist. c. 25.*

(b) *Concil. Matiscon. Can. 6. apud Tom. 5. Conc. Labb. p. 982.* Quacunque reliquiæ Sacrificiorum, post peractam Missam in Sacrario superfederint, quarta & sexta feria innocentes, ab illo cujus interest, ad Ecclesiam adducantur & indicto eis jejunio easdem reliquias consperfas vino percipiant.

reserved) be conveyed from one of their Altars to such sick Persons.

But whatsoever is pretended, they intend other things more suitable to that *Presence*, which they suppose to be there included; stately Tabernacles they prepare upon the Altars for his repose, with lighted Torches burning Day and Night before it; they come thither, even out of the Times of the Assemblies, to make their Prostrations; for so Card. *Bellarmine* (*c*), among the Encouragements to make private Prayers in Temples, gives this as one Reason, *because ordinarily in them, besides the Presence of God which is every where, there is also the Presence of Christ our Mediator corporally in the Eucharist, which increases the Hope and Trust of him that prays.*

(*c*) *De cultu Sanct. l. 3. c. 4. S. Quinta ratio.*
Quia in Templis ordinariè præter Dei præsentiam, quæ est ubique, est etiam præsentia Mediatoris Christi corporaliter in Eucharista, quæ certè auget spem & fiduciam orantis.

This is a new way of increasing Faith and Hope, which the *Ancients* were not acquainted with; they waited indeed at the Altar for that end, when the Eucharist was administred, and the evident representation and *setting forth of Christ before their Eyes as crucified*, was very proper to increase their Faith and Hope: And there in a *Sacramental* Sense, while they thus received, in the Phrase of *Optatus* (*d*), the *Body and Blood of Christ did inhabit for certain Moments.* But these *certain Moments* will not do the Business of this Church, which requires a more *constant* and *fixed Residence*. They do not think their very Temples holy and venerable enough without it; for among the things that make a Temple so, and moreover endue it with a kind of a *Divine Virtue*, the forenamed Cardinal (*e*) reckons the *presence of the Body of Christ in the Eucharist*. So that it seems by their Opinions and Practice, the *reserved parts* of the Sacrament, are as necessary as those that are *received*.

(*d*) *Lib. 6. adv. D* Quid vos offenderat stus, cujus illic *per cert menta* corpus & sanguis tabat?

(*e*) *Ibid. ca, sec. Tertio p. batur.*

Especially if you remember that these *reserved Parts* are designed, not only to receive their *Adorations*, when they come to *say their Prayers before it* in the Churches, but also when it *travels abroad*, as it do's upon many occasions, when none have occasion to receive it, nor think of saying their Prayers, being engaged in the Streets about their Secular Affairs; yet

yet even there, when they happen to meet the Eucharist going in a solemn Procession, they must kneel and adore it. We know also that there is a peculiar Feast instituted (tho' of a late Date, *An.* 1264.) on *Corpus-Christi* Day, on which, with the greatest pomp and state imaginable, it is carried about the Streets and publick Places to be seen and worshipped. Not to mention some extraordinary contingences, such as the breaking out of a great Fire suddenly, occasioning the drawing it out of its Retirement, to oppose against and stop its fury.

Besides, the Pope himself has often need of the *reserved Host*, not to *Take and eat* (according to the Institution) but to *take along with him* when he, in his Pontificals, rides to any Church, or takes a Journey to a City, this always accompanies him; and the *Book of Sacred Ceremonies*, will give you an account of the Horse, and the colour of it, upon which it is set, with the Bell about his Neck, and the pompous Train, the Canopy carried over it, and lighted Torches before it, &c.

Let me only add farther, That in that case which is pretended to be the great occasion for the reservation of the Eucharist, I mean, to be in readiness for sick Persons, yet even here the Procession, and the Pomp, and the Magnificence in the conveying it to such Places, and the Receiving the Adorations of all it meets, seems to be as much designed, as the communicating those sick Persons; which they will be contented as soon to let alone, as to abate those attending Ceremonies.

The *Ancient Church* had very *homely practices*; they used and suffered, in cases of great necessity, things that *this Church* would account incongruous if not profane. Such as that which *Dionysius* of *Alexandria* (*f*) relates concerning *old Serapion*, who when he lay a-dying, sent a young Grand-child of his to call one of the Presbyters of *Alexandria* to give him the Sacrament: Who by reason of Illness, not being able to go along with him, he made no more ado, but took a little portion of the Eucharist, and gave it into the Youth's Hand, and directed him to moisten it, and so to infuse it into his Mouth; which he did, and immediately upon the swallowing

(*f*) Apud Eu-
seb. Hist. Eccles.
l. 6. c. 44.

ing it, the old Man expired: I Question, whether the Gentlemen of the Roman Church will *allow* this to be a *true Communion*; but I believe, with their perswasions, they would not *follow* it for a World.

We may more than guess so, by a remarkable Story *Nic. Trigautius* tells us of what was resolved upon by the skilful *Jesuits*, in a Case exactly like the former (*g*), at *Pekin* in *China*; One *Fabius* who had been converted and baptized, being above Eighty Years old, fell sick to Death; and having been confess'd of his Sins, with great earnestness, desired to receive the Sacrament for his *Viaticum*; but there being no convenient place at his House to celebrate it in, nor liberty to carry it through the Streets in Pomp and requisite State, they comforted him with the consideration of his having made confession of his Sins, which was necessary; and told him that he might, without taking the Sacrament, when he was lawfully hindred, go to Heaven; and so they left him. These admirable Casuists, you see, determine against communicating the dying Person, when it could not be performed with the *majestick Ceremonies* they desired.

(*g*) *Nic. Trigautii exped. apud Sinas, l. 5. c. 7. p.* 503. Neque domi loco convenienti celebrari poterat, neque pro majestate per vicos deferri: solabantur igitur illum socii necessaria peccatorum confessione perfunctum, posse sine viatico, quod legitime impeditus minimè susciperet, cœlestem gloriam introire.

The Priest of *Alexandria*, and the Fathers in *China*, differ very widely in their Practice, and you may be sure their Perswasions in this matter were as different; the Man himself indeed, he tells us, found a way to get the Communion at last, by throwing himself into *their House*, but it was not till they had made a little Procession within doors; till the Tapestry was spread on the Floors, and the Tapers lighted, nothing could be done.

In a word, to perswade People of the necessity of these Pomps and Solemnities in conveying the Sacrament to the Sick, they produce several Miracles *, how when the Priests have carried the Eucharist through Fields without attendance, Troops of Asses and Mares have run to supply this defect, and having first fallen down on their Knees to worship the Deity he carried, they have accompanied him to the Place, waited at the sick Man's Door till all was over, and then marched back again in good order with him; God shewing, by these

* *See the School of the Eucharist, Title, Asses and Mares,* &c.

respects

respects paid to it by Beasts, what he expected much more from Men.

2. *Difference*, relates to what was received in the Eucharist; wherein we also see a plain disagreement in the usages of the *Primitive*, and the *present Roman Church*. Which is this; The *Ancient Church allowed great Liberty privately to reserve what had been publickly received in the Eucharist*: Which would be now a great Crime in the Roman Church; so far from being allowed.

It is undeniable, that anciently this was allowed, (whether they did well or ill in it is not at all the question, but concerning the Matter of Fact.) S. *Basil* (*h*) thinks that the Custom took its rise from Times of Persecution, when Christians were forced to flee into Desarts, and live in solitude, having not the presence of a Priest to communicate them, they had the Sacrament reserved by them, and communicated themselves. But he says (even when this Reason ceased) this became afterwards an inveterate Custom. And in *Alexandria* and *Egypt*, the *Laicks commonly had the Sacrament by them in their own Houses* (*i*); and, he says expresly, this which they so reserved μετ' ἐξουσίας ἁπάσης, *with all liberty* (as his Phrase is) *was a Particle received from the Priest's Hand in the Church*.

(*h*) Epist. 289.

(*i*) Ibid. Καὶ τῆς ἐν λαῷ τυλύντων, ὡς ὅτι τὸ πλεῖςτν ἔχει κοινωνίαν ἐν τῷ οἴκῳ αὑτοῦ.
—ἐν τῇ ἐκκλησίᾳ ὁ ἱερεὺς ἐπιδίδωσι τὴν μερίδα, &c.

(*k*) Orat. 11.
Καὶ εἴ πυ τι τῆς ἀντιτύπου τοῦ τιμίν σώματος, ἢ τοῦ αἵματος ἡ χεὶρ ἐθησαύρισεν, &c.

So *Nazianzen* (*k*) says of his Sister *Gorgonia*; *Whatsoever of the Antitypes of the precious Body and Blood of Christ her Hand had treasured up*, &c.

Which very phrase intimates, that at several times she had reserved and made a collection of the Consecrated Elements.

Tertullian supposes it a common practice in his time, when he says (*l*), *Thy Husband will not know what it is thou tastest secretly before all other Meat*, &c.

(*l*) Lib. 2. ad Uxor.
Non sciet maritus quid secretò ante omnem cibum gustes, &c.

It is true indeed that in the Councils of *Saragosa* and *Toledo* in *Spain*, this was prohibited in the 4th Century, upon occasion of the *Priscillianists*, who did receive the communion as others did, and reserved it, and so could not be discovered, tho'

t'

they never took it; againſt whom Learned Men think thoſe Councils made thoſe Canons, which anathematized thoſe that received, but did not take it down, but reſerved it. However the foreſaid Cuſtom ſtill prevailed in other Places, as might be ſhewn, if it were needful, as far as the 11*th* Century. As for the *preſent Church* this is wholly a Stranger to them; they will have no Remains kept any where but upon the publick Altars, where no Hand muſt touch them but the Prieſt's. The Council of *Trent* (*m*) will not allow the *Sanctimoniales*, the very *Nuns* in their Quires, or in any places within their Cloiſter (*intra chorum vel ſepta Monaſterii*) to keep it by them, but only *in publica Eccleſia*, notwithſtanding any former Grants and Privileges. And a Great Man (*n*) ſpeaking of the former Uſages, ſays, *If any Lay-man now ſhould dare to do ſo, he would be accounted guilty of a Crime to be expiated by a grievous puniſhment, as a profane Violator of the moſt Holy Sacrament.*

(*m*) *Seſſ.* 25. *cap.* 10.

(*n*) *Petavius de Pœnit.l.*1.*c.*7. Si quis nunc Laicus ſimile quid auderet, is apud nos cenſeretur gravi pœna exp andi criminis reus, veluti ſanctiſſimi Sacramenti profanus temerator.

But if it be ſo great a Crime with them to reſerve it when they have received it; What will they ſay to the next Difference I ſhall now mention?

3. *Difference.* That *among the Ancients, what was ſo privately reſerved, was put to ſuch uſes as the preſent Roman Church muſt abhor, becauſe they are direct Affronts to the belief of Tranſubſtantiation, and the corporal Preſence.*

It appears by *S. Cyprian*, (*libr. de Lapſis*) that the very Women in his Time had liberty to take the Euchariſt home with them, and diſpoſe of it as they pleaſed; and the Woman he there ſpeaks of, that *lock'd it up in her Cheſt*, had not the Roman Opinion of a Latent Deity, which ſuch uſage ill agrees with, or rather affronts.

Neither had *Cyril* of *Jeruſalem* (*o*) their Perſwaſions, when he adviſes his Communicant, *whilſt his Lips were wet and dewy*, with what he had drank in the Cup, with his Hands to touch his Eyes and Forehead, and the reſt of the Organs of his Senſes for their Sanctification.

(*o*) Catech. Myſtag. 5. Ἔτι δὲ νοτίδος ἐνούσης τοῖς χείλεσί σου.

But what *Gorgonia, Nazianzen*'s Siſter, did with the Remains of the Antitypes of Chriſt's Body and Blood, exceeds it; when

when as he reports of her, to her commendation (p), she mixed them with her Tears, and anointed her whole Body with it, for the recovery out of a grievous Disease.

(p) Orat. 11. Φαρμάκῳ τύτῳ τὸ πᾶν σῶμα ἐπαλείψασα, &c.

A like Story to which, S. *Austin* gives us (q) of the Mother of one *Acatius*, who was born with closed Eyes, which a Physician advised should be opened with an Instrument of Iron; but she refused, and cured him with a *Cataplasm, or Plaster made of the Eucharist*.

(q) Lib. 3. secundi op. adv. Jul.
Neq; hoc permisisse religiosam matrem suam, sed id effecisse ex *Eucharistiæ cataplasmate*.

In honour to our Saviour, we find a Woman anointing his Body; but to make his Body an Ointment for hers, or to make it into a Medicine, is but course usage of it, and such as none would adventure upon that was perswaded it was a deified Body.

The old Custom which *Eusebius* mentions (r) of sending the Sacrament from one Bishop to another, as a Token of Peace and Communion, seems to argue but little good Manners, (with the Church of *Rome*'s Opinions concerning it); for tho' God sent his Son on a blessed Errand and Embassy, it looks too saucy for us to send him on ours.

(r) Lib. 5. Hist. Ecclef. c. 24. Ἀλλὰ αὐτοὶ μὴ παρόντες οἱ περὶ οὗ πρεσβύτεροι, τοῖς ἀπὸ τῶν παροικιῶν πρῶσι ἔπεμπον εὐχαριστίαν.

What Indecencies would *this Church* justly fear the Body of Christ would be subject to, if there were that permission that was granted of old to carry the Eucharist along with them in their Voyages at Sea? Yet this P. *Gregory* the Great tells us was practised by *Maximianus* and his Companions returning from *Constantinople* to *Rome*; and being in a Tempest in the *Adriatick* Sea (s), *They gave one another the* Pax, *received the Body and Blood of their Redeemer, recommending every one himself to God.*

(s) Dial. l. 3. c. 35.—Sibimet pacem dedisse, corpus & sanguinem Redemptoris accepisse; Deo se singulos commendantes.

But that which S. *Ambrose* informs us (t) of his Brother *Satyrus*, was still more bold; *Who being Shipwrack'd at Sea, and not yet having been baptized, lest he should die without the Mystery, he beg'd of some of those that were baptized, to let*

(t) Orat. de obitu fratris.
Priusquamperfectioribus esset initiatus mysteriis, in naufragio constitutus—— ne vacuus mysterii exiret è vita, quos initiatos esse cognoverat, ab his Divinum illud fidelium sacramentum poposcit,——ligari fecit in orario, & orarium involvit in collo, atq; ita se dejecit in mare.

him

of the Ancient Church, relating to the Eucharist.

him have that *Divine Sacrament of the Faithful*, (the Custom then being to have it reserved about them) which they granting, he put it up in his *Handkerchief* which he then tied about his *Neck*, and so threw himself into the Sea.

Whatsoever Conceits *Satyrus* might have when he borrowed it, yet those that bestowed it, could never think fit (with the foresaid belief) to deliver it into the Hands of one not yet a perfect Christian, nor to be tied about his Neck in a cloth that I suppose was no Corporal (as they call it) to be exposed to the dashing of Sea-waves, like a Bladder or a Cork to keep him from drowning.

But there is a more irreconcileable Practice of the Ancients with the present Belief, with which I shall end this Particular about *reservation* of the Sacrament. It *is the Custom* of burying the *reserved* parts of it with their dead Bodies. The Author of the Life of S. *Basil* (*u*), tells us, That *he kept a Particle of the Eucharist to be buried with him* ; and left it so to be by his last Will.

St. *Gregory* (*x*) tells a strange Story of a Youth that was a *Monk*, who going out of S. *Benet*'s Monastery without his Benediction, suddenly was found dead ; and being buried, the next day was forced out of his Grave, and a second Time was found so after Burial : Whereupon, says he, they ran weeping to S. *Benet*, praying him to bestow his Blessing upon him. To whom that Man of God gave the Communion of the Lord's Body, saying, Go and lay this Body of our Lord upon his Breast, and so bury him. They did so, and then he kept in his Grave, and the Earth threw him out no more.

I know that there are several *Canons of Councils*, made against this Practice, (as the 20*th Canon* of the *Council of Carthage*, and the 83 *Canon* of the 6*th General Council at Constantinople* in *Trullo*) ; upon which *last Canon*, *Zonaras* observes, ἐθ۞ ἰῶ παλαιὸν, &c. *That it was an ancient Custom to deliver the Lord's Body to Dead Bodies.*

But then methinks it's very observable, that the reason why the *Fathers* prohibit it, is not such a one as would be given in

---

(*u*) Vita Basil. c. 6. Τὴν δὲ (μερίδα) ἐφύλαξεν συνταφῆναι αὐτῷ.

(*x*) Dialog. l. 2. c. 24. —Quibus vir Dei manu sua protenus communionem Dominici corporis dedit, dicens, Ite atq; hoc Dominicum corpus super pectus ejus ponite, & sic sepulturæ cum tradite. Quod dum factum fuisset, susceptum corpus ejus terra tenuit, nec ultra projecit.

in the *Roman Church*, from the horrible Profanation and contumely in thus ufing the Lord's Body (as it would be if it were truly and properly there, and no Bread remaining): But their Reafon is from hence, *Becaufe it is written, Take and eat*; *But dead Carcafes can neither take nor eat.*

But notwithftanding all thefe Prohibitions, the old Cuftom continued afterwards; for thofe that write the Lives of Saints, and tell us of the tranflating of their Bodies from one place to another, inform us that they have found pieces of the Euchariſt uncorrupted lying in their Grave: As *Surius* (y) tells us in the Life of *Othmarus*, That when he came to be tranflated fome Years after he was buried, they found under his Head, and about his Breaft, little pieces of Bread, which were with much reverence laid by his Body again.

(y) *Surius cit. Othmar. ad Nov. 16.*
as venerabiliter aſſumens o corpori appoſuit.

The like do's *Amalarius* (z) report, (citing *Bede* for it) that the fame was practifed when S. *Cutberd* was buried, *his Head bound with a Napkin, the Euchariſt laid upon his Holy Breaſt, with his Sacerdotal Habit upon him*, &c.

(z) *De div. Offic. l.4. c.41.*
Oblata fuper pectus Sanctum pofita, veftimento Sacerdotali indutum, &c.

It is little leſs than a Demonftration, that they that thus treated the Sacrament, did not believe it contained a *hidden Deity* under the *fpecies of Bread and Wine*; for fure they would not then have thus ufed the Lord of Life and Glory, to imprifon him, as it were, and fuffer him to lie buried with the putrid Carcafes of the Dead.

8. Inſtance.

The laſt Inſtance of differing Practices in the two Churches, ſhall be, *In their over-follicitoufnefs to prevent any Accidents that might happen in the Adminiſtration of the Euchariſt; their Frights when any ſuch thing do's happen, and the Expiations required for negligence to purge ſuch Crimes*; ſuch as we have no foot-ſteps of in any of thofe cafes, in the Ancient Church.

As to the firſt of thofe Cafes, I have fomewhat prevented my felf, in what I before have ſhown, of their Devices of *Intinction*, fucking the Sacrament *through Pipes*; and, which is worſt of all (out of this abundant caution) *denying the People the Cup*. Here therefore I ſhall mention *other Cautions*, ſuch as thofe which tend to prevent any *Fragments* falling off

from

from the *Bread of the Eucharist*, that no *Crumbs* may have any dishonour done to them, by being left unregarded, but either may be received or reserved.

To this end, they have altered the *Ancient Custom* of providing *common Bread*, such as is of ordinary use, for the Sacrament, and required that it be *unleavened*, because this is less apt to break into *Crumbs*, and cleaves better together in its Parts. And tho' they do not say that there is no Sacrament where leavened Bread is used, yet the *Missal* (*a*) affirms, That he *that consecrates in this, do's grievously Sin*; and herein they have raised (since the days that Transubstantiation was forming into a Doctrine of Faith) and maintained a great Controversy with the *Greek Church*, which do's not use their *Azyms*, no more than the *Ancient Church* did. They have also invented, about the same Time, and still use, those little *round Wafers* (as they are commonly called) which is that which they consecrate for the Bread of the Sacrament, and take care hereby to prevent breaking into *Crumbs*; for they never break them for distribution, but put them whole into the Communicants Mouths; whereas the *Ancient Practice* was, to provide one whole Loaf of Substantial Bread, and to divide this into parts, and break it for to be distributed among them all. But these *Hostiola*, little Hosts, are brought to such a tenuity, that they are the next door to what they call *species*, having scarce any substance, and *deserve not properly* the name of Bread, as a learned Man (*b*) has shown. The very *Missal* (*Loc. citat. n. 7.*) supposes, that they may easily disappear, and that a *Wind may* carry them away, for that is one of the cases it mentions, (*aut vento, aut miraculo, vel ab aliquo animali accepta.*)

It is easy to show, that all this caution to prevent *falling Crumbs*, is perfect nonsense, according to their principles, since the True Body of Christ cannot be broken or crumbled into Bits, which is the only substance remaining; the rest, which they call *Species*, being Mathematical Lines and Colours only, and no matter under them; a *whole World* of them can never make up a *Crumb of Bread*, or any Fragment. And yet these are they about which such superabundant Caution is used; which are mentioned in the *Missal*.

(*a*) *De defectibus, c. 3. n. 3.* Conficiens graviter peccat.

(*b*) *Vossius in Thes. Theol. Disp. 19. de S. Cœnæ Symb.*

Y To

A full View of the Doctrines and Practices

To name a few. When the Priest that celebrates do's communicate himself, it is then only that he breaks the Host into three parts, one of which he puts into the Cup; and after he has taken the other two which are upon the Patin, he is directed (c) *to take the Patin, to view the Corporal,* (or Cloth spread under it) *to gather up the Fragments with the Patin, if there be any on it, and with his Thumb and Fore-finger of his right Hand, to wipe the Patin carefully over the Chalice, and also his Fingers, lest any Fragments remain on them.*

(c) *Missal.Rom. ritus celebr. Missam, c.* 10. *Sect.* 4.

Then for the Hosts that are reserved to another time, after the Priest has taken them off from the Corporal, and put them into the Vessel appointed for them, he is directed *to mind carefully* (d), *lest any Fragment, the left imaginable, remain upon the Corporal; and if there be any, carefully to put them into the Chalice.*

(d) Ibid. Sect. 15.

When he has taken the Cup, with the 3d Particle of the Host put into it (e), *he must purify himself, drinking some wine poured into the Cup by the Minister that attends; then with Wine and Water must wash his Thumbs and Fore-fingers over the Cup, and must wipe them with the Purificatory; then he must drink off the Oblation* (wherein he washed) *and wipe his Mouth and the Chalice with the Purificatory.*

(e) Ibid. Sect. 5.

Such-like also are the Cautions given when the People have communicated *. *If the Hosts were laid upon the Corporal, the Priest wipes it* (or sweeps it) *with the Patin; and if there were any Fragments on it, he puts them into the Chalice. The Minister also holding in his right Hand a Vessel with Wine and Water in it, and in his left a little Napkin* (Mappulam), *do's reach the Purification* (to wash their Mouths) *to them, a little after the Priest, and the little Napkin to wipe their Mouths.*

† Ibid. Sect. 6.

The Communicants also are directed (f), *after receiving, not presently to go out of the Church, or talk, or look about carelesly; nor to spit, nor read aloud Prayers out of a Book, lest the Species of the Sacrament should fall out of their Mouths.*

(f) *See the Rom. Ritual, de S. Eucharist.*

All this is preventing Care: But now when Accidents do happen, they seem, by their ordering Matters, to be in a *frightful Concern*; and strange things are to be done, if possible, to make an honorable amends.

of the Ancient Church, relating to the Eucharist.

In the last Chapter I have given the Reader some Instances of those strange Things, and will here only add two Cases which the Roman Missal provides for.

The first is, *If a Consecrated Host, or any part of it, should fall to the Ground,* the direction is (g), *That it be reverently taken up, and the place where it fell must be cleansed, and a little scraped away, and such dust or scrapings must be put in the Holy Repository. If it fell without the Corporal upon the Napkin* (Mappam) *or any ways upon any Linen Cloth, such Napkin, or Linen, must be carefully washed, and that Water poured out into the Holy Repository.*

(g) *Missal. Rom. de defect..Missæ, c.* 10. *Sect.* 15.

The second Case is, *When by negligence* (h) *any thing of the Blood is Spilt. If it fell upon the Earth, or upon a Board, it must be licked up with the Tongue, and the place scraped sufficiently, and such scraping be burnt, and the Ashes laid up in the Repository. But if it fell upon the Altar-stone, the Priest must sup up the Drop, and the place be well washed, and that water cast into the Repository. If it fell upon the Altar-Cloths, and the Drop sunk as far as the second or third Cloth, those Cloths must be thrice washed where the Drop fell, putting the Cup underneath to receive the Water, and that Water thrown into the foresaid place.* And so it directs to such washing when it falls upon the Corporal alone, or the Priest's Garments, &c.

(h) *Ibid. c.* 10. *Sect.* 12.

I cannot but here annex also the Constitution which the Reader may find in the *Appendix* to the *History of the Church of Peterburgh,* Pag. 344. (being the first of two there set down) directing what is to be done, when any negligence happens about the Lord's Body and Blood, and how to expiate the Crime.

" When there is so great negligence about the Lord's Body
" and Blood, that it happens to fall downward, or into any
" place where it cannot be fully perceived, whether it fell,
" and whether any of it came to the Ground ; Let the Mat-
" ter be discovered as soon as may be to the Abbot or Prior,
" who taking some of the Friars with him, let him come to
" the place where this has happened ; And if the Body shall
" have fallen, or the Blood have been spilt upon Stone, or
" Earth, or Wood, or Mat, or Tapestry, or such like, let
" the dust of the Earth be gathered, part of that Stone be
" scraped, part of that Wood, Mat, Tapestry, or the like,

"be cut away and cast into the Holy Repository. But if the
"place where it fell cannot be plainly discovered, and yet it
"appear that it fell downwards, in that place, and about the
"place where it is thought chiefly to have fallen, let there be
"the like gathering, Scraping, cutting away, and casting in-
"to the Holy Repository. Then they by whose negligence
"this has happened in the next Chapter shall humbly declare
"their Fault, and on their naked Bodies receive Judgment
"(*judicium nudi suscipiant*) and Penance be enjoined them,
"either of Fasting, or Whipping, or Rehearsing so many
"Psalms, or such like. Which Persons going back to their
"places, from their Punishment (*de judicio*) all the priests
"then present shall rise up, and with all devotion offer them-
"selves to receive Punishment. Then he that holds the
"Chapter, shall detain seven of them, which he pleases to
"chuse, to receive the Judgment (of *whipping*) and command
"the rest to go away. The Chapter being ended, all pro-
"strating themselves together, shall say seven Penitential
"Psalms in the Monastery, beginning to sing them as they go
"out from the Chapter. Then shall follow after the Psalms,
"the *Pater Noster*, with these Chapters and Collects. *Let
"thy Mercy, O Lord, be upon us. Remember not our Iniquities.
"The Lord be with you. Let us pray. Hear, O Lord, our
"Prayers, and Spare the Sins of those that confess themselves to
"thee; that they whose guilty Consciences do accuse them, thy mer-
"ciful Pardon may absolve them.* Or that other Collect. *O God,
"whose property is always to have Mercy*; or such other collect
"for Sins.

"But if the Blood fell upon the Corporal, or upon any
"clean Cloth, and it be certain whether it fell, let that part
"of the Cloth be washed in some Chalice, and the first Wa-
"ter it was wash'd in be drunk off by the Friars; the other two
"washings be cast into the Repository. The said Fault
"must be discovered in the first Chapter, but they alone, by
"whose negligence this has happened, shall receive the fore-
"said Discipline, but all the Friars shall say over in the Mona-
"stery all the seven Psalms, with the Chapters and Collects,
"as was said before. If that day, the short one for the Dead
"shall be read in the Chapter, let them first sing my words
"going into the Church.: After that the seven Psalms, as
aforesaid.

" aforesaid. But if in any other manner a lighter negli-
' gence shall happen relating to this Sacrament, the Friar,
" by whose Fault it happened, shall be punished with a ligh-
" ter Revenge at the discretion of the Abbot or Prior.

Thus I have given a sufficient Specimen of the strange Caution and Fears the Roman Church are under, lest any thing
should happen, even to the very least Particle or Drop of the
Sacrament, that is dishonourable: And indeed, their Caution
is very agreeable to their Perswasions, as I have before often
hinted.

But now if we turn our Eyes upon the *Ancient Church*,
tho' we cannot question, either their Devotion or reverent
Behaviour in all Acts of Religious Worship, and particularly
in this great One; yet there is not to be found any such
scrupulosities about *minute things*; nor such *frightful apprehensions* in the case of unforeseen Accidents, nor such *Expiations*
as we have before heard of. They did not forbear to use the
Common Bread (as I said before) tho' it might be more liable to crumble; they took their Share from one *Common Loaf*;
they received the Wine without *intinction*, or *sucking it through
Pipes*, &c. Which are all later Inventions, since the Faith
was innovated concerning the Eucharist.

But because this is only a Negative Argument, I will therefore add a Positive one, to demonstrate that the *Ancients*
were far from these Scrupulosities; and also that they came
into the Church with Transubstantiation, and not before;
viz. The Practice of Communicating Infants. It is not my Business here to prove, that this was the common Usage in the
Church, from the Times of S. *Cyprian* at least, even to later
Ages, which has been done effectually by o-
thers (i), and is acknowledged by our Adver- (i) See Mr. Chillingworth's
saries. *Additional Treatises, in* 4to.

Maldonate (k) the Jesuit owns, that it con- (k) *Comm. in Joan.* 6. 53.
tinued in the Church for six hundred Years.

And Card. *Perron* (l) grants, *That the Primitive* (l) *De loc. August. c.* 10.
*Church gave the Eucharist to Infants as soon as they
were baptized:* And that *Charles the Great*, and *Lewis the Pious*,
both testify that this Custom remained in the West in their *Age*,
that is, in the 9th Century in which they lived. But it went
down lower, even to two Ages after *Charles the Great*. For
that

that Epistle of P. *Paschal* 2. (which I mentioned in another Chapter) given us by *Baronius*, at the end of his *last Tome*, (*Ad Ann.* 1118. when that Pope died) wherein he forbids *Intinction* of the Bread in the Wine, and requires that the Bread and Wine should be *taken separately*; gives us also this exception, (*præter in parvulis ac omnino infirmis qui panem absorbere non possunt*) that *it may be allowed to little Children, and those extreamly weak, that cannot get down the Bread:* Which had been a needless provision for them, if Infants had not then received the Sacrament.

This being then a certain and confessed thing, that Infants received the Eucharist, I refer it to the Conscience of any *Romanist*, whether he can think the *Ancients* had any of their aforesaid Fears, and nice Scrupulosities, about the Accidents that might happen to the consecrated Elements, which in that Practice could not be prevented; it being impossible, where sucking Children receive either Bread or Wine, to hinder the happening of something which the Church of *Rome* will call highly dishonourable to the Sacrament. For to instance in a Case which S. *Cyprian* (m) mentions, of a Christian little Girl, that by her Nurses Wickedness had receiv'd polluted Bread in an Idol's Temple, and afterwards was brought by the Mother, knowing nothing, into the Church to receive the Communion. He relates how the Child, when its turn came to receive the Cup, turned away its Face, shut its Lips, and refused the Cup. *But the Deacon* (n) *persisted, and though it strove against it, did infuse into it of the Sacrament of the Cup. Then followed sighing and vomiting; the Eucharist could not remain in a Body and Mouth that had been prophaned.*

How would a Romanist start at the thoughts of pouring the Sacrament, as this Deacon did (who sure was a *Zuinglian*) into the Mouth of a strugling Child? But here is no mention of any concern about that, or what happened upon it; from whence it is natural to conclude, that the *Ancients* in this common Case having none of this Church's *Scruples* and *Fears*, that they had none of their *Faith*; for they must have had more *Caution*, if they had had their *Opinion* about the Eucharist.

(m) *Liv. de Lapsis.*

(n) *Ibid.* Perstitit Diaconus, & reluctanti licet de Sacramento Calicis infudit. Tunc sequitur singultus & vomitus; in Corpore atq; ore violato Eucharistia permanere non potuit.

It

It is also very observable, to confirm what I have said, that though we can trace the Custom of *Communicating Infants*, as far as to the Age when the Transubstantiating Doctrine was set on foot, and ready to be formed into an Article of Faith; yet here we are at a full stop, and can go no further, for this begat such Scruples and Fears, that made this quickly give place and vanish, which had so many Hazards attending it, and we hear no more of it since that in the *Latin Church*; but other great Churches, that have not made This an Article of their Faith, still retain the old Custom (though they err therein) of Communicating Infants. As the *Greek Churches*, the *Muscovites*, *Armenians*, *Habassins*, *Jacobites*, &c. concerning which see *Dallée de Cultib. Latin.* l. 5. c. 4. *Thomas à Jesu de Convers. gentium*, l. 7. c. 5. & c. 18. *Ludolfi Histor. Æthiop.* l. 3. c. 6. Sect. 37, 38. *Histor. Jacobitarum, Oxon.* cap. 9. See also *Father Simons* Critical History of Religions, concerning the *Georgians*, cap. 5. p. 67, 71. *Nestorians*, p. 101. *Cophties*, p. 114. *Armenians*, c. 12. p. 128.

CHAP.

CHAP. XV.

The Fifteenth Difference.

The Old Prayers in the Canon of the Mass concerning the Sacrament, agree not with the present Faith of the Roman Church: And their New Prayers to the Sacrament have no countenance from the Ancient Church.

IT is to no purpose to enquire, who was the Author of the Canon of the Mass, when *Wallafridus Strabo* (*o*) (who lived in the middle of the 9th Century) tells us, *It was a thing to him unknown.* Seeing also he adds, *That it had been enlarged, not only once but often*; it is as vain to ask after its Age.

The same also the Abbot *Berno* (*p*) says, *It was not one Man that composed the Canon all of it, but at several times another interposed and added another thing.*

And as they added, so also I doubt not but they altered many things, as we may guess by that remarkable Difference, betwixt what the Author of the Book of Sacraments, under the name of S. *Ambrose* (*q*), cites as the Prayer in his Time, and what we now find in it. (speaking of the Oblation) it was, then, Make this Oblation to us allowable, rational, acceptable, *Which is the Figure of the Body and Blood of Christ our Lord:* Which now is turned into this Prayer, That the *Oblation may be made to us the Body and Blood of thy dear Son our Lord.*

But yet to take the *Canon* as now it is, we shall find the Prayers of it, not capable of being reconciled with the present Faith of the Roman Church, and with Transubstantiation.
To

(*o*) *De reb. Ecclesiast. cap.* 22. Quis primus ordinaverit nobis ignotum est.
Auctum tamen fuisse, non semel sed sæpius ex partibus additis intelligimus.

(*p*) *Berno Ab. Augiens. de rebus ad Missam spectant. c.* 1. Attamen ipsum Canonem non unus solus composuit totum, sed per tempora aliud alius interposuit vel adjecit.

(*q*) *Lib.* 4. *de Sacram. cap.* 5. Fac nobis hanc Oblationem adscriptam, rationabilem, acceptabilem, *Quod est Figura corporis & sanguinis Domini nostri Jesu Christi.*
Quam Oblationem tu Deus in omnibus quæsumus benedictam, adscriptam, &c. facere digneris, *Ut nobis corpus & sanguis fiat dilectissimi tui Filii D. N. J. Christi.*

To give some Instances.

Thus they pray in the *Canon*, immediately after the words of Consecration.

Wherefore we, O Lord, thy Servants, and yet thy Holy People, being mindful, as well of the Blessed Passion, as also of the Resurrection from the Dead, and of the glorious Ascension into Heaven, of the same thy Son our Lord Jesus Christ; do offer to thy most excellent Majesty, out of thy own Donations and Gifts, a pure Sacrifice, an Immaculate Sacrifice, the Holy Bread of Eternal Life, and the Cup of Everlasting Salvation.

Upon which (Gifts) vouchsafe to look, with a propitious and serene Aspect: and to accept them, as thou didst vouchsafe to accept the Gifts of thy Child, the Righteous Abel, *and the Sacrifice of our Patriarch* Abraham; *and the Holy Sacrifice, the immaculate Hostie, which thy High Priest* Melchisedeck *did offer to thee.*

Almighty God, we humbly beseech thee, command these things to be carried by the Hands of thy Holy Angel to thy High Altar, before thy Majesty, that as many of us, as by this partaking of the Altar, have received the most holy Body and Blood of thy Son, may be filled with all Heavenly Benediction and Grace, by the same Jesus Christ our Lord.

Vouchsafe also to bestow on us Sinners ——— some part and society with thy Holy Apostles, &c. ——— *into whose society we intreat thee to admit us, not weighing our Merit, but bestowing Pardon on us. Through Christ our Lord.*

By whom, O Lord, thou dost always create, sanctify, quicken, bless, and bestow on us all these good things.

Can. Miss. Unde & memores, Domine, nos servi tui, sed & plebs tua sancta ejusd. Christi Filii tui D.N. tam beatæ passionis, necnon & ab inferis resurrectionis, sed & in cœlos gloriosæ ascensionis; Offerimus præclaræ majestati tuæ de tuis donis ac datis, Hostiam puram, hostiam immaculatam, Panem sanctum vitæ æternæ, & Calicem salutis perpetuæ.

Supra quæ propitio ac sereno vultu respicere digneris: & accepta habere, sicuti accepta habere dignatus es munera pueri tui justi Abel, & sacrificium Patriarchæ nostri Abrahæ, & quod tibi obtulit summus Sacerdos tuus Melchisedeck, sanctum Sacrificium, immaculatam Hostiam.

Supplices te rogamus, omnipotens Deus, jube hæc perferri per manus sancti Angeli tui in sublime Altare tuum, in conspectu Majestatis tuæ, ut quotquot ex hac altaris participatione Sacrosanctum Filii tui corpus & sanguinem sumpserimus, omni benedictione cœlesti & gratia repleamur. Per eundem J. Christum D. N.

Nobis quoque peccatoribus — partem aliquam & societatem donare digneris cum tuis sanctis Apostolis — intra quorum nos consortium, non estimator meriti sed veniæ, quæsumus, largitor admitte. Per Christum D. N.

Per quem hæc omnia, Domine, semper bona creas, sanctificas, vivificas, benedicis & præstas nobis.

Immediately after all have communicated, this follows.

What we have taken with our Mouth, O Lord, may we receive with a pure Heart: and of a temporal Gift, may it be made to us an Eternal Remedy.

Quod ore sumpsimus, Domine, purâ mente capiamus: & de munere temporali fiat nobis remedium sempiternum.

While the Priest is washing his Thumbs and Fore-fingers over the Cup, with Wine and Water, and wiping of them, he is bid to say;

Let thy Body, O Lord, which I have taken, and thy Blood which I have drunk, cleave to my Entrals, and grant that the stain of my Crimes may not remain in me, whom pure and Holy Sacraments have refreshed.

Corpus tuum, Domine, quod sumpsi, & sanguis quem potavi, adhereat visceribus meis: & præsta ut in me non remaneat scelerum macula, quem pura & sancta refocrunt Sacramenta.

Qui vivis, &c.   Who livest, &c.

All these Prayers I have cited, the Reader must remember are *after Consecration*; upon which immediately, according to the present Faith of the Roman Church, the Substance of Bread and Wine is destroyed, and nothing but the Species and Shadows of them remain; and now Christ, instead of them, becomes present there in his Body, and Soul, and Divinity. This is their Faith. But it is impossible to reconcile this to those foregoing Prayers. For at the beginning of the *Canon*, they pray, * *That God would accept and bless these Donations and Gifts, these holy undefiled Sacrifices*; that is, the Oblations of Bread and Wine, which are no more than so, till the words of Consecration.

* Supplices rogamus ac petimus uti accepta habeas & benedicas, hæc dona, hæc munera, hæc sancta sacrificia illibata.

After this (as you heard) they pray, That *this Oblation may be made to us, the Body and Blood of thy dear Son Jesus Christ*. Which do not imply a change of Substances; for those words (*fiat nobis*) *be made to us*, may very well consist with the Oblations remaining in Substance what they were before, only beging the Communication of the Virtue and Efficacy of Christ's Passion to themselves.

And that this is the sense of the *Canon*, appears by those words after Consecration, when they say, *We offer to thy Majesty a pure Sacrifice of thy Donations and Gifts*. Which words plainly

plainly suppose, that they are in Nature what they were, *God's Creatures* still, not the appearance and shadow of them only. But they call them now the *Bread of Eternal Life, and the Cup of Salvation*; because, after they are blessed and made Sacraments, they are not now to be look'd upon as bodily Food, but as the Food of our Souls, as representing that Body of Christ, and his Passion, which is the Bread of Eternal Life.

If they had understood nothing to remain now after consecration, but Christ's *Natural Body*, they would not have called this *thy Gifts* in the Plural Number, but expressed it in the Singular, *thy Gift*. Neither can they refer to the remaining Accidents, because they are no *real Things*, and rather tell us what God has *taken away*, (the whole Substance of them) than what he has given.

But then what follows, puts it out of all doubt *; *Upon which* (still in the Plural) *look propitiously*. If it had been, *Look upon us propitiously for the sake of Christ*, it had been well enough. Or, to desire of God to look *upon these things propitiously which they offer*; if they mean (as he that made the Prayer did) that God would accept this Oblation of Bread and Wine, as he did of *Abel* and *Melchisedeck*, (which latter was indeed Bread and Wine) this had been very proper. But to make that which we offer to be Christ himself, (as they that believe Transubstantiation must expound it) and to desire God to look propitiously and benignly *upon him*, when there can be *no fear* that he should ever be unacceptable to his Father, nor none can be *so foolish* as to think that Christ stands in need of our recommendation to God for acceptance, this sense can never be agreeable to the Prayer. Therefore the most Ancient of all the *spurious Liturgies*, I mean, that attributed to *Clemens* in his *Constitutions* (r), has given us the true sense of it; *We offer to thee this Bread and this Cup —— and we beseech thee to look favourably upon these Gifts set before thee, O God, who standest in need of nothing ; and be well pleased with them for the honour of thy Christ,* &c.

* Supra quæ propitio ac sereno vultu respicere digneris.

(r) Lib. 8. c. 12.
Προσφέρομέν σοι ——τὸν ἄρτον τοῦτον κ͂ τὸ ποτήριον τοῦτο.—— κ͂ ἀξιοῦμέν σε, ὅπως εὐμενῶς ἐπιβλέψῃς ἐπὶ τὰ προκείμενα δῶρα ταῦτα ἐνώπιόν σε ὁ ἀνενδεὴς Θεὸς κ͂ εὐδοκήσῃς ἐπ᾽ αὐτοῖς εἰς τιμὴν τοῦ Χριςοῦ σε, &c.

Would it not run finely, to pray that God would be well pleased with Christ, for the honour of his Christ?

But besides the Petition, that God would look propitiously upon them, it follows in *the Canon, That God would accept them, as he did the Gifts of* Abel, *and* Abraham, *and* Melchisedeck. How unagreeable is this (if Christ himself be understood here) to make the Comparison for acceptance, betwixt a Lamb and a Calf, or Bread and Wine, and Christ the Son of God, with whom he was always highly pleased.

But then what follows still entangles Matters more in the *Church of Rome*'s Sense. The Prayer, That God *would command these things to be carried by the hands of his Holy Angel to the High Altar above.* For how can the Body of Christ be carried by Angels to Heaven, which never left it since his Ascension, but is always there? Besides the *High Altar above,* in the Sense of the *Ancients,* is Christ himself. And *Remigius* of *Auxerre* tells us (s), That S. *Gregory*'s Opinion of the Sacrament was, That *it was snatched into Heaven by Angels, to be joined to the Body of Christ there.* But then in the sense of Transubstantiation, what absurd stuff is here to pray, that Christ's Body may be joined to his own Body? So that there can be no sense in the Prayer, but ours, to understand it of the Elements offered devoutly, first at this Altar below, which by being blessed become Christ's Representative Body, and obtain acceptance above through his Intercession there. And thus it is fully explained, by the Author of the *Constitutions* (t); *Let us entreat God, through his Christ, for the Gift offered to the Lord God, that the good God, by the mediation of his Christ, would receive it to his Cœlestial Altar, for a sweet smelling Savour.*

To put the Matter further out of all doubt, it is observable, that the *Liturgies* that go under the name of S. *James,* and S. *Mark,* do both of them mention the acceptance of the Gifts of *Abel* and *Abraham,* and the admitting them to the *Cœlestial Altar,* before the reciting the words of the *Institution,*

(s) *De celebrat. Missa in Bibl. Pat.* 2dæ *Edit. Tom.* 6. *p.* 1164.
In Cœlo rapitur ministerio Angelorum consociandum corpori Christi.

(t) Lib. 8. c. 13. in initio.
Δεηθῶμέν τῦ Θεῦ διὰ τῦ Χριςῦ αὐτῦ, ὑπὲρ τῦ δώρε τῦ προσκομιθέντ@ κυρίῳ τῷ Θεῷ· ὅπως ὁ ἀγαθὸς Θεὸς προσδέξηται αὐτὸ διὰ τῆς μεσιτείας τῦ Χριςῦ αὐτῦ εἰς τὸ ἐπουράνιον αὐτῦ θυσιαςήριον εἰς ὀσμὴν εὐωδίας.

stitution, or *Consecration*, (as the Roman Church calls them, by which they say the Change is made). That the *Liturgy* of S. *Chrysostom* prays, That *God would receive the Oblations proposed to his Supercelestial Altar*, almost in the same words, both *before* and *after Consecration*; and that he look'd upon them to be the same in substance that they were before, plainly appears by an expression after all, where he prays (*u*), That *the Lord would make an equal division of the proposed Gifts to every one for good, according to every Man's particular need*. Which cannot be understood of Christ's proper Body, (but of the consecrated Bread and Wine) which cannot admit of shares or Portions, equal or unequal.

(*u*) Σὺ ἓν δεσπότα τὰ προκείμενα πᾶσιν ἡμῖν εἰς ἀγαθὸν ἐξομάλισον, κατ᾽ τὴν ἑκάστε ἰδίαν χρείαν.

Lastly, That S. *Basil's Liturgy* also, *before the Consecration*, prays, That the Oblations may be carried unto the *supercelestial Altar*, and be accepted as the Gifts of *Abel*, *Noah*, *Abraham*, &c. And to shew that even *after* the words of Institution, he did not believe them to be other things than they were before, he still calls them the *Antitypes* (*x*) *of the Body and Blood of Christ*; and prays, That *the Spirit may come upon us and upon the Gifts proposed, to bless and sanctify them, and to make this Bread the venerable Body of our Lord God and Saviour Jesus Christ, and this Cup his Blood, the Spirit working the change*.

(*x*) Προσθέντες τὰ ἀντίτυπα τῦ ἁγίε σώματ۞ κὴ αἷματ۞ τῦ Χριστῦ. — ἐλθεῖν τὸ πνεῦμα σε τὸ ἅγιον ἐφ᾽ ἡμᾶς κὴ ἐπὶ τὰ προκείμενα δῶρα ταῦτα, κὴ εὐλογῆσαι αὐτὰ, κὴ ἁγιάσαι κὴ ἀναδεῖξαι τ̄ μ̄ ἄρτον τῦτον αὐτὸ τὸ τίμιον σῶμα, &c.

And afterwards the Priest prays (*y*), That by *reason of his Sins, he would not divert the Grace of his Holy Spirit from the proposed Gifts*. A needless fear, if the Gifts were already Christ's Body, that the Spirit should be hindred from coming upon that, where all the Fulness of the God-head dwells bodily, by any Man's Sins.

(*y*) Μὴ διὰ τὰς ἡμᾶς ἁμαρτίας κωλύσῃς τὴν χάριν τῦ ἁγίε σε πνεύματ۞, ὑπὸ τ̄ν προκειμένων δώρων.

The next Passage of the *Canon* increases still the difficulty to them that believe Transubstantiation. When it says, *Through Jesus Christ our Lord, by whom, O Lord, thou dost always create, sanctify, quicken, bless and bestow all these good things on us*. If there be no good thing remaining in the Eucharist besides Christ, when these words are said, What Sense or Truth is there in them? Can Christ, or his Body that already exists, be created anew, and be always created?

Can

Can that be always *sanctified*, that was never *common*? Or, is he to be raised and quickned anew daily, that once being so raised, can die no more? *&c.* But that which makes the Absurdity of this Interpretation the greater, is, that they say that all this is done *to Christ by Christ* himself; as if God *by Christ* did *create Christ*; and *by Christ*, did *bless*, and *quicken*, and *sanctify Christ*; which none but he that is forsaken of common Sense can affirm.

(z) *In Bibl. Patr. Tom. 6. p. 1165.* Per Christum Deus Pater hæc omnia non solum in exordio creavit condendo, sed etiam *semper creat* præparando & reparando: *bona*, quia omnia à Deo creata valdè bona: creata & suis conspectibus oblata *sanctificat*, ut quæ erant simplex creatura, fiant Sacramenta: *vivificat*, ut sint mysteria vitæ: *Benedicit*, quia omni benedictione cœlesti & gratiâ accumulat. *Præstat nobis*, per eundem secum sanctificantem, qui de corpore suo & sanguine suo nobis tam salubrem dedit refectionem.

The old Interpreters of the Canon made other work of it, and supposed that the *Creatures offered* to God, *remained Creatures* still; for thus the forecited *Remigius* (z) comments upon them. *God the Father not only in the beginning,* created all these things *by Christ, but also always creates them, by preparing and repairing them.* Good, *because all things created by God are very good.* He sanctifies *those things so created and offered in his sight, when the things that were a simple Creature, are made Sacraments:* he quickens them, *so that they become Mysteries of Life:* He blesses them, *because he heaps all Celestial Benediction and Grace on them.* He bestows them on us, *by the same Christ sanctifying them with him, who has given to us so wholsom a repast from his Body and Blood.*

What can be also more plain than the words of the next Prayer I mentioned, *That what we have taken with our Mouth, may of a Temporal Gift be made an Eternal Remedy?* Did ever any one call Christ a *Temporal Gift,* in distinction from an *Eternal Remedy?* Is it not certain that the *Oblata,* the things offered, are the *Temporal Gift,* which by our due receiving them, become eternally beneficial to us?

The last Prayer also, which begs, That *the Body and Blood of Christ may cleave to their Bowels or Entrals,* cannot be interpreted of his *proper* and *natural Body*; since, as the Romanists confess, this Body can neither touch us, nor be touched by us, as it exists in the Sacrament, much less can *cleave or stick* to our Bodies. But the *representative* Body of Christ may; and he that made this Petition first, seems to tell us his *own Sense,* (tho' no very wise one) that he would not have this Holy Food to pass through him, as other Meats did (and which many

many of the Ancients thought this also did) but might remain and be confumed (as S. *Chryfoftom*'s phrafe is) with the Subftance of his Body.

Thus I think I have demonftrated fufficiently the firft thing I afferted at the beginning of this Chapter, *That the old Prayers in the Canon of the Mafs, concerning the Sacrament, agree not with the prefent Faith of the Roman Church.*

I proceed now to fhew the other thing, That *their New Prayers and Devotions to the Sacrament, have no countenance from the Ancient Church.*

I told the Reader before of their New Feftival, which the *Miffal* calls the *Feaft and Solemnity of the Body of Chrift.* They have fuited all things anfwerably to it; *New Prayers, New Hymns*; and their allowed *Books of Devotion*, have an *Office of the Bleffed Sacrament*, for one day of the Week, and a *New Litany*, &c. Which I fhall give now fome account of, and tho' all of them are not direct Prayers to it, yet they are fuch ftrains concerning it, and in fuch a new Stile, as has no old Example.

Thus tranflated in the Manual of Godly Prayers.

Miffal. Rom. in Solemn. corporis Chrifti.

O God, which under the Admirable Sacrament, haft left unto us the Memory of thy Paffion: grant, we befeech thee, that we may fo worfhip the Sacred Myfteries of thy Body and Blood, that continually we may feel in us the fruit of thy Redemption.
Who liveft, &c.

Oratio.
Deus qui nobis fub Sacramento mirabili paffionis tuæ memoriam reliquifti: tribue, quæfumus, ita nos corporis & fanguinis tui facra Myfteria venerari, ut redemptionis tuæ fructum in nobis jugiter fentiamus. Qui vivis, &c.

I believe the *Ancient Church* never thus prayed, that by the *worfhip of the Sacred Myfteries*, they *might feel the Fruit of Chrift's Redemption*; but that *they might fo receive the Sacred Myfteries*, &c. for they laid the ftrefs upon *worthy receiving*, as this Church do's upon *worfhipping*.

In an *Office of the Venerable Sacrament*, printed at *Colen*, 1591. they are still more particular.

Ibid. p. 72. ad completor.
Deus qui gloriosum corporis & sanguinis tui mysterium nobiscum manere voluisti: præsta, quæsumus, ita nos corporalem præsentiam tuam venerari in terris, ut ejus visione gaudere mereamur in cœlis. Qui vivis, &c.

O God, who wouldst have the glorious *Mystery* of thy Body and Blood to remain with us; grant, we pray thee, that we may so worship thy corporal Presence on Earth, that we may be worthy to enjoy the Vision of it in Heaven. Who liveft, &c.

Ibid. p. 44. ad primam.
Deus qui in passionis tuæ memoriam panem & vinum in corpus & sanguinem tuum mirabiliter transmutasti; concede propitius, ut qui in venerabili Sacramento tuam præsentiam corporalem credimus, ad contemplandam speciem tuæ celsitudinis perducamur. Qui vivis, &c.

Again thus;
O God, who in memory of thy Passion didst wonderfully change Bread and Wine into thy Body and Blood; mercifully grant, that we who believe thy Corporal Presence in the Venerable Sacrament, may be brought to the beholding of the appearance of thy Highness.

Who liveft, &c.

Rithmus S. Thomæ ad Sacram Euchariftiam; *Or a Rithm of Tho. Aquinas to the Holy Eucharift.*

In Missal. Rom. ad finem Orat. post Missam.
Adoro te devote latens Deitas,
Quæ sub his figuris vere latitas.
Tibi se cor meum totum subjicit,
Quia te contemplans totum deficit.
Visus, tactus, gustus in te fallitur,
Sed auditu solo tuto creditur.
Credo quicquid dixit Dei Filius.
Nil hoc verbo veritatis verius.
In cruce latebat sola Deitas,
At hic latet simul & humanitas:
Ambo tamen credens atque confitens,
Peto quod petivit Latro penitens.
Plagas, sicut Thomas, non intueor,
Deum tamen meum te confiteor.
Fac me tibi semper magis credere,
In te spem habere, te diligere.
O Memoriale Mortis Domini,
Panis vivus, vitam præstans homini;

I devoutly adore thee, O latent Deity,
Who under these Figures truly lieft hid.
My Heart submits it self wholly to thee, (me.
For when it contemplates thee, it wholly fails
Sight, tast, and touch, is deceived in thee,
Hearing alone a Man may safely trust.
Whatsoe'er the Son of God said, I believe.
Nothing is truer than this Word of Truth.
The Deity only on the Cross was hid,
Here the Humanity also is conceal'd:
But both believing and confessing both,
I ask what the Repenting Thief desir'd.
I do not see, as *Thomas* did, thy Wounds,
Yet I acknowledg thee to be my God.
O make me still more to believe in thee,
On thee to place my Hope, and thee to love.
O thou Memorial of my dying Lord,
Thou living Bread, and giving Life to Men,

Præsta   Grant

of the Ancient Church, relating to the Eucharist. 177

Præsta meæ menti de te vivere,
Et te illi semper dulcè sapere, &c.

Grant that my Soul on thee may ever live,
And thou to it mayst always sweetly tast, &c.

Another Sequence of Tho. Aquinas, which begins,
Lauda Sion Salvatorem.

In Missal. Rom. in festo Corp. Christi.
Docti Sacris institutis,
  Panem vinum in salutis
      Consecramus hostiam.
Dogma datur Christianis,
  Quod in carnem transit panis
      Et vinum in sanguinem.
Quod non capis, quod non vides,
  Animosa firmat fides
      Præter rerum ordinem.
Sub diversis speciebus,
  Signis tantum & non rebus
      Latent res eximiæ.
Caro cibus, sanguis potus;
  Manet tamen Christus totus
      Sub utrâq; specie.
A sumente non concisus,
  Non confractus, non divisus,
      Integer accipitur.
Sumit unus, sumunt mille,
  Quantum isti, tantum ille;
      Nec sumptus consumitur.
Sumunt boni, sumunt mali;
  Sorte tamen inequali
      Vitæ vel interitus.
Mors est malis, vita bonis;
  Vide paris sumptionis
      Quàm sit dispar exitus.
Fracto demum Sacramento,
  Ne vacilles, sed memento,
  Tantum esse sub fragmento,
      Quantum toto tegitur.
Nulla rei fit scissura,
  Signi tantum fit fractura;
  Qua nec status, nec statura
      Signati minuitur, &c.

Being taught by holy Lessons, we consecrate Bread and Wine for a saving Host.

It's a Maxim to Christians, that Bread is changed into Flesh, and Wine into Blood.

What thou dost not comprehend, or see, a strong Faith confirms it, besides the order of Nature.

Precious Things lie hid under different Species, which are Signs only, not Things.

The Flesh is Meat, and the Blood Drink, yet Christ remains whole under each Kind.

Uncut, unbroken, undivided, he is received whole by him that takes him.

When a thousand take him, one takes as much as they; nor is he consumed in taking.

The Good and Bad both take him, but their Lot is unequal in Life and Death.

He is Death to the Bad, and Life to the Good; behold an unlike end of a like taking.

When the Sacrament is broken,
Be not stagger'd, but remember,
There is as much in a Particle
As the whole covers.
Here is no division of the thing,
Only a breaking of the Sign;
Whereby neither the State nor Stature of the thing signified is diminished, &c.

Another Hymn of the same Author, which begins,
Pange lingua gloriosi.

In Breviar. Rom. in festo Corp. Christi.	*Thus translated in the Manual of Godly Prayers.*
In supremæ nocte cœnæ	At his last Supper made by Night,
Recumbens cum fratribus,	He with his Brethren takes his Seat,
Observata lege plenè	And having kept the Ancient rite
Cibis in legalibus ;	Using the Laws prescribed Meat ;
Cibum turbæ duodenæ	His twelve Disciples doth invite,
Se dat suis manibus.	From his own Hands himself to eat.
Verbum caro, panem verum	The Word made Flesh, to words imparts
Verbo carnem efficit,	Such strength, that Bread his Flesh is made,
Fitq; sanguis Christi merum,	He Wine into his Blood converts ;
Et si sensus deficit	And if our Sense here fail and fade,
Ad firmandum cor sincerum	To satisfy Religious Hearts,
Sola fides sufficit.	Faith only can the Truth perswade.
Tantum ergo Sacramentum	Then to this Sacrament so high,
Veneremur cernui :	Low rev'rence let us now direct,
Et antiquum documentum	Old Rites must yield in dignity
Novo cedat ritui :	To this, with such great Graces deckt :
Præstet fides supplementum	And Faith will all those Wants supply,
Sensuum defectui, &c.	Wherein the Senses feel defect, &c.

In another Hymn of Th. Aquinas, *which begins,* Verbum supernum prodiens, *they pray thus to the Sacrament.*

In Breviar. Rom. in Festo Corp. Christi.	
O salutaris Hostia,	O saving Host, that openest Heaven's Door,
Quæ Cœli pandis ostium:	Th' Arms of our Foes, do us enclose :
Bella premunt hostilia,	Thy strength we need ; O help with speed,
Da robur, fer auxilium.	We humbly thee implore.

There was published at *Paris,* with the approbation of three *Doctors of the Faculty* there, *An.* 1669. a little Book in French, called, *Practique pour Adorer le tres Saint Sacrament de l' Autel :* Or, *A Form for the Adoration of the most Holy Sacrament of the Altar.* Which begins thus :
Praised and adored be the most Holy Sacrament of the Altar.
And then adds ;
Whosoever shall say these Holy Words, [*Praised be the most Holy Sacrament of the Altar*] shall gain an hundred days
of

of Indulgences; and he that do's reverence, hearing them repeated, as much. He that, being confessed and communicated, shall say the above-said words, shall gain a Plenary Indulgence; and the first five times that he shall say them, after his having been Confessed and Communicated, he shall deliver five of his Friends-souls, whom he pleases, out of Purgatory.

Then follows the *Form for honouring the Holy Sacrament*, consisting of two Prayers, as follows, (which I shall set down in Latin and English, because I find them in the Hours of *Sarum*, Fol. 66. and in the S. *Litaniæ variæ*, p. 44. printed at *Colen*, 1643. The first of them has this Rubrick before it in the *Hours of Salisbury*. *Our Holy Father the Pope*, John xxii. *hath granted to all them that devoutly say this Prayer after the Elevation of our Lord Jesu Christ, three thousand days of Pardon for deadly Sins*).

Anima Christi sanctifica me.	Soul of Christ, sanctify me.
Corpus Christi salva me.	Body of Christ, save me.
Sanguis Christi inebria me.	Blood of Christ, inebriate me.
Aqua lateris Christi lava me.	Water of Christ's Side, wash me.
(Hor. Sar. *Splendor vultus Christi illumina me.*)	
Passio Christi conforta me.	Passion of Christ, comfort me.
(H.Sar.*Sudor vultus Christi virtuosissime sana me.*)	
O bone Jesu exaudi me.	O good Jesus hear me.
Intra vulnera tua absconde me.	Within thy Wounds hide me.
Ne permittas me separari à te.	Suffer me not to be separated from thee.
Ab hoste maligno defende me.	From the malicious Enemy defend me.
In hora mortis meæ voca me,	In the Hour of my Death call me,
Et jube me venire ad te;	And command me to come to thee,
Ut cum sanctis tuis laudem te	That with thy Saints I may praise thee,
In sæcula sæculorum. Amen.	For evermore. Amen.

At the Elevation of the Mass.

Hor. sec. us. Sar. Ibid. — *Thus translated in the Manual of Godly Prayers.*

Ave verum corpus natum De Maria Virgine;	All hail true Body, born of the Blessed Virgin *Mary*;
Vere passum, immolatum In cruce pro homine:	Truly suffered and offered upon the Cross for Mankind:
Cujus latus perforatum Unda fluxit sanguine.	Whose Side, pierced with a Spear, yielded Water and Blood.
Esto nobis præguslatum Mortis in examine.	Vouchsafe to be received of us in the Hour of Death.
O Clemens, O pie, O dulcis Fili Mariæ.	O good, O Jesu, Son of the Blessed Virgin, have mercy on me.

After this, the *French Form* adds what follows.

"These two good Prayers were found in the Sepulchre of our Lord Jesus Christ in *Jerusalem*; and whosoever carries them about him with Devotion, and in Honour of our Lord Jesus Christ, shall be delivered from the Devil, and from suddain Death, and shall not die of an ill Death. He shall be preserved from Pestilence, and all infectious Diseases. No Sorcerer, nor Sorcery, shall be able to hurt him or her, that has these two good Prayers about them. The Fire from Heaven shall not fall upon the House where these Prayers are rehearsed with devotion. A Woman with Child, saying them devoutly, shall be brought to Bed, without any danger of her own, or her Child's Death. Lightnings and Thunders shall not fall upon the Houses where these Prayers are rehearsed with Devotion. Such a one shall not die without Confession, and God will give him Grace to repent of his Sins.

Now I will add a Specimen of Litanies of the Sacrament.

Litaniæ de Sacramento: S. Litaniæ variæ p. 30.		*The Litany of the Sacrament in the Manual aforesaid.*	
——— Panis vivus qui de Cœlo descendisti		——— Living Bread that didst descend from Heaven	
Deus absconditus & Salvator		God hidden, and my Saviour	
Frumentum Electorum		Bread-Corn of the Elect	
Vinum germinans Virgines		Wine budding forth Virgins	
Panis pinguis & deliciæ Regum		Fat Bread, and the delight of Kings	
Juge Sacrificium	*Miserere nobis.*	Continual Sacrifice	*Have mercy on us.*
Oblatio munda		Pure Oblation	
Agnus absq; macula		Lamb without spot	
		(Manual adds) *Table of Proposition*	
Mensa purissima		Most pure Table	
Angelorum Esca		Food of Angels	
Manna absconditum		Hidden Manna	
Memoria mirabilium Dei		Memorial of God's wonderful Works	
Panis Supersubstantialis		Supersubstantial Bread	
Verbum caro factum habitans in nobis		Word made Flesh and dwelling in us	
Hostia Sancta		Holy Host	
Calix Benedictionis		Chalice of Benediction	
Mysterium		*Mystery*	

Mysterium fidei	Mystery of Faith
Præcelsum & venerabile Sacramentum	Most high and venerable Sacrament
Sacrificium omnium Sanctissimum	Sacrifice of all other most Holy
Vere propitiatorium pro vivis & defunctis	Truly propitiatory for the Quick and Dead
Cœleste Antidotum, quo à peccatis præservamur	Heavenly Antidote, whereby we are preserved from Sin
Stupendum supra omnia miraculum	Miracle above all other astonishing
Sacratissima Dominicæ passionis commemoratio	Most sacred Commemoration of our Lord's Death
Donum transcendens omnem plenitudinem	Gift surpassing all Fulness
Memoriale præcipuum divini amoris	Chief Memorial of Divine Love
Divinæ affluentia largitatis	Abundance of Divine Bounty
Sacrosanctum & augustissimum mysterium	Holy and most Majestical Mystery
Pharmacum immortalitatis	Medicine of Immortality
Tremendum ac vivificum Sacramentum	Dreadful and Life-giving Sacrament
Panis omnipotentia verbi caro factus	Bread by the Word's Omnipotence made Flesh
Incruentum Sacrificium	Unbloody Sacrifice
Cibus & conviva	Meat and Guest (*Manual omits*)
Dulcissimum convivium, cui assistunt Angeli ministrantes	Most sweet Banquet, whereat the Ministring Angels attend
Sacramentum Pietatis	Sacrament of Piety
Vinculum Charitatis	Bond of Charity
Offerens & Oblatio	Offerer and Oblation
Spiritualis dulcedo in proprio fonte degustata	Spiritual sweetness tasted in its proper Fountain
Refectio animarum Sanctarum	Refection of Holy Souls
Viaticum in Domino morientium	Viaticum of those who die in our Lord
Pignus futuræ gloriæ, &c.	Pledge of future Glory, *&c.*

Miserere nobis. — *Have mercy on us.*

This is enough to shew into what strains of Devotion the present *Roman Church* now runs, since Transubstantiation is an Article of its Faith. I deny not that these Prayers are very natural if that Doctrine were true; and I would fain have a good Reason assigned, why, if this Doctrine was believed of old, this was not the way of the *Primitive Devotion:* If they affirm that it was, it lies upon them to produce the evidence. But then let me tell them before-hand, that we will not be shamm'd off with *a Rhetorical Prosopopœia* of an Author, under the name of S. *Denis the Areopagite* (which has been the only thing I have seen alledged, and as often answered) whose Authority neither cannot be considerable to us, who remember that he was first produced and shown to the World by Hereticks, and rejected by the Orthodox. CHAP.

CHAP. XVI.

The Sixteenth Difference.

Our Ancient Roman-Saxon Church differred from the present Roman Church, in the Article of Transubstantiation and Corporal Presence.

THis is the Last Difference I shall mention, tho' not the least; but a very material confirmation of what I have been all along proving, That there is no consent of the Ancient Church with the present Roman Church, in their Faith and Opinions about the Eucharist; when we shall find, that even our own *Old English Church*, that had received most of its Instructions in Christianity from the Roman, and in many other things agreed with what it now professes, yet in this widely differ'd from it.

This plainly argues one of these two things, either that the *then Roman Church*, had not the Opinions of the present Church in these Matters and so did not propagate them to us; (which cannot be said, when we remember the busy Disputes about these Matters in the 9th Century, tho' they were not yet come to a determination); or else, that when the Roman Church warped, and generally espoused a New Doctrine which the Ancient Fathers were strangers to, we still kept our Ground, and did not suffer our selves to be perverted, but held to the Ancient Belief.

This is the Truth of our Case, as appears by a noble Remain of an *Easter Sermon* (about 700 Years old) in the Saxon Tongue, among other Catholick Homilies that were to be read yearly in the Church. It was produced in the last Age in the Saxon with a Translation in our English Tongue; (printed by *John Day*) it was since put, with the same Translation, by Mr. *Fox* into his Martyrology *, and has been set forth with a Latin Translation by the Learned *Abr. Whelock*, in his *Saxon Edition* of *Bede's* Ecclesiastical History, p. 462.

* *Vol. 2. p. 380. last Edition.*

printed at *Cambridg* 1644. out of which I shall transcribe as much as will serve to prove our Assertion, softning the harshness of the Phrases of the last Age, and expressing the sense in words more easily understood.

The Easter Sermon begins thus:

"MEN Beloved, you have been often discoursed to,
" concerning our Saviour's Resurrection, how he, after
" his Passion on this Day, rose powerfully from the Dead.
" Now we shall, by God's Grace explain something to you
" about the Holy Eucharist, which this day we are bound to
" frequent, and instruct your understanding about this My-
" stery, both according to the Old and New Testament, that
" no doubting may disturb you concerning this Life-giving
" Banquet.———

The Sermon goes on with an account of the Jewish Passover, and the Application of those things to the Eucharist, which I omit;

"————Christ, before his suffering, consecrated Bread, P. 469.
" and distributed it to his Disciples, saying thus, *Eat this*
" *Bread, it is my Body, and do this in remembrance of me*: Also
" he Consecrated Wine in a Cup, and said, *Drink ye all of*
" *this, This is my Blood which is shed for many for the Remission of*
" *Sins.* The Apostles did, as Christ commanded, they con-
" secrated Bread and Wine for the Eucharist: And to his
" memory also afterward every one of their Successors, and
" all Christ's Priests, According to Christ's Command, by the
" Apostolical Benediction, did consecrate Bread and Wine
" in his Name. Now Men have often disputed, and do it P. 470.
" still, How that Bread which is prepared of Corn, and is ba-
" ked by the heat of Fire, can be changed into Christ's Body;
" and how that Wine which is pressed out of many Grapes,
" by any blessing of it, can be changed into our Lord's Blood?
" Now to such Men, I answer, that some things are spoken
" of Christ *by signification*, some others by a *known thing*: It
" is a true thing, and known, that Christ was born of a Vir-
" gin, and voluntarily suffered Death, and was buried, and
this

"this Day rose from the Dead. He is called *Bread*, and a
"*Lamb*, and *a Lion*, and otherwise, by *signification*. He is
"called *Bread*, because he is our Life, and the Life of Angels.
"He is called a *Lamb*, for his Innocency. A *Lion*, for his
"Strength, whereby he overcame the strong Devil. Yet
"notwithstanding, according to true Nature, Christ is nei-
"ther *Bread*, nor a *Lamb*, nor a *Lion*. Wherefore then is
"that Holy Eucharist called *Christ's Body*, or *his Blood*, if it
"be not truly what it is called? Truly the Bread and Wine,
"which are consecrated by the Mass of the Priests, show one
"thing outwardly to Mens Senses, and another thing they de-
"clare inwardly to believing Minds. Outwardly, Bread and
"Wine are seen both in appearance, and in tast; yet they
"are truly after Consecration Christ's Body and Blood,
"by *a Spiritual Sacrament*. An Heathen Child is Baptized,
"yet he altereth not his outward shape, though he be chan-
"ged within. He is brought to the Font full of Sin through
"*Adam's* Disobedience, but he is washed from all his Sins in-
"wardly, tho' he has not changed his outward Shape. So al-
"so that Holy Font-Water, which is called the Well-spring
"of Life, is like in Nature *(in specie)* to other Waters, and
"is subject to corruption; but the Power of the Holy Ghost,
"by the Priest's Blessing, comes upon that corruptible Wa-
"ter; and after that, it can wash both Body and Soul from

p. 471.

"all Sins, by spiritual Power. We see now in this one Crea-
"ture two things: that, whereby, according to true Nature,
"it is corruptible Water, and that whereby, according to
"the Spiritual Mystery, it has a saving Power. So also, if
"we look upon that Holy Eucharist according to a corporeal
"Sense, then we see that it is a Creature corruptible and
"changeable; but if we own a spiritual Power there, then
"we understand that Life is in it, and that it confers Im-
"mortality on those that tast it by Faith. There is a great
"difference betwixt the insible Vertue (and Power) of this
"Holy Eucharist, and the visible appearance of its proper
"Nature. By its Nature it is corruptible Bread, and corrup-
"tible Wine; and by the Virtue of the Divine Word, it
"is *truly* the Body and Blood of Christ; yet not *corporally* so,
"but *spiritually*. There is much differencce betwixt that Bo-
"dy which Christ suffer'd in, and that Body which is consecrated

" secrated for the Eucharist. The Body that Christ suffer'd
" in, was Born of the Flesh of *Mary*, with Blood and Bones,
" with Skin and Nerves; animated by a rational Spirit in hu-
" mane Members: but his *Spiritual Body*, which we call the
" Eucharist, is collected from many grains of Corn, without
" Blood and Bone, without Member or Soul: wherefore
" there is nothing in it to be understood *Corporeally*, but all
" is to be understood *Spiritually*. Whatsoever is in that Eu-
" charist which restores Life to us, this is from Spiritual Vir-
" tue, and from invisible Operation. Therefore that Holy
" Eucharist is called a Sacrament, because one thing is there
" seen, and another thing understood: that which is there seen
" has a *bodily Nature*, that which we understand in it has *a*
" *spiritual Virtue*. The Body of Christ, that suffered Death, P. 472.
" and rose from the Dead, henceforth dies no more, but is
" eternal and impassible. That Eucharist is Temporary, not
" Eternal; it is corruptible, and capable of division into mi-
" nute Parts; it is chewed with the Teeth, and sent into the
" draught; yet it will be true, that *according to spiritual Vir-*
" *tue*, it is whole in every part: Many receive that Holy Bo-
" dy, yet according to the spiritual Mystery, it will be whole
" in every part. Tho' some receive a lesser part of it, yet
" there will not be more virtue in the greater part than in the
" lesser, because it will be whole in all Men according to the
" invisible virtue. This Sacrament is a *Pledg*, and a *Type*; the
" Body of Christ is *the Truth:* We keep this Pledg Sacra-
" mentally, till we come to the Truth it self; and then is
" the Pledg at an end. It is indeed, as we said before, Christ's
" Body and his Blood, but not *Corporally*, but *Spiritually*. Do
" not dispute, how this can be effected, but believe it firmly,
" that so it is.

*Here follow some idle Visions, which that credulous Age were
fond of, but are nothing to the purpose, and therefore I omit
them.*

" ———— *Paul* the Apostle speaketh of the old Israelites P. 473.
" writing thus in his Epistle to the Faithful. *All our Fore-fa-*
" *thers were baptized in the Cloud and in the Sea; and all ate the*
" *same spiritual Meat, and all drank the same spiritual Drink*,
" *for*

B b

"for they drank of that spiritual Rock, and that Rock was
"Christ. That Rock, from whence the Water then flowed,
"was not Christ in a *Corporal Sense*, but it signified Christ,
"who declared thus to the Faithful, *Whosoever thirsteth, let him*
"*come to me and drink, and from his belly shall flow living Wa-*
"*ter.* This he said of the Holy Ghost, which they that Believed
"on him, should receive. The Apostle *Paul* said, that the Peo-
"ple of *Israel ate the same spiritual Meat, and drank the same Spi-*
"*ritual Drink*, because the heavenly Food that fed them for
"forty Years, and that Water that flowed from the Rock,
"signified Christ's Body and Blood, which are now dayly of-
"fered in the Church of God. It was the same which we
"offer to day, not *corporally*, but *spiritually*. We told you
"before, that Christ consecrated Bread and Wine for the
"Eucharist before his Passion, and said, This is my Body, and
"my Blood: he had not yet suffered, and yet he changed,
"by his invisible Power, that Bread into his Body, and that
"Wine into his Blood; as he did before in the Wilderness,
"before he was born Man, when he turned the heavenly Food
"into his Flesh, and that Water flowing from the Rock into his

P. 474.

"Blood. Many Persons ate of the Heavenly Food in the Desart,
"and drank of the Spiritual Drink, and yet, as Christ said, are
"dead. Christ meant not that Death which no Man can avoid,
"but he understood eternal Death, which several of that Peo-
"ple, for their Unbelief, had deserved. *Moses* and *Aaron*, and
"several others of the People that pleased God, ate that hea-
"venly Bread, and did not die that everlasting Death, tho'
"they died the common Death. They saw that the heavenly
"Food was visible and Corruptible; but they understood
"that visible thing *spiritually*, and they tasted *it spiritually*.
"Jesus said, *Whoso eateth my Flesh, and drinketh my Blood,*
"*hath Eternal Life:* He did not command them to eat that
"Body which he had assumed, nor to drink that Blood which
"he shed for us; but by that Speech, he meant the Holy Eu-
"charist, which is *Spiritually* his Body, and his Blood; and who-
"soever tasteth this, with a believing Heart, shall have that
"Eternal Life. Under the old Law, the Faithful offered di-
"vers Sacrifices to God, which had a future signification
"of the Body of Christ, which he hath offered in Sacrifice
"to his heavenly Father for our Sins. This Eucharist which
"is

of the Ancient Church, relating to the Eucharist.

"is now confecrated at God's Altar, is a Commemoration of the Body of Chrift which he offered for us, and of his Blood which he fhed for us: As he himfelf commanded, *Do this in remembrance of me.* Chrift once fuffered by himfelf; but yet his Paffion by the Sacrament of this Holy Euchariſt, is daily renewed at the Holy Maſs. Wherefore the Holy Maſs is profitable very much both for the Living, and alſo for the Dead, as it hath been often declared, &c.

The reſt of the Sermon being of a moral and allegorical Nature, I omit.

Befides this Sermon in Publick, we have alſo two other Remains of *Elfrike* the Abbot in the Saxon Tongue*, which fpeak the very fame Senſe, and deferve to be inferted as far as they concern this Argument of the Eucharist, and the change made in it.

* *Publiſhed at the end of the foreſaid Sermon, printed by* John Day. *Alſo in the Notts on* Bede's *Eccl. Hiſt.* p. 332, 333, 334.

The firſt is *an Epiſtle to* Wulffine *Biſhop of Shyrburn*, in which is this Paſſage.

"―――― The Euchariſt is not the Body of Chrift *corporally*, but *ſpiritually*: not the Body in which he fuffered, but that Body when he confecrated Bread and Wine for the Euchariſt, the night before his Paffion, and faid of the Bread he Bleffed, *This is my Body*; and again of the Wine he bleffed, *This is my Blood, which is ſhed for many for the Remiſſion of Sins.* Now then underſtand, that the Lord, who was able to change that Bread before his Paffion into his Body, and that Wine into his Blood, *Spiritually*; that the fame *(Lord)* by the Hands of the Prieſts, daily confecrates Bread and Wine for his Spiritual Body, and for his Spiritual Blood.

The second, an *Epistle of Elfricke to Wulfstane Arch-Bishop of York*, in which, among other things (against too long reserving the Eucharist,) he says thus:

Vid. p. 334.
Hist. Eccles.
Sax.Lat.Beds.

"Christ himself consecrated the Eucharist before his Passion; he blessed Bread, and brake it, saying thus to his Apostles, *Eat this Bread, it is my Body:* and again he blessed the Cup, filled with Wine, and spake thus to them, *Drink ye all of this, it is my Blood of the New Testament, which is shed for many for the Remission of Sins.* Our Lord, who consecrated the Eucharist before his Passion, and said; that Bread was his Body, and Wine truly his Blood, he also daily consecrates, by the Priests hands, Bread for his Body, and Wine for his Blood, in a Spiritual Mystery, as we read in Books. [Yet notwithstanding that Lively Bread is not the same Body in which Christ suffered, nor that Holy Wine the Blood of our Saviour (which was shed for us) in bodily thing *(or sence, in re corporali)* but in a Spiritual sence *(in ratione Spirituali.)* That Bread indeed was his Body, and also that Wine his Blood, just as that heavenly Bread which we call Manna (which fed God's People forty Years) *viz. was his Body*, and that clear Water was his Blood that then flowed from the Rock in the Wilderness.] As *Paul* writes in his Epistle, They all ate the same spiritual Meat and drank the same spiritual Drink, &c. The Apostle that says, what you have heard, They all ate &c. he do's not say, *corporally*, but spiritually. Christ was not as yet born, nor his Blood shed: then it was the People of *Israel* did eat that Spiritual Meat, and drank of that Rock; neither was that Rock Christ Corporeally tho' he spake so. The Sacraments of the Old Law were the same, and did spiritually signify that Sacrament (or Eucharist) of our Saviour's Body, which we now consecrate."

This Last Epistle *Elfricke* wrote first in the Latin Tongue to *Wulfstane*, containing, tho' not word for word, yet the whole Sence of the English Epistle; and that Paragraph of it which I have inclosed between two Brackets, was look'd upon as so disagreeable to the present Faith of the Roman Church,

of the Ancient Church, relating to the Eucharist.

Church, that some had rased them out of the *Worcester* Book; but the same Latin Epistle being found in *Exeter* Church, it was restored.

I was once about to have added some Citations here out of *Bertram*'s Book, (*de corpore & sanguine Domini*) out of which many passages in the Saxon Sermon foregoing, were taken. But they are so many, that I must have transcribed, and the Book it self is small, and so well worth the reading, especially with the late Translation of it into English, and a Learned Historical Dissertation before it, giving a large account of the Difference betwixt his Opinion, and that of Transubstantiation (printed *An* 1686) that I shall rather refer the Reader to it, where he may abundantly satisfy himself.

Instead of it, I will only add one Testimony more out of *Rabanus* Arch-bishop of *Mentz*, in an Epistle to *Heribaldus* *. Which we are beholden to the Learned *Baluzius* for giving it us entire, (*in Appendice ad Reginonem*, p. 516.) a Passage having been rased out of the *Manuscript*, out of which it was first published. Thus he says;

* Epist. ad Heribrib. c. 33. de Eucharist.

As for the Question you put, Whether the Eucharist, after it is consumed and sent into the Draught as other Meats are, do's return again into its former Nature, which it had before it was consecrated on the Altar; This Question is superfluous, when our Saviour himself has said in the Gospel, *Every thing that entreth into the Mouth, goeth into the Belly, and is cast out into the Draught.* The Sacrament of the Body and Blood, is made up of things Visible and Corporeal, but effects the Invisible Sanctification both of Body and Soul. And what reason is there, that what is digested in the Stomach,

Quod autem interrogastis, utrum Eucharistia postquam consumitur & in secessum emittitur, more aliorum ciborum, iterum redeat in naturam pristinam quam habuerat, antequam in Altari consecraretur, superflua est hujusmodi Quæstio, cùm ipse Salvator dixerit in Evangelio, *Omne quod intrat in os, in ventrem vadit, & in secessum emittitur.* Sacramentum Corporis & Sanguinis ex rebus visibilibus & corporalibus conficitur, sed invisibilem tàm corporis quàm animæ efficit sanctificationem. Quæ est enim ratio, ut hoc quod stomacho digeritur, & in secessum emittitur, iterum in statum pristinum redeat, cum nullus hoc unquam fieri asseruerit? Nam quidam nuper de ipso Sacramento corporis & sanguinis Domini non rite sentientes dixerunt, hoc ipsum corpus & sanguinem Domini quod de Maria Virgine natum est, & in quo ipse Dominus passus est in Cruce, & resurrexit de sepulchro, [*Idem esse quod sumitur de altari*] cui errori quantum potuimus, ad *Egilonem Abbatem* scribentes, de corpore ipso quid verè credendum sit, aperuimus.

and

and sent into the Draught, shou'd return into its pristine State, seeing none has ever asserted that this was done? Some indeed of late, not thinking rightly of the Sacrament of our Lord's Body and Blood have said *(which are the very words of* Paschasius, *whom he opposes)* that the very Body and Blood of our Lord, which was born of the *Virgin Mary*, and in which our Lord suffered on the Cross, and rose again out of the Grave, [*is the same that is taken from the Altar*]; which Error we having opposed as we were able, writing to the Abbot *Egilo*, and declared what ought truly to be believed concerning the Body it self.

That which he calls here an *Error*, is an *Article* now of the *Romish Faith*, which some *Zealous Monk* meeting withal, and not enduring it should be condemned as an Error, that the same Body which was born of the Virgin, *&c.* is the same that we receive at the Altar, scraped out those words which I have inclosed between the Brackets; and we may securely trust our Adversaries in this Matter, who have skill enough to know what Assertions make for them, and what against them.

C H A P.

CHAP. XVII.

The CONCLUSION.

That the Doctrine of Transubstantiation has given a new occasion to the Enemies of Christian Religion to blaspheme. It is so great a stumbling-block to the Jews, that their Conversion is hopeless, whilst this is believed by them to be the Common Faith of Christians. That tho' the Church of Rome will not hearken to us, yet they may be provoked to emulation by the Jews themselves, who have given a better account of Christ's Words of Institution, and more agreeable to the Fathers, than this Church has; and raised unanswerable Objections against its Doctrine.

HAving considered, in the foregoing Chapters, the Sense of the Ancient Church about Matters relating to the Eucharist, and Transubstantiation, from their own Writings; and found that their Assertions are inconsistent with the Belief of the present Roman Church; and that their Practices are not to be reconciled thereunto. Having also made an Enquiry into the Ancient forms of Devotion, relating to the Eucharist, remaining still in this Church, and found them to speak a Language, which has a Sence agreeing indeed with that of the Ancients, but no Sence at all, when the Doctrine of Transubstantiation is supposed, and those Prayers to be interpreted by it, &c.

I shall now, for a Conclusion, take a view also of the principal Enemies of the Christian Faith; which will afford a convincing Evidence, that the Roman Doctrine is Novel, and a stranger to the Ancient Christians.

It is sufficiently known, that the Adversaries of Christianity took all the occasions possible, and whatsoever gave them any colour to reproach the *Faith* and *Worship* of Christians, and to make their Names odious. Nothing that looked strange and absurd in either, escaped, being taken notice of by such as *Celsus* and *Porphyry*, *Lucian* and *Julian*, among the Heathens,

Heathens, and such as *Trypho* among the Jews. They curiously examined and surveyed what they taught and practised, and whatsoever they thought to be foolish and incredible, they, with all their wit and cunning, endeavoured to expose it. So, they did with the Doctrines of the *Trinity*, the *Eternal Generation of the Son of God*, his *Incarnation*, his *Crucifixion* especially, and *our Resurrection*. Neither were they less praying into the Christian *Mysteries* and *Worship*, which they could not be ignorant of, there being so many Deserters and Apostates in those Times of Persecution, who were well acquainted with them; and by threatnings and fear of torment if there were any thing secret were likely to betray them. Not to insist upon this, that the great Traducer of Christians, I mean *Julian*, was himself once initiated in their Mysteries, and so could not be Ignorant of what any of them were; and has in particular laught at their Baptism, that Christians should fansy a purgation thereby from Great Crimes.

Yet, after all this, they took no occasion from the Eucharist to traduce them; tho, if Christians then had given that adoration to it, that is now paid in the Roman Church, and if they had declared, either for a *Corporal Presence*, or an *oral Manducation* of him that was their God, they had the fruitfullest Subject in the World given them, both to turn off all the Objections of the Christians against themselves, for worshipping senseless and inanimate things; and also to lay the most plausible Charge of folly and madness against them, which their great Orator * had pronounced, before Christianity was a Religion in the World. *Can any Man be supposed so mad to believe that to be a God which he eats?*

A Learned Romanist † affirms, of the Ancient Christians, *That they did testify their eating the Flesh, and drinking the Blood of their Lord God in their Discourses of the Eucharist*. Which is true indeed, taking this eating and drinking in the Sacramental Sence we do; and so their Adversaries must needs understand their meaning. Otherwise (without a Miracle to hinder it) what he acknowledges in the same place, could never

---

* *Cicero, l. 3. de Nat. Deorum.* Ecquem tam amentem esse putas, qui illud quo vescatur, Deum credat esse?

† *Rigaltius notis ad Tertul. lib. 2. c. 5. ad Uxorem.* Se id facere in Eucharisticis suis testarentur.

of the Ancient Church, relating to the Eucharist. 193

never be true, (a) *That among so many Reproaches of those that accused Christians of Impiety, for not having Altars nor Sacrifices, and among so many false Brethren that were Turn-coats, yet there were none that made this an Accusation against them, that they ate the Flesh of their God and Lord, and drank his Blood.*

We have this ingenuous confession of *Bellarmine* himself (*), *That we might be accounted truly Fools, if without the Word of God, we believed the true Flesh of Christ to be eaten with the Mouth of our Bodies.* But whether *with* or *without* the Word of God they believed such a corporal eating of Christ's Flesh, had been all one to the Heathens, if they knew that this was their Belief, and it would rather have strengthned their Reproach, if they knew that they were bound thus to believe. But then what he adds is very remarkable, *That Infidels always counted this a most foolish Paradox, as appears from* Averroes *and others.* I believe indeed, that they must always count this a foolish Paradox, which *Averroes* charged Christians withal, in that known Saying of his (b). *That he found no Sect worse, or more foolish, than the Christians, who tear with their Teeth, and devour that God whom they worship.* But why was not this cast always in the Teeth of Christians, if this was always their professed Doctrine? Was *Celsus*, or *Julian*, or *Lucian*, less sagacious, or less malicious than *Averroes*, that not a word of this *foolish Paradox* was ever so much as hinted by them to the reproach of Christians then?

But the *Cardinal* has instanced the most unluckily in the World, in naming only *Averroes* for this Calumny, when all acknowledg that this *Philosopher*, & P. *Innocent* 3. (who establish'd *Transubstantiation*) lived in the same Age; and some very learned Men prove, from the *Arabian* Accounts, that those two were Contemporaries. And as for his [*& aliis*] *others,* I should be glad

(a) *Ibid.* Observandum vero, inter tot probra & convitia accusantium Christianos impietatis, eò quod neq; aras haberent neq; sacrificarent, interq; tot fratrum perfidorum transfugia, non extitisse qui Christianos criminarentur, quod Dei ac Domini sui carnes ederent, sanguinem potarent.

(*) *De Eucharist.* l.2. c. 12. Verè stulti haberi possemus, si absq; Verbo Dei crederemus veram Christi carnem ore corporali manducari.

Nam id semper infideles stultissimum paradoxum æstimârunt, ut notum est de A-verroe & aliis.

(b) Se Sectam Christianâ deteriorem aut ineptiorem nullam reperire, quam qui sequuntur, ii quem colunt Deum dentibus ipsi suis discerpunt ac devorant.

Cc

to see any named, that urged what *Averroes* did to the Christians reproach, before the days of *Berengarius*.

After that indeed, we can meet with a Follower of *Mahomet*; who (as a Learned Man (c) gives us his words) says thus, *Those words of Christ*, He that eateth my Flesh, and drinketh my Blood, he is in me, and I in him, &c. *Christians understand them literally, and so Christians are more cruel against Christ, than Jews; for they left Christ when they had slain him, but these eat his Flesh, and drink his Blood, which as experience testifies, is more savage.*

(c) *Hottinger* in *Eucharistia Rijensa*, S. II. 14. p. 220. *Aomed bin Edris* ita scribit, verba autem *Isa* (sic Arabes Christum vocant) super quo pax, *Qui edit carnem meam & bibit sanguinem*, &c. Christiani literaliter intelligunt. Atq; sic Christiani atrociores sunt in Christum quàm Judæi. Illi enim Christum occisum reliquerunt; hi carnem ejus edunt & sanguinem bibunt, quod ipso teste experientia, truculentius est.

. .

After the Roman Church's declaring for Transubstantiation, (though not before) we meet with the Oppositions of *Jews*, testifying their abhorrency (d) of a Doctrine, which talks of a Sacrifice, and *makes Bread to be the Body of their God*, (which he means in the sence of Transubstantiation, by being turned into it, and cloathed with its Accidents) *whose Body that is in Heaven, comes upon the Altar; and upon the pronouncing these words*, For this is my Body, *by the Priest, whether good or wicked is all one, all things are made one Body with the Body of the Messias*, &c.
——*Which things are all repugnant to the first Principles of Reason, and to our very Senses themselves.*
As he afterwards shows in several Instances.

(d) *Ibid. Joseph. Albo de Ikkarim*, lib. 3. cap. 25. Nam panis est corpus Dei ipsorum. Aiunt enim corpus Jesu quod est in Cœlis, venire in Altare & vestiri pane & vino, post pronunciata verba, *Hoc enim est Corpus meum*, à sacrificulo, qualiscunque ille demum fuerit, sive pius sive impius, & omnia fieri Corpus unum cum corpore Messiæ, &c.
—— Repugnant hic omnia Intelligibilibus primis, & ipsis etiam sensibus.

And now we are told that it is a *common Bye-word* to reproach a Christian by among the Turks, to call him *Mange Dieu*.

All these took their rise plainly from *Transubstantiation*, and not from the *Faith of the Ancient Church:* For if one of it (e) may speak for the rest, the *Old Christians* agreed in the Abhorrence, and called it, *the extreamest stupidity to worship that which is eaten.*

(e) *Theodoret. Interrog.* 55. in *Genes.* Ἀθεότητος ἐσχάτης προσκυνεῖν τὸ ἐσθιόμενον.

And

of the Ancient Church, relating to the Eucharist. 195

And again;
How can any one of a sound Mind call that a God, which being offered to the True God, is afterwards eaten by him?

Id. qu. 11. in Levit. Πῶς γὰρ ἄν τις σωφρονῶν τ— ὀνομάσοι Θεὸν—τὸ τῷ ἀληθινῷ Θεῷ προσφερόμενον, καὶ παρ᾽ αὐτοῦ ἐσθιόμενον;

But now, after all, the saddest Consideration is, that the Prejudices are so great against this, (and another *Twin-Doctrine* of the Roman Church, about the *worship of Images*) that a perpetual Stumbling-block seems to be laid before the Jews; and it may be look'd upon as the τὸ κατέχον, that which *will* always *hinder* and obstruct their Conversion, whilst it is believed by them to be the common Sence and Faith of Christians; and they have too great a Temptation to believe so, when they have seen this Church, which has got the most worldly Power into its hands, persecuting not only *Jews*, but *Hereticks* (as they call all other Christians that deny this Doctrine) to the Death for gainsaying it; and when that Work will cease, God only knows. The Jews can never be supposed to get over this hard Chapter, whilst they who call themselves the only Catholick Christians, hold such things about the *Body of Christ*, (and remember that it is about a Body) which as the forenamed *Jos. Albo* (*f*) speaks, *No Man's Mind can conceive, nor Tongue utter, nor any Ear can hear.* He means, by reason of their absurdity.

(*f*) *Ibid.* Ista talia sunt quæ mens non potest concipere, neq; os eloqui, neq; auris audire.

So that the Case of the Jews, and their Conversion, seems to be hopeless and desperate, according to all humane guesses, till there be a change wrought (not in the substance of the Bread and Wine this Church dreams of, but) in the *Romanist's* Belief. And though this also may seem, upon many accounts, to be as hopeless as the former, yet, for a Conclusion, I will try, whether, as once the Great Apostle thought it a wise method (*Rom.* 11. 14.) by the Example of the Gentiles, παραζηλῶσαι, to provoke the Jews to *Emulation*; so it may not be as proper, to propose the Example of the *Jews* themselves to the *Romanists*, to provoke their Emulation, whom they may see better explaining (as blind as they are) Christ's

Cc 2   words

words of Inftitution; and agreeing better with the Ancient Church in the matter of the Eucharift, than themfelves; and raifing fuch Arguments and Objections againft the Tranfubftantiating Doctrine, as can never, to any purpofe, be anfwered.

The Inftances of this are very remarkable, in a Book called *Fortalitium Fidei contra Judeos*, &c. printed *An.* 1494. but written, as the Author himfelf tells us *(fol.* 61.*)* in the Year 1458. where he gives us the Arguments of a Jew againft Tranfubftantiation; fome of which I fhall out of him faithfully tranflate.

(*g*) *Vid. l. 3.*
confid. 6. fol. 130
impoffibl. 10.

The Jew (*g*) begins with Chrift's words of Inftitution, and fhows, that they cannot be interpreted otherwife than figuratively, and fignificatively, as the Fathers, we have heard, have afferted.

"1. Vos Chriftiani dicitis, &c. Ye Chriftians fay in that
"Sacrament *(of the Eucharift)* there is really the Body and
"Blood of Chrift. This is impoffible. Becaufe when your
"Chrift, fhowing the Bread, faid, *This is my Body*, he fpake
"*fignificatively*, and not *really*; as if he had faid, this is the
"Sign or Figure of my Body. After which way of fpea-
"king, Paul faid, 1 *Cor.* 10. *The Rock was Chrift*; that is,
"a Figure of Chrift. And it appears evidently, that this
"was the Intention of your Chrift, becaufe when he had dif-
"courfed about the eating his Body, and drinking his Blood,
"to lay the offence that rofe upon it among the Difciples, he
"fays, as it were, expounding himfelf, *The words that I have
"fpoken to you are Spirit and Life*: denoting, that what he
"had faid, was to be underftood, not according to the Let-
"ter, but according to the Spiritual Sence. And when Chrift
"faid, *This is my Body*, holding Bread in his Hands, he
"meant, that that Bread was his Body *(in potentia propin-
"qua)* in a near poffibility, *viz.* after he had eaten it, for
"then it would be turned into his Body, or into his Flefh;
"and fo likewife the Wine. And after this manner we Jews
"do, on the day of Unleavened Bread; for we take unlea-
"vened Bread in memory of that time, when our Fathers
"were brought out of the Land of *Egypt*, and were not per-
"mitted

of the Ancient Church, relating to the Eucharist.

"mitted to stay so long there, as whilst the Bread might be
"leavened, that was the Bread of the Passover; and we say,
"*This is the Bread which our Fathers ate*, though that be not
"present, since it is past and gone; and so this unleavened
"Bread, minds us of the Bread of *Egypt*, and *this Bread is
"not that*; so is that Bread of which the Sacrifice of the Al-
"tar is made. It is sufficient for Christians to say, that it is
"in memory of that Bread of Christ, though *this Bread be
"not that*. And because it was impossible that one Bit of his
"Flesh should be preserved in memory of him, he command-
"ed, that that Bread should be made, and that Wine, which
"was his Flesh and Blood in the next remove to come into
"act; as we Jews do, (*and Christ borrowed his Phrases and
"the Elements from their Supper*) at the Passover with the un-
"leavened Bread, as we said before. When therefore your
"Christ at the Table took Bread, and the Cup, and gave
"them to his Disciples, he did not bid them believe that the
"Bread and Wine were turned into his Body and Blood, but
"that as often as they did that, they should do it in remem-
"brance of him, *viz.* in memory of that past Bread: and
"if you Christians did understand it so, no impossibility
"would follow; but to say the contrary, as you assert, is
"to say an impossible thing, and against the intention of your
"Christ, as we have show'd.

This is what the Jew urges with great reason. But the Catholick Author makes a poor Answer to it, and has nothing to say, in effect, but this, *That the Tradition of the Catholick Church concerning this Sacrament is true.* viz. *That in this Sacrament there is really, and not by way of Signification, the True Body and True Blood of Christ.*

2. Whereas the Roman Church flies to Miracles in this case of Transubstantiation, the Jew encounters that next of all, thus.

"You Christians say that the Body and Blood of Christ *Ibid.* 11. *Im-*
"is in the Sacrament of the Altar by a Miracle; this I prove *possib. p.* 131.
"to be impossible. Because if there were any Miracle in the
"case, it would appear to the Eye; as when *Moses* turned
"the Rod into a Serpent; that was performed evidently to
the

"the Eye, though Men knew not how it was done. So also "in the case of the Ark of the Covenant of Old, mighty "Miracles were wrought; and those not only sensible Mira- "cles, but also publick, and apparent to all the People; (in- "somuch that Infidels were terrifyed at the very report of "such Miracles) Men seeing before their Eyes the Divine "Power brightly shining in Reverence of the Ark of his "Covenant, as appears in his Dividing the Waters of *Jor-* "*dan,* while the People of *Israel* passed over dry-shod, the "Waters on one side swelling like a Mountain, and on the "other flowing down as far as the dead Sea, till the Priests "with the Ark went over the Chanel of *Jordan,* and then "*Jordan* returned to its wonted course. But the Kings of "the *Amorites* and *Canaanites* hearing of so great and pub- "lick a Miracle, were so confounded with the terror of "God, that no Spirit remained in them (*Josu.* c. 4. & 5.) "and so I might instance in many other Evident Miracles, "which to avoid tediousness, I omit. And yet in that Ark, "neither God nor Christ was really contained, but only the "Tables of Stone containing the Precepts of the Decalogue, "and the Pot of Manna, *&c.* (*Exod.* 16.) and the Rod of "*Aaron* that flourished in the House of *Levi* (*Numb.* 17.) If "therefore by the Ark (that carried only the foresaid Bo- "dies that were inanimate, how sacred soever they were) "God wrought in Honour of it such evident far-spreading "and publick Miracles, how much more powerfully should "they have been wrought by him, if it were true, that in "your Sacrament of the Altar the true God or Christ were "really contained, whom you affirm that he ought to be wor- "shipped and venerated infinitely above all. Since therefore "no such thing do's appear there to the Eye, it follows that "it is impossible for any Miracle to be done there, since this "is against the Nature of a Miracle.

The answer to this is so weak, and so the rest, are generally such an unintelligible School-jargon, that I shall not tire the Reader with them. But shall go on with the Jew.

Ibid. 12. Im-*possib. fol.* 132.

3. "You Christians do assert, that the true Body of Christ "begins to be on the Altar. This seems to be impossible; "For

"For a thing begins to be where it was not before, two ways.
"Either by Local Motion, or by the conversion of another
"thing into it; as appears in Fire, which begins to be any
"where, either because it is kindled there anew, or is
"brought thither *de novo*.

"But it is manifest, that the true Body of Christ was not
"always on the Altar; because the Christians assert, that
"Christ ascended in his Body to Heaven. It seems also im-
"possible to be said, that any thing here is converted anew
"into Christ's Body; because nothing seems convertible into
"that which existed before; since that into which another
"thing is turned, by such a change, begins to exist. Now
"it is manifest, that Christ's Body did praeexist, seeing it
"was conceived in the Womb of *Mary*. It seems therefore
"impossible, that it should begin to be on the Altar anew, by
"the Conversion of another thing into it.

"In like manner, neither by a change of Place, because
"every thing that is locally moved, do's so begin to be in one
"place, that it ceases to be in that other in which it was be-
"fore. We must therefore say, that when Christ begins to
"be on this Altar on which the Sacrament is perform'd, he
"ceases to be in Heaven whither he ascended. It is also
"plain, that this Sacrament is in like manner celebrated on
"divers Altars. Therefore it is impossible that the Body of
"Christ should begin to be there by a Local Motion.

4. "You Christians affirm, that your Christ is whole in *Ibid.* 13. *Impoff.*
"the Sacrament, under the Species of Bread and Wine. *fol.* 134.
"This I prove thus to be impossible. Because never are the
"Parts of any Body contained in divers Places, the Body it
"self remaining whole. But now it is manifest, that in this
"Sacrament the Bread and Wine are asunder in separate Pla-
"ces. If therefore the Flesh of Christ be under the Species
"of Bread, and his Blood under the Species of Wine, it
"seems to follow, that Christ do's not remain whole, but
"that always when this Sacrament is celebrated, his Blood is
"separated from his Body.

5. "You

Ibid. 14. *Imposs.*
fol. eod.

5. "You Christians say, that in that little Host, the Body of Christ is contained. This I prove to be impossible. Because it is impossible that a greater Body should be included in the place of a lesser Body. But it is manifest, that the True Body of Christ is of a greater Quantity than the Bread that is offered on the Altar. Therefore it seems impossible, that the true Body of Christ should be whole and entire there, where the Bread seems to be. But if the whole be not there, but only some part of it, then the foresaid Inconvenience returns, that always when this Sacrament is perform'd, the Body of Christ is Differenced (or *separated*) by Parts."

I will only here set down what the Catholick Author replies to this (after the unintelligible distinctions of the Schools) and seems most to trust to, even such wise Similitudes as these, that the Soul is greater than the Body, and yet is contained within it; that a great Mountain is contained in the little Apple of the Eye; and the greatest Bodies in a little Looking-glass, and great Virtues in little precious Stones, and in the Little Body of the Pope great Authority, &c.

Ibid. 15. *Imposs.*
fol. 135.

6. "The Jew says, you Christians affirm that your Christ is in like manner on more Altars where Masses are celebrated. This seems to be impossible, because it is impossible for one Body to exist in more places than one. But it is plain that this Sacrament is celebrated in more Places. Therefore it seems impossible that the Body of Christ should be truly contained in this Sacrament. Unless perhaps any should say, that according to one part of it, it is here, and according to another Part elsewhere. But from thence it would again follow, that by the Celebration of this Sacrament the Body of Christ is divided into Parts; when yet the Quantity of the Body of Christ seems not to suffice for the dividing so many Particles out of it, as there are Places in which this Sacrament is performed."

7. "You

7. "You Christians say, that after Consecration, all the *Ibid.* 16. *Imposs.*
"Accidents of Bread and Wine are manifestly perceived in *fol.* 135.
"this Sacrament, *viz.* the Colour, Tast, Smell, Figure,
"Quantity and Weight. About which you cannot be de-
"ceived, because Sense is not deceived about its proper Ob-
"jects. Now these Accidents, as you assert, cannot be in
"the Body of Christ as in their Subject. —— Nor can they
"subsist by themselves, seeing the Nature and Essence of an
"Accident is to be in another thing (7. *Metaphys.*) For Ac-
"cidents seeing they are Forms, cannot be individuated but
"by their Subject; and if the Subject were taken away,
"would be universal Forms. It remains therefore that these
"Accidents are in their determinate Subjects, *viz.* In the
"substance of Bread and Wine. Wherefore there is there
"the substance of Bread and Wine, and not the substance
"of Christ's Body; for it seems impossible that two Bodies
"should be together, *(in one place.)*

8. "The Jews say, It is certain that if that Wine in your *Ibid.* 17. *Imposs.*
"Sacrament were taken in great Quantity, that it would heat *fol.* 137.
"*(the Body)* and intoxicate, as before it was a Sacrament:
"and also that the Bread would strengthen and nourish. It
"seems also, that if it be kept long and carelesly, it will cor-
"rupt; and it may be eaten of Mice; the Bread and Wine
"also may be burnt and turned into Vapours; all which can-
"not agree to the Body of Christ, seeing your Faith declares
"it to be impassible. It seems therefore impossible, that the
"Body of Christ should be contained substantially in this Sa-
"crament.

9. "The Jew says, That you Christians break that Sacra- *Ibid.* 18. *Imposs.*
"ment into Parts; Therefore it is impossible that the Body *fol.* 137.
"of Christ should be there. The Consequence is thus pro-
"ved: Because, that Fraction which do's sensibly appear,
"cannot be without a Subject. For it seems to be absurd
"to say, That the Subject of this Fraction is Christ's Body.
"Therefore it is impossible Christ's Body should be there, but
"only the Substance of Bread and Wine.

D d   There

There is a great deal more of what the Jews say against this Doctrine, in that Author: but this is enough, for the purposes I before mentioned (and so I leave it to the Consciences of those concerned) to show, that even the Jews have better explained the words whereby Christ instituted this Sacrament, than the Romanists have, by making it a Figure of Christ's Body, and not the Body it self, spoken more agreeably to the Faith of the *Ancient Church*, that did so; and have confuted the Errors of *this Church*, by Maximes consonant to the Sense and Reason of all Man-kind. Which God grant they may be sensible of, who have so manifestly swerved from them all, that so *their Words* may never rise up in Judgment against them.

THE END.

Books lately printed for Richard Chiswell.

A Dissertation concerning the Government of the *Ancient Church*: more particularly of the Encroachments of the *Bishops of Rome* upon other *Sees*. By WILLIAM CAVE, D. D. *Octavo*.

An Answer to Mr. *Serjeant*'s [Sure Footing in Christianity] concerning the Rule of Faith: With some other Discourses. By *WILLIAM FALKNER*, D. D. 4o.

A Vindication of the Ordinations of the *Church of England*; in Answer to a Paper written by one of the *Church of Rome*, to prove the Nullity of our Orders. By GILBERT BURNET, D. D. *Octavo*.

An Abridgment of the History of the Reformation of the *Church of England*. By GILB. BURNET, D. D. *Octavo*.

The APOLOGY of the *Church of England*; and an Epistle to one Signior *Scipio*, a *Venetian* Gentleman, concerning the Council of *Trent*. Written both in Latin, by the Right Reverend Father in God, *JOHN JEWEL* Lord Bishop of *Salisbury*: Made English by a Person of Quality. To which is added, The Life of the said Bishop: Collected and written by the same Hand. *Octavo*.

The Life of *WILLIAM BEDEL*, D. D. Bishop of *Kilmore* in *Ireland*. Together with *Certain Letters* which passed betwixt him and *James Waddesworth* (a late Pensioner of the Holy Inquisition of *Sevil*) in Matters of Religion, concerning the General Motives to the *Roman Obedience*. *Octavo*.

The Decree made at *ROME* the Second of *March*, 1679. condemning some Opinions of the *Jesuits*, and other *Casuists*. *Quarto*.

A Discourse concerning the Necessity of Reformation, with respect to the Errors and Corruptions of the *Church of Rome*. *Quarto*. First and Second Parts.

A Discourse concerning the Celebration of Divine Service in an Unknown Tongue. *Quarto*.

A Papist not Misrepresented by Protestants. Being a Reply to the Reflections upon the Answer to [A Papist Misrepresented and Represented]. *Quarto*.

An Exposition of the Doctrine of the *Church of England*, in the several Articles proposed by the late BISHOP of *CONDOM*; [in his Exposition of the Doctrine of the *Catholick Church*]. *Quarto*.

A Defence of the Exposition of the Doctrine of the *Church of England*; against the Exceptions of Monsieur de *Meaux*, late Bishop of *Condom*, and his Vindicator. 4o.

A CATECHISM explaining the Doctrine and Practices of the *Church of Rome*. With an Answer thereunto. By a *Protestant* of the *Church of England*. 8o.

A Papist Represented and not Misrepresented, being an Answer to the First, Second, Fifth and Sixth Sheets of the Second Part of the [Papist Misrepresented and Represented]; and for a further Vindication of the *CATECHISM*, truly representing the Doctrines and Practices of the *Church of Rome*. *Quarto*.

The *Lay-Christian*'s Obligation to read the Holy Scriptures. *Quarto*.

The *Plain Man*'s Reply to the *Catholick Missionaries*. 24o.

An Answer to THREE PAPERS lately printed, concerning the Authority of the *Catholick Church* in Matters of Faith, and the Reformation of the *Church of England*. *Quarto*.

A Vindication of the Answer to THREE PAPERS concerning the Unity and Authority of the *Catholick Church*, and the Reformation of the *Church of England*. *Quarto*.

BOOKS lately Printed for *Richard Chiswell*.

Mr. *Chillingworth*'s Book, called [*The Religion of Protestants a safe way to Salvation*] made more generally useful by omitting Personal Contests, but inserting whatsoever concerns the common Cause of *Protestants*, or defends the *Church of England*, with an exact Table of Contents; and an Addition of some genuine Pieces of Mr. *Chillingworth*'s, never before Printed, *viz.* against the *Infallibility* of the *Roman* Church, *Transubstantiation, Tradition*, &c. And an Account of what moved the Author to turn Papist, with his Confutation of the said Motives.

The Pillar and Ground of Truth. A Treatise shewing that the *Roman Church* falsly claims to be *That Church*, and the Pillar of *That Truth* mentioned by S. *Paul* in his first Epistle to *Timothy, Chap.* 3. *Vers.* 15. 4°.

The Peoples Right to read the Holy Scripture Asserted. 4°.

A Short Summary of the principal Controversies between the Church of *England* and the Church of *Rome*; being a Vindication of several Protestant Doctrines, in Answer to a Late Pamphlet, Intituled, [*Protestancy destitute of Scripture Proofs.*] 4°.

Two Discourses; Of Purgatory, and Prayers for the Dead.

An Answer to a Late Pamphlet, Intituled, [The Judgment and Doctrine of the Clergy of the Church of *England* concerning one Special Branch of the King's Prerogative, viz. *In dispensing with the Penal Laws.*] 4°.

The *Notes* of the *Church*, as laid down by Cardinal *Bellarmin*, examined and confuted. 4°. With a Table to the Whole.

Preparation for Death: Being a Letter sent to a young Gentlewoman in *France*, in a dangerous Distemper of which she died. By W. W. 12°.

The Difference between the *Church of England* and the *Church of Rome*, in opposition to a late Book, Intituled, *An Agreement between the Church of England and Church of Rome*.

A *PRIVATE PRAYER* to be used in Difficult Times.

A True Account of a Conference held about Religion at *London, Sept.* 29. 1687. between *A. Pulton*, Jesuit, and *Tho. Tennison*, D. D. as also of that which led to it, and followed after it. 4°.

The Vindication of *A. Cressener*, Schoolmaster in *Long-Acre*, from the Aspersions of *A. Pulton*, Jesuit, Schoolmaster in the *Savoy*, together with some Account of his Discourse with Mr. *Meredith*.

A Discourse shewing that Protestants are on the safer Side, notwithstanding the uncharitable Judgment of their Adversaries; and that *Their Religion* is the surest Way to Heaven. 4°.

Six Conferences concerning the *Eucharist*, wherein is shewed, that the Doctrine of *Transubstantiation* overthrows the Proofs of Christian Religion.

A Discourse concerning the pretended Sacrament of *Extream Unction*; with an account of the Occasions and Beginnings of it in the Western Church. In Three Parts. With a Letter to the Vindicator of the Bishop of *Condom*.

The Pamphlet entituled, *Speculum Ecclesiasticum*, or an Ecclesiastical Prospective-Glass, considered, in its False Reasonings and Quotations. There are added, by way of Preface, two further Answers, the First, to the Defender of the *Speculum*; the Second to the Half-sheet against the *Six Conferences*.